THE BEDFORD READER

SEVENTH EDITION

X. J. Kennedy • Dorothy M. Kennedy
Jane E. Aaron

BEDFORD/ST. MARTIN'S   BOSTON • NEW YORK

For Bedford/St. Martin's
Developmental Editor: Aron Keesbury
Production Editor: Deborah Baker
Production Supervisor: Joe Ford
Marketing Manager: Brian Wheel
Editorial Assistant: Amy Thomas
Production Assistants: Helaine Denenberg, Coleen O'Hanley
Copyeditor: Paula Woolley
Text Design: Anna George
Cover Design: Donna Lee Dennison
Cover Photos: Ginkgo, fossil, and leaf photographs by Masao Ota. Courtesy Photonica.
Composition: Stratford Publishing Services
Printing and Binding: Haddon Craftsmen, Inc.

President: Charles H. Christensen
Editorial Director: Joan E. Feinberg
Editor in Chief: Karen Henry
Director of Marketing: Karen Melton
Director of Editing, Design, and Production: Marcia Cohen
Managing Editor: Elizabeth M. Schaaf

Library of Congress Catalog Card Number: 99-65145

Manufactured in the United States of America.

4 3 2
f e

For information, write: Bedford/St. Martin's, 75 Arlington Street, Boston, MA 02116 (617-399-4000)

ISBN: 0–312–19770–5

ACKNOWLEDGMENTS

Maya Angelou, "Champion of the World," from *I Know Why the Caged Bird Sings* by Maya Angelou. Copyright © 1969 and renewed 1997 by Maya Angelou. Reprinted by permission of Random House, Inc. "Maya Angelou on Writing," excerpts from Sheila Weller, "Work in Progress/Maya Angelou," in *Intellectual Digest*, June 1973. Reprinted by permission.

Acknowledgments and copyrights are continued at the back of the book on pages 698–704, which constitute an extension of the copyright page. It is a violation of the law to reproduce these selections by any means whatsoever without the written permission of the copyright holder.

PREFACE
FOR INSTRUCTORS

"A writer," says Saul Bellow, "is a reader moved to emulate." In a nutshell, the aim of *The Bedford Reader* is to move students to be writers, through reading and emulating the good writing of others.

Like its predecessor, this seventh edition of *The Bedford Reader* works toward its aim both rhetorically and thematically. We present the rhetorical methods realistically, as we ourselves use them — as natural forms that assist invention and fruition *and* as flexible forms that mix easily for any purpose a writer may have. Further, we forge scores of thematic connections among selections, both in paired selections in each rhetorical chapter and in writing topics after all the selections.

For the seventh edition, we asked teachers how we could improve this framework and the myriad elements that contribute to it. Our users urged us to leave many features unchanged, but they also offered excellent suggestions for improvement. In response, we have emphasized the connections between purpose and method, followed ten students as they draw on the methods in real-life writing situations, and provided an alphabetical anthology of essays that show how writers mix the methods to achieve their purposes. These and other changes are highlighted on the next pages with bullets.

REALISTIC TREATMENT OF THE RHETORICAL METHODS.   At the core of *The Bedford Reader,* ten chapters treat ten methods of development not as boxes to be stuffed full of verbiage but as tools for inventing, for shaping, and, ultimately, for accomplishing a purpose.

In this edition, we have stressed even more the connections between purpose and method:

- In every rhetorical chapter, a new case study shows how a student arrived at the method to achieve a practical writing goal, such as reporting an accident, advertising an apartment for sublet, crafting a résumé, developing an association's mission statement, or disputing a parking ticket. Appearing on pages with gray borders, these case studies demonstrate the methods' relevance in real-life writing situations as well as in papers for school.
- The headnote for every selection now explicity relates the writer's purpose to his or her choice of method.
- On the book's front endpapers, an overview of the methods links a range of purposes for writing with the strategies that can help achieve those purposes.

EMPHASIS ON MIXING METHODS.   Taking the realistic approach to the methods even further, we show how writers freely combine the methods to achieve their purposes: Each rhetorical introduction discusses how that method might work with others, at least one "Other Methods" question after every selection helps students analyze how methods work together, and Part Two provides a range of essays that specifically illustrate mixed methods.

This emphasis, too, has been bolstered in the seventh edition:

- Every rhetorical chapter includes a list of essays elsewhere in *The Bedford Reader* that also rely heavily on the same method. These lists both reinforce the methods' flexibility and expand the range of models for each method.
- Part Two offers a more noteworthy and flexible collection of mixed-method essays by very well-known writers, such as Sandra Cisneros, Joan Didion, Annie Dillard, Martin Luther King, Jr., George Orwell, and Virginia Woolf. Arranged alphabetically, the fifteen essays may be integrated into the preceding chapters (following the many rhetorical and thematic links we provide) or may be used independently for their exemplary writing.
- For each essay in Part Two, the headnote not only connects the author's methods and purpose but also lists each significant method used and the paragraphs it develops.

VARIED SELECTIONS BY WELL-KNOWN AUTHORS.   The selections in *The Bedford Reader* vary in authorship, topics, even length. We offer clear models of the methods of development whose authors are noted for their lively writing. Half the selections are by women, and a quarter touch on cultural diversity. They range from one to eleven pages and deal with family, place, gender, language, history, science, ethics, disability, capital punishment, the Internet, and many other subjects.

We continue to freshen the book's selections:

- Of seventy-one pieces, one-third are new. Joining selections by proven favorites such as Maya Angelou, Jessica Mitford, and E. B. White are new pieces by Merrill Markoe, K. C. Cole, Richard Ford, Chitra Divakaruni, Stephen L. Carter, and others.
- The ten new case studies add ten new student works to the five retained from the previous edition.
- For literary works, a new poem by Elizabeth Bishop accompanies stories by Edgar Allan Poe and Jamaica Kincaid.

EXTENSIVE THEMATIC CONNECTIONS.   *The Bedford Reader* provides substantial topics for class discussion and writing. A pair of essays in each rhetorical chapter addresses the same subject, from the ordinary (housekeeping) to the controversial (the death penalty). At least one "Connections" writing topic after every selection suggests links to other selections. And an alternate thematic table of contents arranges the book's selections under more than two dozen topics.

THOROUGH COVERAGE OF CRITICAL READING AND WRITING.   As before, *The Bedford Reader*'s general introduction offers detailed advice on developing a critical response to reading, including a sample of a student's annotations on a text and practical guidelines for summarizing, analyzing, and interpreting texts. A work-in-progress shows a student's developing response to an essay by M. F. K. Fisher, from annotations on the essay through journal entries and drafts to a final paper. And a "Critical Writing" topic after every selection helps students formulate their own critiques.

The introduction's discussion of the writing process also emphasizes journals, freewriting, and other techniques that can help students write fluently, creatively, and confidently; offers detailed advice on thesis sentences, setting up the parallel coverage in each rhetorical chapter; provides checklists for revising and editing; and discusses collaboration in writing and revising, with advice on giving and receiving criticism.

UNIQUE COMMENTS BY WRITERS ON WRITING. After their essays, fifty-five of the book's writers offer comments on everything from grammar to revision to how they developed the reprinted piece. Besides providing rock-solid advice, these comments also prove that for the pros, too, writing is usually a challenge.

For easy access, the Writers on Writing are listed in the book's index under the topics they address. Look up "Revision," for instance, and find that Russell Baker, Dave Barry, Annie Dillard, and Gore Vidal, among others, have something to say about this crucial stage of the writing process.

HELP WITH USING AND DOCUMENTING SOURCES. We have retained the previous edition's appendix with extensive guidance on the use of sources: paraphrasing, summarizing, and quoting; integrating quotations into one's own text; and documenting sources (including electronic sources) in the latest MLA style. The book also offers a researched argument by a student, Curtis Chang, that is fully documented in MLA style.

ABUNDANT EDITORIAL APPARATUS. As always, we've surrounded the selections with a wealth of material designed to get students reading, thinking, and writing. To help structure students' critical approach to the selections, each one comes with two headnotes (on the author and the selection itself), three sets of questions (on meaning, writing strategy, and language), and at least four writing topics. Of these topics, one encourages students to explore their responses in their journals and then develop their ideas into essays, another emphasizes critical writing, and another draws connections to other selections.

Besides the aids with every selection, the book also includes additional writing topics for every rhetorical chapter, a glossary ("Useful Terms") that defines all terms used in the book (including all those printed in SMALL CAPITAL LETTERS), and an index that alphabetizes authors and titles and important topics (including, as noted above, those covered in the Writers on Writing).

INSTRUCTOR'S MANUAL. Available as a separate manual or bound with the book, *Notes and Resources for Teaching The Bedford Reader* includes suggestions for integrating journal writing and collaboration into writing classes along with a discussion of every method, every selection (with possible answers to all questions), and every Writer on Writing.

Two features of the instructor's manual are new to this edition:

- The overview of the book's general introduction includes a complete outline along with tips for using the material in class.

- A discussion of the student case studies elaborates on the rationale for this new feature and suggests ways to build the case studies into a course.

TWO VERSIONS. *The Bedford Reader* has a sibling. A shorter edition, *The Brief Bedford Reader*, features forty-seven selections instead of seventy-one, including five rather than fifteen essays in Part Two.

ACKNOWLEDGMENTS

Hundreds of the teachers and students using *The Bedford Reader* over the years have helped us shape the book. For this edition, the following teachers offered insights from their experiences that encouraged worthy changes: Thomas E. Fish, Cumberland College; Tom Hoberg, Northeastern Illinois University; Jocelyn Ladner, St. Louis Community College; Ruby Lightsem, Central Florida Community College; Phyliss Lotchin, North Carolina Central University; Nanci Love, Day de Noc Community College; Tom Lugo, University of Illinois, Urbana-Champaign; Jeanne Mauzy, Valencia Community College; Todd McCann, Bay de Noc Community College; Kevin Mebergall, Kirkwood Community College; Julie Morgan, Volunteer State Community College; Bill O'Boyle, Nash Community College; Kay L. Smith, Valencia Community College; Susan Stock, Union County College; David J. Tietge, Seton Hall University; James E. Van Sickle, Muskegon Community College; Debra Vazquez, Central Florida Community College; Katheryn White, Saint Peter's College; and Donald Zurack, Henry Ford Community College.

As always, the creative staff of Bedford/St. Martin's supported the authors brilliantly, enthusiastically, and patiently. Charles Christensen, Joan Feinberg, and Karen Henry contributed their astute understanding of the needs of composition teachers and students. Throughout the book's development, Aron Keesbury served as idea factory, project manager, and hand holder, all with unflagging charm and wit. The editorial assistants Ellen Thibault and Amy Thomas ably fielded any request. Jill McDonough, Debra Spark, and Donna Ashley helped to shape the apparatus and instructor's manual. Donna Dennison designed and coordinated the striking cover. And Deborah Baker deftly transformed a difficult manuscript into the book you hold. We are, as ever, grateful for such partners.

CONTENTS

An incident in the writer's childhood proves the occasion for a revelation about her father's past and a lesson in the nature of violence.

A student questions M. F. K. Fisher's acceptance of physical punishment as a justifiable form of violence.

PART ONE
THE METHODS
37

1   NARRATION: Telling a Story   39

She didn't dare ring up a sale while that epic battle was on. A noted African American writer remembers from her early childhood the night when a people's fate hung on a pair of boxing gloves.

PAIRED SELECTIONS

The writer remembers her teenaged angst when the minister and his cute blond son attended her family's Christmas Eve dinner, an elaborate Chinese feast.

PAIRED
SELECTIONS

Contents

3 EXAMPLE: Pointing to Instances   137

Contents

8   CAUSE AND EFFECT: Asking Why   361

GORE VIDAL   •   *Drugs*   373

A critic and novelist presents a radical idea for dealing with drug abuse: Legalize drugs. The effects will be less addiction and less crime.

Gore Vidal on Writing   376

K. C. COLE   •   *The Arrow of Time*   378

It may seem an irrelevant scientific concept, but entropy—the natural tendency toward disorder—affects our everyday lives. A noted science writer explains why.

K. C. Cole on Writing   382

MEGHAN DAUM   •   *Safe-Sex Lies*   384

According to a twenty-something writer, those who grew up in the age of AIDS have learned some unintended lessons, among them "chronic dishonesty and fear."

SCOTT RUSSELL SANDERS   •   *Homeplace*   390

Our culture "nudges everything into motion," this essayist holds, but staying put has much richer benefits for us and for the earth we inhabit.

Scott Russell Sanders on Writing   397

**PAIRED
SELECTIONS**

RICHARD FORD   •   *I Must Be Going*   399

A well-known fiction writer and frequent mover resists the view that he should settle down. Transience has its own rewards, among them independence, experience, and the enlargement of one's mind.

Richard Ford on Writing   404

ADDITIONAL WRITING TOPICS   406

PART TWO
MIXING THE METHODS
523

THEMATIC
TABLE OF CONTENTS

AUTOBIOGRAPHY

ENVIRONMENT

ETHICS

FRIENDSHIP

HEALTH AND DISABILITY

HISTORY

HOMELESSNESS

HUMOR AND SATIRE

LAW

MANNERS AND MORALS

MARRIAGE

MEDIA

MEMORY

MINORITY EXPERIENCE

READING, WRITING, AND LANGUAGE

SCIENCE AND TECHNOLOGY

SELF-DISCOVERY

SEXUALITY

SOCIAL CUSTOMS

SPORTS AND LEISURE

INTRODUCTION

WHY READ? WHY WRITE?
WHY NOT PHONE?

Many prophets have forecast the doom of the word on paper. Soon, they have argued, books and magazines will be read on pocket computers. Newspapers will be found only in attics, supplanted by interactive television. The mails will be replaced by electronic message boards.

The prophets have been making such forecasts for many decades, but book sales remain high, magazines and newspapers keep publishing, and the Postal Service has trouble keeping up with volume. In the electronic office, the computer workstation is often an island in a sea of paper. Evidently, the permanent, word-on-paper record still has its advantages.

Even if the day comes when we throw away pens and paper, it is doubtful that the basic aims and methods of writing will completely change. Whether on paper or on screens, we will need to arrange our thoughts in a clear order. We will still have to explain them to others plainly and forcefully.

That is why, in almost any career or profession you may enter, you will be expected to read continually and also to write. This book assumes that reading and writing are a unity. Deepen your mastery of one, and you deepen your mastery of the other. The experience of carefully reading an excellent writer, noticing not only what the writer has to say but also the quality of its saying, rubs off (if you are patient and perceptive) on your own writing. "We go to college," said the poet Robert Frost, "to be given one more chance to learn to read in case we haven't learned in high school. Once we have learned to read, the rest can be trusted to add itself *unto us*."

For any writer, reading is indispensable. It turns up fresh ideas; it stocks the mind with information, understanding, examples, and illustrations; it instills critical awareness of one's surroundings. When you have a well-stocked and girded mental storehouse, you tell truths, even small and ordinary truths. Instead of building shimmering spires of words in an attempt to make a reader think, "Wow, what a grade A writer," you write what most readers will find worth reading. Thornton Wilder, playwright and novelist, put this advice memorably: "If you write to *impress* it will always be bad, but if you write to *express* it will be good."

USING *THE BEDFORD READER*

The Essays

In this book, we trust, you'll find at least a few selections you will enjoy and care to remember. *The Bedford Reader* features work by many of the finest nonfiction writers and even a few sterling fiction writers.

The essays deal with more than just writing and literature and such usual concerns of English courses; they cut broadly across a college curriculum. You'll find writings on science, history, business, religion, popular culture, women's studies, sociology, education, communication, the environment, technology, sports, politics, the media, and minority experience. Some writers recall their childhoods, their families, their problems and challenges. Some explore matters likely to spark controversy: drug use, funerals, sex roles, race relations, conservation, the death penalty. Some writers are intently serious; others, funny. In all, these seventy-one selections—including two stories and one poem—reveal kinds of reading you will meet in other college courses. Such reading is the usual diet of well-informed people with lively minds—who, to be sure, aren't found only on campuses.

The essays have been chosen with one main purpose in mind: to show you how good writers write. Don't feel glum if at first you find an immense gap in quality between E. B. White's writing and yours. Of course there's a gap: White is an immortal with a unique style that he perfected over half a century. You don't have to judge your efforts by comparison. The idea is to gain whatever writing techniques you can. If you're going to learn from other writers, why not go to the best of them? Do you want to know how to define an idea so that the definition is vivid and clear? Read Marie Winn's "TV Addiction." Do you want to know how to tell a story about your childhood and make it stick in someone's memory? Read Maya Angelou. Incidentally, not all the selections in this book are the work of professional writers: Students, too, write essays worth studying, as Christine D'Angelo, Brad Manning, Linnea Saukko, Christine Leong, and Curtis Chang prove.

This book has another aim: to encourage you in critical reading, meaning thoughtful, open-minded, questioning reading. Like everyone else, you face a daily barrage of words—from the information and advertisements on television, from online newsgroups and Web sites, from course texts and lectures, even from relatives and friends. Mulling over the views of the writers in this book, figuring out their motives and strategies, agreeing or disagreeing with their ideas, will help you learn to manage, digest, and use, in your own writing, what you read and hear.

The Organization

As a glance over the table of contents will show, the essays in *The Bedford Reader* fall into two parts. In Part One each of the ten chapters explains a familiar method of developing ideas, such as DESCRIPTION or CLASSIFICATION or DEFINITION, and the essays illustrate the method. Then Part Two offers an anthology of essays by well-known writers that illustrate how, most often, the methods work together.

These methods of development aren't empty jugs to pour full of any old, dull words. Neither are they straitjackets woven by fiendish English teachers to pin your writing arm to your side and keep you from expressing yourself naturally. The methods are tools for achieving your PURPOSE in writing, whatever that purpose may be. They can help you discover what you know, what you need to know, how to think critically about your subject, and how to shape your writing.

Suppose, for example, that you set out to explain what makes a certain popular singer unique. You want to discuss her voice, her music, her lyrics, her style. While putting your ideas down on paper, it strikes you that you can best illustrate the singer's distinctions by showing the differences between her and another popular singer, one she is often compared with. To achieve your purpose, then, you draw on the method of COMPARISON AND CONTRAST, and as you proceed the method prompts you to notice differences between the two singers that you hadn't dreamed of noticing. Using the methods, such little miracles of focusing and creating take place with heartening regularity. Give the methods a try. See how they help you reach your writing goals by giving you more to say, more that you think is worth saying.

You may wonder about the value of the methods in every sort of writing, not just essays. Each chapter includes a case study showing how a student used a method to solve an actual writing problem, such as crafting a cover letter and a résumé for a job application or composing an ad to sublet an apartment. You'll learn of each student's thinking and writing process as he or she figured out a purpose for writing and worked through the best method to achieve that purpose.

Reading *The Bedford Reader*'s case studies and selections, you'll discover two important facts about the methods of development. First, they are flexible: Two writers can use the same method for quite different ends, and just about any method can point a way into just about any subject. To prove this flexibility, in every method chapter we offer a pair of essays on the same general subject but with different purposes, and we provide two sample paragraphs, one about television and one drawn from a college textbook.

The sample paragraphs illustrate another point about the methods of development: A writer never sticks to just one method all the way through a piece of writing. Even when one method predominates, as in all the essays in Part One, you'll see the writer pick up another method, let it shape a paragraph or more, and then move on to yet another method—all to achieve some overriding aim. In "TV Addiction," Marie Winn mainly defines the term in her title, but she also compares TV addiction with drug and alcohol addiction, gives EXAMPLES of TV addiction that include description, and examines the CAUSES AND EFFECTS of the addiction. The point is that Winn employs whatever methods suit her dual purpose of explaining what TV addiction is and convincing readers that it is, in fact, an addiction.

So the methods are like oxygen, iron, and other elements that make up substances in nature: all around us, indispensable to us, but seldom found alone and isolated, in laboratory-pure states. When you read an essay in a chapter called "Description" or "Classification," don't expect it to describe or classify in every line, but do notice how the method is central to the writer's purpose. Then, when you read the essays in Part Two, notice how the "elements" of description, example, comparison, definition, and so on rise to prominence and recede as the writer's need dictates.

The Questions, Writing Topics, and Glossary

Following every essay, you'll find questions on meaning, writing strategy, and language that can help you analyze the selection and learn from it. (You can see a sample of how these questions work when we analyze M. F. K. Fisher's "The Broken Chain," starting on p. 9.) These questions are followed by at least four suggestions for writing, including one that proposes a journal exercise, one that links the essay with one or two others in the book, and one that asks you to read the essay and write about it with your critical faculties alert (more on this in a moment). More writing topics conclude each chapter.

In the material surrounding the essays, certain terms appear in CAPITAL LETTERS. These are words helpful in discussing both the essays in this book and the essays you write. If you'd like to see such a term defined and illustrated, you can find it in the glossary, Useful Terms, at the back of this book. This section offers more than just brief definitions. It is there to provide you with further information and support.

Writers on Writing

We have tried to give this book another dimension. We want to show that the writers represented here do not produce their readable and informative prose on the first try, as if by magic, leaving the rest of us to cope with writer's block, awkward sentences, and all the other difficulties of writing. Take comfort and cheer: These writers, too, struggled to make themselves interesting and clear. In proof, we visit their workshops littered with crumpled paper and forgotten coffee cups. Later in this introduction, when we discuss the writing process briefly and include an essay by a student, Christine D'Angelo, we also include her drafts and her thoughts about them. Then following most of the other essays are statements by the writers, revealing how they write (or wrote), offering their tricks, setting forth things they admire about good writing.

No doubt you'll soon notice some contradictions in these statements: The writers disagree about when and how to think about their readers, about whether outlines have any value, about whether style follows subject or vice versa. The reason for the difference of opinion is, simply, that no two writers follow the same path to finished work. Even the same writer may take the left instead of the customary right fork if the writing situation demands a change. A key aim of providing D'Angelo's drafts and the other writers' statements on writing, then, is to suggest the sheer variety of routes open to you, the many approaches to writing and strategies for succeeding at it. At the very end of the book, an index points you toward the writers' comments on such practical matters as drafting, finding your point, and revising sentences.

READING AN ESSAY

Whatever career you enter, much of the reading you will do—for business, not for pleasure—will probably be hasty. You'll skim: glance at words here and there, find essential facts, catch the drift of an argument.

To cross oceans of print, you won't have time to paddle: You'll need to hop a jet. By skimming, you'll be able to tear through screens full of electronic mail or quickly locate the useful parts of a long report.

But other reading that you do for work, most that you do in college, and all that you do in this book call for reading word for word. You may be trying to understand how a new company policy affects you, or researching a complicated historical treaty, or (in using this book) looking for pointers to sharpen your reading and writing skills. To learn from the essays here how to write better yourself, expect to spend an hour or two in the company of each one. Does the essay assigned for today remain unread, and does class start in five minutes? "I'll just breeze through this little item," you might tell yourself. But no, give up. You're a goner.

Good writing, as every writer knows, demands toil, and so does CRITICAL READING — reading that looks beneath the surface of the writing, that seeks to understand how the piece works and whether it succeeds. Never try to gulp down a rich and potent essay without chewing; all it will give you is indigestion. When you're going to read an essay in depth, seek out some quiet place — a library, a study cubicle, your room (provided it doesn't also hold a cranky baby or two roommates playing poker). Flick off the radio, stereo, or television. What writer can outsing Aretha Franklin or Luciano Pavarotti, or outshout a kung fu movie? The fewer the distractions, the easier your task will be and the more you'll enjoy it.

How do you read an essay? Exactly how, that is, do you read it critically, master its complexities, learn how a good writer writes, and so write better yourself? To find out, we'll be taking a close look at an actual essay, M. F. K. Fisher's "The Broken Chain." You'll find it rewards the time you spend on it.

The Preliminaries

Critical reading starts before you read the first word of the essay. Like a pilot circling an airfield, you take stock of what's before you, locating clues to the essay's content and the writer's biases.

The Title

Often the title will tell you the writer's subject, as in Barbara Ehrenreich's "In Defense of Talk Shows" or H. L. Mencken's "The Penalty of Death." Sometimes the title immediately states the THESIS, the main point the writer will make: "I Want a Wife." The title may set forth the subject as a question: "Why Don't We Complain?" Some titles spell out the method a writer proposes to follow: "Grant and Lee:

A Study in Contrasts." The TONE of the title may also reveal the writer's attitude toward the material. "Live Free and Starve" gives you an impression of the writer's approach, and so does "Confessions of a Shusher." You, in turn, approach each work in a different way—with serious intent, perhaps, or set to be amused.

Some titles reveal more than others. M. F. K. Fisher's title, "The Broken Chain," is a bit mysterious. We may suspect that the author does not mean "chain" literally (a bicycle chain) but figuratively (like a chain of events or a chain reaction). The title hints at change (a chain breaks), so we may guess that this broken chain lies at the heart of a story. The rest is for us to find out.

Whatever it does, a title sits atop its essay like a neon sign. It tells you what's inside or makes you want to venture in. To pick an alluring title for an essay of your own is a skill worth cultivating.

The Author

Whatever you know about a writer—background, special training, previous works, outlook, or ideology—often will help you guess something about the essay before you read a word of it. Is the writer on new taxes a political conservative? Expect an argument against added "revenue enhancement." Is the writer a liberal? Expect an argument that new social programs are worth the price. Is the writer a feminist? an athlete? an internationally renowned philosopher? a popular television comedian? By knowing something about a writer's background or beliefs, you may know beforehand a little of what he or she will say.

To help provide such knowledge, this book supplies biographical notes. The one on M. F. K. Fisher before "The Broken Chain" (p. 9) tells us that Fisher often wrote about food but that she told other stories as well. You won't know until you read it whether "The Broken Chain" is about food. But if you guess from the note that the essay will be thought provoking, enjoyable, and readily understandable, you will be right.

Where the Essay Was First Published

Clearly, it matters to a writer's credibility whether an article called "Living Mermaids: An Amazing Discovery" first saw print in *Scientific American,* a magazine for scientists and interested nonscientists, or in a popular tabloid weekly, sold at supermarket checkout counters, that is full of eye-popping sensations. But no less important, finding out where an essay first appeared can tell you for whom the writer was writing. In this book we'll strongly urge you as a writer to think of your AUDIENCE, your readers, and to try looking at what you write as if through their eyes. To help you develop this ability, we tell you something about the sources and thus the original readers of each essay you study, in a note just before the essay. (Such a note precedes "The Broken Chain" on p. 9.) After you have read the sample essay, we'll further consider how having a sense of your readers helps you write.

When the Essay Was First Published

Knowing in what year an essay was first printed may give you another key to understanding it. A 1988 essay on mermaids will contain statements of fact more recent and more reliable than an essay printed in 1700—although the older essay might contain valuable information, too, and perhaps some delectable language, folklore, and poetry. In *The Bedford Reader*, the brief introductory note on every essay tells you not only where but also when the essay was originally printed. If you're reading an essay elsewhere—say, in one of the writer's books— you can usually find this information on the copyright page.

The First Reading

On first reading an essay, you don't want to bog down over every troublesome particular. "The Broken Chain" is written for an educated audience, and that means the author may use a few large words when they seem necessary. If you meet any words that look intimidating, take them in your stride. When, in reading a rich essay, you run into an unfamiliar word or name, see if you can figure it out from its surroundings. If a word stops you cold and you feel lost, circle it in pencil; you can always look it up later. (In a little while we'll come back to the helpful habit of reading with a pencil. Indeed, some readers feel more confident with pencil in hand from the start.)

The first time you read an essay, size up the forest; later, you can squint at the acorns all you like. Glimpse the essay in its entirety. When you start to read "The Broken Chain," don't even think about dissecting it. Just see what Fisher has to say.

M. F. K. FISHER

MARY FRANCES KENNEDY FISHER was born in 1908 and began telling stories at age four. Raised in California and educated there and in Illinois and France, Fisher became renowned for her writing about food. Her first book, *Serve It Forth* (1937), was followed by more than sixteen others before her death at eighty-three in 1992. Not all of them concerned eating, and even those on food, such as *How to Cook a Wolf* (1942), expanded the subject to encompass needs and pleasures of all sorts. Besides writing her books, Fisher produced essays, poetry, and a screenplay, kept house, tended a vineyard in Switzerland, and translated a French gastronomical classic, Brillat-Savarin's *The Physiology of Taste*. Her works reveal a keen sense of story, a sharply observant, independent mind, and a search for the truths in her own and others' lives.

The Broken Chain

"The Broken Chain" was written in 1983 and first published in Fisher's last book, *To Begin Again* (1992). Taking her lead from news headlines, Fisher flashes back to an incident in 1920 that transformed her and her father, Rex, and could perhaps help others as well.

1   There has been more talk than usual lately about the abuse and angry beating of helpless people, mostly children and many women. I think about it. I have never been beaten, so empathy is my only weapon against the ugliness I know vicariously. On the radio someone talks about a chain of violence. When is it broken? he asks. How?

2   When I was growing up, I was occasionally spanked and always by my father. I often had to go upstairs with him when he came home from the *News* for lunch, and pull down my panties and lay myself obediently across his long bony knees, and then steel my emotions against the ritualistic whack of five or eight or even ten sharp taps from a wooden hairbrush. They were counted by my age, and by nine or ten he began to use his hand, in an expert upward slap that stung more than the hairbrush. I often cried a little, to prove that I had learned my lesson.

3   I knew that Rex disliked this duty very much, but that it was part of being Father. Mother could not or would not punish us. Instead, she always said, by agreement with him and only when she felt that things were serious enough to drag him into it, that she would have to speak with him about the ugly matter when he came home at noon.

4   This always left me a cooling-off period of thought and regret and conditioned dread, even though I knew that I had been the cause, through my own stupidity, of involving both my parents in the plot.

Maybe it was a good idea. I always felt terrible that it was dragged   5
out. I wished that Mother would whack me or something and get it
over with. And as I grew older I resented having to take several unde-
served blows because I was the older child and was solemnly expected
to be a model to my younger sister, Anne. She was a comparatively
sickly child, and spoiled and much cleverer than I, and often made it
bitterly clear to me that I was an utter fool to take punishment for her
own small jaunty misdoings. I continued to do this, far past the fatherly
spankings and other parental punishments, because I loved her and
agreed that I was not as clever as she.

Once Rex hit me. I deserved it, because I had vented stupid petu-   6
lance on my helpless little brother David. He was perhaps a year old,
and I was twelve. We'd all left the lunch table for the living room and
had left him sitting alone in his high chair, and Father spotted him
through the big doors and asked me to get him down. I felt sulky about
something, and angered, and I stamped back to the table and pulled up
the wooden tray that held the baby in his chair, and dumped him out
insolently on the floor. David did not even cry out, but Rex saw it and
in a flash leapt across the living room toward the dining table and the
empty high chair and gave me a slap across the side of my head that
sent me halfway across the room against the big old sideboard. He
picked up David and stood staring at me. Mother ran in. A couple of
cousins came, looking flustered and embarrassed at the sudden ugliness.

I picked myself up from the floor by the sideboard, really raging   7
with insulted anger, and looked disdainfully around me and then went
silently up the stairs that rose from the dining room to all our sleeping
quarters. Behind me I could hear Mother crying, and then a lot of talk.

I sat waiting for my father to come up to the bedroom that Anne   8
and I always shared, from her birth until I was twenty, in our two family homes in Whittier, and in Laguna in the summers, and then when
we went away to three different schools. I knew I was going to be punished.

Finally Father came upstairs, looking very tired. "Daughter," he   9
said, "your mother wants you to be spanked. You have been bad. Pull
down your panties and lie across my knees."

I was growing very fast and was almost as tall as I am now, with   10
small growing breasts. I looked straight at him, not crying, and got into
the old position, all long skinny arms and legs, with my bottom bared
to him. I felt insulted and full of fury. He gave me twelve expert upward
stinging whacks. I did not even breathe fast, on purpose. Then I stood
up insolently, pulled up my sensible Munsingwear panties, and stared
down at him as he sat on the edge of my bed.

"That's the last time," he said.   11

"Yes," I said. "And you hit me."   12

"I apologize for that," he said, and stood up slowly, so that once   13
again I had to look up into his face as I had always done. He went out
of the room and downstairs, and I stayed alone in the little room under
the eaves of the Ranch house, feeling my insult and anger drain slowly
out and away forever. I knew that a great deal had happened, and I felt
ashamed of behaving so carelessly toward my helpless little brother and
amazed at the way I had simply blown across the room and into the
sideboard under my own father's wild stinging blow across my cheek. I
wished that I would be maimed, so that he would feel shame every time
he looked at my poor face. I tried to forget how silly I'd felt, baring my
pubescent bottom to his heavy dutiful slaps across it. I was full of scowling puzzlements.

My mother came into the room, perhaps half an hour later, and   14
wrapped her arms around me with a tenderness I had never felt from
her before, although she had always been quietly free with her love and
her embraces. She had been crying but was very calm with me, as she
told me that Father had gone back to the *News* and that the cousins
were playing with the younger children. I wanted to stay haughty and
abused with her, but sat there on the bed quietly, while she told me
about Father.

She said that he had been beaten when he was a child and then as   15
a growing boy, my age, younger, older. His father beat him, almost every
Saturday, with a long leather belt. He beat all four of his boys until they
were big enough to tell him that it was the last time. They were all of
them tall strong people, and Mother said without any quivering in her
voice that they were all about sixteen before they could make it clear
that if it ever happened again, they would beat their father worse than
he had ever done it to them.

He did it, she said, because he believed that he was ridding them of   16
the devil, of sin. Grandfather, she said quietly, was not a brute or a
beast, not sinful, not a devil. But he lived in the wild prairies and raised
strong sons to survive, as he had, the untold dangers of frontier life.
When he was starting his family, as a wandering newspaperman and
printer of political broadsides, he got religion. He was born again. He
repented of all his early wildness and tried to keep his four sons from
"sinning," as he came to call what he had done before he accepted God
as his master.

I sat close to Mother as she explained to me how horrible it had   17
been only a few minutes or hours before in my own short life, when Rex
had broken a long vow and struck his own child in unthinking anger.
She told me that before they married, he had told her that he had
vowed when he was sixteen to break the chain of violence and that
never would he strike anyone in anger. She must help him. They
promised each other that they would break the chain. And then today

he had, for the first time in his whole life, struck out, and he had struck his oldest child.

I could feel my mother trembling. I was almost overwhelmed by pity for the two people whom I had betrayed into this by my stupidity. "Then why did he hit me?" I almost yelled suddenly. She said that he hardly remembered doing it, because he was so shocked by my dumping the helpless baby out onto the floor. "Your father does not remember," she repeated. "He simply had to stop you, stop the unthinking way you acted toward a helpless baby. He was . . . He suddenly acted violently. And it is dreadful for him now to see that, after so long, he can be a raging animal. He thought it would never happen. That is why he has never struck any living thing in anger. Until today."

We talked for a long time. It was a day of spiritual purging, obviously. I have never been the same—still stupid but never unthinking, because of the invisible chains that can be forged in all of us, without our knowing it. Rex knew of the chain of violence that was forged in him by his father's whippings, brutal no matter how mistakenly committed in the name of God. I learned of what violence could mean as I sat beside my mother, that day when I was twelve, and felt her tremble as she put her arm over my skinny shoulders and pulled me toward her in an embrace that she was actually giving to her husband.

It is almost certain that I stayed aloof and surly, often, in the next years with my parents. But I was never spanked again. And I know as surely as I do my given name that Rex no longer feared the chain of violence that had bound him when he was a boy. Perhaps it is as well that he hit me, the one time he found that it had not been broken for him.

Rereadings

When first looking into an essay, you are like a person who arrives at the doorway of a large and lively room, surveying a party going on inside. Glancing around the room, you catch the overall picture: the locations of the food and the drinks, of people you know, of people you don't know but would certainly like to. You have just taken such an overview of Fisher's essay. Now, stepping through the doorway of the essay, you can head for whatever beckons most strongly.

Well, what will it be? If it is writing skills you want, then go for those elements that took skill or flair or thoughtful decision on the writer's part. Most likely, you'll need to reread the essay more than once, go over the difficult parts several times, with all the care of someone combing a snag from the mane of an admirable horse.

Writing While Reading

In giving an essay this going-over, many students—some of the best—find a pencil in hand as good as a currycomb for a horse's mane. The pencil (or pen or computer keyboard) concentrates the attention wonderfully, and, as often happens with writing, it can lead you to unexpected questions and connections. (Some readers favor markers that roll pink or yellow ink over a word or line, making the eye jump to that spot, but you can't use a highlighter to note *why* a word or idea is important.) You can annotate your own books, underlining essential ideas, scoring key passages with vertical lines, writing questions in the margins about difficult words or concepts, venting feelings ("Bull!" "Yes!" "Says who?"). Here, as an example, are the jottings of one student, Christine D'Angelo, on a paragraph of Fisher's essay:

"I apologize for that," he said, and stood up slowly, so that once again I had to look up into his face as I had always done. He went out of the room and downstairs, and I stayed alone in the little room under the eaves of the Ranch house, feeling my insult and anger drain slowly out and away forever. I knew that a great deal had happened, and I felt ashamed of behaving so carelessly toward my helpless little brother and amazed at the way I had simply blown across the room and into the sideboard under my own father's wild stinging blow across my cheek. I wished that I would be maimed, so that he would feel shame every time he looked at my poor face. I tried to forget how silly I'd felt, baring my pubescent bottom to his heavy dutiful slaps across it. I was full of scowling puzzlements.

What was his expression?

already forgives father?

difference in blow and spanking (to author and father)

Good phrase for child's mixed emotions

If a book is borrowed, you can accomplish the same thing by making notes on a separate sheet of paper or on your computer.

Whether you own the book or not, you'll need separate notes for responses that are lengthier and more substantial than the margins can contain, such as the informal responses, summaries, detailed analyses, and evaluations discussed below. For such notes, you may find a JOURNAL handy. It can be a repository of your ideas, a comfortable place to record meandering or direct thoughts about what you read. You may be surprised to find that the more you write in an unstructured way, the more you'll have to say when it's time to write a structured essay. (For more on journals, see p. 24.)

Writing and reading help you behold the very spine of an essay, as if in an X-ray view, so that you, as much as any expert, can judge its curves and connections. You'll develop an opinion about what you read, and you'll want to express it. While reading this way, you're being a writer. Your pencil tracks or keystrokes will jog your memory, too, when you review for a test, when you take part in class discussion, or when you want to write about what you've read.

Summarizing

It's usually good practice, especially with more difficult essays, to SUMMARIZE the content in writing to be sure you understand it or, as often happens, to come to understand it. We use summary all the time to fill friends in on the gist of a story—shrinking a two-hour movie to a single sentence, "This woman is recruited to be a spy, and she stops a ring of double agents." In summarizing a work of writing, you digest, *in your own words*, what the author says: You take the essence of the author's meaning, without the supporting evidence and other details that make that gist convincing or interesting. When you are practicing reading and the work is short (the case with the reading you do in this book), you may want to make this a two-step procedure: First write a summary sentence for every paragraph or related group of paragraphs; then summarize those sentences in two or three others that capture the heart of the author's meaning.

Here is a two-step summary of "The Broken Chain." (The numbers in parentheses refer to paragraph numbers in the essay.) First, the longer version:

> (1) Fisher wonders about the "chain of violence" against children and women. (2–3) As a child, she was sometimes spanked on her bare bottom by her father, who carried out the job reluctantly as a father's responsibility. (4–5) The spanking did not occur immediately after the bad behavior, and the delay left Fisher feeling sorry and afraid and often resentful of her younger sister, who escaped such punishment. (6) Then once Fisher peevishly dropped her baby brother on the floor, and her father struck her suddenly and violently in anger. (7–13) She was simply furious at first, but she became remorseful, vindictive, and embarrassed as well when her father later spanked her for her deed and apologized for striking her. (14–16) Her mother then comforted her and explained that her father had been regularly beaten by his own father. (17–18) Her father had sworn that he would "break the chain of violence" by never hitting another person out of anger, and now he was horrified to discover that he, too, could be violent. (19) The incident helped Fisher understand her father and violence. (20) It also broke the chain by releasing her father from his fear that any violence in him must control him as it had his own father.

Now the short summary:

> Fisher's father sometimes reluctantly spanked her as punishment, but once when she deliberately dropped her baby brother he struck her

suddenly and violently. Her father had not escaped the "chain of violence" begun by his own father's regular beatings, but the incident released him from his fear that the chain must control him.

(We're suggesting that you write summaries for yourself, but the technique is also useful when you discuss other people's works in your writing. Then you must use your own words or use quotation marks for the author's words, and either way you must acknowledge the source in a citation. See pp. 672–82.)

Reading Critically

Summarizing will start you toward understanding the author's meaning, but it won't take you as far as you're capable of going, or as far as you'll need to go in school or work or just to live well in our demanding Information Age. Passive, rote learning (such as memorizing the times tables in arithmetic) won't do. You require techniques for comprehending what you encounter. But more: You need tools for discovering what's beneath the surface of an essay or case study or business letter or political message. You need ways to discriminate between the trustworthy and the not so and to apply what's valid in your own work and life.

We're talking here about critical thinking, reading, and writing—not "negative," the common conception of *critical*, but "thorough, thoughtful, question-asking, judgment-forming." When you approach something critically, you harness your faculties, your fund of knowledge, and your experiences to understand, appreciate, and evaluate the object. Using this book—guided by questions on meaning, writing strategy, and language—you'll read an essay and ask what the author's purpose and main idea are, how clear they are, and how well supported. You'll isolate which writing techniques the author has used to special advantage, what hits you as particularly fresh, clever, or wise—and what *doesn't* work, too. You'll discover exactly what the writer is saying, how he or she says it, and whether, in the end, it was worth saying. In class discussions and in writing, you'll tell others what you think and why.

Critical reading is a process involving several overlapping operations: analysis, inference, synthesis, and evaluation.

Analysis.   Say you're listening to a new album by a band called the Alley Cats. Without thinking much about it, you isolate melodies, song lyrics, and instrumentals—in other words, you ANALYZE the album by separating it into its parts. Analysis is a way of thinking so basic to us that it has its own chapter (6) in this book. For reading in this book, you'll consciously analyze essays by looking at the author's main idea, support for the idea, special writing strategies, and other elements.

Analysis underlies many of the other methods of development discussed in this book, so that while you are analyzing a subject you might also (even unconsciously) begin classifying it, or comparing it with something else, or figuring out what caused it. For instance, you might compare the Alley Cats' new instrumentals with those on their earlier albums, or you might notice that the lyrics seem to be influenced by another band's. Similarly, in analyzing a poem you might compare several images of water, or in analyzing a journal article in psychology you might consider how the author's theories affect her interpretations of behavior.

Inference.   Say that after listening to the Alley Cats' new album, you conclude that it reveals a preoccupation with traditional blues music and themes. Now you are using INFERENCE, drawing conclusions about a work based on your store of information and experience, your knowledge of the creator's background and biases, and your analysis. When you infer, you add to the work, making explicit what was only implicit.

In critical reading, inference is especially important in discovering a writer's ASSUMPTIONS: opinions or beliefs, often unstated, that direct the writer's choices of ideas, support, writing strategies, and language. A writer who favors gun control may assume without saying so that some individual rights (such as the right to bear arms) may be infringed for the good of the community. A writer who opposes gun control may assume the opposite—that in this case the individual's right is superior to the community's.

Synthesis.   What are the Alley Cats trying to accomplish with their new album? Is it different from their previous album in its understanding of the blues? Answering such questions leads you into SYNTHESIS, linking elements into a whole, or linking two or more wholes. During synthesis, you use your special aptitudes, interests, and training to reconstitute the work so that it now contains not just the original elements but also your sense of their underpinnings and relationships. About an essay you might ask why the author elicits contradictory feelings from readers, or what this essay has to do with that other essay, or what this essay has to do with your life.

Analysis, inference, and synthesis overlap—so much so that it's often impossible to distinguish one from the other during critical reading. To stave off confusion, in this book we use the word *analysis* to cover all of these operations: identifying elements, drawing conclusions about them, *and* reconstituting them.

Evaluation.   Not all critical reading involves EVALUATION, or judging the quality of the work. You'll probably form a judgment of the Alley Cats' new album (is the band getting better or just standing still?), but often you (and your teachers) will be satisfied with a nonjudgmental reading of a work. ("Nonjudgmental" does not mean "uncritical": You will still be expected to analyze, infer, and synthesize.) When you *do* evaluate, you determine adequacy, significance, value. You answer a question such as whether an essay moves you as it was intended to, or whether the author has proved a case, or whether the argument is even worthwhile.

The following comments on M. F. K. Fisher's "The Broken Chain" show how a critical reading can work. The headings "Meaning," "Writing Strategy" (p. 19), and "Language" (p. 21) correspond to those organizing the questions at the end of each essay.

Meaning

"No man but a blockhead," declared Samuel Johnson, "ever wrote except for money." Perhaps the eighteenth-century critic, journalist, and dictionary maker was remembering his own days as a literary drudge in London's Grub Street; but surely most people who write often do so for other reasons.

When you read an essay, you'll find it rewarding to ask, "What is this writer's PURPOSE?" By purpose, we mean the writer's apparent reason for writing: what he or she was trying to achieve with readers. A purpose is as essential to a good, pointed essay as a destination is to a trip. It affects every choice or decision the writer makes. (On vacation, of course, carefree people sometimes climb into a car without a thought and go happily rambling around; but if a writer rambles like that in an essay, the reader may plead, "Let me out!")

In making a simple statement of a writer's purpose, we might say that the writer writes *to entertain* readers, or *to explain* something to them, or *to persuade* them. To state a purpose more fully, we might say that a writer writes not just to persuade but "to tell readers a story to illustrate the point that when you are being cheated it's a good idea to complain," or not just to entertain but "to tell a horror story to make chills shoot down readers' spines." If the essay is an argument meant to convince, a fuller statement of its writer's purpose might be "to win readers over to the writer's opinion that San Antonio is the most livable city in the United States," or "to persuade readers to take action by writing their representatives and urging more federal spending for the rehabilitation of criminals."

"But," the skeptic might object, "how can I know a writer's purpose? I'm no mind reader, and even if I were, how could I tell what E. B. White was trying to do? He's dead and buried." And yet writers living and dead have revealed their purposes in their writing, just as visibly as a hiker leaves footprints.

What is M. F. K. Fisher's purpose in writing? If you want to be more exact, you can speak of her *main purpose* or *central purpose*, for "The Broken Chain" fulfills more than one. Fisher clearly wants to tell her readers something about her parents and herself as a child. She is not averse to entertaining readers with details capturing the fierce moodiness of a twelve-year-old. But Fisher's main purpose is larger than these and encompasses them. She has heard much lately of child abuse, and a recollection from her own childhood might throw some light on the problem. She wants to help.

How can you tell a writer's purpose? This is where analysis, inference, and synthesis come in. Fisher hints at her purpose in the first paragraph, asking "When is [the chain of violence] broken? . . . How?" The rest of her essay answers these questions: At least for her father, the chain broke when he no longer feared it (para. 20). The opening questions and last paragraph form the THESIS of the essay — the point made for a purpose, the overwhelming idea that the writer communicates. Some writers will come right out and sum up this central idea in a sentence or two (the THESIS SENTENCE). In her response to M. F. K. Fisher's essay titled "Has the Chain Been Broken?" (p. 34), the student Christine D'Angelo states her gist in her opening paragraph:

> The answer [to the difference Fisher sees between spanking and hitting] lies in her distinction between justified and unjustified violence.

D'Angelo's thesis is obvious early on. Sometimes, however, like Fisher, a writer will introduce and conclude the thesis at the beginning and end. Other writers won't come out and state their theses in any neat capsule at all. Even so, the main point of a well-written essay will make itself clear to you — so clear that you can sum it up in a sentence or two of your own. What might that sentence be for Fisher's essay? Perhaps this: The chain of violence against children may be broken when a former victim understands that violence need not take control even when it is expressed.

It's part of your job as an active reader to answer questions like these: What is the writer's purpose? How does it govern the writer's choices? Is it actually achieved? Does the thesis come through? How is it supported? Is the support adequate to convince you of the author's sincerity and truthfulness? (Such conviction is a basic transaction between writer and reader, even when the writer isn't seeking the reader's outright agreement or action.) Sometimes you'll be confused by a writer's point — "What *is* this about?" — and sometimes your confusion won't yield to repeated careful readings. That's when you'll want to toss the book or magazine aside in exasperation, but you won't always have the choice: A school or work assignment or just an urge to figure out the writer's problem may keep you at it. Then it'll be up to you to figure out why the writer fails — in essence, to clarify what's unclear — by, say, digging for buried assumptions that you may not agree with or by spotting where facts and examples fall short.

With some reservations, we think M. F. K. Fisher achieves her purpose. Her essay is engaging. She gives plenty of details to place us in her shoes, to experience what she experienced. Her story about her father rings true, as does the lesson to be learned from it. The story and the lesson do lean on certain assumptions, though, and these are bound to influence a reader's response. One is that the father's spankings are justified and, because they are reluctant and unemotional, do not constitute violence—at least not the abusive violence that concerns Fisher. (This is the assumption that D'Angelo examines in "Has the Chain Been Broken?") Even if the spankings are justified, a second, more ticklish assumption is that their manner is appropriate. Fisher describes herself merely as feeling "silly . . . baring my pubescent bottom" for the spanking (para. 13), but these days many readers might condemn her father for expecting her to undress. If you are one of these readers, the essay may be hard to accept. For us, such objections are understandable but ultimately irrelevant because Fisher was writing of a time (1920) when spankings and whippings (even on bare bottoms) were common methods of disciplining children.

Analyzing writers' purposes and their successes and failures makes you an alert and critical reader. Applied to your own writing, this analysis also gives you a decided advantage, for when you write with a clear-cut purpose in mind, aware of your assumptions, you head toward a goal. Of course, sometimes you just can't know what you are going to say until you say it, to echo the English novelist E. M. Forster. In such a situation, your purpose emerges as you write. But the earlier and more exactly you define your purpose, the easier you'll find it to fulfill.

Writing Strategy

To the extent that M. F. K. Fisher holds our interest and engages our sympathies, it pays to ask, "How does she succeed?" (When a writer bores or angers us, we ask why he or she fails.) As we've already hinted, success and failure lie in the eye of the beholder: The reader knows. Almost all writing is a *transaction* between a writer and an audience, maybe one reader, maybe millions. Conscious writers make choices intended to get their audience on their side so that they can achieve their purpose. These choices are what we mean by STRATEGY in writing.

Fisher's audience was the readers of her memoir, *To Begin Again*. She might have assumed that many of these readers would be familiar with her earlier writing and predisposed to like her work. But even for such an appreciative audience, and certainly for newcomers, Fisher would have to be interesting and focused, making readers (us) care about

this piece. She grabs our attention right at the start by connecting with
the disturbing and controversial issue of physical abuse. She doesn't
oversell, though—she hasn't been abused herself—so she whets our appetites without setting us up for disappointment. When she begins her
story, she keeps involving us by referring to common feelings and experiences in memorably specific terms. Even if we've never been spanked, we
can feel her father's "long bony knees" and the "sharp taps" of the brush
(para. 2). We share Fisher's resentment of her sister, who "made it bitterly clear to me that I was an utter fool to take punishment for her own
small jaunty misdoings" (5). We know that adolescent feeling of "stupid petulance" that caused Fisher to drop her brother (6) and her "raging with insulted anger" at being struck by her father (7). We see that
"little room under the eaves" where Fisher found herself "full of scowling puzzlements" (13). We submit as her mother "wrapped her arms
around me with a tenderness I had never felt from her before" (14), "an
embrace that she was actually giving to her husband" (19). We believe
Fisher because of how vivid and precise she is all along.

Part of a writer's strategy—Fisher's, too—is in the methods used
to elicit and arrange details such as these. Fisher draws mainly on two
methods: narration (telling a story) and description (conveying the evidence of the senses). But she also gives examples of spankings and her
feelings about them (2–5), contrasts the "heavy dutiful slaps" of a
spanking with the "wild stinging blow" of being struck (13), analyzes
her own reactions (13), defines the "chain of violence" (17, 19), and
examines the causes and effects of child abuse (15–20). In short, Fisher
uses nearly every method discussed in this book, asking each one to
perform the work it's best suited for. As we noted earlier, one method or
another may predominate in an essay (as narration and description do
in Fisher's), but other methods will help the writer explore the subject
in paragraphs or shorter passages.

Aside from the details and the methods used to develop them,
probably no writing strategy is as crucial to success as finding an appropriate structure. Writing that we find interesting and clear and convincing almost always has UNITY (everything relates to the main idea)
and COHERENCE (the relations between parts are clear). When we find an
essay wanting, it may be because the writer got lost in digressions or
couldn't make the parts fit together.

Sometimes structure almost takes care of itself. When she chose
the method of narration, for instance, Fisher also chose a chronological
sequence (reporting events as they occurred in time). But she still had
to emphasize certain events and de-emphasize others. She lingers over
the important moments: dropping her brother and being struck by her
father (6–7), the following encounters with her father (8–13) and her
mother (14–18). She compresses all the events that contribute back-

ground but are not the heart of the story, notably the previous spankings (2–4) and taking the blame for her sister (5).

This kind of handiwork will be even more evident in essays where the method of development doesn't dictate an overall structure. Then the writer must mold and shape ideas and details to pique, hold, and direct our interest. One writer may hit us with the big idea right at the start and then fill us in on the details. Another writer may gradually unfold the idea, leading to a surprise. One writer may arrange information in order of increasing importance; another may do the opposite. Like all other choices in writing, these come out of the writer's purpose: What is the aim? What do I want readers to think or feel? What's the best way to achieve that? As you'll see in this book, there are as many options as there are writers.

Language

To examine the element of language is often to go even more deeply into an essay and how it was made. Fisher, you'll notice, is a writer whose language is rich and varied. It isn't bookish. Many expressions from common speech lend her prose vigor and naturalness. "I always felt terrible that it was dragged out," she writes (5). Her father "gave me a slap across the side of my head that sent me halfway across the room against the big old sideboard" (6). When spanked, she says, "I did not even breathe fast, on purpose" (10). "I have never been the same—" she concludes, "still stupid but never unthinking" (19). These relaxed sentences suit the material: Fisher's recollections of herself as a fresh, moody adolescent. At the same time, Fisher is an adult addressing adults, and her vocabulary reflects as much. Consult a dictionary if you need help defining *vicariously* (1), *ritualistic* (2), *conditioned* (4), *petulance, insolently* (6), *disdainfully* (7), *pubescent* (13), or *haughty* (14).

Fisher's words and sentence structures not only sharpen and animate her meaning but also convey her attitudes and elicit them from readers. They create a TONE, the equivalent of tone of voice in speaking. Whether it's angry, sarcastic, or sad, joking or serious, tone carries almost as much information about a writer's purpose as the words themselves do. Fisher's tone is sincere, matter-of-fact. In true adolescent fashion, she occasionally veers into indignation or embarrassment or compassion; but she never indulges in histrionics, which would overwhelm the sensations and make her account untrustworthy.

With everything you read, as with "The Broken Chain," it's instructive to study the writer's tone so that you are aware of whether and how it affects you. Pay particular attention to the CONNOTATIONS of words — their implied meanings, their associations. We sympathize when Fisher takes those "twelve expert upward stinging whacks" (10) — stinging whacks *hurt*. We identify with her "scowling puzzlements" (13)—the anger and hurt are there and also the confusion. When one writer calls the homeless "society's downtrodden" and another calls them "human refuse," we know something of their attitudes and can use that knowledge to analyze and evaluate what they say about homelessness.

One other use of language is worth noting in Fisher's essay and in many others in this book: FIGURES OF SPEECH, bits of colorful language not meant to be taken literally. In one instance, Fisher makes her adolescent gangliness vivid with *hyperbole*, or exaggeration, describing herself as "all skinny arms and legs" (10). Most memorable is the extended *metaphor* of the "chain of violence" (17, 19–20)—not an actual, physical chain, of course, but a pattern of behavior passed from generation to generation. This chain is "invisible"; it had "bound" Fisher's father since childhood; and finally, as the title tells us, it was "broken." Such a colorful comparison—a chain and a destructive behavior—gives Fisher's essay flavor and force. (More examples of figures of speech can be found under Useful Terms, p. 683.)

Many questions in this book point to such figures, to oddities of tone, or to troublesome or unfamiliar words. We don't wish to swamp you in details or make you a slave to your dictionary; we only want to get you thinking about how meaning and effect begin at the most basic level, with the word. As a writer, you can have no traits more valuable to you than a fondness and respect for words and a yen to experiment with them.

WRITING

Suggestions for Writing

Throughout this book every essay is followed by several "Suggestions for Writing." The first of these encourages you to respond to the essay in two ways: by approaching it in your journal (especially useful if you feel shy or blocked about responding) and by transforming that journal entry into an essay for an audience. One of the other writing suggestions, labeled "Critical Writing," asks you to take a deliberate, critical look at the essay. And a final suggestion, labeled "Connections," helps you relate the essay to one or two other essays in the book. You may not wish to take these suggestions exactly as worded; they may merely urge your own thoughts toward what you want to say. Here are four possibilities for M. F. K. Fisher's "The Broken Chain."

1. **JOURNAL WRITING.** Write about a moment in your childhood or adolescence that changed you or someone you know or both. Try to capture the details of the incident: where, why, and how it happened; how the participants looked and behaved; actual dialogue.

FROM JOURNAL TO ESSAY. Following Fisher's example, shape your journal writing into an essay full of concrete, specific details so that your readers understand the incident and its effects. Use a chronological organization, and take advantage of your distance from the incident to evaluate how it changed you or someone else.

2. If you have had some experience with physical abuse (as a counselor, bystander, victim, abuser) and you care to write about it, compose an essay that develops a thesis about the problem. You do not have to write in the first person (*I*) unless you want to. Draw on personal experience, observation, or reading as needed to support your thesis. (If you draw on reading, be sure to acknowledge your sources.)

3. **CRITICAL WRITING.** Write an essay in which you analyze and evaluate Fisher's attitudes toward physical punishment. Consider what Fisher actually says about spanking and what her words convey about her feelings. (You will have to infer some of her assumptions.) When you are sure you understand Fisher's point of view, explain it and then evaluate it, using specific evidence from the essay and from your own sources (experience, observation, reading). Do you agree with Fisher? Does she omit any important considerations? In your view, do her attitudes toward physical punishment weaken or strengthen the essay? Why?

4. **CONNECTIONS.** Both Fisher's "The Broken Chain" and Brad Manning's "Arm Wrestling with My Father" (p. 100) address the ways love and standards of behavior are passed from one generation to another. Compare and contrast these two essays, looking closely at how Fisher's and Manning's parents love and educate their children. Be specific in your analysis, using evidence from the essays and, if you wish, your own experience. (If you need help with the method of comparison and contrast, see Chap. 4.)

The Writing Process

To complete an assignment like those above, you need in a way to duplicate the reading process, moving from sketchy impressions to rich understandings as you gain mastery over your material. Like critical reading, writing is no snap: As this book's Writers on Writing attest, even professionals do not produce thoughtful, detailed, attention-getting essays in a single draft. Writing well demands, and rewards, a willingness to work recursively—to begin tentatively, perhaps, and then to double back, to welcome change and endure frustration, to recognize and exploit progress. Something of this recursive process is captured in the essay-in-progress beginning on page 29. A student, Christine D'Angelo, wrote this piece for *The Bedford Reader* in response to M. F. K. Fisher's essay. D'Angelo provided us with her notes and drafts, along with her comments on her progress at each stage.

For you, as for D'Angelo and most writers, the recursive writing process may proceed through three rough stages: discovery, drafting, and revision.

Discovery

During the first phase of the writing process, DISCOVERY, you'll feel your way into an assignment. This is the time when you critically read any text that is part of the assignment and begin to generate ideas for writing. When writing about essays in this book, you'll be reading and rereading and writing, coming to understand the work, figuring out what you think of it, figuring out what you have to *say* about it. From notes during reading to jotted phrases, lists, or half-finished paragraphs after reading, this stage should always be a writing stage. You may even produce a rough draft. The important thing is to let yourself go: Do not, above all, concern yourself with making beautiful sentences or correcting errors. Such self-consciousness at this stage will only jam the flow of thoughts. If your idea of "audience" is "teacher with sharp pencil" (not, by the way, a fair picture), then temporarily blank out your audience, too.

A few techniques can help you let go and open up during the discovery stage.

Keeping a journal.   A JOURNAL is a notebook or tablet or computer file where you record your thoughts *for yourself*. (Teachers sometimes assign journals and periodically collect them to see how students are doing, but even in these situations the journal is for yourself.) In keeping a journal, you don't have to worry about being understood by a reader or making mistakes: You are free to write however you want to get your thoughts down.

Kept faithfully—say, for ten or fifteen minutes a day—a journal can limber up your writing muscles, giving you more confidence and flexibility as a writer. It can also provide a place to work out personal difficulties, explore half-formed ideas, make connections between courses, or respond to reading. Here, for instance, is Christine D'Angelo's initial journal entry on M. F. K. Fisher's "The Broken Chain":

> I liked this—the writer makes me remember what it's like to be really mad at my parents for being mean, even when part of me knows they might be right (like the time I stole the car and got grounded!). But I don't get why Fisher makes such a big deal about the difference between a slap from her father when she dropped the baby and the regular spankings she got from him. She's getting hit either way, right? Got to get at the difference Fisher sees.

Freewriting.   Another technique for limbering up, but more in response to specific writing assignments than as a regular habit, is *freewriting*. When freewriting, you write without stopping for ten or fifteen minutes, not halting to reread, criticize, edit, or admire. You can use partial sentences, abbreviations, question marks for uncertain words. If you can't think of anything to write about, jot "can't think" over and over until new words come (they will).

You can use this technique to find a subject for writing or to explore ideas on a subject you already have. Of course, when you've finished, you'll need to separate the promising passages from the dead ends, using those promising bits as the starting place for more freewriting or perhaps a freely written first draft.

Using the methods of development.   Since each method of development provides a different perspective on your subject, you can use the methods singly or together to discover possible ideas or directions. Say you already have a sense of your purpose for writing: Then you can search the methods for one or more that will help you achieve that purpose by revealing and focusing your ideas. Or say you're still in the dark about your purpose: Then you can apply each method of development systematically to throw light on your subject, as a headlight illuminates a midnight road, so that you see its possible angles.

The introductions to Chapters 1–10 suggest the purposes each method is suited for and some specific ways the method can open up your subject. For now, we've given some examples of how the methods can reveal responses, either direct or indirect, to Fisher's "The Broken Chain."

- *Narration:* Tell a story about the subject, possibly to enlighten or entertain readers or to explain something to them. Answer the journalist's questions: who, what, when, where, why, how? For instance, consider an incident in your own life that changed you, as Fisher's experience changed her and her father.
- *Description:* To explain or evoke the subject, focus on its look, sound, feel, smell, taste—the evidence of the senses. For instance, examine Fisher's use of language to evoke sensation.
- *Example:* Point to instances, or illustrations, of the subject that clarify and support your idea about it. For instance, give examples that illustrate Fisher's use of language to portray herself as an adolescent.
- *Comparison and contrast:* Set the subject beside something else, noting similarities or differences or both, for the purpose of either explaining or evaluating. For instance, compare and contrast Fisher's views of spanking and hitting.
- *Process analysis:* Explain step by step how to do something or how something works—in other words, how a sequence of actions leads to a particular result. For instance, explain a process for disciplining children that does not involve physical punishment.
- *Division or analysis:* Slice the subject into its parts or elements in order to show how they relate and to explain your conclusions about the subject. For instance, analyze Fisher's tone and its relation to her purpose.

- *Classification:* To show resemblances and differences among many related subjects, or the many forms of a subject, sort them into kinds or groups. For example, classify different kinds of family discipline, physical and otherwise.
- *Cause and effect:* Explain why or what if, showing reasons for or consequences of the subject. For instance, explain why parents strike their children.
- *Definition:* Trace a boundary around the subject to pin down its meaning. For instance, define *violence* or *child abuse*.
- *Argument and persuasion:* Formulate an opinion or make a proposal about the subject. For instance, argue that Fisher's father did (or did not) abuse her by spanking her.

Drafting

Sooner or later, the discovery stage yields to DRAFTING: arranging ideas in sequence, filling in their details, spelling out their relationships. For most, this is the occasion for further exploration, but with a sharper focus. Here you may be concerned with clarifying your purpose. You may experiment with tone. You may try out different structures. It's best to stay fairly loose during drafting so that you're free to wander down intriguing avenues or consider changing direction altogether. As during discovery, you'll want to keep your eyes on what's ahead, not obsess over the pebbles underfoot—the possible mistakes, "wrong" words, and bumpy sentences that you can attend to later. This is an important message that many inexperienced writers miss: It's okay to make mistakes. You can fix them later.

One important element that should receive some attention during drafting, or shortly after, is the THESIS, often stated in a THESIS SENTENCE or two. The thesis, to recap page 18, is the main idea of a piece of writing, its focus. Without a focus, either expressed or implied, an essay wanders and irritates and falls flat. With a focus, an essay is much more likely to click.

We've already given one example of a thesis sentence from Christine D'Angelo's "Has the Chain Been Broken?" (see p. 18). Here are some other examples from the essays in this book:

> These were two strong men, these oddly different generals [Ulysses S. Grant and Robert E. Lee], and they represented the strengths of two conflicting currents that, through them, had come into final collision. (Bruce Catton, "Grant and Lee: A Study in Contrasts")

> Inanimate objects are classified into three major categories—those that don't work, those that break down and those that get lost. (Russell Baker, "The Plot Against People")

It is possible to stop most drug addiction in the United States within a very short time. Simply make all drugs available and sell them at cost. (Gore Vidal, "Drugs")

These three diverse examples share a few important qualities:

- First, in these thesis sentences the authors assert opinions, taking positions on their subjects. They do not merely state facts, as in "Grant and Lee both signed the document ending the Civil War" or "Grant and Lee were different men."
- Second, each thesis sentence projects a single idea. The thesis may have parts (such as Baker's three categories of objects), but the parts fit under a single umbrella idea.
- Third (as you will see when you read the essays themselves), each thesis sentence accurately forecasts the scope of its essay, neither taking on too much nor leaving out essential parts.
- Finally, these thesis statements hint about each writer's purpose — we can tell that Catton and Baker want to explain, whereas Vidal wants mainly to persuade. (Explaining and persuading overlap a great deal; we're talking here about the writer's *primary* purpose.)

Every single essay in this book has a *thesis* because a central, controlling idea is a requirement of good writing. But we can give no rock-hard rules about the *thesis sentence*—how long it must be or where it must appear in an essay or even whether it must appear. Indeed, the essays in this book demonstrate that writers have great flexibility in these areas. For your own writing, we advise stating your thesis explicitly and putting it near the beginning of your essay—at least until you've gained experience as a writer. The stated thesis will help you check that you have that necessary focus, and the early placement will tell your readers what to expect from your writing.

Revision

If it helps you produce writing, you may want to view your draft as a kind of dialogue with readers, fulfilling their expectations, answering the questions you imagine they would ask. But some writers save this kind of thinking for the next stage, REVISION. Literally "re-seeing," revision is the price you pay for the freedom to experiment and explore. Initially the work centers on you and your material, but gradually it shifts into that transaction we spoke of earlier between you and your reader. And that means stepping outside the intense circle of you-and-the-material to see the work as a reader will, with whatever qualities you imagine that reader to have. Questions after most essays in this book ask you to analyze how the writers' ideas of their readers have influenced their writing strategies, and how you as a reader react to the writers' choices. These analyses will teach you much about responding to your own readers.

Like many writers, you will be able to concentrate better if you approach revision as at least a two-step process. First you question fundamental matters, using a checklist like this one:

QUESTIONS FOR REVISION

Will my purpose be clear to readers? Have I achieved it?
What is my thesis? Have I proved it?
Is the essay unified (all parts relate to the thesis)?
Is the essay coherent (the parts relate clearly)?
Will readers be able to follow the organization?
Have I given enough details, examples, and other specifics for readers to understand me and stay with me?
Is the tone appropriate for my purpose?
Have I used the methods of development to full advantage?

When these deeper issues are resolved, you then look at the surface of the writing in the step also called *editing*:

QUESTIONS FOR EDITING

Do PARAGRAPH breaks help readers grasp related information?
Do TRANSITIONS tell readers where I am making connections, additions, and other changes?
Are sentences smooth and concise? Do they use PARALLELISM, EMPHASIS, and other techniques to clarify meaning?
Do words say what I mean, and are they as vivid as I can make them?
Are my grammar and punctuation correct?
Are any words misspelled?

Two-step revision is like inspecting a ship before it sails. First check under the water for holes to make sure the boat will stay afloat. Then look above the water at what will move the boat and please the passengers: intact sails, sparkling hardware, gleaming decks.

A Note on Collaboration

Your writing teacher may ask you to spend some time talking with your classmates, as a whole class or in small groups or pairs. You may analyze the essays in this book (perhaps answering the end-of-essay questions), read each other's journals or drafts, or plot revision strategies. Such conversation and collaboration—voicing, listening to, and arguing about ideas—can help you develop more confidence in your writing and give you a clearer sense of audience. One classmate may show you that your introduction, which you thought was lame, really worked to get her involved in your essay. Another classmate may question you in a way that helps you see how the introduction sets up expectations in the reader, expectations you're obliged to fulfill.

You may at first be anxious about collaboration: How can I judge others' writing? How can I stand others' criticism of my own writing? These are natural worries, and your teacher will try to help you with both of them—for instance, by providing a checklist to guide your critique of your classmates' writing. (The first checklist on the opposite page works for reading others' drafts as well as your own.) With practice and plentiful feedback, you'll soon appreciate how much you're learning about writing and what a good effect that knowledge has on your work. You're writing for an audience, after all, and you can't beat the immediate feedback of a live one.

An Essay-in-Progress

In the following pages, you have a chance to watch Christine D'Angelo as she develops an essay through journal notes and several drafts. Her topic is the third one on page 23, about M. F. K. Fisher's attitudes toward physical punishment—a topic she had already started exploring in her journal (p. 24). D'Angelo's journal notes during each stage enlighten us about her thinking as she proceeds through the writing process.

Journal Notes on Reading

"I have never been beaten"—she doesn't consider her father's punishment as beating. (¶ 1)

Very conscious of how to play role of victim (excellent description of kids that age).

> *—"I often cried a little, to prove that I had learned my lesson" (¶ 2)*
> *—wishes she were maimed (¶ 13)*
> *—"I wanted to stay haughty and abused with her" (¶ 14)*

"Your mother wants you to be spanked" (¶ 9): typical of fathers' tendency not to take responsibility for feelings. More common when trying to express tenderness: "Your mother was worried sick about you," "Your mother and I are going to miss you," "You know we love you," etc. The potentially embarrassing feelings are diluted.

She doesn't seem to consider spankings as violent:

> *"<u>Once</u> Rex hit me" (¶ 6)*
> *"<u>And</u> you hit me" (¶ 12)*

Calling father by first name: distancing?
("Father" vs. "Rex")

Justifies father's actions

> —he *"disliked this duty very much"* (¶ 3)
> —*"fatherly spankings"* (¶ 5)
> —*"two people whom I had betrayed into this"* (¶ 18)

Is father's reaction justified by narrator's act? Both are acts of violence. It's easy to understand his anger.

"Once Rex hit me" and "And you hit me" literally confusing until you become aware that she doesn't count spanking as "hitting."

Mother shares same refusal to see spanking as violent.

Fisher's ideas about physical punishment outdated. These days many people would consider spanking abusive.

I think I have a lot of evidence here to answer question 3, about Fisher's attitudes toward physical punishment and whether they weaken or strengthen the essay.
It's clear that she doesn't think of the spankings as violent. I like the idea of talking about how Fisher's assumptions confuse the reader who doesn't share them. I was confused that she opened with "I have never been beaten" and then recounted many spankings. (This could be a good introduction.)
Even though they're interesting ideas, I don't think I'll be able to use anything about the narrator knowing how to play the victim or fathers' inability to express their emotions. (Not in this paper at least.)

First Draft

How is the reader of "The Broken Chain" to reconcile the narrator's account of the physical punishment she suffered from her father up to the age of twelve with her assumption in the very first paragraph that "I have never been beaten"?

Knowing that the father has a history of spanking the narrator, the reader has a hard time interpreting her statement "Once Rex hit me." Why does she say "once" if he actually hit her quite often? In the key scene in which the narrator is spanked for having dropped her baby brother on the floor, her father says "That's the last time," after he has finished spanking her. To which she responds, "And you hit me." "Once" and "And" make no sense. Until we realize that spanking seems to fall under the realm of just punishment but on the other hand violence outside the clear realm of punishment is unjustifiable.

The narrator's mother shares this distinction. Describing her husband's history of violence in the family, she maintains that up until now he had succeeded in breaking the chain. "He has never struck any living thing in anger," she says, "Until today." In other words, the spankings have never counted as part of the chain of violence.

It is interesting to note that the narrator never questions why it should be the father who struggles constantly to keep his violence in check, who has this "duty" rather than the mother. After all, isn't such a choice rather like putting a dieter in charge of guarding the refrigerator?

When we understand that the narrator does not consider her father's spankings to be violent, we can only call this assumption into question, in fact it is easier to justify the father's response to the dumping of the baby on the floor, itself a violent act that could have been deadly, than his more calculated, repeated capital punishment. If the father is so concerned with breaking the "chain of violence" in his family, why can he not look to alternative methods of punishment? And again, why is it him and not the mother who must carry out this punishment?

I can only speculate on Fisher's reasons for not classifying her father's spankings as violent. But capital punishment is no longer considered an acceptable form of punishment--it is recognized as violence in its own right. In writing this essay, Fisher's purpose was to expose in a family the "chain of violence" against children passed down from generation to generation. But she herself is too blind to see that spanking is a form of violence too.

Journal Notes for Revision

This gets at what I want to say pretty well, but there are some big holes. I need an explicit thesis sentence — an answer to the question I pose in the first paragraph — to tie the whole thing together. The last sentence of the second paragraph is really my thesis: that the narrator makes a distinction between two kinds of violence — one kind (the spankings) being OK, the other (the slap) unjustified. The rest of the paper goes on to explain this distinction and call it into question. I just need to make this thesis clearer and bring it up into the first paragraph.

The second paragraph needs to be developed more, probably expanded into two paragraphs. I think the first paragraph can pretty much stay the way it is, talking about readers' confusion. But the idea of the last sentence — now the thesis — needs to be fleshed out, expanded into an entire paragraph. Need to define the narrator's distinction between justified and unjustified violence.

What to do with the fourth paragraph asking why only the father, not the mother, has the duty of spanking? It's an interesting point, but it goes nowhere and doesn't fit in with the rest of the paper. Think it's going to have to be cut. (Same for last sentence of the next paragraph.)

The last sentence of the conclusion is too angry and judgmental. Instead, I could say something about how the very fact that Fisher doesn't see the spankings as violent just goes to show how subtle the "chain" is.

Title??? It should work in the thesis somehow.

Big mistake: spanking is corporal, *not* capital, *punishment.*

Revised Draft

Has the Chain Been Broken?
Two Ideas of Violence in "The Broken Chain"

How is the reader of "The Broken Chain" to reconcile the narrator's account of the physical punishment she suffered from her father up to the
age of twelve with her assumption in the very first paragraph that "I have
never been beaten"? *The answer lies in the difference she makes between what is
in her view justified and unjustified violence.*
        ¶ *This distinction is never made explicit in the essay and is apt to lead to
confusion on the readers' part.*
    ∧ Knowing that the father has a history of spanking the narrator,
the reader has a hard time interpreting her statement "Once Rex hit me."
                                              Likewise,   i
~~Why does she say "once" if he actually hit her quite often?~~ ~~I~~n the key
scene in which the narrator is spanked for having dropped her baby
brother on the floor, her father says "That's the last time," after he has
finished spanking her. To which she responds, "And you hit me."
What does she mean by "And"?
~~"Once" and "And" make no sense. Until we realize that spanking seems to~~
~~fall under the realm of just punishment but on the other hand violence out-~~
~~side the clear realm of punishment is unjustifiable.~~

*The "Once" and "And" make no sense until we realize that they do not refer to
the fathers spankings. They refer to his violent, immediate reaction to the
narrator's dropping the baby. It becomes clear that "spanking" and "hitting" have
different values for the narrator depending on the intention behind it. Spanking, in
her eyes, falls under the realm of just punishment, unpleasant though it may be,
she sees it as an appropriate response to her own crime. On the other hand,
violence outside the clear realm of punishment, in this case the blow, is
unjustifiable, despite the fact that both are responses to the same wrongdoing
(and each probably hurts about as much as the other!).*
                        between "just" and "unjust" violence.
The narrator's mother shares this distinction∧ ~~D~~escribing her
husband's history of violence in the family, she maintains that up until now
he had succeeded in breaking the chain. "He has never struck any living
thing in anger," she says, "Until today." In other words, the spankings have
never counted as part of the chain of violence.

~~It is~~ interesting to note that the narrator never questions ~~why it~~ should
be the father who struggles ~~constantly~~ to ~~keep his~~ violence in check, who
has this "duty" rather ~~than~~ the mother. After ~~all,~~ ~~isn't~~ such a choice rather
~~like putting~~ a dieter in charge of guarding the refrigerator?

When we understand that the narrator does not consider her father's
spankings to be violent, we can only call this assumption into question, in

fact it is easier to justify the father's response to the dumping of the baby

on the floor, itself a violent act that could have been deadly, than his more

corporal
calculated, repeated ~~capital~~ punishment. If the father is so concerned

with breaking the "chain of violence" in his family, why can he not look to

In law, a premeditated crime is more
alternative methods of punishment? ~~And again, why is it him and not the~~
serious than one committed on the spur of the moment.
~~mother who must carry out this punishment?~~

I can only speculate on Fisher's reasons for not classifying her father's

spankings as violent. *Perhaps she loved and respected her parents too much to
judge them objectively, even sixty years after the essay.*
corporal
But ~~capital~~ punishment is no longer considered an acceptable form

of punishment -- it is recognized as violence in its own right. In writing

this essay, Fisher's purpose was to expose in a family the "chain of

violence" against children passed down from generation to generation. But
her refusal to recognize corporal punishment as a form of violence is a good example
~~she herself is too blind to see that spanking is a form of violence too.~~
of how subtle the chain is, and why it is so hard to break.

Journal Notes for Editing and Final Draft

*This hangs together much better now; more coherent. Every paragraph has
something to do with the distinction between "good" and "bad" violence. The new
title incorporates both the thesis (the two standards of violence) and the hint in
the conclusion about the chain not necessarily being broken.*

*The first sentence is abrupt. Need a "cushion" to ease the reader into the
paper.*

*I think saying "the narrator" is too impersonal for an autobiographical essay.
Since this is a personal essay, not fiction, I could just say "Fisher." And since the
events in the essay really happened, I should change them to the past tense,
keeping present tense when referring to Fisher as writer, in 1983. This will help
make it clear that there are really two "Fishers" in question.*

*Conclusion: Last sentence is still too angry. I could change "refusal" to
"inability," taking some of the blame off Fisher.*

*Need to edit for rough or awkward sentences, spelling and grammar mistakes,
and poor word choice.*

Edited Paragraph

The "Once" and "And" make no sense until we realize that they ~~do not~~
not , *but*
refer∧to the fathers spankings∧ ~~They refer~~ to his violent, immediate
Fisher's
reaction to ~~the narrator's~~ dropping the baby. It becomes clear that
Fisher
"spanking" and "hitting" have different values for ~~the narrator~~ depending
them.
on the intention behind ~~it.~~ Spanking, in her eyes, falls under the realm
. U *have been,*
of just punishment/ ~~U~~npleasant though it may ~~be,~~ she sees it as an
misconduct. *But*
appropriate response to her own ~~crime. On the other hand,~~ violence outside

well-defined   ——   ——
the ~~clear~~ realm of punishment/ in this case the blow/ is unjustifiable,

despite the fact that both are responses to the same wrongdoing/(and
                         the same!).
~~each~~ probably hurt$ ~~about as much as the other!).~~

Final Draft

  We have annotated D'Angelo's final draft to show you something
of how it works. D'Angelo's purpose is to explain and dispute the contradiction she sees in Fisher's essay. For this purpose, she draws heavily
on DIVISION or ANALYSIS, examining the elements of the essay (especially
Fisher's words) and how they work together. Throughout, D'Angelo
provides EXAMPLES from Fisher's essay to illustrate her points.
  Within the two primary methods of division or analysis and example, D'Angelo also uses other methods to develop her ideas, especially CAUSE AND EFFECT, DEFINITION, and COMPARISON AND CONTRAST.

     Has the Chain Been Broken?

    Two Ideas of Violence in "The Broken Chain"

  There is a problem of definition in "The Broken   *Introduction sets up the*

Chain." How is the reader to reconcile M. F. K. Fisher's   *contradiction to be*
                                                    examined.
account of the physical punishment she suffered from her

father up to the age of twelve with her assertion in the

very first paragraph that "I have never been beaten"?

The answer lies in her distinction between justified and   *Thesis sentence*
                                                       establishes the main idea.
unjustified violence.

  This distinction is never made explicit in the essay.   *Division or analysis, with*
                                                   examples, structures the
Knowing that the father had a history of spanking Fisher,   *entire essay.*

the reader has a hard time interpreting her statement

"Once Rex hit me." Then after Fisher was spanked for

dropping her baby brother on the floor and her father

said, "That's the last time," she responded, "And you hit

me." What did she mean by "And"?

  The "Once" and "And" make no sense until we realize

that they refer not to the father's spankings but to his vi-

olent, immediate reaction to Fisher's dropping the baby. It

becomes clear that "spanking" and "hitting" have differ-   *Cause and effect explains*
                                                  why Fisher makes the
ent values for Fisher depending on the intention behind   *distinction. Definition*
                                                  and comparison and
them. Spanking, in her eyes, falls under the realm of just   *contrast clarify the*
                                                  distinction.
punishment. Unpleasant though it may have been, she

sees it as an appropriate response to her own misconduct.

But violence outside the well-defined realm of punishment--in this case the blow--is unjustifiable, despite the fact that both are responses to the same wrongdoing (and probably hurt the same!).

The mother shared Fisher's distinction between "just" and "unjust" violence. Describing the "chain of violence" passed down from generation to generation in her husband's family, she maintained that up until then he had succeeded in breaking the chain. "He has never struck any living thing in anger," she said. "Until today." In other words, the spankings never counted.

Comparison and contrast likens Fisher's and her mother's responses.

Once we understand that Fisher does not consider her father's spankings to be violent, we can only call this assumption into question. In fact, it is easier to justify the father's heated response to the dumping of the baby on the floor, a violent act that could have been deadly, than his more calculated, repeated corporal punishment. In law, a premeditated crime is more serious than one committed on the spur of the moment. If the father was so concerned with breaking the "chain of violence," why didn't he look into alternative methods of punishment?

Comparison and contrast supports D'Angelo's view.

One can only speculate on Fisher's reasons for not classifying her father's spankings as violent. Perhaps she loves and respects her parents too much to judge them objectively, even sixty years after the events of the essay. But physical punishment is no longer universally considered acceptable; it is recognized as violence in its own right. In writing this essay, Fisher intends to expose the "chain of violence" against children passed from generation to generation in a family. But her inability to recognize corporal punishment as a form of violence is a good example of how subtle the chain is, and why it is so hard to break.

Cause and effect proposes a reason for Fisher's view.

Comparison and contrast distinguishes past and present attitudes.

Conclusion ties together elements of Fisher's essay and D'Angelo's critique, ending with implications for the present.

PART ONE

THE METHODS

1

NARRATION
Telling a Story

THE METHOD

"What happened?" you ask a friend who sports a luminous black eye. Unless he merely grunts, "A golf ball," he may answer you with a narrative—a story, true or fictional.

"Okay," he sighs, "you know The Tenth Round? That nightclub down by the docks that smells of formaldehyde? Last night I heard they were giving away $500 to anybody who could stand up for three minutes against this karate expert, the Masked Samurai. And so..."

You lean forward. At least, you lean forward *if* you love a story. Most of us do, particularly if the story tells us of people in action or in conflict, and if it is told briskly, vividly, and with insight into the human heart. NARRATION, or storytelling, is therefore a powerful method by which to engage and hold the attention of listeners—readers as well. A little of its tremendous power flows to the public speaker who starts off with a joke, even a stale joke ("A funny thing happened to me on my way over here..."), and to the preacher who at the beginning of a sermon tells of some funny or touching incident. In its opening paragraph, an article in a popular magazine ("Vampires Live Today!") will give us a brief, arresting narrative: perhaps the case history of a car dealer who noticed, one moonlit night, his incisors strangely lengthening.

The term *narrative* takes in abundant territory. A narrative may be short or long, factual or imagined, as artless as a tale told in a locker room or as artful as a novel by Henry James. A narrative may instruct and inform, or simply divert and regale. It may set forth some point or message, or it may be no more significant than a horror tale that aims to curdle your blood.

At least a hundred times a year, you probably resort to narration, not always for the purpose of telling an entertaining story, but often to explain, to illustrate a point, to report information, to argue, or to persuade. That is, although a narrative can run from the beginning of an essay to the end, more often in your writing (as in your speaking) a narrative is only a part of what you have to say. It is there because it serves a larger purpose. In truth, because narration is such an effective way to put across your ideas, the ability to tell a compelling story — on paper, as well as in conversation — may be one of the most useful skills you can acquire.

A novel is a narrative, but a narrative doesn't have to be long. Sometimes an essay will include several brief stories. See, for instance, "Why Don't We Complain?" by William F. Buckley, Jr. (p. 496). A type of story often used to illustrate a point is the ANECDOTE, a short, entertaining account of a single incident. Anecdotes add color and specifics to history and to every issue of *People* magazine, and they often help support an ARGUMENT by giving it the flesh and blood of real life. Besides being vivid, an anecdote can be deeply revealing. In a biography of Samuel Johnson, the great eighteenth-century critic and scholar, W. Jackson Bate uses an anecdote to show that his subject was human and lovable. As Bate tells us, Dr. Johnson, a portly and imposing gentleman of fifty-five, had walked with some friends to the crest of a hill, where the great man,

> delighted by its steepness, said he wanted to "take a roll down." They tried to stop him. But he said he "had not had a roll for a long time," and taking out of his pockets his keys, a pencil, a purse, and other objects, lay down parallel at the edge of the hill, and rolled down its full length, "turning himself over and over till he came to the bottom."

However small the event it relates, this anecdote is memorable — partly because of its attention to detail, such as the exact list of the contents of Johnson's pockets. In such a brief story, a superhuman figure comes down to human size. In one stroke, Bate reveals an essential part of Johnson: his boisterous, hearty, and boyish sense of fun.

An anecdote may be used to explain a point. Asked why he had appointed to a cabinet post Josephus Daniels, the harshest critic of his policies, President Woodrow Wilson replied with an anecdote of a woman he knew. On spying a strange man urinating through her picket fence into her flower garden, she invited the offender into her yard because, as she explained to him, "I'd a whole lot rather have you inside pissing out than have you outside pissing in." By telling this story, Wilson made clear his situation in regard to his political enemy more succinctly and pointedly than if he had given a more abstract explanation.

THE PROCESS

Purpose and Shape

Every good story has a purpose, and we've suggested several on the preceding pages. A narrative without a purpose is bound to irritate readers, as a young child's rambling can vex an unsympathetic adult.

Whatever the reason for its telling, an effective story holds the attention of readers or listeners; and to do so, the storyteller shapes that story to appeal to its audience. If, for instance, you plan to tell a few friends of an embarrassing moment you had on your way to campus—you tripped and spilled a load of books into the arms of a passing dean—you know how to proceed. Simply to provide a laugh is your purpose, and your listeners, who need no introduction to you or the dean, need to be told only the bare events of the story. Perhaps you'll use some vivid words to convey the surprise on the dean's face when sixty pounds of literary lumber hit her. Perhaps you'll throw in a little surprise of your own. At first, you didn't take in the identity of this passerby on whom you'd dumped a load of literary lumber. Then you realized: It was the dean!

The Narrator in the Story

Such simple, direct storytelling is so common and habitual that we do it without planning in advance. The NARRATOR (or teller) of such a personal experience is the speaker, the one who was there. (All the selections in this chapter tell of such experiences. All except Ralph Ellison use the first PERSON *I*.) The telling is usually SUBJECTIVE, with details and language chosen to express the writer's feelings. Of course, a personal experience told in the first person can use some artful telling and some structuring. (In the course of this discussion, we'll offer advice on telling stories of different kinds.)

When a story isn't your own experience but a recital of someone else's, or of events that are public knowledge, then you proceed differently as narrator. Without expressing opinions, you step back and report, content to stay invisible. Instead of saying, "I did this; I did that," you use the third person, *he, she, it,* or *they*: "The runner did this; he did that." You may have been on the scene; if so, you will probably write as a spectator, from your own POINT OF VIEW (or angle of seeing). If you put together what happened from the testimony of others, you tell the story from the point of view of a nonparticipant (a witness who didn't take part). Generally, a nonparticipant is OBJECTIVE in setting forth events: unbiased, as accurate and dispassionate as possible.

When you narrate a story in the third person, you aren't a character central in the eyes of your audience. Unlike the first-person writer of a personal experience, you aren't the main actor; you are the camera operator, whose job is to focus on what transpires. Most history books and news stories are third-person narratives, and so is much fiction. In narrating actual events, writers stick to the facts and do not invent the thoughts of participants (historical novels, though, do mingle fact and fancy in this way). And even writers of fiction and anecdote imagine the thoughts of their characters only if they want to explore psychology. Note how much Woodrow Wilson's anecdote would lose if the teller had gone into the thoughts of his characters: "The woman was angry and embarrassed at seeing the stranger...."

A final element of the narrator's place in the story is verb tense, whether present (*I stare, he stares*) or past (*I stared, he stared*). Telling a story in the present tense (instead of the past, traditionally favored) gives events a sense of immediacy. Presented as though everything were happening right now, Wilson's story might have begun, "Peering out her window, a woman spies a strange man...." You can try the present tense, if you like, and see how immediate it seems to you. Be warned, however, that it can seem artificial (because we're used to reading stories in the past tense), and it can be difficult to sustain throughout an entire narrative. The past tense may be more removed, but it is still powerful: Just look at Edgar Allan Poe's toe-curling story "The Tell-Tale Heart," at the end of this chapter.

What to Emphasize

Discovery and Choice of Details

Whether you tell of your own experience or of someone else's, even if it is brief, you need a whole story to tell. If the story is complex, do some searching and discovering in writing. One trusty method to test your memory (or to make sure you have all the necessary elements of a story) is that of a news reporter. Ask yourself:

1. *What* happened?
2. *Who* took part?

3. *When?*
4. *Where?*
5. *Why* did this event (or these events) take place?
6. *How* did it (or they) happen?

That last *how* isn't merely another way of asking what happened. It means: In exactly what way or under what circumstances? If the event was a murder, how was it done—with an ax or with a bulldozer? Journalists call this handy list of questions "the five *W*'s and the *H*."

Well-prepared storytellers, those who first search their memories (or do some research and legwork), have far more information on hand than they can use. The writing of a good story calls for careful choice. In choosing, remember your purpose and your audience. If you're writing that story of the dean and the books to give pleasure to readers who are your friends, delighted to hear about the discomfort of a pompous administrator, you will probably dwell lovingly on each detail of her consternation. You would tell the story differently if your audience were strangers who didn't know the dean from Eve. They would need more information on her background, reputation for stiffness, and appearance. If, suspected of having deliberately contrived the dean's humiliation, you were writing a report of the incident for the campus police, you'd want to give the plainest possible account of the story—without drama, without adornment, without background, and certainly without any humor whatsoever.

Scene Versus Summary

Your purpose and your audience, then, clearly determine which of the two main strategies of narration you're going to choose: to tell a story by SCENE or to tell it by SUMMARY. When you tell a story in a scene, or in scenes, you visualize each event as vividly and precisely as if you were there—as though it were a scene in a film, and your reader sat before the screen. This is the strategy of most fine novels and short stories—and of much excellent nonfiction as well. Instead of just mentioning people, you portray them. You recall dialogue as best you can, or you invent some that could have been spoken. You include DESCRIPTION (a mode of writing to be dealt with fully in our next chapter).

For a lively example of a well-drawn scene, see Maya Angelou's account of a tense crowd's behavior as, jammed into a small-town store, they listen to a fight broadcast (in "Champion of the World," beginning on p. 52). Angelou prolongs one scene for almost her entire essay. Sometimes, though, a writer will draw a scene in only two or three sentences. This is the brevity we find in W. Jackson Bate's glimpse of the hill-rolling Johnson (p. 40). Unlike Angelou, Bate evidently seeks not to weave a tapestry of detail but to show, in telling of one brief event, a trait of his hero's character.

When, on the other hand, you tell a story by the method of summary, you relate events concisely. Instead of depicting people and their surroundings in great detail, you set down just the essentials of what happened. Most of us employ this method in most stories we tell, for it takes less time and fewer words. A summary is to a scene, then, as a simple stick figure is to a portrait in oils. This is not to dismiss simple stick figures as inferior. The economy of a story told in summary may be as effective as the lavish detail of a story told in scenes.

Again, your choice of a method depends on your answer to the questions you ask yourself: What is my purpose? Who is my audience? How fully to flesh out a scene, how much detail to include—these choices depend on what you seek to do, and on how much your audience needs to know to follow you. Read the life of some famous person in an encyclopedia, and you will find the article telling its story in summary form. Its writer's purpose, evidently, is to recount the main events of a whole life in a short space. But glance through a book-length biography of the same celebrity, and you will probably find scenes in it. A biographer writes with a different purpose: to present a detailed portrait roundly and thoroughly, bringing the subject vividly to life.

To be sure, you can use both methods in telling a single story. Often, summary will serve a writer who passes briskly from one scene to the next, or hurries over events of lesser importance. Were you to write, let's say, the story of a man's fiendish passion for horse racing, you might decide to give short shrift to most other facts of his life. To emphasize what you consider essential, you might begin a scene with a terse summary: "Seven years went by, and after three marriages and two divorces, Lars found himself again back at Hialeah." (A detailed scene might follow.)

Good storytellers know what to emphasize. They do not fall into a boring drone: "And then I went down to the club and I had a few beers and I noticed this sign, Go 3 Minutes with the Masked Samurai and Win $500, so I went and got knocked out and then I had pizza and went home." In this lazily strung-out summary, the narrator reduces all events to equal unimportance. A more adept storyteller might leave out the pizza and dwell in detail on the big fight.

In *The Bedford Reader*, we are concerned with the kind of writing you do every day in college: nonfiction writing in which you generally explain ideas, organize information you have learned, analyze other people's ideas, or argue a case. In fiction, though, we find an enormously popular and appealing use of narration and certain devices of storytelling from which all storytellers can learn. For these reasons, this chapter includes one celebrated short story by a master storyteller,

Edgar Allan Poe. But fiction and fact barely separate Poe's story and the equally compelling true memoirs in this chapter. All the authors strive to make people and events come alive for us. All of them also use a tool that academic writers generally do not: dialogue. Reported speech, in quotation marks, is invaluable for revealing characters' feelings.

Organization

In any kind of narration, the simplest approach is to set down events in CHRONOLOGICAL ORDER, the way they happened. To do so is to have your story already organized for you. A chronological order is therefore an excellent sequence to follow unless you can see some special advantage in violating it. Ask: What am I trying to do? If you are trying to capture your readers' attention right away, you might begin *in medias res* (Latin, "in the middle of things") and open with a colorful, dramatic event, even though it took place late in the chronology. If trying for dramatic effect, you might save the most exciting or impressive event for last, even though it actually happened early. By this means, you can keep your readers in suspense for as long as possible. (You can return to earlier events by a FLASHBACK, an earlier scene recalled.) Let your purpose be your guide.

The writer Calvin Trillin has recalled why, in a narrative titled "The Tunica Treasure," he deliberately chose not to follow a chronology:

> I wrote a story on the discovery of the Tunica treasure which I couldn't begin by saying, "Here is a man who works as a prison guard in Angola State Prison, and on his weekends he sometimes looks for buried treasure that is rumored to be around the Indian village." Because the real point of the story centered around the problems caused when an amateur wanders onto professional territory, I thought it would be much better to open with how momentous the discovery was, that it was the most important archeological discovery about Indian contact with the European settlers to date, and *then* to say that it was discovered by a prison guard. So I made a conscious choice *not* to start with Leonard Charrier working as a prison guard, not to go back to his boyhood in Bunkie, Louisiana, not to talk about how he'd always been interested in treasure hunting—hoping that the reader would assume I was about to say that the treasure was found by an archeologist from the Peabody Museum at Harvard.

Trillin, by saving the fact that a prison guard made the earthshaking discovery, effectively took his reader by surprise. (For an example of Trillin's narrative style, see "Spelling Yiffniff" in this chapter.)

No matter what order you choose, either following chronology or departing from it, make sure your audience can follow it. The sequence of events has to be clear. This calls for TRANSITIONS of time, whether they are brief phrases that point out exactly when each event happened ("Seven years later," "A moment earlier"), or whole sentences that announce an event and clearly locate it in time ("If you had known Leonard Charrier ten years earlier, you would have found him voraciously poring over every archeology text he could lay his hands on in the public library"). See "Transitions" in Useful Terms for a list of possibilities.

The Point

In writing a news story, a reporter often begins with the conclusion, placing the main event in the opening paragraph (called the lead) so that readers get the essentials up front. Similarly, in using an anecdote to explain something or to argue a point, you'll want to tell readers directly what you think the story demonstrates. But in most other kinds of narration, whether fiction or nonfiction, whether to entertain or to make an idea clear, the storyteller refrains from revealing the gist of the story, its point, right at the beginning. In fact, many narratives do not contain a THESIS SENTENCE, a statement of the idea behind the story, because such a statement can rob the reader of the very pleasure of narration, the excitement of seeing a story build. That doesn't mean the story lacks a focal point—far from it. The writer has every obligation to construct the narrative as if a thesis sentence showed the way at the start, even when it didn't.

By the end of the story, that focal point should become obvious, as the writer builds toward a memorable CONCLUSION. In a story Mark Twain liked to tell aloud, a woman's ghost returns to claim her artificial arm made of gold, which she wore in life and which her greedy husband had unscrewed from her corpse. Carefully, Twain would build up suspense as the ghost pursued the husband upstairs to his bedroom, stood by his bed, breathed her cold breath on him, and intoned, *"Who's got my golden arm?"* Twain used to end his story by suddenly yelling at a member of the audience, *"You've got it!"*—and enjoying the victim's shriek of surprise. That final punctuating shriek may be a technique that will work only in oral storytelling; yet, like Twain, most storytellers like to end with a bang if they can. For another example, take specific notice of Edgar Allan Poe's ending for "The Tell-Tale Heart" (*after* you've read the whole story, that is). The final impact need not be as dramatic as Twain's and Poe's, either. As Maya Angelou and Barbara Huttmann demonstrate in their narratives in this chapter, you can achieve a lot just by leading to your point, stating your thesis sentence at the very end. You can sometimes make your point just by saving the best incident—the most dramatic or the funniest—for last.

CHECKLIST FOR REVISING A NARRATIVE

✔ **POINT OF VIEW.** Is your narrator's position in the story appropriate for your purpose and consistent throughout the story? Check for awkward or confusing shifts in point of view (participant or nonparticipant; first, second, or third person) and in the tenses of verbs (present to past or vice versa).

✔ **SELECTION OF EVENTS.** Have you selected and emphasized events to suit your audience and fulfill your purpose? Tell the important parts of the story in the greatest detail. Summarize the less important, connective events.

✔ **ORGANIZATION.** If your organization is not strictly chronological (first event to last), do you have a compelling reason for altering it? If you start somewhere other than the beginning of the story or use flashbacks at any point, will your readers benefit from your creativity?

✔ **TRANSITIONS.** Have you used transitions to help clarify the order of events and their duration?

✔ **DIALOGUE.** If you have used dialogue, quoting participants in the story, is it appropriate for your purpose? Is it concise, telling only the important, revealing lines? Does the language sound like spoken English?

✔ **THE POINT.** What is the point of your narrative? Will it be clear to readers by the end? Even if you haven't stated it in a thesis sentence, your story should focus on a central idea. If you can't risk readers' misunderstanding—if, for instance, you're using narration to support an argument or explain a concept—then have you stated your thesis outright?

NARRATION IN A PARAGRAPH: TWO ILLUSTRATIONS

Using Narration to Write About Television

The following paragraph was written for *The Bedford Reader* as a kind of mini-essay. But it is easy to see how it might have worked in the context of a full essay about, say, the emotional effects of television on children. Recounting events vividly, moment by moment, the writer gives evidence for a rather dramatic effect on one little girl.

Oozing menace from beyond the stars or from the deeps, televised horror powerfully stimulates a child's already frisky imagination. As parents know, a "Creature Double Feature" has an impact that lasts long after the click of

Claim to be supported by narrative

the *off* button. Recently a neighbor reported the strange case of her eight-year-old. Discovered late at night in the game room watching *The Exorcist*, the girl was promptly sent to bed. An hour later, her parents could hear her chanting something in the darkness of her bedroom. On tiptoe, they stole to her door to listen. The creak of springs told them that their daughter was swaying rhythmically to and fro, and the smell of acrid smoke warned them that something was burning. At once, they shoved open the door to find the room flickering with shadows cast by a lighted candle. Their daughter was sitting in bed, rocking back and forth as she intoned over and over, "Fiend in human form... Fiend in human form..." This case may be unique; still, it seems likely that similar events take place each night all over the screen-watching world.

Transitions (underlined) clarify sequence and pace of events

Anecdote builds suspense:

   Mystery

   Warnings

   Crisis

Conclusion broadens claim

Using Narration in an Academic Discipline

In this paragraph from a geology textbook, the authors use narration to illustrate a powerful geological occurrence. Following another paragraph that explains landslides more generally, the narrative places the reader at an actual event.

The news media periodically relate the terrifying and often grim details of landslides. On May 31, 1970, one such event occurred when a gigantic rock avalanche buried more than 20,000 people in Yungay and Ranrahirca, Peru. There was little warning of the impending disaster; it began and ended in just a matter of a few minutes. The avalanche started 14 kilometers from Yungay, near the summit of 6,700-meter-high Nevados Huascaran, the loftiest peak in the Peruvian Andes. Triggered by the ground motion from a strong offshore earthquake, a huge mass of rock and ice broke free from the precipitous north face of the mountain. After plunging nearly one kilometer, the material pulverized on impact and immediately began rushing down the mountainside, made fluid by trapped air and melted ice. The initial mass ripped loose additional millions of tons of debris as it roared downhill. The shock waves produced by the event created thunderlike noise and stripped nearby hillsides of vegetation. Although the material followed a previously eroded gorge, a portion of the debris jumped a 200–300-meter-high bedrock ridge that had protected Yungay from past rock avalanches and buried the entire city. After inundating another town in its path, Ranrahirca, the mass of debris finally reached the bottom of the valley where its momentum carried it across the Rio Santa and tens of meters up the opposite bank.

Generalization illustrated by narrative

Anecdote helps explain landslides:

   Sudden beginning

   Fast movement

   Irresistible force

Transitions (underlined) clarify sequence and pace of events

—Edward J. Tarbuck and Frederick K. Lutgens,
The Earth: An Introduction to Physical Geology

NARRATION ELSEWHERE IN *THE BEDFORD READER*

Besides the selections in this chapter, almost every other essay in *The Bedford Reader* includes some narrative. In the selections below, the authors use narration throughout their essays, together with one or more other dominant methods.

PART ONE

Brad Manning, "Arm Wrestling with My Father"
Itabari Njeri, "When Morpheus Held Him"
Merrill Markoe, "Bob the Dog (1974–1988)"
Judith Ortiz Cofer, "Silent Dancing"
John McPhee, "Silk Parachute"
Roy Blount, Jr., "As Well as I Do My Own"
Brent Staples, "Black Men and Public Space"
Dave Barry, "Batting Clean-Up and Striking Out"
Michael Kroll, "The Unquiet Death of Robert Harris"
William F. Buckley, Jr., "Why Don't We Complain?"

PART TWO

Stephen L. Carter, "The Insufficiency of Honesty"
Sandra Cisneros, "Only Daughter"
Joan Didion, "In Bed"
Annie Dillard, "Lenses"
Maxine Hong Kingston, "No Name Woman"
N. Scott Momaday, "The Way to Rainy Mountain"
George Orwell, "Shooting an Elephant"
Richard Rodriguez, "Aria: A Memoir of a Bilingual Childhood"
E. B. White, "Once More to the Lake"
Virginia Woolf, "The Death of the Moth"

CASE STUDY
Using Narration

Robert Guzman was on his way to class at Cañada College when his car was hit at an intersection. He reported the accident to his insurance company, and the claims adjuster asked him to supplement the standard police report with a letter explaining what happened.

"What happened?" prompted Guzman to write the following narrative. Since the accident was uncomplicated, he had little difficulty getting the events down in chronological order. In editing, though, he did add some clarifying TRANSITIONS, such as "After the light turned green" and "When I was midway through the intersection."

Robert Guzman
415 Washington St., Apt. 5
San Carlos, CA 94070
June 7, 1999

David McClure
MDN Insurance
2716 El Camino Real
San Carlos, CA 94072

Dear Mr. McClure:

Thanks for your call about my claim. Here is the report you requested about the accident I was involved in.

At about 7:30 on the morning of June 4, I was driving south on Laurel Street in San Carlos. The traffic light at the corner of Laurel and San Carlos Avenue was red and I stopped at it, the first car in the stop line.

After the light turned green, I looked to my left and right. Although I saw a car approaching from the right on San Carlos, it seemed to be slowing for the light. Since my light was green, I proceeded through the intersection.

The car, which I later found out was driven by Mr. Henry, did not stop for its red light. When I was midway through the intersection, I heard its tires squeal and felt an impact. Mr. Henry's car hit the rear fender and bumper on my passenger side. My car spun clockwise and came to a stop facing north, in the northbound lane of Laurel.

Mr. Henry parked in a lot across the street, and I pulled in after him. I called the police on my cell phone, and we waited for the police to arrive. No one was injured, but my passenger-side rear fender is severely dented and my bumper is twisted like a pretzel.

As you can see, I was not at fault in this accident. I believe Mr. Henry will confirm as much. Please let me know if you have any questions or if I can help my claim in any other way.

Sincerely,

Robert Guzman

Robert Guzman

MAYA ANGELOU

MAYA ANGELOU was born Marguerite Johnson in Saint Louis in 1928. After an unpleasantly eventful youth by her account ("from a broken family, raped at eight, unwed mother at sixteen"), she went on to join a dance company, star in an off-Broadway play (*The Blacks*), write six books of poetry, produce a series on Africa for PBS-TV, act in the television-special series *Roots*, serve as a coordinator for the Southern Christian Leadership Conference, and accept several honorary doctorates. She is best known, however, for the five books of her searching, frank, and joyful autobiography—beginning with *I Know Why the Caged Bird Sings* (1970), which she adapted for television, through *All God's Children Need Traveling Shoes* (1986). Her latest books are collections of essays, *Wouldn't Take Nothing for My Journey Now* (1993) and *Even the Stars Look Lonesome* (1997). In 1998 Angelou directed her first feature film, *Down in the Delta*. She is Reynolds Professor of American Studies at Wake Forest University.

Champion of the World

"Champion of the World" is the nineteenth chapter in *I Know Why the Caged Bird Sings;* the title is a phrase taken from the chapter. Remembering her childhood, the writer tells how she and her older brother, Bailey, grew up in a town in Arkansas. The center of their lives was Grandmother and Uncle Willie's store, a gathering place for the black community. On the night when this story takes place, Joe Louis, the "Brown Bomber" and the hero of his people, defends his heavyweight boxing title against a white contender. Angelou's telling of the event both entertains us and explains what it was like to be African American in a certain time and place.

Amy Tan's "Fish Cheeks," following Angelou's essay, also explores the experience of growing up an outsider in mainly white America.

The last inch of space was filled, yet people continued to wedge 1
themselves along the walls of the Store. Uncle Willie had turned the radio up to its last notch so that youngsters on the porch wouldn't miss a word. Women sat on kitchen chairs, dining-room chairs, stools, and upturned wooden boxes. Small children and babies perched on every lap available and men leaned on the shelves or on each other.

The apprehensive mood was shot through with shafts of gaiety, as 2
a black sky is streaked with lightning.

"I ain't worried 'bout this fight. Joe's gonna whip that cracker like 3
it's open season."

"He gone whip him till that white boy call him Momma." 4

52

At last the talking finished and the string-along songs about razor   5
blades were over and the fight began.

"A quick jab to the head." In the Store the crowd grunted. "A left   6
to the head and a right and another left." One of the listeners cackled
like a hen and was quieted.

"They're in a clinch, Louis is trying to fight his way out."   7

Some bitter comedian on the porch said, "That white man don't   8
mind hugging that niggah now, I betcha."

"The referee is moving in to break them up, but Louis finally   9
pushed the contender away and it's an uppercut to the chin. The contender is hanging on, now he's backing away. Louis catches him with a
short left to the jaw."

A tide of murmuring assent poured out the door and into the yard.   10

"Another left and another left. Louis is saving that mighty right . . ."   11
The mutter in the Store had grown into a baby roar and it was pierced
by the clang of a bell and the announcer's "That's the bell for round
three, ladies and gentlemen."

As I pushed my way into the Store I wondered if the announcer   12
gave any thought to the fact that he was addressing as "ladies and gentlemen" all the Negroes around the world who sat sweating and praying, glued to their "Master's voice."[1]

There were only a few calls for RC Colas, Dr Peppers, and Hires   13
root beer. The real festivities would begin after the fight. Then even
the old Christian ladies who taught their children and tried themselves
to practice turning the other cheek would buy soft drinks, and if the
Brown Bomber's victory was a particularly bloody one they would order
peanut patties and Baby Ruths also.

Bailey and I laid the coins on top of the cash register. Uncle Willie   14
didn't allow us to ring up sales during a fight. It was too noisy and might
shake up the atmosphere. When the gong rang for the next round
we pushed through the near-sacred quiet to the herd of children outside.

"He's got Louis against the ropes and now it's a left to the body and   15
a right to the ribs. Another right to the body, it looks like it was
low . . . Yes, ladies and gentlemen, the referee is signaling but the contender keeps raining the blows on Louis. It's another to the body, and it
looks like Louis is going down."

My race groaned. It was our people falling. It was another lynching,   16
yet another Black man hanging on a tree. One more woman ambushed
and raped. A Black boy whipped and maimed. It was hounds on the
trail of a man running through slimy swamps. It was a white woman
slapping her maid for being forgetful.

---

[1]"His master's voice," accompanied by a picture of a little dog listening to a
phonograph, was a familiar advertising slogan. (The picture still appears on some RCA
recordings.) — EDS.

The men in the Store stood away from the walls and at attention.   17
Women greedily clutched the babes on their laps while on the porch
the shufflings and smiles, flirtings and pinching of a few minutes before
were gone. This might be the end of the world. If Joe lost we were back
in slavery and beyond help. It would all be true, the accusations that we
were lower types of human beings. Only a little higher than apes. True
that we were stupid and ugly and lazy and dirty and, unlucky and worst
of all, that God Himself hated us and ordained us to be hewers of wood
and drawers of water, forever and ever, world without end.

We didn't breathe. We didn't hope. We waited.   18

"He's off the ropes, ladies and gentlemen. He's moving towards the   19
center of the ring." There was no time to be relieved. The worst might
still happen.

"And now it looks like Joe is mad. He's caught Carnera with a left   20
hook to the head and a right to the head. It's a left jab to the body and
another left to the head. There's a left cross and a right to the head.
The contender's right eye is bleeding and he can't seem to keep his
block up. Louis is penetrating every block. The referee is moving in,
but Louis sends a left to the body and it's an uppercut to the chin and
the contender is dropping. He's on the canvas, ladies and gentlemen."

Babies slid to the floor as women stood up and men leaned toward   21
the radio.

"Here's the referee. He's counting. One, two, three, four, five, six,   22
seven...Is the contender trying to get up again?"

All the men in the store shouted, "NO."   23

"—eight, nine, ten." There were a few sounds from the audience, but   24
they seemed to be holding themselves in against tremendous pressure.

"The fight is all over, ladies and gentlemen. Let's get the micro-   25
phone over to the referee...Here he is. He's got the Brown Bomber's
hand, he's holding it up...Here he is..."

Then the voice, husky and familiar, came to wash over us—"The   26
winnah, and still heavyweight champeen of the world...Joe Louis."

Champion of the world. A Black boy. Some Black mother's son.   27
He was the strongest man in the world. People drank Coca-Colas like
ambrosia and ate candy bars like Christmas. Some of the men went behind the Store and poured white lightning in their soft-drink bottles,
and a few of the bigger boys followed them. Those who were not chased
away came back blowing their breath in front of themselves like proud
smokers.

It would take an hour or more before the people would leave the   28
Store and head for home. Those who lived too far had made arrangements to stay in town. It wouldn't do for a Black man and his family to
be caught on a lonely country road on a night when Joe Louis had
proved that we were the strongest people in the world.

QUESTIONS ON MEANING

1. What do you take to be the author's PURPOSE in telling this story?
2. What connection does Angelou make between the outcome of the fight and the pride of African Americans? To what degree do you think the author's view is shared by the others in the store listening to the broadcast?
3. To what extent are the statements in paragraphs 16 and 17 to be taken literally? What function do they serve in Angelou's narrative?
4. Primo Carnera was probably *not* the Brown Bomber's opponent on the night Maya Angelou recalls. Louis fought Carnera only once, on June 25, 1935, and it was not a title match; Angelou would have been no more than seven years old at the time. Does the author's apparent error detract from her story?

QUESTIONS ON WRITING STRATEGY

1. What details in the opening paragraphs indicate that an event of crucial importance is about to take place?
2. How does Angelou build up SUSPENSE in her account of the fight? At what point were you able to predict the winner?
3. Comment on the IRONY in Angelou's final paragraph.
4. What EFFECT does the author's use of direct quotation have on her narrative?
5. **OTHER METHODS.** Besides narration, Angelou also relies heavily on the method of DESCRIPTION. Analyze how narration depends on description in paragraph 27 alone.

QUESTIONS ON LANGUAGE

1. Explain what the author means by "string-along songs about razor blades" (para. 5).
2. How does Angelou's use of NONSTANDARD ENGLISH contribute to her narrative?
3. Be sure you know the meanings of these words: apprehensive (para. 2); assent (10); ambushed, maimed (16); ordained (17); ambrosia, white lightning (27).

SUGGESTIONS FOR WRITING

1. **JOURNAL WRITING.** What groups do you belong to, and how do you know you're a member? Consider groups based on race, ethnic background, religion, sports, hobbies, politics, friendship, kinship, or any other ties. **FROM JOURNAL TO ESSAY.** Choose one of the groups from your journal entry, and explore your sense of membership through a narrative that tells of an incident when that sense was strong. Try to make the incident come alive for your readers with vivid details, dialogue, and tight sequencing of events.

2. Write an essay based on some childhood experience of your own, still vivid in your memory.

3. **CRITICAL WRITING.** Angelou does not directly describe relations between African Americans and whites, yet her essay implies quite a lot. Write a brief essay about what you can INFER from the exaggeration of paragraphs 16–17 and the obliqueness of paragraph 28. Focus on Angelou's details and the language she uses to present them.

4. **CONNECTIONS.** Angelou's "Champion of the World" and the next essay, Amy Tan's "Fish Cheeks," both tell stories of children who felt like outsiders in predominantly white America. COMPARE AND CONTRAST the two writers' perceptions of what sets them apart from the dominant culture. How does the event each reports affect that sense of difference? Use specific examples from both essays as your EVIDENCE.

MAYA ANGELOU ON WRITING

Maya Angelou's writings have shown great variety: She has done notable work as an autobiographer, poet, short-story writer, screenwriter, journalist, and song lyricist. Asked by interviewer Sheila Weller, "Do you start each project with a specific idea?" Angelou replied:

It starts with a definite subject, but it might end with something entirely different. When I start a project, the first thing I do is write down, in longhand, everything I know about the subject, every thought I've ever had on it. This may be twelve or fourteen pages. Then I read it back through, for quite a few days, and find—given that subject—what its rhythm is. 'Cause everything in the universe has a rhythm. So if it's free form, it still has a rhythm. And once I hear the rhythm of the piece, then I try to find out what are the salient points that I must make. And then it begins to take shape.

I try to set myself up in each chapter by saying: "This is what I want to go from—from B to, say, G-sharp. Or from D to L." And then I find the hook. It's like the knitting, where, after you knit a certain amount, there's one thread that begins to pull. You know, you can see it right along the cloth. Well, in writing, I think: "Now where is that one hook, that one little thread?" It may be a sentence. If I can catch that, then I'm home free. It's the one that tells me where I'm going. It may not even turn out to be in the final chapter. I may throw it out later or change it. But if I follow it through, it leads me right out.

FOR DISCUSSION

1. How would you define the word *rhythm* as Maya Angelou uses it?
2. What response would you give a student who said, "Doesn't Angelou's approach to writing waste more time and thought than it's worth?"

AMY TAN

Amy Tan is a gifted storyteller whose first novel, *The Joy Luck Club* (1989), met with critical acclaim and huge success. The relationships it details between immigrant Chinese mothers and their Chinese American daughters came from Tan's firsthand experience. She was born in 1952 in Oakland, California, the daughter of immigrants who had fled China's Cultural Revolution in the late 1940s. She majored in English and linguistics at San Jose State University, where she received a B.A. in 1973 and an M.A. in 1974. After two more years of graduate work, Tan became a consultant in language development for disabled children and then started her own company writing reports and speeches for business corporations. Tan began writing fiction to explore her ethnic ambivalence and to find a voice for herself. After *The Joy Luck Club*, she published *The Kitchen God's Wife* (1991), a fictional account of her mother's harrowing life in China, and *The Hundred Secret Senses* (1995), a novel. Tan has also written children's books and contributed essays to *McCall's*, *Life*, *Glamour*, *The Atlantic Monthly*, and other magazines.

Fish Cheeks

"Fish Cheeks" is a very brief narrative, almost an anecdote, but still it deftly portrays the contradictory feelings and the advantages of a girl with feet in different cultures. The essay first appeared in *Seventeen*, a magazine for teenage girls and young women, in 1987.

For a complementary view of growing up "different," read the preceding essay, Maya Angelou's "Champion of the World."

I fell in love with the minister's son the winter I turned fourteen. He 1 was not Chinese, but as white as Mary in the manger. For Christmas I prayed for this blond-haired boy, Robert, and a slim new American nose.

When I found out that my parents had invited the minister's fam- 2 ily over for Christmas Eve dinner, I cried. What would Robert think of our shabby Chinese Christmas? What would he think of our noisy Chinese relatives who lacked proper American manners? What terrible disappointment would he feel upon seeing not a roasted turkey and sweet potatoes but Chinese food?

On Christmas Eve I saw that my mother had outdone herself in 3 creating a strange menu. She was pulling black veins out of the backs of fleshy prawns. The kitchen was littered with appalling mounds of raw food: A slimy rock cod with bulging eyes that pleaded not to be thrown into a pan of hot oil. Tofu, which looked like stacked wedges of rubbery white sponges. A bowl soaking dried fungus back to life. A

plate of squid, their backs crisscrossed with knife markings so they resembled bicycle tires.

And then they arrived—the minister's family and all my relatives   4
in a clamor of doorbells and rumpled Christmas packages. Robert
grunted hello, and I pretended he was not worthy of existence.

Dinner threw me deeper into despair. My relatives licked the ends   5
of their chopsticks and reached across the table, dipping them into the
dozen or so plates of food. Robert and his family waited patiently for
platters to be passed to them. My relatives murmured with pleasure
when my mother brought out the whole steamed fish. Robert grimaced.
Then my father poked his chopsticks just below the fish eye and
plucked out the soft meat. "Amy, your favorite," he said, offering me
the tender fish cheek. I wanted to disappear.

At the end of the meal my father leaned back and belched loudly,   6
thanking my mother for her fine cooking. "It's a polite Chinese custom
to show you are satisfied," explained my father to our astonished guests.
Robert was looking down at his plate with a reddened face. The minister managed to muster up a quiet burp. I was stunned into silence for
the rest of the night.

After everyone had gone, my mother said to me, "You want to be the   7
same as American girls on the outside." She handed me an early gift. It
was a miniskirt in beige tweed. "But inside you must always be Chinese.
You must be proud you are different. Your only shame is to have shame."

And even though I didn't agree with her then, I knew that she   8
understood how much I had suffered during the evening's dinner. It
wasn't until many years later—long after I had gotten over my crush
on Robert—that I was able to fully appreciate her lesson and the true
purpose behind our particular menu. For Christmas Eve that year, she
had chosen all my favorite foods.

QUESTIONS ON MEANING

1. Why does Tan cry when she finds out that the boy she is in love with is
   coming to dinner?
2. Why does Tan's mother go out of her way to prepare a disturbingly
   traditional Chinese dinner for her daughter and guests? What one sentence best sums up the lesson Tan was not able to understand until years
   later?
3. How does the fourteen-year-old Tan feel about her Chinese background?
   about her mother?
4. What is Tan's PURPOSE in writing this essay? Does she just want to entertain
   readers, or might she have a weightier goal?

QUESTIONS ON WRITING STRATEGY

1. How does Tan draw the reader into her story right from the beginning?
2. How does Tan use TRANSITIONS both to drive and to clarify her narrative?
3. What is the IRONY of the last sentence of the essay?
4. **OTHER METHODS.** Paragraph 3 is a passage of pure DESCRIPTION. Why does Tan linger over the food? What is the EFFECT of this paragraph?

QUESTIONS ON LANGUAGE

1. The simile about Mary in the second sentence of the essay is surprising. Why? Why is it amusing? (See "Figures of Speech" in Useful Terms for a definition of *simile*.)
2. How does the narrator's age affect the TONE of this essay? Give EXAMPLES of language particularly appropriate to a fourteen-year-old.
3. Make sure you know the meanings of the following words: prawns, tofu (para. 3); clamor (4); grimaced (5); muster (6).

SUGGESTIONS FOR WRITING

1. **JOURNAL WRITING.** Think of an occasion when, for whatever reason, you were ashamed of being different. How did you react? Did you try to hide your difference in order to fit in, or did you reveal or celebrate your uniqueness?

   FROM JOURNAL TO ESSAY. Using Tan's essay as a model, write a brief narrative based on the sketch from your journal. Try to imitate the way Tan integrates the external events of the dinner with her own feelings about what is going on. Your story may be humorous, like Tan's, or more serious.
2. Take a perspective like that of the minister's son, Robert: Write a narrative essay about a time when you had to adjust to participating in a culture different from your own. It could be a meal, a wedding or other rite of passage, a religious ceremony, a trip to another country. What did you learn from your experience, about yourself and others?
3. **CRITICAL WRITING.** From this essay one can INFER two very different sets of ASSUMPTIONS about the extent to which immigrants should seek to integrate themselves into the culture of their adopted country. Take either of these positions, in favor of or against assimilation (cultural integration), and make an ARGUMENT for your case.
4. **CONNECTIONS.** Both Tan and Maya Angelou, in "Champion of the World" (p. 52), write about difference from white Americans, but their POINTS OF VIEW are not the same: Tan's is a teenager's lament about not fitting in; Angelou's is an oppressed child's excitement about proving the injustice of oppression. In an essay, ANALYZE the two authors' uses of narration to convey their perspectives. What details do they focus on? What internal thoughts do they report? Is one essay more effective than the other? Why, or why not?

AMY TAN ON WRITING

In 1989 Amy Tan delivered a lecture titled "Mother Tongue" at the State of the Language Symposium in San Francisco. The lecture, later published in *The Threepenny Review* in 1990, addresses Tan's own experience as a bilingual child speaking both Chinese and English. "I do think that the language spoken in the family, especially in immigrant families, which are more insular, plays a large role in shaping the language of the child. And I believe that it affected my results on achievement tests, IQ tests, and the SAT. While my English skills were never judged as poor, compared to math English could not be considered my strong suit.... This was understandable. Math is precise; there is only one correct answer. Whereas, for me at least, the answers on English tests were always a judgment call, a matter of opinion and personal experience."

Tan goes on to say that the necessity of adapting to different styles of expression may affect other children from bilingual households. "I've been asked, as a writer, why there are not more Asian-Americans represented in American literature. Why are there few Asian-Americans enrolled in creative-writing programs? Why do so many Chinese students go into engineering? Well, these are broad sociological questions I can't begin to answer. But I have noticed in surveys...that Asian students, as a whole, always do significantly better on math achievement tests than in English. And this makes me think that there are other Asian-American students whose English spoken in the home might also be described as 'broken' or 'limited.' And perhaps they also have teachers who are steering them away from writing and into math and science, which is what happened to me."

Tan admits that when she first began writing fiction, she wrote "what I thought to be wittily crafted sentences, sentences that would finally prove I had mastery over the English language." But they were awkward and self-conscious, so she changed her tactic. "I later decided I should envision a reader for the stories I would write. And the reader I decided upon was my mother, because these were stories about mothers. So with this reader in mind—and in fact, she did read my early drafts—I began to write stories using all the Englishes I grew up with: the English I spoke to my mother,... the English she used with me,... my translation of her Chinese,... and what I imagined to be her translation of her Chinese if she could speak in perfect English, her internal language, and for that I sought to preserve the essence, but not either an English or a Chinese structure. I wanted to capture what language ability tests can never reveal: her intent, her passion, her imagery, the rhythms of her speech and the nature of her thoughts.

"Apart from what any critic had to say about my writing, I knew I had succeeded where it counted when my mother finished reading my book and gave me her verdict: 'So easy to read.'"

FOR DISCUSSION

1. How could growing up in a household of "broken" English be a handicap for a student taking an achievement test?
2. What does the author suggest is the reason why more Asian Americans enter engineering than English?
3. Why did Amy Tan's mother make a good reader?

CALVIN TRILLIN

CALVIN TRILLIN, a distinguished and often funny commentator on American life, was born in 1935 in Kansas City, Missouri, where he grew up. After earning his B.A. from Yale in 1957, he worked as a reporter and writer for *Time*. In 1963 he joined *The New Yorker* as a staff writer and ever since has been a contributor to that lively weekly magazine. From 1978 until 1985 Trillin wrote a column on political affairs for *The Nation* (he now writes a weekly humorous poem for the magazine), and in 1986 he became a syndicated newspaper columnist. His essays and commentary have been gathered in *Uncivil Liberties* (1982), *With All Disrespect* (1985), *If You Can't Say Something Nice* (1987), *Enough's Enough (And Other Rules of Life)* (1990), and other volumes. Trillin has also written two novels and (with appetite) the essays on food and drink that appear in *American Fried* (1974), *Alice, Let's Eat* (1978), and *Third Helpings* (1983).

Spelling Yiffniff

Trillin's wry humor comes to the fore in "Spelling Yiffniff," a narrative about, yes, spelling that brightens even such a mundane subject. One of Trillin's syndicated columns, the essay was collected in *If You Can't Say Something Nice*.

My father used to offer an array of prizes for anyone who could spell 1 yiffniff. That's not how to spell it, of course — yiffniff. I'm just trying to let you know what it sounds like, in case you'd like to take a crack at it yourself. Don't get your hopes up: this is a spelling word that once defied some of the finest twelve-year-old minds Kansas City had to offer.

The prizes were up for grabs any time my father drove us to a Boy 2 Scout meeting. After a while, all he had to say to start the yiffniff attempts was "Well?"

"Y-i..." some particularly brave kid like Dogbite Davis would say. 3

"Wrong," my father would say, in a way that somehow made it 4 sound like "Wrong, dummy."

"How could I be wrong already?" Dogbite would say. 5

"Wrong," my father would repeat. "Next." 6

Sometimes he would begin the ride by calling out the prizes he was 7 offering: "...a new Schwinn three-speed, a trip to California, a lifetime pass to Kansas City Blues baseball games, free piano lessons for a year, a new pair of shoes." No matter what the other prizes were, the list always ended with "a new pair of shoes."

Some of the prizes were not tempting to us. We weren't interested   8
in shoes. We would have done anything to avoid free piano lessons for
a year. Still, we were desperate to spell yiffniff.

"L-l..." Eddie Williams began one day.   9

"Wrong," my father said. "Next."   10

"That's Spanish," Eddie said, "the double L that sounds like a y."   11

"This is English," my father said. "Next."   12

Sometimes someone would ask what yiffniff meant.   13

"You don't have to give the definition to get the prizes," my father   14
would say. "Just spell it."

As far as I could gather, yiffniff didn't have a definition. It was a   15
word that existed solely to be spelled. My father had invented it for
that purpose.

Occasionally some kid in the car would make an issue out of   16
yiffniff's origins. "But you made it up!" he'd tell my father, in an accusing tone.

"Of course I made it up," my father would reply. "That's why I know   17
how to spell it."

"But it could be spelled a million ways."   18

"All of them are wrong except my way," my father would say. "It's   19
my word."

If you're thinking that my father, who had never shared the secret   20
of how to spell his word, could have simply called any spelling we came
up with wrong and thus avoided handing out the prizes, you never
knew my father. His views on honesty made the Boy Scout position on
that subject seem wishy-washy. There was no doubt among us that my
father knew how to spell yiffniff and would award the prizes to anyone
who spelled it that way. But nobody seemed able to do it.

Finally, we brought in a ringer—my cousin Keith, from Salina,   21
who had reached the finals of the Kansas State Spelling Bee. (Although Keith's memory has always differed from mine on this point,
I'm sure I was saying even then that the word he missed in the finals
was *hayseed*.) We told my father that Keith, who was visiting Kansas
City, wanted to go to a Scout meeting with us to brush up on some of
his knots.

"Well?" my father said, when the car was loaded.   22

"Yiffniff," my cousin Keith said clearly, announcing the assigned   23
word in the spelling bee style. "Y-y..."

Y-y! Using y both as a consonant and as a vowel! What a move!   24
We looked at my father for a response. He said nothing. Emboldened,
Keith picked up the pace: "Y-y-g-h-k-n-i-p-h."

For a few moments the car was silent. Then my father said,   25
"Wrong. Next."

Suddenly the car was bedlam as we began arguing about where our 26
plans had gone wrong. "Maybe we should have got the guy who knew
how to spell *hayseed*," Dogbite said. We argued all the way to the Scout
meeting, but it was the sort of argument that erupts on a team that has
already lost the game. We knew Keith had been our best shot.

Keith now teaches English to college students. He presumably has 27
scholarly credentials that go beyond spelling, but he still worries about
yiffniff. Not long ago, while we were talking about something else, he
suddenly said, "Maybe I should have put a hyphen between yiff and niff."

"No, it doesn't have a hyphen," I said.   28

"How do you know?"   29

"Because the other day one of my kids spelled it your way except   30
with a hyphen, and I had to tell her she was wrong," I said. "It's a
shame. She's really had her eye on winning that new pair of shoes."

QUESTIONS ON MEANING

1. What do you take to be the author's PURPOSE in telling this story? Is there more than one purpose?
2. How do you interpret the sentence in paragraph 20, in which Trillin writes of his father, "His views on honesty made the Boy Scout position on that subject seem wishy-washy"?
3. How do you think Trillin knows how to spell *yiffniff*? Where in the text is it implied that he knows at all?
4. What are some possible lessons Trillin's father was teaching the boys with his spelling contest?

QUESTIONS ON WRITING STRATEGY

1. What is the EFFECT of the use of the word *you* in the first paragraph?
2. How does the dialogue contribute to the story's TONE?
3. How does Trillin's narration make a TRANSITION between events of the past and of the present?
4. What effect does Trillin gain by withholding the actual spelling of *yiffniff* from the reader?
5. **OTHER METHODS.** The final paragraph suggests a COMPARISON AND CONTRAST between Trillin's daughter and his friends when they were children. How is the daughter like the boys? How is she different?

QUESTIONS ON LANGUAGE

1. How many spellings for *yiffniff* can you think of, besides those offered (and rejected) in Trillin's essay?

2. What is implied about cousin Keith in paragraph 21 by Trillin's joke that "the word he missed in the [spelling bee] finals was *hayseed*"?
3. Consult a dictionary if you need help in defining the following: ringer (para. 21); emboldened (24); bedlam (26).

SUGGESTIONS FOR WRITING

1. **JOURNAL WRITING.** Make up a word like *yiffniff* that could have many possible spellings. (Some sounds in English with varying spellings include *f/ff/pf/ph/gh; ow/ou/au; ough/ew; uff/ough; k/ck/c; tch/ch.*)
   FROM JOURNAL TO ESSAY. From your journal entry, build a narrative in which you imagine yourself as a parent driving a car, offering prizes for the spelling of your imagined word, and your children guessing spellings.
2. Trillin's essay focuses on time spent in the car with his friends and his father. Write an essay based on a vivid memory you have of being in a car as a child.
3. **CRITICAL WRITING.** What can you INFER about Trillin's father from this essay? Look especially at paragraphs 4, 7, 14–15, 17, 19, 20, and 25. Use specific examples and quotations as EVIDENCE.
4. **CONNECTIONS.** Compare "Spelling Yiffniff" with Amy Tan's "Fish Cheeks" (p. 57). Both authors write humorously about childhood experiences with their parents, but there are some differences in tone and purpose. Write a COMPARISON AND CONTRAST essay in which you examine both the similarities between the two essays and the differences.

CALVIN TRILLIN ON WRITING

In an interview conducted by his wife, Alice Trillin, and published in the *Journal of Basic Writing,* Calvin Trillin described his drafting process:

I do a kind of predraft—what I call a "vomit-out." I don't even look at my notes to write it. It...starts out, at least, in the form of a story. But it degenerates fairly quickly, and by page four or five sometimes the sentences aren't complete. I write almost the length of the story in this way. The whole operation takes no more than an hour at the typewriter, but it sometimes takes me all day to do it because I'm tired and I've put it off a bit. Sometimes I don't even look at the vomit-out for the rest of the week and I have an absolute terror of anybody seeing it. It's a very embarrassing document. I tear it up at the end of the week.

I don't write a predraft for fiction or for humor, but I can't seem to do without one for nonfiction. I've tried to figure out why I need it, what purpose it serves. I think it gives me an inventory of what I want to say and an opportunity to see which way the tone of the story is going to go, which is very important. Also, this is about the time that I begin to see technical problems that will come up—for example, that one part of the story doesn't lead into the next, or that I should write the story in the first person, or start it in a different way.

FOR DISCUSSION

1. The term "vomit-out" is Trillin's own—not one you're likely to find in another text that explains the writing process. Why is the term appropriate for the kind of drafting Trillin describes?
2. What, according to Trillin, are the advantages of writing a "vomit-out"?

RALPH ELLISON

Ralph Waldo Ellison is best known for his award-winning novel *Invisible Man* (1952), about a black man who seeks his identity somewhere beyond white and black stereotypes. Born in 1919, Ellison studied music and read literature at Tuskegee Institute in Alabama but left before graduating for lack of money. He began publishing stories in the late 1930s and wrote essays of autobiography, criticism, and cultural history that were collected in *Shadow and Act* (1964) and *Going to the Territory* (1986). At New York University, Ellison was Albert Schweitzer Professor in Humanities for almost a decade, and he lectured at Rutgers, Yale, and many other universities. Ellison died in 1994, but his words continue to be published: *Collected Essays* and *Conversations with Ralph Ellison* both appeared in 1995, and *Juneteenth*, a novel extracted by his literary executor, John F. Callahan, from more than two thousand pages of drafts, appeared in 1999.

On Being the Target of Discrimination

Ellison grew up in Oklahoma, where he felt that "relationships between the races were more fluid and thus more human than in the old slave states." Still, as a boy he knew discrimination in "brief impersonal encounters, stares, vocal inflections, hostile laughter, or public reversals of private expectations." He uses narration to recount some of these slights in this essay, which first appeared in 1989 in *A World of Difference*, a special *New York Times* supplement devoted to reducing racial and ethnic prejudice.

It got to you first at the age of six, and through your own curiosity. 1
With kindergarten completed and the first grade ahead, you were eagerly anticipating your first day of public school. For months you had been imagining your new experience and the children, known and unknown, with whom you would study and play. But the physical framework of your imagining, an elementary school in the process of construction, lay close at hand on the block-square site across the street from your home. For over a year you had watched it rise and spread in the air to become a handsome structure of brick and stone, then seen its broad encircling grounds arrayed with seesaws, swings, and baseball diamonds. You had imagined this picture-book setting as the scene of your new experience, and when enrollment day arrived, with its grounds astir with bright colors and voices of kids like yourself, it did, indeed, become the site of your very first lesson in public schooling—though not within its classrooms, as you had imagined, but well

outside its walls. For while located within a fairly mixed neighborhood this new public school was exclusively for whites.

It was then you learned that you would attend a school located far to the south of your neighborhood, and that reaching it involved a journey which took you over, either directly or by way of a viaduct which arched head-spinning high above, a broad expanse of railroad tracks along which a constant traffic of freightcars, switch engines, and passenger trains made it dangerous for a child to cross. And that once the tracks were safely negotiated you continued past warehouses, factories, and loading docks, and then through a notorious red-light district where black prostitutes in brightly colored housecoats and Mary Jane shoes supplied the fantasies and needs of a white clientele. Considering the fact that you couldn't attend school with white kids this made for a confusion that was further confounded by the giggling jokes which older boys whispered about the district's peculiar form of integration. For you it was a grown-up's mystery, but streets being no less schools than routes to schools, the district would soon add a few forbidden words to your vocabulary.

It took a bit of time to forget the sense of incongruity aroused by your having to walk *past* a school to get *to* a school, but soon you came to like your school, your teachers, and most of your schoolmates. Indeed, you soon enjoyed the long walks and anticipated the sights you might see, the adventures you might encounter, and the many things not taught in school that could be learned along the way. Your school was not nearly so fine as that which faced your home but it had its attractions. Among them its nearness to a park, now abandoned by whites, in which you picnicked and played. And there were the two tall cylindrical fire-escapes on either wing of its main building down which it was a joy to lie full-length and slide, spiraling down and around three stories to the ground—providing no outraged teacher was waiting to strap your legs once you sailed out of its chute like a shot off a fireman's shovel. Besides, in your childish way you were learning that it was better to take self-selected risks and pay the price than be denied the joy or pain of risk-taking by those who begrudged your existence.

Beginning when you were four or five you had known the joy of trips to the city's zoo, but one day you would ask your mother to take you there and have her sigh and explain that it was now against the law for Negro kids to view the animals. Had someone done something bad to the animals? No. Had someone tried to steal them or feed them poison? No. Could white kids still go? Yes! So why? Quit asking questions, it's the law and only because some white folks are out to turn this state into a part of the South.

This sudden and puzzling denial of a Saturday's pleasure was disappointing and so angered your mother that later, after the zoo was moved north of the city, she decided to do something about it. Thus one warm Saturday afternoon with you and your baby brother dressed in your best she took you on a long streetcar ride which ended at a strange lakeside park, in which you found a crowd of noisy white people. Having assumed that you were on your way to the integrated cemetery where at the age of three you had been horrified beyond all tears or forgetting when you saw your father's coffin placed in the ground, you were bewildered. But now as your mother herded you and your brother in to the park you discovered that you'd come to the zoo and were so delighted that soon you were laughing and babbling as excitedly as the kids around you.

Your mother was pleased and as you moved through the crowd of   6
white parents and children she held your brother's hand and allowed as much time for staring at the cages of rare animals as either of you desired. But once your brother began to tire she herded you out of the park and toward the streetcar line. And then it happened.

Just as you reached the gate through which crowds of whites were   7
coming and going you had a memorable lesson in the strange ways of segregated-democracy as instructed by a guard in civilian clothes. He was a white man dressed in a black suit and a white straw hat, and when he looked at the fashion in which your mother was dressed, then down to you and your brother, he stiffened, turned red in the face, and stared as though at something dangerous.

"Girl," he shouted, "where are your *white* folks!"   8

"*White* folks," your mother said. "What white folks? I don't *have* any   9
white folks, I'm a Negro!"

"Now don't you get smart with me, colored gal," the white man   10
said. "I mean where are the white folks you come *out* here with!"

"But I just told you that I didn't come here with any white people,"   11
your mother said. "I came here with my boys..."

"Then what are you doing in this park," the white man said.   12

And now when your mother answered you could hear the familiar   13
sound of anger in her voice.

"I'm here," she said, "because I'm a *taxpayer*, and I thought it was   14
about time that my boys have a look at those animals. And for that I didn't *need* any *white* folks to show me the way!"

"Well," the white man said, "*I'm* here to tell you that you're break-   15
ing the law! So now you'll have to leave. Both you and your chillun too. The rule says no niggers is allowed in the zoo. That's the law and I'm enforcing it!"

"Very well," your mother said, "we've seen the animals anyway and   16
were on our way to the streetcar line when you stopped us."

"That's fine," the white man said, "and when that car comes you be   17
sure that you get on it, you hear? You and your chillun too!"

So it was quite a day. You had enjoyed the animals with your baby   18
brother and had another lesson in the sudden ways good times could be
turned into bad when white people looked at your color instead of *you.*
But better still, you had learned something of your mother's courage
and were proud that she had broken an unfair law and stood up for her
right to do so. For while the white man kept staring until the streetcar
arrived she ignored him and answered your brother's questions about
the various animals. Then the car came with its crowd of white parents
and children, and when you were entrained and rumbling home past
the fine lawns and houses your mother gave way to a gale of laughter;
in which, hesitantly at first, and then with assurance and pride, you
joined. And from that day the incident became the source of a family
joke that was sparked by accidents, faux pas, or obvious lies. Then one
of you was sure to frown and say, "Well, I think you'll have to go now,
both you and your chillun too!" And the family would laugh hilari-
ously. Discrimination teaches one to discriminate between discrimina-
tors while countering absurdity with black (Negro? Afro-American?
African-American?) comedy.

When you were eight you would move to one of the white sections   19
through which you often passed on the way to your father's grave and
your truly last trip to the zoo. For now your mother was the custodian
of several apartments located in a building which housed on its street
floor a drug store, a tailor shop, a Piggly Wiggly market, and a branch
post office. Built on a downward slope, the building had at its rear a
long driveway which led from the side street past an empty lot to a
group of garages in which the apartments' tenants stored their cars.
Built at an angle with wings facing north and east, the structure supported a servant's quarters which sat above its angle like a mock watch-
tower atop a battlement, and it was there that you now lived.

Reached by a flight of outside stairs, it consisted of four small   20
rooms, a bath, and a kitchen. Windows on three of its sides provided a
view across the empty frontage to the street, of the back yards behind
it, and of the back wall and windows of the building in which your
mother worked. It was quite comfortable but you secretly disliked the
idea of your mother living in service and missed your friends who now
lived far away. Nevertheless, the neighborhood was pleasant, served by
a sub-station of the streetcar line, and marked by a variety of activities
which challenged your curiosity. Even its affluent alleys were more exciting to explore than those of your old neighborhood, and the one
white friend you were to acquire in the area lived nearby.

This friend was a brilliant but sickly boy who was tutored at home,   21
and with him you shared your new interest in building radios, a hobby
at which he was quite skilled. Your friendship eased your loneliness and
helped dispel some of the mystery and resentment imposed by segrega-

tion. Through access to his family, headed by an important Episcopalian minister, you learned more about whites and thus about yourself. With him you could make comparisons that were not so distorted by the racial myths which obstructed your thrust toward self-perception; compare their differences in taste, discipline, and manners with those of Negro families of comparable status and income; observe variations between your friend's boyish lore and your own, and measure his intelligence, knowledge, and ambitions against your own. For you this was a most important experience and a rare privilege, because up to now the prevailing separation of the races had made it impossible to learn how you and your Negro friends compared with boys who lived on the white side of the color line. It was said by word of mouth, proclaimed in newsprint, and dramatized by acts of discriminatory law that you were inferior. You were barred from vying with them in sports and games, competing in the classroom or the world of art. Yet what you saw, heard, and smelled of them left irrepressible doubts. So you ached for objective proof, for a fair field of testing.

Even your school's proud marching band was denied participation   22
in the statewide music contests so popular at the time, as though so airy and earth-transcending an art as music would be contaminated if performed by musicians of different races.

Which was especially disturbing because after the father of a friend   23
who lived next door in your old neighborhood had taught you the beginner's techniques required to play valved instruments you had decided to become a musician. Then shortly before moving among whites your mother had given you a brass cornet, which in the isolation of the servant's quarters you practiced hours on end. But you yearned to play with other musicians and found none available. Now you lived less than a block from a white school with a famous band, but there was no one in the neighborhood with whom to explore the mysteries of the horn. You could hear the school band's music and watch their marching, but joining in making the thrilling sounds was impossible. Nor did it help that you owned the scores to a few of their marches and could play with a certain facility and fairly good tone. So there, surrounded by sounds but unable to share a sound, you went it alone. You turned yourself into a one-man band.

You played along as best you could with the phonograph, read the   24
score to *The Carnival of Venice* while listening to Del Steigers executing triple-tongue variations on its themes; played the trumpet parts of your bandbook's marches while humming in your head the supporting voices of horns and reeds. And since your city was a seedbed of Southwestern jazz you played Kansas City riffs, bugle calls, and wha-wha-muted imitations of blues singers' pleas. But none of this made up for your lack of fellow musicians. And then, late one Saturday afternoon

when your mother and brother were away, and when you had dozed off while reading, you awoke to the nearby sound of live music. At first you thought you were dreaming, and then that you were listening to the high school band, but that couldn't be the source because, instead of floating over building tops and bouncing off wall and windowpane, the sounds you heard rose up, somewhat muffled, from below.

With that you ran to a window which faced the driveway, and 25 looking down through the high windowpane of the lighted post office you could see the metal glint of instruments. Then you were on your feet and down the stairs, keeping to the shadows as you drew close and peeped below. And there you looked down upon a room full of men and women postal workers who were playing away at a familiar march. It was like the answer to a silent prayer because you could tell by the sound that they were beginners like yourself and the covers of the thicket of bandbooks revealed that they were of the same set as yours. For a while you listened and hummed along, unseen but shaking with excitement in the dimming twilight. And then, hardly before the idea formed in your head, you were skipping up the stairs to grab your cornet, lyre, and bandbook and hurtling down again to the drive.

For a while you listened, hearing the music come to a pause and the 26 sound of the conductor's voice. Then came a rap on a music stand and once again the music. And now turning to the march by the light from the window, you snapped score to lyre, raised horn to lip, and began to play; at first silently tonguing the notes through the mouthpiece and then, carried away with the thrill of stealing a part of the music, you tensed your diaphragm and blew. And as you played, keeping time with your foot on the concrete drive, you realized that you were a better cor-netist than some in the band and grew bold in the pride of your sound. Now in your mind you were marching along a downtown street to the flying of flags, the tramping of feet, and the cheering of excited crowds. For at last by an isolated act of brassy cunning you had become a mem-ber of the band.

Yes, but unfortunately you then let yourself become so carried away 27 that you forgot to listen for the conductor's instructions which you were too high and hidden to see. Suddenly the music faded and you opened your ears to the fact that you were now rendering a lonely solo in the startled quietness. And before you could fully return to reality there came the sound of table legs across a floor and a rustle of move-ment ending in the appearance of a white startled face in the opened window. Then you heard a man's voice exclaim, "I'll be damn, it's a little nigger!" whereupon you took off like quail at the sound of sud-den shotgun fire.

Next thing you knew, you were up the stairs and on your bed, cry- 28 ing away in the dark your guilt and embarrassment. You cried and cried, asking yourself how could you have been so lacking in pride as to shame yourself and your entire race by butting in where you weren't wanted. And this just to make some amateur music. To this you had no answers but then and there you made a vow that it would never happen again. And then, slowly, slowly, as you lay in the dark, your earlier lessons in the absurd nature of racial relations came to your aid. And suddenly you found yourself laughing, both at the way you'd run away and the shock you'd caused by joining unasked in the music.

Then you could hear yourself intoning in your eight-year-old's imitation of a white Southern accent. "Well boy, you broke the law, so you have to go, and that means you and your chillun too!"　　29

QUESTIONS ON MEANING

1. What do you see as Ellison's PURPOSE in writing this essay?
2. What does the phrase "You and your chillun too" mean in paragraph 17? What does it come to mean in the writer's family? What does it mean at the end of the essay?
3. How does the writer's self-image change from the beginning of the narrative to the end?

QUESTIONS ON WRITING STRATEGY

1. What is the narrator's POINT OF VIEW? What PERSON does the narrator use? What EFFECT does this choice of person have on you as reader?
2. Why do you think this essay was published in a newspaper supplement designed to reduce discrimination (see the note on the essay, p. 67)? How did the essay affect your understanding of or attitude toward discrimination?
3. Why does Ellison narrate several events instead of just one? What is the point of each incident?
4. How do we learn that the narrator's father is dead? Is this fact important to the narrative? Is the narrator's handling of it effective?
5. **OTHER METHODS.** Comment on Ellison's use of EXAMPLES in paragraphs 3 and 24. What do they add?

QUESTIONS ON LANGUAGE

1. What do the DESCRIPTION and dialogue in paragraphs 7–17 tell you about Ellison's attitude toward the white zoo guard?
2. What is generally meant by "black comedy" or "black humor"? What joke is Ellison making at the end of paragraph 18?
3. Define: astir (para. 1); viaduct, clientele (2); incongruity, begrudged (3); faux pas (18); battlement (19); lore, vying (21); intoning (29).

SUGGESTIONS FOR WRITING

1. **JOURNAL WRITING.** Have you ever broken a code (whether an unwritten rule or a recorded law) to do something? How did the experience make you feel? Did you get caught?

   FROM JOURNAL TO ESSAY. Write an essay that EVALUATES the worth of breaking the code you described in your journal. What did you risk and gain (or lose)? Make sure to use concrete details to narrate both the incident and the outcome.

2. Write a narrative about a childhood event in which you discovered something about your place in the world. Give careful consideration to point of view and the use of dialogue.

3. Relate an incident from your childhood that illustrates how you felt about a particular environment — a house, rooftop, school, neighborhood, clearing in the woods. Use description to create a clear picture of the place.

4. **CRITICAL WRITING.** Ellison's use of *you* for the participant in his story is unusual; we might expect *I* or, less commonly, *he*. To ANALYZE this strategy, rewrite paragraph 28 twice, first substituting *I/my* and then *he/his* for *you/your*. (You'll need to change verbs to match the new pronouns.) Read the paragraphs aloud, analyzing the effect of each pronoun: Does it create distance or immediacy? Does it elicit more or less sympathy for the narrator? Is it clear or confusing? What can you INFER about Ellison's reasons for choosing *you*? In an essay, evaluate Ellison's choice, supporting your ideas with examples from the essay or your rewrites.

5. **CONNECTIONS.** If you haven't already, read Maya Angelou's "Champion of the World" (p. 52). COMPARE AND CONTRAST the ways the African Americans in Ellison's and Angelou's essays find their value as human beings.

RALPH ELLISON ON WRITING

In his introduction to his essay collection *Shadow and Act* (1964), Ralph Ellison talks about how he came to be a writer. "When the first of these essays [reprinted in *Shadow and Act*] was published I regarded myself — in my most secret heart at least — a musician.... Writing was far from a serious matter.... Nor had I invested in writing any long hours of practice and study. Rather it was a reflex of reading, an extension of a source of pleasure, escape, and instruction.... It was not, then, the *process* of writing which initially claimed my attention, but the finished creations, the artifacts — poems, plays, novels.... The pleasure I derived from reading had long been a necessity, and in the *act* of reading, that marvelous collaboration between the writer's artful vision and the reader's sense of life, I had become acquainted with other possible selves — freer, more courageous and ingenuous and, during the course of the narrative at least, even wise."

The process of writing did not attract Ellison as strongly until he actually started writing. "Once involved," he says, "I soon became consciously concerned with craft, with technique.... I was gradually led, often reluctantly, to become consciously concerned with the nature of the culture and the society out of which American fiction is fabricated."

For Ellison, "the act of writing requires a constant plunging back into the shadow of the past where time hovers ghostlike.... [It is] the agency of my efforts to answer the question: Who am I, what am I, how did I come to be? What shall I make of the life around me, what celebrate, what reject, how confront the snare of good and evil which is inevitable? What does American society *mean* when regarded out of my *own* eyes, when informed by my *own* sense of the past and viewed by my *own* complex sense of the present? How, in other words, should I think of myself and my pluralistic sense of the world, how express my vision of the human predicament?"

FOR DISCUSSION

1. How did reading prepare Ellison for writing?
2. What connection does Ellison see between writing and personal identity?

BARBARA HUTTMANN

BARBARA HUTTMANN is a registered nurse, a health-care administrator, and a writer on health-care issues. Born in 1935, she received a B.S. in nursing and an M.S. in nursing administration. She has directed a consulting firm for hospitals, nursing organizations, and health-care consumers, and she is currently a technical writer for a medical software company. Huttmann has also published two books, *The Patient's Advocate* (1981) and *Code Blue: A Nurse's True-Life Story* (1982). She lives in California.

A Crime of Compassion

As a nurse, Huttmann has had to care for many people who are dying. In this essay from a 1983 *Newsweek*, Huttmann tells of one such patient, Mac, whose rapid decline she witnessed and whose death she finally did nothing to prevent. She uses narration to explain herself and to argue that patients like Mac have the right to choose death.

"Murderer," a man shouted. "God help patients who get *you* for a nurse."

"What gives you the right to play God?" another one asked.

It was the Phil Donahue show where the guest is a fatted calf and the audience a 200-strong flock of vultures hungering to pick at the bones. I had told them about Mac, one of my favorite cancer patients. "We resuscitated him 52 times in just one month. I refused to resuscitate him again. I simply sat there and held his hand while he died."

There wasn't time to explain that Mac was a young, witty, macho cop who walked into the hospital with 32 pounds of attack equipment, looking as if he could single-handedly protect the whole city, if not the entire state. "Can't get rid of this cough," he said. Otherwise, he felt great.

Before the day was over, tests confirmed that he had lung cancer. And before the year was over, I loved him, his wife, Maura, and their three kids as if they were my own. All the nurses loved him. And we all battled his disease for six months without ever giving death a thought. Six months isn't such a long time in the whole scheme of things, but it was long enough to see him lose his youth, his wit, his macho, his hair, his bowel and bladder control, his sense of taste and smell, and his ability to do the slightest thing for himself. It was also long enough to watch Maura's transformation from a young woman into a haggard, beaten old lady.

When Mac had wasted away to a 60-pound skeleton kept alive by liquid food we poured down a tube, i.v. solutions we dripped into his veins, and oxygen we piped to a mask on his face, he begged us: "Mercy...for God's sake, please just let me go."

The first time he stopped breathing, the nurse pushed the button 7 that calls a "code blue" throughout the hospital and sends a team rushing to resuscitate the patient. Each time he stopped breathing, sometimes two or three times in one day, the code team came again. The doctors and technicians worked their miracles and walked away. The nurses stayed to wipe the saliva that drooled from his mouth, irrigate the big craters of bedsores that covered his hips, suction the lung fluids that threatened to drown him, clean the feces that burned his skin like lye, pour the liquid food down the tube attached to his stomach, put pillows between his knees to ease the bone-on-bone pain, turn him every hour to keep the bedsores from getting worse, and change his gown and linen every two hours to keep him from being soaked in perspiration.

At night I went home and tried to scrub away the smell of decay- 8 ing flesh that seemed woven into the fabric of my uniform. It was in my hair, the upholstery of my car—there was no washing it away. And every night I prayed that Mac would die, that his agonized eyes would never again plead with me to let him die.

Every morning I asked his doctor for a "no-code" order. Without 9 that order, we had to resuscitate every patient who stopped breathing. His doctor was one of several who believe we must extend life as long as we have the means and knowledge to do it. To not do it is to be liable for negligence, at least in the eyes of many people, including some nurses. I thought about what it would be like to stand before a judge, accused of murder, if Mac stopped breathing and I didn't call a code.

And after the fifty-second code, when Mac was still lucid enough 10 to beg for death again, and Maura was crumbled in my arms again, and when no amount of pain medication stilled his moaning and agony, I wondered about a spiritual judge. Was all this misery and suffering supposed to be building character or infusing us all with the sense of humility that comes from impotence?

Had we, the whole medical community, become so arrogant that 11 we believed in the illusion of salvation through science? Had we become so self-righteous that we thought meddling in God's work was our duty, our moral imperative and our legal obligation? Did we really believe that we had the right to force "life" on a suffering man who had begged for the right to die?

Such questions haunted me more than ever early one morning 12 when Maura went home to change her clothes and I was bathing Mac. He had been still for so long, I thought he at last had the blessed relief of coma. Then he opened his eyes and moaned, "Pain...no more...Barbara...do something...God, let me go."

The desperation in his eyes and voice riddled me with guilt. "I'll   13
stop," I told him as I injected the pain medication.

I sat on the bed and held Mac's hands in mine. He pressed his bony   14
fingers against my hand and muttered, "Thanks." Then there was one
soft sigh and I felt his hands go cold in mine. "Mac?" I whispered, as I
waited for his chest to rise and fall again.

A clutch of panic banded my chest, drew my finger to the code but-   15
ton, urged me to do something, anything…but sit there alone with
death. I kept one finger on the button, without pressing it, as a waxen
pallor slowly transformed his face from person to empty shell. Nothing
I've ever done in my 47 years has taken so much effort as it took *not* to
press that code button.

Eventually, when I was as sure as I could be that the code team   16
would fail to bring him back, I entered the legal twilight zone and
pushed the button. The team tried. And while they were trying, Maura
walked into the room and shrieked, "No…don't let them do this to
him…for God's sake…please, no more."

Cradling her in my arms was like cradling myself, Mac, and all   17
those patients and nurses who had been in this place before, who do
the best they can in a death-denying society.

So a TV audience accused me of murder. Perhaps I am guilty. If a   18
doctor had written a no-code order, which is the only *legal* alternative,
would he have felt any less guilty? Until there is legislation making it a
criminal act to code a patient who has requested the right to die, we
will all of us risk the same fate as Mac. For whatever reason, we developed the means to prolong life, and now we are forced to use it. We do
not have the right to die.

QUESTIONS ON MEANING

1. Is Huttmann's PURPOSE in this essay personal (wanting to justify her act) or
   social (wanting to establish the right to die) or both? Explain.
2. What is the contradiction in the title of the essay?
3. What personal risk does Huttmann assume when she decides not to press
   the button? What does she mean by "legal twilight zone" (para. 16)?
4. Is Huttmann confident that she made the right decision?
5. Where does Huttmann state her THESIS?

QUESTIONS ON WRITING STRATEGY

1. Why does Huttmann begin the essay the way she does? What do we AS-
   SUME about the nurse referred to in the first sentence, and at what point do
   we begin to question that assumption?

2. What is the TONE of this piece? How does Huttmann manage to avoid the SENTIMENTALITY one might expect of an essay on this subject? (Cite specific EXAMPLES from the text.)
3. How does the detail about resuscitating Mac fifty-two times in one month (para. 3) contribute to the effectiveness of Huttmann's ARGUMENT?
4. **OTHER METHODS.** This essay illustrates how narrative can help promote an argument. Summarize Huttmann's argument. What does she gain by supporting it with a story?

QUESTIONS ON LANGUAGE

1. Consult a dictionary for any of the following words whose meanings you are unsure of: resuscitate (para. 3); haggard (5); irrigate, suction, feces, lye, bedsores (7); lucid, infusing, impotence (10); imperative (11); riddled (13); banded, pallor (15).
2. Some of the words in the vocabulary list above are medical terminology, but perhaps fewer than one would expect, given the subject. What about her AUDIENCE (originally readers of *Newsweek* magazine) would influence Huttmann's use of terms?
3. Find words in the essay that illustrate Huttmann's particular fondness for Mac. What difference does the closeness of their relationship make to her argument?
4. Explain the METAPHOR in paragraph 3.

SUGGESTIONS FOR WRITING

1. **JOURNAL WRITING.** What do you think of Huttmann's essay? Does a terminally ill patient have a right to choose death? Should a doctor or anyone else be legally empowered to overrule a patient's wish for death? **FROM JOURNAL TO ESSAY.** After exploring your opinions and beliefs in your journal, write an essay arguing for or against the right of a terminally ill patient to choose death. You may, like Huttmann, support your argument with a narrative of personal experience. Or you may argue on other grounds — religious, moral, humanitarian, medical, and so on. In your argument, be sure to acknowledge the views of those who might oppose you, as you understand those views. This acknowledgment will help show your fairness and reach out to more readers.
2. Think back to a moment in your life when you had to make a difficult choice, one with important consequences. (The stakes need not have been as high as in Huttmann's essay.) What were the circumstances? What was the result of the decision you made? In a narrative essay, start by stating the choice you had to make and its implications; then go back and relate the circumstances; and, finally, conclude by explaining the results of your choice and its effectiveness.
3. Huttmann presents two opposed ideas of God's role in human life and death. For the member of Phil Donahue's audience, only God can decide to stop someone's life; anyone who tries to make that decision is "play[ing] God" (para. 2). For Huttmann, in contrast, sustaining life artificially is

"meddling in God's work" (para. 11). Which view do you agree with, and why? (If you'd rather not debate the role of God, try "nature" instead.)

4. **CRITICAL WRITING.** When they take the Hippocratic oath, physicians promise to "do no harm." It could be argued that neither choice available to Huttmann avoids harm to her patient. Given the circumstances of the patient she describes, did she choose the less harmful alternative? Why, or why not? Can your argument be generalized: Is it applicable in every case?

5. **CONNECTIONS.** Barbara Huttmann and Barbara Lazear Ascher, in "On Compassion" (p. 145), both examine, as Ascher puts it, "the conditions that finally give birth to empathy, the mother of compassion." Write a well-detailed narrative about a time when you helped someone or were helped by someone. Use this essay as an opportunity to examine your own ideas about compassion: How do you define the word? What causes compassionate feelings?

EDGAR ALLAN POE

EDGAR ALLAN POE (1809–49) was the first American writer to gain a reputation outside the United States. His short stories and poems, famously mysterious or frightening, were popular both at home and in Europe, and his literary criticism helped shape the course of French poetry. Poe was born in Boston, grew up in England and Virginia, and died in Baltimore at only forty years of age. His short life was often clouded by family troubles, disciplinary problems (he was expelled from West Point), and heavy drinking; yet he held jobs on magazines, wrote volumes of criticism, published collections of poetry, and crafted immortal stories. Poe is perhaps best known for such stories as "The Tell-Tale Heart" (printed here), "The Pit and the Pendulum" (1843), and "The Cask of Amontillado" (1846), as well as for his poems "Annabel Lee" (1849, addressed to his recently deceased wife) and "The Raven" (1845). In honor of the famous poet who died there, the city of Baltimore in 1996 named its football team the Baltimore Ravens, thus making Poe, as the humorist Russell Baker observed, "the first literary man to break into professional sports."

The Tell-Tale Heart

This masterpiece of paranoid terror, first published in 1843, uses narration not only to entertain us but also to tell us something of human nature. If you've never read the story before, bear with the occasionally old-fashioned style until you swing into the narrator's groove (as you certainly will). If you have read the story, read it again just for the pleasure, noticing how Poe's narrative technique pulls you in and along.

True!—nervous—very, very dreadfully nervous I had been and am; but why *will* you say that I am mad? The disease had sharpened my senses—not destroyed—not dulled them. Above all was the sense of hearing acute. I heard all things in the heaven and in the earth. I heard many things in hell. How, then, am I mad? Hearken! and observe how healthily—how calmly I can tell you the whole story. 1

It is impossible to say how first the idea entered my brain; but once conceived, it haunted me day and night. Object there was none. Passion there was none. I loved the old man. He had never wronged me. He had never given me insult. For his gold I had no desire. I think it was his eye! yes, it was this! One of his eyes resembled that of a vulture—a pale blue eye, with a film over it. Whenever it fell upon me, my blood ran cold; and so by degrees—very gradually—I made up my mind to take the life of the old man, and thus rid myself of the eye for ever. 2

Now this is the point. You fancy me mad. Madmen know nothing.   3
But you should have seen *me*. You should have seen how wisely I proceeded—with what caution—with what foresight—with what dissimulation I went to work! I was never kinder to the old man than
during the whole week before I killed him. And every night, about
midnight, I turned the latch of his door and opened it—oh, so gently!
And then, when I had made an opening sufficient for my head, I put in
a dark lantern, all closed, closed, so that no light shone out, and then I
thrust in my head. Oh, you would have laughed to see how cunningly I
thrust it in! I moved it slowly—very, very slowly, so that I might not
disturb the old man's sleep. It took me an hour to place my whole head
within the opening so far that I could see him as he lay upon his bed.
Ha—would a madman have been so wise as this? And then, when my
head was well in the room, I undid the lantern cautiously—oh, so cautiously—cautiously (for the hinges creaked)—I undid it just so much
that a single thin ray fell upon the vulture eye. And this I did for seven
long nights—every night just after midnight—but I found the eye always closed; and so it was impossible to do the work; for it was not the
old man who vexed me, but his Evil Eye. And every morning, when the
day broke, I went boldly into the chamber, and spoke courageously to
him, calling him by name in a hearty tone, and inquiring how he had
passed the night. So you see he would have been a very profound old
man, indeed, to suspect that every night, just at twelve, I looked in
upon him while he slept.

Upon the eighth night I was more than usually cautious in opening   4
the door. A watch's minute hand moves more quickly than did mine.
Never before that night had I *felt* the extent of my own powers—of my
sagacity. I could scarcely contain my feelings of triumph. To think that
there I was, opening the door, little by little, and he not even to dream
of my secret deeds or thoughts. I fairly chuckled at the idea; and perhaps he heard me; for he moved on the bed suddenly, as if startled. Now
you may think that I drew back—but no. His room was as black as
pitch with the thick darkness (for the shutters were close fastened,
through fear of robbers), and so I knew that he could not see the opening of the door, and I kept pushing it on steadily, steadily.

I had my head in, and was about to open the lantern, when my   5
thumb slipped upon the tin fastening, and the old man sprang up in the
bed, crying out—"Who's there?"

I kept quite still and said nothing. For a whole hour I did not move   6
a muscle, and in the meantime I did not hear him lie down. He was still
sitting up in the bed listening;—just as I have done, night after night,
hearkening to the death watches in the wall.

Presently I heard a slight groan, and I knew it was the groan of mor- 7
tal terror. It was not a groan of pain or of grief—oh, no!—it was the

low stifled sound that arises from the bottom of the soul when over-charged with awe. I knew the sound well. Many a night, just at mid-night, when all the world slept, it has welled up from my own bosom, deepening with its dreadful echo, the terrors that distracted me. I say I knew it well. I knew what the old man felt, and pitied him, although I chuckled at heart. I knew that he had been lying awake ever since the first slight noise, when he had turned in the bed. His fears had been ever since growing upon him. He had been trying to fancy them cause-less, but could not. He had been saying to himself—"It is nothing but the wind in the chimney—it is only a mouse crossing the floor," or "it is merely a cricket which has made a single chirp." Yes, he has been try-ing to comfort himself with these suppositions; but he had found all in vain. *All in vain;* because Death, in approaching him, had stalked with his black shadow before him, and enveloped the victim. And it was the mournful influence of the unperceived shadow that caused him to feel—although he neither saw nor heard—to *feel* the presence of my head within the room.

When I had waited a long time, very patiently, without hearing him lie down, I resolved to open a little—a very, very little crevice in the lantern. So I opened it—you cannot imagine how stealthily, stealthily—until, at length, a single dim ray, like the thread of the spi-der, shot from out the crevice and full upon the vulture eye. 8

It was open—wide, wide open—and I grew furious as I gazed upon it. I saw it with perfect distinctness—all a dull blue, with a hideous veil over it that chilled the very marrow in my bones, but I could see noth-ing else of the old man's face or person: for I had directed the ray as if by instinct, precisely upon the damned spot. 9

And now have I not told you that what you mistake for madness is but over-acuteness of the senses?—now, I say, there came to my ears a low, dull, quick sound, such as a watch makes when enveloped in cot-ton. I knew *that* sound well too. It was the beating of the old man's heart. It increased my fury, as the beating of a drum stimulates the sol-dier into courage. 10

But even yet I refrained and kept still. I scarcely breathed. I held the lantern motionless. I tried how steadily I could maintain the ray upon the eye. Meantime the hellish tattoo of the heart increased. It grew quicker and quicker, and louder and louder every instant. The old man's terror *must* have been extreme! It grew louder, I say, louder every moment!—do you mark me well? I have told you that I am nervous: so I am. And now at the dead hour of the night, amid the dreadful silence of that old house, so strange a noise as this excited me to uncontrol-lable terror. Yet, for some minutes longer I refrained and stood still. But the beating grew louder, louder! I thought the heart must burst. And now a new anxiety seized me—the sound would be heard by a neigh- 11 bor! The old man's hour had come! With a loud yell, I threw open the lantern and leaped into the room. He shrieked once — once only. In an instant I dragged him to the floor, and pulled the heavy bed over him. I then smiled gaily, to find the deed so far done. But, for many minutes, the heart beat on with a muffled sound. This, however, did not vex me; it would not be heard through the wall. At length it ceased. The old man was dead. I removed the bed and examined the corpse. Yes, he was stone, stone dead. I placed my hand upon the heart and held it there many minutes. There was no pulsation. He was stone dead. His eye would trouble me no more.

If still you think me mad, you will think so no longer when I describe the wise precautions I took for the concealment of the body. The night waned, and I worked hastily, but in silence. First of all I dismembered the corpse. I cut off the head and the arms and the legs. 12

I then took up three planks from the flooring of the chamber, and deposited all between the scantlings. I then replaced the boards so cleverly, so cunningly, that no human eye — not even *his* — could have detected anything wrong. There was nothing to wash out — no stain of any kind — no blood-spot whatever. I had been too wary for that. A tub had caught all — ha! ha! 13

When I had made an end of these labors, it was four o'clock — still dark as midnight. As the bell sounded the hour, there came a knocking at the street door. I went down to open it with a light heart — for what had I *now* to fear? There entered three men, who introduced themselves, with perfect suavity, as officers of the police. A shriek had been heard by a neighbor during the night; suspicion of foul play had been aroused; information had been lodged at the police office, and they (the officers) had been deputed to search the premises. 14

I smiled — for *what* had I to fear? I bade the gentlemen welcome. The shriek, I said, was my own in a dream. The old man, I mentioned, was absent in the country. I took my visitors all over the house. I bade them search — search *well*. I led them, at length, to *his* chamber. I showed them his treasures, secure, undisturbed. In the enthusiasm of my confidence, I brought chairs into the room, and desired them *here* to rest from their fatigues, while I myself, in the wild audacity of my perfect triumph, placed my own seat upon the very spot beneath which reposed the corpse of the victim. 15

The officers were satisfied. My *manner* had convinced them. I was singularly at ease. They sat, and while I answered cheerily, they chatted familiar things. But, ere long, I felt myself getting pale and wished them gone. My head ached, and I fancied a ringing in my ears: but still they sat and still chatted. The ringing became more distinct: — it continued and became more distinct: I talked more freely to get rid of the feeling: 16

but it continued and gained definitiveness—until, at length, I found that the noise was *not* within my ears.

No doubt I now grew *very* pale;—but I talked more fluently, and   17
with a heightened voice. Yet the sound increased—and what could I do? It was *a low, dull, quick sound—much such a sound as a watch makes when enveloped in cotton.* I gasped for breath—and yet the officers heard it not. I talked more quickly—more vehemently; but the noise steadily increased. I arose and argued about trifles, in a high key and with violent gesticulations, but the noise steadily increased. Why *would* they not be gone? I paced the floor to and fro with heavy strides, as if excited to fury by the observation of the men—but the noise steadily increased. Oh God! what *could* I do? I foamed—I raved—I swore! I swung the chair upon which I had been sitting, and grated it upon the boards, but the noise arose over all and continually increased. It grew louder—louder—*louder!* And still the men chatted pleasantly, and smiled. Was it possible they heard not? Almighty God—no, no! They heard!—they suspected!—they *knew!*—they were making a mockery of my horror—this I thought, and this I think. But any thing was better than this agony! Any thing was more tolerable than this derision! I could bear those hypocritical smiles no longer! I felt that I must scream or die—and now—again!—hark! louder! louder! louder! *louder!*—

"Villains!" I shrieked, "dissemble no more! I admit the deed!—tear   18
up the planks—here, here!—it is the beating of his hideous heart!"

QUESTIONS ON MEANING

1. On what basis does the narrator claim to be sane? Is he convincing?
2. In paragraph 7 the narrator empathizes with his victim's fears. How does he know so much of what the old man feels?
3. Why does the narrator choose to sit directly above the buried heart during his interview with the police?
4. Why does the narrator unnecessarily give himself away in the end?
5. What, in your opinion, was Poe's PURPOSE in writing this story?

QUESTIONS ON WRITING STRATEGY

1. What is the purpose of the opening paragraph? Why does Poe delay the opening of the story?
2. What is the EFFECT of the narrator's addressing the reader directly as *you* (for example, para. 3)?

3. What is the IRONY in the fact that the old man's shutters were always closed (para. 4)?

4. Note the conciseness of the narration in the second half of paragraph 14. From whose POINT OF VIEW is the story being told here? How do you know?

5. **OTHER METHODS.** The narrator complains that he suffers from "over-acuteness of the senses" (para. 10), an affliction that gives Poe an opportunity for rich DESCRIPTION. ANALYZE Poe's treatment of the sense of sound in paragraph 11. How does Poe play on the contrast between sound and silence, stillness and movement, in this paragraph?

QUESTIONS ON LANGUAGE

1. What effect is created by Poe's frequent use of repetition—for instance, "slowly—very, very slowly" (para. 3); "stealthily, stealthily" (8); "The old man was dead.... Yes, he was stone, stone dead.... He was stone dead" (11)? Is this bad prose? Why, or why not?

2. Poe is a master of forceful FIGURES OF SPEECH. In paragraph 4 he writes, "A watch's minute hand moves more quickly than did mine." Substitute the word *hour* for *minute*. Which is more effective, and why? What other powerful figures of speech can you find in the story?

3. What is the effect of Poe's use of italics throughout the story, especially in paragraph 17? Do any of the choices of italicized words seem strange or arbitrary?

4. This story contains a number of words that may be unfamiliar, including a couple of familiar words used in unfamiliar ways (these are asterisked). Look up any words you're unsure of: hearken (para. 1); foresight, dissimulation, cunningly, vexed (3); sagacity (4); stifled, suppositions, mournful (7); crevice, stealthily (8); refrained, tattoo,* mark* (11); dismembered (12); scantlings (13); suavity, deputed (14); bade, fatigues, audacity (15); ere (16); vehemently, gesticulations, derision, hypocritical, hark (17); dissemble (18).

SUGGESTIONS FOR WRITING

1. **JOURNAL WRITING.** Write about an actual crime you know of, setting down the facts as completely and OBJECTIVELY as you can. (If you need ideas for crimes, try looking in a tabloid newspaper or watching a true-crime program on television.)

   FROM JOURNAL TO ESSAY. Retell the events of the crime you have written about from the point of view of the criminal. Choose any psychology you like for the criminal: articulate but mad (like the narrator of Poe's story), guilt-ridden, unjustly accused—use your imagination. Like Poe, you will need to add IMAGES and details to spice up the objective account in your journal.

2. Look up the clinical DEFINITIONS of *obsessive-compulsive disorder* and *paranoia* in an encyclopedia or a psychology textbook. How well does Poe's narrator fit either of these definitions? Make a case for a clinical basis to the narrator's madness, drawing on both the narrator's own descriptions of

his mental states and faculties and the textbook definitions of the two mental disorders.

3. **CRITICAL WRITING.** Notice how much effort Poe devotes to recounting an event as simple as the opening of a door or lantern. How does Poe manage to keep readers on the edge of their seats while working on such a microscopic level? How does he indicate the passing of time? How does he create SUSPENSE? In a brief essay, ANALYZE the rhythm of Poe's narrative, paying close attention to TRANSITIONS.

4. **CONNECTIONS.** In "Safe-Sex Lies" (p. 384) Meghan Daum writes about a very different kind of paranoia from that of Poe's narrator—what she sees as the unreasonable fear of AIDS among low-risk groups. Although it will be easier to CONTRAST than to COMPARE the two selections, try to find as many common points as you can between the paranoia of Poe's narrator and that described by Daum.

EDGAR ALLAN POE ON WRITING

Writing in *Graham's Magazine* in 1842, Edgar Allan Poe commented on the stories of his contemporary Nathaniel Hawthorne and in the process revealed much about his own views of narration. What he says could apply equally to fiction and to nonfiction. (It could also apply equally to female and to male writers. Poe uses the generalized *he*, once universally understood to mean "he or she.")

Poe emphasizes that "in almost all classes of composition, the unity of effect or impression is a point of the greatest importance," something achievable in "the short prose narrative, requiring from a half-hour to one or two hours in its perusal.... In the brief tale,... the author is enabled to carry out the fullness of his intention, be it what it may. During the hour of perusal the soul of the reader is at the writer's control...."

"A skillful literary artist has constructed a tale. If wise, he has not fashioned his thoughts to accommodate his incidents; but having conceived, with deliberate care, a certain unique or single *effect* to be wrought out,... he then combines such events as may best aid him in establishing this preconceived effect. If his very initial sentence tends not to the outbringing of this effect, then he has failed in his first step. In the whole composition there should be no word written, of which the tendency, direct or indirect, is not to the one pre-established design. And by such means, with such care and skill, a picture is at length painted which leaves in the mind of him who contemplates it with a kindred art, a sense of the fullest satisfaction."

FOR DISCUSSION

1. Why, according to Poe, is the "unity of effect" so important to a narrative?
2. What role do you see for revision in Poe's narrative process? Do you think he means that the first sentence must be perfect the first time it's written? Why, or why not?

ADDITIONAL WRITING TOPICS

Narration

1. Write a narrative with one of the following as your subject. It may be (as your instructor may advise) either a first-PERSON memoir or a story written in the third person, observing the experience of someone else. Decide before you begin what your PURPOSE is and whether you are writing (1) an anecdote; (2) an essay consisting mainly of a single narrative; or (3) an essay that includes more than one story.

   A memorable experience from your early life
   A lesson you learned the hard way
   A trip into unfamiliar territory
   An embarrassing moment that taught you something
   A monumental misunderstanding
   An accident
   An unexpected encounter
   A story about a famous person, or someone close to you
   A conflict or contest
   A destructive storm
   An assassination attempt
   A historical event of significance

2. Tell a true story of your early or recent school days, either humorous or serious, relating a struggle you experienced (or still experience) in school.

Note: Writing topics combining narration and description appear on pages 135–36.

2

DESCRIPTION
Writing with Your Senses

THE METHOD

Like narration, DESCRIPTION is a familiar method of expression, already a working part of you. In any talk-fest with friends, you probably do your share of describing. You depict in words someone you've met by describing her clothes, the look on her face, the way she walks. You describe somewhere you've been, something you admire, something you just can't abide. In a diary or in a letter to a friend, you describe your college (cast concrete buildings, crowded walks, pigeons rattling their wings); or perhaps you describe your brand-new secondhand car, from the snakelike glitter of its hubcaps to the odd antiques in its trunk, bequeathed by its previous owner. You hardly can live a day without describing (or hearing described) some person, place, or thing. Small wonder that, in written discourse, description is almost as indispensable as paper.

Description reports the testimony of your senses. It invites your readers to imagine that they, too, not only see but perhaps also hear, taste, smell, and touch the subject you describe. Usually, you write a description for either of two PURPOSES: (1) to convey information without bias or emotion; or (2) to convey it with feeling.

In writing with the first purpose in mind, you write an OBJECTIVE (or *impartial, public,* or *functional*) description. You describe your subject so clearly and exactly that your reader will understand it or recognize it, and you leave your emotions out. Technical or scientific descriptive writing is usually objective: a manual detailing the parts of an internal combustion engine, a biology report on a species of frog. You write this kind of description in sending a friend directions for finding your house: "Look for the green shutters on the windows and a new garbage can at the front door." Although in a personal letter describing your house you might very well become emotionally involved with it (and call it, perhaps, a "fleabag"), in writing an objective description your purpose is not to convey your feelings. You are trying to make the house easily recognized.

The other type of descriptive writing is SUBJECTIVE (or *emotional, personal,* or *impressionistic*). This is the kind included in a magazine advertisement for a new car. It's what you write in your e-mail to a friend setting forth what your college is like—whether you are pleased or displeased with it. In this kind of description, you may use biases and personal feelings—in fact, they are essential. Let us consider a splendid example: a subjective description of a storm at sea. Charles Dickens, in his memoir *American Notes*, conveys his passenger's-eye view of an Atlantic steamship on a morning when the ocean is wild:

> Imagine the ship herself, with every pulse and artery of her huge body swollen and bursting ... sworn to go on or die. Imagine the wind howling, the sea roaring, the rain beating; all in furious array against her. Picture the sky both dark and wild, and the clouds in fearful sympathy with the waves, making another ocean in the air. Add to all this the clattering on deck and down below; the tread of hurried feet; the loud hoarse shouts of seamen; the gurgling in and out of water through the scuppers; with every now and then the striking of a heavy sea upon the planks above, with the deep, dead, heavy sound of thunder heard within a vault; and there is the head wind of that January morning.
>
> I say nothing of what may be called the domestic noises of the ship; such as the breaking of glass and crockery, the tumbling down of stewards, the gambols, overhead, of loose casks and truant dozens of bottled porter, and the very remarkable and far from exhilarating sounds raised in their various staterooms by the seventy passengers who were too ill to get up to breakfast.

Notice how many *sounds* are included in this primarily ear-minded description. We can infer how Dickens feels about the storm. It is a terrifying event that reduces the interior of the vessel to chaos; and yet the writer (in hearing the loose barrels and beer bottles merrily gambol, in finding humor in the seasick passengers' plight) apparently delights in it. Writing subjectively, he intrudes his feelings. Think of what a starkly different description of the very same storm the captain might set down—objectively—in the ship's log: "At 0600 hours, watch reported a wind from due north of 70 knots. Whitecaps were noticed, in height two ells above the bow. Below deck, much gear was reported adrift, and ten casks of ale were broken and their staves strewn about. Mr. Liam Jones, chief steward, suffered a compound fracture of the left leg...." But Dickens, not content simply to record information, strives to ensure that the mind's eye is dazzled and the mind's ear regaled.

Description is usually found in the company of other methods of writing. Often, for instance, it will enliven NARRATION and make the people in the story and the setting unmistakably clear. Writing an ARGUMENT in his essay "Why Don't We Complain?" (p. 496), William F. Buckley, Jr., begins with a description of eighty suffering commuters perspiring in an overheated train; the description makes the argument more powerful. Description will help a writer in examining the EFFECTS of a flood, or in COMPARING AND CONTRASTING two towns. Keep the method of description in mind when you come to try expository and argumentative writing.

THE PROCESS

Purpose, Audience, and Dominant Impression

Understand, first of all, why you are writing about your subject and thus what kind of description is called for. Is it appropriate to perceive and report without emotion or bias—and thus write an objective description? Or is it appropriate to express your personal feelings as well as your perceptions—and thus write a subjective description?

Give a little thought to your AUDIENCE. What do your readers need to be told, if they are to share the perceptions you would have them share, if they are clearly to behold what you want them to? If, let's say, you are describing a downtown street on a Saturday night for an audience of fellow students who live in the same city and know it well, then you need not dwell on the street's familiar geography. What must you tell? Only those details that make the place different on a Saturday night. But if you are remembering your home city, and writing for readers who don't know it, you'll need to establish a few central landmarks to sketch (in their minds) an unfamiliar street on a Saturday night.

Before you begin to write a description, go look at your subject. If that is not possible, your next best course is to spend a few minutes imagining the subject until, in your mind's eye, you can see every flyspeck on it.

Then, having fixed your subject in mind, ask yourself which of its features you'll need to report to your particular audience, for your particular purpose. Ask, "What am I out to accomplish? What main impression of my subject am I trying to give?" Let your description, as a whole, convey this one DOMINANT IMPRESSION. If you plan to write a sub-jective description of an old house, laying weight on its spooky atmos-phere for readers you wish to make shiver, then you might mention its squeaking bats and its shadowy halls, leaving out any reference to its busy swimming pool and the stomping dance music that billows from its interior. If, however, you are describing the house in a classified ad, for an audience of possible buyers, you might focus instead on its eat-in kitchen, working fireplace, and proximity to public transportation. De-tails have to be carefully selected. Feel no grim duty to include every perceptible detail. To do so would only invite chaos—or perhaps, for the reader, mere tedium. Pick out the features that matter most.

Your dominant impression is like the THESIS of your description—the main idea about your subject that you want readers to take away with them. When you use description to explain or to argue, it's usually a good strategy to state that dominant impression outright, tying it to your es-say's thesis or a part of it. In a biology report on a species of frog, for in-stance, you might preface your description with a statement like this one:

> A number of unique features distinguish this frog from others in the order Anura.

Or in an argument in favor of cleaning a local toxic-waste site, you might begin with a description of the site and then state your point about it:

> This landscape is as poisonous as it looks, for underneath its barren crust are enough toxic chemicals to sicken a small village.

When you use subjective description more for its own sake—to show the reader a place or a person, to evoke feelings—you needn't al-ways state your dominant impression as a THESIS SENTENCE, as long as the impression is there dictating the details. Sometimes, though, stating your dominant impression can bring your writing to a climax. That's what Merrill Markoe does at the end of "Bob the Dog," her humorous essay about an unruly pet:

> Yes, we shared a lot of special moments, my dog Bob and I.... So it's a pretty fair tribute to his charisma as a dog that I miss him as much as I do. I miss him a lot.

Organization

You can organize a description in several ways. In depicting the storm at sea—a subjective description—Charles Dickens sorts out the pandemonium for us. He groups the various sounds into two classes: those of sea and sailors, and the "domestic noises" of the ship's passen-gers—their smashing dishes, their rolling bottles, the crashing of stew-ards who wait on them.

Other writers of description rely on their POINT OF VIEW to help them arrange details—the physical angle from which they're perceiving and describing. In the previous chapter, on narration, we spoke of point of view: how essential it is for a story to have a narrator—one who, from a certain position, reports what takes place. A description, too, needs a consistent point of view: that of an observer who stays put and observes steadily. From this point of view, you can make a carefully planned inspection tour of your subject, moving spatially (from left to right, from near to far, from top to bottom, from center to periphery), or perhaps moving from prominent objects to tiny ones, from dull to bright, from commonplace to extraordinary—or vice versa.

The plan for you is the one that best fulfills your purpose, arranging details so that the reader firmly receives the impression you mean to convey. If you were to describe, for instance, a chapel in the middle of a desert, you might begin with the details of the lonely terrain. Then, as if approaching the chapel with the aid of a zoom lens, you might detail its exterior and then go on inside. That might be a workable method to write a description *if* you wanted to create the dominant impression of the chapel as an island of beauty and feeling in the midst of desolation. Say, however, that you had a different impression in mind: to emphasize the spirituality of the chapel's interior. You might then begin your description inside the structure, perhaps with its most prominent feature, the stained glass windows. You might mention the surrounding desert later in your description, but only incidentally.

Whatever method you follow in arranging details, stick with it all the way through. Don't start out describing a group of cats by going from old cats to kittens, then switch in the middle of your description and line up the cats according to color. If your arrangement would cause any difficulty for the reader, you need to rearrange your details. If a writer, in describing a pet shop, should skip about wildly from clerks to cats to customers to cat food to customers to cat food to clerks, the reader may quickly be lost. Instead, the writer might group clerks together with customers, and cats together with cat food (or in some other clear order). But suppose (the writer might protest) it's a wildly confused pet shop I'm trying to describe? No matter—the writer nevertheless has to write in an orderly manner, if the reader is to understand. Dickens describes a scene of shipboard chaos, yet his prose is orderly.

Details

Luckily, to write a memorable description, you don't need a storm at sea or any other awe-inspiring subject. As Judith Ortiz Cofer demonstrates in "Silent Dancing" later in this chapter, you can write about your family as effectively as you write about a tornado. The secret is in the vividness, the evocativeness of the details. Like most good describers, Cofer uses many IMAGES (language calling up concrete sensory experiences), including FIGURES OF SPEECH (expressions that do not mean literally what they say, often describing one thing in terms of another). Cofer writes of radiator hisses that disturbed her sleep "like a nonhuman presence in the room—a dragon sleeping at the entrance of my childhood" (a *simile*), and she describes apartment living as "beehive life" (a *metaphor*). Another writer, the humorist S. J. Perelman, uses metaphor to convey the garish brightness of a certain low-rent house. Notice how he makes clear the spirit of the place: "After a few days, I could have sworn that our faces began to take on the hue of Kodachromes, and even the dog, an animal used to bizarre surroundings, developed a strange, off-register look, as if he were badly printed in overlapping colors."

When you, too, write an effective description, you'll convey your sensory experience as exactly as possible. Find vigorous, specific words, and you will enable your reader to behold with the mind's eye—and to feel with the mind's fingertips.

CHECKLIST FOR REVISING A DESCRIPTION

✔ **SUBJECTIVE OR OBJECTIVE.** Given your purpose and audience, is your description appropriately subjective (emphasizing feelings) or objective (unemotional)?

✔ **DOMINANT IMPRESSION.** What is the dominant impression of your subject? If you haven't stated it, will your readers be able to express it accurately to themselves?

✔ **POINT OF VIEW AND ORGANIZATION.** Do your point of view and organization work together to make your subject clear in readers' minds? Are they consistent?

✔ **DETAILS.** Have you provided all the details—and just those— needed to convey your dominant impression? What needs expanding? What needs condensing or cutting?

✔ **CONCRETE LANGUAGE.** Have you used words that appeal to the senses of sight, hearing, touch, taste, and smell? A vague word such as *loud* does little for readers; a concrete word such as *screeching* works harder, and a fresh figure of speech such as *a screech like a 747 directly overhead* does even more.

DESCRIPTION IN A PARAGRAPH: TWO ILLUSTRATIONS

Using Description to Write About Television

In this paragraph written especially for *The Bedford Reader*, description works with narration to create suspense. Without even knowing the cause of the suspense, we gather tension from the details. Such a paragraph might pull us into an essay on the subject that is finally revealed only in the last sentence.

At 2:59 this Monday afternoon, a thick hush settles like cigarette smoke inside the sweat-scented TV room of Harris Hall. First to arrive, freshman Lee Ann squashes down into the catbird seat in front of the screen. Soon she is flanked by roommates Lisa and Kate, silent, their mouths straight lines, their upturned faces lit by the nervous flicker of a detergent ad. To the left and right of the couch, Pete and Anse crouch on the floor, leaning forward like runners awaiting a starting gun. Behind them, stiff standees line up at attention. Farther back still, English majors and jocks compete for an unobstructed view. Fresh from class, shirttail flapping, arm crooking a bundle of books, Dave barges into the room demanding, "Has it started? Has it started yet?" He is shushed. Somebody shushes a popped-open can of Dr Pepper whose fizz is distractingly loud. What do these students so intently look forward to—the announcement of World War III? A chord of music signals the opening of a soap opera.

Dominant impression (not stated): tense expectation of something vital

Details (underlined) contribute to dominant impression

Organization proceeds from front of room (at TV) to back

Using Description in an Academic Discipline

Description interprets a familiar painting in the following paragraph from a text on art history. The details "translate" the painting, creating a bridge between the reader and the text's reproduction of the great work.

While working on *The Battle of Anghiari*, Leonardo painted his most famous portrait, the *Mona Lisa*. The delicate *sfumato* already noted in the *Madonna of the Rocks* is here so perfected that it seemed miraculous to the artist's contemporaries. The forms are built from layers of glazes so gossamer-thin that the entire panel seems to glow with a gentle light from within. But the fame of the *Mona Lisa* comes not from this pictorial subtlety alone; even more intriguing is the psychological fascination of the sitter's personality. Why, among all the smiling faces ever painted, has this particular one been singled out as "mysterious"? Perhaps the reason is that, as a portrait, the picture does not fit our expectations.

(Sfumato: soft gradations of light and dark)

Main idea (topic sentence) of the paragraph, supported by description of "pictorial subtlety" (above) and "psychological fascination" (below)

The features are too individual for Leonardo to have simply depicted an ideal type, yet the element of idealization is so strong that it blurs the sitter's character. Once again the artist has brought two opposites into harmonious balance. The smile, too, may be read in two ways: as the echo of a momentary mood, and as a timeless, symbolic expression (somewhat like the "Archaic smile" of the Greeks...). Clearly, the *Mona Lisa* embodies a quality of maternal tenderness which was to Leonardo the essence of womanhood. Even the landscape in the background, composed mainly of rocks and water, suggests elemental generative forces.

Details (underlined) contribute to dominant impression

—H. W. Janson, *History of Art*

DESCRIPTION ELSEWHERE IN *THE BEDFORD READER*

Description is such an effective way of building details into writing that every author in this book uses it. Besides the selections in this chapter, the following essays, though developed by at least one other method as well, are largely descriptive.

PART ONE

Maya Angelou, "Champion of the World"
Amy Tan, "Fish Cheeks"
Ralph Ellison, "On Being the Target of Discrimination"
Barbara Huttmann, "A Crime of Compassion"
Edgar Allan Poe, "The Tell-Tale Heart"
Barbara Lazear Ascher, "On Compassion"
Anna Quindlen, "Homeless"
Jeff Greenfield, "The Black and White Truth About Basketball"
Emily Prager, "Our Barbies, Ourselves"
Michael Kroll, "The Unquiet Death of Robert Harris"

PART TWO

Joan Didion, "In Bed"
Annie Dillard, "Lenses"
Maxine Hong Kingston, "No Name Woman"
N. Scott Momaday, "The Way to Rainy Mountain"
George Orwell, "Shooting an Elephant"
Richard Rodriguez, "Aria: A Memoir of a Bilingual Childhood"
E. B. White, "Once More to the Lake"
Virginia Woolf, "The Death of the Moth"

CASE STUDY
Using Description

Edward Johnson was leaving campus for the summer and wanted to sublet his apartment. Scouting around, he discovered that the best place to advertise his apartment was with his college's online "Housing Connection," which served as a network for students, staff, and faculty seeking short- or long-term rentals.

Johnson looked through many of the ads at "The Housing Connection," especially in his category of one-bedrooms, to see how he could make his place seem irresistible compared with the others listed. He noticed that other ads tended to be bare-bones, just the basics on rooms and rent, so he decided to use the twelve lines allotted to him to portray the special qualities of his apartment. In just a couple of drafts, he summoned the descriptive details that would attract a tenant. Here is the actual online posting:

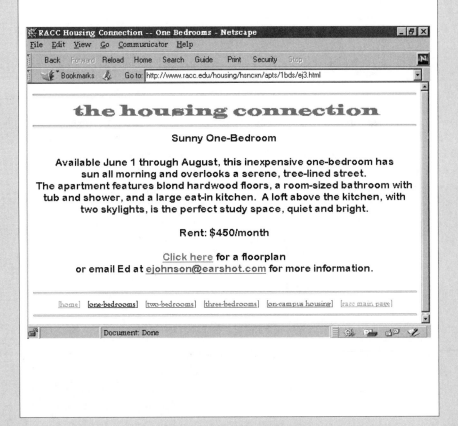

BRAD MANNING

BRAD MANNING was born in Little Rock, Arkansas, in 1967 and grew up near Charlottesville, Virginia. He attended Harvard University, graduating in 1990 with a B.A. in history and religion. At Harvard he played intramural sports and wrote articles and reviews for the *Harvard Independent*. After graduation Manning wrote features and news stories for the *Charlotte Observer* and then attended law school at the University of Virginia, graduating in 1995. Now living in Charlottesville with his wife and son, Manning is in medical school at the University of Virginia, training to be a family physician.

Arm Wrestling with My Father

In this essay written for his freshman composition course, Manning explores his physical contact with his father over the years, perceiving gradual changes that are, he realizes, inevitable. For Manning, description provides a way to express his feelings about his father and to comment on relations between sons and fathers. In the essay after Manning's, Itabari Njeri uses description for similar ends, but her subject is a daughter and her father.

Manning's essay has been published in a Harvard collection of students' writing; in *Student Writers at Work: The Bedford Prizes*; and in *Montage*, a collection of Russian and American stories published in Russian.

"Now you say when" is what he always said before an arm-wrestling   1
match. He liked to put the responsibility on me, knowing that he would always control the outcome. "When!" I'd shout, and it would start. And I would tense up, concentrating and straining and trying to push his wrist down to the carpet with all my weight and strength. But Dad would always win; I always had to lose. "Want to try it again?" he would ask, grinning. He would see my downcast eyes, my reddened, sweating face, and sense my intensity. And with squinting eyes he would laugh at me, a high laugh, through his perfect white teeth. Too bitter to smile, I would not answer or look at him, but I would just roll over on my back and frown at the ceiling. I never thought it was funny at all.

That was the way I felt for a number of years during my teens, after   2
I had lost my enjoyment of arm wrestling and before I had given up that same intense desire to beat my father. Ours had always been a physical relationship, I suppose, one determined by athleticism and strength. We never communicated as well in speech or in writing as in a strong hug, battling to make the other gasp for breath. I could never find him at one of my orchestra concerts. But at my lacrosse games, he would be

there in the stands, with an angry look, ready to coach me after the game on how I could do better. He never helped me write a paper or a poem. Instead, he would take me outside and show me a new move for my game, in the hope that I would score a couple of goals and gain confidence in my ability. Dad knew almost nothing about lacrosse and his movements were all wrong and sad to watch. But at those times I could just feel how hard he was trying to communicate, to help me, to show the love he had for me, the love I could only assume was there.

His words were physical. The truth is, I have never read a card or a   3
letter written in his hand because he never wrote to me. Never. Mom wrote me all the cards and letters when I was away from home. The closest my father ever came, that I recall, was in a newspaper clipping Mom had sent with a letter. He had gone through and underlined all the important words about the dangers of not wearing a bicycle helmet. Our communication was physical, and that is why we did things like arm wrestle. To get down on the floor and grapple, arm against arm, was like having a conversation.

This ritual of father-son competition in fact had started early in my   4
life, back when Dad started the matches with his arm almost horizontal, his wrist an inch from defeat, and still won. I remember in those battles how my tiny shoulders would press over our locked hands, my whole upper body pushing down in hope of winning that single inch from his calm, unmoving forearm. "Say when," he'd repeat, killing my concentration and causing me to squeal, "I did, I did!" And so he'd grin with his eyes fixed on me, not seeming to notice his own arm, which would begin to rise slowly from its starting position. My greatest efforts could not slow it down. As soon as my hopes had disappeared I'd start to cheat and use both hands. But the arm would continue to move steadily along its arc toward the carpet. My brother, if he was watching, would sometimes join in against the arm. He once even wrapped his little legs around our embattled wrists and pulled back with everything he had. But he did not have much and, regardless of the opposition, the man would win. My arm would lie at rest, pressed into the carpet beneath a solid, immovable arm. In that pinned position, I could only giggle, happy to have such a strong father.

My feelings have changed, though. I don't giggle anymore, at least   5
not around my father. And I don't feel pressured to compete with him the way I thought necessary for years. Now my father is not really so strong as he used to be and I am getting stronger. This change in strength comes at a time when I am growing faster mentally than at any time before. I am becoming less my father and more myself. And as a result, there is less of a need to be set apart from him and his command. I am no longer a rebel in the household, wanting to stand up against the master with clenched fists and tensing jaws, trying to impress him

with my education or my views on religion. I am no longer a challenger, quick to correct his verbal mistakes, determined to beat him whenever possible in physical competition.

I am not sure when it was that I began to feel less competitive with   6
my father, but it all became clearer to me one day this past January. I was home in Virginia for a week between exams, and Dad had stayed home from work because the house was snowed in deep. It was then that I learned something I never could have guessed.

I don't recall who suggested arm wrestling that day. We hadn't   7
done it for a long time, for months. But there we were, lying flat on the carpet, face to face, extending our right arms. Our arms were different. His still resembled a fat tree branch, one which had leveled my wrist to the ground countless times before. It was hairy and white with some pink moles scattered about. It looked strong, to be sure, though not so strong as it had in past years. I expect that back in his youth it had looked even stronger. In high school he had played halfback and had been voted "best-built body" of the senior class. Between college semesters he had worked on road crews and on Louisiana dredges. I admired him for that. I had begun to row crew in college and that accounted for some small buildup along the muscle lines, but it did not seem to be enough. The arm I extended was lanky and featureless. Even so, he insisted that he would lose the match, that he was certain I'd win. I had to ignore this, however, because it was something he always said, whether or not he believed it himself.

Our warm palms came together, much the same way we had shaken   8
hands the day before at the airport. Fingers twisted and wrapped about once again, testing for a better grip. Elbows slid up and back making their little indentations on the itchy carpet. My eyes pinched closed in concentration as I tried to center as much of my thought as possible on the match. Arm wrestling, I knew, was a competition that depended less on talent and experience than on one's mental control and confidence. I looked up into his eyes and was ready. He looked back, smiled at me, and said softly (did he sound nervous?), "You say when."

It was not a long match. I had expected him to be stronger, faster. I   9
was conditioned to lose and would have accepted defeat easily. However, after some struggle, his arm yielded to my efforts and began to move unsteadily toward the carpet. I worked against his arm with all the strength I could find. He was working hard as well, straining, breathing heavily. It seemed that this time was different, that I was going to win. Then something occurred to me, something unexpected. I discovered that I was feeling sorry for my father. I wanted to win but I did not want to see him lose.

It was like the thrill I had once experienced as a young boy at my   10
grandfather's lake house in Louisiana when I hooked my first big fish.

There was that sudden tug that made me leap. The red bobber was sucked down beneath the surface and I pulled back against it, reeling it in excitedly. But when my cousin caught sight of the fish and shouted out, "It's a keeper," I realized that I would be happier for the fish if it were let go rather than grilled for dinner. Arm wrestling my father was now like this, like hooking "Big Joe," the old fish that Lake Quachita holds but you can never catch, and when you finally think you've got him, you want to let him go, cut the line, keep the legend alive.

Perhaps at that point I could have given up, letting my father win. But it was so fast and absorbing. How could I have learned so quickly how it would feel to have overpowered the arm that had protected and provided for me all of my life? His arms have always protected me and the family. Whenever I am near him I am unafraid, knowing his arms are ready to catch me and keep me safe, the way they caught my mother one time when she fainted halfway across the room, the way he carried me, full grown, up and down the stairs when I had mononucleosis, the way he once held my feet as I stood on his shoulders to put up a new basketball net. My mother may have had the words or the touch that sustained our family, but his were the arms that protected us. And his were the arms now that I had pushed to the carpet, first the right arm, then the left. 11

I might have preferred him to be always the stronger, the one who carries me. But this wish is impossible now; our roles have begun to switch. I do not know if I will ever physically carry my father as he has carried me, though I fear that someday I may have that responsibility. More than once this year I have hesitated before answering the phone late at night, fearing my mother's voice calling me back to help carry his wood coffin. When I am home with him and he mentions a sharp pain in his chest, I imagine him collapsing onto the floor. And in that second vision I see me rushing to him, lifting him onto my shoulders, and running. 12

A week after our match, we parted at the airport. The arm-wrestling match was by that time mostly forgotten. My thoughts were on school. I had been awake most of the night studying for my last exam, and by that morning I was already back into my college-student manner of reserve and detachment. To say goodbye, I kissed and hugged my mother and I prepared to shake my father's hand. A handshake had always seemed easier to handle than a hug. His hugs had always been powerful ones, intended I suppose to give me strength. They made me suck in my breath and struggle for control, and the way he would pound his hand on my back made rumbles in my ears. So I offered a handshake; but he offered a hug. I accepted it, bracing myself for the impact. Once our arms were wrapped around each other, however, I sensed a different message. His embrace was softer, longer than before. 13

I remember how it surprised me and how I gave an embarrassed laugh as if to apologize to anyone watching.

I got on the airplane and my father and mother were gone. But as   14
the plane lifted my throat was hurting with sadness. I realized then that Dad must have learned something as well, and what he had said to me in that last hug was that he loved me. Love was a rare expression between us, so I had denied it at first. As the plane turned north, I had a sudden wish to go back to Dad and embrace his arms with all the love I felt for him. I wanted to hold him for a long time and to speak with him silently, telling him how happy I was, telling him all my feelings, in that language we shared.

In his hug, Dad had tried to tell me something he himself had dis-   15
covered. I hope he tries again. Maybe this spring, when he sees his first crew match, he'll advise me on how to improve my stroke. Maybe he has started doing pushups to rebuild his strength and challenge me to another match — if this were true, I know I would feel less challenged than loved. Or maybe, rather than any of this, he'll just send me a card.

QUESTIONS ON MEANING

1. In paragraph 3 Manning says that his father's "words were physical." What does this mean?
2. After his most recent trip home, Manning says, "I realized then that Dad must have learned something as well" (para. 14). What is it that father and son have each learned?
3. Manning says in the last paragraph that he "would feel less challenged than loved" if his father challenged him to a rematch. Does this statement suggest that he did not feel loved earlier? Why, or why not?
4. What do you think is Manning's PURPOSE in this essay? Does he want to express love for his father, or is there something more as well?

QUESTIONS ON WRITING STRATEGY

1. Why does Manning start his essay with a match that leaves him "too bitter to smile" and then move backward to earlier bouts of arm wrestling?
2. In the last paragraph Manning suggests that his father might work harder at competing with him and pushing him to be competitive, or he might just send his son a card. Why does Manning present both of these options? Are we supposed to know which will happen?
3. Explain the fishing ANALOGY Manning uses in paragraph 10.
4. **OTHER METHODS.** Manning's essay is as much a NARRATIVE as a description: The author gives brief stories, like video clips, to show the dynamic of his relationship with his father. Look at the story in paragraph 4. How does Manning mix elements of both methods to convey his powerlessness?

QUESTIONS ON LANGUAGE

1. Manning uses the word *competition* throughout this essay. Why is this a more accurate word than *conflict* to describe Manning's relationship with his father?
2. What is the EFFECT of "the arm" in this line from paragraph 4: "But the arm would continue to move steadily along its arc toward the carpet"?
3. In paragraph 9 Manning writes, "I wanted to win but I did not want to see him lose." What does this apparent contradiction mean?
4. If any of these words is unfamiliar, look it up in a dictionary: embattled (para. 4); dredges, crew (7); conditioned (9); mononucleosis (11).

SUGGESTIONS FOR WRITING

1. **JOURNAL WRITING.** When have you felt strongly conflicting emotions over a person or an event: a relative, friend, breakup, ceremony, move? **FROM JOURNAL TO ESSAY.** Expand your journal entry into a descriptive essay that brings your feelings to life for your reader. Focus less on the circumstances and events than on emotions, both positive and negative.
2. Write an essay that describes your relationship with a parent or another close adult. You may want to focus on just one aspect of your relationship, or one especially vivid moment, in order to give yourself the space and time to build many sensory details into your description.
3. **CRITICAL WRITING.** In paragraph 12 Manning writes, "our roles have begun to switch." Does this seem like an inevitable switch, or one that this father and son have been working to achieve? Use EVIDENCE from Manning's essay to support your answer. Also consider whether Manning and his father would respond the same way to this question.
4. **CONNECTIONS.** Like "Arm Wrestling with My Father," the next essay, Itabari Njeri's "When Morpheus Held Him," depicts a struggle for communication between child and parent. In an essay, COMPARE AND CONTRAST the two essays on this point. What impedes positive communication between the two authors and their fathers? In what circumstances are they able to communicate?

BRAD MANNING ON WRITING

For *The Bedford Reader,* Brad Manning offered some valuable concrete advice on writing as a student.

You hear this a lot, but writing takes a long time. For me, this is especially true. The only difference between the "Arm Wrestling" essay and all the other essays I wrote in college (and the only reason it's in this book and not thrown away) is that I rewrote it six or seven times over a period of weeks.

If I have something to write, I need to start early. In college, I had a bad habit of putting off papers until 10 P.M. the night before they were due and spending a desperate night typing whatever ideas the coffee inspired. But putting off papers didn't just lower my writing quality; it robbed me of a good time.

I like starting early because I can jot down notes over a stretch of days; then I type them up fast, ignoring typos; I print the notes with narrow margins, cut them up, and divide them into piles that seem to fit together; then it helps to get away for a day and come back all fresh so I can throw away the corny ideas. Finally, I sit on the floor and make an outline with all the cutouts of paper, trying at the same time to work out some clear purpose for the essay.

When the writing starts, I often get hung up most on trying to "sound" like a good writer. If you're like me and came to college from a shy family that never discussed much over dinner, you might think your best shot is to sound like a famous writer like T. S. Eliot and you might try to sneak in words that aren't really your own like *ephemeral* or *the lilacs smelled like springtime*. But the last thing you really want a reader thinking is how good or bad a writer you are.

Also, in the essay on arm wrestling, I got hung up thinking I had to make my conflict with my father somehow "universal." So in an early draft I wrote in a classical allusion—Aeneas lifting his old father up onto his shoulders and carrying him out of the burning city of Troy.[1] I'd read that story in high school and guessed one classical allusion might make the reader think I knew a lot more. But Aeneas didn't help the essay much, and I'm glad my teacher warned me off trying to universalize. He told me to write just what was true for me.

But that was hard, too, and still is—especially in the first draft. I don't know anyone who enjoys the first draft. If you do, I envy you. But in my early drafts, I always get this sensation like I have to impress somebody and I end up overanalyzing the effects of every word I am about to write. This self-consciousness may be unavoidable (I get self-conscious calling L. L. Bean to order a shirt), but, in this respect, writing is great for shy people because you can edit all you want, all day long, until it finally sounds right. I never feel that I am being myself until the third or fourth draft, and it's only then that it gets personal and starts to be fun.

When I said that putting off papers robbed me of a good time, I really meant it. Writing the essay about my father turned out to be a high point in my life. And on top of having a good time with it, I now

---

[1] In the *Aeneid*, by the Roman poet Vergil (70–19 B.C.), the mythic hero Aeneas escaped from the city of Troy when it was sacked by the Greeks and went on to found Rome. —EDS.

have a record of what happened. And my ten-month-old son, when he grows up, can read things about his grandfather and father that he'd probably not have learned any other way.

FOR DISCUSSION

1. What did Manning miss by writing his college papers at the last minute?
2. Why does Manning say that "writing is great for shy people"? Have you ever felt that you could express yourself in writing better than in speech?

ITABARI NJERI

ITABARI NJERI was born Jill Stacey Moreland in Brooklyn, New York. Though she began her professional life as a singer and actor, she eventually turned to journalism. She received a B.S. from Boston University's School of Public Communication and an M.S. from Columbia University's Graduate School of Journalism. She worked as a reporter and producer for National Public Radio and then as a writer for the *Miami Herald* and the *Los Angeles Times*. Njeri is the author of three books: *Every Good-Bye Ain't Gone: Family Portraits and Personal Escapades* (1990), *Sushi & Grits: The Challenge of Diversity* (1993), and *The Last Plantation: Color, Conflict and Identity; Reflections of a New World Black* (1997). Currently writer-in-residence at Washington University in Saint Louis, Njeri often speaks at universities and on TV and radio about memoir, multiculturalism, and ethnic conflict.

When Morpheus Held Him

Like the previous essay, Brad Manning's "Arm Wrestling with My Father," Njeri's "When Morpheus Held Him" explores the relationship between child and father. Describing her father's personal struggles and their effect on her as a girl, Njeri creates an indelible portrait of a troubled and difficult man. The essay was first published in *Harper's* magazine in 1990.

Daddy wore boxer shorts when he worked; that's all. He'd sit for hours reading and writing at a long, rectangular table covered with neat stacks of *I. F. Stone's Weekly, The Nation, The New Republic,* and the handwritten pages of his book in progress, *The Tolono Station and Beyond.* A Mott's applesauce jar filled with Teacher's scotch was a constant, and his own forerunner of today's wine coolers was the ever-present chaser: ginger ale and Manischewitz Concord grape wine in a tall, green iced-tea glass.

As he sat there, his beer belly weighing down the waistband of his shorts, I'd watch. I don't know if he ever saw me. I hid from him at right angles. From the bend of the hallway, at the end of a long, dark, L-shaped corridor in our Harlem apartment, it was at least thirty feet to the living room where my father worked, framed by the doorway. I sat cross-legged on the cold linoleum floor and inspected his seated, six-foot-plus figure through a telescope formed by my forefinger and thumb: bare feet in thonged sandals, long hairy legs that rose toward the notorious shorts (I hated those shorts, wouldn't bring my girlfriends home because of those shorts), breasts that could fill a B cup, and a long neck on which a balding head rested. Viewed in isolation, I thought perhaps I'd see him clearer, know him better.

Daddy was a philosopher, a Marxist historian, an exceptional teacher, and a fine tenor. He had a good enough voice to be as great a concert artist as John McCormack, one of his favorites. The obstacles to that career couldn't have been much greater than the ones he actually overcame. ³

The state of Georgia, where my father grew up, established its version of the literacy test in 1908, the year he was born. If you substituted Georgia for Mississippi in the story that Lerone Bennett, Jr., relates in *Before the Mayflower: A History of Black America,* the main character could easily have been my father: A black teacher, a graduate of Eton and Harvard, presents himself to a Mississippi registrar. The teacher is told to read the state constitution and several books. He does. The registrar produces a passage in Greek, which the teacher reads. Then another in Latin. Then other passages in French, German, and Spanish, all of which the teacher reads. The registrar finally holds up a page of Chinese characters and asks: "What does this mean?" The teacher replies: "It means you don't want me to vote." ⁴

Apocryphal, perhaps, but the tale exemplified enough collective experience that I heard my father tell virtually the same story about a former Morehouse College classmate to a buddy over the phone one afternoon. At the punch line, he fell into a fit of laughter, chuckling hard into a balled fist he held at his mouth. Finally, he said, "Fred, I'll have to call you back," then fell back on the bed, in his boxer shorts, laughing at the ceiling. ⁵

He claimed he burst out laughing like this once in a class at Harvard. A law professor, discussing some constitutional issue in class, singled out my father and said, "In this matter, regarding men of your race —" ⁶

"Which race is that?" my father boomed, cutting him off, "the 50 yard or the 100?" But it seemed to me he always related that particular tale with a sneer on his lips. ⁷

He'd been at Harvard studying law on a postdoctoral scholarship from 1942 to 1943. After receiving his Ph.D. in philosophy from the University of Toronto ten years earlier, he had headed toward the dust bowls others were escaping in the mid-1930s and became the editor of a black newspaper, the *Oklahoma Eagle,* in Tulsa. He eventually returned to academia and by 1949 was the head of the philosophy department at Morgan State University in Baltimore. That's where he met my mother, a nurse many years his junior. ⁸

My mother—who commits nothing to paper, speaks of the past cryptically, and believes all unpleasantries are best kept under a rug— once leaked the fact that she and my father took me to a parade in ⁹

Brooklyn when I was about three. We were standing near the arch at Grand Army Plaza when he suddenly hauled off and punched her in the mouth, with me in her arms. My mother, a very gentle and naive woman, said the whole thing left her in a state of shock. My father had never been violent before.

They separated, and I seldom saw my father again until my parents   10 reunited when I was seven. We moved into my father's six-room apartment on 129th Street, between Convent Avenue and St. Nicholas Terrace. It was certainly far more spacious than the apartment I'd lived in with my mother on St. James Place in Brooklyn. The immediate neighborhood was an attractive, hilly section of Harlem, just a few blocks from City College. All things considered, I hated it. More precisely, I hated my father, so I hated it all.

Because of his past leftist political affiliations, Daddy had lost his   11 government and university jobs. Now, out of necessity but also desire, he decided to devote his time to teaching younger people. He wanted to reach them at a stage in their lives when he felt he could make a difference. He joined the faculty of a Jersey City high school and began teaching journalism, history, and English. He also taught English at night to foreign-born students at City College. His students, I came to learn, loved him; his daughter found it hard to. I made the mistake of calling him Pop—once. He said, "Don't ever call me that again. If you don't like calling me Daddy, you can call me Dr. Moreland."

Once, my mother deserted me, leaving me alone with him. She   12 went to Atlanta for several weeks with my baby brother to tend my ailing Grandma Hattie, my father's mother. Since I hadn't known this man most of my seven years on the planet, and didn't like him much now that I did, I asked him if I could stay around the corner with a family friend, Aunt Pearl. "If she asks you to stay, fine. But don't ask her," he told me. Naturally I asked her.

When he asked me if I had asked her, I hesitated. But I was not a   13 child inclined to lie. So I said, "I don't want to lie. I asked her." I got a beating for that, a brutal beating with a belt that left welts and bruises on my legs for months.

My father felt children should be hit for any infraction. Further,   14 they should be seen and not heard, speak only when spoken to, etc. From the day he hit me, the latter became my philosophy, too. I never consciously decided to stop speaking to my father, but for the next ten years, I rarely initiated a conversation with him. Later he would tell me, "You were a very strange child."

But if I would not accept him as a father, my curiosity would not let   15 me deny him as a teacher. One day, a question about the nature of truth compelled a thaw in my emotional cold war—nothing less could have.

Truth changes, a classmate in the seventh grade had insisted that day. It is constant, I argued, and went to my father for confirmation.

People's perceptions change, I explained. New information de-   16
bunks the lies of the past, but the truth was always there. And I told my father what I had told my mostly white classmates in a Bronx junior high school at the height of the civil rights movement: Black people were always human beings worthy of the same rights other Americans enjoyed, but it took hundreds of years of a slave system that dehuman-ized the master as well as the slave and a social revolution before most white Americans would accept that truth.

My father turned from his worktable, took off his glasses, with their   17
broken right temple piece, and released a long and resonant "Yesssss." And then he spoke to me of a rational cosmos and what Lincoln had to do with Plato. When our philosophical discussion ended, we each went to our separate corners.

My father had a beaten, black upright piano in the parlor, badly out   18
of tune. But its bench was a treasure of ancient sheet music: Vincent Youman's "Through the Years," with a picture of Gladys Swarthout on the frayed cover. And I loved the chord changes to "Spring Is Here."

I ventured from the sanctuary of my blue-walled room one summer   19
afternoon, walking down the long hallway toward the kitchen, then stopped abruptly. I heard my father in the kitchen several feet away; he was making an ice-cream soda, something as forbidden to him as alco-hol since he was a diabetic. I heard the clink of a metal spoon against a glass as he sang, "For I lately took a notion for to cross the briny ocean, and I'm off to Philadelphia in the morning." It was an Irish folk song made famous by John McCormack. I backed up. Too late. He danced across the kitchen threshold in his boxer shorts, stopped when he spot-ted me in the shadows, then shook his head. He smiled, lifted one leg and both arms in a Jackie Gleason "and away we go" motion, then slid off.

Minutes later he called me. "Jill the Pill, you know this song?" I knew   20
all the songs and wrote down the words to "Moon River" for him. Then he asked me to sing it. I was always ready to sing, even for my father.

He sat on the edge of his bed with the lyrics in his hand as I sang.   21
When I finished the phrase "We're after the same rainbow's end, waitin' round the bend, my huckleberry friend," my daddy looked at me and said what others would tell me years later but with far less poetry: "My girl, you have the celestial vibration." And then he asked me to sing it again and told me it was "wonderful." Then I left him.

For days, maybe weeks, a tense calm would reign in the apartment.   22
Then, without warning, the hall would fill with harsh voices. My father

stood in the narrow, shadowy space hitting my mother. "Put it down," he yelled. "Put it down or I'll..."

My mother had picked up a lamp in a lame effort to ward off his blows. His shouting had awakened me. I'd been sick in bed with the flu and a high fever. When he saw me open my bedroom door he yelled, "Get back in your room." I did, my body overtaken by tremors and the image of my mother branded on my eyeballs. I swore that I would never let anyone do that to me or to anyone else I had the power to help. I had no power to help my mother. It was an oath with terrible consequences, one I'd have to disavow to permit myself the vulnerability of being human.

I know my father's fury was fueled by his sense of insignificance. He felt himself to be an intellectual giant boxed in by mental midgets. Unlike Ralph Ellison, Paul Robeson, or Richard Wright—all contemporaries and acquaintances of my father's—he was never acknowledged by the dominant culture whose recognition he sought. He could be found, Ellison once told me, pontificating in Harlem barbershops, elucidating the dialogues of Plato for a captive audience of draped men, held prone, each with a straight-edge razor pressed against his cheek.

My father's unreconciled identities—the classic schizophrenia of being black and an American, the contradictions of internalizing whole the cultural values of a society that sees you, when it sees you at all, as life in one of its lower forms—stoked his alcoholism. And since my father at once critiqued the society that denied him and longed for its approbation, he lived with the pain-filled consciousness of one who knows he is a joke. I think sometimes he laughed the hardest, so often did I stumble upon him alone, chuckling into his balled fist at some silent, invisible comedian.

When his drunken rages ended, he slept for days, spread out on the bed wearing only his boxer shorts. I watched him on those days, too, daring to come closer, safe with the knowledge that Morpheus[1] held him. I examined his face, wondering who he was and why he was. As I watched, he'd lift his head off the pillow, then fall back muttering: "Truth and justice will prevail."

QUESTIONS ON MEANING

1. What seems to be the author's PURPOSE in describing her father?
2. How do you interpret the story about Mississippi's literacy test in paragraph 4?

[1]Morpheus, a figure of Greek and Roman mythology, was the god of dreams, the son of sleep. —EDS.

3. What is the significance of the fact that Njeri's mother "commits nothing to paper, speaks of the past cryptically, and believes all unpleasantries are best kept under a rug" (para. 9)?
4. Reread paragraphs 15–17. How does this exchange between Njeri and her father about the nature of truth affect their relationship? Why is it important to her portrait of her father?

QUESTIONS ON WRITING STRATEGY

1. In paragraph 10, Njeri uses words such as "spacious" and "attractive" to describe a new home. What is the EFFECT of the PARADOX that follows: "All things considered, I hated it"?
2. Discuss Njeri's POINT OF VIEW. Is her perspective that of a young girl or of an adult looking back on childhood experiences? What EVIDENCE supports your answer?
3. What is the dominant impression of Njeri's description of her father? What details give you this impression?
4. **OTHER METHODS.** Njeri's description of her father relies on other methods as well. What are some EXAMPLES she uses to paint a picture of her father? Where does she use NARRATION to demonstrate her father's behavior?

QUESTIONS ON LANGUAGE

1. What does the title suggest to you? (You may want to consult the footnote to the essay's last paragraph for information about Morpheus.) Why does Njeri take the image from the last paragraph as her title?
2. Paragraph 11 tells us, "His students, I came to learn, loved him; his daughter found it hard to." How is this sentence given additional meaning by the rest of the paragraph?
3. Consult a dictionary if you need help in defining the following: notorious (para. 2); apocryphal, exemplified, virtually (5); cryptically (9); infraction (14); celestial (21); pontificating, elucidating (24).

SUGGESTIONS FOR WRITING

1. **JOURNAL WRITING.** Njeri's essay includes several examples that work together to build a picture of her father: his appearance when working (paras. 1–2), his laughter (5), his experience at Harvard (6–7), his violence against Njeri's mother (9), and more. Write down at least five telling examples—more if you can—about someone close to you.
   FROM JOURNAL TO ESSAY. Elaborate on your journal entry, drawing a portrait of the person you chose by filling out at least three of your examples. Use plenty of descriptive details to bring your subject to life for your reader.
2. In a detailed paragraph or two, describe someone's appearance. Look to Njeri's first two paragraphs for a model of such physical description, though your own may of course be more flattering.
3. **CRITICAL WRITING.** What can you tell about Njeri's attitudes toward her father now that she is an adult? How are they resolved or unresolved? Are

they mean or kind, hating or loving? In a brief essay, ANALYZE her attitudes, using specific examples as evidence.

4. **CONNECTIONS.** Both Njeri and Brad Manning, in "Arm Wrestling with My Father," describe their fathers. In an essay, examine how the words Manning and Njeri use convey their feelings of distance from their fathers. Use quotations from both essays to support your analysis.

ITABARI NJERI ON WRITING

Itabari Njeri's path to being a writer was not conventional. She began by studying music and actually worked as a studio and back-up singer. "But," she told Toyomi Igus for an article in *American Visions*, "I was frustrated by my colleagues at school who were devoted to music to the exclusion of everything else.... Music wasn't political enough for me. I had to do something directly political to be part of the [African American] struggle, so I felt that, to make a statement, I'd become part of the communications industry."

Njeri obtained a journalism degree and became a reporter. She also began writing fiction but soon turned to the autobiography *Every Good-Bye Ain't Gone*. "Memoir is a tradition among African American writers," she asserted in an interview with Gene Seymour of *Newsday*. "It's also a way of documenting not only the personal experience, but also the group experience of people who have been rendered invisible or marginalized by the larger culture. We write the memoir first, then the novel."

Speaking later to *Contemporary Authors*, Njeri said, "I was not thinking of the great African American autobiographical tradition when I first started my memoir, but I knew instinctively that by telling key aspects of my family's story, I would be illuminating important aspects of black life. And I'm always thinking about the larger political picture when I write. To impose order on the chaos of memory is a universal impulse fueling the desire to write autobiography. But first and foremost, I hoped to create a work of art out of my experience as a woman of color in the New World at the end of the twentieth century. I wanted to illuminate the beauty, pain and complexity of a particular piece of the African diaspora [dispersion of a once homogeneous people], a piece central to the American experience. I wanted to tell the truth and make it sing."

FOR DISCUSSION

1. What were Njeri's goals in writing about her family and herself? To what extent does each aim seem to influence her essay "When Morpheus Held Him"?

2. On the occasions when you have written about your own experiences, has the writing helped you, as Njeri puts it, "impose order on the chaos of memory"?

MERRILL MARKOE

A comedian and comedy writer, MERRILL MARKOE was born in New York City in 1950 and received an M.F.A. from the University of California at Berkeley in 1974. She worked for one year as a drawing teacher and then tried stand-up comedy. While performing in Los Angeles in 1977, she met David Letterman and went on to win four Emmy Awards as a writer for *Late Night with David Letterman*. She wrote and starred in several cable TV specials, including *This Week Indoors* and *Merrill Markoe's Guide to Glamorous Living*. She won Writers' Guild and Ace awards for *Not Necessarily the News*. Markoe's essays for *New York Woman* are collected in *What the Dogs Have Taught Me* (1992). Her latest books are *Merrill Markoe's Guide to Love* (1997) and a children's story, *The Day My Dogs Became Guys* (1998). The creator of Stupid Pet Tricks lives in Malibu, California, with several dogs.

Bob the Dog
(1974–1988)

People magazine once called Markoe "the funniest woman in America." In this essay from *What the Dogs Have Taught Me*, Markoe wittily describes an unruly but somehow still lovable pet.

About a month ago my older boy, Bob, started acting sick. He was 1 fourteen (which, of course, is ninety-eight to you, me and Lorne Greene), but his problems weren't only about being an old guy. Suddenly he just wasn't what he used to be. At first this was kind of a blessing because what he used to be was a dog who would stop at *nothing* in his quest for things he felt might possibly turn out to be food.

Bob wasn't content to wait until that part of the day when the 2 green plastic dish full of gelatinous glop would descend. On more than one occasion he actually stole and flattened several sealed cans of food from a not-quite-unpacked case in the kitchen. By the time I discovered the remains, he had extracted all the contents in such a way as to leave the empty containers looking like overworked summer-camp copper-tooling projects.

For Bob, the word *edible* had the broadest definition. Where food 3 was concerned, he was a freethinker. Earlier this year, for example, I came home to find that my art portfolio had been removed from where I had wedged it between a filing cabinet and a dresser. It had been opened carefully, and several of my graduate school watercolors, including my self-portrait (which took me quite a few weeks to paint), had been removed and partially consumed. For a brief moment I wondered if a uniquely frightening psychotic criminal had begun a fiendish campaign of terror against me. On the bright side, Bob was able to bring an interesting new visual metaphor to what had been kind of a traditional painting.

Looking back on his life, I would have to say that this was his most   4
creative phase. It was during this period that he ate my Scrabble board, a lot of my dictionary and about a third of Joseph Heller's *Good as Gold*. (Perhaps he would have eaten more if he'd had a chance to eat *Catch-22* first.)[1] In fact, Bob got so creative with eating that it was hard to guess what things to try to keep away from him. He ate a Prestolog. He opened a closet door and removed a sealed box from the second shelf, deciding for reasons of his own to eat my antique Christmas ornaments. In the process he also managed to get a decorative fishing lure lodged in his front paw, which meant that I had to get in the car and haul him into town to an emergency room at 2:00 A.M. to have this particular snack item surgically removed.

All this was tame compared with the time I found him relaxing in   5
the backyard, gnawing on what looked like an amazingly lifelike cat hand puppet. I still don't know if the skunk met the same fate, but I do remember with clarity the end result. After we'd drenched Bob in many, many cans of tomato juice, which everyone said would neutralize the odor, he looked and smelled like an Italian *marinara* dish from hell. And of course he spent the rest of the day trying to drink his own back. These were truly the magical times—rationalizing the death of some small creature that never imagined itself as somebody's hors d'oeuvre. Bob's life was, on occasion, devoted to murder as well as mayhem and dinner.

Happily, he sometimes resorted to ingenuity rather than cold-   6
blooded homicide. He even figured out how to open the refrigerator. One night we found him cheerfully seated in the corner opposite the fridge, doing the doggie equivalent of a smile and wave, several inches from an empty Styrofoam steak tray and a piece of plastic that had once held a giant block of cheddar cheese. Bob was calmly finishing off an apple core. Not far away was a plastic supermarket sack containing two untouched zucchinis. Apparently when he was constructing his dinner menu, he decided to forgo the vegetable dish.

Bob wasn't a great-looking dog, and for most of his life he had a   7
weight problem. Vets listed his breed as "German shepherd mix," although it always seemed to me that he had less shepherd than German

---

[1]Joseph Heller (born 1923) is an American writer. *Catch-22* (1961), a satire of World War II, is his first novel and by far his most successful. (Heller's expression *catch-22* has entered the language to describe a problem that cannot be resolved because of illogical rules or conditions.)—Eds.

waiter or chef. Once when I went out to the store, he removed a pot of split-pea soup from the front burner of the stove, carried it into the living room and ate it without spilling a drop. If we lived in a more perfect world, he might have had the chance to make a very fine busboy for some restaurant. At least they never would've worried about scraping the dishes off before loading them into the dishwasher.

He did goofy things in his short life—such as jump at birds who   8
were circling several hundred feet above him. But he wasn't a stupid dog, if you define dog intelligence as the ability to solve problems (and if you can define dog problems as worth solving at all). When he and I first started living together, I intended to keep him in the backyard—a situation he rectified the first day. By the time I got home from work he had removed the lower five panes of glass on a jalousie window and made himself a very handsome doggie door. That was the last time I bothered trying to lock him out. It was futile. He would eat through wood. He would break through glass or screen. No Cyclone fence could hold his big fat body. He was driven, ever driven, by the insatiable need to get from wherever he was to the other side of everything and anything. It cost me several thousand dollars in fence repairs when he escaped from the backyard to a place in the front yard where he sat patiently waiting to be let back into the house so he could eventually get into the backyard again. I like to think he appreciated the Zen truth of this.

And then there were the Manhattan days, beginning with that first   9
early-morning walk down Sixth Avenue to the park when Bob came to a screeching halt to take a dump right in front of the Magic Pan. Dog ownership in the Big Apple is unlike dog ownership in any, less complicated, suburb. In the deepest, darkest part of the night I would awake to find him gently nuzzling my neck—a signal that in California would simply mean I had to open the back door but that in Manhattan meant that I had to get up and put on all my clothes, including shoes and socks (not to mention appropriate seasonal gear), and accompany him down to the street to deal with an emergency I dared not question but that sometimes turned out to be that he thought he had heard something.

On the plus side, being a dog owner in New York brought a new in-   10
timacy to the relationship between owner and dog, as I found myself relating to details of the dog's digestion in ways I'd never before dreamed of. I'm ashamed to admit it, but in California I never accompanied my dogs out after dinner (although I guess the opportunity was always mine for the taking), but once in New York I was able to see really close up just how well the dogs were enjoying—and digesting—their meals. There were other benefits too, such as interaction with the neighbors. It can be a real icebreaker when someone calls from two to twenty stories above, "Get your damn dog away from there!"

It was during our years in New York City that I came home one 11
evening to find that Bob had eaten a jar of pills the vet had prescribed
for my other dog, Stan. I never knew if the pressures of city life were responsible for this sudden drug problem, only that I had to pour hydrogen peroxide down his throat to induce vomiting and then follow him
around for the rest of the evening, cleaning up after him. (I'm told this
is also the procedure they used on Liz Taylor at the Betty Ford Center.)

It was in Manhattan that the dogs decided no apartment was big 12
enough for the two of them and set out methodically to reduce the indoor dog population to one. The hired dog-walker would call with the
news that skirmishes had broken out and all parties were waiting for me
at the hospital. It was amazing to think of Bob in a fight of any sort because, quite frankly, he wasn't much of an athlete. Stan always enjoyed
a rousing game of fetch, but Bob preferred to play "I'll Just Get the Ball
and Eat It."

Bob forced me to learn some hard lessons, such as: Bob should 13
never be let off the leash. I learned that when I took him running with
me in the park. It had seemed so idyllic — a girl and her dog. Until I
turned back to check on him and discovered that he was nowhere to be
seen. After three long hours wandering the environs, calling his name
in increasingly panicky tones, I headed back to my car, some six blocks
away. It was sunset, and I felt sure he was dead or gone. Until I actually
got right up next to my Honda and, of course, there he was, sitting in
the front seat, with a trail of doggie toenail marks all the way up the
door to the window. I guess he'd just figured, Screw this exercise stuff!
and decided to leave me to it.

Which reminds me of the other time he disappeared, before I in- 14
stalled the second layer of fence in the backyard. I live near a highway,
and as the evening wore on and things were beginning to look grim, I
got out the big guns. I stood out in the street and yelled, "Dinner! Bob!
Dinner!" When he wasn't home by dawn, I was sure he was now just an
area rug. But bright and early the next morning the neighbor who had
accidentally trapped him in her backyard released him. I realized that
he must have lived through a very peculiar kind of torture that night.
There he was, only a few feet from me yelling "Dinner!" and probably
thinking to himself, *Damn! I can't believe it. The one time that she has a
second seating and I can't make it.*

Yes, we shared a lot of special moments, my dog Bob and I. Or at 15
least I shared them. I was never sure if he was paying attention, which
is similar to the problem I often have with men. But I cut Bob a lot
more slack because he was a dog. I mean, after all those years he still
didn't know what I did for a living. So it's a pretty fair tribute to his
charisma as a dog that I miss him as much as I do. I miss him a lot.
Though reading back over this piece, it's pretty hard to say why.

QUESTIONS ON MEANING

1. What is the THESIS of this essay? Where is it stated? How does this thesis relate to Markoe's PURPOSE?
2. How do you know that Bob is dead?
3. What does "cold-blooded homicide" refer to in paragraph 6?
4. What does Markoe mean in paragraph 15 by Bob's "charisma as a dog"? What is *charisma*? How is Bob charismatic?

QUESTIONS ON WRITING STRATEGY

1. What is the dominant impression of Markoe's description of Bob? Cite four or five passages in which it is most evident.
2. What is the EFFECT of Markoe's calling Bob her "older boy" in the first sentence?
3. ANALYZE the author's use of IRONY in paragraph 10. How does it contribute to the humor?
4. **OTHER METHODS.** Markoe's description of Bob depends on EXAMPLES of his behavior. Pick out the two or three examples that you found funniest or most illuminating. What does each one illustrate?

QUESTIONS ON LANGUAGE

1. How do you understand the simile in paragraph 2: "he had extracted all the contents in such a way as to leave the empty containers looking like overworked summer-camp copper-tooling projects"? (See "Figures of speech" in Useful Terms if you need a definition of *simile*.)
2. How do phrases like "the broadest definition" and "freethinker" (para. 3) work to develop humor and an affectionate understanding of Bob's appetite?
3. Consult a dictionary if you need help in defining the following: gelatinous (para. 2); fiendish (3); hors d'oeuvre, mayhem (5); ingenuity (6); rectified (8).

SUGGESTIONS FOR WRITING

1. **JOURNAL WRITING.** Choose something you care about that simultaneously annoys or angers you—perhaps a pet, a younger sibling, a troublesome friend, your car, your computer. Sketch some ideas about your chosen subject's good and bad points.
   FROM JOURNAL TO ESSAY. From your journal entry, build a description that, like "Bob the Dog," conveys your affection for your subject while also explaining the difficulties you have with it. You may take a serious approach or a humorous one.
2. Markoe CONTRASTS living with Bob in the city and living with him in "any, less complicated, suburb" (paras. 9–12). If you have lived both in a city

and in a suburb (or in the country), think of some other activity that is different in each place, such as shopping for food, eating out, getting around, parking, or making friends. (If you haven't lived in both kinds of environments, maybe you can imagine the differences.) Write an essay in which you contrast the activity in the two places. Use humor if it serves your purpose.

3. **CRITICAL WRITING.** Why do you think Markoe misses Bob? What were his good qualities? What was it about even his bad behavior that seems to have made him lovable? In two or three paragraphs, analyze Markoe's essay within this framework, using specific examples from the essay as EVIDENCE.

4. **CONNECTIONS.** In an essay, COMPARE the use of irony in "Bob the Dog" and in Dave Barry's "Batting Clean-Up and Striking Out" (p. 191). How do both Markoe and Barry achieve humor through irony? How does their irony differ?

MERRILL MARKOE ON WRITING

In "The Day I Turned Sarcastic," an essay also collected in *What the Dogs Have Taught Me*, Merrill Markoe tells of rereading old pages in her diary:

"It is a strangely pleasurable thing to read your own words from widely varying periods and phases in your life," she writes. "You can hear not just how you thought but how you sounded at the moment you were thinking it. It's so much clearer and more specific than when your memory plays it back."

Markoe analyzes the entries she wrote between the ages of nine and thirteen "in an attempt," she says, "to discover the primitive roots of my need for self-expression." What she finds is records of mostly trivial (and hilarious) events and feelings, but she does detect an important shift. At first she wrote just for herself, assured of her privacy by the diary's lock and key. But when she learned that the lock could be opened by just about anything, her view turned outward, toward an audience. Now she focused on "gaining a readership. Suddenly I was dropping asides to 'whoever is reading this' or an invisible 'you' (as in 'In case you want to know')." It was, Markoe says, the beginning of "writerly awareness" and "the birth of a writer."

FOR DISCUSSION

1. What, according to Markoe (but in your own words), can be gained from rereading one's own past diary entries? Could the same be said of journal entries you may have written?

2. How does considering an audience launch Markoe as "a writer"? What important changes occur when we write not just for ourselves but for others?

JUDITH ORTIZ COFER

A native of Puerto Rico who has lived most of her life in the United States, JUDITH ORTIZ COFER writes poetry, fiction, and essays about her heritage and the balancing of two cultures. Born in Hormigueros, Puerto Rico, in 1952, she earned a B.A. from Augusta College in 1974 and an M.A. from Florida Atlantic University in 1977. Cofer started out as a bilingual teacher in the schools of Palm Beach County, Florida, and she is now a professor of English and creative writing at the University of Georgia. Her publications include collections of poetry, among them *Peregrina* (1986) and *Terms of Survival* (1987); a novel, *The Line of the Sun* (1989); a book of essays, *Silent Dancing* (1990); a book of stories for young people, *An Island Like You: Stories of the Barrio* (1995); and a collection of stories and poems, *The Year of Our Revolution* (1998). As a native Spanish speaker who challenged herself to learn English, she is always experimenting, she says, with "the 'infinite variety' and power of language."

Silent Dancing

Cofer immigrated to New Jersey from Puerto Rico when she was three years old. In this much-reprinted essay, she links views of old home movies and bits of dreams with her adult recollections to describe her family's and her own immigrant experience. The essay first appeared in *The Georgia Review* and then as the title essay in Cofer's collection *Silent Dancing*.

We have a home movie of this party. Several times my mother and I have 1
watched it together, and I have asked questions about the silent revelers coming in and out of focus. It is grainy and of short duration, but it's a great visual aid to my memory of life at that time. And it is in color—the only complete scene in color I can recall from those years.

We lived in Puerto Rico until my brother was born in 1954. Soon 2
after, because of economic pressures on our growing family, my father joined the United States Navy. He was assigned to duty on a ship in Brooklyn Yard—a place of cement and steel that was to be his home base in the States until his retirement more than twenty years later. He left the Island first, alone, going to New York City and tracking down his uncle who lived with his family across the Hudson River in Paterson, New Jersey. There my father found a tiny apartment in a huge tenement that had once housed Jewish families but was just being taken over and transformed by Puerto Ricans, overflowing from New York City. In 1955 he sent for us. My mother was only twenty years old, I was

not quite three, and my brother was a toddler when we arrived at El Building, as the place had been christened by its newest residents.

My memories of life in Paterson during those first few years are all in shades of gray. Maybe I was too young to absorb vivid colors and details, or to discriminate between the slate blue of the winter sky and the darker hues of the snow-bearing clouds, but that single color washes over the whole period. The building we lived in was gray, as were the streets, filled with slush the first few months of my life there. The coat my father had bought for me was similar in color and too big; it sat heavily on my thin frame.

I do remember the way the heater pipes banged and rattled, startling all of us out of sleep until we got so used to the sound that we automatically shut it out or raised our voices above the racket. The hiss from the valve punctuated my sleep (which has always been fitful) like a nonhuman presence in the room—a dragon sleeping at the entrance of my childhood. But the pipes were also a connection to all the other lives being lived around us. Having come from a house designed for a single family back in Puerto Rico—my mother's extended-family home—it was curious to know that strangers lived under our floor and above our heads, and that the heater pipe went through everyone's apartment. (My first spanking in Paterson came as a result of playing tunes on the pipes in my room to see if there would be an answer.) My mother was as new to this concept of beehive life as I was, but she had been given strict orders by my father to keep the doors locked, the noise down, ourselves to ourselves.

It seems that Father had learned some painful lessons about prejudice while searching for an apartment in Paterson. Not until years later did I hear how much resistance he had encountered with landlords who were panicking at the influx of Latinos into a neighborhood that had been Jewish for a couple of generations. It made no difference that it was the American phenomenon of ethnic turnover which was changing the urban core of Paterson, and that the human flood could not be held back with an accusing finger.

"You Cuban?" one man had asked my father, pointing at his name tag on the navy uniform—even though my father had the fair skin and light brown hair of his northern Spanish background, and the name Ortiz is as common in Puerto Rico as Johnson is in the United States.

"No," my father had answered, looking past the finger into his adversary's angry eyes. "I'm Puerto Rican."

"Same shit." And the door closed.

My father could have passed as European, but we couldn't. My brother and I both have our mother's black hair and olive skin, and so we lived in El Building and visited our great-uncle and his fair children on the next block. It was their private joke that they were the German branch of the family. Not many years later that area too would be mainly Puerto Rican. It was as if the heart of the city map were being gradually colored brown—*café con leche*[1] brown. Our color.

The movie opens with a sweep of the living room. It is "typical" immi- 10 *grant Puerto Rican decor for the time: The sofa and chairs are square and hard-looking, upholstered in bright colors (blue and yellow in this instance) and covered with the transparent plastic that furniture salesmen then were so adept at convincing women to buy. The linoleum on the floor is light blue; where it had been subjected to spike heels, as it was in most places, there were dime-size indentations all over it that cannot be seen in this movie. The room is full of people dressed up: dark suits for the men, red dresses for the women. When I have asked my mother why most of the women are in red that night, she has shrugged and said, "I don't remember. Just a coincidence." She doesn't have my obsession for assigning symbolism to everything.*

The three women in red sitting on the couch are my mother, my eighteen- 11 *year-old cousin, and her brother's girlfriend. The novia[2] is just up from the Island, which is apparent in her body language. She sits up formally, her dress pulled over her knees. She is a pretty girl, but her posture makes her look in-secure, lost in her full-skirted dress, which she has carefully tucked around her to make room for my gorgeous cousin, her future sister-in-law. My cousin has grown up in Paterson and is in her last year of high school. She doesn't have a trace of what Puerto Ricans call la mancha (literally, the stain: the mark of the new immigrant—something about the posture, the voice, or the humble demeanor that makes it obvious to everyone the person has just arrived on the mainland). My cousin is wearing a tight, sequined, cocktail dress. Her brown hair has been lightened with peroxide around the bangs, and she is holding a cigarette expertly between her fingers, bringing it up to her mouth in a sensuous arc of her arm as she talks animatedly. My mother, who has come up to sit between the two women, both only a few years younger than herself, is somewhere between the poles they represent in our culture.*

It became my father's obsession to get out of the barrio, and thus we 12 were never permitted to form bonds with the place or with the people who lived there. Yet El Building was a comfort to my mother, who never got over yearning for *la isla.*[3] She felt surrounded by her language: The walls were thin, and voices speaking and arguing in Spanish could be heard all day. *Salsas* blasted out of radios, turned on early in the morning and left on for company. Women seemed to cook rice and

---

[1]Spanish for "coffee with milk."—Eds.
[2]Fiancée, or a girl just arrived from Puerto Rico.—Eds.
[3]The island.—Eds.

beans perpetually—the strong aroma of boiling red kidney beans permeated the hallways.

Though Father preferred that we do our grocery shopping at the su-   13
permarket when he came home on weekend leaves, my mother insisted
that she could cook only with products whose labels she could read.
Consequently, during the week I accompanied her and my little
brother to La Bodega—a hole-in-the-wall grocery store across the
street from El Building. There we squeezed down three narrow aisles
jammed with various products. Goya and Libby's—those were the
trademarks that were trusted by her *mamá*, so my mother bought many
cans of Goya beans, soups, and condiments, as well as little cans of
Libby's fruit juices for us. And she also bought Colgate toothpaste and
Palmolive soap. (The final *e* is pronounced in both these products in
Spanish, so for many years I believed that they were manufactured on
the Island. I remember my surprise at first hearing a commercial on
television in which "Colgate" rhymed with "ate.") We always lingered
at La Bodega, for it was there that Mother breathed best, taking in the
familiar aromas of the foods she knew from Mamá's kitchen. It was also
there that she got to speak to the other women of El Building without violating outright Father's dictates against fraternizing with our neighbors.

Yet Father did his best to make our "assimilation" painless. I can   14
still see him carrying a real Christmas tree up several flights of stairs to
our apartment, leaving a trail of aromatic pine. He carried it formally,
as if it were a flag in a parade. We were the only ones in El Building that
I knew of who got presents on both Christmas and *día de Reyes*, the day
when the Three Kings brought gifts to Christ and to Hispanic children.

Our supreme luxury in El Building was having our own television   15
set. It must have been a result of Father's guilt feelings over the isolation he had imposed on us, but we were among the first in the barrio to
have one. My brother quickly became an avid watcher of Captain Kan-
garoo and Jungle Jim, while I loved all the series showing families. By
the time I started first grade, I could have drawn a map of Middle
America as exemplified by the lives of characters in *Father Knows Best,
The Donna Reed Show, Leave It to Beaver, My Three Sons,* and (my favorite) *Bachelor Father,* where John Forsythe treated his adopted
teenage daughter like a princess because he was rich and had a Chinese
houseboy to do everything for him. In truth, compared to our neighbors
in El Building, *we* were rich. My father's navy check provided us with
financial security and a standard of living that the factory workers en-
vied. The only thing his money could not buy us was a place to live
away from the barrio—his greatest wish, Mother's greatest fear.

In the home movie the men are shown next, sitting around a card table   16
set up in one corner of the living room, playing dominoes. The clack of the

ivory pieces was a familiar sound. I heard it in many houses on the Island and in many apartments in Paterson. In Leave It to Beaver, *the Cleavers played bridge in every other episode; in my childhood, the men started every social occasion with a hotly debated round of dominoes. The women would sit around and watch, but they never participated in the games.*

Here and there you can see a small child. Children were always brought   17
to parties and, whenever they got sleepy, were put to bed in the host's bedroom. Babysitting was a concept unrecognized by the Puerto Rican women I knew: A responsible mother did not leave her children with any stranger. And in a culture where children are not considered intrusive, there was no need to leave the children at home. We went where our mother went.

Of my preschool years I have only impressions: the sharp bite of the   18
wind in December as we walked with our parents toward the brightly lit stores downtown; how I felt like a stuffed doll in my heavy coat, boots, and mittens; how good it was to walk into the five-and-dime and sit at the counter drinking hot chocolate. On Saturdays our whole family would walk downtown to shop at the big department stores on Broadway. Mother bought all our clothes at Penney's and Sears, and she liked to buy her dresses at the women's specialty shops like Lerner's and Diana's. At some point we'd go into Woolworth's and sit at the soda fountain to eat.

We never ran into other Latinos at these stores or when eating out,   19
and it became clear to me only years later that the women from El Building shopped mainly in other places—stores owned by other Puerto Ricans or by Jewish merchants who had philosophically accepted our presence in the city and decided to make us their good customers, if not real neighbors and friends. These establishments were located not downtown but in the blocks around our street, and they were referred to generically as La Tienda, El Bazar, La Bodega, La Botánica. Everyone knew what was meant. These were the stores where your face did not turn a clerk to stone, where your money was as green as anyone else's.

One New Year's Eve we were dressed up like child models in the   20
Sears catalogue: my brother in a miniature man's suit and bow tie, and I in black patent-leather shoes and a frilly dress with several layers of crinoline underneath. My mother wore a bright red dress that night, I remember, and spike heels; her long black hair hung to her waist. Father, who usually wore his navy uniform during his short visits home, had put on a dark civilian suit for the occasion: We had been invited to his uncle's house for a big celebration. Everyone was excited because my mother's brother—Hernan—a bachelor who could indulge him-

self with luxuries—had bought a home movie camera, which he would be trying out that night.

Even the home movie cannot fill in the sensory details such a gathering left imprinted in a child's brain. The thick sweetness of women's perfumes mixing with the ever-present smells of food cooking in the kitchen: meat and plantain *pasteles,* as well as the ubiquitous rice dish made special with pigeon peas—*gandules*—and seasoned with precious *sofrito* sent up from the Island by somebody's mother or smuggled in by a recent traveler. *Sofrito* was one of the items that women hoarded, since it was hardly ever in stock at La Bodega. It was the flavor of Puerto Rico. 21

The men drank Palo Viejo rum, and some of the younger ones got weepy. The first time I saw a grown man cry was at a New Year's Eve party: He had been reminded of his mother by the smells in the kitchen. But what I remember most were the boiled *pasteles,* plantain or yucca rectangles stuffed with corned beef or other meats, olives, and many other savory ingredients, all wrapped in banana leaves. Everybody had to fish one out with a fork. There was always a "trick" *pastel*—one without stuffing—and whoever got that one was the "New Year's Fool." 22

There was also the music. Long-playing albums were treated like precious china in these homes. Mexican recordings were popular, but the songs that brought tears to my mother's eyes were sung by the melancholy Daniel Santos, whose life as a drug addict was the stuff of legend. Felipe Rodríguez was a particular favorite of couples, since he sang about faithless women and brokenhearted men. There is a snatch of one lyric that has stuck in my mind like a needle on a worn groove: *De piedra ha de ser mi cama, de piedra la cabezera . . . la mujer que a mi me quiera . . . ha de quererme de veras. Ay, Ay, Ay, corazón, porque no amas . . .* I must have heard it a thousand times since the idea of a bed made of stone, and its connection to love, first troubled me with its disturbing images. 23

The five-minute home movie ends with people dancing in a circle—the creative filmmaker must have set it up, so that all of them could file past him. It is both comical and sad to watch silent dancing. Since there is no justification for the absurd movements that music provides for some of us, people appear frantic, their faces embarrassingly intense. It's as if you were watching sex. Yet for years, I've had dreams in the form of this home movie. In a recurring scene, familiar faces push themselves forward into my mind's eye, plastering their features into distorted close-ups. And I'm asking them: "Who is *she?* Who is the old woman I don't recognize? Is she an aunt? Somebody's wife? Tell me who she is." 24

"See the beauty mark on her cheek as big as a hill on the lunar [25] landscape of her face—well, that runs in the family. The women on your father's side of the family wrinkle early; it's the price they pay for that fair skin. The young girl with the green stain on her wedding dress is *la novia*—just up from the Island. See, she lowers her eyes when she approaches the camera, as she's supposed to. Decent girls never look at you directly in the face. *Humilde*, humble, a girl should express humility in all her actions. She will make a good wife for your cousin. He should consider himself lucky to have met her only weeks after she arrived here. If he marries her quickly, she will make him a good Puerto Rican–style wife; but if he waits too long, she will be corrupted by the city, just like your cousin there."

[26]

"She means me. I do what I want. This is not some primitive island I live on. Do they expect me to wear a black mantilla on my head and go to mass every day? Not me. I'm an American woman, and I will do as I please. I can type faster than anyone in my senior class at Central High, and I'm going to be a secretary to a lawyer when I graduate. I can pass for an American girl anywhere—I've tried it. At least for Italian, anyway—I never speak Spanish in public. I hate these parties, but I wanted the dress. I look better than any of these *humildes* here. My life is going to be different. I have an American boyfriend. He is older and has a car. My parents don't know it, but I sneak out of the house late at night sometimes to be with him. If I marry him, even my name will be American. I hate rice and beans—that's what makes these women fat."

[27]

"Your *prima*[4] is pregnant by that man she's been sneaking around with. Would I lie to you? I'm your *tía política*,[5] your great-uncle's common-law wife—the one he abandoned on the Island to go marry your cousin's mother. *I* was not invited to this party, of course, but I came anyway. I came to tell you that story about your cousin that you've always wanted to hear. Do you remember the comment your mother made to a neighbor that has always haunted you? The only thing you heard was your cousin's name, and then you saw your mother pick up your doll from the couch and say: 'It was as big as this doll when they flushed it down the toilet.' This image has bothered you for years, hasn't it? You had nightmares about babies being flushed down the toilet, and you wondered why anyone would do such a horrible thing. You didn't dare ask your mother about it. She would only tell you that you had not heard her right, and yell at you for listening to adult conversations. But later, when you were old enough to know about abortions, you suspected. [28]

"I am here to tell you that you were right. Your cousin was growing an *americanito* in her belly when this movie was made. Soon after, she put something long and pointy into her pretty self, thinking

4Cousin. —EDS.
5Aunt-in-law. —EDS.

maybe she could get rid of the problem before breakfast and still make it to her first class at the high school. Well, *niña*,[6] her screams could be heard downtown. Your aunt, her *mamá*, who had been a midwife on the Island, managed to pull the little thing out. Yes, they probably flushed it down the toilet. What else could they do with it—give it a Christian burial in a little white casket with blue bows and ribbons? Nobody wanted that baby—least of all the father, a teacher at her school with a house in West Paterson that he was filling with real children, and a wife who was a natural blonde.   29

"Girl, the scandal sent your uncle back to the bottle. And guess where your cousin ended up? Irony of ironies. She was sent to a village in Puerto Rico to live with a relative on her mother's side: a place so far away from civilization that you have to ride a mule to reach it. A real change in scenery. She found a man there—women like that cannot live without male company—but believe me, the men in Puerto Rico know how to put a saddle on a woman like her. *La gringa*,[7] they call her. Ha, ha, ha. *La gringa* is what she always wanted to be..."   30

The old woman's mouth becomes a cavernous black hole I fall into. And as I fall, I can feel the reverberations of her laughter. I hear the echoes of her last mocking words: *la gringa, la gringa!* And the conga line keeps moving silently past me. There is no music in my dream for   31 the dancers.

When Odysseus visits Hades to see the spirit of his mother,[8] he makes an offering of sacrificial blood, but since all the souls crave an audience with the living, he has to listen to many of them before he can ask questions. I, too, have to hear the dead and the forgotten speak in my dream. Those who are still part of my life remain silent, going around and around in their dance. The others keep pressing their faces   32 forward to say things about the past.

My father's uncle is last in line. He is dying of alcoholism, shrunken and shriveled like a monkey, his face a mass of wrinkles and broken arteries. As he comes closer I realize that in his features I can see my whole family. If you were to stretch that rubbery flesh, you could find my father's face, and deep within *that* face—my own. I don't want to look into those eyes ringed in purple. In a few years he will retreat into silence, and take a long, long time to die. *Move back, Tío, I tell him. I don't want to hear what you have to say. Give the dancers room to move. Soon it will be midnight. Who is the New Year's Fool this time?*

[6]Child. —Eds.

[7]Anglo-Saxon. —Eds.

[8]An episode in the *Odyssey*, usually attributed to Homer, who flourished in the ninth or eighth century B.C. In Greek mythology, Hades rules the underworld. —Eds.

QUESTIONS ON MEANING

1. What do you think is Cofer's PURPOSE in this description? Does she have something specific she wants the reader to understand?
2. Of her father, Cofer writes, "The only thing his money could not buy us was a place to live away from the barrio—his greatest wish, Mother's greatest fear" (para. 15). Why was moving her father's greatest wish? Why did her mother fear it? What passages from the essay support your answer?
3. Are the quoted speeches in paragraphs 25–29 real or imagined? Use EVIDENCE from the essay to support your answer.

QUESTIONS ON WRITING STRATEGY

1. What are the contents of the passages in italics (paras. 1, 10–11, 16–17) and the ones in smaller type (25–29)? How do these passages work with those in regular type? What is their EFFECT?
2. How well does the observation in paragraph 24, "It is both comical and sad to watch silent dancing," convey the dominant impression of Cofer's essay? What, if anything, would you add to "comical and sad"?
3. What does the dialogue contribute to Cofer's TONE?
4. What does Cofer's description of Paterson and her childhood apartment (paras. 3–4) tell us about Cofer herself as a child?
5. **OTHER METHODS.** Paragraph 11 offers three EXAMPLES of Puerto Rican women: Cofer's mother, her assimilated cousin, and the cousin's brother's girlfriend. How does her description of these three women illustrate a cultural shift Puerto Rican immigrants were experiencing at the time the home movie was made?

QUESTIONS ON LANGUAGE

1. How might "silent dancing" serve as a metaphor for memory? (See "Figures of speech" in Useful Terms for a definition of *metaphor*.)
2. What larger meaning can we infer from this sentence in paragraph 23: "Long-playing albums were treated like precious china in these homes"?
3. Consult a dictionary if you need help in defining the following: influx (5); adept (10); animatedly (11); barrio (12); assimilation (14); avid (15); plantain (22); mantilla (26).

SUGGESTIONS FOR WRITING

1. **JOURNAL WRITING.** Think of a dream you've had that stays with you for some reason. Write down as many details of the dream as you can.
   FROM JOURNAL TO ESSAY. In an essay, describe the dream you wrote about in your journal, but also do more: Try to interpret the dream in the context of your life when you had it. What do you think it meant? Why did you have it when you did? What did it tell you?

2. Have you had the experience of being isolated from your surroundings, whether because of language or culture or because of some other barrier— being new in town, feeling friendless, or even just having to study when everyone else was having fun? Describe the experience in an essay, using plenty of details to help your readers understand your feelings.
3. **CRITICAL WRITING.** ANALYZE the different tones of Cofer herself, her cousin (para. 26), and her *tía política* (25, 27–29). How do their tones convey the different experiences and expectations of these three women?
4. **CONNECTIONS.** Cofer and Itabari Njeri, in "When Morpheus Held Him" (p. 108), both describe their fathers. COMPARE AND CONTRAST the characters of these two men, focusing especially on the way they coped with the isolation of being "different" in the dominant culture.

JUDITH ORTIZ COFER ON WRITING

In the 1980s Cofer told *Contemporary Authors* why she so often chooses her family as her writing subject. She was speaking of her poetry, but the same could be said of her stories and essays as well. "My family is one of the main topics of my poetry," Cofer explained, "the ones left behind on the island of Puerto Rico, and the ones who came to the United States. In tracing their lives, I discover more about mine. The place of birth itself becomes a metaphor for the things we all must leave behind; the assimilation of a new culture is the coming into maturity by accepting the terms necessary for survival. My poetry is the study of this process of change, assimilation, and transformation."

FOR DISCUSSION

1. What does Cofer mean when she says that "the assimilation of a new culture is the coming into maturity by accepting the terms necessary for survival"? Does this statement apply only to immigrants or to nonimmigrants as well? Why?
2. If you have ever written about your family or a relative, what did the experience tell you about your kin? What did it tell you about yourself?

ELIZABETH BISHOP

Known for poems of dense detail and personal reticence, ELIZABETH BISHOP is one of the most admired writers of the twentieth century. Born in Worcester, Massachusetts, in 1911, she was orphaned at an early age and spent her childhood in Nova Scotia, Canada. In 1934, she received her B.A. from Vassar College, where she met her life-long friend and mentor, the poet Marianne Moore. Bishop traveled extensively and lived in New York, Florida, Massachusetts, and Brazil; the themes of travel and loss figure prominently in her poems and stories. Most of her published work is gathered in two volumes: *The Complete Poems, 1929–1979* (1983) and *The Collected Prose, 1911–1979* (1984). She translated the famous Portuguese memoir *The Diary of Helena Morley* (1957, 1977, 1991) and cotranslated *An Anthology of Contemporary Brazilian Poetry* (1972). Bishop received numerous awards for her poetry, including the Pulitzer Prize for her first two books, *North and South* (1946) and *A Cold Spring* (1955); National Book Awards for *Questions of Travel* (1965) and an earlier *Complete Poems* (1969); and the National Book Critics Circle Award for *Geography III* (1976). In 1976, she was the first woman and first American to receive the Books Abroad/Neustadt Prize for Literature. Bishop taught at Harvard University from 1970 until 1977, and she died in Cambridge in 1979.

Filling Station

In this poem, first published in 1965, Bishop illuminates the minutest details of a roadside fixture to find a universal truth. As this sort of gas station-with-garage fast succumbs to shiny "convenience marts" selling gas and snacks, Bishop's description reminds contemporary readers of the color (not to mention the care) we may soon miss altogether.

Oh, but it is dirty!
— this little filling station,
oil-soaked, oil-permeated
to a disturbing, over-all
black translucency.   5
Be careful with that match!

Father wears a dirty,
oil-soaked monkey suit
that cuts him under the arms,
and several quick and saucy   10
and greasy sons assist him

(it's a family filling station),
all quite thoroughly dirty.

Do they live in the station?
It has a cement porch   15
behind the pumps, and on it
a set of crushed and grease-
impregnated wickerwork;
on the wicker sofa
a dirty dog, quite comfy.   20

Some comic books provide
the only note of color—
of certain color. They lie
upon a big dim doily
draping a taboret[1]   25
(part of the set), beside
a big hirsute begonia.

Why the extraneous plant?
Why the taboret?
Why, oh why, the doily?   30
(Embroidered in daisy stitch
with marguerites, I think,
and heavy with gray crochet.)

Somebody embroidered the doily.
Somebody waters the plant,   35
or oils it, maybe. Somebody
arranges the rows of cans
so that they softly say:
ESSO—SO—SO—SO
to high-strung automobiles.   40
Somebody loves us all.

QUESTIONS ON MEANING

1. "Some comic books provide / the only note of color— / of certain color"
   (lines 21–23). What does Bishop imply by qualifying her statement with
   the afterthought "of certain color"?
2. What is the EFFECT of "ESSO—SO—SO—SO" in the third to last line? (Esso
   is the former name of what is now Exxon.)
3. How do the details of the filling station help Bishop come to her conclusion, "Somebody loves us all" (line 41)?
4. What seems to be this poem's PURPOSE?

[1] A low stool. — EDS.

QUESTIONS ON WRITING STRATEGY

1. The spaces between sections of the poem divide it into six stanzas. Why do you think Bishop created these stanzas? How would the poem have been different if it were one uninterrupted strip of language?
2. How would you characterize Bishop's TONE in this poem? How and where does it subtly shift? Use specific passages as EVIDENCE to support your answer.
3. At several points in the poem (lines 12, 26, 31–33), Bishop encloses thoughts in parentheses. What is the effect of these parenthetical asides?
4. **OTHER METHODS.** Bishop CONTRASTS the dirty father and his sons, and the dirty surroundings they have evidently created (lines 1–23), with the meticulous care taken by someone (someone else?) to decorate the place (lines 23–40). Why is this contrast especially effective for Bishop's purpose — more effective than, say, a description that recorded all the details of the place together, without creating distinctions among them?

QUESTIONS ON LANGUAGE

1. Bishop uses just a few words that may be unfamiliar. Make sure you know the meanings of permeated (line 3); translucency (5); saucy (10); hirsute (27); extraneous (28); marguerites (32).
2. How is the language in this poem different from that you've encountered in essays?
3. What is the effect of restating "oil-soaked" as "oil-permeated" in the first stanza?

SUGGESTIONS FOR WRITING

1. **JOURNAL WRITING.** Think of a place or situation that gives you a definite feeling. It may be a surprising feeling, such as the one Bishop encountered in the dirty filling station, or it may be an expected one: comfort at home, serenity at a lakeside, anxiety in the dentist's office, anger in traffic. Describe the place or situation and the feeling.
   FROM JOURNAL TO ESSAY. Using plenty of details, develop the ideas in your journal entry into an essay that describes the place or situation and the feeling it evokes. In your writing, also try to explain why one causes the other.
2. Have you ever tried writing a poem? Try it now, choosing, like Bishop, a place. (It could be the same place you consider in the previous assignment.) Don't worry too much about the technical aspects of poetry (meter, rhyme, and the rest). Instead, think carefully about your choice of words and IMAGES, building the poem through description.
3. **CRITICAL WRITING.** Write an essay in which you examine Bishop's use of the word somebody four times in the last stanza. Does the word refer to the same somebody each time? How does the anonymity of the somebody or somebodies contribute to Bishop's certainty that "Somebody loves us all"?
4. **CONNECTIONS.** COMPARE AND CONTRAST Bishop's poem and John McPhee's "Silk Parachute" (p. 155). What sort of assurance does each author arrive at? How are each author's EXAMPLES connected to her or his conclusion?

ADDITIONAL WRITING TOPICS

Description

1. This is an in-class writing experiment. Describe another person in the room so clearly and unmistakably that when you read your description aloud, your subject will be recognized. (Be OBJECTIVE. No insulting descriptions, please!)
2. Write a paragraph describing one subject from *each* of the following categories. It will be up to you to make the general subject refer to a particular person, place, or thing. Write at least one paragraph as an OBJECTIVE description and at least one as a SUBJECTIVE description.

PERSON

A friend or roommate
A typical rap, heavy metal, or country musician
One of your parents
An elderly person you know
A prominent politician
A historical figure

PLACE

An office
A classroom
A college campus
A vacation spot
A hospital emergency room
A forest

THING

A car
A dentist's drill
A painting or photograph
A foggy day
A season of the year
A musical instrument

3. In a brief essay, describe your ideal place: an apartment, a bookstore, a dorm room, a vacation spot, a classroom, a restaurant, a gym, a supermarket or convenience store, a garden, a golf course. With concrete details, try to make the ideal seem actual.

Narration and Description

4. Use a combination of narration and description to develop any one of the
   following topics:

   Your first day on the job
   Your first day at college
   Returning to an old neighborhood
   Getting lost
   A brush with a celebrity
   Delivering bad (or good) news

3

EXAMPLE

Pointing to Instances

THE METHOD

"There have been many women runners of distinction," a writer begins, and quickly goes on, "among them Joan Benoit, Grete Waitz, Florence Griffith Joyner...."

You have just seen examples at work. An EXAMPLE (from the Latin *exemplum*: "one thing selected from among many") is an instance that reveals a whole type. By selecting an example, a writer shows the nature or character of the group from which it is taken. In a written essay, examples will often serve to illustrate a general statement, or GENERAL- IZATION. Here, for instance, the writer Linda Wolfe makes a point about the food fetishes of Roman emperors (Domitian and Claudius ruled in the first century A.D.).

> The emperors used their gastronomical concerns to indicate their contempt of the country and the whole task of governing it. Domitian humiliated his cabinet by forcing them to attend him at his villa to help solve a serious problem. When they arrived he kept them waiting for hours. The problem, it finally appeared, was that the emperor had just purchased a giant fish, too large for any dish he owned, and he needed the learned brains of his ministers to decide

whether the fish should be minced or whether a larger pot should be sought. The emperor Claudius one day rode hurriedly to the Senate and demanded they deliberate the importance of a life without pork. Another time he sat in his tribunal ostensibly administering justice but actually allowing the litigants to argue and orate while he grew dreamy, interrupting the discussions only to announce, "Meat pies are wonderful. We shall have them for dinner."

Wolfe might have allowed the opening sentence of her paragraph—the TOPIC SENTENCE—to remain a vague generalization. Instead, she supports it with three examples, each a brief story of an emperor's contemptuous behavior. With these examples, Wolfe not only explains and supports her generalization but also animates it.

The method of giving examples—of illustrating what you're saying with a "for instance"—is not merely helpful to practically all kinds of writing, it is indispensable. Bad writers—those who bore us, or lose us completely—often have an ample supply of ideas; their trouble is that they never pull their ideas down out of the clouds. A dull writer, for instance, might declare, "The emperors used food to humiliate their governments," and then, instead of giving examples, go on, "They also manipulated their families," or something—adding still another large, unillustrated idea. Specific examples are *needed* elements in effective prose. Not only do they make ideas understandable, but they also keep readers awake. (The previous paragraphs have tried—by giving examples from Linda Wolfe and from "a dull writer"—to illustrate this point.)

THE PROCESS

The Generalization

Examples illustrate a generalization, such as Linda Wolfe's opening statement about the Roman emperors, and any example essay is bound to have a generalization as its THESIS STATEMENT. Here are a few examples from the essays in this chapter:

> Sometimes I think we would be better off [in dealing with social problems] if we forgot about the broad strokes and concentrated on the details. (Anna Quindlen, "Homeless")

> That first encounter, and those that followed, signified that a vast, unnerving gulf lay between nighttime pedestrians—particularly women—and me. (Brent Staples, "Black Men and Public Space")

Such a generalization forms the backbone, the central idea, of an essay developed by example. Then the specifics bring the idea down to earth for readers.

Example   **139**

The Examples

An essay developed by example will often start with an example or two. That is, you'll see something—a man pilfering a quarter for bus fare from a child's Kool-Aid stand, a friend dating another friend's fiancé (or fiancée)—and your observation will suggest a generalization (perhaps a statement about how people mishandle ethical dilemmas). But a mere example or two probably won't demonstrate your generalization for readers and thus won't achieve your PURPOSE. For that you'll need a range of instances.

Where do you find more? In anything you know—or care to learn. Start close to home. Seek examples in your own immediate knowledge and experience. Explore your conversations with others, your studies, and the storehouse of information you have gathered from books, newspapers, magazines, radio, and TV and from popular hearsay: proverbs and sayings, bits of wisdom you've heard voiced in your family, folklore, popular song.

Now and again, you may feel an irresistible temptation to make up an example out of thin air. This procedure is risky, but can work wonderfully—if, that is, you have a wonder-working imagination. When Henry David Thoreau, in *Walden*, attacks Americans' smug pride in the achievements of nineteenth-century science and industry, he wants to illustrate that kind of invention or discovery "which distracts our attention from serious things." And so he makes up the examples—farfetched at the time, but pointed—of a transatlantic speaking tube and what it might convey: "We are eager to tunnel under the Atlantic and bring the Old World some weeks nearer to the New; but perchance the first news that will leak through into the broad, flapping American ear will be that the Princess Adelaide has the whooping cough." (Thoreau would be appalled at our immersion in the British Royal Family via just the sort of communication he imagined.)

Thoreau's examples (and the sarcastic phrase about the American ear) bespeak genius; but, of course, not every writer can be a Thoreau—or needs to be. A hypothetical example may well be better than no example at all; yet, as a rule, an example from fact or experience is likely to carry more weight. Suppose you have to write about the benefits—any benefits—that recent science has conferred upon the nation. You might imagine one such benefit: the prospect of one day being able to vacation in outer space and drift about in free-fall like a soap bubble. That imagined benefit would be all right, but it is obviously a conjecture that you dreamed up without going to the library. Do a little digging in recent books and magazines (for the latter, with the aid of the *Readers' Guide to Periodical Literature*). Your reader will feel better informed to be told that science — specifically, the NASA space program — has produced useful inventions. You add:

> Among these are the smoke detector, originally developed as Skylab equipment; the inflatable air bag to protect drivers and pilots, designed to cushion astronauts in splashdowns; a walking chair that enables paraplegics to mount stairs and travel over uneven ground, derived from the moonwalkers' surface buggy; the technique of cryosurgery, the removal of cancerous tissue by fast freezing.

By using specific examples like these, you render the idea of "benefits to society" more concrete and more definite. Such examples are not prettifications of your essay; they are necessary if you are to hold your readers' attention and convince them that you are worth listening to.

When giving examples, you'll find other methods useful. Sometimes, as in the paragraph by Linda Wolfe, an example takes the form of a NARRATIVE (Chap. 1): a brief story, an ANECDOTE, or a case history. Sometimes an example embodies a vivid DESCRIPTION of a person, place, or thing (Chap. 2).

Lazy writers think, "Oh well, I can't come up with any example here — I'll just leave it to the reader to find one." The flaw in this ASSUMPTION is that the reader may be as lazy as the writer. As a result, a perfectly good idea may be left suspended in the stratosphere. The linguist and writer S. I. Hayakawa tells the story of a professor who, in teaching a philosophy course, spent a whole semester on the theory of beauty. When students asked him for a few examples of beautiful paintings, symphonies, or works of nature, he refused, saying, "We are interested in principles, not in particulars." The professor himself may well have been interested in principles, but it is a safe bet that his classroom resounded with snores. In written EXPOSITION, it is undoubtedly the particulars — the pertinent examples — that keep a reader awake and having a good time, and taking in the principles besides.

CHECKLIST FOR REVISING AN EXAMPLE ESSAY

- ✔ **GENERALIZATION.** What general statement do your examples illustrate? Will it be clear to readers what ties the examples together?
- ✔ **SUPPORT.** Do you have enough examples to establish your generalization, or will readers be left needing more?
- ✔ **SPECIFICS.** Are your examples detailed? Does each capture some aspects of the generalization?
- ✔ **RELEVANCE.** Do all your examples relate to your generalization? Should any be cut because they go off-track?

Example   **141**

EXAMPLE IN A PARAGRAPH: TWO ILLUSTRATIONS

Using Example to Write About Television

This paragraph appears in an essay maintaining that television merely simulates, or imitates, real problems, events, activities, and institutions. The essay offers many examples of programming that only seems to represent what's real, such as morning news shows, small-claims courts (*The People's Court* and *Judge Judy*), and wrestling. Here the author uses further examples of TV wrestling to show how it simulates televised football, basketball, and other sports.

To sustain the simulation, wrestling must construct and maintain a little universe of the simulated. To do this, its discourse refers in its every enunciation to the apparatus *Generalization to be illustrated* used to broadcast conventional sport. Wrestling features the same style of ringside commentary, the same interpolation of interviews, the same mystification of sporting expertise, the same freeze-frame and instant replay formats, the same *Six examples* faintly prurient interest in the wrestlers' private lives (not to mention parts), the same cults of personality, and so on. This system of understanding, however, is marshaled in the service of an event which is a parody of its originating source: "real" sport.

> —Michael Sorkin, "Faking It,"
> in *Watching Television*, ed. Todd Gitlin

Using Example in an Academic Discipline

The following paragraph from an economics textbook appears amid the author's explanation of how markets work. To dispel what might seem clouds of theory, the author here brings an abstract principle down to earth with a concrete and detailed example.

The primary function of the market is to bring together suppliers and demanders so that they can trade with one another. Buyers and sellers do not necessarily have to be in face-to-face contact; they can signal their desires and in- *Generalization to be illustrated* tentions through various intermediaries. For example, the demand for green beans in California is not expressed directly by the green bean consumers to the green bean growers. People who want green beans buy them at a grocery store; the store orders them from a vegetable wholesaler; *Single extended example* the wholesaler buys them from a bean cooperative, whose manager tells local farmers of the size of the current demand for green beans. The demanders of green beans are able to

signal their demand schedule to the original suppliers, the
farmers who raise the beans, without any personal communication between the two parties.

—Lewis C. Solmon, *Microeconomics*

EXAMPLE ELSEWHERE IN *THE BEDFORD READER*

Every selection in this book uses examples: They are, as we have
said, a mainstay of clear, specific writing. In the essays listed below, the
authors depend on a single extended example or a series of examples
while also developing their ideas by other methods.

PART ONE

Ralph Ellison, "On Being the Target of Discrimination"
Barbara Huttmann, "A Crime of Compassion"
Merrill Markoe, "Bob the Dog (1974–1988)"
Suzanne Britt, "Neat People vs. Sloppy People"
Dave Barry, "Batting Clean-Up and Striking Out"
Jeff Greenfield, "The Black and White Truth About Basketball"
Judy Brady, "I Want a Wife"
Armin A. Brott, "Not All Men Are Sly Foxes"
Russell Baker, "The Plot Against People"
Deborah Tannen, "But What Do You Mean?"
Stephanie Ericsson, "The Ways We Lie"
William Lutz, "The World of Doublespeak"
Gloria Naylor, "The Meanings of a Word"
Christine Leong, "Being a Chink"
Michael Kroll, "The Unquiet Death of Robert Harris"
Heidi Pollock, "Welcome to Cyberbia"
William F. Buckley, Jr., "Why Don't We Complain?"

PART TWO

Stephen L. Carter, "The Insufficiency of Honesty"
Annie Dillard, "Lenses"
George Orwell, "Shooting an Elephant"
Tom Wolfe, "Pornoviolence"

CASE STUDY
Using Examples

As a college sophomore, Kharron Reid was applying for a summer internship implementing computer networks for businesses. He put together a résumé structured to present his previous work experience and his education for this kind of job. (See the résumé on pp. 317–18.)

In drafting a cover letter for the résumé, Reid at first found himself repeating all his background in a very long letter. On the advice of his school's placement office, he rewrote the letter to emphasize just what the prospective employer would most need to know: the work, courses, and computer skills that qualified him for the opening it had. The rewritten letter, below, focuses on examples from the résumé to support the statement (in the second-to-last paragraph) that "my education and my hands-on experience with networking prepare me for the opening you have."

Kharron Reid
137 Chester St., Apt. E
Allston, MA 02134
February 23, 1999

Ms. Dolores Jackson
Human Resources Director
E-line Systems
75 Arondale Avenue
Boston, MA 02114

Dear Ms. Jackson:

I am applying for the networking internship in your information technology department, advertised in the career services office of Boston University.

I have considerable experience in networking from summer internships at NBS Systems and at Pioneer Networking. At NBS I planned and laid the physical platforms and configured the software for seven WANs on a Windows NT server. At Pioneer, I laid the physical platforms and configured the software to connect eight workstations into a LAN. Both internships gave me experience in every stage of networking.

In the fall I will be entering my third year in Boston University's School of Management, majoring in business administration and information systems. I have completed courses in computers (including programming), information systems, and business. In addition to my experience and coursework, I am proficient in Unix, NT, and Linux.

As the enclosed résumé indicates, my education and my hands-on experience with networking prepare me for the opening you have.

I am available for an interview at your convenience. Please call me at (617) 555-4009 or e-mail me at kreid@bu.edu.

Sincerely,

Kharron Reid

Kharron Reid

BARBARA LAZEAR ASCHER

BARBARA LAZEAR ASCHER was born in 1946 and educated at Bennington College and Cardozo School of Law. She practiced law for two years in a private firm, where she found herself part of a power structure in which those on top resembled "the two-year-old with the biggest plastic pail and shovel on the beach. It's a life of nervous guardianship." Ascher quit the law to devote herself to writing, to explore, as she says, "what really matters." Her essays have appeared in the *New York Times*, the *Yale Review*, *Vogue*, and other periodicals and have been collected in *Playing After Dark* (1986) and *The Habit of Loving* (1989). She is a contributing editor of *Self* magazine. Her most recent books are *Landscape Without Gravity: A Memoir of Grief* (1993), about her brother's death from AIDS; and *Dancing in the Dark: Romance, Yearning, and the Search for the Sublime* (1999), about our search for romance in our lives.

On Compassion

Ascher often writes about life in New York City, where human problems sometimes seem larger and more stubborn than in other places. In this essay Ascher uses examples from the city to address a universal need: compassion for those who require help. First published in *Elle* magazine in 1988, the essay was later reprinted in *The Habit of Loving*. The essay following this one, Anna Quindlen's "Homeless," addresses the same issue.

The man's grin is less the result of circumstance than dreams or 1
madness. His buttonless shirt, with one sleeve missing, hangs outside the waist of his baggy trousers. Carefully plaited dreadlocks bespeak a better time, long ago. As he crosses Manhattan's Seventy-ninth Street, his gait is the shuffle of the forgotten ones held in place by gravity rather than plans. On the corner of Madison Avenue, he stops before a blond baby in an Aprica stroller. The baby's mother waits for the light to change and her hands close tighter on the stroller's handle as she sees the man approach.

The others on the corner, five men and women waiting for the 2
crosstown bus, look away. They daydream a bit and gaze into the weak rays of November light. A man with a briefcase lifts and lowers the shiny toe of his right shoe, watching the light reflect, trying to catch and balance it, as if he could hold and make it his, to ease the heavy gray of coming January, February, and March. The winter months that will send snow around the feet, calves, and knees of the grinning man as he heads for the shelter of Grand Central or Pennsylvania Station.

But for now, in this last gasp of autumn warmth, he is still. His eyes   3
fix on the baby. The mother removes her purse from her shoulder and
rummages through its contents: lipstick, a lace handkerchief, an address book. She finds what she's looking for and passes a folded dollar
over her child's head to the man who stands and stares even though the
light has changed and traffic navigates about his hips.

His hands continue to dangle at his sides. He does not know his   4
part. He does not know that acceptance of the gift and gratitude are
what make this transaction complete. The baby, weary of the unwaver-
ing stare, pulls its blanket over its head. The man does not look away.
Like a bridegroom waiting at the altar, his eyes pierce the white veil.

The mother grows impatient and pushes the stroller before her,   5
bearing the dollar like a cross. Finally, a black hand rises and closes
around green.

Was it fear or compassion that motivated the gift?   6

Up the avenue, at Ninety-first Street, there is a small French bread   7
shop where you can sit and eat a buttery, overpriced croissant and wash
it down with rich cappuccino. Twice when I have stopped here to stave
hunger or stay the cold, twice as I have sat and read and felt the warm
rush of hot coffee and milk, an old man has wandered in and stood inside the entrance. He wears a stained blanket pulled up to his chin, and
a woolen hood pulled down to his gray, bushy eyebrows. As he stands,
the scent of stale cigarettes and urine fills the small, overheated room.

The owner of the shop, a moody French woman, emerges from the   8
kitchen with steaming coffee in a Styrofoam cup, and a small paper bag
of...of what? Yesterday's bread? Today's croissant? He accepts the offering as silently as he came, and is gone.

Twice I have witnessed this, and twice I have wondered, what com-   9
pels this woman to feed this man? Pity? Care? Compassion? Or does she
simply want to rid her shop of his troublesome presence? If expulsion
were her motivation she would not reward his arrival with gifts of food.
Most proprietors do not. They chase the homeless from their midst
with expletives and threats.

As winter approaches, the mayor of New York City is moving the   10
homeless off the streets and into Bellevue Hospital. The New York
Civil Liberties Union is watchful. They question whether the rights of
these people who live in our parks and doorways are being violated by
involuntary hospitalization.

I think the mayor's notion is humane, but I fear it is something else   11
as well. Raw humanity offends our sensibilities. We want to protect
ourselves from an awareness of rags with voices that make no sense and
scream forth in inarticulate rage. We do not wish to be reminded of the
tentative state of our own well-being and sanity. And so, the troublesome presence is removed from the awareness of the electorate.

Like other cities, there is much about Manhattan now that resem- 12
bles Dickensian London. Ladies in high-heeled shoes pick their way
through poverty and madness. You hear more cocktail party complaints
than usual, "I just can't take New York anymore." Our citizens dream of
the open spaces of Wyoming, the manicured exclusivity of Hobe Sound.

And yet, it may be that these are the conditions that finally give 13
birth to empathy, the mother of compassion. We cannot deny the existence of the helpless as their presence grows. It is impossible to insulate
ourselves against what is at our very doorstep. I don't believe that one
is born compassionate. Compassion is not a character trait like a sunny
disposition. It must be learned, and it is learned by having adversity at
our windows, coming through the gates of our yards, the walls of our
towns, adversity that becomes so familiar that we begin to identify and
empathize with it.

For the ancient Greeks, drama taught and reinforced compassion 14
within a society. The object of Greek tragedy was to inspire empathy in
the audience so that the common response to the hero's fall was:
"There, but for the grace of God, go I." Could it be that this was the response of the mother who offered the dollar, the French woman who
gave the food? Could it be that the homeless, like those ancients, are
reminding us of our common humanity? Of course, there is a difference.
This play doesn't end—and the players can't go home.

QUESTIONS ON MEANING

1. What do the two men in Ascher's essay exemplify?
2. What is Ascher's THESIS? What is her PURPOSE?
3. What solution to homelessness is introduced in paragraph 10? What does
   Ascher think of this possibility?
4. How do you interpret Ascher's last sentence? Is she optimistic or pes-
   simistic about whether people will learn compassion?

QUESTIONS ON WRITING STRATEGY

1. Which comes first, the GENERALIZATIONS or the supporting examples? Why
   has Ascher chosen this order?
2. What assumptions does the author make about her AUDIENCE?
3. Why do the other people at the bus stop look away (para. 2)? What does
   Ascher's description of their activities say about them?
4. **OTHER METHODS.** Ascher explores CAUSES AND EFFECTS. Do you agree with
   her that exposure to others' helplessness increases our compassion? Why,
   or why not?

QUESTIONS ON LANGUAGE

1. What is the difference between empathy and compassion? Why does Ascher say that "empathy [is] the mother of compassion" (para. 13)?
2. Find definitions for the following words: plaited, dreadlocks, bespeak (para. 1); stave, stay (7); expletives (9); inarticulate, electorate (11).
3. What are the implications of Ascher's ALLUSION to "Dickensian London" (para. 12)?
4. Examine the language Ascher uses to describe the two homeless men. Is it OBJECTIVE? sympathetic? negative?

SUGGESTIONS FOR WRITING

1. **JOURNAL WRITING.** Write about a personal experience with misfortune. Have you needed to beg on the street, been evicted from an apartment, had to scrounge for food? Have you worked in a soup kitchen, been asked for money by beggars, helped out in a city hospital?
   FROM JOURNAL TO ESSAY. Write an essay on the experience you explored in your journal, using examples to convey the effect the experience had on you.
2. Write an essay on the problem of homelessness in your town or city. Use examples to support your view of the problem and a possible solution.
3. Ascher refers to the efforts of New York City to move the homeless off the streets (para. 10). In October 1987, one of New York's homeless, Joyce Brown, was taken off the sidewalk where she lived to Bellevue Hospital. The American Civil Liberties Union sued on her behalf, claiming that she was not a danger to herself or to others — the grounds for involuntary hospitalization. Although Brown was eventually released in January 1988, the issue of the city's right to hospitalize her was never resolved. Consult the *New York Times Index* and the *Times* itself for news articles and editorials on this situation. Write an essay arguing for or against Joyce Brown's freedom to live on the street, supporting your argument with EVIDENCE from the newspaper and from your own experience.
4. **CRITICAL WRITING.** In her last paragraph, Ascher mentions but does not address another key difference between the characters in Greek tragedy and the homeless on today's streets: The former were "heroes" — gods and goddesses, kings and queens — whereas the latter are placeless, poor, anonymous, even reviled. Does this difference negate Ascher's comparison between Greek theatergoers and ourselves or her larger point about how compassion is learned? Answer in a brief essay, saying why or why not.
5. **CONNECTIONS.** The next essay, Anna Quindlen's "Homeless," also uses examples to make a point about homelessness. What are some of the differences in the examples each writer uses? In a brief essay, explore whether and how these differences create different TONES in the two works.

BARBARA LAZEAR ASCHER ON WRITING

A lawyer before she was a full-time writer, Barbara Lazear Ascher thinks that her legal training helped her become a stronger writer.

"I believe there is a kind of legal thinking that becomes part of your own thinking," she told Jean W. Ross of *Contemporary Authors*. "What it did for me was help me to become quite a tight writer. My pieces are very short, and I think a lot of that has to do with the training in law, which is to tell the facts and the theories, and then put it all together and close it up. I might have been a more excessive writer if I hadn't had the legal training."

For Ascher, the essay is the ideal form of expression. "I'm quite impatient, so it's very satisfying to have a small space in which to tell what it was you wanted to tell. You get to the point right away instead of having to drag it out and slowly reveal it."

FOR DISCUSSION

1. How did her legal training help Ascher when she became a writer? How does a "tight writer" help readers as well?
2. How might an "excessive writer" have trouble with the essay form? What, in your view, is "excessive" writing?

ANNA QUINDLEN

A<small>NNA</small> Q<small>UINDLEN</small> was born in 1952 and graduated from Barnard College in 1974. She worked as a reporter for the *New York Post* and the *New York Times* before taking over the *Times*'s "About New York" column, serving as the paper's deputy metropolitan editor, and in 1986 creating her own weekly column, "Life in the Thirties." Many of the essays from this popular column were collected in *Living Out Loud* (1988). Between 1989 and 1994 Quindlen wrote a twice-weekly op-ed column for the *Times*, on social and political issues. The columns earned her the Pulitzer Prize in 1992, and many of them were collected in *Thinking Out Loud: On the Personal, the Political, the Public, and the Private* (1993). Quindlen has also published two books about children, one for children, and three successful novels: *Object Lessons* (1991), *One True Thing* (1994), and *Black and Blue: A Novel* (1998). *One True Thing* was made into a movie starring Meryl Streep.

Homeless

In this essay from *Living Out Loud*, Quindlen uses examples to explore the same topic as Barbara Lazear Ascher (p. 145), but with a different slant. Typically for Quindlen, she mingles a reporter's respect for details with a passionate regard for life.

Her name was Ann, and we met in the Port Authority Bus Terminal several Januarys ago. I was doing a story on homeless people. She said I was wasting my time talking to her; she was just passing through, although she'd been passing through for more than two weeks. To prove to me that this was true, she rummaged through a tote bag and a manila envelope and finally unfolded a sheet of typing paper and brought out her photographs.

They were not pictures of family, or friends, or even a dog or cat, its eyes brown-red in the flashbulb's light. They were pictures of a house. It was like a thousand houses in a hundred towns, not suburb, not city, but somewhere in between, with aluminum siding and a chain-link fence, a narrow driveway running up to a one-car garage and a patch of backyard. The house was yellow. I looked on the back for a date or a name, but neither was there. There was no need for discussion. I knew what she was trying to tell me, for it was something I had often felt. She was not adrift, alone, anonymous, although her bags and her raincoat with the grime shadowing its creases had made me believe she was. She had a house, or at least once upon a time had had one. Inside were curtains, a couch, a stove, potholders. You are where you live. She was somebody.

I've never been very good at looking at the big picture, taking the ³ global view, and I've always been a person with an overactive sense of place, the legacy of an Irish grandfather. So it is natural that the thing that seems most wrong with the world to me right now is that there are so many people with no homes. I'm not simply talking about shelter from the elements, or three square meals a day or a mailing address to which the welfare people can send the check—although I know that all these are important for survival. I'm talking about a home, about precisely those kinds of feelings that have wound up in cross-stitch and French knots on samplers over the years.

Home is where the heart is. There's no place like it. I love my home ⁴ with a ferocity totally out of proportion to its appearance or location. I love dumb things about it: the hot-water heater, the plastic rack you drain dishes in, the roof over my head, which occasionally leaks. And yet it is precisely those dumb things that make it what it is—a place of certainty, stability, predictability, privacy, for me and for my family. It is where I live. What more can you say about a place than that? That is everything.

Yet it is something that we have been edging away from gradually ⁵ during my lifetime and the lifetimes of my parents and grandparents. There was a time when where you lived often was where you worked and where you grew the food you ate and even where you were buried. When that era passed, where you lived at least was where your parents had lived and where you would live with your children when you became enfeebled. Then, suddenly where you lived was where you lived for three years, until you could move on to something else and something else again.

And so we have come to something else again, to children who do ⁶ not understand what it means to go to their rooms because they have never had a room, to men and women whose fantasy is a wall they can paint a color of their own choosing, to old people reduced to sitting on molded plastic chairs, their skin blue-white in the lights of a bus station, who pull pictures of houses out of their bags. Homes have stopped being homes. Now they are real estate.

People find it curious that those without homes would rather sleep ⁷ sitting up on benches or huddled in doorways than go to shelters. Certainly some prefer to do so because they are emotionally ill, because they have been locked in before and they are damned if they will be locked in again. Others are afraid of the violence and trouble they may find there. But some seem to want something that is not available in shelters, and they will not compromise, not for a cot, or oatmeal, or a shower with special soap that kills the bugs. "One room," a woman with a baby who was sleeping on her sister's floor, once told me, "painted blue." That was the crux of it; not size or location, but pride of ownership. Painted blue.

This is a difficult problem, and some wise and compassionate   8
people are working hard at it. But in the main I think we work around
it, just as we walk around it when it is lying on the sidewalk or sitting
in the bus terminal—the problem, that is. It has been customary to take
people's pain and lessen our own participation in it by turning it into an
issue, not a collection of human beings. We turn an adjective into a
noun: the poor, not poor people; the homeless, not Ann or the man who
lives in the box or the woman who sleeps on the subway grate.

Sometimes I think we would be better off if we forgot about the   9
broad strokes and concentrated on the details. Here is a woman without a bureau. There is a man with no mirror, no wall to hang it on.
They are not the homeless. They are people who have no homes. No
drawer that holds the spoons. No window to look out upon the world.
My God. That is everything.

QUESTIONS ON MEANING

1. What is Quindlen's THESIS?
2. What distinction is Quindlen making in her CONCLUSION with the sentences "They are not the homeless. They are people who have no homes"?
3. Why does Quindlen believe that having a home is important?

QUESTIONS ON WRITING STRATEGY

1. Why do you think Quindlen begins with the story of Ann? How else
   might Quindlen have begun her essay?
2. What is the EFFECT of Quindlen's examples of her own home?
3. What key ASSUMPTIONS does the author make about her AUDIENCE? Are the
   assumptions reasonable? Where does she specifically address an assumption that might undermine her view?
4. **OTHER METHODS.** Quindlen uses examples to support an ARGUMENT. What
   position does she want readers to recognize and accept?

QUESTIONS ON LANGUAGE

1. What is the effect of "My God" in the last paragraph?
2. How might Quindlen be said to give new meaning to the old CLICHÉ
   "Home is where the heart is" (para. 4)?
3. What is meant by "crux" (para. 7)? Where does the word come from?

SUGGESTIONS FOR WRITING

1. **JOURNAL WRITING.** What does the word *home* mean to you? Does it involve material things, privacy, family, a sense of permanence? Explore your idea of the word in your journal.

   FROM JOURNAL TO ESSAY. Write an essay that gives a detailed DEFINITION of *home* by using your own home(s), hometown(s), or experiences with home(s) as supporting examples. See Chap. 9 if you need help with definition.)

2. Have you ever moved from one place to another? What sort of experience was it? Write an essay about leaving an old home and moving to a new one. Was there an activity or a piece of furniture that helped ease the transition?

3. Address Quindlen's contention that turning homelessness into an issue avoids the problem, that we might "be better off if we forgot about the broad strokes and concentrated on the details."

4. **CRITICAL WRITING.** Write a brief essay in which you agree or disagree with Quindlen's assertion that a home is "everything." Can one, for instance, be a fulfilled person without a home? In your answer, take account of the values that might underlie an attachment to home; Quindlen mentions "certainty, stability, predictability, privacy" (para. 4), but there are others, including some (such as fear) that are less positive.

5. **CONNECTIONS.** COMPARE AND CONTRAST the views of homelessness and its solution in Quindlen's "Homeless" and Barbara Lazear Ascher's "On Compassion" (p. 145). Use specific passages from each essay to support your comparison.

ANNA QUINDLEN ON WRITING

Anna Quindlen started her writing career as a newspaper reporter. "I had wanted to be a writer for most of my life," she recalls in the introduction to her book *Living Out Loud*, "and in the service of the writing I became a reporter. For many years I was able to observe, even to feel, life vividly, but at secondhand. I was able to stand over the chalk outline of a body on a sidewalk dappled with black blood; to stand behind the glass and look down into an operating theater where one man was placing a heart in the yawning chest of another; to sit in the park on the first day of summer and find myself professionally obligated to record all the glories of it. Every day I found answers: who, what, when, where, and why."

Quindlen was a good reporter, but the business of finding answers did not satisfy her personally. "In my own life," she continues, "I had only questions." Then she switched from reporter to columnist at the *New York Times*. It was "exhilarating," she says, that "my work became a reflection of my life. After years of being a professional observer of other people's lives, I was given the opportunity to be a professional observer of my own. I was permitted—and permitted myself—to write a column, not about my answers, but about my questions. Never did I make so much sense of my life as I did then, for it was inevitable that as a writer I would find out most clearly what I thought, and what I only thought I thought, when I saw it written down....After years of feeling second-hand, of feeling the pain of the widow, the joy of the winner, I was able to allow myself to feel those emotions for myself."

FOR DISCUSSION

1. What were the advantages and disadvantages of news reporting, according to Quindlen?
2. What did Quindlen feel she could accomplish in a column that she could not accomplish in a news report? What evidence of this difference do you see in her essay "Homeless"?

JOHN McPHEE

The acclaimed nonfiction writer JOHN MCPHEE creates an elegantly detailed bridge between specialists and nonspecialists on subjects as diverse as basketball, orange growing, the Alaskan frontier, and the environmental problem of discarded tires. McPhee was born in 1931 in Princeton, New Jersey, and graduated from Princeton University in 1953. He has been a staff writer for *The New Yorker* since 1964 and Ferris Professor of Journalism at Princeton since 1975. In more than two dozen books, McPhee has provided readers, in the words of the critic T. H. Watkins, with "swift, lucid, authoritative stuff produced with a reporter's sure eye and a writer's love of language." His best-known books include *Coming into the Country* (1977), *The Control of Nature* (1989), and *Annals of the Former World* (1998), the last two exploring a favorite subject of McPhee's, the ever-changing earth. Described by McPhee as "three pounds of literary geology," *Annals of the Former World* won the Pulitzer Prize in 1999.

Silk Parachute

In this uncharacteristic piece of autobiography, McPhee leads us through the process of seeking a generalization in examples: To sum up his mother, he offers incidents in his life with her. The essay originally appeared in *The New Yorker* in May 1997.

When your mother is ninety-nine years old, you have so many   1
memories of her that they tend to overlap, intermingle, and blur. It is extremely difficult to single out one or two, impossible to remember any that exemplify the whole.

It has been alleged that when I was in college she heard that I had   2
stayed up all night playing poker and wrote me a letter that used the word "shame" forty-two times. I do not recall this.

I do not recall being pulled out of my college room and into the   3
church next door.

It has been alleged that on December 24, 1936, when I was five   4
years old, she sent me to my room at or close to 7 P.M. for using four-letter words while trimming the Christmas tree. I do not recall that.

The assertion is absolutely false that when I came home from high   5
school with an A-minus she demanded an explanation for the minus.

It has been alleged that she spoiled me with protectionism, because   6
I was the youngest child and therefore the most vulnerable to attack from overhead—an assertion that I cannot confirm or confute, except to say that facts don't lie.

We lived only a few blocks from the elementary school and rou-   7
tinely ate lunch at home. It is reported that the following dialogue and
ensuing action occurred on January 22, 1941:

"Eat your sandwich."   8

"I don't want to eat my sandwich."   9

"I made that sandwich, and you are going to eat it, Mister Man.   10
You filled yourself up on penny candy on the way home, and now you're
not hungry."

"I'm late. I have to go. I'll eat the sandwich on the way back to   11
school."

"Promise?"   12

"Promise."   13

Allegedly, I went up the street with the sandwich in my hand and   14
buried it in a snowbank in front of Dr. Wright's house. My mother,
holding back the curtain in the window of the side door, was watching.
She came out in the bitter cold, wearing only a light dress, ran to the
snowbank, dug out the sandwich, chased me up Nassau Street, and
rammed the sandwich down my throat, snow and all. I do not recall
any detail of that story. I believe it to be a total fabrication.

There was the case of the missing Cracker Jack at Lindel's corner   15
store. Flimsy evidence pointed to Mrs. McPhee's smallest child. It has
been averred that she laid the guilt on with the following words: "'Like
mother like son' is a saying so true, the world will judge largely of
mother by you." It has been asserted that she immediately repeated
that proverb three times, and also recited it on other occasions too numerous to count. I have absolutely no recollection of her saying that
about the Cracker Jack or any other controlled substance.

We have now covered everything even faintly unsavory that has   16
been reported about this person in ninety-nine years, and even those
items are a collection of rumors, half-truths, prevarications, false alle-
gations, inaccuracies, innuendos, and canards.

This is the mother who—when Alfred Knopf[1] wrote her twenty-   17
two-year-old son a letter saying, "The readers' reports in the case of your
manuscript would not be very helpful, and I think might discourage you
completely"—said, "Don't listen to Alfred Knopf. Who does Alfred
Knopf think he is, anyway? Someone should go in there and k-nock his
block off." To the best of my recollection, that is what she said.

I also recall her taking me, on or about March 8th, my birthday, to   18
the theatre in New York every year, beginning in childhood. I remember those journeys as if they were today. I remember *A Connecticut Yankee*. Wednesday, March 8, 1944. Evidently, my father had written for

---

[1]Alfred A. Knopf (pronounced "K-nopf") published distinguished fiction and
nonfiction under the imprint bearing his name. He lived from 1892 to 1984.—EDS.

the tickets, because she and I sat in the last row of the second balcony. Mother knew what to do about that. She gave me for my birthday an elegant spyglass, sufficient in power to bring the Connecticut Yankee back from Vermont. I sat there watching the play through my telescope, drawing as many guffaws from the surrounding audience as the comedy on the stage.

On one of those theatre days—when I was eleven or twelve—I asked her if we could start for the city early and go out to LaGuardia Field to see the comings and goings of airplanes. The temperature was well below the freeze point and the March winds were so blustery that the wind-chill factor was forty below zero. Or seemed to be. My mother figured out how to take the subway to a stop in Jackson Heights and a bus from there—a feat I am unable to duplicate to this day. At La-Guardia, she accompanied me to the observation deck and stood there in the icy wind for at least an hour, maybe two, while I, spellbound, watched the DC-3s coming in on final, their wings flapping in the gusts. When we at last left the observation deck, we went downstairs into the terminal, where she bought me what appeared to be a black rubber ball but on closer inspection was a pair of hollow hemispheres hinged on one side and folded together. They contained a silk parachute. Opposite the hinge, each hemisphere had a small nib. A piece of string wrapped round and round the two nibs kept the ball closed. If you threw it high into the air, the string unwound and the parachute blossomed. If you sent it up with a tennis racquet, you could put it into the clouds. Not until the development of the ten-megabyte hard disk would the world ever know such a fabulous toy. Folded just so, the parachute never failed. Always, it floated back to you—silkily, beautifully—to start over and float back again. Even if you abused it, whacked it really hard—gracefully, lightly, it floated back to you.

19

QUESTIONS ON MEANING

1. Why did the proverb that McPhee's mother recites in paragraph 15 induce guilt in her son?
2. What qualities are we meant to understand about McPhee's mother from her statement, "Don't listen to Alfred Knopf. Who does Alfred Knopf think he is, anyway? Someone should go in there and k-nock his block off" (para. 17)?
3. What does McPhee's response to the parachute (para. 19)—especially the final sentence—tell about his feelings for his mother?

QUESTIONS ON WRITING STRATEGY

1. McPhee's impression of his mother accumulates through examples, but he does not explicitly generalize about what the examples add up to. In a sentence or two, provide your own generalization about McPhee's mother. What is the EFFECT of McPhee's leaving this work to the reader?
2. In the first half of the essay, McPhee uses a kind of legal language in commenting on his examples—for instance, "It has been alleged" (paras. 2, 4, 6); "I do not recall" (2, 3, 4); "The assertion is absolutely false" (5); "I believe it to be a total fabrication" (14). What does he convey with this language?
3. McPhee presents his recollections of the "dialogue and ensuing action . . . on January 22, 1941," with meticulous detail, including specifics such as "Dr. Wright's house" and "Nassau Street" (paras. 8–14). How do these details and his reporting of later events contradict his assertion that "I believe [the story] to be a total fabrication"?
4. **OTHER METHODS.** McPhee's essay CONTRASTS two kinds of memories of his mother—the ones reported before paragraph 16 and the ones reported after that point. How does McPhee's TONE shift at paragraph 17 to support this contrast?

QUESTIONS ON LANGUAGE

1. What does a phrase like "Mister Man" in paragraph 10 evoke?
2. Study these words McPhee uses to describe the silk parachute (para. 19): "silkily," "gracefully," "lightly." How do the words have different CONNOTATIONS when applied to the parachute and to McPhee's mother?
3. Consult a dictionary if you need help defining the following: alleged (para. 2); protectionism, confute (6); averred (15); prevarications, innuendos, canards (16); guffaws (18).

SUGGESTIONS FOR WRITING

1. **JOURNAL WRITING.** Write down as many examples as you can that typify your interaction with someone important to you. He or she could be a parent, another relative, a friend, a teacher, a boss.
   FROM JOURNAL TO ESSAY. Develop the best examples from your journal entry into a detailed portrait of the person. You may, like McPhee, opt to leave your generalization about the person—your THESIS—unstated, but make sure readers will be able to form the generalization themselves.
2. As an alternative to the assignment above, NARRATE a single extended event that illustrates the character of a significant person in your life and your relationship with that person. Use dialogue and plenty of DESCRIPTION to make your narrative vivid and to make it clear what your extended example illustrates.
3. **CRITICAL WRITING.** Write an essay that ANALYZES McPhee's use of legal language in the first half of "Silk Parachute" (question 2 on writing strategy can give you a start). What does this language convey about McPhee's relationship with his mother and about the writer as an adult? How would the essay be different if McPhee had not used the language? To support your analysis, use specific examples, including quotations, from the essay.

4. **CONNECTIONS.** Read "Silk Parachute" along with Itabari Njeri's "When Morpheus Held Him" (p. 108). Both essays describe a parent through examples from memory. Write an essay COMPARING AND CONTRASTING the language each author uses to characterize his or her parent. Narrow your discussion to, say, three to five words in each essay that seem most central to the author's portrait, and use examples from the essays to show why these words are central.

JOHN McPHEE ON WRITING

A teacher of writing himself, John McPhee has often shared his ideas and experiences with interviewers. In a 1991 article published in the journal *College Composition and Communication,* Douglas Vipond and Russell A. Hunt quote McPhee on his conception of audience:

"As I am sitting composing a sentence, my primary thought is not imagining a reader, and whether the reader is grasping this. I think that what I'm doing is trying to put it in the way that seems most effective to *me.* Not that I'm 'writing for myself,' in that old cliché, but since I have nothing to go on but what's in my own head — in terms of selection of things that I'm going to set on the paper, and all the choices that go with that — I listen to the sentence until I both hear it and see it as something that I want. And it would be a given that a person reading it would *share* the effect that the sentence has earlier had on me."

McPhee has often been classed as a "literary journalist" because of his skill at sifting and conveying factual information with a distinctive grace and flow. (At Princeton he teaches a course called "The Literature of Fact.") Speaking to Vipond and Hunt, McPhee explained something of his technique with details:

"If you can find a specific, firm, and correct image, it's always going to be better than a generality, and hence I tend, for example, to put in trade names and company names.... You'd say 'Sony' instead of 'tape recorder' if the context made it clear you meant to say tape recorder. It's not because you're on the take from Sony, it's because the image, at least to this writer or reader, strikes a clearer note."

FOR DISCUSSION

1. How does McPhee's practice of writing "something that I want" differ from "writing for [him]self"? What role does CRITICAL READING seem to play in his writing process?
2. Visualize a tape recorder. Then visualize a Sony tape recorder. What does the second image conjure up that the first one doesn't? How does this contrast illuminate McPhee's point that a "specific, firm, and correct image" is "better than a generality"?

ROY BLOUNT, JR.

Sometimes compared with Mark Twain, ROY BLOUNT, JR., is among the wittiest writers in America today. He was born in 1941 in Indiana, grew up in Georgia, attended Vanderbilt University (B.A., 1963) and Harvard University (M.A., 1964), and served as a lieutenant in the U.S. Army. Blount (pronounced "blunt") began writing for newspapers while still in school; after the army, he worked at the *Atlanta Journal* and at *Sports Illustrated* for a decade before going freelance. He has written plays and contributed to more than a hundred periodicals. Covering sports, politics, food, parents, and culture, and even branching into fiction, Blount's many books include *About Three Bricks Shy of a Load* (1974), *One Fell Soup; or, I'm Just a Bug on the Windshield of Life* (1982), *Camels Are Easy, Comedy's Hard* (1991), and *Be Sweet: A Conditional Love Story* (1998). Though he describes himself as "singing impaired," Blount also performs his own songs, notably on PBS radio's *Prairie Home Companion*.

As Well as I Do My Own

The critic Deborah Mason places Blount's humor in "the genre of earnest, plain-spoken bumpkinhood,...brilliantly loopy, reassuringly subversive." In this essay from a 1985 *Atlantic*, Blount's cagey bumpkinhood shines through as he collects examples to illustrate his terrible difficulty remembering people's names.

1   When someone takes too authoritative a tone with my friend Slick Lawson, the Nashville photographer, he will say, "Well, I go along with what Donald Wilson Breland said about that."

2   Then he will proceed to snap pictures. After a few moments, the person who has taken too authoritative a tone will say, "Well...I don't *know* Breland. Of course I know his *work*..."

3   Then Slick will go on to mention that Donald Wilson Breland was a kid who sat in front of him in the fourth grade and ate paste. And what Donald Wilson Breland said, about everything, was "Whutcha wawnt *me* t'do uhbout it?"

4   Someone is going to catch me out like that someday. And only because I am trying to be gracious.

5   At my twenty-fifth high school reunion, last year, you would have been proud of me. The way I called those names up, with seldom even a quick half-glance at a tag, you would have thought they were Ajax, Salome, Mrs. Miniver, and Jackie Robinson. I hadn't seen Steve Fladger or Mickey Wallis in a quarter of a century, and they were the

only two returning class members whose bone structure had changed (late night spurts) since graduation. But their names came to me like the list of vowels, because I had learned them when I was fresh, back before I had met or heard of 375,000 other Americans. By the time anyone gets to be forty-three, if he has followed current events and been out of town a few times, two-thirds of the names he hears sound vaguely, but only vaguely, familiar.

People ask me, "Do you know Mason Swint?"   6

And I am not sure whether: 7

(a) I certainly do.

(b) I don't personally, but I do know *of* him, because he is the one who just won an Emmy or Oscar or Grammy or Tony or Obie or Golden Globe or Golden Gloves or Olympic gold or Nobel or National Book Award or that other thing that's like the National Book Award or one of the three or four world junior light-heavyweight championships.

(c) I don't personally, but I do know *of* him, because he is that petting-zoo operator who was charged with lambkin, piglet, and duckling abuse.

(d) I am thinking of Morgan Swift, Morris Wilt, Milton Sweet, Marion Sweat, Morton Swing, Martin Short, or Myron Smart, some of whom I am sure I do know, or know of, and some of whom I believe I do, unless I am thinking of Mason Swint.

I should cut down on my name intake. But I don't want anyone to   8
think that I don't know who's who in my field. And I don't know what my field is. Furthermore, I love names too much, for their own sake. How can I close my eyes to the fact that Stanford University has professors named Condoleezza Rice, an arms-control specialist, and Jon Roughgarden, an ecologist? All those *z*'s and *g*'s, on one faculty! Roughgarden should be a common term, like roughhouse or rough fish. Condoleezza Rice, according to the *Stanford Observer,* is from Birmingham, Alabama, and "her unusual name of Condoleezza is derived from the Italian musical term *con dolce,* which means 'with sweetness.'" Ah.

Does Condoleezza rhyme with Louisa, pizza, mezza? In this country,   9
names can ring a range of bells. My friend Walter Iooss, the Flemish-American sports photographer, pronounces his name like "Yost" only with another *s* in place of the *t.* When Iooss took his marital vows, he did not say "I do." He said what New York Knicks announcer Marv Albert says when a Knick hits a shot: "Yesss!" Iooss and I once rode in a Chicago cab driven by Rosetta Shinboom.

Cabdrivers, as a class, have the most noteworthy names in Amer-   10
ica. There was one in the *New York Daily News* the other day named

Just Ackah. And yet they are quite often quoted anonymously. This strikes me as fishy. The way I look at journalistic ethics, license to cite a cogent cabdriver should not be extended to anyone who cannot also make up a credible name:

> "Well," observed U Gonxha, the Burmese-Albanian hackie who drove me in from the airport, "what most folks around here are saying is…"

Most folks are not cabdrivers. But when I was younger, I could re- 11 member their names anyway. One weekend in Pittsburgh I must have introduced my wife to two hundred people, flawlessly except for a set of twins. (With twins I have always tried too hard. I get them down pat, and then I look at one or the other, and it's not as though I don't know which one it is, but I think, "Pat. Is this the one I am determined to re- member is Pat, or isn't Pat?") That was ten years ago. Now names come to me like dreams: at first so vivid (Oh, I'll have no trouble holding on to this!) and then gone.

I fault not only my age, which is advancing, but also the one we 12 live in, which isn't. Names today are like dollars: There are far more of them than there used to be, and they amount to less. Baseball players should all be mythical. But today there must be, among the Minnesota Twins alone, four or five semi-phenoms who have moved right on into budding sort-of-stardom without ever quite registering. There is a Puckett—or am I flashing back to Howie Pollet or Duane Pilette or General Pickett? And there is a Teufel. If you held a knife to my throat, I couldn't tell you whether Teufel is pronounced as in

> *Teufel, Teufel,*
> *We adore thee*

or to rhyme with *rueful*. I just don't know. I don't know whether I ever will know.

But I can live with that. What bothers me is finding myself face-to- 13 face with an actual human being who looks familiar and who seems to know me (and why would he lie?) but whose name I am afraid I will not be able to dredge up until sometime next week, if then. Recently I spoke with my old college friend Lamar Alexander, who is now the governor of Tennessee. (Which means that I can name one American governor. Didn't governors used to be more vivid?) I asked him how he managed to remember all the people he must shake hands with. His an- swer was he didn't. He said that when somebody comes up to him with a certain sly grin and says, "I bet you don't remember my name," he of- ten replies, "No, I bet I don't."

Why can't I do that? Why must I bluff and flounder? Why in the 14 name of all that is holy do I say things like, "Oh! Hi! Great to see you again, ah, Hmblmbl"? What possesses me to plunge into "Well! If it isn't..." at the same time that I am thinking to myself, What if, in fact, it's *not*?

It is time for me to face up to the fact that I can no longer place im-   15
plicit trust in the tip of my tongue. I can no longer assume that I *virtually* remember the name in question and that if I just plunge forward
with an honest heart... After your mind reaches saturation, an honest
heart can't carry it.

Not long ago I was autographing books in a city where I had   16
worked some years before. No matter how bad your handwriting, you
can't fake an inscription: "For Mmnlnnln—those were the days!" And
if you say, "For the life of me, I can't remember the *spelling*...," then the
answer will be:

"C-U-N..."   17
"Right, right..."   18
"...N-I-N..."   19
"Oh, yeah, uh..."   20
"...G...H..."   21
"Ohh, sure,...uh..."   22
"...A..."   23
"Oh! No! Of course! I don't mean the *Cunningham* part! I mean   24
your *first*..."
"J-I-M."   25

So I was delighted to see none other than old Greer Chastain (not   26
his real name) in front of me. "Hey, Greer!" I sang out.

"This is old Greer Chastain," I informed the bookstore's proprietor.   27
"Hell of a fisherman. Used to come into the office with a string that
long of bass and bream and crappies and..."

"Shea Whislet," Greer said.   28
"What say, Greer?" I said.   29
"I'm Shea Whislet," he said. (Not his real name.)   30
"Oh," I said. "I...What's wrong with me! Thing is, I guess because   31
you used to hang around so much with Greer Chastain, and..."

"Noo," he said, frowning.   32
"That's right! That's right! I don't know what made me... *Nobody*   33
used to hang around with Greer Chastain! Nobody even *liked* Greer
Chastain! He stuck in my mind I guess because he was *so* unmemo-
rable. Here, Shea, let me..."

Even though I made a point of not having to ask him how to spell   34
Shea, our grins were forced when he moved away and the next person
came forward.

"I'm Greer Chastain," he said.   35
The other day I was playing tennis with my friend Lois Betts when   36
a mutual acquaintance stopped by with his dog. I was almost entirely
sure that this man was the one I thought he was, whose name I had

heard many times, with whom I had chatted several times, and to whom I had often said, "Hi, how you doing?" I felt that if I strained for about five minutes I would know his name from Adam.

Furthermore, I felt that I would be able to stall for five minutes by fo- 37
cusing on the dog, whom I heard Lois call Bob. Unfortunately I am unable
to focus *casually* on something I am not actually focusing on in my mind.

"Bob? Hey, that's a good name for a big old orange dog," I said, tou- 38
sling Bob's ears. "What caused you to name him Bob?"

"No...it's Hobbit, actually," said the man. 39

"Oh," I said heartily. "Thought Lois said Bob. Well, you're a fine 40
dog, Hobbit. Yes, sir. Never knew a dog named Hobbit."

Meanwhile, I was thinking: *Don't babble. Concentrate. Wait a* 41
minute, it's coming. Is it...? No, no it probably isn't. Don't blurt it out! It
probably isn't!

"I had a dog named Bob when I was a kid," I went on. "Because of 42
his tail. And then, too, I had read *Bob, Son of Battle.* You know, that
book by...Oh, you know. What's his name? I *know* his name, it's..."

Meanwhile, I was thinking: *Drop it. You've got enough to worry* 43
about. This man's name. Concentrate.

"Old Bob, yep. I guess whenever I think of dogs, Bob's name comes 44
to mind. He was my favorite dog."

Meanwhile, I was thinking: *He was not! You're lying about who your* 45
favorite dog was! Bob was no-account! Used to get lost all the time! Chipper
was your favorite, and you know it! Somewhere in dog heaven, Bob is prob-
ably saying, "Hey, he never seemed to think I was all that great a dog when
I was alive. Truth is, I wasn't all that great a dog. I was always getting lost.
He knows that. I never realized he was so shallow."

After perhaps four and a half minutes, Hobbit and the man trotted 46
off. I gazed after them, relieved and yet vexed. "Lois," I said, "what is..."

"Now *that*," said Lois, "was *awful.*" 47

"Well," I said, "I was trying..." 48

"The *guy's* name is Bob," she said. 49

I could, I guess, call all men Colonel or Big Fella. That doesn't ad- 50
dress the problem of what to call women. Sister? I don't think it would
go over.

For that matter, you have to be a certain kind of person to carry off 51
calling people Colonel or Big Fella. You have to be a person on the order of Babe Ruth, who never made any pretense of remembering anyone's name, even longtime teammates'. Ruth called everyone Jidge, a
sort of affectionym for George, which was Ruth's real first name. I believe that Bobo Newsom, the old pitcher, called everyone Bobo. Or
maybe it was Bobo Olson, the old fighter. I don't think I want to call
everyone Roy.

I am reminded, however, that Byron Sahm, the Philadelphia   52
Phillies' announcer, is said to have opened his broadcast once by exclaiming, *"Hello,* Byron Sahm! This is everybody!"

If only one were, in fact, everyone else. Then the burden would be   53
on them.

QUESTIONS ON MEANING

1. What do you think is this essay's PURPOSE? How do the names Blount recalls—Slick Lawson (para. 1), Mason Swint (6), Condoleezza Rice (8),
   and Just Ackah (10), among others—help the essay achieve this purpose?
2. Blount COMPARES his high school classmates to "Ajax, Salome, Mrs.
   Miniver, and Jackie Robinson" (para. 5). What do you think he means by
   these comparisons?
3. What does Blount mean when he writes, "I fault not only my age, which
   is advancing, but also the one we live in, which isn't" (para. 12)?
4. What is the point of Blount's CONCLUSION (para. 53)?

QUESTIONS ON WRITING STRATEGY

1. Discuss how Blount uses examples in his essay. What kinds of examples
   does he select? Can you locate a generalization that the examples illustrate?
2. The sentences in paragraph 9 may seem almost disconnected from each
   other. How are they, in fact, related?
3. Blount moves from cabbie names to his strong memory in youth with this
   transition: "Most folks are not cabdrivers. But when I was younger, I could
   remember their names anyway" (para. 11). What is the EFFECT of this transition?
4. **OTHER METHODS.** Where in the essay does Blount use NARRATIVE most effectively, in your view? Why do you think so?

QUESTIONS ON LANGUAGE

1. What meaning can you infer for Blount's made-up term "affectionym"
   (para. 51)?
2. How do the passages of dialogue—for example, in paragraphs 16–35 and
   38–49—affect the TONE of the essay?
3. Give definitions of the following words: cogent (para. 10); bluff, flounder
   (14); implicit, virtually (15); bream, crappies (27).
4. What does Blount mean when he writes, "Names today are like dollars:
   There are far more of them than there used to be, and they amount to
   less" (para. 12)?

SUGGESTIONS FOR WRITING

1. **JOURNAL WRITING.** At one time or another, most of us have been in Blount's shoes, desperately trying to recall a name while demonstrating all too clearly that we cannot. Write about one or more such experiences of your own, or (if you've been lucky enough to avoid that particular embarrassment) write about another kind of memory lapse that got you in trouble.

   FROM JOURNAL TO ESSAY. Develop your journal writing into a narrative relating the event or events when your memory failed. You may, like Blount, wish to write humorously, or you could take a more serious approach. In either case, use dialogue to enliven the narrative. And be sure the narrative has a point, whether you state it or not.

2. What are some good ways to deal with a situation like the one Blount encounters in paragraphs 36–49? Imagine you're writing the section in an etiquette book titled "Forgetting Names." In a short PROCESS ANALYSIS, explain step by step one or more polite and effective approaches to the problem.

3. **CRITICAL WRITING.** Citing examples from "As Well as I Do My Own," write a brief essay that explains why you think Blount is unwilling to admit he's forgotten a name. In paragraph 4 he says he's "trying to be gracious." What other reasons does he provide or can you INFER?

4. **CONNECTIONS.** Read K. C. Cole's essay "The Arrow of Time" (p. 378) and consider the differences between Cole's scientifically based pessimism about order in the world and Blount's persistent optimism that he will remember the names he struggles with. Do you find that you relate to the world more with optimism or with pessimism? Using examples from your experience, write an essay that illustrates your basic outlook.

ROY BLOUNT, JR., ON WRITING

In a 1998 interview with Katie Bacon of *Atlantic Unbound*, the on-line version of *The Atlantic* magazine, Roy Blount, Jr. talked about his writing process:

I don't work at being funny; I work at writing as clearly, fluidly, and interestingly as I can, which is a struggle. In baseball you have scientific hitters who try to out-think the pitcher, and then you have hitters who just see the ball and hit it. Some equivalent to that — seeing the ball and hitting it — is my approach to being funny. But that doesn't mean I'm just up there hacking. One reason I am a writer instead of a baseball player (which is what I wanted to be as a boy) is that as a writer you can foul a pitch off and then go back and change your swing, over and over, until it hits the same pitch squarely. You can even change the pitch to some extent. You've got to have an instinctive sense of what it feels like to make good contact—you have to have a lust for that, in fact—but you also have to get your mechanics down, which is to say you have to write a good sentence, pick the right words.

FOR DISCUSSION

1. What does Blount mean by "as a writer you can foul a pitch off and then go back and change your swing"? What part of the writing process is he referring to?
2. How can a writer "even change the pitch to some extent"? What does the pitch stand for in this ANALOGY between baseball and writing?
3. Compare Blount's comments on writing humor with Dave Barry's on pages 194–95. How do the two writers seem to approach humorous writing similarly or differently?

BRENT STAPLES

BRENT STAPLES is a member of the editorial board of the *New York Times*. Born in 1951 in Chester, Pennsylvania, Staples has a B.A. in behavioral science from Widener University in Chester and a Ph.D. in psychology from the University of Chicago. Before joining the *New York Times* in 1985, he worked for the *Chicago Sun-Times*, the *Chicago Reader*, *Chicago* magazine, and *Down Beat* magazine. At the *Times*, Staples writes on culture and politics. He has also contributed to the *New York Times Magazine*, *New York Woman*, *Ms.*, *Harper's*, and other magazines. His memoir, *Parallel Time: Growing Up in Black and White*, appeared in 1994.

Black Men and Public Space

"Black Men and Public Space" appeared in the December 1986 issue of *Harper's* magazine and was then published, in a slightly different version, in Staples's memoir, *Parallel Time*. To explain a recurring experience of African American men, Staples relates incidents when he has been "a night walker in the urban landscape."

My first victim was a woman—white, well dressed, probably in her late twenties. I came upon her late one evening on a deserted street in Hyde Park, a relatively affluent neighborhood in an otherwise mean, impoverished section of Chicago. As I swung onto the avenue behind her, there seemed to be a discreet, uninflammatory distance between us. Not so. She cast back a worried glance. To her, the youngish black man—a broad six feet two inches with a beard and billowing hair, both hands shoved into the pockets of a bulky military jacket—seemed menacingly close. After a few more quick glimpses, she picked up her pace and was soon running in earnest. Within seconds she disappeared into a cross street.

That was more than a decade ago. I was twenty-two years old, a graduate student newly arrived at the University of Chicago. It was in the echo of that terrified woman's footfalls that I first began to know the unwieldy inheritance I'd come into—the ability to alter public space in ugly ways. It was clear that she thought herself the quarry of a mugger, a rapist, or worse. Suffering a bout of insomnia, however, I was stalking sleep, not defenseless wayfarers. As a softy who is scarcely able to take a knife to a raw chicken—let alone hold one to a person's throat—I was surprised, embarrassed, and dismayed all at once. Her flight made me feel like an accomplice in tyranny. It also made it clear that I was indistinguishable from the muggers who occasionally seeped into the area from the surrounding ghetto. That first encounter, and those that followed, signified that a vast, unnerving gulf lay between nighttime pedestrians—particularly women—and me. And I soon gathered that being perceived as dangerous is a hazard in itself. I only needed to turn a corner into a dicey situation, or crowd some frightened, armed person in a foyer somewhere, or make an errant move after being pulled over by a policeman. Where fear and weapons meet—and they often do in urban America—there is always the possibility of death.

In that first year, my first away from my hometown, I was to become   3
thoroughly familiar with the language of fear. At dark, shadowy intersections, I could cross in front of a car stopped at a traffic light and elicit the *thunk, thunk, thunk, thunk* of the driver—black, white, male, or female—hammering down the door locks. On less traveled streets after dark, I grew accustomed to but never comfortable with people crossing to the other side of the street rather than pass me. Then there were the standard unpleasantries with policemen, doormen, bouncers, cabdrivers, and others whose business it is to screen out troublesome individuals *before* there is any nastiness.

I moved to New York nearly two years ago and I have remained an   4
avid night walker. In central Manhattan, the near-constant crowd cover minimizes tense one-on-one street encounters. Elsewhere—in SoHo, for example, where sidewalks are narrow and tightly spaced buildings shut out the sky—things can get very taut indeed.

After dark, on the warrenlike streets of Brooklyn where I live, I   5
often see women who fear the worst from me. They seem to have set their faces on neutral, and with their purse straps strung across their chests bandolier-style, they forge ahead as though bracing themselves against being tackled. I understand, of course, that the danger they perceive is not a hallucination. Women are particularly vulnerable to street violence, and young black males are drastically overrepresented among the perpetrators of that violence. Yet these truths are no solace against the kind of alienation that comes of being ever the suspect, a fearsome entity with whom pedestrians avoid making eye contact.

It is not altogether clear to me how I reached the ripe old age of   6
twenty-two without being conscious of the lethality nighttime pedestrians attributed to me. Perhaps it was because in Chester, Pennsylvania, the small, angry industrial town where I came of age in the 1960s, I was scarcely noticeable against a backdrop of gang warfare, street knifings, and murders. I grew up one of the good boys, had perhaps a half-dozen fistfights. In retrospect, my shyness of combat has clear sources.

As a boy, I saw countless tough guys locked away; I have since   7
buried several, too. They were babies, really—a teenage cousin, a brother of twenty-two, a childhood friend in his mid-twenties—all gone down in episodes of bravado played out in the streets. I came to

doubt the virtues of intimidation early on. I chose, perhaps unconsciously, to remain a shadow—timid, but a survivor.

The fearsomeness mistakenly attributed to me in public places often has a perilous flavor. The most frightening of these confusions occurred in the late 1970s and early 1980s, when I worked as a journalist in Chicago. One day, rushing into the office of a magazine I was writing for with a deadline story in hand, I was mistaken for a burglar. The office manager called security and, with an ad hoc posse, pursued me through the labyrinthine halls, nearly to my editor's door. I had no way of proving who I was. I could only move briskly toward the company of someone who knew me.   8

Another time I was on assignment for a local paper and killing time before an interview. I entered a jewelry store on the city's affluent Near North Side. The proprietor excused herself and returned with an enormous red Doberman pinscher straining at the end of a leash. She stood, the dog extended toward me, silent to my questions, her eyes bulging nearly out of her head. I took a cursory look around, nodded, and bade her good night.   9

Relatively speaking, however, I never fared as badly as another black male journalist. He went to nearby Waukegan, Illinois, a couple of summers ago to work on a story about a murderer who was born there. Mistaking the reporter for the killer, police officers hauled him from his car at gunpoint and but for his press credentials would probably have tried to book him. Such episodes are not uncommon. Black men trade tales like this all the time.   10

Over the years, I learned to smother the rage I felt at so often being taken for a criminal. Not to do so would surely have led to madness. I now take precautions to make myself less threatening. I move about with care, particularly late in the evening. I give a wide berth to nervous people on subway platforms during the wee hours, particularly when I have exchanged business clothes for jeans. If I happen to be entering a building behind some people who appear skittish, I may walk by, letting them clear the lobby before I return, so as not to seem to be following them. I have been calm and extremely congenial on those rare occasions when I've been pulled over by the police.   11

And on late-evening constitutionals I employ what has proved to be an excellent tension-reducing measure: I whistle melodies from Beethoven and Vivaldi and the more popular classical composers. Even steely New Yorkers hunching toward nighttime destinations seem to relax, and occasionally they even join in the tune. Virtually everybody seems to sense that a mugger wouldn't be warbling bright, sunny selections from Vivaldi's *Four Seasons*. It is my equivalent of the cowbell that hikers wear when they know they are in bear country.   12

QUESTIONS ON MEANING

1. What is the PURPOSE of this essay? Do you think Staples believes that he (or other African American men) will cease "to alter public space in ugly ways" in the near future? Does he suggest any long-term solution for "the kind of alienation that comes of being ever the suspect" (para. 5)?
2. In paragraph 5 Staples says he understands that the danger women fear when they see him "is not a hallucination." Do you take this to mean that Staples perceives himself to be dangerous? Explain.
3. Staples says, "I chose, perhaps unconsciously, to remain a shadow— timid, but a survivor" (para. 7). What are the usual CONNOTATIONS of the word *survivor*? Is "timid" one of them? How can you explain this apparent discrepancy?

QUESTIONS ON WRITING STRATEGY

1. The concept of altering public space is relatively abstract. How does Staples convince you that this phenomenon really takes place?
2. The author employs a large number of examples in a fairly small space. He cites three specific instances that involved him, several general situations, and one incident involving another African American man. How does Staples avoid having the piece sound like a list? How does he establish CO-HERENCE among all these examples? (Look, for example, at details and TRANSITIONS.)
3. **OTHER METHODS.** Many of Staples's examples are actually ANECDOTES— brief NARRATIVES. The opening paragraph is especially notable. Why is it so effective?

QUESTIONS ON LANGUAGE

1. What does the author accomplish by using the word *victim* in the essay's first paragraph? Is the word used literally? What TONE does it set for the essay?
2. Be sure you know how to define the following words, as used in this essay: affluent, uninflammatory (para. 1); unwieldy, tyranny, pedestrians (2); intimidation (7); congenial (11); constitutionals (12).
3. The word *dicey* (para. 2) comes from British slang. Without looking it up in your dictionary, can you figure out its meaning from the context in which it appears?

SUGGESTIONS FOR WRITING

1. **JOURNAL WRITING.** Have you ever felt as if *you* altered public space—in other words, as if you changed people's attitudes or behavior just by being in a place or entering a situation? If not, have you seen someone else alter public space in this way?

FROM JOURNAL TO ESSAY. Write an essay narrating either your experience of altering public space yourself or your experience of being a witness when someone else altered public space. What changes did you observe in the behavior of the people around you? Was your behavior similarly affected? In retrospect, do you think your reactions were justified?

2. Write an essay using examples to show how a trait of your own or of someone you know well always seems to affect people, whether positively or negatively.

3. **CRITICAL WRITING.** Consider, more broadly than Staples does, what it means to alter public space. Staples would rather not have the power to do so, but it *is* a power, and it could perhaps be positive in some circumstances (wielded by a street performer, for instance, or the architect of a beautiful new building on campus). Write an essay expanding on Staples's essay in which you examine the pros and cons of altering public space. Use specific examples as your EVIDENCE.

4. **CONNECTIONS.** Like Staples, Barbara Lazear Ascher, in "On Compassion" (p. 145), considers how people regard and respond to "the Other," the one who is viewed as different. In an essay, COMPARE AND CONTRAST the POINTS OF VIEW of these two authors. How does point of view affect each author's selection of details and tone?

BRENT STAPLES ON WRITING

In comments written especially for *The Bedford Reader*, Brent Staples talks about the writing of "Black Men and Public Space." "I was only partly aware of how I felt when I began this essay. I knew only that I had this collection of experiences (facts) and that I felt uneasy with them. I sketched out the experiences one by one and strung them together. The bridge to the essay—what I wanted to say, but did not know when I started—sprang into life quite unexpectedly as I sat looking over these experiences. The crucial sentence comes right after the opening anecdote, in which my first 'victim' runs away from me: 'It was in the echo of that terrified woman's footfalls that I first began to know the unwieldy inheritance I'd come into—the ability to alter public space in ugly ways.' 'Aha!' I said. 'This is why I feel bothered and hurt and frustrated when this happens. I don't want people to think I'm stalking them. I want some fresh air. I want to stretch my legs. I want to be as anonymous as any other person out for a walk in the night.'"

A news reporter and editor by training and trade, Staples sees much similarity between the writing of a personal essay like "Black Men and Public Space" and the writing of, say, a murder story for a daily newspaper. "The newspaper murder," he says, "begins with standard newspaper information: the fact that the man was found dead in an alley in such-and-such a section of the city; his name, occupation, and where he lived; that he died of gunshot wounds to such-and-such a part of his body; that arrests were or were not made; that such-and-such a weapon was found at the scene; that the police have established no motive; etc.

"Personal essays take a different tack, but they, too, begin as assemblies of facts. In 'Black Men and Public Space,' I start out with an anecdote that crystallizes the issue I want to discuss — what it is like to be viewed as a criminal all the time. I devise a sentence that serves this purpose and also catches the reader's attention: 'My first victim was a woman — white, well dressed, probably in her late twenties.' The piece gives examples that are meant to illustrate the same point and discusses what those examples mean.

"The newspaper story stacks its details in a specified way, with each piece taking a prescribed place in a prescribed order. The personal essay begins often with a flourish, an anecdote, or the recounting of a crucial experience, then goes off to consider related experiences and their meanings. But both pieces rely on reporting. Both are built of facts. Reporting is the act of finding and analyzing facts.

"A fact can be a state of the world — a date, the color of someone's eyes, the arc of a body that flies through the air after having been struck by a car. A fact can also be a feeling — sorrow, grief, confusion, the sense of being pleased, offended, or frustrated. 'Black Men and Public Space' explores the relationship between two sets of facts: (1) the way people cast worried glances at me and sometimes run away from me on the streets after dark, and (2) the frustration and anger I feel at being made an object of fear as I try to go about my business in the city."

Personal essays and news stories share one other quality as well, Staples thinks: They affect the writer even when the writing is finished. "The discoveries I made in 'Black Men and Public Space' continued long after the essay was published. Writing about the experiences gave me access to a whole range of internal concerns and ideas, much the way a well-reported news story opens the door onto a given neighborhood, situation, or set of issues."

FOR DISCUSSION

1. In recounting how his essay developed, what does Staples reveal about his writing process?
2. How, according to Staples, are essay writing and news writing similar? How are they different?
3. What does Staples mean when he says that "writing about the experiences gave me access to a whole range of internal concerns and ideas"?

ADDITIONAL WRITING TOPICS

Example

1. Select one of the following general statements, or set forth a general statement of your own that one of these inspires. Making it your central idea (or THESIS), support it in an essay full of examples. Draw your examples from your reading, your studies, your conversation, or your own experience.

   Voice mail is a great convenience (or a great inconvenience) for the caller.

   Electronic mail provides a form of communication that letters and the telephone don't.

   People one comes to admire don't always at first seem likable.

   Fashions this year are loonier than ever before.

   Good (or bad) habits are necessary to the nation's economy.

   Each family has its distinctive lifestyle.

   Certain song lyrics, closely inspected, promote violence.

   Comic books are going to the dogs.

   At some point in life, most people triumph over crushing difficulties.

   Churchgoers aren't perfect.

   TV commercials suggest that buying the advertised product will improve your love life like crazy.

   Home cooking can't win over fast food.

   Ordinary lives sometimes give rise to legends.

   Some people I know are born winners (or losers).

   Books can change our lives.

   Certain machines *do* have personalities.

   Some road signs lead drivers astray.

2. In a brief essay, make a GENERALIZATION about either the terrors or the joys that members of minority groups seem to share. To illustrate your generalization, draw examples from personal experience, from outside reading, or from two or three of the following essays in this book: Maya Angelou's "Champion of the World" (p. 52), Amy Tan's "Fish Cheeks" (p. 57), Ralph Ellison's "On Being the Target of Discrimination" (p. 67), Itabari Njeri's "When Morpheus Held Him" (p. 108), Judith Ortiz Cofer's "Silent Dancing" (p. 122), Brent Staples's "Black Men and Public Space" (p. 168), Nancy Mairs's "Disability" (p. 207), Gloria Naylor's "The Meanings of a Word" (p. 418), Christine Leong's "Being a Chink" (p. 424), Curtis Chang's "Streets of Gold" (p. 509), Martin Luther King, Jr.'s "I Have a Dream" (p. 567), Richard Rodriguez's "Aria" (p. 606), and Alice Walker's "In Search of Our Mothers' Gardens" (p. 632).

4

COMPARISON
AND CONTRAST
Setting Things Side by Side

THE METHOD

Should we pass laws to regulate pornography, or just let pornography run wild? Which team do you place your money on, the Cowboys or the Forty-Niners? To go to school full-time or part-time: What are the rewards and drawbacks of each way of life? How do the Republican and the Democratic platforms stack up against each other? How is the work of Picasso like or unlike that of Matisse? These are questions that may be addressed by the dual method of COMPARISON AND CONTRAST. In comparing, you point to similar features of the subjects; in contrasting, to different features. (The features themselves you identify by the method of DIVISION or ANALYSIS; see Chap. 6.)

With the aid of comparison and contrast, you can show why you prefer one thing to another, one course of action to another, one idea to another. In an argument in which you support one of two possible choices, a careful and detailed comparison and contrast of the choices may be extremely convincing. In an expository essay, it can demonstrate that you understand your subjects thoroughly. That is why, on exams that call for essay answers, often you will be asked to compare and contrast. Sometimes the examiner will come right out and say,

"Compare and contrast nineteenth-century methods of treating drug addiction with those of the present day." Sometimes, however, comparison and contrast won't even be mentioned by name; instead, the examiner will ask, "What resemblances and differences do you find between John Updike's short story 'A & P' and the Grimm fairy tale 'Godfather Death'?" Or, "Explain the relative desirability of holding a franchise as against going into business as an independent proprietor." But those—as you realize when you begin to plan your reply—are just other ways of asking you to compare and contrast.

In practice, the two methods are usually inseparable. A little reflection will show you why you need both. Say you intend to write a portrait-in-words of two people. No two people are in every respect exactly the same or entirely dissimilar. Simply to compare them or to contrast them would not be true to life. To set them side by side and portray them accurately, you must consider both similarities and differences.

A good essay in comparing and contrasting serves a PURPOSE. Most of the time, the writer of such an essay has one of two purposes in mind:

1. *The purpose of showing each of two subjects distinctly by considering both, side by side.* Writing with such a purpose, the writer doesn't necessarily find one of the subjects better than the other. In "The Black and White Truth About Basketball" in this chapter, Jeff Greenfield details two styles of playing the game; and his conclusion is not that either "black" or "white" basketball is the more beautiful, but that the two styles can complement each other on the same court.

2. *The purpose of choosing between two things.* In daily life, we often EVALUATE two possibilities to choose between them: which college course to elect, which movie to see, which luncheon special to take—chipped beef over green noodles or fried smelt on a bun? Our thinking on a matter such as the last is quick and informal: "Hmmmm, the smelt *looks* better. Red beef, green noodles—ugh, what a sight! Smelt has bones, but the beef is rubbery. Still, I don't like the smell of that smelt. I'll go for the beef (or maybe just grab a hamburger after class)." In essays, too, a writer, by comparing and evaluating points, decides which of two things is more admirable: "Organic Gardening, Yes; Gardening with Chemical Fertilizers, No!"—or "Skydiving Versus the Safe, Sane Life." In writing, as in thinking, you need to consider the main features of both subjects, the positive features and the negative, and to choose the subject whose positive features more clearly predominate.

THE PROCESS

Subjects for Comparison

When you find yourself considering two subjects side by side or preferring one subject over another, you have already embarked on comparison and contrast. Just be sure that your two subjects display a clear basis for comparison. In other words, they should have something significant in common. Comparison usually works best with two of a kind: two means of reading for the visually impaired, two ways of gardening, two California wines, two mystery writers, two schools of political thought.

It can sometimes be effective to find similarities between evidently unlike subjects — a city and a country town, say — and a special form of comparison, ANALOGY, always equates two very unlike things, explaining one in terms of the other. (In an analogy you might explain how the human eye works by comparing it to a simple camera, or you might explain the forces in a thunderstorm by comparing them to armies in battle.) In any comparison of unlike things, you must have a valid reason for bringing the two together. In his essay "Grant and Lee," Bruce Catton compares the characters of the two Civil War generals. But in an essay called "General Grant and Mick Jagger" you would be hard-pressed to find any real basis for comparison. Although you might wax ingenious and claim, "Like Grant, Jagger posed a definite threat to Nashville," the ingenuity would wear thin and soon the yoking together of general and rock star would fall apart.

Basis for Comparison

Beginning to identify the shared and dissimilar features of your subjects will get you started, but the comparison won't be manageable for you or interesting to your readers unless you also limit it. You would be overly ambitious to try to compare and contrast the Russian way of life with the American way of life in five hundred words; you couldn't include all the important similarities and differences. In a brief paper, you would be wise to select a single basis for comparison: to show, for instance, how day-care centers in Russia and the United States are both like and unlike each other.

This basis for comparison will eventually underpin the THESIS of your essay — the claim you have to make about the similarities and dissimilarities of two things or about one thing's superiority over another. Here, from essays in this chapter, are THESIS SENTENCES that clearly lay out what's being compared and why:

> Neat people are lazier and meaner than sloppy people. (Suzanne Britt, "Neat People vs. Sloppy People")

These were two strong men, these oddly different generals, and they represented the strengths of two conflicting currents that, through them, had come into collision. (Bruce Catton, "Grant and Lee: A Study in Contrasts")

Notice that each author not only identifies his or her subjects (neat and sloppy people, two generals) but also previews the purpose of the comparison, whether to evaluate (Britt) or to explain (Catton).

Organization

Even with a limited basis for comparison, the method of comparison and contrast can be tricky without some planning. We suggest that you make an outline (preferably in writing), using one of two organizations described below. Say you're writing an essay on two banjo-pickers, Jed and Jake. Your purpose is to explain the distinctive identities of the two players, and your thesis sentence might be the following:

> Jed and Jake are both excellent banjo-pickers whose differences reflect their training.

Here are the two ways you might arrange your comparison:

1. *Subject by subject.* Set forth all your facts about Jed, then do the same for Jake. Next, sum up their similarities and differences. In your conclusion, state what you think you have shown.

   1. *Jed*
      Training
      Choice of material
      Technical dexterity
      Playing style

   2. *Jake*
      Training
      Choice of material
      Technical dexterity
      Playing style

   SUMMARY
   CONCLUSION

   This procedure works for a paper of a few paragraphs, but for a longer one, it has a built-in disadvantage: Readers need to remember all the facts about subject 1 while they read about subject 2. If the essay is long and lists many facts, this procedure may be burdensome.

2. *Point by point.* Usually more workable in writing a long paper than the first method, the second scheme is to compare and contrast as you go. You consider one point at a time, taking up your two sub-

jects alternately. In this way, you continually bring the subjects to-gether, perhaps in every paragraph. Notice the differences in the outline:

1. *Training*
   Jed: studied under Earl Scruggs
   Jake: studied under Bela Fleck

2. *Choice of material*
   Jed: bluegrass
   Jake: jazz-oriented

3. *Technical dexterity*
   Jed: highly skilled
   Jake: highly skilled

4. *Playing style*
   Jed: rapid-fire
   Jake: impressionistic

For either the subject-by-subject or the point-by-point scheme, your conclusion might be: Although similar in skill, the two differ greatly in aims and in personalities. Jed is better suited to the Grand Ol' Opry; Jake, to a concert hall.

No matter how you group your points, they have to balance; you can't discuss Jed's on-stage manner without discussing Jake's too. If you have nothing to say about Jake's on-stage manner, then you might as well omit the point. A surefire loser is the paper that proposes to compare and contrast two subjects but then proceeds to discuss quite different elements in each: Jed's playing style and Jake's choice of material, Jed's fondness for smelt on a bun and Jake's hobby of antique-car collecting. The writer of such a paper doesn't compare and contrast the two musicians at all, but provides two quite separate discussions.

By the way, a subject-by-subject organization works most efficiently for a *pair* of subjects. If you want to write about *three* banjo-pickers, you might first consider Jed and Jake, then Jake and Josh, then Josh and Jed—but it would probably be easiest to compare and contrast all three point by point.

Flexibility

As you write, an outline will help you see the shape of your paper and keep your procedure in mind. But don't be the simple tool of your outline. Few essays are more boring to read than the long comparison and contrast written mechanically. The reader comes to feel like a weary tennis spectator whose head has to swivel from side to side: now Jed, now Jake; now Jed again, now back to Jake. You need to mention the same features of both subjects, it is true, but no law decrees *how* you must mention them. You need not follow your outline in lockstep order, or cover similarities and differences at precisely the same length, or spend a hundred words on Jed's banjo-picking skill just because you spend a hundred words on Jake's. Your essay, remember, doesn't need to be as symmetrical as a pair of salt and pepper shakers. What is your outline but a simple means to organize your account of a complicated reality? As you write, keep casting your thoughts upon a living, particular world—not twisting and squeezing that world into a rigid scheme, but moving through it with open senses, being patient and faithful and exact in your telling of it.

CHECKLIST FOR REVISING A COMPARISON AND CONTRAST

✔ **PURPOSE.** What is the aim of your comparison: to explain two subjects or evaluate them? Will the purpose be clear to readers from the start?

✔ **SUBJECTS.** Are the subjects enough alike, sharing enough features, to make comparison worthwhile?

✔ **THESIS.** Does your thesis establish a limited basis for comparison so that you have room and time to cover all the relevant similarities and differences?

✔ **ORGANIZATION.** Does your arrangement of material, whether subject by subject or point by point, do justice to your subjects and help readers follow the comparison?

✔ **BALANCE AND FLEXIBILITY.** Have you covered the same features of both subjects? At the same time, have you avoided a rigid back-and-forth movement that could bore or exhaust a reader?

COMPARISON AND CONTRAST
IN A PARAGRAPH: TWO ILLUSTRATIONS

Using Comparison and Contrast
to Write About Television

The following example, written especially for *The Bedford Reader*, uses point-by-point comparison for a clear purpose: to evaluate television drama then and now, and to express a preference for one over the other. Notice that the writer is fair—acknowledging (toward the end) that today's dramas also have fine actors and have none of the primitiveness of yesterday's dramas.

Though written to be freestanding, this paragraph on drama might do good work in a full essay about, say, the chief differences between TV programming in the medium's early days and programming now.

Seen on aged 16-millimeter film, the original production of Paddy Chayevsky's *Marty* makes clear the differences between television drama of 1953 and that of today. <u>Today</u> there's no weekly Goodyear Playhouse to showcase original one-hour plays by important authors; most scriptwriters collaborate, all but anonymously, on serials about familiar characters. *Marty* features no bodice ripping, no drug busts, no deadly illness, no laugh track. <u>Instead</u>, it simply shows the awakening of love between a heavyset butcher and a mousy high-school teacher: both single, lonely, and shy, never twice dating the same person. <u>Unlike the writer of today</u>, Chayevsky couldn't set scenes outdoors or on location. In one small studio, in slow lingering takes (some five minutes long—not eight to twelve seconds, <u>as we now expect</u>), the camera probes the faces of two seated characters as Marty and his pal Angie plan Saturday night ("What do you want to do?"—"I dunno, what do *you*?"). Oddly, the effect is spellbinding. To bring such scenes to life, the actors must project with vigor; and <u>like the finer actors of today</u>, Rod Steiger as Marty exploits each moment. <u>In 1953</u>, plays were telecast live. <u>Today</u>, well-edited videotape may eliminate blown lines, but a chill slickness prevails. Technically, *Marty* is primitive, yet it probes souls. Most televised drama <u>today</u> displays a physically larger world—only to nail a box around it.

Point-by-point comparison supporting this topic sentence

1. Original plays vs. serials

2. Simple love story vs. violence and sex

3. Studio sets with long takes vs. locations with short takes

4. Good acting vs. good acting

5. Live vs. videotaped

6. Primitive and probing vs. big and limited

Transitions (underlined) clarify the comparison

Using Comparison and Contrast in an Academic Discipline

Taken from a textbook on architectural history, this subject-by-subject comparison explains the differences between two competing theories of architecture in Russia in the 1920s and 1930s. The paragraph is one of several in which the author shows how modernist architects divided into those concerned mainly with form and those concerned mainly with social progress.

In Russia, too, modernists fell into two camps. They squared off against each other in public debate and in Vkhutemas, a school of architecture organized in 1920 along lines parallel to the Bauhaus. "The measure of architecture is architecture," went the motto of one camp. They believed in an unfettered experimentalism of form. The rival camp had a problem-solving orientation. The architect's main mission, in their view, was to share in the common task of achieving the transformation of society promised by the October Revolution [of 1917]. They were keen on standardization, user interviews, and ideological prompting. They worked on new building programs that would consolidate the social order of communism. These they referred to as "social condensers."

— Spiro Kostof, *A History of Architecture*

Subject-by-subject comparison supporting this topic sentence

1. First camp: experimental

2. Second camp: problem-solving (receives more attention because it eventually prevailed)

COMPARISON AND CONTRAST
ELSEWHERE IN *THE BEDFORD READER*

In the essays in this chapter, the writers develop their ideas mainly by comparison and contrast. But the method figures prominently in many other of the book's selections as well, helping the authors organize and detail their ideas.

PART ONE

Brad Manning, "Arm Wrestling with My Father"
Anna Quindlen, "Homeless"
Armin A. Brott, "Not All Men Are Sly Foxes"
Deborah Tannen, "But What Do You Mean?"
Scott Russell Sanders, "Homeplace"
Richard Ford, "I Must Be Going"
Gloria Naylor, "The Meanings of a Word"
Christine Leong, "Being a Chink"
Marie Winn, "TV Addiction"
Barbara Kingsolver, "Stone Soup"
Curtis Chang, "Streets of Gold: The Myth of the Model Minority"

PART TWO

Stephen L. Carter, "The Insufficiency of Honesty"
Annie Dillard, "Lenses"
Maxine Hong Kingston, "No Name Woman"
Richard Rodriguez, "Aria: A Memoir of a Bilingual Childhood"
E. B. White, "Once More to the Lake"

CASE STUDY
Using Comparison and Contrast

In the fall of her sophomore year in college, Susan Wheeler was running for president of her dormitory. She prepared a campaign statement for the student newspaper's coverage of the election, and she also created the flier on the next page for posting throughout the dorm.

Wheeler believed that her campaign platform was much stronger than her opponent's, and she decided to highlight the differences by showing her ideas alongside her opponent's (in a point-by-point arrangement). But her draft needed work to make the points more concise and to give them PARALLEL wording that would clarify and stress the contrasts. Originally, the first three points read as follows:

Susan Wheeler	*Matt Parker*
• A supporter of all extra-curricular activities	• Supports mainly sports and cheerleading
• Actively participates in student government association	• He is not in the student government association
• The food plans should be more flexible for all students	• Does not mention the food plans

In Wheeler's final draft (next page), the parallel wording (each point beginning with a verb) is both easier to read and more emphatic.

Susan Wheeler

for

Dorm President

Here are the reasons why:

Susan Wheeler	*Matt Parker*
• Supports all extracurricular activities	• Supports mainly sports and cheerleading
• Participates actively in student government association	• Does not participate in student government association
• Wants to make food plans more flexible for all students	• Does not mention the food plans
• Wants to extend bookstore hours	• Does not mention extending bookstore hours
• Wants to increase quantity and accessibility of copiers	• Does not mention copier problems
• Wants a 24-hour computer lab in the dorm	• Does not mention a computer lab
• Has made Dean's List every semester	• Has not made Dean's List

Vote May 2

SUSAN WHEELER FOR PRESIDENT . . . WE'LL DO IT TOGETHER!

SUZANNE BRITT

Suzanne Britt was born in Winston-Salem, North Carolina, and studied at Salem College and Washington University, where she earned an M.A. in English. She writes a regular column for a newsletter, *Authors Ink*. Britt has written for *Sky Magazine*, the *New York Times*, *Newsweek*, the *Boston Globe*, and many other publications. She teaches English part-time at Meredith College in North Carolina and has published a history of the college and two English textbooks. Her other books are collections of her essays: *Skinny People Are Dull and Crunchy like Carrots* (1982) and *Show and Tell* (1983).

Neat People
vs.
Sloppy People

"Neat People vs. Sloppy People" appears in Britt's collection *Show and Tell*. Mingling humor with seriousness (as she often does), Britt has called the book a report on her journey into "the awful cave of self: You shout your name and voices come back in exultant response, telling you their names." In this essay, Britt uses comparison mainly to entertain by showing us aspects of our own selves, awful or not. For another approach to a similar subject, see the next essay, by Dave Barry.

I've finally figured out the difference between neat people and sloppy people. The distinction is, as always, moral. Neat people are lazier and meaner than sloppy people.

Sloppy people, you see, are not really sloppy. Their sloppiness is merely the unfortunate consequence of their extreme moral rectitude. Sloppy people carry in their mind's eye a heavenly vision, a precise plan, that is so stupendous, so perfect, it can't be achieved in this world or the next.

Sloppy people live in Never-Never Land. Someday is their métier. Someday they are planning to alphabetize all their books and set up home catalogs. Someday they will go through their wardrobes and mark certain items for tentative mending and certain items for passing on to relatives of similar shape and size. Someday sloppy people will make family scrapbooks into which they will put newspaper clippings, postcards, locks of hair, and the dried corsage from their senior prom. Someday they will file everything on the surface of their desks, including the cash receipts from coffee purchases at the snack shop. Someday they will sit down and read all the back issues of *The New Yorker*.

For all these noble reasons and more, sloppy people never get neat. 4
They aim too high and wide. They save everything, planning someday
to file, order, and straighten out the world. But while these ambitious
plans take clearer and clearer shape in their heads, the books spill from
the shelves onto the floor, the clothes pile up in the hamper and closet,
the family mementos accumulate in every drawer, the surface of the
desk is buried under mounds of paper, and the unread magazines
threaten to reach the ceiling.

Sloppy people can't bear to part with anything. They give loving 5
attention to every detail. When sloppy people say they're going to
tackle the surface of a desk, they really mean it. Not a paper will go un-
turned; not a rubber band will go unboxed. Four hours or two weeks
into the excavation, the desk looks exactly the same, primarily because
the sloppy person is meticulously creating new piles of papers with new
headings and scrupulously stopping to read all the old book catalogs before he throws them away. A neat person would just bulldoze the desk.

Neat people are bums and clods at heart. They have cavalier atti- 6
tudes toward possessions, including family heirlooms. Everything is just
another dust-catcher to them. If anything collects dust, it's got to go
and that's that. Neat people will toy with the idea of throwing the children out of the house just to cut down on the clutter.

Neat people don't care about process. They like results. What they 7
want to do is get the whole thing over with so they can sit down and
watch the rasslin' on TV. Neat people operate on two unvarying principles: Never handle any item twice, and throw everything away.

The only thing messy in a neat person's house is the trash can. The 8
minute something comes to a neat person's hand, he will look at it, try
to decide if it has immediate use and, finding none, throw it in the
trash.

Neat people are especially vicious with mail. They never go 9
through their mail unless they are standing directly over a trash can. If
the trash can is beside the mailbox, even better. All ads, catalogs, pleas
for charitable contributions, church bulletins, and money-saving
coupons go straight into the trash can without being opened. All letters from home, postcards from Europe, bills, and paychecks are opened,
immediately responded to, then dropped in the trash can. Neat people
keep their receipts only for tax purposes. That's it. No sentimental salvaging of birthday cards or the last letter a dying relative ever wrote.
Into the trash it goes.

Neat people place neatness above everything, even economics. 10
They are incredibly wasteful. Neat people throw away several toys
every time they walk through the den. I knew a neat person once who
threw away a perfectly good dish drainer because it had mold on it. The
drainer was too much trouble to wash. And neat people sell their fur-

niture when they move. They will sell a La-Z-Boy recliner while you are reclining in it.

Neat people are no good to borrow from. Neat people buy every-   11
thing in expensive little single portions. They get their flour and sugar in two-pound bags. They wouldn't consider clipping a coupon, saving a leftover, reusing plastic nondairy whipped cream containers, or rinsing off tin foil and draping it over the unmoldy dish drainer. You can never borrow a neat person's newspaper to see what's playing at the movies. Neat people have the paper all wadded up and in the trash by 7:05 A.M.

Neat people cut a clean swath through the organic as well as the   12
inorganic world. People, animals, and things are all one to them. They are so insensitive. After they've finished with the pantry, the medicine cabinet, and the attic, they will throw out the red geranium (too many leaves), sell the dog (too many fleas), and send the children off to boarding school (too many scuff-marks on the hardwood floors).

QUESTIONS ON MEANING

1. "Suzanne Britt believes that neat people are lazy, mean, petty, callous, wasteful, and insensitive." How would you respond to this statement?
2. Is the author's main PURPOSE to make fun of neat people, to assess the habits of neat and sloppy people, to help neat and sloppy people get along better, to defend sloppy people, to amuse and entertain, or to prove that neat people are morally inferior to sloppy people? Discuss.
3. What is meant by "as always" in the sentence "The distinction is, as always, moral" (para. 1)? Does the author seem to be suggesting that any and all distinctions between people are moral?

QUESTIONS ON WRITING STRATEGY

1. What is the general TONE of this essay? What words and phrases help you determine that tone?
2. Britt mentions no similarities between neat and sloppy people. Does that mean this is not a good comparison and contrast essay? Why might a writer deliberately focus on differences and give very little or no time to similarities?
3. Consider the following GENERALIZATIONS: "For all these noble reasons and more, sloppy people never get neat" (para. 4) and "The only thing messy in a neat person's house is the trash can" (8). How can you tell that these statements are generalizations? Look for other generalizations in the essay. What is the EFFECT of using so many?
4. **OTHER METHODS.** Although filled with generalizations, Britt's essay does not lack for EXAMPLES. Study the examples in paragraph 11, and explain

how they do and don't work the way examples are supposed to, to bring the generalizations about people down to earth.

QUESTIONS ON LANGUAGE

1. Consult your dictionary for definitions of these words: rectitude (para. 2); métier, tentative (3); accumulate (4); excavation, meticulously, scrupulously (5); salvaging (9).
2. How do you understand the use of the word *noble* in the first sentence of paragraph 4? Is it meant literally? Are there other words in the essay that appear to be written in a similar tone?

SUGGESTIONS FOR WRITING

1. **JOURNAL WRITING.** Although Britt is writing tongue-in-cheek when she says, "Neat people are lazier and meaner than sloppy people," her essay suggests that grouping people according to oppositions like neat/sloppy reveals other things about them. What oppositions do you use to evaluate people? Smart/dumb? Fit/out of shape? Rich/poor? Outgoing/shy?
   FROM JOURNAL TO ESSAY. Choose your favorite opposition for evaluating people, and write an essay in which you compare and contrast those who pass your "test" with those who fail it. You may choose to write your essay tongue-in-cheek, as Britt does, or seriously.
2. Write an essay in which you compare and contrast two apparently dissimilar groups of people: for example, blue-collar workers and white-collar workers, people who write a lot of e-mail and people who don't bother with it, runners and football players, readers and TV watchers, or any other variation you choose. Your approach may be either lighthearted or serious, but make sure you come to some conclusion about your subjects. Which group do you favor? Why?
3. ANALYZE the similarities and differences between two characters in your favorite novel, story, film, or television show. Which aspects of their personalities make them work well together, within the context in which they appear? Which characteristics work against each other, and therefore provide the necessary conflict to hold the reader's or viewer's attention?
4. **CRITICAL WRITING.** Britt's essay is remarkable for its exaggeration of the two types. Write a brief essay analyzing and contrasting the ways Britt characterizes sloppy people and neat people. Be sure to consider the CONNOTATIONS of the words, such as "moral rectitude" for sloppy people (para. 2) and "cavalier" for neat people (6).
5. **CONNECTIONS.** Neither Suzanne Britt nor the author of the next essay, Dave Barry, seems to have much sympathy for neat people. Write a brief essay in which you explain why neatness matters. Or if you haven't a clue why, then write a brief essay in which you explain the benefits of dirt and disorder.

SUZANNE BRITT ON WRITING

Asked to tell how she writes, Suzanne Britt contributed the following comment to *The Bedford Reader*.

The question "How do you write?" gets a snappy, snappish response from me. The first commandment is "Live!" And the second is like unto it: "Pay attention!" I don't mean that you have to live high or fast or deep or wise or broad. And I certainly don't mean you have to live true and upright. I just mean that you have to suck out all the marrow of whatever you do, whether it's picking the lint off the navy-blue suit you'll be wearing to Cousin Ione's funeral or popping an Aunt Jemimah frozen waffle into the toaster oven or lying between sand dunes, watching the way the sea oats slice the azure sky. The ominous question put to me by students on all occasions of possible accountability is "Will this count?" My answer is rock bottom and hard: "Everything counts," I say, and silence falls like prayers across the room.

The same is true of writing. Everything counts. Despair is good. Numbness can be excellent. Misery is fine. Ecstasy will work—or pain or sorrow or passion. The only thing that won't work is indifference. A writer refuses to be shocked and appalled by anything going or coming, rising or falling, singing or soundless. The only thing that shocks me, truth to tell, is indifference. How dare you not fight for the right to the crispy end piece on the standing-rib roast? How dare you let the fragrance of Joy go by without taking a whiff of it? How dare you not see the old woman in the snap-front housedress and the rolled-down socks, carrying her Polident and Charmin in a canvas tote that says, simply, elegantly, Le Bag?

After you have lived, paid attention, seen connections, felt the harmony, writhed under the dissonance, fixed a Diet Coke, popped a big stick of Juicy Fruit in your mouth, gathered your life around you as a mother hen gathers her brood, as a queen settles the folds in her purple robes, you are ready to write. And what you will write about, even if you have one of those teachers who makes you write about, say, Guatemala, will be something very exclusive and intimate—something just between you and Guatemala. All you have to find out is what that small intimacy might be. It is there. And having found it, you have to make it count.

There is no rest for a writer. But there is no boredom either. A Sunday morning with a bottle of extra-strength aspirin within easy reach and an ice bag on your head can serve you very well in writing. So can a fly buzzing at your ear or a heart-stopping siren in the night or an interminable afternoon in a biology lab in front of a frog's innards.

All you need, really, is the audacity to believe, with your whole being, that if you tell it right, tell it truly, tell it so we can all see it, the
"it" will play in Peoria, Poughkeepsie, Pompeii, or Podunk. In the
South we call that conviction, that audacity, an act of faith. But you
can call it writing.

FOR DISCUSSION

1. What advice does Britt offer a student assigned to write a paper about, say,
   Guatemala? If you were that student, how would you go about taking her
   advice?
2. Where in her comment does the author use colorful and effective FIGURES
   OF SPEECH?
3. What is the TONE of Britt's remarks? Sum up her attitude toward her subject, writing.

DAVE BARRY

DAVE BARRY is a humorist whom the *New York Times* has called "the funniest man in America." Barry was born in 1947 in Armonk, New York, and graduated from Haverford College in 1969. He worked as a journalist for five years and lectured businesspeople on writing for eight years while he began to establish himself as a columnist. His humor writing now appears in several hundred newspapers and has been collected in more than twenty books, including *Bad Habits: A 100% Fact Free Book* (1985), *The World According to Dave Barry* (1994), *Dave Barry in Cyberspace* (1996), *Dave Barry Turns 50* (1998), and *Big Trouble* (1999). In 1988 Barry received the Pulitzer Prize for "distinguished commentary," although, he says, "nothing I've ever written fits the definition." (He thinks he won because his columns stood out from the "earthshakingly important" competition.) Barry lives in Miami with his family.

Batting Clean-Up and Striking Out

This essay from *Dave Barry's Greatest Hits* (1988) illustrates Barry's gift, in the words of critic Alison Teal, "for taking things at face value and rendering them funny on those grounds alone, for rendering every ounce of humor out of a perfectly ordinary experience." Like Suzanne Britt in the previous essay, Barry contrasts two styles of dealing with a mess.

The primary difference between men and women is that women can see extremely small quantities of dirt. Not when they're babies, of course. Babies of both sexes have a very low awareness of dirt, other than to think it tastes better than food.

But somewhere during the growth process, a hormonal secretion takes place in women that enables them to see dirt that men cannot see, dirt at the level of *molecules*, whereas men don't generally notice it until it forms clumps large enough to support agriculture. This can lead to tragedy, as it did in the ill-fated ancient city of Pompeii, where the residents all got killed when the local volcano erupted and covered them with a layer of ash twenty feet deep.[1] Modern people often ask, "How come, when the ashes started falling, the Pompeii people didn't just *leave?*" The answer is that in Pompeii, it was the custom for the men to do the housework. They never even *noticed* the ash until it had for the most part covered the children. "Hey!" the men said (in Latin).

[1] Pompeii, in what is now southern Italy, was buried in the eruption of Mount Vesuvius in A.D. 79. — EDS.

"It's mighty quiet around here!" This is one major historical reason why, to this very day, men tend to do extremely little in the way of useful housework.

What often happens in my specific family unit is that my wife will 3 say to me: "Could you clean Robert's bathroom? It's filthy." So I'll gather up the Standard Male Cleaning Implements, namely a spray bottle of Windex and a wad of paper towels, and I'll go into Robert's bathroom, and it *always looks perfectly fine*. I mean, when I hear the word "filthy" used to describe a bathroom, I think about this bar where I used to hang out called Joe's Sportsman's Lounge, where the men's room had bacteria you could enter in a rodeo.

Nevertheless, because I am a sensitive and caring kind of guy, I 4 "clean" the bathroom, spraying Windex all over everything including the six hundred action figures each sold separately that God forbid Robert should ever take a bath without, and then I wipe it back off with the paper towels, and I go back to whatever activity I had been engaged in, such as doing an important project on the Etch-a-Sketch, and a little while later my wife will say: "I hate to rush you, but could you do Robert's bathroom? It's really *filthy*." She is in there looking at the very walls I *just Windexed*, and she is seeing *dirt! Everywhere!* And if I tell her I already *cleaned* the bathroom, she gives me this look that she has perfected, the same look she used on me the time I selected Robert's outfit for school and part of it turned out to be pajamas.

The opposite side of the dirt coin, of course, is sports. This is an 5 area where men tend to feel very sensitive and women tend to be extremely callous. I have written about this before and I always get irate letters from women who say they are the heavyweight racquetball champion of some place like Iowa and are sensitive to sports to the point where they could crush my skull like a ripe grape, but I feel these women are the exception.

A more representative woman is my friend Maddy, who once in- 6 vited some people, including my wife and me, over to her house for an evening of stimulating conversation and jovial companionship, which sounds fine except that this particular evening occurred *during a World Series game*. If you can imagine such a social gaffe.

We sat around the living room and Maddy tried to stimulate a con- 7 versation, but we males could not focus our attention on the various suggested topics because we could actually *feel* the World Series television and radio broadcast rays zinging through the air, penetrating right into our bodies, causing our dental fillings to vibrate, and all the while the women were behaving *as though nothing were wrong*. It was exactly like that story by Edgar Allan Poe where the murderer can hear the victim's heart beating louder and louder even though he (the murder victim) is dead, until finally he (the murderer) can't stand it anymore, and he just *has* to watch the World Series on television.[2] That was how we felt.

Maddy's husband made the first move, coming up with an ab-   8
solutely brilliant means of escape: *He used their baby.* He picked up Jus-
tine, their seven-month-old daughter, who was fussing a little, and
announced: "What this child needs is to have her bottle and watch the
World Series." And just like that he was off to the family room, moving very quickly for a big man holding a baby. A second male escaped
by pretending to clear the dessert plates. Soon all four of us were in
there, watching the Annual Fall Classic, while the women prattled
away about human relationships or something. It turned out to be an
extremely pivotal game.

QUESTIONS ON MEANING

1. What is the PURPOSE of Barry's essay? How do you know?
2. How OBJECTIVE is Barry's portrayal of men and women? Does he seem to
   understand one sex better than the other? Does he seek to justify and excuse male sloppiness and antisocial behavior?
3. What can you INFER about Barry's attitude toward the differences between
   the sexes? Does he see a way out?

QUESTIONS ON WRITING STRATEGY

1. Barry's comparison is organized point by point — differences in sensitivity
   to dirt, then differences in sensitivity to sports. What is the EFFECT of this
   organization? Or, from another angle, what would have been the effect of
   a subject-by-subject organization — just men, then just women (or vice
   versa)?
2. How does Barry set the TONE of this piece from the very first paragraph?
3. The first sentence looks like a THESIS SENTENCE but turns out not to be complete. Where does Barry finish his statement of the essay's thesis? Does it
   hurt or help the essay that the thesis is divided? Why?
4. How does Barry's ALLUSION to Poe's "The Tell-Tale Heart" enhance Barry's
   own story?
5. **OTHER METHODS.** How persuasive is the historical EXAMPLE cited in paragraph 2 as EVIDENCE for Barry's claims about men's and women's differing
   abilities to perceive dirt? Must examples always be persuasive?

---

[2] Barry refers to Poe's story "The Tell-Tale Heart" (1843). The story (minus Barry's
World Series ending) appears on page 81 of this book. — EDS.

QUESTIONS ON LANGUAGE

1. Define these words: hormonal (para. 2); implements (3); callous, irate (5); jovial, gaffe (6); prattled, pivotal (8).
2. Paragraph 4 begins with a textbook example of a run-on sentence. Does Barry need a better copy editor, or is he deliberately going for an effect here? If so, what is it?
3. What effect does Barry achieve through his frequent use of italics (for example, *just Windexed*," para. 4) and capital letters ("Standard Male Cleaning Implements," 3)?
4. Why does Barry use the word *males* instead of *men* in paragraphs 7 and 8?

SUGGESTIONS FOR WRITING

1. **JOURNAL WRITING.** Make a list of traits of the opposite sex you find foreign or bewildering. (They would rather talk to you on the phone than in person. They would rather watch sports on TV than play them....)
   FROM JOURNAL TO ESSAY. Choose the trait on your list about the opposite sex that seems to have the most potential for humor. Write an essay similar to Barry's, exaggerating the difference to the point where it becomes the defining distinction between men and women.
2. How well do you conform to Barry's GENERALIZATIONS about your gender? In what ways are you stereotypically male or female? Do such generalizations amuse or merely annoy you? Why?
3. **CRITICAL WRITING.** Barry is obviously not afraid of offending women: He claims to have already done so (para. 5), and yet he persists. Do you take offense at any of this essay's stereotypes of women and men? If so, explain the nature of the offense as coolly as you can. Whether you take offense or not, can you see any virtue in using such stereotypes for humor? For instance, does the humor help undermine the stereotypes or merely strengthen them? Write an essay in which you address these questions, using quotations from Barry as examples and evidence.
4. **CONNECTIONS.** Write an essay about the humor gained from exaggeration, relying on Barry's essay and the previous one, Suzanne Britt's "Neat People vs. Sloppy People." Consider why exaggeration is often funny and what qualities humorous exaggeration has. Use quotations and PARA-PHRASES from Barry's and Britt's essays as your support.

DAVE BARRY ON WRITING

For Dave Barry, coming up with ideas for humorous writing is no problem. "Just about anything's a topic for a humor column," he told an interviewer for *Contemporary Authors* in 1990, "any event that occurs in the news, anything that happens in daily life—driving, shopping, reading, eating. You can look at just about anything and see humor in it somewhere."

Writing challenges, for Barry, occur after he has his idea. "Writing has always been hard for me," he says. "The hard part is getting the jokes to come, and it never happens all at once for me. I very rarely have any idea where a column is going to go when it starts. It's a matter of piling a little piece here and a little piece there, fitting them together, going on to the next part, then going back and gradually shaping the whole piece into something. I know what I want in terms of reaction, and I want it to have a certain feel. I know when it does and when it doesn't. But I'm never sure when it's going to get there. That's what writing is. That's why it's so painful and slow. But that's more technique than anything else. You don't rely on inspiration — I don't, anyway, and I don't think most writers do. The creative process is just not an inspirational one for most people. There's a little bit of that and a whole lot of polishing."

A humor writer must be sensitive to readers, trying to make them smile, but Barry warns against catering to an audience. "I think it's a big mistake to write humor for anybody but yourself, to try to adopt any persona other than your own. If I don't at some point think something is funny, then I'm not going to write it." Not that his own sense of humor will always make a piece fly. "Thinking of it in rough form is one thing," Barry confesses, "and shaping and polishing it so that you like the way it reads is so agonizingly slow that by the time you're done, you don't think anything is funny. You think this is something you might use to console a widow."

More often, though, the shaping and polishing — the constant revision — do work. "Since I know how to do that," Barry says, "since I do it every day of the week and have for years and years, I'm confident that if I keep at it I'll get something."

FOR DISCUSSION

1. Do you agree with Barry that "[y]ou can look at just about anything and see humor in it somewhere"? What topics do you think would be off-limits for humor?
2. What does successful writing depend on, according to Barry? What role does inspiration play?
3. How might Barry's views on writing be relevant to your own experiences as a writer? What can a humor writer teach a college writer?

BRUCE CATTON

BRUCE CATTON (1899–1978) became America's best-known historian of the Civil War. As a boy in Benzonia, Michigan, Catton acted out historical battles on local playing fields. In his memoir *Waiting for the Morning Train* (1972), he recalls how he would listen by the hour to the memories of Union Army veterans. His studies at Oberlin College interrupted by service in World War I, Catton never finished his bachelor's degree. Instead, he worked as a reporter, columnist, and editorial writer for the *Cleveland Plain Dealer* and other newspapers, then became a speechwriter and information director for government agencies. Of Catton's eighteen books, seventeen were written after his fiftieth year. *A Stillness at Appomattox* (1953) won him both a Pulitzer Prize for history and a National Book Award; other notable works include *This Hallowed Ground* (1956) and *Gettysburg: The Final Fury* (1974). From 1954 until his death, Catton edited *American Heritage*, a magazine of history. President Gerald Ford awarded him a Medal of Freedom for his life's accomplishment.

Grant and Lee: A Study in Contrasts

"Grant and Lee: A Study in Contrasts" first appeared in *The American Story*, a book of essays written by eminent historians for interested general readers. Contrasting the two great Civil War generals allows Catton to portray not only two very different men but also the conflicting traditions they represented. Catton's essay builds toward the conclusion that, in one outstanding way, the two leaders were more than a little alike.

When Ulysses S. Grant and Robert E. Lee met in the parlor of a 1
modest house at Appomattox Court House, Virginia, on April 9, 1865, to work out the terms for the surrender of Lee's Army of Northern Virginia, a great chapter in American life came to a close, and a great new chapter began.

These men were bringing the Civil War to its virtual finish. To be 2
sure, other armies had yet to surrender, and for a few days the fugitive confederate government would struggle desperately and vainly, trying to find some way to go on living now that its chief support was gone. But in effect it was all over when Grant and Lee signed the papers. And the little room where they wrote out the terms was the scene of one of the poignant, dramatic contrasts in American history.

They were two strong men, these oddly different generals, and they   3
represented the strengths of two conflicting currents that, through
them, had come into final collision.

Back of Robert E. Lee was the notion that the old aristocratic con-   4
cept might somehow survive and be dominant in American life.

Lee was tidewater Virginia, and in his background were family, cul-   5
ture, and tradition...the age of chivalry transplanted to a New World
which was making its own legends and its own myths. He embodied a
way of life that had come down through the age of knighthood and the
English country squire. America was a land that was beginning all over
again, dedicated to nothing much more complicated than the rather
hazy belief that all men had equal rights, and should have an equal
chance in the world. In such a land Lee stood for the feeling that it was
somehow of advantage to human society to have a pronounced inequality in the social structure. There should be a leisure class, backed
by ownership of land; in turn, society itself should be keyed to the land
as the chief source of wealth and influence. It would bring forth (according to this ideal) a class of men with a strong sense of obligation to
the community; men who lived not to gain advantage for themselves,
but to meet the solemn obligations which had been laid on them by the
very fact that they were privileged. From them the country would get
its leadership; to them it could look for the higher values—of thought,
of conduct, of personal deportment—to give it strength and virtue.

Lee embodied the noblest elements of this aristocratic ideal.   6
Through him, the landed nobility justified itself. For four years, the
Southern states had fought a desperate war to uphold the ideals for
which Lee stood. In the end, it almost seemed as if the Confederacy
fought for Lee; as if he himself was the Confederacy...the best thing
that the way of life for which the Confederacy stood could ever have to
offer. He had passed into legend before Appomattox. Thousands of
tired, underfed, poorly clothed Confederate soldiers, long-since past
the simple enthusiasm of the early days of the struggle, somehow considered Lee the symbol of everything for which they had been willing
to die. But they could not quite put this feeling into words. If the Lost
Cause, sanctified by so much heroism and so many deaths, had a living
justification, its justification was General Lee.

Grant, the son of a tanner on the Western frontier, was everything   7
Lee was not. He had come up the hard way, and embodied nothing in
particular except the eternal toughness and sinewy fiber of the men
who grew up beyond the mountains. He was one of a body of men who
owed reverence and obeisance to no one, who were self-reliant to a
fault, who cared hardly anything for the past but who had a sharp eye
for the future.

These frontier men were the precise opposites of the tidewater aris-   8
tocrats. Back of them, in the great surge that had taken people over the
Alleghenies and into the opening Western country, there was a deep,
implicit dissatisfaction with a past that had settled into grooves. They
stood for democracy, not from any reasoned conclusion about the
proper ordering of human society, but simply because they had grown
up in the middle of democracy and knew how it worked. Their society
might have privileges, but they would be privileges each man had won
for himself. Forms and patterns meant nothing. No man was born to
anything, except perhaps to a chance to show how far he could rise.
Life was competition.

Yet along with this feeling had come a deep sense of belonging to a   9
national community. The Westerner who developed a farm, opened
a shop, or set up in business as a trader could hope to prosper only as
his own community prospered—and his community ran from the Atlantic to the Pacific and from Canada down to Mexico. If the land was
settled, with towns and highways and accessible markets, he could
better himself. He saw his fate in terms of the nation's own destiny. As
its horizons expanded, so did his. He had, in other words, an acute
dollars-and-cents stake in the continued growth and development of
his country.

And that, perhaps, is where the contrast between Grant and Lee   10
becomes most striking. The Virginia aristocrat, inevitably, saw himself
in relation to his own region. He lived in a static society which could
endure almost anything except change. Instinctively, his first loyalty
would go to the locality in which that society existed. He would fight
to the limit of endurance to defend it, because in defending it he was
defending everything that gave his own life its deepest meaning.

The Westerner, on the other hand, would fight with an equal   11
tenacity for the broader concept of society. He fought so because everything he lived by was tied to growth, expansion, and a constantly
widening horizon. What he lived by would survive or fall with the nation itself. He could not possibly stand by unmoved in the face of an attempt to destroy the Union. He would combat it with everything he
had, because he could only see it as an effort to cut the ground out from
under his feet.

So Grant and Lee were in complete contrast, representing two di-   12
ametrically opposed elements in American life. Grant was the modern
man emerging; beyond him, ready to come on the stage, was the great
age of steel and machinery, of crowded cities and a restless, burgeoning
vitality. Lee might have ridden down from the old age of chivalry, lance
in hand, silken banner fluttering over his head. Each man was the perfect champion of his cause, drawing both his strengths and his weaknesses from the people he led.

Yet it was not all contrast, after all. Different as they were — in 13
background, in personality, in underlying aspiration — these two great
soldiers had much in common. Under everything else, they were marvelous fighters. Furthermore, their fighting qualities were really very
much alike.

Each man had, to begin with, the great virtue of utter tenacity and 14
fidelity. Grant fought his way down the Mississippi Valley in spite of
acute personal discouragement and profound military handicaps. Lee
hung on in the trenches at Petersburg after hope itself had died. In each
man there was an indomitable quality...the born fighter's refusal to
give up as long as he can still remain on his feet and lift his two fists.

Daring and resourcefulness they had, too; the ability to think faster 15
and move faster than the enemy. These were the qualities which gave
Lee the dazzling campaigns of Second Manassas and Chancellorsville
and won Vicksburg for Grant.

Lastly, and perhaps greatest of all, there was the ability, at the end, 16
to turn quickly from war to peace once the fighting was over. Out of the
way these two men behaved at Appomattox came the possibility of
a peace of reconciliation. It was a possibility not wholly realized, in
the years to come, but which did, in the end, help the two sections to
become one nation again...after a war whose bitterness might have
seemed to make such a reunion wholly impossible. No part of either
man's life became him more than the part he played in their brief meeting in the McLean house at Appomattox. Their behavior there put all
succeeding generations of Americans in their debt. Two great Americans, Grant and Lee — very different, yet under everything very much
alike. Their encounter at Appomattox was one of the great moments of
American history.

QUESTIONS ON MEANING

1. What is Bruce Catton's PURPOSE in writing: to describe the meeting of two
   generals at a famous moment in history; to explain how the two men
   stood for opposing social forces in America; or to show how the two differed in personality?
2. SUMMARIZE the background and the way of life that produced Robert E.
   Lee; then do the same for Ulysses S. Grant. According to Catton, what
   ideals did each man represent?
3. In the historian's view, what essential traits did the two men have in common? Which trait does Catton think most important of all? For what reason?
4. How does this essay help you understand why Grant and Lee were such
   determined fighters?

QUESTIONS ON WRITING STRATEGY

1. From the content of this essay, and from knowing where it first appeared, what can you infer about Catton's original AUDIENCE? At what places in his essay does the writer expect of his readers a familiarity with United States history?
2. What effect does the writer achieve by setting both his INTRODUCTION and his CONCLUSION in Appomattox?
3. For what reasons does Catton contrast the two generals *before* he compares them? Suppose he had reversed his outline, and had dealt first with Grant's and Lee's mutual resemblances. Why would his essay have been less effective?
4. Pencil in hand, draw a single line down the margin of every paragraph in which you find the method of contrast. Then draw a *double* line next to every paragraph in which you find the method of comparison. How much space does Catton devote to each method? Why didn't he give comparison and contrast equal time?
5. Closely read the first sentence of every paragraph and underline each word or phrase in it that serves as a TRANSITION. Then review your underlinings. How much COHERENCE has Catton given his essay?
6. What is the TONE of this essay—that is, what is the writer's attitude toward his two subjects? Is Catton poking fun at Lee by imagining the Confederate general as a knight of the Middle Ages, "lance in hand, silken banner fluttering over his head" (para. 12)?
7. **OTHER METHODS.** In identifying "two conflicting currents," Catton uses CLASSIFICATION to sort Civil War–era Americans into two groups represented by Lee and Grant. Catton then uses ANALYSIS to tease out the characteristics of each current, each type. How do classification and analysis serve Catton's comparison and contrast?

QUESTIONS ON LANGUAGE

1. In his opening paragraph, Catton uses a metaphor: American life is a book containing chapters. Find other FIGURES OF SPEECH in his essay (consulting Useful Terms if you need help). What do the figures of speech contribute?
2. Look up *poignant* in the dictionary. Why is it such a fitting word in paragraph 2? Why wouldn't *touching, sad,* or *teary* have been as good?
3. What information do you glean from the sentence "Lee was tidewater Virginia" (para. 5)?
4. Define *aristocratic* as Catton uses it in paragraphs 4 and 6.
5. Define *obeisance* (para. 7); *indomitable* (14).

SUGGESTIONS FOR WRITING

1. **JOURNAL WRITING.** During the American Civil War, nearly every citizen had an opinion and chose sides. Do you think Americans today are generally as interested in political issues? Why, or why not?
   FROM JOURNAL TO ESSAY. Write an essay that offers an explanation for public participation in or commitment to political and social causes

today. What fires people up or turns them off? To help focus your essay, zero in on a specific issue, such as education, government spending, health insurance, or gun control.

2. In a brief essay full of specific examples, discuss: Do the "two diametrically opposed elements in American life" (as Catton calls them) still exist in the country today? Are there still any "landed nobility"?

3. In your thinking and your attitudes, whom do you more closely resemble—Grant or Lee? Compare and contrast your outlook with that of one famous American or the other. (A serious tone for this topic isn't required.)

4. **CRITICAL WRITING.** Although slavery, along with other issues, helped precipitate the Civil War, Catton in this particular essay does not deal with it. Perhaps he assumes that his readers will supply the missing context themselves. Is this a fair ASSUMPTION? If Catton had recalled the facts of slavery, would he have undermined any of his assertions about Lee? (Though the general of the pro-slavery Confederacy, Lee was personally opposed to slavery.) In a brief essay, judge whether or not the omission of slavery weakens the essay, and explain why.

5. **CONNECTIONS.** In "The Penalty of Death" (p. 470), H. L. Mencken maintains that capital punishment satisfies the need "to destroy the concrete scoundrels whose act has alarmed everyone, and thus made everyone unhappy." Mencken also says, "I do not argue that this yearning is noble; I simply argue that it is almost universal among human beings." How do Mencken's assertions illuminate Catton's final paragraph? In a brief essay, explain just what Grant and Lee accomplished at Appomattox.

BRUCE CATTON ON WRITING

Most of Bruce Catton's comments on writing, those that have been preserved, refer to the work of others. As editor of *American Heritage*, he was known for his blunt, succinct comments on unsuccessful manuscripts: "This article can't be repaired and wouldn't be much good if it were." Or: "The high-water mark of this piece comes at the bottom of page one, where the naked Indian nymph offers the hero strawberries. Unfortunately, this level is not maintained."

In a memoir published in *Bruce Catton's America* (1979), Catton's associate Oliver Jensen marvels that, besides editing *American Heritage* for twenty-four years (and contributing to nearly every issue), Catton managed to produce so many substantial books. "Concentration was no doubt the secret, that and getting an early start. For many years Catton was always the first person in the office, so early that most of the staff never knew when he did arrive. On his desk the little piles of yellow sheets grew slowly, with much larger piles in the wastebasket. A neat and orderly man, he preferred to type a new page than correct very much in pencil."

His whole purpose as a writer, Catton once said, was "to reexamine [our] debt to the past."

FOR DISCUSSION

1. To which of Catton's traits does Oliver Jensen attribute the historian's impressive output?
2. Which characteristics of Catton the editor would you expect to have served him well as a writer?

NANCY MAIRS

A self-described "radical feminist, pacifist, and cripple," NANCY MAIRS aims to "speak the 'unspeakable.'" Her poetry, memoirs, and essays deal with many sensitive subjects, including her struggles with the debilitating disease of multiple sclerosis. Born in Long Beach, California, in 1943, Mairs grew up in New Hampshire and Massachusetts. She received a B.A. from Wheaton College in Massachusetts (1964) and an M.F.A. in creative writing (1975) and a Ph.D. in English literature (1984) from the University of Arizona. While working on her advanced degrees, Mairs taught high school and college writing courses and served as project director at the Southwest Institute for Research on Women. Her second book of poetry, *In All the Rooms of the Yellow House* (1984), received a Western States Arts Foundation book award. Her essays are published in *Plaintext* (1986), *Remembering the Bone-House* (1988), *Carnal Acts* (1990), *Ordinary Time* (1993), and *Waist High in the World: A Life Among the Nondisabled* (1996).

Disability

As a writer afflicted with multiple sclerosis, Nancy Mairs is in a unique position to examine how the culture responds to people with disabilities. In this essay from *Carnal Acts*, she draws two contrasts involving the media's depiction of disability and argues with her usual unsentimental candor that the media must treat disability as normal. The essay was first published in 1987 as a "Hers" column in the *New York Times*.

For months now I've been consciously searching for representation 1
of myself in the media, especially television. I know I'd recognize this self because of certain distinctive, though not unique, features: I am a forty-three-year-old woman crippled with multiple sclerosis; although I can still totter short distances with the aid of a brace and a cane, more and more of the time I ride in a wheelchair. Because of these appliances and my peculiar gait, I'm easy to spot even in a crowd. So when I tell you I haven't noticed any women like me on television, you can believe me.

Actually, last summer I did see a woman with multiple sclerosis 2
portrayed on one of those medical dramas that offer an illness-of-the-week like the daily special at your local diner. In fact, that was the whole point of the show: that this poor young woman had MS. She was terribly upset (understandably, I assure you) by the diagnosis, and her response was to plan a trip to Kenya while she was still physically capable of making it, against the advice of the young, fit, handsome doctor

who had fallen in love with her. And she almost did it. At least, she got as far as a taxi to the airport, hotly pursued by the doctor. But at the last she succumbed to his blandishments and fled the taxi into his manly protective embrace. No escape to Kenya for this cripple.

Capitulation into the arms of a man who uses his medical powers 3 to strip one of even the urge toward independence is hardly the sort of representation I had in mind. But even if the situation had been sensitively handled, according to the woman her right to her own adventures, it wouldn't have been what I'm looking for. Such a television show, as well as films like *Duet for One* and *Children of a Lesser God*, in taking disability as its major premise, excludes the complexities that round out a character and make her whole. It's not about a woman who happens to be physically disabled; it's about physical disability and the determining factor of a woman's existence.

Take it from me, physical disability looms pretty large in one's life. 4 But it doesn't devour one wholly. I'm not, for instance, Ms. MS, a walking, talking embodiment of a chronic incurable degenerative disease. In most ways I'm just like every other woman of my age, nationality, and socioeconomic background. I menstruate, so I have to buy tampons. I worry about smoker's breath, so I buy mouthwash. I smear my wrinkling skin with lotions. I put bleach in the washer so my family's undies won't be dingy. I drive a car, talk on the telephone, get runs in my pantyhose, eat pizza. In most ways, that is, I'm the advertisers' dream: Ms. Great American Consumer. And yet the advertisers, who determine nowadays who will get represented publicly and who will not, deny the existence of me and my kind absolutely.

I once asked a local advertiser why he didn't include disabled 5 people in his spots. His response seemed direct enough: "We don't want to give people the idea that our product is just for the handicapped." But tell me truly now: If you saw me pouring out puppy biscuits, would you think these kibbles were only for the puppies of the cripples? If you saw my blind niece ordering a Coke, would you switch to Pepsi lest you be struck sightless? No, I think the advertiser's excuse masked a deeper and more anxious rationale: To depict disabled people in the ordinary activities of daily life is to admit that there is something ordinary about disability itself, that it may enter anybody's life. If it is effaced completely, or at least isolated as a separate "problem," so that it remains at a safe distance from other human issues, then the viewer won't feel threatened by her or his own physical vulnerability.

This kind of effacement or isolation has painful, even dangerous 6 consequences, however. For the disabled person, these include self-degradation and a subtle kind of self-alienation not unlike that experienced by other minorities. Socialized human beings love to conform, to study others and then mold themselves to the contours of those whose images, for good reasons or bad, they come to love. Imagine a life in which feasible others—others you can hope to be like—don't exist. At the least you might conclude that there is something queer about you, something ugly or foolish or shameful. In the extreme, you might feel as though you don't exist, in any meaningful social sense, at all. Everyone else is "there," sucking breath mints and splashing cologne and swigging wine coolers. You're "not there." And if not there, nowhere.

But this denial of disability imperils even you who are able-bodied, and not just by shrinking your insight into the physically and emotionally complex world you live in. Some disabled people call you TAPs, or Temporarily Abled Persons. The fact is that ours is the only minority you can join involuntarily, without warning, at any time. And if you live long enough, as you're increasingly likely to do, you may well join it. The transition will probably be difficult from a physical point of view no matter what. But it will be a good bit easier psychologically if you are accustomed to seeing disability as a normal characteristic, one that complicates but does not ruin human existence. Achieving this integration, for disabled and able-bodied people alike, requires that we insert disability daily into our field of vision: quietly, naturally, in the small and common scenes of our ordinary lives.

QUESTIONS ON MEANING

1. Why does Mairs object to the TV movie about the woman with multiple sclerosis (paras. 2–3)?
2. What does Mairs mean by the phrase "Ms. Great American Consumer" (para. 4)?
3. Why, according to Mairs, should there be images of people with disabilities on television?
4. Restate Mairs's THESIS in your own words.
5. What is this essay's PURPOSE?

QUESTIONS ON WRITING STRATEGY

1. What does Mairs compare and contrast in this essay? How does the comparison help her achieve her purpose?
2. What key GENERALIZATIONS does Mairs make to support her thesis? Do you find them valid? Why, or why not?
3. How does Mairs use her INTRODUCTION to lay the groundwork for her essay? How does she make the TRANSITION from her introduction into the TV drama?

4. How would you characterize Mairs's TONE in this essay? Point out specific sentences and words that establish it. What is the EFFECT?

5. **OTHER METHODS.** Discuss how Mairs uses EXAMPLE to help build her case. What kinds of examples does she select? What are their effects?

QUESTIONS ON LANGUAGE

1. What is the function of IRONY in this essay (for example, "If you saw my blind niece ordering a Coke, would you switch to Pepsi lest you be struck sightless?")?

2. Look up *multiple sclerosis* in an encyclopedia or medical dictionary. What is the precise meaning of the term? How might advancing multiple sclerosis affect someone's ease of motion in a world designed for people who are not physically disabled?

3. Give definitions of the following words: gait (para. 1); blandishments (2); capitulation (3); degenerative (4); rationale, effaced (5); feasible (6).

4. What are the CONNOTATIONS of the words "crippled," "totter," appliances," and "peculiar gait" (para. 1)? What is the effect of these words in the essay's introduction?

5. What do people with disabilities mean when they refer to "Temporarily Abled Persons" (para. 7)? Why might they use this phrase?

SUGGESTIONS FOR WRITING

1. **JOURNAL WRITING.** What do you feel when you see a stranger using a wheelchair: pity? sympathy? curiosity? uncertainty? admiration? fear? something else? As honestly as you can, set down your responses. What do you think causes them? Consider whether they are colored by your experiences with disability—for instance, whether you are disabled yourself, know someone who is disabled, or have no experience with disability (whether in person or in the media).

   FROM JOURNAL TO ESSAY. Based on your journal reflections, write an essay that explains how your own responses to people with disabilities lead you to accept or dispute Mairs's call for depicting "disabled people in the ordinary activities of daily life."

2. Choose another group you think has been "effaced" in television advertising and programming—a racial, ethnic, or religious group, for instance. Write an essay detailing how and why that group is overlooked. How could representations of the group be incorporated into the media? What effects might such representation have?

3. Write an essay discussing how people with disabilities are treated in our society. You could NARRATE a day in the life of someone with a disability; you could COMPARE AND CONTRAST the access and facilities your school provides physically average versus disabled students; you could CLASSIFY social attitudes toward disabilities, with examples of each type.

4. **CRITICAL WRITING.** Reread this essay carefully. Mairs tells us about herself through details and through tone (for example, through irony, intensity, and humor). Write an essay on how Mairs's self-revelations do or do not help further her thesis.

5. **CONNECTIONS.** Read Joan Didion's "In Bed" (p. 540) and compare Didion's experience with Mairs's. How do their conditions affect them? What are the most difficult effects? How do the two authors portray migraines and multiple sclerosis as positive parts of their lives? Compare how they work to communicate their conditions to those whom Didion calls "the unafflicted."

NANCY MAIRS ON WRITING

Nancy Mairs frequently writes about the calamities in her life, and she ponders why in an essay appearing in the *New York Times Book Review* in February 1993. Why, for instance, did she record the details of her husband's grave illness? Perhaps because writing about one's misery is a way to overcome the isolation it creates. "There must have been millions keeping bedside vigils, whispering as I whispered over and over, 'Come back. Don't leave me. I need you,' each of us trapped in this profound and irrational solitude, as though walls of black glass had dropped on every side, shutting out the light, deadening all sound but the loved one's morphine-drugged breathing. I was not, in truth, alone."

In addition to this sense of kinship, Mairs also gains personal power from writing about illness. "The impulse, at least for someone of a writerly persuasion, is not to bemoan this condition but to remark on it in detail. Initially, one's motives for translating happenstance into acts of language may be quite private. Catastrophe tends to be composed not of a monolithic event but of a welter of little incidents, many of which bear no apparent relationship to one another, and language, in ordering these into recognizable patterns, counteracts disorientation and disintegration. This process of making sense of a flood of random data also produces the impression—generally quite groundless—of control, which may save one's sanity even though it can't save one's own or anyone else's life."

These therapeutic results, Mairs maintains, provide reason enough for keeping a private journal. However, going public "is an intrinsically social act, 'I' having no reason to speak aloud unless I posit 'you' there listening." The presence of the reader is especially important, Mairs says, "if I am seeking…to reconnect my self, now so utterly transformed by events unlike any I've experienced before as to seem a stranger even to myself, to the human community." The human community is no stranger to pain. "All of us who write out of calamity know this above all else: There is nothing exceptional about our lives, however they may differ in their particulars. What we can offer you, when the time comes, is companionship in a common venture. It's not a lot, I know, but it may come in handy. The narrator of personal disaster, I think, wants not to whine, not to boast, but to comfort."

But, Mairs finds, perhaps the most compelling reason of all to record personal afflication is to show "the spiritual maturation that suffering can force." "The writing about personal disaster that functions as literature tends not to be 'about' disaster at all," Mairs observes. Rather, it delineates a "progress toward sympathetic wisdom." The best writers "transcend their separate ordeals to speak generally, and generously, of the human condition." They write about "going on. All the way. To our common destination.

"To which none of us wants to go ignorant and alone," Mairs adds. "Hence, into the dark, we write."

FOR DISCUSSION

1. Why does Mairs believe that writing about one's own misery is valuable, both for the writer and for readers?
2. How does Mairs distinguish between journal writing and writing with a reader in mind?

JEFF GREENFIELD

JEFF GREENFIELD, born in 1943, graduated from the University of Wisconsin and Yale University School of Law. Early in his career, Greenfield served as a staff aide and writer of speeches for both John V. Lindsay, former mayor of New York City, and the late attorney general Robert F. Kennedy. Since then, he has been a sportswriter, a media commentator for CBS-TV, a political and media analyst for ABC News, and a regular guest on the news show *Nightline*. He now serves as senior analyst for CNN, cohosts a news show for that network, and writes a column for *Time* magazine. His books include *A Populist Manifesto* (1972), *Where Have You Gone, Joe DiMaggio?* (1973), *The World's Greatest Team* (history of the Boston Celtics, 1976), *Television: The First 50 Years* (1977), *Playing to Win: An Insider's Guide to Politics* (1980), *The Real Campaign* (1982), and *The People's Choice* (1995).

The Black and White Truth About Basketball

In this essay Greenfield uses comparison and contrast to explain "A Skin-Deep Theory of Style" (the essay's original subtitle). A survey of "black" and "white" styles of basketball play, the essay provoked immediate interest and controversy when it was first published in *Esquire* in 1975. Greenfield updated the essay for *The Bedford Reader*, most recently in 1993. (His thesis remains unchanged.)

The dominance of black athletes over professional basketball is beyond dispute. Two-thirds of the players are black, and the number would be greater were it not for the continuing practice of picking white bench warmers for the sake of balance. Over the last two decades, no more than three white players have been among the ten starting players on the National Basketball Association's All-Star team, and in the last quarter century, only two white players—Dave Cowens and Larry Bird of the Boston Celtics—have ever been chosen as the NBA's Most Valuable Player.

And at a time when a baseball executive can lose his job for asserting that blacks lack "the necessities" to become pro sports executives and when the National Football League only in 1989 had its first black head coach, the NBA stands as a pro sports league that hired its first black head coach in 1968 (Bill Russell) and its first black general manager in the early 1970s (Wayne Embry of the Milwaukee Bucks). What discrimination remains—lack of equal opportunity for speaking engagements

209

and product endorsements—has more to do with society than with basketball.

This dominance reflects a natural inheritance: Basketball is a pastime of the urban poor. The current generation of black athletes are heirs to a tradition more than half a century old. In a neighborhood without the money for bats, gloves, hockey sticks and ice skates, or shoulder pads, basketball is an eminently accessible sport. "Once it was the game of the Irish and Italian Catholics in Rockaway and the Jews on Fordham Road in the Bronx," writes David Wolf in his brilliant book, *Foul!* "It was recreation, status, and a way out." But now the ethnic names have been changed: Instead of the Red Holzmans, Red Auerbachs, and the McGuire brothers, there are the Michael Jordans and Charles Barkleys, the Shaquille O'Neals and Patrick Ewings. And professional basketball is a sport with national television exposure and million-dollar salaries.

But the mark on basketball of today's players can be measured by more than money or visibility. It is a question of style. For there is a clear difference between "black" and "white" styles of play that is as clear as the difference between 155th Street at Eighth Avenue and Crystal City, Missouri. Most simply (remembering we are talking about culture, not chromosomes), "black" basketball is the use of superb athletic skill to adapt to the limits of space imposed by the game. "White" ball is the pulverization of that space by sheer intensity.[1]

It takes a conscious effort to realize how constricted the space is on a basketball court. Place a regulation court (ninety-four by fifty feet) in a football field, and it will reach from the back of the end zone to the twenty-one-yard line; its width will cover less than a third of the field. On a baseball diamond, a basketball court will reach from home plate to first base. Compared to its principal indoor rival, ice hockey, basketball covers about one-fourth the playing area. Moreover, during the normal flow of the game, most of the action takes place on the third of the court nearest the basket. It is in this dollhouse space that ten men, each of them half a foot taller than the average man, come together to battle each other.

There is, thus, no room; basketball is a struggle for the edge: the half step with which to cut around the defender for a lay-up, the half second of freedom with which to release a jump shot, the instant a head

[1] This distinction has nothing to do with the question of whether whites can play as "well" as blacks. In 1987, the Detroit Pistons' Isiah Thomas quipped that the Celtics' Larry Bird was "a pretty good player," but would be much less celebrated and wealthy if he were black. As Thomas later said, Bird was one of the greatest pro players in history. Nor is this distinction about "smart," although the ex–Los Angeles Laker great Magic Johnson was right when he said that too many journalists attribute brilliant strategic moves by black players to "innate" ability.

turns allowing a pass to a teammate breaking for the basket. It is an arena for the subtlest of skills: the head fake, the shoulder fake, the shift of body weight to the right and the sudden cut to the left. Deception is crucial to success; and to young men who have learned early and painfully that life is a battle for survival, basketball is one of the few pursuits in which the weapon of deception is a legitimate tactic rather than a source of trouble.

If there is, then, the need to compete in a crowd, to battle for the   7
edge, then the surest strategy is to develop the *unexpected*: to develop a shot that is simply and fundamentally different from the usual methods of putting the ball in the basket. Drive to the hoop, but go under it and come up the other side; hold the ball at waist level and shoot from there instead of bringing the ball up to eye level; leap into the air, but fall away from the basket instead of toward it. All these tactics, which a fan can see embodied in the astonishing play of the Chicago Bulls' Michael Jordan, take maximum advantage of the crowding on the court. They also stamp uniqueness on young men who may feel it nowhere else.

"For many young men in the slums," David Wolf writes, "the   8
school yard is the only place they can feel true pride in what they do, where they can move free of inhibitions and where they can, by being spectacular, rise for the moment against the drabness and anonymity of their lives. Thus, when a player develops extraordinary 'school yard' moves and shots...[they] become his measure as a man."

So the moves that begin as tactics for scoring soon become calling   9
cards. You don't just lay the ball in for an uncontested basket; you take the ball in both hands, leap as high as you can, and slam the ball through the hoop. When you jump in the air, fake a shot, bring the ball back to your body, and throw up a shot, all without coming back down, you have proven your worth in uncontestable fashion.

This liquid grace is an integral part of "black" ball, almost exclu-   10
sively the province of the playground player. Some white stars like Bob Cousy, Billy Cunningham, Doug Collins, and Kevin McHale had it; John Stockton of the Utah Jazz has it now: the body control, the moves to the basket, the free-ranging mobility. Most of them also possessed the surface ease that is integral to the "black" style; an incorporation of the ethic of mean streets—to "make it" is not just to have wealth but to have it without strain. Whatever the muscles and organs are doing, the face of the "black" star almost never shows it. Magic Johnson of the Lakers could bring the ball downcourt with two men on him, whip a pass through an invisible opening, cut to the basket, take a return pass, and hit the shot all with no more emotion than a quick smile. So stoic was San Antonio Spurs great George Gervin that he earned the nickname "Ice Man." (Interestingly, a black coach like San Antonio's John

Lucan exhibits far less emotion on the bench than a white counterpart like Portland's Rick Adelman.)

If there is a single trait that characterizes "black" ball it is leaping   11
ability. Bob Cousy, ex-Celtic great and former pro coach, says that "when coaches get together, one is sure to say, 'I've got the one black kid in the country who can't jump.' When coaches see a white boy who can jump or who moves with extraordinary quickness, they say, 'He should have been born black, he's that good.'" This pervasive belief was immortalized by the title of the hit film *White Men Can't Jump*.

Don Nelson, now a top executive with the Golden State Warriors,   12
recalls that back in 1970, Dave Cowens, then a relatively unknown graduate of Florida State, prepared for his rookie pro season by playing in the Rucker League, an outdoor competition in Harlem playgrounds that pits pros against college kids and playground stars. So ferocious was Cowens's leaping ability, Nelson says, that "when the summer was over, everyone wanted to know who the white son of a bitch was who could jump so high." That's another way to overcome a crowd around the basket—just go over it.

Speed, mobility, quickness, acceleration, "the moves"—all of   13
these are catch-phrases that surround the "black" playground athlete, the style of play. So does the most racially tinged of attributes, "rhythm." Yet rhythm is what the black stars themselves talk about: feeling the flow of the game, finding the tempo of the dribble, the step, the shot. It is an instinctive quality (although it stems from hundreds of hours of practice), and it is one that has led to difficulty between system-oriented coaches and free-form players. "Cats from the street have their own rhythm when they play," said college dropout Bill Spivey, onetime New York high school star. "It's not a matter of somebody setting you up and you shooting. You *feel* the shot. When a coach holds you back, you lose the feel and it isn't fun anymore."

When legendary Brooklyn playground star Connie Hawkins was   14
winding up his NBA career under Laker coach Bill Sharman, he chafed under the methodical style of play. "He's systematic to the point where it begins to be a little too much. It's such an action-reaction type of game that when you have to do everything the same way, I think you lose something."

There is another kind of basketball that has grown up in America.   15
It is not played on asphalt playgrounds with a crowd of kids competing for the court; it is played on macadam driveways by one boy with a ball and a backboard nailed over the garage; it is played in gyms in the frigid winter of the rural Midwest and on Southern dirt courts. It is a mechanical, precise development of skills (when Don Nelson was an Iowa farm boy, his incentive to make his shots was that an errant rebound would land in the middle of chicken droppings). It is a game without

frills, without flow, but with effectiveness. It is "white" basketball: jagged, sweaty, stumbling, intense. Where a "black" player overcomes an obstacle with finesse and body control, a "white" player reacts by outrunning or overpowering the obstacle.

By this definition, the Boston Celtics have been classically "white"   16 regardless of the pigmentation of the players. They have rarely suited up a player with dazzling moves; indeed, such a player would probably have made Red Auerbach swallow his cigar. Instead, the Celtic philosophy has been to wear you down with execution, with constant running, with the same play run again and again. The rebound by Bill Russell (or Dave Cowens or Robert Parrish) triggers the fast break, as everyone races downcourt; the ball goes to Bob Cousy (or John Havlicek or Larry Bird), who pulls up and takes the shot, or who drives and then finds Sam Jones (or Kevin McHale or M. L. Carr) free for an easy basket.

Perhaps the most definitively "white" position is that of the quick   17 forward, one without great moves to the basket, without highly developed shots, without the height and mobility for rebounding effectiveness. So what does he do?

He runs. He runs from the opening jump to the final buzzer. He   18 runs up and down the court, from base line to base line, back and forth under the basket, looking for the opening, the pass, the chance to take a quick step, the high-percentage shot. To watch Detroit's Bill Laimbeer or the Suns' Dan Majerle, players without speed or obvious moves, is to wonder what they are doing in the NBA—until you see them swing free and throw up a shot that, without demanding any apparent skill, somehow goes in the basket more frequently than the shots of many of their more skilled teammates. And to have watched the New York Knicks' (now U.S. Senator) Bill Bradley, or the Celtics' John Havlicek, is to have watched "white" ball at its best.

Havlicek or Laimbeer or the Phoenix Suns' Danny Ainge stands in   19 dramatic contrast to Michael Jordan or to the Philadelphia 76ers legend Julius Erving. Erving had the capacity to make legends come true, leaping from the foul line and slam-dunking the ball on his way down; going up for a lay-up, pulling the ball to his body, and driving under and up the other side of the rim, defying gravity and probability with impossible moves and jumps. Michael Jordan of the Chicago Bulls has been seen by thousands spinning a full 360 degrees in midair before slamming the ball through the hoop.

When John Havlicek played, by contrast, he was the living em-   20 bodiment of his small-town Ohio background. He would bring the ball downcourt, weaving left, then right, looking for a path. He would swing the ball to a teammate, cut behind the pick, take the pass, and release the shot in a flicker of time. It looked plain, unvarnished. But it was a blend of skills that not more than half a dozen other players in the league possessed.

To former pro Jim McMillian, a black who played quick forward   21
with "white" attributes, "it's a matter of environment. Julius Erving grew up in a different environment from Havlicek. John came from a very small town in Ohio. There everything was done the easy way, the shortest distance between two points. It's nothing fancy; very few times will he go one-on-one. He hits the lay-up, hits the jump shot, makes the free throw, and after the game you look up and say, 'How did he hurt us that much?'"

"White" ball, then, is the basketball of patience, method, and   22
sometimes brute strength. "Black" ball is the basketball of electric self-expression. One player has all the time in the world to perfect his skills, the other a need to prove himself. These are slippery categories, because a poor boy who is black can play "white" and a white boy of middle-class parents can play "black." Charles Oakley of the New York Knicks and John Paxson of the Chicago Bulls are athletes who seem to defy these categories.

And what makes basketball the most intriguing of sports is how   23
these styles do not necessarily clash; how the punishing intensity of "white" players and the dazzling moves of the "blacks" can fit together, a fusion of cultures that seems more and more difficult in the world beyond the out-of-bounds line.

QUESTIONS ON MEANING

1. According to Greenfield, how did black athletes come to dominate professional basketball?
2. What differences does the author discern between "black" and "white" styles of play? How do exponents of the two styles differ in showing emotion?
3. Explain the author's reference to the word *rhythm* as "the most racially tinged of attributes" (para. 13).
4. Does Greenfield stereotype black and white players? Where in his essay does he admit there are players who don't fit neatly into his two categories?

QUESTIONS ON WRITING STRATEGY

1. How much do we have to know about professional basketball to appreciate Greenfield's essay? Is it written only for basketball fans, or for a general AUDIENCE?

2. In what passage in his essay does Greenfield begin comparing and contrasting? What is the function of the paragraphs that come before this passage?
3. In paragraph 5, the author compares a basketball court to a football field, a baseball diamond, and an ice hockey arena. What is the basis for his comparison?
4. **OTHER METHODS.** In addition to comparison and contrast and a good deal of DESCRIPTION, Greenfield uses CAUSE AND EFFECT when he accounts for the differences in playing style. In your own words, SUMMARIZE the author's point about school yards (para. 8) and his point about macadam driveways, gyms, and dirt courts (15). Explain "the ethic of mean streets" (10).

QUESTIONS ON LANGUAGE

1. Consult the dictionary if you need help in defining the following words: ethnic (para. 3); constricted (5); inhibitions, anonymity (8); uncontestable (9); finesse (15); execution (16); embodiment (20).
2. Talk to someone who knows basketball if you need help in understanding the head fake, the shoulder fake (para. 6); the fast break (16); the high-percentage shot (18); the jump shot (21). What kind of DICTION do you find in these instances?
3. When Greenfield says that "we are talking about culture, not chromosomes" (para. 4), how would you expect him to define these terms?

SUGGESTIONS FOR WRITING

1. **JOURNAL WRITING.** Is it a problem that Greenfield's argument relies on GENERALIZATIONS about groups of people? Why, or why not?
   FROM JOURNAL TO ESSAY. Write an essay that discusses how well (or not) Greenfield has surmounted the difficulties facing any writer who makes generalizations about people. Consider as background what makes a generalization reasonable or responsible.
2. Compare and contrast a college basketball and professional basketball team, or the styles of two athletes in any sport.
3. Compare and contrast the styles of two people in the same line of work, showing how their work is affected by their different personalities. You might take, for instance, two singers, two taxi drivers, two bank tellers, two evangelists, two teachers, or two symphony orchestra conductors.
4. **CRITICAL WRITING.** Do you agree with Greenfield's observations about basketball styles? Consider the exceptions Greenfield cites (paras. 10, 21, 22), and muster any of your own. In an essay, EVALUATE whether Greenfield's essay can withstand these exceptions: In your opinion, are Greenfield's ideas valid?
5. **CONNECTIONS.** Both Jeff Greenfield and Maya Angelou, in "Champion of the World" (p. 52), explore racial themes through sports. In your mind, what role does sports play in relations between African Americans and white Americans? In an essay using plenty of EXAMPLES, consider whether African American sports heroes such as Joe Louis and Michael Jordan contribute to improved race relations, have no effect on them, or perhaps actually undermine them.

JEFF GREENFIELD ON WRITING

For *The Bedford Reader,* Jeff Greenfield told how he gathered his information for "The Black and White Truth About Basketball" from basketball professionals, and how he tried to contrast the two styles of play with humor and goodwill.

In the early 1970s, I was spending a good deal of time playing hooky from my work as a political consultant writing books and magazine articles; and no writing was more enjoyable than sports reporting. Coming from the world of politics where everything was debatable — who would win, whose position was right, who was engaging in "desperation smear tactics" — I relished the world of sports, where winners and losers were clearly identifiable.

It was while writing about various star basketball players of the time — men like the New York Knicks' Willis Reed, the Boston Celtics' Dave Cowens — that I first began noticing how often offhand, utterly unmalicious racial references were being thrown about. A white player in practice would miss a rebound, and a black teammate would joke, "Come on, man, jump like a brother." A black player would lose a footrace for a ball, and someone would quip, "Looks black, plays white." It slowly became clear to me that many of those in the basketball world freely acknowledged that there were different styles of play that broke down, roughly speaking, into black and white characteristics.

At first, it did not even occur to me that this would make a publishable magazine piece. For one thing, I came from a typical postwar liberal family, repulsed by the racial stereotypes which still dominated "respectable" conversation. In a time when black Americans were heavily portrayed as happy-go-lucky, shiftless, childlike adults, consigned to success as athletes and tap-dancers, the idea that there was anything like a "black" or "white" way to play basketball would have seemed something out of a segregationist manifesto.

For another, I have always been an enthusiastic follower of the sports pages and had never seen any such analysis in the many newspapers I read. Apparently, most sportswriters felt equally uncomfortable with a foray into race; it had, after all, taken baseball more than a half a century to admit blacks into its ranks. Indeed, one of the more common assertions of bigots in the 1930s and 1940s was that blacks could not be great athletes because "they couldn't take the pressure." It is easy to understand why race was not a comfortable basis on which to analyze athletic grace.

In the end, I decided to write about "black" and "white" basketball because it made the game more enjoyable to me. Clearly, there *were* different ways to play the game; clearly the kind of self-assertion represented by the spectacular moves of black schoolyard ball was a reflection of how important the game was to an inner-city kid, for whom the asphalt court was the cheapest—maybe the only—release from a nasty, sometimes brutish, existence. And books such as Pete Axthelm's *The City Game* and David Wolf's *Foul!* had brilliantly explored the significance of basketball in the urban black world of modern America.

I talked with players and sportswriters alike when I wrote the article; without exception, they approached the subject as I did: with humor, un-self-consciously. Perhaps it is a measure of the progress we have made in racial matters that no one—black or white—thought it insulting or offensive to remark on the different styles of play, to note that the gravity-defying slam-dunks of a Michael Jordan and the carefully calibrated shots of a Dan Majerle are two facets of the same game.

FOR DISCUSSION

1. What gave Greenfield the idea for his essay?
2. What aspects of his topic made Greenfield hesitant to write about it? What persuaded him to go ahead?

ADDITIONAL WRITING TOPICS

Comparison and Contrast

1. In an essay replete with examples, compare and contrast the two subjects in any one of the following pairs:

   The main characters of two films, stories, or novels
   Women and men as consumers
   The styles of two runners
   Liberals and conservatives: their opposing views of the role of government
   How city dwellers and country dwellers spend their leisure time
   The presentation styles of two television news commentators

2. Approach a comparison and contrast essay on one of the following general subjects by explaining why you prefer one thing to the other:

   Computers: Macs and PCs
   Two buildings on campus or in town
   Two football teams
   German-made cars and Detroit-made cars
   Two horror movies
   Television when you were a child and television today
   City life and small-town or rural life
   Malls and main streets
   Two neighborhoods
   Two sports

3. Write an essay in which you compare a reality (what actually exists) with an ideal (what should exist). Some possible topics:

   The affordable car
   Available living quarters
   A job
   The college curriculum
   Public transportation
   Financial aid to college students

5

PROCESS ANALYSIS
Explaining Step by Step

THE METHOD

A chemist working for a soft-drink firm is asked to improve on a competitor's product, Orange Quench. First, she chemically tests a sample to figure out what's in the drink. This is the method of DIVISION or ANALYSIS, the separation of something into its parts in order to understand it (see the following chapter). Then the chemist writes a report telling her boss how to make a drink like Orange Quench, but better. This recipe is a special kind of analysis, called PROCESS ANALYSIS: explaining step by step how to do something or how something is done.

Like any type of analysis, process analysis divides a subject into its components: It divides a continuous action into stages. Processes much larger and more involved than the making of an orange drink also may be analyzed. When geologists explain how a formation such as the Grand Canyon occurred—a process taking several hundred million years—they describe the successive layers of sediment deposited by oceans, floods, and wind; then the great uplift of the entire region by underground forces; and then the erosion, visible to us today, by the Colorado River and its tributaries, by little streams and flash floods, by crumbling and falling rock, and by wind. Exactly what are the geologists doing in this explanation? They are taking a complicated event (or process) and dividing it into parts. They are telling us what happened first, second, and third, and what is still happening today.

Because it is useful in explaining what is complicated, process analysis is a favorite method of scientists such as geologists. The method, however, may be useful to anybody. Two PURPOSES of process analysis are very familiar to you:

- A *directive process analysis* explains how to do something or make something. You meet it when you read a set of instructions for assembling newly purchased stereo components, or follow the directions to a stereo store ("Turn right at the blinker and follow Patriot Boulevard for 2.4 miles...").
- An *informative process analysis* explains how something is done or how it takes place. This is the kind we often read out of curiosity. Such an essay may tell of events beyond our control: how atoms behave when split, how lions hunt, how a fertilized egg develops into a child.

In this chapter, you will find examples of both kinds of process analysis—both the "how to" and the "how." For instance, Tibor Kalman and Lulu Kalman offer a funny directive on how to open a CD package, while Jessica Mitford spellbindingly informs us of how corpses are embalmed (but, clearly, she doesn't expect us to rush down to our basements and give her instructions a try).

Sometimes process analysis is used very imaginatively. Foreseeing that the sun eventually will cool, the earth shrink, the oceans freeze, and all life perish, an astronomer who cannot possibly behold the end of the world nevertheless can write a process analysis of it. An exercise in learned guesswork, such an essay divides a vast and almost inconceivable event into stages that, taken one at a time, become clearer and more readily imaginable.

Whether it is useful or useless (but fun to imagine), an effective process analysis can grip readers and even hold them fascinated. Say you were proposing a change in the procedures for course registration at your school. You could argue your point until you were out of words, but you would get nowhere if you failed to tell your readers exactly how the new process would work: That's what makes your proposal sing. Leaf through a current issue of a newsstand magazine, and you will find that process analysis abounds. You may meet, for instance, articles telling you how to tenderize cuts of meat, sew homemade designer jeans, lose fat, cut hair, play the money markets, arouse a bored mate, and search the World Wide Web. Less practical, but not necessarily less interesting, are the informative articles: how brain surgeons work, how diamonds are formed, how cities fight crime. Readers, it seems, have an unslakable thirst for process analysis. In every issue of the *New York Times Book Review*, we find an entire best-seller list devoted to "Advice, How-to, and Miscellaneous," including books on how to make money in real estate, how to lose weight, how to find a good mate, and how to lose a bad one. Evidently, if anything will still make an American crack open a book, it is a step-by-step explanation of how he or she, too, can be a success at living.

THE PROCESS

Here are suggestions for writing an effective process analysis of your own. (In fact, what you are about to read is itself a process analysis.)

1. *Understand clearly the process you are about to analyze.* Think it through. This preliminary survey will make the task of writing far easier for you.

2. *Consider your thesis.* What is the point of your process analysis: Why are you bothering to tell readers about it? The THESIS SENTENCE for a process analysis need do no more than say what the subject is and maybe outline its essential stages. For instance:

   The main stages in writing a process analysis are listing the steps in the process, drafting to explain the steps, and revising to clarify the steps.

   But your readers will surely appreciate something livelier and more pointed, something that says "You can use this" or "This may surprise you" or "Listen up." Here are two examples from essays in this chapter:

   [In a mortuary the body] is in short order sprayed, sliced, pierced, pickled, trussed, trimmed, creamed, waxed, painted, rouged, and neatly dressed — transformed from a common corpse into a Beautiful Memory Picture. (Jessica Mitford, "Behind the Formaldehyde Curtain")

   Poisoning the earth can be difficult because the earth is always trying to cleanse and renew itself. (Linnea Saukko, "How to Poison the Earth")

3. *Think about preparatory steps.* If the reader should do something before beginning the process, list these steps. For instance, you might begin, "Remove the packing from the components," or, "First, lay out three eggs, one pound of Sheboygan bratwurst...."

4. *List the steps or stages in the process.* Try setting them down in chronological order, one at a time — if this is possible. Some processes,

however, do not happen in an orderly sequence, but occur all at once. If, for instance, you are writing an account of a typical earthquake, what do you mention first? The shifting of underground rock strata? Cracks in the earth? Falling houses? Bursting water mains? Toppling trees? Mangled cars? Casualties? Here is a subject for which the method of CLASSIFICATION (Chap. 7) may come to your aid. You might sort out apparently simultaneous events into categories: injury to people; damage to homes, to land, to public property.

5. *Check the completeness and order of the steps.* Make sure your list includes *all* the steps in the right order. Sometimes a stage of a process may contain a number of smaller stages. Make sure none has been left out. If any seems particularly tricky or complicated, underline it on your list to remind yourself when you write your essay to slow down and detail it with extra care.

6. *Define your terms.* Ask yourself, "Do I need any specialized or technical terms?" If so, be sure to define them. You'll sympathize with your reader if you have ever tried to work a Malaysia-made VCR that comes with an instruction booklet written in translatorese, full of unexplained technical JARGON, or if you have ever tried to assemble a plastic tricycle according to a directive that begins, "Position sleeve casing on wheel center in fork with shaft in tong groove, and gently but forcibly tap in medium pal nut head."

7. *Use time-markers or* TRANSITIONS. These words or phrases indicate *when* one stage of a process stops and the next begins, and they greatly aid your reader in following you. Here, for example, is a paragraph of plain medical prose that makes good use of the helpful time-markers printed in *italics*. (The paragraph is adapted from Alan F. Guttmacher's *Pregnancy and Birth*.)

> In the human, *thirty-six hours after* the egg is fertilized, a two-cell egg appears. A twelve-cell development takes place *in seventy-two hours*. The egg is *still* round and has increased little in diameter. In this respect it is like a real estate development. *At first* a road bisects the whole area, *then* a cross road divides it into quarters, and *later* other roads divide it into eighths and twelfths. This happens without the taking of any more land, simply by subdivision of the original tract. *On the third or fourth day*, the egg passes from the Fallopian tube into the uterus. *By the fifth day* the original single large cell has subdivided into sixty small cells and floats about the slitlike uterine cavity *a day or two longer*, *then* adheres to the cavity's inner lining. *By the twelfth day* the human egg is already firmly implanted. Impregnation is *now* completed, *as yet* unbeknown to the woman. *At present*, she has not even had time to miss her first menstrual period, and other symptoms of pregnancy are *still several days distant*.

Brief as these time-markers are, they define each stage of the human egg's journey. Note how the writer, after declaring in the second sentence that the egg forms twelve cells, backtracks for a moment and retraces the process by which the egg has subdivided, comparing it (by a brief ANALOGY) to a piece of real estate. When using time-markers, vary them so that they won't seem mechanical. If you can, avoid the monotonous repetition of a fixed phrase (*In the fourteenth stage...*, *In the fifteenth stage...*). Even boring time-markers, though, are better than none at all. As in any chronological narrative, words and phrases such as *in the beginning, first, second, next, after that, three seconds later, at the same time,* and *finally* can help a process to move smoothly in the telling and lodge firmly in the reader's mind.

8. *Be specific.* When you write a first draft, state your analysis in generous detail, even at the risk of being wordy. When you revise, it will be easier to delete than to amplify.

9. *Revise.* When your essay is finished, reread it carefully against the checklist below. You might also enlist a friend's help. If your process analysis is a directive ("How to Eat an Ice Cream Cone Without Dribbling"), see if the friend can follow your instructions without difficulty. If your process analysis is informative ("How a New Word Enters the Dictionary"), ask the friend whether the process unfolds as clearly in his or her mind as it does in yours.

CHECKLIST FOR REVISING A PROCESS ANALYSIS

✔ **THESIS.** Does your process analysis have a point? Have you made sure readers know what it is?

✔ **ORGANIZATION.** Have you arranged the steps of your process in a clear chronological order? If steps occur simultaneously, have you grouped them so that readers perceive some order?

✔ **COMPLETENESS.** Have you included all the necessary steps and explained each one fully? Is it clear how each one contributes to the result?

✔ **DEFINITIONS.** Have you explained the meanings of any terms your readers may not know?

✔ **TRANSITIONS.** Do time-markers distinguish the steps and clarify their sequence?

PROCESS ANALYSIS IN A PARAGRAPH: TWO ILLUSTRATIONS

Using Process Analysis to Write About Television

The following paragraph, written especially for *The Bedford Reader*, explains the process of setting the timer on a particular VCR. Though composed to be freestanding, the paragraph (ideally with an accompanying illustration) could easily be dropped into a complete set of instructions on how to operate the VCR.

The timer on your videocassette recorder permits you to record up to eight programs over a two-week period even when you are not at home. For each program you wish to record in your absence, locate an empty program number by pushing the *P* button until a flashing number appears on the TV screen. The next four steps set the information for the program. First, push the *Day* button until the day and date show on the screen. The screen will flash *On*. Next set the starting time (be sure the time is set correctly for A.M. or P.M.). Then push the *Off* button and set the ending time (again, watching A.M. or P.M.). When the times have been set, push the *Chan* button and set the channel using the unit's channel selector. You may review the program information by pushing the *Check* button. When you are satisfied that the settings are correct, push *Timer* to set the timer to operate. (The unit cannot be operated manually while the timer is on.)

Process to be explained with directive analysis
Step 1
Preview of steps 2–5
Step 2
Step 3
Step 4
Step 5
Step 6
Step 7
Transitions (underlined) clarify steps

Using Process Analysis in an Academic Discipline

This paragraph on our descent into sleep comes from a psychology textbook's section on "the most perplexing of our biological rhythms." Before this paragraph the authors review the history of sleep research; after it they continue to analyze the night-long process that follows this initial descent.

When you first climb into bed, close your eyes, and relax, your brain emits bursts of *alpha waves* in a regular, high-amplitude, low-frequency rhythm of 8–12 cycles per second. Alpha is associated with relaxing or not concentrating on anything in particular. Gradually these waves slow down even further and you drift into the Land of Nod, passing through four stages, each deeper than the previous one.

Steps preceding process

Process to be explained with informative analysis

1. *Stage 1.* Your brain waves become small and irregular, indicating activity with low voltage and mixed frequencies. You feel yourself drifting on the edge of consciousness, in a state of light sleep. If awakened, you may recall fantasies or a few visual images.

Step 1

2. *Stage 2.* Your brain emits occasional short bursts of   *Step 2*
rapid, high-peaking waves called *sleep spindles.* Light
sounds or minor noises probably won't disturb you.

3. *Stage 3.* In addition to the waves characteristic of stage   *Step 3*
2, your brain occasionally emits very slow waves of about
1–3 cycles per second, with very high peaks. These *delta
waves* are a sure sign that you will be hard to arouse. Your
breathing and pulse have slowed down, your temperature
has dropped, and your muscles are relaxed.

4. *Stage 4.* Delta waves have now largely taken over, and   *Step 4*
you are in deep sleep. It will take vigorous shaking or a
loud noise to awaken you, and you won't be very happy
about it. Oddly enough, though, if you talk or walk in
your sleep, this is when you are likely to do so.

—Carole Wade and Carol Tavris, *Psychology*

PROCESS ANALYSIS ELSEWHERE
IN *THE BEDFORD READER*

Although process analysis is one of the most specialized methods of
development, the writers of the following essays do find a need to explain how to do something or how something is done, even as they develop their ideas by other methods as well.

PART ONE

Brad Manning, "Arm Wrestling with My Father"
Jeff Greenfield, "The Black and White Truth About Basketball"
Gail Sheehy, "Predictable Crises of Adulthood"
Deborah Tannen, "But What Do You Mean?"
Stephanie Ericsson, "The Ways We Lie"
William Lutz, "The World of Doublespeak"
K. C. Cole, "The Arrow of Time"
Marie Winn, "TV Addiction"
Esther Dyson, "Cyberspace for All"
Heidi Pollock, "Welcome to Cyberbia"

PART TWO

Joan Didion, "In Bed"
Annie Dillard, "Lenses"
Stephen Jay Gould, "Sex, Drugs, Disasters, and the Extinction of
Dinosaurs"
Jonathan Swift, "A Modest Proposal"

CASE STUDY
Using Process Analysis

As a sophomore at Mary Washington College in Virginia, Jennifer Meska was a resident assistant in a freshman dormitory, responsible for students' welfare and, when necessary, for establishing dormitory rules.

In the following memo to the dorm's residents, Meska explained what students must do in the three-times-yearly fire drills. Meska's aim in drafting the memo was to outline the drill procedure so that students could remember and follow it—in other words (though she didn't think of the task this way), to write a clear directive process analysis. In her first draft, Meska ran the steps of the process together in a paragraph, and for some steps she omitted explanations that might motivate residents to follow them. The bulleted list in her revision and the added explanations make the steps more distinct and memorable.

TO: Residents of Russell Hall
FROM: Jennifer Meska
DATE: September 6, 1998
SUBJECT: Fire-drill procedure

To prepare for the possibility of a fire in our residence hall, we will run three unannounced fire drills throughout the year. These drills will familiarize you with the potentially lifesaving procedures to be used during a real fire.

A loud buzzing noise and flashing lights will signal the start of a fire drill. Each resident has three minutes to complete the following tasks and exit the building:

- Close all bedroom and bathroom windows to prevent additional oxygen from feeding the fire.

- Turn off all electrical appliances, including computers, televisions, fans, radios, and lights. Turning off appliances will prevent electrical surges from starting additional fires.

- Grab a towel to cover your mouth in case you come across any smoke-filled passages, and wear shoes to protect your feet from any dangerous debris.

- Don't take anything else with you. In a real fire, delay could cost you your life.

- Close your door behind you to retard the spread of the fire.

- Go immediately to the nearest exit.

The fire drills are mandated by the state, and all residence halls must pass them in the required three minutes. If you have any questions, please let me know.

LINNEA SAUKKO

LINNEA SAUKKO was born in Warren, Ohio, in 1956. After receiving a degree in environmental quality control from Muskingum Area Technical College, she spent three years as an environmental technician, developing hazardous waste programs and acting as adviser on chemical safety at a large corporation. Concerned about the lack of safe methods for disposing of hazardous waste, Saukko went back to school to earn a B.A. in geology (Ohio State University, 1985) so that she could help address this issue. She currently lives in Hilliard, Ohio, and works as a groundwater manager at the Ohio Environmental Protection Agency, evaluating various sites for possible contamination of the groundwater. She is also researching the links between routine spraying in workplaces, workers' chemical sensitivities, and so-called sick-building syndrome.

How to Poison the Earth

"How to Poison the Earth" was written in response to an assignment given in a freshman composition class and was awarded a Bedford Prize in Student Writing. It was subsequently published in *Student Writers at Work: The Bedford Prizes* (1984). Saukko's essay is largely a directive process analysis, but it is also a SATIRE: By outwardly showing us one way to guarantee the fate of the earth, the author implicitly urges us not to do it.

Poisoning the earth can be difficult because the earth is always try- 1
ing to cleanse and renew itself. Keeping this in mind, we should generate as much waste as possible from substances such as uranium-238, which has a half-life (the time it takes for half of the substance to decay) of one million years, or plutonium, which has a half-life of only 0.5 million years but is so toxic that if distributed evenly, ten pounds of it could kill every person on the earth. Because the United States generates about eighteen tons of plutonium per year, it is about the best substance for long-term poisoning of the earth. It would help if we would build more nuclear power plants because each one generates only 500 pounds of plutonium each year. Of course, we must include persistent toxic chemicals such as polychlorinated biphenyl (PCB) and dichlorodiphenyl trichloroethane (DDT) to make sure we have enough toxins to poison the earth from the core to the outer atmosphere. First, we must develop many different ways of putting the waste from these nuclear and chemical substances in, on, and around the earth.

Putting these substances in the earth is a most important step in 2
the poisoning process. With deep-well injection we can ensure that the

earth is poisoned all the way to the core. Deep-well injection involves drilling a hole that is a few thousand feet deep and injecting toxic substances at extremely high pressures so they will penetrate deep into the earth. According to the Environmental Protection Agency (EPA), there are about 360 such deep injection wells in the United States. We cannot forget the groundwater aquifers that are closer to the surface. These must also be contaminated. This is easily done by shallow-well injection, which operates on the same principle as deep-well injection, only closer to the surface. The groundwater that has been injected with toxins will spread contamination beneath the earth. The EPA estimates that there are approximately 500,000 shallow injection wells in the United States.

Burying the toxins in the earth is the next best method. The toxins from landfills, dumps, and lagoons slowly seep into the earth, guaranteeing that contamination will last a long time. Because the EPA estimates there are only about 50,000 of these dumps in the United States, they should be located in areas where they will leak to the surrounding ground and surface water.

Applying pesticides and other poisons on the earth is another part of the poisoning process. This is good for coating the earth's surface so that the poisons will be absorbed by plants, will seep into the ground, and will run off into surface water.

Surface water is very important to contaminate because it will transport the poisons to places that cannot be contaminated directly. Lakes are good for long-term storage of pollutants while they release some of their contamination to rivers. The only trouble with rivers is that they act as a natural cleansing system for the earth. No matter how much poison is dumped into them, they will try to transport it away to reach the ocean eventually.

The ocean is very hard to contaminate because it has such a large volume and a natural buffering capacity that tends to neutralize some of the contamination. So in addition to the pollution from rivers, we must use the ocean as a dumping place for as many toxins as possible. The ocean currents will help transport the pollution to places that cannot otherwise be reached.

Now make sure that the air around the earth is very polluted. Combustion and evaporation are major mechanisms for doing this. We must continuously pollute because the wind will disperse the toxins while rain washes them from the air. But this is good because a few lakes are stripped of all living animals each year from acid rain. Because the lower atmosphere can cleanse itself fairly easily, we must explode nuclear tests bombs that shoot radioactive particles high into the upper atmosphere where they will circle the earth for years. Gravity must pull some of the particles to earth, so we must continue exploding these bombs.

So it is that easy. Just be sure to generate as many poisonous sub-   8
stances as possible and be sure they are distributed in, on, and around
the entire earth at a greater rate than it can cleanse itself. By following
these easy steps we can guarantee the poisoning of the earth.

QUESTIONS ON MEANING

1. Is the author's main PURPOSE to amuse and entertain, to inform readers of
   ways they can make better use of natural resources, to warn readers about
   threats to the future of our planet, or to make fun of scientists? Support
   your answer with EVIDENCE from the essay.
2. Describe at least three of the earth's mechanisms for cleansing its land,
   water, and atmosphere, as presented in this essay.
3. According to Saukko, many of our actions are detrimental, if not outright
   destructive, to our environment. Identify these practices and discuss
   them. If these activities are harmful to the earth, why are they permitted?
   Do they serve some other important goal or purpose? If so, what? Are
   there other ways that these goals might be reached?

QUESTIONS ON WRITING STRATEGY

1. How detailed and specific are Saukko's instructions for poisoning the
   earth? Which steps in this process would you be able to carry out, once
   you finished reading the essay? In what instances might an author choose
   not to provide concrete, comprehensive instructions for a procedure? Relate your answer to the TONE and purpose of this essay.
2. How is Saukko's essay organized? Follow the process carefully to determine whether it happens chronologically, with each step depending on
   the one before it, or whether it follows another order. How effective is this
   method of organization and presentation?
3. For what AUDIENCE is this essay intended? How can you tell?
4. What is the tone of this essay? Consider especially the title and the last
   paragraph as well as examples from the body of the essay. How does the
   tone contribute to Saukko's SATIRE?
5. **OTHER METHODS.** Saukko doesn't mention every possible pollutant but
   instead focuses on certain EXAMPLES. Why do you think she chooses these
   particular examples? What serious pollutants can you think of that
   Saukko doesn't mention specifically?

QUESTIONS ON LANGUAGE

1. How do the phrases "next best method" (para. 3), "another part of the
   poisoning process" (4), and "lakes are good for long-term storage of pollutants" (5) signal the tone of this essay? Should they be read literally, IRON-
   ICALLY, metaphorically, or some other way?

2. Be sure you know how to define the following words: generate, nuclear, toxins (para. 1); lagoons, contamination (3); buffering, neutralize (6); combustion (7).

SUGGESTIONS FOR WRITING

1. **JOURNAL WRITING.** In everyday conversations, we often use satire or SARCASM to suggest solutions to problems that seem ridiculous or overwhelming. For example, we suggest breaking all the dishes so that we don't have to wash them again or barring pedestrians from city streets so that they don't interfere with cars. What kinds of situations drive you to make suggestions like these? Are the suggestions ever serious?
   FROM JOURNAL TO ESSAY. Choose one of the solutions you wrote about in your journal, or propose a solution to a problem that your journal entry has suggested. Write an essay detailing this satirical solution, paying careful attention to explaining each step of the process and to maintaining your satiric tone throughout.
2. Write an essay defending and justifying the use of nuclear power plants, pesticides, or another pollutant Saukko mentions. This essay will require some research because you will need to argue that the benefits of these methods outweigh their hazardous and destructive effects. Be sure to support your claims with factual information and statistics. Or approach the issue from the same point of view that Saukko did, and argue against the use of nuclear power plants or pesticides. Substantiate your argument with data and facts, and be sure to propose alternative sources of power or alternative methods of insect control.
3. **CRITICAL WRITING.** What does Saukko gain or lose by using satire and irony to make her point? What would be the comparative strengths and weaknesses of an essay that approached the same pollution problems straightforwardly and sincerely, perhaps urging or pleading with readers to stop polluting?
4. **CONNECTIONS.** Saukko is not the only writer of irony in this book: Merrill Markoe (p. 116), Suzanne Britt (p. 185), Dave Barry (p. 191), Jessica Mitford (p. 244), Horace Miner (p. 255), Judy Brady (p. 275), Emily Prager (p. 288), H. L. Mencken (p. 470), and Jonathan Swift (p. 621) also employ it. Based on Saukko's essay and essays by at least two of these others, define *irony*. If you need a boost, supplement the definition in this book's Useful Terms with one in a dictionary of literary or rhetorical terms. But go beyond others' definitions to construct one of your own, using quotations from the essays as your support.

LINNEA SAUKKO ON WRITING

"After I have chosen a topic," says Linnea Saukko, "the easiest thing for me to do is to write about how I really feel about it. The goal of 'How to Poison the Earth' was to inform people, or more specifically, to open their eyes.

"As soon as I decided on my topic, I made a list of all the types of pollution and I sat down and basically wrote the paper in less than two hours. The information seemed to pour from me onto the page. Of course I did a lot of editing afterward, but I never changed the idea and the tone that I started with."

FOR DISCUSSION

When have you had the experience of writing on a subject that compelled your words to pour forth with little effort? What was the subject? What did you learn from this experience?

TIBOR KALMAN
AND
LULU KALMAN

TIBOR KALMAN (1949–99) was a graphic designer renowned for his innovative ideas and social consciousness. He was born in Hungary and with his family immigrated to Poughkeepsie, New York, in 1957. Kalman attended New York University and later became the first creative director of Barnes & Noble. In 1980, he founded the New York design firm M&Co and was credited with being a social prod as well as an imaginative, even radical, resource for his clients. He worked for magazines as well, serving as art director for *Artforum*, creative director for *Interview*, and founding editor-in-chief of *Colors*, a magazine published by the clothing chain Benetton. A monograph of Kalman's work, *Tibor Kalman: Perverse Optimist*, was published shortly before his death from cancer at age 49.

LULU BODONI KALMAN, Tibor Kalman's daughter, was born in 1982. A photographer, writer, and snowboarder, she is a senior at the Nightingale Bamford High School in New York City.

How to Open a CD Box

"To me," Tibor Kalman once said, "design is a matter of solving problems." Lulu Kalman sought a solution to a problem that she found especially "nerve-wracking": opening compact-disc packages. For a 1998 *New York Times Magazine*, father and daughter collaborated on this process analysis to help others reach the music inside.

1. Remove the plastic wrap. How? With a knife? Better yet, buy a special 99-cent EZ-CD opener tool designed precisely for this purpose. Ain't America grand? (Now, where did you put that thing?)

2. Peel off the special sticker that seals the CD case. Don't bother with the little pull tab—it'll tear off and become useless if you dare touch it. Just start peeling the plastic off with your nails instead. The pieces are superglued, so they will stick to your fingers. Roll them into a ball and flick it against the wall. Then ask a neighbor to remove the little ball of sticky plastic and throw it away.

3. Open the plastic box. It's snapped tight on itself. Insert your index finger at the opening opposite the hinge and pry carefully. Try very hard not to break the box. The box, called a jewel box probably because of the jewels that the packaging executives were able to purchase with their profits, is five-sixteenths of an inch thick. You can fit about fifty into a foot of drawer space. A CD that is slipped into a cardboard sleeve

the way LP's were packaged is about one-sixteenth of an inch thick. You can fit nearly two hundred in a foot of drawer space.

4. Ah. Now you can see the CD! Try to remove it. Go ahead. It's plugged onto that little plastic thing with the little plastic fingers— plugged on really tight to secure it for shipping. In the next two weeks, those little, tiny plastic fingers will break off, one at a time, and fall on the floor. Your dog will eat them. ("It might be food. If not, I'll just throw up.")

5. The CD itself has a colorful label with a stunning color photo of a boot. No artist's name, no title, no song list, just this beautiful, shiny boot. The back cover of the CD box has the other boot. To find the song list, you must try to remove the CD booklet. This will take considerable ingenuity because it is wedged into position by several cleverly designed plastic tabs and a special device that is a last-ditch attempt to block you when you try to remove it. This will cost you a cuticle.

6. Open the CD booklet. Turn to the last page. There, among the copyright notices, publishing credits and assistant tape-engineer credits, you'll find the song list. Isn't it fun reading with a magnifying glass?

7. Enjoy the CD.

8. Return the CD to its shelf. Since the boxes are slippery, carry them one at a time and never stack them, to avoid the consequences of No. 9. Make appointments with your optometrist and chiropractor if you amass a shelved collection.

9. In two weeks, you'll drop the plastic box while trying to open it. Its hinges will break, challenging you to find another solution to the problem of storing your now naked CD.

10. In a couple of years, you'll put them in the basement, next to your LP's, replacing them with mini-CCDVDCVDX's, the new state-of-the-art format. The guys with the jewels have the packaging already figured out. Just fourteen steps.

QUESTIONS ON MEANING

1. What is this essay's PURPOSE? Is there more than one?
2. What do the authors imply by instructing the reader to "ask a neighbor to remove the little ball of sticky plastic and throw it away" (para. 2)?
3. What is meant by the theory that CD cases are called jewel boxes "because of the jewels that the packaging executives were able to purchase with their profits" (para. 3)?
4. What ASSUMPTIONS do the authors make about their AUDIENCE?

QUESTIONS ON WRITING STRATEGY

1. Kalman and Kalman provide a directive process analysis. How helpful is it in meeting the goal stated in the title, "How to Open a CD Box"? What else does the analysis accomplish?
2. The authors omit a conventional INTRODUCTION, a paragraph or so that would draw readers in and let them know where they are headed. Is the absence of an introduction a plus or a minus, in your view? Why? If you think it is a minus, try drafting an introduction that you think would be appropriate.
3. What is the effect of the RHETORICAL QUESTIONS in the essay: "How?... Ain't America grand?" (para. 1) and "Isn't it fun reading with a magnifying glass?" (6).
4. How does the numbering of paragraphs affect your reading of the essay? Does it add to the humor of the instructions for you?
5. **OTHER METHODS.** Where in the essay do Kalman and Kalman use COMPARISON AND CONTRAST? What is implied by the comparison?

QUESTIONS ON LANGUAGE

1. What do the authors imply when they predict the development of "mini-CCDVDCVDX's" (para. 10)?
2. Where do the authors do more than imply that the designers of CD packaging deliberately want to frustrate us? Does this aim seem feasible to you? What else might explain the packaging?
3. Give definitions of the following words: ingenuity (5); optometrist, chiropractor (8).

SUGGESTIONS FOR WRITING

1. **JOURNAL WRITING.** Think of everyday things that annoy you: voice mail, your roommate's snoring, a toaster oven that persists in burning your breakfast. Write down as many such sources of annoyance as you can in five minutes of freewriting.
   FROM JOURNAL TO ESSAY. Choose one of the annoying things from your journal entry. How do you deal with the presence of this difficulty in your life? Mimic Kalman and Kalman's directive process analysis to instruct your readers how to overcome this trouble.
2. Write a letter of complaint to the manufacturers of CD packages. Use as many details from the essay as you like, and feel free to elaborate with specifics from your own experience. Instead of using the humorous, biting tone of the essay, though, show yourself to be calm, thoughtful, reasonable. Try to convince the packagers to make changes.
3. **CRITICAL WRITING.** The Kalmans' essay humorously attacks the design of CD packaging, especially the plastic case (the "jewel box"). From the perspective of the CD case's designers, write an essay in response, defending all of the features that the Kalmans criticize.
4. **CONNECTIONS.** Look at "How to Open a CD Box" together with Linnea Saukko's "How to Poison the Earth" (p. 228). Both essays use directive

process analysis to criticize, to draw attention to a situation their authors find wrong. Write a directive process analysis of your own that seeks not simply to explain a process, but also to express a view about the process. The subject could be anything from a school's needlessly confusing registration procedure to a company's unfair hiring practices. (You may, but need not, use humor like the Kalmans or IRONY like Saukko's.)

PHILLIP LOPATE

Through his own writing and his editing of the anthology *The Art of the Personal Essay* (1994), PHILLIP LOPATE has focused the interest of contemporary readers and writers on the essay form. His own essay collections include *Bachelorhood* (1981), *Against Joie de Vivre* (1989), *Portrait of My Body* (1996), and *Totally, Tenderly, Tragically: Essays and Criticism from a Lifelong Love Affair with the Movies* (1998). In his essays Lopate writes frankly and wryly about subjects ranging from romantic relationships to cities to self-awareness to fatherhood. He has also written poetry (*The Eyes Don't Always Stay Open* and *The Daily Round*, both 1976) and novels (*Confessions of Summer*, 1979, and *The Rug Merchant*, 1987). A longtime New Yorker, Lopate was born in 1943 in Jamaica Heights, New York, and educated at Columbia University, where he received a B.A. in 1964. He is a professor of English at Hofstra University, where he holds the Adams Chair.

Confessions of a Shusher

Phillip Lopate likes movies, and he likes to watch them in movie theaters. But he doesn't like to be disturbed by the chatter of others around him. In defense, as he tells us in this essay from *Portrait of My Body*, he has devised a process for trying to silence his seatmates. Are you a shusher like Lopate or a shushee?

I am a shusher, which is to say a self-appointed sergeant-at-arms who tells noisemakers in the theater to be quiet. You take your life in your hands when you shush a stranger, since he may turn out to be a touchy psychopath who is reminded of an admonishing schoolteacher he detested. But having been in the past a grade-school teacher, I cannot shake the idea that I am somehow responsible for the correction of these breakdowns in the assembly.

My usual procedure is to start with a glare at the offender. Glares are unfortunately quite ineffective when the noisemakers sit in front of you. Even if they are to the side or behind, a glare may be misinterpreted as rubbernecking. I then proceed to clear my throat, hoping that this signal of civilized discomfit will be understood as a reproach. It almost never is. I then usually undergo an internal struggle, asking myself, Who am I to set myself up as a policer of public behavior? Can't I simply ignore the nuisance? Is it really worth it to emit an ugly sound, which grates on my ears as well, which may distract others from the movie and may draw on my head some physical retaliation against which I am ill-prepared to defend myself, or else some unpleasant curse? These questions are merely a way of biding my time in the hope that the problem will disappear by itself. If it doesn't, I am compelled to graduate to Stage 2: a good hearty "Shhh!" Much as I might want to soften the aggressiveness of this susurration, experience has taught me that a tentative shush is a waste of time—too easily mistaken for some private sigh.

But then, even a lusty shush is frequently ignored. Perhaps it is too comic-sounding, has too much of the sneeze about it, the hyperactive radiator or the ready kettle. In any event, a shush does not obligate its target to recognize that he or she has been addressed, the way normal speech does. What shushes do have in their favor is that, being such a universal signal, they make the reprimand seem less a personal confrontation and more the bubbling up of a communal superego. However, if the offenders continue to talk after several shushes (perhaps even issuing some derisive mimicking shush of their own as a witty riposte), then there is no choice but to come out from behind the anonymity of the shush and, heart in mouth, escalate to a crisp verbal "Please stop talking." This is sometimes followed by "You're not in your living room, you know," if one is feeling pedagogically self-righteous. Whatever statement one makes is likely to produce a furious twisting in the chair by the chief gabbler, to see what puritanical nerd has had the temerity to question his freedom of speech. It is necessary to return the fellow's look with a cool, frowning stare of one's own. Sometimes the shusher senses a small ripple of curiosity among those nearby, like schoolchildren drawn to a playground fight. Their lack of support for law and order is not the least irritating facet of the situation, since you had thought you were intervening at least partly for everyone's sake, and now realize that to them you are merely one more lunatic releasing commands into the indifferent dark.

By now the movie's spell has been broken. I sit boiling, feeling helplessly angry and at the same time frightened of the offender's potential rage. If he falls into a resentful silence, I can calm my heartbeat and tell myself that I have struck a blow for moviegoers everywhere. The problem is that the request to shut up is often taken rather personally. It seems to touch a sore spot in the requestee's dignity. Particularly, I have noticed, if the chief talker is showing off for his date, or his group of buddies, he may continue to jaw all night as a point of machismo, so that what had started out as unconscious rudeness graduates, via shushing, to defiant policy.

At such turns I compose speeches to myself, along the lines of "We did not pay good money to listen to your asinine conversation" or "How can we expect to have a democracy if…" But I usually spare them the civics lesson, because by this point I decide to write these people off as hopeless morons. I sweep up my coat and belongings, ignoring the victorious hoots, and allow myself a slow, censorious abandonment of the row. Perhaps a grain of guilt, I tell myself, will lodge itself in their subconsciousness and come to ripening next time.

It would be agreeable to report that the problem ends there. But 6 many times my newly chosen section is also contaminated with talkers, so that I may be forced to move three times in the course of a feature film. In doing so, I incur the risk of being mistaken for a restless flasher, but it is a small price to pay for cinematic peace of mind.

The crux of the problem is that I want to watch movies in movie 7 theaters, as they were designed to be seen, and I like having the company of other bodies, other spectators around me; but at the same time, I have become preternaturally sensitive, during years of devoted filmgoing, to distractions: not just to the conversationalists but to the foot-kickers or those who nervously cross and uncross their legs behind me, each time pressing into the back of my seat; the latecomer who compounds the first fault by making what seems like a deliberately elaborate coming to rest, removing her coat slowly and rearranging her department store bags; the doting parent who keeps feeding his child sourball candy wrapped in maximally crackling cellophane.... I don't even like to sit behind baldheaded men, because their domes reflect too much light and detract from the screen's luminescence. (The fact that my own hairline is receding at a rapid pace makes me hope that others are not so pathologically picky.)

The truth is, I can live with the kickers, the candy-unwrappers, the 8 baldies, etc., but I draw the line at prattlers. Is it just my luck to attract them, or have today's movie audiences declined across the board in their capacity to keep silent?

We can always blame television for altering movie-viewing habits. 9 A good many people who attend movies today do seem convinced that they are sitting on the couch at home; others must believe they are in the bedroom, as they snore or make love. You would expect that young people, who have grown up in the channel-hopping, short-attention-span era, would be the worst offenders. But the noisiest, from my observation, are elderly couples, who keep comparing notes on what is happening and why. Maybe hearing loss makes them talk louder, but it is also as if submission to the film experience were a threat to their dyadic bond, and in the end they choose togetherness over immersion.

Audiences of the twenties and thirties were famous—indeed, they 10 were so criticized by intellectuals—for their mass somnambulism as the lights dimmed. Today's audiences are like patients hard to hypnotize; they resist the oneiric plunge. Accustomed to seeing modest-sized images in the convivial, lamp-lit surround of family life, they do not fully participate in the ritual of a sudden, engulfing nightfall. And today's theater owners further dilute the darkness by letting in considerably more ambient light—usually for security reasons—and scaling down the grandeur with smaller, multiplexed screens. The result is an uneasy suspension above the film narrative, the equivalent of a light sleep.

Audience chatter has also been affected by a shifting perception of 11 when a movie actually begins. I was sitting in a movie house recently, waiting for the show to start (I like to get there early, to absorb the atmosphere and compose myself for the descent), and in front of me were two women having a discussion about apples. Granny Smith versus Macintosh, fresh versus baked. It was one of those tedious conversations you cannot help but eavesdrop in on. The lights lowered, the coming attractions started, the women chatted on. Now they were discussing which restaurant they would go to after the show. Coming attractions can be fascinating cultural artifacts, and, in any case, I have a fondness for their tantalizing promise, but I recognize that they are, in a sense, only advertisements, and so the audience has the right to talk through them, resisting these solicitations with skeptical remarks, such as "They couldn't pay me to see that one." However, the titles of the feature film started to appear, and the women continued conversing. Should they go to a French bistro or eat Chinese? But—you will say— it was only during the titles. *Only* the titles? I am curious who is in the cast, who wrote the screenplay, produced it; and even if I were not, I would still think the labor of these collaborators deserved a respectful silence as their names passed before my eyes. Then there is the choice of typeface, no small matter. Above all, the title sequence often introduces the key visual and musical leitmotifs in the film. One school of criticism even argues that the title sequence is a miniature model—encoded, of course—of the movie to follow. All right, I see I haven't convinced you about the significance of the title sequence; but surely you will agree that the first shot of the film is highly important in arousing our expectations—as important, say, as the first sentence of a novel. Yet the women kept talking. This particular opening shot panned across the rooftops of a Sicilian city huddled in the landscape, establishing the drama's larger social context while at the same time expressing certain aesthetic choices (camera movement, angle, lighting) that allowed us to sense the tempo at which Fate would be distributed to the characters. It was a particularly engrossing, well-composed, mood-setting shot, undermined by the chatter of my neighbors, and I felt I had no option but to shush. One of the women replied, "Nothing's happening yet!" Mood, location—this was nothing. It was only during the first *dialogue* sequence that they decided something was happening, and finally fell silent.

I want to make a distinction here between what I regard as justifi- 12 able audience noise and the kind of chatter I have been describing. I do not expect utter silence in a theater, nor do I necessarily want it. Comedies obviously gain from being seen in a packed, roaring house. If

I am at a horror movie and during a frightening sequence some teenagers start yelling "Watch out!" or "Oh, gross!" it's in the spirit of the occasion. If my fellow moviegoers rejoice at a chainsaw dismemberment or at so-called "street slime" being blown away in *Death Wish IX*, I may fear for their souls and their politics, but I do not fault them for improper audience behavior. They are still reacting as a public to the events on-screen, are swept up in the drama. What I cannot accept is the selfishness of private conversation. Even when nothing is audible from a nearby tête-à-tête but a whispering buzz, the mere knowledge that my neighbors are not watching with their full attention dilutes and spoils my own concentration.

For all that one is still a crowd member, moviegoing is essentially a 13 solitary process. To refuse that solitude is to violate the social contract that should be written on each ticket stub. If, indeed, movie audiences of today chatter more during films than they used to, I can only surmise that it has something to do with, on the one hand, a spreading fear of solitude and, on the other, an erosion of what it means to be a member of the public.

There have been times, over the years, when my roles as cinephile 14 and swain have come into conflict. I have had to make it clear to my date, however much I may have doted on her, that I actually did want to watch the movie. I have made it clear to the gabblers around us as well, though one woman who was a perfect lady and to whom I was especially devoted, hated my shushing, which she found an embarrassment and a breach of manners. One time I went so far as to shush *her* when she was talking to a friend who had come with us to the movies, and afterward she let me know, with uncharacteristic directness, that if I ever did that to her again, she would break my arm. She was right, of course — or at least I pretended she was right, because I knew that if I attempted to defend my quixotic position, it would only make things worse. Nobody loves a shusher.

QUESTIONS ON MEANING

1. How do shushes differ from verbal reproaches for Lopate?
2. What does Lopate imply when he writes that, if his shushing fails, he allows himself "a slow, censorious abandonment of the row" (para. 5)?
3. What does Lopate see as the key difference between objectionable and unobjectionable audience noise in a movie theater (para. 12)?
4. What is this essay's THESIS? What do you think is its PURPOSE?

QUESTIONS ON WRITING STRATEGY

1. Lopate's process analysis is informative, not directive. What parts of the process would another person have trouble duplicating?
2. How do paragraphs 7 and 8 create a TRANSITION from the process analysis, preparing us for the rest of the essay?
3. How would you categorize Lopate's TONE? Is it deferential? self-mocking? arrogant? something else? Cite passages from the essay to support your answer.
4. What is the EFFECT of *you* in Lopate's defense of himself for insisting on silence during a film's opening titles (para. 11): "But—you will say—it was only during the titles. *Only* the titles?...All right, I see I haven't convinced you about the significance of the title sequence...."
5. **OTHER METHODS.** This essay is partly process analysis and partly CAUSE AND EFFECT. What does Lopate think causes "audience chatter"?

QUESTIONS ON LANGUAGE

1. Lopate uses a number of words that may be unfamiliar to you. Consult your dictionary for definitions of psychopath, admonishing (para. 1); discomfit, susurration (2); lusty, derisive, riposte, pedagogically, gabbler, puritanical, temerity (3); machismo (4); asinine, censorious (5); preternaturally, luminescence, pathologically (7); prattlers (8); dyadic (9); somnambulism, oneiric, convivial, ambient (10); tantalizing, solicitations, leitmotifs (11); tête-à-tête (12); surmise (13); cinephile, swain, quixotic (14).
2. What does the vocabulary in this essay contribute to its tone?
3. ANALYZE the effect of the variations in tone and content within this sentence: "If my fellow moviegoers rejoice at a chainsaw dismemberment or at so-called 'street slime' being blown away in *Death Wish IX*, I may fear for their souls and their politics, but I do not fault them for improper audience behavior" (para. 12).
4. How would you describe Lopate's tone when he refers to a "mimicking shush" as a "witty riposte" (para. 3)?

SUGGESTIONS FOR WRITING

1. **JOURNAL WRITING.** Make a list of guilty pleasures or annoying activities that you engage in—perhaps correcting your friends when they mispronounce words, singing off-key with the radio, drinking milk from the carton, chewing your cuticles. Write down as many as you can think of in four or five minutes.
   FROM JOURNAL TO ESSAY. Lopate's step-by-step process analysis involves the reader in his motives and the struggles his actions cause him. Write an informative process analysis of your own about one of the activities you listed in your journal, stopping along the way to help readers understand your thought process.
2. Write a NARRATIVE about a conflict you had with a stranger in public. It could have resulted from talking in a theater, a traffic accident, a rude comment, an unfounded accusation, anything. Use plenty of concrete details to make the incident lively for readers.

3. **CRITICAL WRITING.** What can you INFER about Lopate as a person from his essay? Is he polite, rude, considerate, arrogant, thoughtful, brash, shy, outspoken? In an essay, use passages from "Confessions of a Shusher" to portray its author.
4. **CONNECTIONS.** Look at Lopate's essay together with Barbara Huttmann's "A Crime of Compassion" (p. 76). Both authors use the first person (*I*) and defend their actions to readers. Write a COMPARISON AND CONTRAST essay examining similarities and differences in the ways Lopate and Huttmann present their own ambivalence or confidence. What writing strategies does each employ to gain readers' sympathies?

PHILLIP LOPATE ON WRITING

In an interview with Richard E. Ziegfield of *Contemporary Authors*, Phillip Lopate discussed his aims as a writer, and his frustrations.

My style is not that kind of style that stands on its own shoulders and discovers something much larger and different through the alchemical[1] combination of words. I don't—I can't—create an...explosion of meaning beyond meaning. I don't want to fool people into thinking I know more than I know. I want to tell them, "This is all I know." Like a scientist: "This is my preliminary report."...

I have always started with the incredibly simple and humble idea that I wanted to write down reality as I experienced it. The deviations from reality that occur in my books have less to do with my Mozartian playing around and more to do with the problem of transferring from a three-dimensional to a two-dimensional medium. Just as in photographs, a photographer is faced with the problem of photographing something that is real, but having to transfer to a two-dimensional medium. In writing, something is always going to be lost.

FOR DISCUSSION

1. How does Lopate avoid "fool[ing] people into thinking I know more than I know"?
2. What does Lopate mean by "the problem of transferring from a three-dimensional to a two-dimensional medium"? When writing, have you also had his experience of losing something in the transfer from reality to the page?·

---

[1]Alchemy was a medieval scientific philosophy, one of whose aims was to turn base metals into gold. —EDS.

JESSICA MITFORD

Born in Batsford Mansion, England, in 1917, the daughter of Lord and Lady Redesdale, JESSICA MITFORD devoted much of her early life to defying her aristocratic upbringing. In her autobiography *Daughters and Rebels* (1960), she tells how she received a genteel schooling at home, then as a young woman moved to Loyalist Spain during the violent Spanish Civil War. Later, she emigrated to America, where for a time she worked in Miami as a bartender. She became one of her adopted country's most noted reporters: *Time* called her "Queen of the Muckrakers." Exposing with her typewriter what she regarded as corruption, abuse, and absurdity, Mitford wrote *The American Way of Death* (1963, revised as *The American Way of Death Revisited* in 1998), *Kind and Unusual Punishment: The Prison Business* (1973), and *The American Way of Birth* (1992). *Poison Penmanship* (1979) collects articles from *The Atlantic*, *Harper's*, and other magazines. *A Fine Old Conflict* (1976) is the second volume of Mitford's autobiography. And a novel, *Grace Had an English Heart* (1989), examines how the media transform ordinary people into celebrities. Jessica Mitford died in 1996.

Behind the Formaldehyde Curtain

The most famous (or infamous) thing Jessica Mitford wrote is *The American Way of Death*, a critique of the funeral industry. In this selection from the book, Mitford analyzes the twin processes of embalming and restoring a corpse, the practices she finds most objectionable. You may need a stable stomach to enjoy the selection, but in it you'll find a clear, painstaking process analysis, written with masterly style and outrageous wit. (For those who want to know, Mitford herself was cremated after her death.)

For a complementary view of cultural practices, read the essay following Mitford's, Horace Miner's "Body Ritual Among the Nacirema."

The drama begins to unfold with the arrival of the corpse at the   1
mortuary.

Alas, poor Yorick! How surprised he would be to see how his coun-   2
terpart of today is whisked off to a funeral parlor and is in short order sprayed, sliced, pierced, pickled, trussed, trimmed, creamed, waxed, painted, rouged, and neatly dressed—transformed from a common corpse into a Beautiful Memory Picture. This process is known in the trade as embalming and restorative art, and is so universally employed in the United States and Canada that the funeral director does it routinely, without consulting corpse or kin. He regards as eccentric those

few who are hardy enough to suggest that it might be dispensed with. Yet no law requires embalming, no religious doctrine commends it, nor is it dictated by considerations of health, sanitation, or even of personal daintiness. In no part of the world but in Northern America is it widely used. The purpose of embalming is to make the corpse presentable for viewing in a suitably costly container; and here too the funeral director routinely, without first consulting the family, prepares the body for public display.

Is all this legal? The processes to which a dead body may be subjected are after all to some extent circumscribed by law. In most states, for instance, the signature of next of kin must be obtained before an autopsy may be performed, before the deceased may be cremated, before the body may be turned over to a medical school for research purposes; or such provision must be made in the decedent's will. In the case of embalming, no such permission is required nor is it ever sought.[1] A textbook, *The Principles and Practices of Embalming,* comments on this: "There is some question regarding the legality of much that is done within the preparation room." The author points out that it would be most unusual for a responsible member of a bereaved family to instruct the mortician, in so many words, to "embalm" the body of a deceased relative. The very term *embalming* is so seldom used that the mortician must rely upon custom in the matter. The author concludes that unless the family specifies otherwise, the act of entrusting the body to the care of a funeral establishment carries with it an implied permission to go ahead and embalm.

Embalming is indeed a most extraordinary procedure, and one must wonder at the docility of Americans who each year pay hundreds of millions of dollars for its perpetuation, blissfully ignorant of what it is all about, what is done, how it is done. Not one in ten thousand has any idea of what actually takes place. Books on the subject are extremely hard to come by. They are not to be found in most libraries or bookshops.

In an era when huge television audiences watch surgical operations in the comfort of their living rooms, when, thanks to the animated cartoon, the geography of the digestive system has become familiar territory even to the nursery school set, in a land where the satisfaction of curiosity about almost all matters is a national pastime, the secrecy sur-

[1] Partly because of Mitford's attack, the Federal Trade Commission now requires the funeral industry to provide families with itemized price lists, including the price of embalming, to state that embalming is not required, and to obtain the family's consent to embalming before charging for it. Shortly before her death, however, Mitford observed that the FTC had "watered down" the regulations and "routinely ignored" consumer complaints about the funeral industry. — EDS.

rounding embalming can, surely, hardly be attributed to the inherent gruesomeness of the subject. Custom in this regard has within this century suffered a complete reversal. In the early days of American embalming, when it was performed in the home of the deceased, it was almost mandatory for some relative to stay by the embalmer's side and witness the procedure. Today, family members who might wish to be in attendance would certainly be dissuaded by the funeral director. All others, except apprentices, are excluded by law from the preparation room.

A close look at what does actually take place may explain in large   6
measure the undertaker's intractable reticence concerning a procedure that has become his major *raison d'être*. Is it possible he fears that public information about embalming might lead patrons to wonder if they really want this service? If the funeral men are loath to discuss the subject outside the trade, the reader may, understandably, be equally loath to go on reading at this point. For those who have the stomach for it, let us part the formaldehyde curtain....

The body is first laid out in the undertaker's morgue — or rather,   7
Mr. Jones is reposing in the preparation room — to be readied to bid the world farewell.

The preparation room in any of the better funeral establish-   8
ments has the tiled and sterile look of a surgery, and indeed the embalmer–restorative artist who does his chores there is beginning to adopt the term *dermasurgeon* (appropriately corrupted by some mortician-writers as "demi-surgeon") to describe his calling. His equipment, consisting of scalpels, scissors, augers, forceps, clamps, needles, pumps, tubes, bowls, and basins, is crudely imitative of the surgeon's, as is his technique, acquired in a nine- or twelve-month post-high-school course in an embalming school. He is supplied by an advanced chemical industry with a bewildering array of fluids, sprays, pastes, oils, powders, creams, to fix or soften tissue, shrink or distend it as needed, dry it here, restore the moisture there. There are cosmetics, waxes, and paints to fill and cover features, even plaster of Paris to replace entire limbs. There are ingenious aids to prop and stabilize the cadaver: a Vari-Pose Head Rest, the Edwards Arm and Hand Positioner, the Repose Block (to support the shoulders during the embalming), and the Throop Foot Positioner, which resembles an old-fashioned stocks.

Mr. John H. Eckels, president of the Eckels College of Mortuary   9
Science, thus describes the first part of the embalming procedure: "In the hands of a skilled practitioner, this work may be done in a comparatively short time and without mutilating the body other than by slight incision — so slight that it scarcely would cause serious inconvenience if made upon a living person. It is necessary to remove the blood, and doing this not only helps in the disinfecting, but removes the principal cause of disfigurements due to discoloration."

Another textbook discusses the all-important time element: "The   10
earlier this is done, the better, for every hour that elapses between
death and embalming will add to the problems and complications encountered...." Just how soon should one get going on the embalming?
The author tells us, "On the basis of such scanty information made
available to this profession through its rudimentary and haphazard system of technical research, we must conclude that the best results are to
be obtained if the subject is embalmed before life is completely extinct—that is, before cellular death has occurred. In the average case,
this would mean within an hour after somatic death." For those who
feel that there is something a little rudimentary, not to say haphazard,
about this advice, a comforting thought is offered by another writer.
Speaking of fears entertained in early days of premature burial, he
points out, "One of the effects of embalming by chemical injection,
however, has been to dispel fears of live burial." How true; once the
blood is removed, chances of live burial are indeed remote.

To return to Mr. Jones, the blood is drained out through the veins   11
and replaced by embalming fluid pumped in through the arteries. As
noted in *The Principles and Practices of Embalming,* "every operator has a
favorite injection and drainage point—a fact which becomes a handicap only if he fails or refuses to forsake his favorites when conditions demand it." Typical favorites are the carotid artery, femoral artery, jugular
vein, subclavian vein. There are various choices of embalming fluid. If
Flextone is used, it will produce a "mild, flexible rigidity. The skin re-
tains a velvety softness, the tissues are rubbery and pliable. Ideal for
women and children." It may be blended with B. and G. Products Company's Lyf-Lyk tint, which is guaranteed to reproduce "nature's own skin
texture...the velvety appearance of living tissue." Suntone comes in
three separate tints: Suntan; Special Cosmetic Tint, a pink shade "especially indicated for female subjects"; and Regular Cosmetic Tint, mod-
erately pink.

About three to six gallons of a dyed and perfumed solution of   12
formaldehyde, glycerin, borax, phenol, alcohol, and water is soon cir-
culating through Mr. Jones, whose mouth has been sewn together with
a "needle directed upward between the upper lip and gum and brought
out through the left nostril," with the corners raised slightly "for a more
pleasant expression." If he should be bucktoothed, his teeth are
cleaned with Bon Ami and coated with colorless nail polish. His eyes,
meanwhile, are closed with flesh-tinted eye caps and eye cement.

The next step is to have at Mr. Jones with a thing called a trocar.   13
This is a long, hollow needle attached to a tube. It is jabbed into the
abdomen, poked around the entrails and chest cavity, the contents of
which are pumped out and replaced with "cavity fluid." This done, and
the hole in the abdomen sewn up, Mr. Jones's face is heavily creamed

(to protect the skin from burns which may be caused by leakage of the chemicals), and he is covered with a sheet and left unmolested for a while. But not for long—there is more, much more, in store for him. He has been embalmed, but not yet restored, and the best time to start the restorative work is eight to ten hours after embalming, when the tissues have become firm and dry.

The object of all this attention to the corpse, it must be remem- 14 bered, is to make it presentable for viewing in an attitude of healthy repose. "Our customs require the presentation of our dead in the semblance of normality... unmarred by the ravages of illness, disease, or mutilation," says Mr. J. Sheridan Mayer in his *Restorative Art*. This is rather a large order since few people die in the full bloom of health, unravaged by illness and unmarked by some disfigurement. The funeral industry is equal to the challenge: "In some cases the gruesome appearance of a mutilated or disease-ridden subject may be quite discouraging. The task of restoration may seem impossible and shake the confidence of the embalmer. This is the time for intestinal fortitude and determination. Once the formative work is begun and affected tissues are cleaned or removed, all doubts of success vanish. It is surprising and gratifying to discover the results which may be obtained."

The embalmer, having allowed an appropriate interval to elapse, 15 returns to the attack, but now he brings into play the skill and equipment of sculptor and cosmetician. Is a hand missing? Casting one in plaster of Paris is a simple matter. "For replacement purposes, only a cast of the back of the hand is necessary; this is within the ability of the average operator and is quite adequate." If a lip or two, a nose, or an ear should be missing, the embalmer has at hand a variety of restorative waxes with which to model replacements. Pores and skin texture are simulated by stippling with a little brush, and over this cosmetics are laid on. Head off? Decapitation cases are rather routinely handled. Ragged edges are trimmed, and head joined to torso with a series of splints, wires, and sutures. It is a good idea to have a little something at the neck—a scarf or a high collar—when time for viewing comes. Swollen mouth? Cut out tissue as needed from inside the lips. If too much is removed, the surface contour can easily be restored by padding with cotton. Swollen necks and cheeks are reduced by removing tissue through vertical incisions made down each side of the neck. "When the deceased is casketed, the pillow will hide the suture incisions... as an extra precaution against leakage, the suture may be painted with liquid sealer."

The opposite condition is more likely to present itself—that of 16 emaciation. His hypodermic syringe now loaded with massage cream, the embalmer seeks out and fills the hollowed and sunken areas by injection. In this procedure the backs of the hands and fingers and the under-chin area should not be neglected.

Positioning the lips is a problem that recurrently challenges the in-   17
genuity of the embalmer. Closed too tightly, they tend to give a stern,
even disapproving expression. Ideally, embalmers feel, the lips should
give the impression of being ever so slightly parted, the upper lip protruding slightly for a more youthful appearance. This takes some engineering, however, as the lips tend to drift apart. Lip drift can sometimes
be remedied by pushing one or two straight pins through the inner margin of the lower lip and then inserting them between the two front upper teeth. If Mr. Jones happens to have no teeth, the pins can just as
easily be anchored in his Armstrong Face Former and Denture Re-
placer. Another method to maintain lip closure is to dislocate the
lower jaw, which is then held in its new position by a wire run through
holes which have been drilled through the upper and lower jaws at the
midline. As the French are fond of saying, *il faut souffrir pour être belle.*[2]

If Mr. Jones has died of jaundice, the embalming fluid will very   18
likely turn him green. Does this deter the embalmer? Not if he has intestinal fortitude. Masking pastes and cosmetics are heavily laid on,
burial garments and casket interiors are color-correlated with particular
care, and Jones is displayed beneath rose-colored lights. Friends will say
"How *well* he looks." Death by carbon monoxide, on the other hand,
can be rather a good thing from the embalmer's viewpoint: "One advantage is the fact that this type of discoloration is an exaggerated form
of a natural pink coloration." This is nice because the healthy glow is
already present and needs but little attention.

The patching and filling completed, Mr. Jones is now shaved,   19
washed, and dressed. Cream-based cosmetic, available in pink, flesh,
suntan, brunette, and blond, is applied to his hands and face, his hair is
shampooed and combed (and, in the case of Mrs. Jones, set), his hands
manicured. For the horny-handed son of toil special care must be
taken; cream should be applied to remove ingrained grime, and the
nails cleaned. "If he were not in the habit of having them manicured in
life, trimming and shaping is advised for better appearance—never
questioned by kin."

Jones is now ready for casketing (this is the present participle of the   20
verb "to casket"). In this operation his right shoulder should be depressed
slightly "to turn the body a bit to the right and soften the appearance of
lying flat on the back." Positioning the hands is a matter of importance,
and special rubber positioning blocks may be used. The hands should be
cupped slightly for a more lifelike, relaxed appearance. Proper placement
of the body requires a delicate sense of balance. It should lie as high as
possible in the casket, yet not so high that the lid, when lowered, will hit

---

[2] You have to suffer to be beautiful. —EDS.

the nose. On the other hand, we are cautioned, placing the body too low "creates the impression that the body is in a box."

Jones is next wheeled into the appointed slumber room where a   21
few last touches may be added—his favorite pipe placed in his hand or, if he was a great reader, a book propped into position. (In the case of little Master Jones a Teddy bear may be clutched.) Here he will hold open house for a few days, visiting hours 10 A.M. to 9 P.M.

All now being in readiness, the funeral director calls a staff confer-   22
ence to make sure that each assistant knows his precise duties. Mr. Wilber Kriege writes: "This makes your staff feel that they are a part of the team, with a definite assignment that must be properly carried out if the whole plan is to succeed. You never heard of a football coach who failed to talk to his entire team before they go on the field. They have drilled on the plays they are to execute for hours and days, and yet the successful coach knows the importance of making even the bench-warming third-string substitute feel that he is important if the game is to be won." The winning of *this* game is predicated upon glass-smooth handling of the logistics. The funeral director has notified the pallbear-ers whose names were furnished by the family, has arranged for the presence of clergyman, organist, and soloist, has provided transporta-tion for everybody, has organized and listed the flowers sent by friends. In *Psychology of Funeral Service* Mr. Edward A. Martin points out, "He may not always do as much as the family thinks he is doing, but it is his helpful guidance that they appreciate in knowing they are proceeding as they should.... The important thing is how well his services can be used to make the family believe they are giving unlimited expression to their own sentiment."

The religious service may be held in a church or in the chapel of   23
the funeral home; the funeral director vastly prefers the latter arrange-ment, for not only is it more convenient for him but it affords him the opportunity to show off his beautiful facilities to the gathered mourn-ers. After the clergyman has had his say, the mourners queue up to file past the casket for a last look at the deceased. The family is *never* asked whether they want an open-casket ceremony; in the absence of their instruction to the contrary, this is taken for granted. Consequently well over 90 per cent of all American funerals feature the open casket—a custom unknown in other parts of the world. Foreigners are astonished by it. An English woman living in San Francisco described her reaction in a letter to the writer:

> I myself have attended only one funeral here—that of an elderly fellow worker of mine. After the service I could not understand why everyone was walking towards the coffin (sorry, I mean casket), but thought I had better follow the crowd. It shook me rigid to get there and find the casket open and poor old Oscar lying there in his brown

tweed suit, wearing a suntan makeup and just the wrong shade of lip-stick. If I had not been extremely fond of the old boy, I have a hor-rible feeling that I might have giggled. Then and there I decided that I could never face another American funeral—even dead.

The casket (which has been resting throughout the service on a   24 Classic Beauty Ultra Metal Casket Bier) is now transferred by a hy-draulically operated device called Porto-Lift to a balloon-tired, Glide Easy casket carriage which will wheel it to yet another conveyance, the Cadillac Funeral Coach. This may be lavender, cream, light green—anything but black. Interiors, of course, are color-correlated, "for the man who cannot stop short of perfection."

At graveside, the casket is lowered into the earth. This office, once   25 the prerogative of friends of the deceased, is now performed by a patented mechanical lowering device. A "Lifetime Green" artificial grass mat is at the ready to conceal the sere earth, and overhead, to conceal the sky, is a portable Steril Chapel Tent ("resists the intense heat and humidity of summer and the terrific storms of winter...avail-able in Silver Gray, Rose, or Evergreen"). Now is the time for the ritual scattering of earth over the coffin, as the solemn words "earth to earth, ashes to ashes, dust to dust" are pronounced by the officiating cleric. This can today be accomplished "with a mere flick of the wrist with the Gordon Leak-Proof Earth Dispenser. No grasping of a handful of dirt, no soiled fingers. Simple, dignified, beautiful, reverent! The modern way!" The Gordon Earth Dispenser (at $5) is of nickel-plated brass construction. It is not only "attractive to the eye and long wearing"; it is also "one of the 'tools' for building better public relations" if pre-sented as "an appropriate non-commercial gift" to the clergyman. It is shaped something like a saltshaker.

Untouched by human hand, the coffin and the earth are now united.   26

It is in the function of directing the participants through this maze of   27 gadgetry that the funeral director has assigned to himself his relatively new role of "grief therapist." He has relieved the family of every detail, he has revamped the corpse to look like a living doll, he has arranged for it to nap for a few days in a slumber room, he has put on a well-oiled per-formance in which the concept of *death* has played no part whatsoever—unless it was inconsiderately mentioned by the clergyman who con-ducted the religious service. He has done everything in his power to make the funeral a real pleasure for everybody concerned. He and his team have given their all to score an upset victory over death.

QUESTIONS ON MEANING

1. What was your emotional response to this essay? Can you analyze your feelings?
2. To what does the author attribute the secrecy that surrounds the process of embalming?
3. What, according to Mitford, is the mortician's intent? What common obstacles to fulfilling it must be surmounted?
4. What do you understand from Mitford's remark in paragraph 10, on dispelling fears of live burial: "How true; once the blood is removed, chances of live burial are indeed remote"?
5. Do you find any implied PURPOSE in this essay? Does Mitford seem primarily out to rake muck, or does she offer any positive suggestions to Americans?

QUESTIONS ON WRITING STRATEGY

1. What is Mitford's TONE? In her opening two paragraphs, exactly what shows her attitude toward her subject?
2. Why do you think Mitford goes into so much grisly detail in analyzing the processes of embalming and restoration? How does the detail serve her purpose?
3. What is the EFFECT of calling the body Mr. Jones (or Master Jones)?
4. Paragraph by paragraph, what TRANSITIONS does the author employ? (If you need a refresher on this point, see the discussion of transitions on p. 697.)
5. Into what stages has the author divided the embalming process?
6. To whom does Mitford address her process analysis? How do you know she isn't writing for an AUDIENCE of professional morticians?
7. Consider one of the quotations from the journals and textbooks of professionals and explain how it serves the author's general purpose.
8. **OTHER METHODS.** In paragraph 8, Mitford uses CLASSIFICATION in listing the embalmer's equipment and supplies. What groups does she identify, and why does she bother sorting the items at all?

QUESTIONS ON LANGUAGE

1. Explain the ALLUSION to Yorick in paragraph 2.
2. What IRONY do you find in this statement in paragraph 7: "The body is first laid out in the undertaker's morgue—or rather, Mr. Jones is reposing in the preparation room"? Pick out any other words or phrases in the essay that seem ironic. Comment especially on those you find in the essay's last two sentences.
3. Why is it useful to Mitford's purpose that she cites the brand names of morticians' equipment and supplies (the Edwards Arm and Hand Positioner, Lyf-Lyk tint)? List all the brand names in the essay that are memorable.

4. Define the following words or terms: counterpart (para. 2); circumscribed, autopsy, cremated, decedent, bereaved (3); docility, perpetuation (4); inherent, mandatory (5); intractable, reticence, *raison d'être*, formaldehyde (6); "dermasurgeon," augers, forceps, distend, stocks (8); somatic (10); carotid artery, femoral artery, jugular vein, subclavian vein, pliable (11); glycerin, borax, phenol, bucktoothed (12); trocar, entrails (13); stippling, sutures (15); emaciation (16); jaundice (18); predicated (22); queue (23); hydraulically (24); cleric (25); therapist (27).

SUGGESTIONS FOR WRITING

1. **JOURNAL WRITING.** Presumably, morticians embalm and restore corpses, and survivors support the work, because the practices are thought to ease the shock of death. Now that you know what goes on behind the scenes, how do you feel about a loved one's undergoing these procedures?

   FROM JOURNAL TO ESSAY. Drawing on your personal response to Mitford's process analysis, write a brief essay that ARGUES either for or against embalming and restoration. Consider the purposes served by these practices, both for the mortician and for the dead person's relatives and friends, as well as their costs and effects.

2. Search the Web or consult the *Readers' Guide to Periodical Literature* for information about the recent phenomenon of quick-freezing the dead. Set forth this process, including its hoped-for result of reviving the corpses in the far future.

3. ANALYZE some other process whose operations may not be familiar to everyone. (Have you ever held a job, or helped out in a family business, that has taken you behind the scenes? How is fast food prepared? How are cars serviced? How is a baby sat? How is a house constructed?) Detail it step by step, including transitions to clarify the steps.

4. **CRITICAL WRITING.** In attacking the funeral industry, Mitford also, implicitly, attacks the people who pay for and comply with the industry's attitudes and practices. What ASSUMPTIONS does Mitford seem to make about how we ought to deal with death and the dead? (Consider, for instance, her statements about the "docility of Americans,...blissfully ignorant" [para. 4] and the funeral director's making "the funeral a real pleasure for everybody concerned" [27].) Write an essay in which you interpret Mitford's assumptions and agree or disagree with them, based on your own reading and experience. If you like, defend the ritual of the funeral, or the mortician's profession, against Mitford's attack.

5. **CONNECTIONS.** Both Jessica Mitford and the author of the following essay, Horace Miner, use process analysis to reveal something about human behavior. How are the two authors' intentions the same or different? What does each want to accomplish with her or his analysis? Use EXAMPLES from both essays to support your claims.

JESSICA MITFORD ON WRITING

"Choice of subject is of cardinal importance," declared Jessica Mitford in *Poison Penmanship*. "One does by far one's best work when besotted by and absorbed in the matter at hand." After *The American Way of Death* was published, Mitford received hundreds of letters suggesting alleged rackets that ought to be exposed, and to her surprise, an overwhelming majority of these letters complained about defective and overpriced hearing aids. But Mitford never wrote a book blasting the hearing aid industry. "Somehow, although there may well be need for such an exposé, I could not warm up to hearing aids as a subject for the kind of thorough, intensive, long-range research that would be needed to do an effective job." She once taught a course at Yale in muckraking, with each student choosing a subject to investigate. "Those who tackled hot issues on campus, such as violations of academic freedom or failure to implement affirmative-action hiring policies, turned in some excellent work; but the lad who decided to investigate 'waste in the Yale dining halls' was predictably unable to make much of this trivial topic." (The editors interject: We aren't sure that the topic is necessarily trivial, but obviously not everyone would burn to write about it!)

The hardest problem Mitford faced in writing *The American Way of Death*, she recalled, was doing her factual, step-by-step account of the embalming process. She felt "determined to describe it in all its revolting details, but how to make this subject palatable to the reader?" Her solution was to cast the whole process analysis in the official JARGON of the mortuary industry, drawing on lists of taboo words and their EUPHEMISMS (or acceptable synonyms), as published in the trade journal *Casket & Sunnyside*: "Mr., Mrs., Miss Blank, not corpse or body; preparation room, not morgue; reposing room, not laying-out room...." The story of Mr. Jones thus took shape, and Mitford's use of jargon, she found, added macabre humor to the proceedings.

FOR DISCUSSION

1. What seem to be Mitford's criteria for an effective essay or book?
2. What is muckraking? Why do you suppose anyone would want to do it?

HORACE MINER

An anthropologist and teacher, HORACE MINER specialized in the cultures of Africa. He was born in 1912 in Saint Paul, Minnesota, and received degrees from the University of Kentucky (B.A., 1933) and the University of Chicago (M.A., 1935; Ph.D., 1937). Miner taught anthropology and sociology at Wayne State University and for many years at the University of Michigan, where he was also a researcher in the Museum of Anthropology. He retired from Michigan in 1980. Based on his field research, Miner wrote numerous journal articles and books, including *St. Denis: A French-Canadian Parish* (1939), *Culture and Agriculture* (1953), *Oasis and Casbah: Algerian Culture and Personality in Change* (1960), and *The City in Modern Africa* (1967). Miner died in 1993.

Body Ritual Among the Nacirema

As an anthropologist, Miner was adept at *ethnography,* studying and reporting on specific cultures. Miner's specialty was African cultures, but here he turned his ethnographer's eye on a North American culture that may seem familiar to you. Like Jessica Mitford in the previous selection, Miner uses process analysis to reveal and also to poke fun at customs. His essay first appeared in the journal *American Anthropologist* in June 1956 and has often been reprinted.

The anthropologist has become so familiar with the diversity of ways in which different peoples behave in similar situations that he is not apt to be surprised by even the most exotic customs. In fact, if all of the logically possible combinations of behavior have not been found somewhere in the world, he is apt to suspect that they must be present in some yet undescribed tribe. This point has, in fact, been expressed with respect to clan organization by Murdock.[1] In this light, the magical beliefs and practices of the Nacirema present such unusual aspects that it seems desirable to describe them as an example of the extremes to which human behavior can go. 1

Professor Linton first brought the ritual of the Nacirema to the attention of anthropologists twenty years ago, but the culture of this people is still very poorly understood. They are a North American group living in the territory between the Canadian Cree, the Yaqui and Tarahumare of Mexico, and the Carib and Arawak of the Antilles. 2

---

[1] George Peter Murdock (1897–1985) was an American anthropologist who attempted to identify and classify the cultures of the world. —EDS.

Little is known of their origin, although tradition states that they came from the east....

Nacirema culture is characterized by a highly developed market economy which has evolved in a rich natural habitat. While much of the people's time is devoted to economic pursuits, a large part of the fruits of these labors and a considerable portion of the day are spent in ritual activity. The focus of this activity is the human body, the appearance and health of which loom as a dominant concern in the ethos of the people. While such a concern is certainly not unusual, its ceremonial aspects and associated philosophy are unique. 3

The fundamental belief underlying the whole system appears to be that the human body is ugly and that its natural tendency is to debility and disease. Incarcerated in such a body, man's only hope is to avert these characteristics through the use of the powerful influences of ritual and ceremony. Every household has one or more shrines devoted to this purpose. The more powerful individuals in the society have several shrines in their houses and, in fact, the opulence of a house is often referred to in terms of the number of such ritual centers it possesses. Most houses are of wattle and daub construction, but the shrine rooms of the more wealthy are walled with stone. Poorer families imitate the rich by applying pottery plaques to their shrine walls. 4

While each family has at least one such shrine, the rituals associated with it are not family ceremonies but are private and secret. The rites are normally only discussed with children, and then only during the period when they are being initiated into these mysteries. I was able, however, to establish sufficient rapport with the natives to examine these shrines and to have the rituals described to me. 5

The focal point of the shrine is a box or chest which is built into the wall. In this chest are kept the many charms and magical potions without which no native believes he could live. These preparations are secured from a variety of specialized practitioners. The most powerful of these are the medicine men, whose assistance must be rewarded with substantial gifts. However, the medicine men do not provide the curative potions for their clients, but decide what the ingredients should be and then write them down in an ancient and secret language. This writing is understood only by the medicine men and by the herbalists who, for another gift, provide the required charm. 6

The charm is not disposed of after it has served its purpose, but is placed in the charm-box of the household shrine. As these magical materials are specific for certain ills, and the real or imagined maladies of the people are many, the charm-box is usually full to overflowing. The magical packets are so numerous that people forget what their purposes were and fear to use them again. While the natives are very vague on this point, we can only assume that the idea in retaining all the old 7 magical materials is that their presence in the charm-box, before which the body rituals are conducted, will in some way protect the worshipper.

Beneath the charm-box is a small font. Each day every member of   8
the family, in succession, enters the shrine room, bows his head before the charm-box, mingles different sorts of holy water in the font, and proceeds with a brief rite of ablution. The holy waters are secured from the Water Temple of the community, where the priests conduct elaborate ceremonies to make the liquid ritually pure.

In the hierarchy of magical practitioners, and below the medicine   9
men in prestige, are specialists whose designation is best translated "holy-mouth-men." The Nacirema have an almost pathological horror of and fascination with the mouth, the condition of which is believed to have a supernatural influence on all social relationships. Were it not for the rituals of the mouth, they believe that their teeth would fall out, their gums bleed, their jaws shrink, their friends desert them, and their lovers reject them. They also believe that a strong relationship exists between oral and moral characteristics. For example, there is a ritual ablution of the mouth for children which is supposed to improve their moral fiber.

The daily body ritual performed by everyone includes a mouth-rite.   10
Despite the fact that these people are so punctilious about care of the mouth, this rite involves a practice which strikes the uninitiated stranger as revolting. It was reported to me that the ritual consists of inserting a small bundle of hog hairs into the mouth, along with certain magical powders, and then moving the bundle in a highly formalized series of gestures.

In addition to the private mouth-rite, the people seek out a holy-   11
mouth-man once or twice a year. These practitioners have an impressive set of paraphernalia, consisting of a variety of augers, awls, probes, and prods. The use of these objects in the exorcism of the evils of the mouth involves almost unbelievable ritual torture of the client. The holy-mouth-man opens the client's mouth and, using the above mentioned tools, enlarges any holes which decay may have created in the teeth. Magical materials are put into these holes. If there are not naturally occurring holes in the teeth, large sections of one or more teeth are gouged out so that the supernatural substance can be applied. In the client's view, the purpose of these ministrations is to arrest decay and to draw friends. The extremely sacred and traditional character of the rite is evident in the fact that the natives return to the holy-mouth-men year after year, despite the fact that their teeth continue to decay.

It is to be hoped that, when a thorough study of the Nacirema is   12
made, there will be careful inquiry into the personality structure of these people. One has but to watch the gleam in the eye of a holy-mouth-man, as he jabs an awl into an exposed nerve, to suspect that a

certain amount of sadism is involved. If this can be established, a very interesting pattern emerges, for most of the population shows definite masochistic tendencies. It was to these that Professor Linton referred in discussing a distinctive part of the daily body ritual which is performed only by men. This part of the rite involves scraping and lacerating the surface of the face with a sharp instrument. Special women's rites are performed only four times during each lunar month, but what they lack in frequency is made up in barbarity. As part of this ceremony, women bake their heads in small ovens for about an hour. The theoretically interesting point is that what seems to be a preponderantly masochistic people have developed sadistic specialists.

The medicine men have an imposing temple, or *latipso*, in every   13
community of any size. The more elaborate ceremonies required to treat very sick patients can only be performed at this temple. These ceremonies involve not only the thaumaturge but a permanent group of vestal maidens who move sedately about the temple chambers in distinctive costume and headdress.

The *latipso* ceremonies are so harsh that it is phenomenal that a fair   14
proportion of the really sick natives who enter the temple ever recover. Small children whose indoctrination is still incomplete have been known to resist attempts to take them to the temple because "that is where you go to die." Despite this fact, sick adults are not only willing but eager to undergo the protracted ritual purification, if they can afford to do so. No matter how ill the supplicant or how grave the emergency, the guardians of many temples will not admit a client if he cannot give a rich gift to the custodian. Even after one has gained admission and survived the ceremonies, the guardians will not permit the neophyte to leave until he makes still another gift.

The supplicant entering the temple is first stripped of all his or her   15
clothes. In everyday life the Nacirema avoids exposure of his body and its natural functions. Bathing and excretory acts are performed only in the secrecy of the household shrine, where they are ritualized as part of the body-rites. Psychological shock results from the fact that body secrecy is suddenly lost upon entry into the *latipso*. A man, whose own wife has never seen him in an excretory act, suddenly finds himself naked and assisted by a vestal maiden while he performs his natural functions into a sacred vessel. This sort of ceremonial treatment is necessitated by the fact that the excreta are used by a diviner to ascertain the course and nature of the client's sickness. Female clients, on the other hand, find their naked bodies are subjected to the scrutiny, manipulation and prodding of the medicine men.

Few supplicants in the temple are well enough to do anything but   16
lie on their hard beds. The daily ceremonies, like the rites of the holy-mouth-men, involve discomfort and torture. With ritual precision, the

vestals awaken their miserable charges each dawn and roll them about on their beds of pain while performing ablutions, in the formal movements of which the maidens are highly trained. At other times they insert magic wands in the supplicant's mouth or force him to eat substances which are supposed to be healing. From time to time the medicine men come to their clients and jab magically treated needles into their flesh. The fact that these temple ceremonies may not cure, and may even kill the neophyte, in no way decreases the people's faith in the medicine men.

There remains one other kind of practitioner, known as a "listener." This witchdoctor has the power to exorcise the devils that lodge in the heads of people who have been bewitched. The Nacirema believe that parents bewitch their own children. Mothers are particularly suspected of putting a curse on children while teaching them the secret body rituals. The counter-magic of the witchdoctor is unusual in its lack of ritual. The patient simply tells the "listener" all his troubles and fears, beginning with the earliest difficulties he can remember. The memory displayed by the Nacirema in these exorcism sessions is truly remarkable. It is not uncommon for the patient to bemoan the rejection he felt upon being weaned as a babe, and a few individuals even see their troubles going back to the traumatic effects of their own birth.   17

In conclusion, mention must be made of certain practices which have their base in native esthetics but which depend upon the pervasive aversion to the natural body and its functions. There are ritual fasts to make fat people thin and ceremonial feasts to make thin people fat. Still other rites are used to make women's breasts larger if they are small, and smaller if they are large. General dissatisfaction with breast shape is symbolized in the fact that the ideal form is virtually outside the range of human variation. A few women afflicted with almost inhuman hyper-mammary development are so idolized that they make a handsome living by simply going from village to village and permitting the natives to stare at them for a fee.   18

Reference has already been made to the fact that excretory functions are ritualized, routinized, and relegated to secrecy. Natural reproductive functions are similarly distorted. Intercourse is taboo as a topic and scheduled as an act. Efforts are made to avoid pregnancy by the use of magical materials or by limiting intercourse to certain phases of the moon. Conception is actually very infrequent. When pregnant, women dress so as to hide their condition. Parturition takes place in secret, without friends or relatives to assist, and the majority of women do not nurse their infants.   19

Our review of the ritual life of the Nacirema has certainly shown them to be a magic-ridden people. It is hard to understand how they have managed to exist so long under the burdens which they have im-   20 posed upon themselves. But even such exotic customs as these take on real meaning when they are viewed with the insight provided by Malinowski[2] when he wrote:

> Looking from far and above, from our high places of safety in the developed civilization, it is easy to see all the crudity and irrelevance of magic. But without its power and guidance early man could not have mastered his practical difficulties as he has done, nor could man have advanced to the higher stages of civilization.

QUESTIONS ON MEANING

1. At what point did you realize what Miner's true subject is? What tipped you off? Did you see the big hint in the spelling of *Nacirema*?
2. One of Miner's purposes is clearly to amuse readers through social SATIRE. But what other purposes does he seem to have?
3. What stereotype does Miner exploit for its humor at the end of paragraph 6?
4. At the beginning and end of the essay, Miner refers to the Nacirema as having "magical beliefs and practices" (para. 1) and as being "magic-ridden" (20). What kinds of cultures are usually described in this way? Why does Miner use such terms to describe the Nacirema?

QUESTIONS ON WRITING STRATEGY

1. Miner explains several processes under the umbrella of "body rituals." What are these processes in Americanese — that is, in the words we commonly use for them?
2. What is the EFFECT of Miner's opening paragraph? What do the academic TONE and mention of the anthropologist Murdock's work accomplish?
3. This essay originally appeared in *American Anthropologist*, a serious academic journal. In what ways are anthropologists the perfect AUDIENCE for Miner's humor? How do you respond differently to this essay than you think an anthropologist would?
4. This essay was first published more than four decades ago. In what ways does it seem dated? What parts of it still seem fresh?
5. **OTHER METHODS.** Miner's humor involves DEFINITIONS of things that ordinarily need no defining: For instance, he refers to a toothbrush as a "small bundle of hog hairs" (para. 10). Find other examples of bizarre definitions of ordinary things. Other than humor, what is the effect of such definitions?

---

[2] Bronislaw Malinowski (1884–1942) was a Polish-born British anthropologist who saw customs in terms of their functions in a culture. — EDS.

QUESTIONS ON LANGUAGE

1. Why do you think Miner chose the name "Nacirema" for his subjects? What associations does this name call up for you?
2. Explain the IRONY of the last paragraph.
3. Make sure you know the definitions of the following words, including some that are specific to the discipline of anthropology: ethos (para. 3); debility, incarcerated, opulence, wattle and daub (4); curative (6); font, ablution (8); hierarchy (9); punctilious (10); augers, awls, gouged, ministrations (11); sadism, masochistic, lacerating, preponderantly (12); thaumaturge (13); indoctrination, supplicant, neophyte (14); excretory, vestal, vessel, excreta, diviner (15); esthetics (18); parturition (19).

SUGGESTIONS FOR WRITING

1. **JOURNAL WRITING.** Think about all the little "rituals" you perform regularly: doing the dishes, walking the dog, going to the movies. Write out all the steps of two or three of these routines, in chronological order, in as much detail as you can.

   FROM JOURNAL TO ESSAY. Imagine that you are an observer from another planet reporting back to your authorities on Earth customs. Write them a letter describing the processes you have detailed in your journal. Remember, you don't understand the language of these earthlings and have no names for the processes you are writing about.
2. Miner satirizes our society's obsession with physical appearance, our hypochondria, our shame over our bodies, our overdependence on psychoanalysis—all in 1956. Evaluate the relevance of this essay today, considering where the concerns with our bodies have brought us. Do you think we are better or worse off, physically and mentally, than we were a hundred or even forty years ago? What's better? What's worse? Be specific.
3. **CRITICAL WRITING.** Anthropologists have sometimes been criticized for turning the people they study into weird and mysterious "others." How does Miner manage to criticize anthropology while working within it, on its own terms, and using its own language and methodology? Focus in particular on the implications of the last paragraph.
4. **CONNECTIONS.** Read or reread Jessica Mitford's "Behind the Formaldehyde Curtain" (p. 244). Taken together, what do Miner's and Mitford's essays say about the importance of the body in our culture? Write an essay either defending or criticizing Americans' obsession with the way they look.

ADDITIONAL WRITING TOPICS

Process Analysis

1. Write a *directive* process analysis (a "how-to" essay) in which, drawing on your own knowledge, you instruct someone in doing or making something. Divide the process into steps, and be sure to detail each step thoroughly. Some possible subjects (any of which may be modified or narrowed):

   How to find games (or another kind of software) on the Internet
   How to enlist people's confidence
   How to bake bread
   How to meditate
   How to teach a child to swim
   How to select a science fiction novel
   How to drive a car in snow or rain
   How to prepare yourself to take an intelligence test
   How to compose a photograph
   How to judge cattle
   How to buy a used motorcycle
   How to enjoy an opera
   How to organize your own rock group
   How to eat an artichoke
   How to groom a horse
   How to bellydance
   How to make a movie or videotape
   How to build (or fly) a kite
   How to start weight training
   How to aid a person who is choking
   How to behave on a first date
   How to get your own way
   How to kick a habit
   How to lose weight
   How to win at poker
   How to make an effective protest or complaint

   Or, if you don't like any of those topics, what else do you know that others might care to learn from you?

2. Step by step, working in chronological order, write a careful *informative* analysis of any one of the following processes. (This is not to be a "how-to" essay, but an essay that explains how something works or happens.) Make use of DESCRIPTION wherever necessary, and be sure to include frequent TRANSITIONS. If one of these topics gives you a better idea for a paper, go with your own subject.

   How a student is processed during orientation or registration
   How the student newspaper gets published
   How a particular Web search engine works

How a professional umpire (or an acupuncturist, or some other professional) does his or her job

How an amplifier (or other stereo component) works

How an air conditioner (or other household appliance) works

How birds teach their young (or some other process in the natural world: how sharks feed, how a snake swallows an egg, how the human liver works)

How police control crowds

How people usually make up their minds when shopping for new cars (or new clothes)

3. Write a directive process analysis in which you use a light TONE. Although you need not take your subject in deadly earnest, your humor will probably be effective only if you take the method of process analysis seriously. Make clear each stage of the process and explain it in sufficient detail. Possible topics:

How to get through the month of November (or March)

How to flunk out of college swiftly and efficiently

How to outwit a pinball machine

How to choose a mate

How to go broke

How to sell something that nobody wants

6

DIVISION OR ANALYSIS
Slicing into Parts

THE METHOD

A chemist working for a soft-drink company is asked to improve on a competitor's product, Orange Quench. (In Chap. 5, the same chemist was working on a different part of the same problem.) To do the job, the chemist first has to figure out what's in the drink. She smells the stuff and tastes it. Then she tests a sample chemically to discover the actual ingredients: water, corn syrup, citric acid, sodium benzoate, coloring. Methodically, the chemist has performed DIVISION or ANALYSIS: She has separated the beverage into its components. Orange Quench stands revealed, understood, ready to be bettered.

Division or analysis (the terms are interchangeable) is a key skill in learning and in life. It is an instrument allowing you to slice a large and complicated subject into smaller parts that you can grasp and relate to one another. With analysis you comprehend—and communicate— the structure of things. And when it works, you find in the parts an idea or conclusion about the subject that makes it clearer, truer, more comprehensive, or more vivid than before you started.

If you have worked with the previous two chapters, you have already used division or analysis in explaining a process (Chap. 5) and in comparing and contrasting (Chap. 4). To make a better Orange Quench (a process), the chemist might prepare a recipe that divides the process into separate steps or actions ("First, boil a gallon of water..."). When the batch was done, she might taste-test the two drinks, analyzing and then comparing their orange flavor, sweetness, and acidity. As you'll see in following chapters, too, division or analysis figures in all the other methods of developing ideas, for it is basic to any concerted thought, explanation, or evaluation.

Kinds of Division or Analysis

Although division or analysis always works the same way—separating a whole, singular subject into its elements, slicing it into parts—the method can be more or less difficult depending on how unfamiliar, complex, and abstract the subject is. Obviously, it's going to be much easier to analyze a chicken (wings, legs, thighs...) than a poem by T. S. Eliot (this image, that allusion...), easier to analyze the structure of a small business than that of a multinational conglomerate. Just about any subject *can* by analyzed and will be the clearer for it. In "I Want a Wife," an essay in this chapter, Judy Brady divides the role of a wife into its various functions or services. In an essay called "Teacher" from his book *Pot Shots at Poetry* (1980), Robert Francis divides the knowledge of poetry he imparted to his class into six pie sections. The first slice is what he told his students that they knew already.

> The second slice is what I told them that they could have found out just as well or better from books. What, for instance, is a sestina?
> The third slice is what I told them that they refused to accept. I could see it on their faces, and later I saw the evidence in their writing.
> The fourth slice is what I told them that they were willing to accept and may have thought they accepted but couldn't accept since they couldn't fully understand. This also I saw in their faces and in their work. Here, no doubt, I was mostly to blame.
> The fifth slice is what I told them that they discounted as whimsy or something simply to fill up time. After all, I was being paid to talk.
> The sixth slice is what I didn't tell them, for I didn't try to tell them all I knew. Deliberately I kept back something—a few professional secrets, a magic formula or two.

There are always multiple ways to divide or analyze a subject, just as there are many ways to slice a pie. Francis could have divided his knowledge of poetry into knowledge of rhyme, knowledge of meter, knowledge of imagery, and so forth—basically following the components of a poem. In other words, the outcome of an analysis depends on the rule or principle used to do the slicing. This fact accounts for some of the differences among academic disciplines: A psychologist, say, may look at the individual person primarily as a bundle of drives and needs, whereas a sociologist may emphasize the individual's roles in society. Even within disciplines, different factions analyze differently, using different principles of division or analysis. Some psychologists are interested mainly in thought, others mainly in behavior; some psychologists focus mainly on emotional development, others mainly on moral development.

Analysis and Critical Thinking

Analysis plays a fundamental role in CRITICAL THINKING, READING, and WRITING, topics discussed in this book's introduction (pp. 15–17). In fact, *analysis* and *criticism* are deeply related: The first comes from a Greek word meaning "to undo," the second from a Greek word meaning "to separate."

Critical thinking, reading, and writing go beneath the surface of the object, word, image, or whatever the subject is. When you work critically, you divide the subject into its elements, INFER the buried meanings and ASSUMPTIONS that define its essence, and SYNTHESIZE the parts into a new whole. Say a campaign brochure quotes a candidate as favoring "reasonable government expenditures on reasonable highway projects." The candidate will support new roads, right? Wrong. As a critical reader of the brochure, you quickly sense something fishy in the use (twice) of "reasonable." As an informed reader, you know (or find out) that the candidate has consistently opposed new roads, so the chances of her finding a highway project "reasonable" are slim. At the same time, her stand has been unpopular, so of course she wants to seem "reasonable" on the issue. Read critically, then, a campaign statement that seems to offer mild support for highways is actually a slippery evasion of any such commitment.

Analysis (a convenient term for the overlapping operations of analysis, inference, and synthesis) is very useful for exposing such evasiveness, but that isn't its only function. It may also help you understand a short story, perceive the importance of a sociological case study, or form a response to an environmental impact report.

If you've read this far in this book, you've already done quite a bit of analytical/critical thinking as you've read and analyzed the essays. In this chapter, three of the essays themselves—by Armin A. Brott, Barbara Ehrenreich, and Emily Prager—show critical thinking about artifacts of popular culture.

THE PROCESS

Subjects and Theses

Keep an eye out for writing assignments requiring division or analysis — in college and work, they won't be few or hard to find. They will probably include the word *analyze* or a word implying analysis such as *evaluate, examine, interpret, discuss,* or *criticize.* Any time you spot such a term, you know your job is to separate the subject into its elements, to infer their meanings, to explore the relations among them, and to draw a conclusion about the subject.

Almost any coherent entity — object, person, place, concept — is a fit subject for analysis *if* the analysis will add to the subject's meaning or significance. Little is deadlier than the rote analytical exercise that leaves the parts neatly dissected and the subject comatose on the page. As a writer, you have to animate the subject, and that means finding your interest. What about your subject seems curious? What's appealing? or mysterious? or awful? And what will be your PURPOSE in writing about the subject: Do you simply want to explain it, or do you want to argue for or against it?

Such questions can help you find the principle or framework you will use to divide the subject into parts. (As we mentioned before, there's more than one way to slice most subjects.) Say you're contemplating a hunk of bronze in the park. Why do you like the sculpture, or why don't you? What elements of its creation and physical form make it art? What is the point of such public art? What does this sculpture do to this park, or vice versa? Any of these questions could suggest a slant on the subject, a framework for analysis, and a purpose for writing, getting your analysis moving.

Finding your principle of analysis will lead you to your essay's THESIS as well — the main point you want to make about your subject. Expressed in a THESIS SENTENCE, this idea will help keep you focused and help your readers see your subject as a whole rather than a bundle of parts. Your essay on the bronze in the park, for instance, might have one of these thesis sentences:

> Though it may not be obvious at first, this bronze sculpture represents the city dweller's relationship with nature.

> Like much public art today, this bronze sculpture seems chiefly intended to make people ignore it.

> The huge bronze sculpture in the middle of McBean Park demonstrates that so-called public art does little for the public interest.

After any of these thesis sentences, you would go on to identify and explain the relevant elements of the sculpture: in the first case, maybe the sculpture's hints of plants and water and connection; in the second case, maybe the sculpture's blandness, lack of a clear message, and lack of artistic rigor; in the third case, maybe the sculpture's cost, uselessness, and ugliness. (Notice that each approach reveals something different in the sculpture, with very different results.)

In developing an essay by analysis, having an outline at your elbow can be a help. You don't want to overlook any parts or elements that should be included in your framework. (You needn't mention every feature in your final essay or give them all equal treatment, but any omissions or variations should be conscious.) And you want to use your framework consistently, not switching carelessly (and confusingly) from, say, the form of the sculpture to the cost of public art. In writing her brief essay "I Want a Wife," Judy Brady must have needed an outline to work out carefully the different activities of a wife, so that she covered them all and clearly distinguished them.

Evidence

Making a valid analysis is chiefly a matter of giving your subject thought, but for the result to seem useful and convincing to your readers, it will have to refer to the concrete world. The method requires not only cogitation, but open eyes and a willingness to provide EVIDENCE. The nature of the evidence will depend entirely on what you are analyzing—physical details for a sculpture, quotations for a poem, financial data for a business case study, statistics for a psychology case study, and so forth. The idea is to supply enough evidence to justify and support your particular slant on the subject.

A final caution: It's possible to get carried away with one's own analysis, to become so enamored of the details that the subject itself becomes dim or distorted. You can avoid this danger by keeping the subject literally in front of you as you work (or at least imagining it vividly) and by maintaining an outline. It often helps to reassemble your subject at the end of the essay: That gives you a chance to place your subject in a larger context, speculate on its influence, or affirm its significance. By the end of the essay, your subject must be a coherent whole truly represented by your analysis, not twisted, diminished, inflated, or obliterated. The reader should be intrigued by your subject, yes, but also able to recognize it on the street.

CHECKLIST FOR REVISING A DIVISION OR ANALYSIS

✔ **PRINCIPLE OF ANALYSIS.** What is your particular slant on your subject, the rule or principle you have used to divide your subject into its elements? Where do you tell readers what it is?

✔ **COMPLETENESS.** Have you considered all the subject's elements required by your principle of analysis?

✔ **CONSISTENCY.** Have you applied your principle of analysis consistently, viewing your subject from a definite slant?

✔ **EVIDENCE.** Is your division or analysis well supported with concrete details, quotations, data, or statistics, as appropriate?

✔ **SIGNIFICANCE.** Why should readers care about your analysis? Have you told them something about your subject that wasn't obvious on its surface?

✔ **TRUTH TO SUBJECT.** Is your analysis faithful to the subject, not distorted, exaggerated, deflated?

DIVISION OR ANALYSIS IN A PARAGRAPH: TWO ILLUSTRATIONS

Using Division or Analysis to Write About Television

The following paragraph analyzes the components of a television laugh track, the recorded chorus that tells us when a comedy is funny. Though written especially for *The Bedford Reader*, not as part of an essay, this brief analysis could itself be one component in an examination of TV comedy. Or, with the related paragraph on pages 315–16, illustrating CLASSIFICATION, it could contribute to an essay on, say, how the producers of TV comedies manipulate viewers.

Most television comedies, even some that boast live audiences, rely on the laugh machine to fill too-quiet moments on the soundtrack. The effect of a canned laugh comes from its four overlapping elements. The first is style, from titter to belly laugh. The second is intensity, the volume, ranging from mild to medium to earsplitting. The third ingredient is duration, the length of the laugh, whether quick, medium, or extended. And finally, there's the number of laughers, from a lone giggler to a roaring throng. According to rumor (for its exact workings are a secret), the machine contains a bank of thirty-two tapes. Furiously working keys and tromping pedals, the operator plays the tapes singly or in combination to blend the four ingredients, as a maestro weaves a symphony out of brass, woodwinds, percussion, and strings.

Principle of analysis: elements creating the effect of a canned laugh

1. Style

2. Intensity

3. Duration

4. Number

Details and examples clarify elements

Using Division or Analysis
in an Academic Discipline

The next paragraph appeared first in a scholarly journal and then in a textbook on medical ethics. The author discusses four possible models for the doctor-patient relationship, ending with the one detailed below. The careful analysis supports his preference for this model over the others.

The model of social relationship which fits these conditions [of realistic equality between patient and doctor] is that of the contract or covenant. The notion of contract should not be loaded with legalistic implications, but taken in its more symbolic form as in the traditional religious or marriage "contract" or "covenant." Here two individuals or groups are interacting in a way where there are obligations and expected benefits for both parties. The obligations and benefits are limited in scope, though, even if they are expressed in somewhat vague terms. The basic norms of freedom, dignity, truth-telling, promise-keeping, and justice are essential to a contractual relationship. The premise is trust and confidence even though it is recognized that there is not a full mutuality of interests. Social sanctions institutionalize and stand behind the relationship, in case there is a violation of the contract, but for the most part the assumption is that there will be a faithful fulfillment of the obligations.

— Robert M. Veatch,
"Models for Medicine in a Revolutionary Age"

Principle of analysis: elements of a contract between doctor and patient

1. Obligations and benefits for both parties

2. Obligations and benefits limited

3. Freedom, dignity, and other norms

4. Trust and confidence

5. Support of social sanctions (meaning that society upholds the relationship)

DIVISION OR ANALYSIS
ELSEWHERE IN *THE BEDFORD READER*

Division or analysis is so fundamental to thinking and writing that it might make more sense to list the essays where the method does *not* make a notable appearance. It underpins all the illustrations of comparison and contrast (Chap. 4), process analysis (Chap. 5), classification (Chap. 7), cause and effect (Chap. 8), and definition (Chap. 9). (These chapters' selections are not listed below.) In addition, the writers of the following essays make extensive use of the method.

PART ONE

Ralph Ellison, "On Being the Target of Discrimination"
Brad Manning, "Arm Wrestling with My Father"
Itabari Njeri, "When Morpheus Held Him"
Merrill Markoe, "Bob the Dog (1974–1998)"
Barbara Lazear Ascher, "On Compassion"
Anna Quindlen, "Homeless"

Brent Staples, "Black Men and Public Space"
H. L. Mencken, "The Penalty of Death"
Esther Dyson, "Cyberspace for All"
Heidi Pollock, "Welcome to Cyberbia"
William F. Buckley, Jr., "Why Don't We Complain?"
Chitra Divakaruni, "Live Free and Starve"
Curtis Chang, "Streets of Gold: The Myth of the Model Minority"

PART TWO

Joan Didion, "In Bed"
Stephen Jay Gould, "Sex, Drugs, Disasters, and the Extinction of
    Dinosaurs"
George Orwell, "Shooting an Elephant"
Richard Rodriguez, "Aria: A Memoir of a Bilingual Childhood"
Jonathan Swift, "A Modest Proposal"
Alice Walker, "In Search of Our Mothers' Gardens"
E. B. White, "Once More to the Lake"
Tom Wolfe, "Pornoviolence"

CASE STUDY
Using Division or Analysis

During her sophomore year at Boston University, Cortney Keim applied for transfer to Pomona College in California. As part of its application, Pomona requested a statement about Keim, her academic goals, and her reasons for wanting to transfer.

Keim tried several approaches to her statement, struggling to present herself as serious and unique. In one draft, she followed the cue of Pomona's request—providing a brief autobiography, a list of goals, and an explanation for choosing Pomona—but that version seemed obvious and dull. In the end, Keim settled on the fresher approach you see here. She first divides herself into parts and then details each one, showing its relevance to Pomona.

Application Statement of Cortney Keim

In applying for transfer to Pomona, I seek to develop the three main components of myself: actor, student, and explorer.

Pomona's strong theater curriculum will give me the background I need to embark on a career in acting. As unstable a career as it may prove to be, acting is my fire. I have always liked entertaining others (in high school, I was voted class clown), even if it involves making a display of myself. As I have had the chance to act in varied plays over the last few years, I have also found that interpreting an author's text allows me paradoxically to express myself and to lose myself. And, yes, I have loved the appreciation of an audience, the sighs or laughs in the right places, the applause at the end.

Yet acting is not all. In high school and for two years at Boston University, I have also relished the liberal arts courses I've taken and the writing I've done in those courses. The courses have introduced me to worlds of information and ideas I wouldn't have known otherwise, and the writing has let me make up my own text, my own version of reality. Liberal arts courses are hard work, harder in many ways than acting, but the work pays off. Pomona's respected liberal arts curriculum will help me become the rounded, thoughtful, disciplined student I hope to be for the rest of my life.

It's also significant to me that Pomona is a small school in California, so different from the huge university I attend now and so far from the East Coast city where I have lived all my life. The explorer in me needs a new horizon. At Pomona I anticipate the opportunity to be more involved in the activities of the college and to get to know a wider variety of people. In southern California, I expect to become familiar with a new climate, geography, and ecosystem.

Pomona promises to help me fulfill my needs to act, learn, and explore. In return, I promise to contribute whatever I can to the college and the larger community.

JUDY BRADY

Judy Brady, born in 1937 in San Francisco, where she now lives, earned a B.F.A. in painting from the University of Iowa in 1962. Drawn into political action by her work in the feminist movement, she went to Cuba in 1973, where she studied class relationships as a way of understanding change in a society. "I am not a 'writer,'" Brady declares, "but really am a disenfranchised (and fired) housewife, now secretary." Despite her disclaimer, Brady has published articles occasionally—on union organizing and education in Cuba, among other topics—and she writes a regular column for the Women's Cancer Research Center. In 1991 she published *1 in 3: Women with Cancer Confront an Epidemic*, an anthology of writings by women. Asked by an interviewer if she had won any awards lately, Brady responded, "People who do what I do don't get awards."

I Want a Wife

"I Want a Wife" first appeared in the Spring 1972 issue of *Ms.* magazine and has been reprinted often. The essay is one of the best-known manifestos in popular feminist writing. In it, Brady trenchantly divides the work of a wife into its multiple duties and functions, leading to an inescapable conclusion. If you find that Brady stereotypes men, read the essay after hers, Armin A. Brott's "Not All Men Are Sly Foxes," for a different view.

1   I belong to that classification of people known as wives. I am A Wife. And, not altogether incidentally, I am a mother.

2   Not too long ago a male friend of mine appeared on the scene fresh from a recent divorce. He had one child, who is, of course, with his ex-wife. He is looking for another wife. As I thought about him while I was ironing one evening, it suddenly occurred to me that I, too, would like to have a wife. Why do I want a wife?

3   I would like to go back to school so that I can become economically independent, support myself, and, if need be, support those dependent upon me. I want a wife who will work and send me to school. And while I am going to school I want a wife to take care of my children. I want a wife to keep track of the children's doctor and dentist appointments. And to keep track of mine, too. I want a wife to make sure my children eat properly and are kept clean. I want a wife who will wash the children's clothes and keep them mended. I want a wife who is a good nurturant attendant to my children, who arranges for their schooling, makes sure that they have an adequate social life with their peers, takes them to the park, the zoo, etc. I want a wife who takes care

of the children when they are sick, a wife who arranges to be around when the children need special care, because, of course, I cannot miss classes at school. My wife must arrange to lose time at work and not lose the job. It may mean a small cut in my wife's income from time to time, but I guess I can tolerate that. Needless to say, my wife will arrange and pay for the care of the children while my wife is working.

I want a wife who will take care of my physical needs. I want a wife who will keep my house clean. A wife who will pick up after my children, a wife who will pick up after me. I want a wife who will keep my clothes clean, ironed, mended, replaced when need be, and who will see to it that my personal things are kept in their proper place so that I can find what I need the minute I need it. I want a wife who cooks the meals, a wife who is a *good* cook. I want a wife who will plan the menus, do the necessary grocery shopping, prepare the meals, serve them pleasantly, and then do the cleaning up while I do my studying. I want a wife who will care for me when I am sick and sympathize with my pain and loss of time from school. I want a wife to go along when our family takes vacation so that someone can continue to care for me and my children when I need a rest and change of scene.

I want a wife who will not bother me with rambling complaints about a wife's duties. But I want a wife who will listen to me when I feel the need to explain a rather difficult point I have come across in my course of studies. And I want a wife who will type my papers for me when I have written them.

I want a wife who will take care of the details of my social life. When my wife and I are invited out by my friends, I want a wife who will take care of the babysitting arrangements. When I meet people at school that I like and want to entertain, I want a wife who will have the house clean, will prepare a special meal, serve it to me and my friends, and not interrupt when I talk about things that interest me and my friends. I want a wife who will have arranged that the children are fed and ready for bed before my guests arrive so that the children do not bother us. I want a wife who takes care of the needs of my guests so that they feel comfortable, who makes sure that they have an ashtray, that they are passed the hors d'oeuvres, that they are offered a second helping of the food, that their wine glasses are replenished when necessary, that their coffee is served to them as they like it. And I want a wife who knows that sometimes I need a night out by myself.

I want a wife who is sensitive to my sexual needs, a wife who makes love passionately and eagerly when I feel like it, a wife who makes sure that I am satisfied. And, of course, I want a wife who will not demand sexual attention when I am not in the mood for it. I want a wife who assumes the complete responsibility for birth control, because I do not want more children. I want a wife who will remain sexually faithful to me so that I do not have to clutter up my intellectual life with jealousies. And I want a wife who understands that *my* sexual needs may entail more than strict adherence to monogamy. I must, after all, be able to relate to people as fully as possible.

If, by chance, I find another person more suitable as a wife than the   8
wife I already have, I want the liberty to replace my present wife with another one. Naturally, I will expect a fresh, new life; my wife will take the children and be solely responsible for them so that I am left free.

When I am through with school and have a job, I want my wife to   9
quit working and remain at home so that my wife can more fully and completely take care of a wife's duties.

My God, who *wouldn't* want a wife?   10

QUESTIONS ON MEANING

1. Sum up the duties of a wife as Brady sees them.
2. To what inequities in the roles traditionally assigned to men and to women does "I Want a Wife" call attention?
3. What is the THESIS of this essay? Is it stated or implied?
4. Is Brady unfair to men?

QUESTIONS ON WRITING STRATEGY

1. What EFFECT does Brady obtain with the title "I Want a Wife"?
2. What do the first two paragraphs accomplish?
3. What is the TONE of this essay?
4. How do you explain the fact that Brady never uses the pronoun *she* to refer to a wife? Does this make her prose unnecessarily awkward?
5. What principle does Brady use to analyze the role of wife? Can you think of some other principle for analyzing the job?
6. Knowing that this essay was first published in *Ms.* magazine in 1972, what can you guess about its intended readers? Does "I Want a Wife" strike a college AUDIENCE today as revolutionary?
7. **OTHER METHODS.** Although she mainly divides or analyzes the role of wife, Brady also uses CLASSIFICATION to sort the many duties and responsibilities into manageable groups. What are the groups?

QUESTIONS ON LANGUAGE

1. What is achieved by the author's frequent repetition of the phrase "I want a wife"?
2. Be sure you know how to define the following words as Brady uses them: nurturant (para. 3); replenished (6); adherence, monogamy (7).

3. In general, how would you describe the DICTION of this essay? How well does it suit the essay's intended audience?

SUGGESTIONS FOR WRITING

1. **JOURNAL WRITING.** Brady addresses the traditional obligations of a wife and mother. What are the parallel obligations of a husband and father? **FROM JOURNAL TO ESSAY.** Write an essay titled "I Want a Husband" in which, using examples as Brady does, you enumerate the roles traditionally assigned to men in our society.
2. Imagining that you want to employ someone to do a specific job, divide the task into its duties and functions. Then, guided by your analysis, write an accurate job description in essay form.
3. **CRITICAL WRITING.** In an essay, SUMMARIZE Brady's view as you understand it and then EVALUATE her essay. Consider: Is Brady fair? (If not, is unfairness justified?) Is the essay relevant today? (If not, what has changed?) Provide specific EVIDENCE from your experience, observation, and reading.
4. **CONNECTIONS.** Both "I Want a Wife" and Armin A. Brott's "Not All Men Are Sly Foxes" (next page) challenge traditional ideas about how men and women are supposed to divide the labor in a marriage. However, Brady's STYLE is fast-paced and her tone is sarcastic, while Brott is more methodical and earnest. Which method of addressing these issues do you find more effective? Why? Write an essay that COMPARES AND CONTRASTS the essays' tones, styles, POINTS OF VIEW, and OBJECTIVE versus SUBJECTIVE language. What conclusions can you draw about the connection between the writers' strategies and their messages?

ARMIN A. BROTT

Armin A. Brott is a freelance writer living in San Francisco. Born in 1958, he received a B.A. in Russian from San Francisco State University and an M.B.A. that he calls "less useful than the degree in Russian" before embarking on a career in marketing. He turned to writing when his first child was born because he "wanted to be an active, involved father." Since that time he has contributed to the *New York Times Magazine*, the *Washington Post*, *Reader's Digest*, *Family Circle*, the *Saturday Evening Post*, *Playboy*, and other magazines. He treats issues that affect men: education, health, and especially fatherhood. His books include *The Expectant Father* (1995, with Jennifer Ash), *The New Father* (1997), *A Dad's Guide to the Toddler Years* (1998), *The Single Father* (1999), and *Throwaway Dads* (1999).

Not All Men Are Sly Foxes

In this essay from a 1992 *Newsweek* magazine, Brott offers a different view of men from that taken by Judy Brady in the previous essay. While acknowledging that women and men are not yet equal in child care, Brott holds that children's books are hardly helping. He uses analysis to show that the Sly Fox remains much more common than the Caring Dad.

If you thought your child's bookshelves were finally free of openly (and not so openly) discriminatory materials, you'd better check again. In recent years groups of concerned parents have persuaded textbook publishers to portray more accurately the roles that women and minorities play in shaping our country's history and culture. *Little Black Sambo* has all but disappeared from library and bookstore shelves; feminist fairy tales by such authors as Jack Zipes have, in many homes, replaced the more traditional (and obviously sexist) fairy tales. Richard Scarry, one of the most popular children's writers, has reissued new versions of some of his classics; now female animals are pictured doing the same jobs as male animals. Even the terminology has changed: Males and females are referred to as mail "carriers" or "firefighters."

There is, however, one very large group whose portrayal continues to follow the same stereotypical lines as always: fathers. The evolution of children's literature didn't end with *Goodnight Moon* and *Charlotte's Web*. My local public library, for example, previews 203 new children's picture books (for the under-five set) each *month*. Many of these books make a very conscious effort to take women characters out of the kitchen and the nursery and give them professional jobs and responsibilities.

Despite this shift, mothers are by and large still shown as the pri-   3
mary caregivers and, more important, as the primary nurturers of their
children. Men in these books—if they're shown at all—still come
home late after work and participate in the child rearing by bouncing
baby around for five minutes before putting the child to bed.

In one of my two-year-old daughter's favorite books, *Mother Goose*   4
and the Sly Fox, "retold" by Chris Conover, a single mother (Mother
Goose) of seven tiny goslings is pitted against (and naturally outwits)
the sly Fox. Fox, a neglectful and presumably unemployed single father,
lives with his filthy, hungry pups in a grimy hovel littered with the
bones of their previous meals. Mother Goose, a successful entrepreneur
with a thriving lace business, still finds time to serve her goslings homemade soup in pretty porcelain cups. The story is funny and the illustrations marvelous, but the unwritten message is that women take better
care of their kids and men have nothing else to do but hunt down and
kill innocent, law-abiding geese.

The majority of other children's classics perpetuate the same nega-   5
tive stereotypes of fathers. Once in a great while, people complain
about *Babar*'s colonialist slant (little jungle-dweller finds happiness in
the big city and brings civilization—and fine clothes—to his backward village). But I've never heard anyone ask why, after his mother is
killed by the evil hunter, Babar is automatically an "orphan." Why can
he find comfort only in the arms of another female? Why do Arthur's
and Celeste's mothers come alone to the city to fetch their children?
Don't the fathers care? Do they even have fathers? I need my answers
ready for when my daughter asks.

I recently spent an entire day on the children's floor of the local li-   6
brary trying to find out whether these same negative stereotypes are
found in the more recent classics-to-be. The librarian gave me a list of
the twenty most popular contemporary picture books and I read every
one of them. Of the twenty, seven don't mention a parent at all. Of the
remaining thirteen, four portray fathers as much less loving and caring
than mothers. In *Little Gorilla*, we are told that the little gorilla's
"mother loves him" and we see Mama gorilla giving her little one a
warm hug. On the next page we're also told that his "father loves him,"
but in the illustration, father and son aren't even touching. Six of the
remaining nine books mention or portray mothers as the only parent,
and only three of the twenty have what could be considered "equal"
treatment of mothers and fathers.

The same negative stereotypes also show up in literature aimed at   7
the *parents* of small children. In *What to Expect the First Year*, the authors answer almost every question the parents of a newborn or toddler
could have in the first year of their child's life. They are meticulous in

alternating between references to boys and girls. At the same time, they refer almost exclusively to "mother" or "mommy." Men, and their feelings about parenting, are relegated to a nine-page chapter just before the recipe section.

Unfortunately, it's still true that, in our society, women do the bulk   8
of the child care, and that thanks to men abandoning their families, there are too many single mothers out there. Nevertheless, to say that portraying fathers as unnurturing or completely absent is simply "a reflection of reality" is unacceptable. If children's literature only reflected reality, it would be like prime-time TV and we'd have books filled with child abusers, wife beaters and criminals.

Young children believe what they hear—especially from a parent   9
figure. And since, for the first few years of a child's life, adults select the reading material, children's literature should be held to a high standard. Ignoring men who share equally in raising their children, and continuing to show nothing but part-time or no-time fathers is only going to create yet another generation of men who have been told since boyhood—albeit subtly—that mothers are the truer parents and that fathers play, at best, a secondary role in the home. We've taken major steps to root out discrimination in what our children read. Let's finish the job.

QUESTIONS ON MEANING

1. What is the THESIS of Brott's essay? Where is it stated succinctly?
2. What does Brott ASSUME about his AUDIENCE in this essay? To what extent do you fit his assumptions?
3. Brott points out a difference between the illustration of the little gorilla with his mother and the one of him with his father (para. 6). Why is this difference significant?
4. What is the EFFECT of Brott's concluding sentences: "We've taken major steps to root out discrimination in what our children read. Let's finish the job"?

QUESTIONS ON WRITING STRATEGY

1. What principle of analysis does Brott use in examining the children's books? What elements does he perceive in these books?
2. What purpose does paragraph 7, with its reference to books for parents, serve in this essay about children's books?
3. **OTHER METHODS.** In paragraph 4, Brott provides vivid DESCRIPTION of Mother Goose's and Sly Fox's homes to show the differences between the two parents. What concrete details help explain these differences?

QUESTIONS ON LANGUAGE

1. What is the difference between "caregivers" and "nurturers" as Brott uses the words in paragraph 3?
2. How would you analyze Brott's TONE? Give specific words and sentences that you think contribute to the tone.
3. If some of the following words are unfamiliar, look them up in a dictionary: discriminatory (para. 1); stereotypical, evolution (2); goslings, neglectful, hovel, entrepreneur, porcelain (4); perpetuate, colonialist (5); meticulous, exclusively, relegated (7); albeit, subtly (9).

QUESTIONS FOR WRITING

1. **JOURNAL WRITING.** Do you remember being read to as a child—either at home or at school? Does a particular book stand out in your memory? What made this book come alive so that you still remember it today— the words, the illustrations, the story?
   FROM JOURNAL TO ESSAY. Write a brief essay that explores the messages sent by one of your childhood books. Did the book contain positive role models? negative ones? moral messages? values that you now embrace or reject? Did you learn anything in particular from this book? Based on your recollections, come to your own conclusions about what's appropriate or not in children's books.
2. Write an essay that analyzes another type of writing by examining its elements. You may choose any kind of writing that's familiar to you: news article, sports article, mystery, romance, science fiction, biography, and so on. Be sure to make your principle of analysis clear to your readers.
3. **CRITICAL WRITING.** "If children's literature only reflected reality," Brott claims, "it would be like prime-time TV and we'd have books filled with child abusers, wife beaters and criminals" (para. 8). However, Brott also suggests that "reality" contains a significant number of responsible, loving fathers. Does the claim about "reality" being "like prime-time TV" detract from Brott's argument on behalf of good fathers? Write an essay in which you explain how (or whether) Brott resolves this contradiction in his essay. It will probably be helpful to DEFINE clearly what *reality* means in this context.
4. **CONNECTIONS.** Look over Judy Brady's "I Want a Wife" (p. 275) and make a list of her implied complaints about the traditional roles of a wife. Now make a list of the responsibilities that Brott implies a good father is happy to take on. How could Brott's essay be viewed as a sort of response or solution to some of the problems Brady raises? Write an essay explaining the changes in traditional gender roles suggested by "I Want a Wife" and "Not All Men Are Sly Foxes" together.

BARBARA EHRENREICH

BARBARA EHRENREICH was born in 1941 in Butte, Montana. After she graduated from Reed College, she took her Ph.D. at Rockefeller University, then taught at the State University of New York in Old Westbury in the early 1970s. She has contributed to many periodicals, among them *The New Republic, Mother Jones, Ms., Time*, and, most recently, *The Progressive*, for which she writes a column. Ehrenreich's range encompasses investigative journalism, popular history, and astute social and political commentary. Her books include *Complaints and Disorders: The Sexual Politics of Sickness* (1973); *For Her Own Good: 150 Years of the Experts' Advice to Women* (with Deirdre English, 1978); *The Hearts of Men: American Dreams and the Flight from Commitment* (1983); *Fear of Falling: The Inner Life of the Middle Class* (1989); *The Worst Years of Our Lives* (1990) and *The Snarling Citizen* (1995), both collections of essays; *Kipper's Game* (1993), a novel; and *Blood Rites: Origins and History of the Passions of War* (1997).

In Defense of Talk Shows

Their popularity may have peaked, but talk shows still prevail on daytime television and still raise people's dander. In this typically lively essay, Ehrenreich uses analysis for cultural criticism, maintaining that talk shows have their merits. This essay first appeared in *Time* magazine in December 1995.

Up until now, the targets of Bill (*The Book of Virtues*) Bennett's[1] crusades have at least been plausible sources of evil. But the latest victim of his wrath—TV talk shows of the *Sally Jessy Raphael* variety— are in a whole different category from drugs and gangsta rap. As anyone who actually watches them knows, the talk shows are one of the most excruciatingly moralistic forums the culture has to offer. Disturbing and sometimes disgusting, yes, but their very business is to preach the middle-class virtues of responsibility, reason and self-control.

Take the case of Susan, recently featured on *Montel Williams* as an example of a woman being stalked by her ex-boyfriend. Turns out Susan is also stalking the boyfriend and—here's the sexual frisson—has slept with him only days ago. In fact Susan is neck deep in trouble without any help from the boyfriend: She's serving a yearlong stretch

---

[1] William Bennett (born 1943) has held posts in Republican administrations and urged moral and cultural reform. In *The Book of Virtues* (1993), Bennett collects the fables, folklore, and stories that he sees as the root of American values.—EDS.

of home incarceration for assaulting another woman, and home is the tiny trailer she shares with her nine-year-old daughter.

But no one is applauding this life spun out of control. Montel   3 scolds Susan roundly for neglecting her daughter and failing to confront her role in the mutual stalking. A therapist lectures her about this unhealthy "obsessive kind of love." The studio audience jeers at her every evasion. By the end Susan has lost her cocky charm and dissolved into tears of shame.

The plot is always the same. People with problems—"husband says   4 she looks like a cow," "pressured to lose her virginity or else," "mate wants more sex than I do"—are introduced to rational methods of problem solving. People with moral failings—"boy crazy," "dresses like a tramp," "a hundred sex partners"—are introduced to external standards of morality. The preaching—delivered alternately by the studio audience, the host and the ever present guest therapist—is relentless. "This is wrong to do this," Sally Jessy tells a cheating husband. "Feel bad?" Geraldo asks the girl who stole her best friend's boyfriend. "Any sense of remorse?" The expectation is that the sinner, so hectored, will see her way to reform. And indeed, a Sally Jessy update found "boy crazy," who'd been a guest only weeks ago, now dressed in schoolgirlish plaid and claiming her "attitude [had] changed"—thanks to the rough-and-ready therapy dispensed on the show.

All right, the subjects are often lurid and even bizarre. But there's   5 no part of the entertainment spectacle, from *Hard Copy* to *Jade*, that doesn't trade in the lurid and bizarre. At least in the talk shows, the moral is always loud and clear: Respect yourself, listen to others, stop beating on your wife. In fact it's hard to see how *The Bill Bennett Show*, if there were to be such a thing, could deliver a more pointed sermon. Or would he prefer to see the feckless Susan, for example, tarred and feathered by the studio audience instead of being merely booed and shamed?

There *is* something morally repulsive about the talks, but it's not   6 anything Bennett or his co-crusader Senator Joseph Lieberman has seen fit to mention. Watch for a few hours, and you get the claustrophobic sense of lives that have never seen the light of some external judgment, of people who have never before been listened to, and certainly never been taken seriously if they were. "What kind of people would let themselves be humiliated like this?" is often asked, sniffily, by the shows' detractors. And the answer, for the most part, is people who are so needy—of social support, of education, of material resources and self-esteem—that they mistake being the center of attention for being actually loved and respected.

What the talks are about, in large part, is poverty and the distor-   7 tions it visits on the human spirit. You'll never find investment bankers bickering on *Rolonda,* or the host of *Gabrielle* recommending therapy to sobbing professors. With few exceptions the guests are drawn from trailer parks and tenements, from bleak streets and narrow, crowded rooms. Listen long enough, and you hear references to unpaid bills, to welfare, to twelve-hour workdays and double shifts. And this is the real shame of the talks: that they take lives bent out of shape by poverty and hold them up as entertaining exhibits. An announcement appearing between segments of *Montel* says it all: The show is looking for "pregnant women who sell their bodies to make ends meet."

This is class exploitation, pure and simple. What next — "homeless   8 people so hungry they eat their own scabs"? Or would the next step be to pay people outright to submit to public humiliation? For $50 would you confess to adultery in your wife's presence? For $500 would you reveal your thirteen-year-old's girlish secrets on *Ricki Lake*? If you were poor enough, you might.

It is easy enough for those who can afford spacious homes and private therapy to sneer at their financial inferiors and label their pathetic   9 moments of stardom vulgar. But if I had a talk show, it would feature a whole different cast of characters and category of crimes than you'll ever find on the talks: "CEOs[2] who rake in millions while their employees get downsized" would be an obvious theme, along with "Senators who voted for welfare and Medicaid cuts" — and, if he'll agree to appear, "well-fed Republicans who dithered about talk shows while trailer-park residents slipped into madness and despair."

QUESTIONS ON MEANING

1. Ehrenreich's essay takes exception to Bill Bennett's criticism of talk shows. In your own words, what is Ehrenreich's THESIS?
2. What does Ehrenreich say is the role of a talk show's studio audience?
3. According to this essay, what are a talk show's main methods of "helping" the people who participate as panelists?
4. Why does Ehrenreich think talk shows are "morally repulsive" (paras. 6–8)?

QUESTIONS ON WRITING STRATEGY

1. What are the four parts of talk shows that Ehrenreich identifies in her analysis?
2. Does Ehrenreich seem to assume that her readers are also watchers of talk shows? What EVIDENCE supports your answer?

---

[2] Chief Executive Officers, the heads of corporations. — EDS.

3. What TONE does Ehrenreich use in paragraph 8? How does this tone reflect the criticisms she is making?

4. **OTHER METHODS.** In her CONCLUSION, Ehrenreich offers alternative talk show topics. What is the point of this COMPARISON AND CONTRAST with real shows? Do you find this conclusion effective?

QUESTIONS ON LANGUAGE

1. How do Ehrenreich's descriptions of the talk show as "lurid and even bizarre" and as an "entertainment spectacle" (para. 5) contribute to her analysis of these shows?

2. Ehrenreich calls the "therapy" on talk shows "rough-and-ready" (para. 4). What are the CONNOTATIONS of this expression?

3. Why does Ehrenreich pose this RHETORICAL QUESTION in paragraph 5: "Or would [Bennett] prefer to see the feckless Susan, for example, tarred and feathered by the studio audience instead of being merely booed and shamed?"

4. Look up the definitions if any of the following words are unfamiliar to you: plausible, wrath, excruciatingly, moralistic, forums (para. 1); frisson, incarceration (2); roundly, jeers, evasion (3); hectored (4); feckless (5); claustrophobic, detractors (6); tenements (7); exploitation (8); vulgar, dithered (9).

SUGGESTIONS FOR WRITING

1. **JOURNAL WRITING.** If you have never watched a talk show, you may want to sample a few programs. Once you are familiar with the shows' format and content, write your reactions to them in your journal.
   FROM JOURNAL TO ESSAY. Using one episode of a talk show as an EXAMPLE, write an essay analyzing the role of the show's "stars." Do you agree with Ehrenreich that the show exploits its participants? Why, or why not?

2. Write an essay that analyzes another kind of television show—perhaps a sports event, a game show, a true-crime program, or a news program. How do the elements of the show come together to send a specific message or achieve certain goals?

3. **CRITICAL WRITING.** Throughout this essay, Ehrenreich uses a number of religious metaphors to help explain what goes on during talk shows. Locate some of these metaphors. (See "Figures of speech" in Useful Terms if you need help.) In light of the arguments against talk shows made by William Bennett and others, why do you think Ehrenreich uses such metaphors? Write an essay explaining how they reinforce her argument about the morality of talk shows.

4. **CONNECTIONS.** Ehrenreich holds that television talk shows exploit their participants. Read Marie Winn's "TV Addiction" (p. 431), in which the author quotes a "heavy viewer" who confesses that watching TV makes him feel "sapped, will-less, enervated" (para. 8). In an essay, consider this assertion by a critic of television: "TV exploits its viewers, rendering them comatose with bland entertainment and continual commercials in order to quell dissent and encourage consumption." To what extent do you agree or disagree with this assertion, and why? Are Ehrenreich's talk-show

participants and Winn's TV addicts solely responsible for their situations, or does the medium also bear some responsibility?

BARBARA EHRENREICH ON WRITING

The printed word, in the view of Barbara Ehrenreich, should be a powerful instrument for reform. In an article in *Mother Jones*, though, she complains about a tacit censorship in American magazines that has sometimes prevented her from fulfilling her purpose as a writer. Ehrenreich recalls the difficulties she had in trying to persuade the editor of a national magazine to assign her a story on the plight of Third World women refugees. "Sorry," said the editor, "Third World women have never done anything for me."

Ehrenreich infers that writers who write for such magazines must follow a rule: "You must learn not to stray from your assigned sociodemographic stereotype." She observes, "As a woman, I am generally asked to write on 'women's topics,' such as cooking, divorce, how to succeed in business, diet fads, and the return of the bustle. These are all fine topics and give great scope to my talents, but when I ask, in faltering tones, for an assignment...on the trade deficit, I am likely to be told that *anyone* (Bill, Gerry, Bob) could cover that, whereas my 'voice' is *essential* for the aerobic toothbrushing story. This is not, strictly speaking, 'censorship'—just a division of labor in which white men cover politics, foreign policy, and the economy, and the rest of us cover what's left over, such as the bustle."

Over the years Ehrenreich has had many manuscripts rejected by editors who comment, "too angry," "too depressing," and "Where's the bright side?" She agrees with writer Herbert Gold, who once deduced that the American media want only "happy stories about happy people with happy problems." She concludes, "You can write about anything—death squads, AIDS...—so long as you make it 'upbeat.'" Despite such discouragements, Ehrenreich continues her battle to "disturb the stupor induced by six straight pages of Calvin Klein ads."

FOR DISCUSSION

1. Is Ehrenreich right about "a tacit censorship in American magazines"? Check a recent issue of a magazine that prints signed articles. How many of the articles *not* on "women's topics" are written by women? How many are written by men?
2. How many women can you name who write serious newspaper and magazine articles reporting on or arguing matters of general interest, as opposed to those meant to appeal chiefly to women?
3. To what extent do you agree with Ehrenreich—and with Herbert Gold—that the American media are interested only in "upbeat" stories?

EMILY PRAGER

EMILY PRAGER was first published at age five when the *Houston Post* released her novel *Cinderella Goes to the Ball and Breaks Her Leg*. Born in 1952, she grew up in Houston, Asia, and New York City and graduated from Barnard College with a degree in anthropology. She wrote for *The National Lampoon Magazine*, cowrote and acted in the films *Mr. Mike's Mondo* and *Arena Brains*, and starred for four years in the soap opera *The Edge of Night*. Prager has written humor and social satire for numerous periodicals, collected in *In the Missionary Position* (1999), and she has published four books of fiction: *A Visit from the Footbinder and Other Stories* (1982), *Clea and Zeus Divorce* (1987), *Eve's Tattoo* (1991), and *Roger Fishbite: A Novel* (1999). She lives in New York City with her daughter.

Our Barbies, Ourselves

The Barbie doll is just a harmless plaything for little girls, right? Prager suspected not, even when she was a child, and some recent information confirmed her hunch. Using division or analysis, she shows here how Barbie represents a twisted ideal of women. The essay first appeared in *Interview* magazine in 1991.

I read an astounding obituary in *The New York Times* not too long ago. It concerned the death of one Jack Ryan. A former husband of Zsa Zsa Gabor, it said, Mr. Ryan had been an inventor and designer during his lifetime. A man of eclectic creativity, he designed Sparrow and Hawk missiles when he worked for the Raytheon Company, and, the notice said, when he consulted for Mattel he designed Barbie.[1]

If Barbie was designed by a man, suddenly a lot of things made sense to me, things I'd wondered about for years. I used to look at Barbie and wonder, What's wrong with this picture? What kind of woman designed this doll? Let's be honest: Barbie looks like someone who got her start at the Playboy Mansion. She could be a regular guest on *The Howard Stern Show*. It is a fact of Barbie's design that her breasts are so out of proportion to the rest of her body that if she were a human woman, she'd fall flat on her face.

If it's true that a woman didn't design Barbie, you don't know how much saner that makes me feel. Of course, that doesn't ameliorate the

---

[1] After Prager wrote this essay, Barbie's thirty-fifth birthday was the occasion for a "biography" asserting that Ryan did not design the doll from scratch but supervised its evolution from a sophisticated adult doll made in Germany. — EDS.

damage. There are millions of women who are subliminally sure that a thirty-nine-inch bust and a twenty-three-inch waist are the epitome of lovability. Could this account for the popularity of breast implant surgery?

I don't mean to step on anyone's toes here. I loved my Barbie. Secretly, I still believe that neon pink and turquoise blue are the only colors in which to decorate a duplex condo. And like many others of my generation, I've never married, simply because I cannot find a man who looks as good in clam diggers as Ken.   4

The question that comes to mind is, of course, Did Mr. Ryan design Barbie as a weapon? Because it *is* odd that Barbie appeared about the same time in my consciousness as the feminist movement—a time when women sought equality and small breasts were king. Or is Barbie the dream date of weapons designers? Or perhaps it's simpler than that: Perhaps Barbie is Zsa Zsa if she were eleven inches tall. No matter what, my discovery of Jack Ryan confirms what I have always felt: There is something indescribably masculine about Barbie—dare I say it, phallic. For all her giant breasts and high-heeled feet, she lacks a certain softness. If you asked a little girl what kind of doll she wanted for Christmas, I just don't think she'd reply, "Please, Santa, I want a hard-body."   5

On the other hand, you could say that Barbie, in feminist terms, is definitely her own person. With her condos and fashion plazas and pools and beauty salons, she is definitely a liberated woman, a gal on the move. And she has always been sexual, even totemic. Before Barbie, American dolls were flat-footed and breastless, and ineffably dignified. They were created in the image of little girls or babies. Madame Alexander was the queen of doll makers in the '50s, and her dollies looked like Elizabeth Taylor in *National Velvet*. They represented the kind of girls who looked perfect in jodhpurs, whose hair was never out of place, who grew up to be Jackie Kennedy—before she married Onassis. Her dolls' boyfriends were figments of the imagination, figments with large portfolios and three-piece suits and presidential aspirations, figments who could keep dolly in the style to which little girls of the '50s were programmed to become accustomed, a style that spasm-ed with the '60s and the appearance of Barbie. And perhaps what accounts for Barbie's vast popularity is that she was also a '60s woman: into free love and fun colors, anti-class, and possessed of a real, molded boyfriend, Ken, with whom she could chant a mantra.   6

But there were problems with Ken. I always felt weird about him. He had no genitals, and, even at age ten, I found that ominous. I mean, here was Barbie with these humongous breasts, and that was O.K. with the toy company. And then, there was Ken with that truncated, unidentifiable lump at his groin. I sensed injustice at work. Why, I wondered, was Barbie designed with such obvious sexual equipment and   7

Ken not? Why was his treated as if it were more mysterious than hers? Did the fact that it was treated as such indicate that somehow his equipment, his essential maleness, was considered more powerful than hers, more worthy of the dignity of concealment? And if the issue in the mind of the toy company was obscenity and its possible damage to children, I still object. How do they think I felt, knowing that no matter how many water beds they slept in, or hot tubs they romped in, or swimming pools they lounged by under the stars, Barbie and Ken could never make love? No matter how much sexuality Barbie possessed, she would never turn Ken on. He would be forever withholding, forever detached. There was a loneliness about Barbie's situation that was always disturbing. And twenty-five years later, movies and videos are still filled with topless women and covered men. As if we're all trapped in Barbie's world and can never escape.

QUESTIONS ON MEANING

1. Why does Prager say that "suddenly a lot of things made sense" when she discovered that Barbie was designed by a man? Is she referring here only to Barbie's looks?
2. Are we supposed to believe the claims that Prager makes in paragraph 4? What is the point she is trying to make?
3. What is Prager's DEFINITION of a *feminist* in this essay? Where do you find this definition?
4. What is Prager's THESIS?

QUESTIONS ON WRITING STRATEGY

1. What elements of Barbie does Prager's analysis identify? What new picture of the doll does Prager arrive at as a result?
2. Prager refers to four famous women by name. What does each reference suggest? What is the EFFECT of her using these famous names?
3. Prager poses several RHETORICAL QUESTIONS, such as "Could this account for the popularity of breast implant surgery?" (para. 3), "Or is Barbie the dream date of weapons designers?" (5), and "Why . . . was Barbie designed with such obvious sexual equipment and Ken not?" (7). What is the PURPOSE of these rhetorical questions?
4. **OTHER METHODS.** In her last paragraph Prager COMPARES AND CONTRASTS the ways the toy company depicted the sexuality of Barbie and Ken. What are the differences? What ideas of CAUSE AND EFFECT emerge from this comparison?

QUESTIONS ON LANGUAGE

1. Prager notes that Barbie is a product of a time when "small breasts were king" (para. 5). What is the significance of the word *king* in this context?
2. Why does Prager call Barbie "masculine" in paragraph 5? Does this description contradict Prager's view of Barbie as an unattainable and inappropriate feminine ideal?
3. Prager describes dolls' boyfriends before Barbie's Ken as "figments with large portfolios and three-piece suits and presidential aspirations" (para. 6). What are the CONNOTATIONS of this description?
4. Consult your dictionary if any of the following words are unfamiliar: eclectic (para. 1); ameliorate, subliminally, epitome (3); phallic (5); totemic, ineffably, jodhpurs (6); humongous, truncated (7).

SUGGESTIONS FOR WRITING

1. **JOURNAL WRITING.** Did you play with Barbie or another kind of doll as a child (for instance, Ken, G.I. Joe, *Star Wars* action figures)? Describe your relationship with this doll, or explain why you never owned one.

   FROM JOURNAL TO ESSAY. Using your own experiences as EVIDENCE, write an essay that explains the influence of a particular doll or of dolls in general. Your essay may be serious or humorous, but it should include plenty of description and focus on cause and effect.
2. Prager asserts that knowing a man designed Barbie *explains* a lot of problems she always had with Barbie, but it does not *excuse* or *solve* the problems. What new knowledge can you think of that provided a reasonable explanation for a personal problem, while doing nothing to repair the situation? For instance, did you come to understand why your taxes or your rent increased, why you received a disappointing grade in a course, why someone dislikes you, or why a friend is depressed? In an essay, explain the situation, what you now understand about it, and finally, what it would take, in addition to the new information, to solve the problem.
3. **CRITICAL WRITING.** In paragraph 6 Prager suggests, with a tinge of IRONY, several ways to think of Barbie as contributing to the liberation rather than the oppression of women. What do *you* think of Barbie as a role model for girls? Write an essay supporting or refuting Prager's thesis. (If you haven't seen a Barbie doll in a while, you might visit a toy store or borrow a child's.) Is Barbie damaging, as Prager maintains, or liberating, or neither?
4. **CONNECTIONS.** Both Prager and Armin A. Brott, in "Not All Men Are Sly Foxes" (p. 279), examine cultural artifacts that could influence children's ideas of their own and the opposite sex. Consider a cultural artifact that affected you as a child, such as a television show, book, movie, toy, sport, or kind of music. (It may have influenced your views of sex roles but could also have influenced you in other ways—for instance, by contributing to your values, your interests, your ideas about friendship or adult life.) Write an essay that analyzes your subject, identifying the elements that made it influential.

EMILY PRAGER ON WRITING

Actually, this section should be titled "Emily Prager on *Reading and Writing*." In the Toronto, Canada, *Globe and Mail*, Prager made a passionate case for both:

As a writer, I worry a lot about literacy in the United States. In part, it's purely selfish. If most U.S. high-school graduates can't read above a Grade 5 level, then I'm out of a job in ten years. Without a young, new audience to keep you on your toes, a writer can go stale. Your arteries can harden. You start writing only for your own generation and then you're like a snake eating its own tail: self-involved to the point of stasis....

Americans, given the problems of drugs and dysfunctional school systems, have been left thoroughly, classically illiterate. This, in my estimation, is a form of spiritual bankruptcy—because the ultimate aim of classical literacy (the ability to read and write) is to be able to think, to form ideas, to fantasize goals, to hope, to imagine, to invent and reinvent, to believe in life.

Drugs in school have, of course, contributed mightily to classical illiteracy. By and large, when kids take drugs they do not read. Reading was itself the drug of my generation's childhood. Before we baby boomers found drugs, we read voraciously, addictively. I always say, only half-joking, that if teachers taught reading as the great drug it truly is, kids would want to do it.

But teachers don't. Reading is taught as some dry, dull, meaningless, academic pursuit. No mention is ever made of the high, the physical euphoria and bliss, the fantastic turn-on of intellectual understanding. It seems amazing now that mothers used to fear our reading. Go outside, they'd shout, threatened by our focus and solitude. Little did they know....

It is interesting that the United States, with its national emphasis on freedom, should have come to this strange pass, but it has. The average American is, at this point, dubious both about the quality of his life and his sense of personal freedom. He is also desperate to rediscover these things, to find his depth, to relocate some magic and meaning in his existence.

This, television, computers and drug addiction cannot do. Only access to the great thought and history and art of the planet through reading, and the formulation of ideas and the sparking of imagination through writing, can feed the emptiness that we feel. Man cannot live by money and real estate alone.

Fortunately, Americans are easily bored. I somehow feel they might take up reading and writing again just because they're bored with everything else and need a new thrill.

Fine by me. Whatever makes them do it. Readers in their teens never read my books now and that saddens me. But I can live with it if, when I'm sixty, there's a whole crop of literate twenty-year-olds to keep my writing young.

FOR DISCUSSION

1. What, according to Prager, has caused today's "classical illiteracy"? What can reading and writing provide that "television, computers and drug addiction" cannot?
2. Prager makes some negative GENERALIZATIONS about the teaching of reading today. On the basis of your own experience as a student, do you agree or disagree with these generalizations? Why?
3. How serious do you think Prager is in hoping for improved literacy because it would benefit her own writing (first and last paragraphs)?

GAIL SHEEHY

A journalist and best-selling author, GAIL SHEEHY was born in 1937. She earned her B.S. degree from the University of Vermont in 1958 and was a fellow in Columbia University's Journalism School in 1970. A contributor to the *New York Times Magazine, Esquire, Mc-Call's, Ms., Cosmopolitan, Rolling Stone*, and other magazines, she has also written a novel, *Lovesounds* (1970), and many popular studies of contemporary life: *Speed Is of the Essence* (1971), *Panthermania* (1971), *Hustling* (1973), *Passages* (1976), *Pathfinders* (1981), *In the Spirit of Survival* (1986), *Character: America's Search for Leadership* (1988), *The Man Who Changed the World: The Lives of Mikhail S. Gorbachev* (1991), *Silent Passage* (1992), *New Passages* (1995), *Understanding Men's Passages* (1998), and *Hillary's Choice* (1999), the last about Hillary Rodham Clinton. Sheehy and her husband, Clay Felker, an editor and journalism teacher, live in New York and California.

Predictable Crises of Adulthood

"Predictable Crises of Adulthood" is adapted from the second chapter of *Passages*. In the essay, Sheehy identifies six stages that most people experience between the ages of eighteen and fifty. The author, as she herself makes clear, is not a theorist or a scholar; she is an artful reporter, in this case of findings in adult development. Not everyone goes through the stages Sheehy traces at exactly the same time, but see whether any of the following crises sound familiar to you.

We are not unlike a particularly hardy crustacean. The lobster 1
grows by developing and shedding a series of hard, protective shells. Each time it expands from within, the confining shell must be sloughed off. It is left exposed and vulnerable until, in time, a new covering grows to replace the old.

With each passage from one stage of human growth to the next we, 2
too, must shed a protective structure. We are left exposed and vulnerable—but also yeasty and embryonic again, capable of stretching in ways we hadn't known before. These sheddings may take several years or more. Coming out of each passage, though, we enter a longer and more stable period in which we can expect relative tranquility and a sense of equilibrium regained....

As we shall see, each person engages the steps of development in 3
his or her own characteristic *step-style*. Some people never complete the whole sequence. And none of us "solves" with one step—by jumping out of the parental home into a job or marriage, for example—the problems in separating from the caregivers of childhood. Nor do we

"achieve" autonomy once and for all by converting our dreams into concrete goals, even when we attain those goals. The central issues or tasks of one period are never fully completed, tied up, and cast aside. But when they lose their primacy and the current life structure has served its purpose, we are ready to move on to the next period.

Can one catch up? What might look to others like listlessness, con-   4
trariness, a maddening refusal to face up to an obvious task may be a person's own unique detour that will bring him out later on the other side. Developmental gains won can later be lost—and rewon. It's plausible, though it can't be proven, that the mastery of one set of tasks fortifies us for the next period and the next set of challenges. But it's important not to think too mechanistically. Machines work by units. The bureaucracy (supposedly) works step by step. Human beings, thank God, have an individual inner dynamic that can never be precisely coded.

Although I have indicated the ages when Americans are likely to   5
go through each stage, and the differences between men and women where they are striking, do not take the ages too seriously. The stages are the thing, and most particularly the sequence.

Here is the briefest outline of the developmental ladder.   6

Pulling Up Roots

Before 18, the motto is loud and clear: "I have to get away from my   7
parents." But the words are seldom connected to action. Generally still safely part of our families, even if away at school, we feel our autonomy to be subject to erosion from moment to moment.

After 18, we begin Pulling Up Roots in earnest. College, military   8
service, and short-term travels are all customary vehicles our society provides for the first round trips between family and a base of one's own. In the attempt to separate our view of the world from our family's view, despite vigorous protestations to the contrary—"I know exactly what I want!"—we cast about for any beliefs we can call our own. And in the process of testing those beliefs we are often drawn to fads, preferably those most mysterious and inaccessible to our parents.

Whatever tentative memberships we try out in the world, the fear   9
haunts us that we are really kids who cannot take care of ourselves. We cover that fear with acts of defiance and mimicked confidence. For allies to replace our parents, we turn to our contemporaries. They become conspirators. So long as their perspective meshes with our own, they are able to substitute for the sanctuary of the family. But that doesn't last very long. And the instant they diverge from the shaky ideals of "our group," they are seen as betrayers. Rebounds to the family are common between the ages of 18 and 22.

The tasks of this passage are to locate ourselves in a peer group role,   10
a sex role, an anticipated occupation, an ideology or world view. As a
result, we gather the impetus to leave home physically and the identity
to *begin* leaving home emotionally.

Even as one part of us seeks to be an individual, another part longs   11
to restore the safety and comfort of merging with another. Thus one of
the most popular myths of this passage is: We can piggyback our development by attaching to a Stronger One. But people who marry during
this time often prolong financial and emotional ties to the family and
relatives that impede them from becoming self-sufficient.

A stormy passage through the Pulling Up Roots years will probably   12
facilitate the normal progression of the adult life cycle. If one doesn't
have an identity crisis at this point, it will erupt during a later transition, when the penalties may be harder to bear.

The Trying Twenties

The Trying Twenties confront us with the question of how to take   13
hold in the adult world. Our focus shifts from the interior turmoils of
late adolescence — "Who am I?" "What is truth?" — and we become almost totally preoccupied with working out the externals. "How do I put
my aspirations into effect?" "What is the best way to start?" "Where do
I go?" "Who can help me?" "How did *you* do it?"

In this period, which is longer and more stable compared with the   14
passage that leads to it, the tasks are as enormous as they are exhilarating: To shape a Dream, that vision of ourselves which will generate energy, aliveness, and hope. To prepare for a lifework. To find a mentor if
possible. And to form the capacity for intimacy, without losing in the
process whatever consistency of self we have thus far mustered. The
first test structure must be erected around the life we choose to try.

Doing what we "should" is the most pervasive theme of the twen-   15
ties. The "shoulds" are largely defined by family models, the press of the
culture, or the prejudices of our peers. If the prevailing cultural instructions are that one should get married and settle down behind one's own
door, a nuclear family is born. If instead the peers insist that one should
do one's own thing, the 25-year-old is likely to harness himself onto a
Harley-Davidson and burn up Route 66 in the commitment to have no
commitments.

One of the terrifying aspects of the twenties is the inner conviction   16
that the choices we make are irrevocable. It is largely a false fear.
Change is quite possible, and some alteration of our original choices is
probably inevitable.

Two impulses, as always, are at work. One is to build a firm,   17
safe structure for the future by making strong commitments, to "be

set." Yet people who slip into a ready-made form without much self-examination are likely to find themselves *locked in*.

The other urge is to explore and experiment, keeping any structure 18 tentative and therefore easily reversible. Taken to the extreme, these are people who skip from one trial job and one limited personal encounter to another, spending their twenties in the *transient* state.

Although the choices of our twenties are not irrevocable, they do 19 set in motion a Life Pattern. Some of us follow the lock-in pattern, others the transient pattern, the wunderkind pattern, the caregiver pattern, and there are a number of others. Such patterns strongly influence the particular questions raised for each person during each passage....

Buoyed by powerful illusions and belief in the power of the will, we 20 commonly insist in our twenties that what we have chosen to do is the one true course in life. Our backs go up at the merest hint that we are like our parents, that two decades of parental training might be reflected in our current actions and attitudes.

"Not me," is the motto, "I'm different." 21

Catch-30

Impatient with devoting ourselves to the "shoulds," a new vitality 22 springs from within as we approach 30. Men and women alike speak of feeling too narrow and restricted. They blame all sorts of things, but what the restrictions boil down to are the outgrowth of career and personal choices of the twenties. They may have been choices perfectly suited to that stage. But now the fit feels different. Some inner aspect that was left out is striving to be taken into account. Important new choices must be made, and commitments altered or deepened. The work involves great change, turmoil, and often crisis—a simultaneous feeling of rock bottom and the urge to bust out.

One common response is the tearing up of the life we spent most of 23 our twenties putting together. It may mean striking out on a secondary road toward a new vision or converting a dream of "running for president" into a more realistic goal. The single person feels a push to find a partner. The woman who was previously content at home with children chafes to venture into the world. The childless couple reconsiders children. And almost everyone who is married, especially those married for seven years, feels a discontent.

If the discontent doesn't lead to a divorce, it will, or should, call for 24 a serious review of the marriage and of each partner's aspirations in their Catch-30 condition. The gist of that condition was expressed by a 29-year-old associate with a Wall Street law firm:

"I'm considering leaving the firm. I've been there four years now; 25 I'm getting good feedback, but I have no clients of my own. I feel weak.

If I wait much longer, it will be too late, too close to that fateful time of decision on whether or not to become a partner. I'm success-oriented. But the concept of being 55 years old and stuck in a monotonous job drives me wild. It drives me crazy now, just a little bit. I'd say that 85 percent of the time I thoroughly enjoy my work. But when I get a screwball case, I come away from court saying, 'What am I doing here?' It's a *visceral* reaction that I'm wasting my time. I'm trying to find some way to make a social contribution or a slot in city government. I keep saying, 'There's something more.'"

Besides the push to broaden himself professionally, there is a wish   26
to expand his personal life. He wants two or three more children. "The concept of a home has become very meaningful to me, a place to get away from troubles and relax. I love my son in a way I could not have anticipated. I never could live alone."

Consumed with the work of making his own critical life-steering   27
decisions, he demonstrates the essential shift at this age: an absolute requirement to be more self-concerned. The self has new value now that his competency has been proved.

His wife is struggling with her own age-30 priorities. She wants to   28
go to law school, but he wants more children. If she is going to stay home, she wants him to make more time for the family instead of taking on even wider professional commitments. His view of the bind, of what he would most like from his wife, is this:

"I'd like not to be bothered. It sounds cruel, but I'd like not to have   29
to worry about what she's going to do next week. Which is why I've told her several times that I think she should do something. Go back to school and get a degree in social work or geography or whatever. Hopefully that would fulfill her, and then I wouldn't have to worry about her line of problems. I want her to be decisive about herself."

The trouble with his advice to his wife is that it comes out of con-   30
cern with *his* convenience, rather than with *her* development. She quickly picks up on this lack of goodwill: He is trying to dispose of her. At the same time, he refuses her the same latitude to be "selfish" in making an independent decision to broaden her horizons. Both perceive a lack of mutuality. And that is what Catch-30 is all about for the couple.

Rooting and Extending

Life becomes less provisional, more rational and orderly in the   31
early thirties. We begin to settle down in the full sense. Most of us begin putting down roots and sending out new shoots. People buy houses and become very earnest about climbing career ladders. Men in particular concern themselves with "making it." Satisfaction with marriage

generally goes downhill in the thirties (for those who have remained together) compared with the highly valued, vision-supporting marriage of the twenties. This coincides with the couple's reduced social life outside the family and the inturned focus on raising their children.

The Deadline Decade

In the middle of the thirties we come upon a crossroads. We have 32 reached the halfway mark. Yet even as we are reaching our prime, we begin to see there is a place where it finishes. Time starts to squeeze.

The loss of youth, the faltering of physical powers we have always 33 taken for granted, the fading purpose of stereotyped roles by which we have thus far identified ourselves, the spiritual dilemma of having no absolute answers—any or all of these shocks can give this passage the character of crisis. Such thoughts usher in a decade between 35 and 45 that can be called the Deadline Decade. It is a time of both danger and opportunity. All of us have the chance to rework the narrow identity by which we defined ourselves in the first half of life. And those of us who make the most of the opportunity will have a full-out authenticity crisis.

To come through this authenticity crisis, we must reexamine our 34 purposes and reevaluate how to spend our resources from now on. "Why am I doing all this? What do I really believe in?" No matter what we have been doing, there will be parts of ourselves that have been suppressed and now need to find expression. "Bad" feelings will demand acknowledgment along with the good.

It is frightening to step off onto the treacherous footbridge leading 35 to the second half of life. We can't take everything with us on this journey through uncertainty. Along the way, we discover that we are alone. We no longer have to ask permission because we are the providers of our own safety. We must learn to give ourselves permission. We stumble upon feminine or masculine aspects of our natures that up to this time have usually been masked. There is grieving to be done because an old self is dying. By taking in our suppressed and even our unwanted parts, we prepare at the gut level for the reintegration of an identity that is ours and ours alone—not some artificial form put together to please the culture or our mates. It is a hard passage at the beginning. But by disassembling ourselves, we can glimpse the light and gather our parts into a renewal.

Women sense this inner crossroads earlier than men do. The time 36 pinch often prompts a woman to stop and take an all-points survey at age 35. Whatever options she has already played out, she feels a "my last chance" urgency to review those options she has set aside and those that aging and biology will close off in the *now foreseeable* future. For all her qualms and confusion about where to start looking for a new future, she usually enjoys an exhilaration of release. Assertiveness begins rising. There are so many firsts ahead.

Men, too, feel the time push in the mid-thirties. Most men respond 37 by pressing down harder on the career accelerator. It's "my last chance" to pull away from the pack. It is no longer enough to be the loyal junior executive, the promising young novelist, the lawyer who does a little *pro bono* work on the side. He wants now to become part of top management, to be recognized as an established writer, or an active politician with his own legislative program. With some chagrin, he discovers that he has been too anxious to please and too vulnerable to criticism. He wants to put together his own ship.

During this period of intense concentration on external advance- 38 ment, it is common for men to be unaware of the more difficult, gut issues that are propelling them forward. The survey that was neglected at 35 becomes a crucible at 40. Whatever rung of achievement he has reached, the man of 40 usually feels stale, restless, burdened, and unappreciated. He worries about his health. He wonders, "Is this all there is?" He may make a series of departures from well-established lifelong base lines, including marriage. More and more men are seeking second careers in midlife. Some become self-destructive. And many men in their forties experience a major shift of emphasis away from pouring all their energies into their own advancement. A more tender, feeling side comes into play. They become interested in developing an ethical self.

Renewal or Resignation

Somewhere in the mid-forties, equilibrium is regained. A new sta- 39 bility is achieved, which may be more or less satisfying.

If one has refused to budge through the midlife transition, the sense 40 of staleness will calcify into resignation. One by one, the safety and supports will be withdrawn from the person who is standing still. Parents will become children; children will become strangers; a mate will grow away or go away; the career will become just a job—and each of these events will be felt as an abandonment. The crisis will probably emerge again around 50. And although its wallop will be greater, the jolt may be just what is needed to prod the resigned middle-ager toward seeking revitalization.

On the other hand... 41

If we have confronted ourselves in the middle passage and found a 42 renewal of purpose around which we are eager to build a more authentic life structure, these may well be the best years. Personal happiness takes a sharp turn upward for partners who can now accept the fact: "I cannot expect *anyone* to fully understand me." Parents can be forgiven for the burdens of our childhood. Children can be let go without leaving us in collapsed silence. At 50, there is a new warmth and mellow-ing. Friends become more important than ever, but so does privacy. Since it is so often proclaimed by people past midlife, the motto of this stage might be "No more bullshit."

QUESTIONS ON MEANING

1. In your own words, SUMMARIZE each of Sheehy's six predictable stages of adult life.
2. According to the author, what happens to people who fail to experience a given stage of growth at the usual time?
3. How would you characterize Sheehy's attitude toward growth and change in adult life?

QUESTIONS ON WRITING STRATEGY

1. Why does Sheehy employ the method of division or analysis? How does it serve her readers, too?
2. What, if anything, does the author gain by writing her essay in the first PERSON plural (*we, us*)?
3. What difficulties go along with making GENERALIZATIONS about human be-ings? To what extent does Sheehy surmount these difficulties?
4. How much knowledge of psychology does Sheehy expect of her AUDIENCE?
5. **OTHER METHODS.** Sheehy relies on CAUSE AND EFFECT to explain why needs and goals change at each stage of adulthood. Summarize the pattern of cause and effect in the "Catch-30" stage (paras. 22–30).

QUESTIONS ON LANGUAGE

1. Consult your dictionary if you need help in defining the following words: crustacean (para. 1); embryonic, tranquility, equilibrium (2); autonomy, primacy (3); plausible (4); inaccessible (8); sanctuary (9); impetus (10); exhilarating, mentor (14); pervasive (15); irrevocable (16); tentative (18); wunderkind (19); visceral (25); mutuality (30); dilemma (33); *pro bono*, chagrin, vulnerable (37); crucible (38); calcify (40).
2. What is a "nuclear family" (para. 15)?
3. The author coins a few phrases of her own. Refer to their context to help you define the following: step-style (para. 3); Stronger One (11); Catch-30 (24); authenticity crisis (33).

SUGGESTIONS FOR WRITING

1. **JOURNAL WRITING.** Did any of the stages outlined by Sheehy ring especially true for you? Describe some of the events in your life that place you in one of Sheehy's stages.

   FROM JOURNAL TO ESSAY. Sheehy focuses each of her six stages on a "crisis." Does the word *crisis* seem appropriate or extreme to you? Choose one of Sheehy's stages that you know firsthand, and write an essay that EVALUATES her account of it. Use the details from your journal to support your evaluation.

2. Following Sheehy's example, look back on your own earlier life or that of a younger person you know, and detail a series of phases in it. Invent names for the phases.

3. **CRITICAL WRITING.** In popularizing scholarly research from developmental psychology, Sheehy eliminates such features as detailed analyses of researchers' methods and results, statistical correlations and other data, source citations, and specialized terminology. Write an essay EVALUATING the advantages and disadvantages of popularizations such as Sheehy's versus scholarly books and articles like those you read for courses in the sciences, social sciences, or humanities.

4. **CONNECTIONS.** You may have noticed the similarity between Sheehy's characterization of the Catch-30 couple (paras. 22–30) and Judy Brady's analysis in "I Want a Wife" (p. 275). Use the information provided by Sheehy (about other stages as well, if you like) to analyze the particular crisis of the "I" who wants a wife in Brady's essay. Support your ideas with EVIDENCE from both essays.

GAIL SHEEHY ON WRITING

With the 1995 publication of a sequel to *Passages,* the book containing "Predictable Crises of Adulthood," Gail Sheehy showed both how a writer's own situation can influence his or her ideas and how time can change those ideas. In the sequel, *New Passages,* Sheehy admitted that when publishing *Passages* at the age of thirty-nine, she "couldn't imagine life beyond fifty. And I certainly couldn't bring myself to consider it a time of potential." But the intervening years brought changes, and not just in Sheehy herself. "People," she wrote, "are taking longer to grow up and much longer to die." Adolescence may now run through the twenties, marriage and children may not come until the forties, and life may not end until the nineties.

New Passages proposes three life stages: provisional adulthood, from ages eighteen to thirty; first adulthood, from ages thirty to forty-five; and second adulthood, from age forty-five to death. In an interview with Regina Weinreich of the *New York Times,* Sheehy said, "After years of interviews, it became apparent that all the age models were off. There were predictable stages but no predictable ages for when we go through them. . . . What I hope people will get out of the book is that there is a second adulthood. They can't carry the roles, identities, dreams of the first adulthood into the second. . . . They're going to live longer. Prepare by thinking what would be the new dream that will enliven the whole vast expanse of life."

FOR DISCUSSION

Should a writer's ideas be as vulnerable to change as Sheehy's were in *Passages*? Do Sheehy's recent observations about the stages of life invalidate "Predictable Crises of Adulthood"? Why, or why not?

JAMAICA KINCAID

JAMAICA KINCAID was born Elaine Potter Richardson in 1949 on the Caribbean island of Antigua. She attended school in Antigua and struggled to become independent of her mother and her place. "I was supposed to be full of good manners and good speech," she has recalled. "Where the hell I was going to go with it I don't know." Kincaid took it to New York, where she went at age seventeen to work as a family helper. She briefly attended Franconia College on a photography scholarship and did odd jobs in New York. In the early 1970s, she became friends with George Trow, a writer for *The New Yorker.* Soon she was contributing to the magazine, and in 1976 she became a staff writer. Soon after, she began writing fiction, producing a collection of stories, *At the Bottom of the River* (1983), and three novels, *Annie John* (1985), *Lucy* (1990), and *The Autobiography of My Mother* (1996)—all based on her own life on Antigua and as an immigrant. Her nonfiction books include *A Small Place* (1988), also about Antigua, and *My Brother* (1997), a National Book Award finalist. An avid gardener, Kincaid has also edited *My Favorite Plants: Writers and Gardeners on the Plants They Love* (1998). She lives in Vermont.

Girl

This very short story was collected in *At the Bottom of the River.* Much like Judy Brady in "I Want a Wife" (p. 275), Kincaid analyzes the domain of the title girl, both the roles she is expected to fill and the condition of being her mother's daughter. The writer Stephanie Vaughn has said that Kincaid's story "spills out in a single breath.... Its exhilarating motion gives me the sense of a writer carried over the precipice by the energy of her own vision."

Wash the white clothes on Monday and put them on the stone heap; wash the color clothes on Tuesday and put them on the clothesline to dry; don't walk barehead in the hot sun; cook pumpkin fritters in very hot sweet oil; soak your little cloths right after you take them off; when buying cotton to make yourself a nice blouse, be sure that it doesn't have gum on it, because that way it won't hold up well after a wash; soak salt fish overnight before you cook it; is it true that you sing benna[1] in Sunday school?; always eat your food in such a way that it won't turn someone else's stomach; on Sundays try to walk like a lady and not like the slut you are so bent on becoming; don't sing benna in

[1] Calypso music. — EDS.

Sunday school; you mustn't speak to wharf-rat boys, not even to give directions; don't eat fruits on the street—flies will follow you; *but I don't sing benna on Sundays at all and never in Sunday school*; this is how to sew on a button; this is how to make a buttonhole for the button you have just sewed on; this is how to hem a dress when you see the hem coming down and so to prevent yourself from looking like the slut I know you are so bent on becoming; this is how you iron your father's khaki shirt so that it doesn't have a crease; this is how you iron your father's khaki pants so that they don't have a crease; this is how you grow okra—far from the house, because okra tree harbors red ants; when you are growing dasheen,[2] make sure it gets plenty of water or else it makes your throat itch when you are eating it; this is how you sweep a corner; this is how you sweep a whole house; this is how you sweep a yard; this is how you smile to someone you don't like too much; this is how you smile to someone you don't like at all; this is how you smile to someone you like completely; this is how you set a table for tea; this is how you set a table for dinner; this is how you set a table for dinner with an important guest; this is how you set a table for lunch; this is how you set a table for breakfast; this is how to behave in the presence of men who don't know you very well, and this way they won't recognize immediately the slut I have warned you against becoming; be sure to wash every day, even if it is with your own spit; don't squat down to play marbles—you are not a boy, you know; don't pick people's flowers—you might catch something; don't throw stones at blackbirds, because it might not be a blackbird at all; this is how to make a bread pudding; this is how to make doukona;[3] this is how to make pepper pot; this is how to make a good medicine for a cold; this is how to make a good medicine to throw away a child before it even becomes a child; this is how to catch a fish; this is how to throw back a fish you don't like, and that way something bad won't fall on you; this is how to bully a man; this is how a man bullies you; this is how to love a man, and if this doesn't work there are other ways, and if they don't work don't feel too bad about giving up; this is how to spit up in the air if you feel like it, and this is how to move quick so that it doesn't fall on you; this is how to make ends meet; always squeeze bread to make sure it's fresh; *but what if the baker won't let me feel the bread?*; you mean to say that after all you are really going to be the kind of woman who the baker won't let near the bread?

[2] Taro, a tropical plant with an edible tuber. —EDS.
[3] A pudding made of plantains, a fruit similar to a banana. —EDS.

QUESTIONS ON MEANING

1. What are the CONNOTATIONS of the phrase "wharf-rat boys"? Why is the girl of the title supposed to avoid them?
2. What does it mean to "be the kind of woman who the baker won't let near the bread" (last line)?
3. What do the elements of the mother's advice add up to: What kind of life does she depict for her daughter?

QUESTIONS ON WRITING STRATEGY

1. Why do you think Kincaid wrote her story as one long sentence? What does she achieve?
2. What does Kincaid convey through the one comment and one question in italics?
3. Toward the end of this story, the mother says, "this is how to spit up in the air if you feel like it, and this is how to move quick so that it doesn't fall on you." What is the EFFECT of this particular piece of advice? What effect would it have if it were the last line of the story?
4. **OTHER METHODS.** The many obligations of a girl/woman can be CLASSIFIED into groups of skills and behaviors. What categories do you see? How do they help organize the story?

QUESTIONS ON LANGUAGE

1. What do the repeated directions about how to "sweep," "smile," and "set a table" suggest?
2. What can you conclude about the girl from the mother's scolding, "don't squat down to play marbles — you are not a boy, you know"?
3. Make sure you know the meanings of the following words: fritters, khaki, okra.
4. The fiction writer Stephanie Vaughn advises reading "Girl" aloud. She says, "I find that it is best to stand up when you read this story aloud, and to take a breath from the deepest region of your belly. When your lungs are full, when your shoulders are back, you begin to speak the story, and then you find that you are singing." Try it yourself. How is reading the story aloud different from reading it to yourself?

SUGGESTIONS FOR WRITING

1. **JOURNAL WRITING.** What warnings or instructions were drilled into you when you were a young adolescent? Who took the responsibility for drilling you? In your journal, describe the advice you remember receiving. **FROM JOURNAL TO ESSAY.** "Adolescents' heads are stuffed with advice intended to make them conform to rigid cultural roles and values." Based on your own experience, do you agree or disagree with this statement? Write

an essay explaining your position, using EXAMPLES from your journal entry as support.

2. It's fair to assume that "Girl" is at least partly autobiographical because Kincaid has often written or spoken about the influence of her mother. In "Jamaica Kincaid on Writing" (following), the author mentions rebelling against her mother's "magic." Elsewhere, she has said that her mother's close attention made Kincaid's past "a kind of museum....Clearly, the way I became a writer is that my mother wrote my life for me and told it to me." What adult has had a large influence on you? How are you different today because of him or her? Write an essay identifying the parts of yourself that you can attribute to this person—in other words, analyzing yourself as the product of this person's interest (or lack of interest) in you.

3. **CRITICAL WRITING.** The story's speaker repeatedly and gloomily connects her daughter and a "slut." Write an essay analyzing Kincaid's use of *slut*. How does the mother seem to be defining this word? Why does she repeat it so often? Should we ASSUME that the daughter actually is a "slut"? What might be the effect of this repetition on the daughter? What is the effect on you, the reader?

4. **CONNECTIONS.** Judy Brady, in "I Want a Wife" (p. 275), and Kincaid both analyze women's traditional roles, although they have different perspectives on those roles. How are the roles they describe similar? What do the speakers' TONES convey about their attitudes toward their roles? Write an essay explaining how Brady and Kincaid use word choice, sentence structures, repetition, and other elements of tone to clarify their speakers' values and feelings.

JAMAICA KINCAID ON WRITING

In a 1990 interview with Louise Kennedy in the *Boston Globe*, Jamaica Kincaid says that making sense of life is what motivates her writing. "I started out feeling alone," she remarks. "I grew up in a place where I was very alone. I didn't know then that I wanted to write; I didn't have that thought. But even if I had, I would have had no one to tell it to. They would have laughed before they threw me in a pond or something." With this beginning, Kincaid came to believe that the point of writing is not to please the reader. "Sometimes I feel—'I've pushed too far, I don't care, I don't care if you don't like this. I know it and it makes sense to me.'" The point, then, is to understand the world through the self. "I'm trying to discover the secret of myself....For me everything passes through the self."

Kincaid's writing helps her come to terms with the conflicts in her life. "I could be dead or in jail. If you don't know how to make sense of what's happened to you, if you see things but can't express them—it's so painful." Part of Kincaid's pain growing up was the "magic" her mother held over her, a power that fueled Kincaid's rebellion. "That feeling of rebellion is doomed," she says. "You can't succeed. But it's worth trying because you find out that you can't. You have to try, or you die."

Although her native Antigua figures strongly in her writing, Kincaid cannot write there. "When I'm in the place where I'm from, I can't really think. I just absorb it; I take it all in. Then I come back and take it out and unpack it and walk through it." Her need for distance has led her to live in Vermont, "the opposite of where I come from. It changes. It's mountainous. It has seasons." As for Antigua, Kincaid says, "I don't know how to live there, but I don't know how to live without there."

FOR DISCUSSION

1. How can not caring about the reader's response liberate a writer?
2. What does Kincaid mean by "everything passes through the self"? Do you experience this process from time to time?
3. How does the author view her place of birth? Do you find her last statement contradictory?

ADDITIONAL WRITING TOPICS

Division or Analysis

Write an essay by the method of division or analysis using one of the following subjects (or choose your own subject). In your essay, make sure your purpose and your principle of division or analysis are clear to your readers. Explain the parts of your subject so that readers know how each relates to the others and contributes to the whole.

1. The slang or technical terminology of a group such as stand-up comedians or computer hackers
2. An especially bad movie, television show, or book
3. A doll, game, or other toy from childhood
4. A typical TV commercial for a product such as laundry soap, deodorant, beer, or a luxury or economy car
5. An appliance or machine, such as a stereo speaker, a motorcycle, a microwave oven, or a camera
6. An organization or association, such as a social club, a sports league, or a support group
7. The characteristic appearance of a rock singer or a classical violinist
8. A year in the life of a student
9. Your favorite poem
10. A short story, essay, or other work that made you think
11. The government of your community
12. The most popular video store (or other place of business) in town
13. The Bible
14. A band or orchestra
15. A painting or statue

7

CLASSIFICATION
Sorting into Kinds

THE METHOD

To CLASSIFY is to make sense of the world by arranging many units—trucks, chemical elements, wasps, students—into more manageable groups. Zoologists classify animals, botanists classify plants—and their classifications help us to understand a vast and complex subject: life on earth. To help us find books in a library, librarians classify books into categories: fiction, biography, history, psychology, and so forth. For the convenience of readers, newspapers run classified advertising, grouping many small ads into categories such as Help Wanted and Cars for Sale.

Subjects and Reasons for Classification

The subject of a classification is always a number of things, such as peaches or political systems. (In contrast, DIVISION or ANALYSIS, the topic of the preceding chapter, usually deals with a solitary subject, a coherent whole, such as *a* peach or *a* political system.) The job of classification is to sort the things into groups or classes based on their similarities and differences. Say, for instance, you're going to write an essay about how people write. After interviewing a lot of writers, you determine that writers' processes differ widely, mainly in the amount of planning and rewriting they entail. (Notice that this determination involves analyzing the process of writing, separating it into steps. See Chap. 5.) On the basis of your findings, you create groups for planners, one-drafters, and rewriters. Once your groups are defined (and assuming they are valid), your subjects (the writers) almost sort themselves out.

Classification is done for a PURPOSE. In a New York City guidebook, Joan Hamburg and Norma Ketay discuss low-priced hotels. (Notice that already they are examining the members of a group: low-priced as opposed to medium- and high-priced hotels.) They cast the low-priced hotels into categories: Rooms for Singles and Students, Rooms for Families, Rooms for Servicepeople, and Rooms for General Occupancy. Always their purpose is evident: to match up the visitor with a suitable kind of room. When a classification has no purpose, it seems a silly and hollow exercise.

Just as you can ANALYZE a subject (or divide a pie) in many ways, you can classify a subject according to many principles. A different New York guidebook might classify all hotels according to price: grand luxury, luxury, commercial, low-priced (Hamburg and Ketay's category), fleabag, and flophouse. The purpose of this classification would be to match visitors to hotels fitting their pocketbooks. The principle you use in classifying things depends on your purpose. A linguist might explain the languages of the world by classifying them according to their origins (Romance languages, Germanic languages, Coptic languages...), but a student battling with a college language requirement might try to entertain fellow students by classifying languages into three groups: hard to learn, harder to learn, and unlearnable.

Kinds of Classification

The simplest classification is binary (or two-part), in which you sort things out into (1) those with a certain distinguishing feature and (2) those without it. You might classify a number of persons, let's say, into smokers and nonsmokers, heavy metal fans and nonfans, runners and nonrunners, believers and nonbelievers. Binary classification is most useful when your subject is easily divisible into positive and negative categories.

Classification can be complex as well. As Jonathan Swift reminds us,

> So, naturalists observe, a flea
> Hath smaller fleas that on him prey,
> And these have smaller yet to bite 'em.
> And so proceed *ad infinitum*.

In being faithful to reality, you will sometimes find that you have to sort out the members of categories into subcategories. Hamburg and Ketay did something of the kind when they subclassified the class of low-priced New York hotels. Writing about the varieties of one Germanic language, such as English, a writer could identify the subclasses of British English, North American English, Australian English, and so on.

As readers, we all enjoy watching a clever writer sort things into categories. We like to meet classifications that strike us as true and familiar. This pleasure may account for the appeal of magazine articles that classify things ("The Seven Common Garden Varieties of Moocher," "Five Embarrassing Types of Social Blunder"). Usefulness as well as pleasure may explain the popularity of classifications that EVALUATE things. In a survey of current movies, a newspaper critic might classify the films into categories: "Don't Miss," "Worth Seeing," "So-So," and "Never Mind." The magazine *Consumer Reports* uses this method of classifying in its comments on different brands of stereo speakers or canned tuna. Products are sorted into groups (excellent, good, fair, poor, and not acceptable), and the merits of each are discussed by the method of description. (Of a frozen pot pie: "Bottom crust gummy, meat spongy when chewed, with nondescript old-poultry and stale-flour flavor.")

THE PROCESS

Purposes and Theses

Classification will usually come into play when you want to impose order on a complex subject that includes many items. In one essay in this chapter, for instance, Deborah Tannen tackles miscommunications among working men and women. Sometimes you may use classification humorously, as Russell Baker does in another essay in this chapter, to give a charge to familiar experiences. Whichever use you make of classification, though, do it for a reason. The files of composition instructors are littered with student essays in which nothing was ventured and nothing gained by classification.

Things can be classified into categories that reveal truth, or into categories that don't tell us a thing. To sort out ten U.S. cities according to their relative freedom from air pollution or their cost of living or the degree of progress they have made in civil rights might prove highly informative and useful. Such a classification might even tell us where we'd want to live. But to sort out the cities according to a superficial feature such as the relative size of their cat and dog populations wouldn't interest anyone, probably, except a veterinarian looking for a job.

Your purpose, your THESIS, and your principle of classification will all overlap at the point where you find your interest in your subject. Say you're curious about how other students write. Is your interest primarily in the materials they use (word processor, typewriter, pencil), in where and when they write, or in how much planning and rewriting they do? Any of these could lead to a principle for sorting the students into groups. And that principle should be revealed in your THESIS SENTENCE (or sentences), letting readers know why you are classifying. Here, from the essays in this chapter, are two examples of classification thesis sentences:

> Inanimate objects are classified into three major categories — those that don't work, those that break down and those that get lost. (Russell Baker, "The Plot Against People")

> Unfortunately, women and men often have different ideas about what's appropriate [in conversation], different ways of speaking. Many of the conversational rituals common among women are designed to take the other person's feelings into account, while many of the conversational rituals common among men are designed to maintain the one-up position, or at least avoid appearing one-down. (Deborah Tannen, "But What Do You Mean?")

Categories

For a workable classification, make sure that the categories you choose don't overlap. If you were writing a survey of popular magazines for adults and you were sorting your subject into categories that included women's magazines and sports magazines, you might soon run into trouble. Into which category would you place *Women's Sports?* The trouble is that both categories take in the same item. To avoid this problem, you'll need to reorganize your classification on a different principle. You might sort out the magazines by their audiences: magazines mainly for women, magazines mainly for men, magazines for both women and men. Or you might group them according to subject matter: sports magazines, literary magazines, astrology magazines, fashion magazines, TV fan magazines, trade journals, and so on. *Women's Sports* would fit into either of those classification schemes, but into only *one* category in each scheme.

When you draw up a scheme of classification, be sure also that you include all essential categories. Omitting an important category can weaken the effect of your essay, no matter how well written it is. It would be a major oversight, for example, if you were to classify the residents of a dormitory according to their religious affiliations and not include a category for the numerous nonaffiliated. Your reader might wonder if your sloppiness in forgetting a category extended to your thinking about the topic as well.

Some form of outline can be helpful to keep the classes and their members straight as you develop and draft ideas. You might experiment with a diagram in which you jot down headings for the groups, with plenty of space around them, and then let each heading accumulate members as you think of them, the way a magnet attracts paperclips. This kind of diagram offers more flexibility than a vertical list or outline, and it may be a better aid for keeping categories from overlapping or disappearing.

CHECKLIST FOR REVISING A CLASSIFICATION

✔ **PURPOSE.** Have you classified for a reason? Will readers see why you bothered?

✔ **PRINCIPLE OF CLASSIFICATION.** Will readers also see what rule or principle you have used for sorting individuals into groups? Is this principle apparent in your thesis sentence?

✔ **CONSISTENCY.** Does each representative of your subject fall into one category only, so that categories don't overlap?

✔ **COMPLETENESS.** Have you mentioned all the essential categories suggested by your principle of classification?

✔ **EVIDENCE.** Have you provided enough examples for each category so that readers can clearly distinguish one from another?

CLASSIFICATION IN A PARAGRAPH: TWO ILLUSTRATIONS

Using Classification to Write About Television

Written for *The Bedford Reader,* the following paragraph uses classification to explain how a TV comedy's taped laugh track combines various laughs to sound like an actual rib-tickled audience. With the related paragraph on page 270, which ANALYZES the elements of any particular kind of laugh, this paragraph could be part of a full behind-the-scenes essay on how TV comedies make us laugh, even despite ourselves.

Most canned laughs produced by laugh machines fall into one of five reliable sounds. There are *titters,* light vocal laughs with which an imaginary audience responds to a comedian's least wriggle or grimace. Some producers rely heavily on *chuckles,* deeper, more chesty responses. Most profound of all, *belly laughs* are summoned to acclaim broader jokes and sexual innuendos. When provided at full level of sound and in longest duration, the belly laugh becomes the Big Boffola. There are also *wild howls* or *screamers,* extreme responses used not more than three times per show, lest they seem fake. These are crowd laughs, and yet the machine also offers	*Thesis sentence names principle of classification* *Categories:* *1. Titters* *2. Chuckles* *3. Belly laughs* *4. Wild howls or screamers*

freaky laughs, the piercing, eccentric screeches of solitary kooks. With them, a producer affirms that even a canned audience may include one thorny individualist.

5. Freaky laughs
Examples clearly
distinguish categories

Using Classification in an Academic Discipline

This paragraph comes from a textbook on human physical and cultural evolution. The author offers a standard classification of hand grips in order to explain one of several important differences between human beings and their nearest relatives, apes and monkeys.

There are two distinct ways of holding and using tools: the *power grip* and the *precision grip,* as John Napier termed them. Human infants and children begin with the power grip and progress to the precision grip. Think of how a child holds a spoon: first in the power grip, in its fist or between its fingers and palm, and later between the tips of the thumb and first two fingers, in the precision grip. Many primates have the power grip also. It is the way they get firm hold of a tree branch. But neither a monkey nor an ape has a thumb long enough or flexible enough to be completely *opposable* through rotation at the wrist, able to reach comfortably to the tips of all the other fingers, as is required for our delicate yet strong precision grip. It is the opposability of our thumb and the independent control of our fingers that make possible nearly all the movements necessary to handle tools, to make clothing, to write with a pencil, to play a flute.

Thesis sentence names principle of classification

Two categories explained side by side

Second category explained in greater detail

— Bernard Campbell, *Humankind Emerging*

CLASSIFICATION ELSEWHERE IN *THE BEDFORD READER*

In a number of essays besides those in this chapter, the authors use classification to help bring order to an otherwise unwieldy subject.

PART ONE

Suzanne Britt, "Neat People vs. Sloppy People"
Bruce Catton, "Grant and Lee: A Study in Contrasts"
Judy Brady, "I Want a Wife"
Armin A. Brott, "Not All Men Are Sly Foxes"
Gloria Naylor, "The Meanings of a Word"
Christine Leong, "Being a Chink"
Esther Dyson, "Cyberspace for All"

PART TWO

Stephen Jay Gould, "Sex, Drugs, Disasters, and the Extinction of Dinosaurs"

CASE STUDY
Using Classification

The summer between his sophomore and junior years of college, Kharron Reid was seeking an internship in computer networking. After seeing several likely openings posted at his school's placement office, he began compiling a résumé that would make him appealing to potential employers.

Part of Reid's challenge in drafting his résumé was to bring order to what seemed a complex and unwieldy subject, his life. The main solution was to classify his activities and interests into clearly defined groups, such as work experience, education, and special skills. Classification wasn't a conscious choice for Reid: He didn't think, "I must classify." Instead, he recognized from advice he'd seen on résumé writing that some sorting was required.

In his first draft, Reid worked to emphasize his qualifications for the internship he sought. The group that gave him the most trouble was work experience: Should he list his jobs with the specifics of each one? Or should he further sort his work experience into skills (such as computer skills, administrative skills, and communication skills) and then list the specifics of his jobs under each subcategory? He tried the résumé both ways and finally opted for the former arrangement, which seemed more straightforward, potentially less confusing to readers.

Before he could prepare his final draft, Reid also needed to decide which to put first, the category of education or the category of work experience. Here, he decided on work experience first because it was directly related to the internships he now sought; his education was more broad-based.

Reid's final résumé appears on the next page. For the cover letter he wrote to go with the résumé, see page 143.

Kharron Reid
137 Chester Street, Apt. E
Allston, MA 02134
(617) 555-4009
kreid@bu.edu

OBJECTIVE

An internship that offers experience in information systems

EXPERIENCE

Pioneer Networking, Damani, MI, May–September 1998

As an intern, worked as a LAN specialist using a Unix-based server.
- Connected eight workstations onto a LAN by laying physical platform and configuring software
- Assisted Network Engineer in monitoring operations of LAN

NBS Systems Corp., Denniston, MI, June–September 1997

As an intern, helped install seven WANs using Windows NT Workstation
- Planned layout for WANs
- Installed physical platform and configured servers

SPECIAL SKILLS

Computer programs:

Windows NT	Windows 3.1, 95, 98	Corel 6.0, 8.0
Unix	Adobe Photoshop and	Html
Linux	Pagemaker	Javascript

Internet research

INTERESTS

Building computers, designing Web sites, wrestling

EDUCATION

Boston University, School of Management, 1997 to present

Current standing: sophomore
Double major: business administration and information systems
Courses: introductory and advanced programming, information systems 1 and 2, basic business courses

Lahser High School, Bloomfield Hills, MI, 1993–1997

Graduated with academic, college-preparatory degree

REFERENCES

Available on request from Office of Career Services, Boston University, 19 Deerfield Street, Boston, MA 02215

RUSSELL BAKER

RUSSELL BAKER is one of America's notable humorists and political satirists. Born in 1925 in Virginia, Baker was raised in New Jersey and Maryland by his widowed mother. After serving in the navy during World War II, he earned a B.A. from Johns Hopkins University in 1947. He became a reporter for the *Baltimore Sun* that year and then joined the *New York Times* in 1954, covering the State Department, the White House, and Congress. From 1962 until his retirement from the *Times* in 1998, he wrote a popular column that ranged over the merely bothersome (unreadable menus) and the serious (the Cold War). Baker has twice received the Pulitzer Prize, once for distinguished commentary and again for the first volume of his autobiography, *Growing Up* (1982). Many of his columns have been collected in books, most recently *There's a Country in My Cellar* (1990). Baker has also written fiction and children's books and edited *Russell Baker's Book of American Humor* (1993). In 1993 he began his television career as host of PBS's *Masterpiece Theatre*.

The Plot Against People

The critic R. Z. Sheppard has commented that Baker can "best be appreciated for doing what a good humorist has always done: writing to preserve his sanity for at least one more day." In this piece from the *New York Times* in 1968, Baker uses classification for that purpose, taking aim, as he has often done, at things.

Inanimate objects are classified into three major categories — those 1 that don't work, those that break down and those that get lost.

The goal of all inanimate objects is to resist man and ultimately to 2 defeat him, and the three major classifications are based on the method each object uses to achieve its purpose. As a general rule, any object capable of breaking down at the moment when it is most needed will do so. The automobile is typical of the category.

With the cunning typical of its breed, the automobile never breaks 3 down while entering a filling station with a large staff of idle mechanics. It waits until it reaches a downtown intersection in the middle of the rush hour, or until it is fully loaded with family and luggage on the Ohio Turnpike.

Thus it creates maximum misery, inconvenience, frustration and ir- 4 ritability among its human cargo, thereby reducing its owner's life span.

Washing machines, garbage disposals, lawn mowers, light bulbs, 5 automatic laundry dryers, water pipes, furnaces, electrical fuses, television tubes, hose nozzles, tape recorders, slide projectors — all are in league with the automobile to take their turn at breaking down whenever life threatens to flow smoothly for their human enemies.

Many inanimate objects, of course, find it extremely difficult to 6 break down. Pliers, for example, and gloves and keys are almost totally incapable of breaking down. Therefore, they have had to evolve a different technique for resisting man.

They get lost. Science has still not solved the mystery of how they 7 do it, and no man has ever caught one of them in the act of getting lost. The most plausible theory is that they have developed a secret method of locomotion which they are able to conceal the instant a human eye falls upon them.

It is not uncommon for a pair of pliers to climb all the way from 8 the cellar to the attic in its single-minded determination to raise its owner's blood pressure. Keys have been known to burrow three feet under mattresses. Women's purses, despite their great weight, frequently travel through six or seven rooms to find hiding space under a couch.

Scientists have been struck by the fact that things that break down 9 virtually never get lost, while things that get lost hardly ever break down.

A furnace, for example, will invariably break down at the depth of 10 the first winter cold wave, but it will never get lost. A woman's purse, which after all does have some inherent capacity for breaking down, hardly ever does; it almost invariably chooses to get lost.

Some persons believe this constitutes evidence that inanimate ob- 11 jects are not entirely hostile to man, and that a negotiated peace is possible. After all, they point out, a furnace could infuriate a man even more thoroughly by getting lost than by breaking down, just as a glove could upset him far more by breaking down than by getting lost.

Not everyone agrees, however, that this indicates a conciliatory at- 12 titude among inanimate objects. Many say it merely proves that furnaces, gloves and pliers are incredibly stupid.

The third class of objects — those that don't work — is the most cu- 13 rious of all. These include such objects as barometers, car clocks, cigarette lighters, flashlights and toy-train locomotives. It is inaccurate, of course, to say that they never work. They work once, usually for the first few hours after being brought home, and then quit. Thereafter, they never work again.

In fact, it is widely assumed that they are built for the purpose of not 14 working. Some people have reached advanced ages without ever seeing some of these objects — barometers, for example — in working order.

Science is utterly baffled by the entire category. There are many 15 theories about it. The most interesting holds that the things that don't work have attained the highest state possible for an inanimate object, the state to which things that break down and things that get lost can still only aspire.

They have truly defeated man by conditioning him never to expect   16
anything of them, and in return they have given man the only peace he
receives from inanimate society. He does not expect his barometer to
work, his electric locomotive to run, his cigarette lighter to light or his
flashlight to illuminate, and when they don't it does not raise his blood
pressure.

He cannot attain that peace with furnaces and keys and cars   17
and women's purses as long as he demands that they work for their keep.

QUESTIONS ON MEANING

1. What is Baker's THESIS?
2. Why don't things that break down get lost, and vice versa?
3. Does Baker have any PURPOSE other than to make his readers smile?
4. How have inanimate objects "defeated man"?

QUESTIONS ON WRITING STRATEGY

1. What is the EFFECT of Baker's principle of classification? What categories
   are omitted here, and why?
2. Find three places where Baker uses hyperbole. (See "Figures of speech" in
   Useful Terms if you need a definition.) What is the EFFECT of the hyperbole?
3. How does the essay's INTRODUCTION help set its TONE? How does the CON-
   CLUSION reinforce the tone?
4. **OTHER METHODS.** How does Baker use NARRATION to portray inanimate
   objects in the act of "resisting" people? Discuss how these mini-narratives
   make his classification more persuasive.

QUESTIONS ON LANGUAGE

1. Look up any of these words that are unfamiliar: plausible, locomotion
   (para. 7); invariably, inherent (10); conciliatory (12).
2. What are the CONNOTATIONS of the word "cunning" (para. 3)? What is its
   effect in this context?
3. Why does Baker use such expressions as "man," "some people," and "their
   human enemies" rather than *I* to describe those who come into conflict
   with inanimate objects? How might the essay have been different if Baker
   had relied on *I*?

SUGGESTIONS FOR WRITING

1. **JOURNAL WRITING.** What other ways can you think of to classify inanimate objects? You may want to expand on Baker's categories or invent

new ones of your own based on a different principle (for example, objects no
student can live without, or objects no student would be caught dead with).
FROM JOURNAL TO ESSAY. Write a brief, humorous essay based on one
classification system from your journal entry. It may be helpful to use narration or DESCRIPTION in your classification. FIGURES OF SPEECH, especially hyperbole and understatement, can help you to establish a comic tone.

2. Think of a topic that would not generally be considered appropriate for a
serious classification (some examples: game-show winners, body odors,
stupid pet tricks, knock-knock jokes). Select a principle of classification
and write a brief essay sorting the subject into categories. You may want
to use a humorous tone; then again, you may want to approach the topic
"seriously," counting on the contrast between subject and treatment to
make your IRONY clear.

3. **CRITICAL WRITING.** In a short essay, discuss the likely AUDIENCE for "The
Plot Against People." (Recall that it was first published in the *New York
Times*.) What can you INFER from his EXAMPLES about Baker's own age and
economic status? Does he ASSUME his audience is similar? How do the con-
nections between author and audience help establish the essay's humor?
Could this humor be seen as excluding some readers?

4. **CONNECTIONS.** Read K. C. Cole's "The Arrow of Time" (p. 382). To what
extent can the behavior of the objects Baker classifies be blamed on entropy? Do any of Baker's classes of objects seem more likely than others to
be subject to the law of entropy? What might be the relationship between
entropy and Baker's theory that things that don't work have conditioned
us "never to expect anything of them" (para. 16)? In an essay that's humorous or serious, explore the answers to these questions.

RUSSELL BAKER ON WRITING

In "Computer Fallout," an essay from the October 11, 1987, *New
York Times Magazine*, Baker sets out to prove that computers make a
writer's life easier, but he ends up somewhere else entirely. The skillful way he takes us along with him is what makes the journey enjoyable — and perhaps familiar.

The wonderful thing about writing with a computer instead of a
typewriter or a lead pencil is that it's so easy to rewrite that you can make
each sentence almost perfect before moving on to the next sentence.
An impressive aspect of using a computer to write with
One of the plusses about a computer on which to write
Happily, the computer is a marked improvement over both the
typewriter and the lead pencil for purposes of literary composition, due
to the ease with which rewriting can be effectuated, thus enabling
What a marked improvement the computer is for the writer over
the typewriter and lead pencil

The typewriter and lead pencil were good enough in their day, but if Shakespeare had been able to access a computer with a good writing program

If writing friends scoff when you sit down at the computer and say, "The lead pencil was good enough for Shakespeare

One of the drawbacks of having a computer on which to write is the ease and rapidity with which the writing can be done, thus leading to the inclusion of many superfluous terms like "lead pencil," when the single word "pencil" would be completely, entirely and utterly adequate.

The ease with which one can rewrite on a computer gives it an advantage over such writing instruments as the pencil and typewriter by enabling the writer to turn an awkward and graceless sentence into one that is practically perfect, although it

The writer's eternal quest for the practically perfect sentence may be ending at last, thanks to the computer's gift of editing ease and swiftness to those confronting awkward, formless, nasty, illiterate sentences such as

Man's quest is eternal, but what specifically is it that he quests, and why does he

Mankind's quest is

Man's and woman's quest

Mankind's and womankind's quest

Humanity's quest for the perfect writing device

Eternal has been humanity's quest

Eternal have been many of humanity's quests

From the earliest cave writing, eternal has been the quest for a device that will forever prevent writers from using the word "quest," particularly when modified by such adjectives as "eternal," "endless," "tireless" and

Many people are amazed at the ease

Many persons are amazed by the ease

Lots of people are astounded when they see the nearly perfect sentences I write since upgrading my writing instrumentation from pencil and typewriter to

Listen, folks, there's nothing to writing almost perfect sentences with ease and rapidity provided you've given up the old horse-and-buggy writing mentality that says Shakespeare couldn't have written those great plays if he had enjoyed the convenience of electronic compositional instrumentation.

Folks, have you ever realized that there's nothing to writing almost

Have you ever stopped to think, folks, that maybe Shakespeare could have written even better if

To be or not to be, that is the central focus of the inquiry.

In the intrapersonal relationships played out within the mind as to the relative merits of continuing to exist as opposed to not continuing to exist

Live or die, a choice as ancient as humanities' eternal quest, is a tough choice which has confounded mankind as well as womankind ever since the option of dreaming was first perceived as a potentially negating effect of the quiescence assumed to be obtainable through the latter course of action.

I'm sick and tired of Luddites saying pencils and typewriters are just as good as computers for writing nearly perfect sentences when they—the Luddites, that is—have never experienced the swiftness and ease of computer writing which makes it possible to compose almost perfect sentences in practically no time at

Folks, are you sick and tired of

Are you, dear reader

Good reader, are you

A lot of you nice folks out there are probably just as sick and tired as I am of hearing people say they are sick and tired of this and that and

Listen, people, I'm just as sick and tired as you are of having writers and TV commercial performers who oil me in cornpone politician prose addressed to "you nice folks out

A curious feature of computers, as opposed to pencils and typewriters, is that when you ought to be writing something more interesting than a nearly perfect sentence

Since it is easier to revise and edit with a computer than with a typewriter or pencil, this amazing machine makes it very hard to stop editing and revising long enough to write a readable sentence, much less an entire newspaper column.

FOR DISCUSSION

1. What is Baker's unstated THESIS? Does he convince you?
2. Do you find yourself ever having the problem Baker finally admits to in the last paragraph?

MARION WINIK

Born in 1958 in New York City, MARION WINIK received a B.A. from Brown University in 1978 and an M.F.A. from Brooklyn College in 1983. She is the author of *The Lunch-Box Chronicles* (1998), which *Child* magazine voted the best parenting book of 1998. A memoir of her marriage, *First Comes Love* (1996), was a New York Times Notable Book. Her essays have appeared in *Redbook, Cosmopolitan,* the *Los Angeles Times,* and other periodicals, and many are collected in *Telling: Confessions, Concessions, and Other Flashes of Light* (1994). Winik has been a commentator on National Public Radio since 1991, broadcasting short essays on NPR's *All Things Considered.* "I think it is unusual and worth noting," Winik says, "that I actually prefer reading out loud to an audience to writing. The act of speaking is central to my work. I am all about voice."

What Are Friends For?

In "What Are Friends For?" Winik uses classification to sort through the varieties of friends we cherish, laugh with, lean on, and even, sometimes, try to avoid. The essay appears in Winik's collection *Telling: Confessions, Concessions, and Other Flashes of Light.*

I was thinking about how everybody can't be everything to each other, but some people can be something to each other, thank God, from the ones whose shoulder you cry on to the ones whose half-slips you borrow to the nameless ones you chat with in the grocery line.

Buddies, for example, are the workhorses of the friendship world, the people out there on the front lines, defending you from loneliness and boredom. They call you up, they listen to your complaints, they celebrate your successes and curse your misfortunes, and you do the same for them in return. They hold out through innumerable crises before concluding that the person you're dating is no good, and even then understand if you ignore their good counsel. They accompany you to a movie with subtitles or to see the diving pig at Aquarena Springs. They feed your cat when you are out of town and pick you up from the airport when you get back. They come over to help you decide what to wear on a date. Even if it is with that creep.

What about family members? Most of them are people you just got stuck with, and though you love them, you may not have very much in common. But there is that rare exception, the Relative Friend. It is your cousin, your brother, maybe even your aunt. The two of you share the same views of the other family members. Meg never should have divorced Martin. He was the best thing that ever happened to her. You can confirm each other's memories of things that happened a long time ago. Don't you remember when Uncle Hank and Daddy had that awful fight in the middle of Thanksgiving dinner? Grandma always hated Grandpa's stamp collection; she probably left the windows open during the hurricane on purpose.

While so many family relationships are tinged with guilt and obli- 4
gation, a relationship with a Relative Friend is relatively worry-free. You don't even have to hide your vices from this delightful person. When you slip out Aunt Joan's back door for a cigarette, she is already there.

Then there is that special guy at work. Like all the other people at 5
the job site, at first he's just part of the scenery. But gradually he starts to stand out from the crowd. Your friendship is cemented by jokes about co-workers and thoughtful favors around the office. Did you see Ryan's hair? Want half my bagel? Soon you know the names of his turtles, what he did last Friday night, exactly which model CD player he wants for his birth-day. His handwriting is as familiar to you as your own.

Though you invite each other to parties, you somehow don't quite 6
fit into each other's outside lives. For this reason, the friendship may not survive a job change. Company gossip, once an infallible source of entertainment, soon awkwardly accentuates the distance between you. But wait. Like School Friends, Work Friends share certain memories which acquire a nostalgic glow after about a decade.

A Faraway Friend is someone you grew up with or went to school 7
with or lived in the same town as until one of you moved away. With-out a Faraway Friend, you would never get any mail addressed in hand-writing. A Faraway Friend calls late at night, invites you to her wedding, always says she is coming to visit but rarely shows up. An ac-tual visit from a Faraway Friend is a cause for celebration and binges of all kinds. Cigarettes, Chips Ahoy, bottles of tequila.

Faraway Friends go through phases of intense communication, 8
then may be out of touch for many months. Either way, the connection is always there. A conversation with your Faraway Friend always helps to put your life in perspective: When you feel you've hit a dead end, come to a confusing fork in the road, or gotten lost in some crackerbox subdivision of your life, the advice of the Faraway Friend—who has the big picture, who is so well acquainted with the route that brought you to this place—is indispensable.

Another useful function of the Faraway Friend is to help you re- 9
member things from a long time ago, like the name of your seventh-grade history teacher, what was in that really good stir-fry, or exactly what happened that night on the boat with the guys from Florida.

Ah, the Former Friend. A sad thing. At best a wistful memory, at 10
worst a dangerous enemy who is in possession of many of your deepest

secrets. But what was it that drove you apart? A misunderstanding, a betrayed confidence, an unrepaid loan, an ill-conceived flirtation. A poor choice of spouse can do in a friendship just like that. Going into business together can be a serious mistake. Time, money, distance, cult religions: all noted friendship killers. You quit doing drugs, you're not such good friends with your dealer anymore.

And lest we forget, there are the Friends You Love to Hate. They 11 call at inopportune times. They say stupid things. They butt in, they boss you around, they embarrass you in public. They invite themselves over. They take advantage. You've done the best you can, but they need professional help. On top of all this, they love you to death and are convinced they're your best friend on the planet.

So why do you continue to be involved with these people? Why do 12 you tolerate them? On the contrary, the real question is, What would you do without them? Without Friends You Love to Hate, there would be nothing to talk about with your other friends. Their problems and their irritating stunts provide a reliable source of conversation for everyone they know. What's more, Friends You Love to Hate make you feel good about yourself, since you are obviously in so much better shape than they are. No matter what these people do, you will never get rid of them. As much as they need you, you need them too.

At the other end of the spectrum are Hero Friends. These people 13 are better than the rest of us, that's all there is to it. Their career is something you wanted to be when you grew up — painter, forest ranger, tireless doer of good. They have beautiful homes filled with special handmade things presented to them by villagers in the remote areas they have visited in their extensive travels. Yet they are modest. They never gossip. They are always helping others, especially those who have suffered a death in the family or an illness. You would think people like this would just make you sick, but somehow they don't.

A New Friend is a tonic unlike any other. Say you meet her at a 14 party. In your bowling league. At a Japanese conversation class, perhaps. Wherever, whenever, there's that spark of recognition. The first time you talk, you can't believe how much you have in common. Suddenly, your life story is interesting again, your insights fresh, your opinion valued. Your various shortcomings are as yet completely invisible.

It's almost like falling in love. 15

QUESTIONS ON MEANING

1. What is this essay's PURPOSE, do you think?
2. To what extent does Winik answer the question she poses in her title?
3. What does the author seem to ASSUME about her AUDIENCE?

QUESTIONS ON WRITING STRATEGY

1. What is Winik's principle of classification: On what basis does she sort friends into groups?
2. How are the types of friends made distinct from one another? What kinds of TRANSITIONS does Winik provide?
3. Winik introduces one category without explaining it: "But wait. Like School Friends, Work Friends share certain memories which acquire a nostalgic glow after about a decade" (para. 6). What is Winik's purpose in mentioning "School Friends"? Is it a flaw in the essay that the author does not explain the category? Why, or why not?
4. How does the first sentence establish the TONE of Winik's essay? How would you describe this tone?
5. **OTHER METHODS.** Locate the EXAMPLES Winik provides just in paragraphs 3, 5, and 10. How well do they clarify the groups Winik is discussing? What, if anything, would we miss if the examples were not included?

QUESTIONS ON LANGUAGE

1. "Buddies, for example, are the workhorses of the friendship world, the people out there on the front lines, defending you from loneliness and boredom" (para. 2). How do the two metaphors in this sentence illustrate Winik's sense of "Buddies"? (If necessary, consult *metaphor* under "Figures of speech" in Useful Terms.)
2. What is the EFFECT of *you* in the descriptions of various friends—for instance, "They feed your cat when you are out of town and pick you up from the airport when you get back" (para. 2)?
3. Winik uses a number of incomplete sentences, or sentence fragments, such as "Even if it is with that creep" (para. 2), "Cigarettes, Chips Ahoy, bottles of tequila" (7), and "Ah, the Former Friend. A sad thing" (10). Do you think these fragments are intentional? How do they affect Winik's tone?
4. Give definitions of the following words: counsel (para. 2); tinged (4); tonic (14).

SUGGESTIONS FOR WRITING

1. **JOURNAL WRITING.** In your journal, sort your friends into the categories Winik presents. You may not have friends in every category, and some of your friends may belong to new categories. Feel free to create new categories if necessary in which to place as many friends as you can.

FROM JOURNAL TO ESSAY. Choose one of the friends you categorized in your journal, and write an essay explaining why this friend fits this category. Whether the category is one of Winik's or a new one you have created, define the category carefully and use plenty of examples to show how your friend illustrates it.

2. Write an essay DEFINING *friendship* in all its varieties. When does an acquaintanceship become a friendship? What are the minimum requirements of a friend? What lines of behavior may a friend not cross and still be a friend? Develop your definition with examples from your own experience. If it serves your purpose, you may also draw on Winik's categories and definitions.

3. **CRITICAL WRITING.** Evaluate the success of Winik's classification. Are her categories well distinguished and well defined? Does she overlook any important categories of friends? Are her examples clear and effective? Offer specific EVIDENCE for your own view, whether positive or negative.

4. **CONNECTIONS.** Look at "What Are Friends For?" alongside Russell Baker's "The Plot Against People" (p. 319). Both authors draw on everyday experience, establishing categories to help make sense of that experience. Write a classification essay of your own about some aspect of everyday experience that interests you — perhaps foods, sports, drivers, roommates, neighbors, teachers, ways of procrastinating, TV talk shows. Make sure your classification has a purpose, and use plenty of examples to make your categories clear to readers.

MARION WINIK ON WRITING

Marion Winik's past has sometimes been rocky — she joined a cult as a teenager, experimented with drugs, was widowed with two small children. "I have an ambiguous, weird story," Winik told David L. Ulin of *Newsday*, "because I've done so many bad things, and I'm okay.... In a lot of ways, actually, I still have to figure out what my story is."

Figuring out her story and what it could mean is part of what makes Winik write. "In a way, all my books have been about how to integrate the mistakes we make, and the dark sides of our lives, into some reasonably positive version of ourselves. I think a lot of life's work is about getting up again. It's about integrity, and, at least for me, integrity has to encompass a lot of downsides."

FOR DISCUSSION

1. How does writing help Winik understand herself?
2. Read Stephen L. Carter's "The Insufficiency of Honesty" (p. 525), which defines *integrity*. How does Winik's view of this term correspond with Carter's? What does writing (Winik's or anyone's) have to do with integrity?

DEBORAH TANNEN

DEBORAH TANNEN is a linguist who is best known for her popular studies of communication between men and women. Born and raised in New York City, Tannen earned a B.A. from Harpur College (now the State University of New York at Binghamton); M.A.s from Wayne State University and the University of California at Berkeley; and a Ph.D. in linguistics from Berkeley. She is University Professor at Georgetown University, has published many scholarly articles and books, and has lectured on linguistics all over the world. But her renown is more than academic: With television talk-show appearances, speeches to businesspeople and senators, and best-selling books like *You Just Don't Understand* (1990) and *Talking from 9 to 5* (1994), Tannen has become, in the words of one reviewer, "America's conversational therapist." Her latest book is *The Argument Culture* (1998).

But What Do You Mean?

Why do men and women so often communicate badly, if at all? This question motivates much of Tannen's research and writing, including the essay here. Excerpted in *Redbook* magazine from Tannen's book *Talking from 9 to 5*, "But What Do You Mean?" classifies the conversational areas where men and women have the most difficulty.

Conversation is a ritual. We say things that seem obviously the 1 thing to say, without thinking of the literal meaning of our words, any more than we expect the question "How are you?" to call forth a detailed account of aches and pains.

Unfortunately, women and men often have different ideas about 2 what's appropriate, different ways of speaking. Many of the conversational rituals common among women are designed to take the other person's feelings into account, while many of the conversational rituals common among men are designed to maintain the one-up position, or at least avoid appearing one-down. As a result, when men and women interact—especially at work—it's often women who are at the disadvantage. Because women are not trying to avoid the one-down position, that is unfortunately where they may end up.

Here, the biggest areas of miscommunication. 3

1. Apologies

Women are often told they apologize too much. The reason they're 4 told to stop doing it is that, to many men, apologizing seems synonymous with putting oneself down. But there are many times when "I'm sorry" isn't self-deprecating, or even an apology; it's an automatic way of keeping both speakers on an equal footing. For example, a well-known columnist once interviewed me and gave me her phone number in case I needed to call her back. I misplaced the number and had to go through the newspaper's main switchboard. When our conversation was winding down and we'd both made ending-type remarks, I added, "Oh, I almost forgot—I lost your direct number, can I get it again?" "Oh, I'm sorry," she came back instantly, even though she had done nothing wrong and I was the one who'd lost the number. But I understood she wasn't really apologizing; she was just automatically reassuring me she had no intention of denying me her number.

Even when "I'm sorry" *is* an apology, women often assume it will be   5
the first step in a two-step ritual: I say "I'm sorry" and take half the blame, then you take the other half. At work, it might go something like this:

> A: When you typed this letter, you missed this phrase I inserted.
>
> B: Oh, I'm sorry. I'll fix it.
>
> A: Well, I wrote it so small it was easy to miss.

When both parties share blame, it's a mutual face-saving device.   6
But if one person, usually the woman, utters frequent apologies and the other doesn't, she ends up looking as if she's taking the blame for mishaps that aren't her fault. When she's only partially to blame, she looks entirely in the wrong.

I recently sat in on a meeting at an insurance company where the   7
sole woman, Helen, said "I'm sorry" or "I apologize" repeatedly. At one point she said, "I'm thinking out loud. I apologize." Yet the meeting was intended to be an informal brainstorming session, and *everyone* was thinking out loud.

The reason Helen's apologies stood out was that she was the only   8
person in the room making so many. And the reason I was concerned was that Helen felt the annual bonus she had received was unfair. When I interviewed her colleagues, they said that Helen was one of the best and most productive workers—yet she got one of the smallest bonuses. Although the problem might have been outright sexism, I suspect her speech style, which differs from that of her male colleagues, masks her competence.

Unfortunately, not apologizing can have its price too. Since so   9
many women use ritual apologies, those who don't may be seen as hard-edged. What's important is to be aware of how often you say you're sorry (and why), and to monitor your speech based on the reaction you get.

2. Criticism

A woman who cowrote a report with a male colleague was hurt   10
when she read a rough draft to him and he leapt into a critical response — "Oh, that's too dry! You have to make it snappier!" She herself would have been more likely to say, "That's a really good start. Of
course, you'll want to make it a little snappier when you revise."

Whether criticism is given straight or softened is often a matter of   11
convention. In general, women use more softeners. I noticed this difference when talking to an editor about an essay I'd written. While going over changes she wanted to make, she said, "There's one more
thing. I know you may not agree with me. The reason I noticed the
problem is that your other points are so lucid and elegant." She went
on hedging for several more sentences until I put her out of her misery:
"Do you want to cut that part?" I asked — and of course she did. But I
appreciated her tentativeness. In contrast, another editor (a man) I
once called summarily rejected my idea for an article by barking, "Call
me when you have something new to say."

Those who are used to ways of talking that soften the impact of   12
criticism may find it hard to deal with the right-between-the-eyes style.
It has its own logic, however, and neither style is intrinsically better.
People who prefer criticism given straight are operating on an assumption that feelings aren't involved: "Here's the dope. I know you're good;
you can take it."

3. Thank-Yous

A woman manager I know starts meetings by thanking everyone   13
for coming, even though it's clearly their job to do so. Her "thank-you"
is simply a ritual.

A novelist received a fax from an assistant in her publisher's office;   14
it contained suggested catalog copy for her book. She immediately
faxed him her suggested changes and said, "Thanks for running this by
me," even though her contract gave her the right to approve all copy.
When she thanked the assistant, she fully expected him to reciprocate:
"Thanks for giving me such a quick response." Instead, he said, "You're
welcome." Suddenly, rather than an equal exchange of pleasantries, she
found herself positioned as the recipient of a favor. This made her feel
like responding, "Thanks for nothing!"

Many women use "thanks" as an automatic conversation starter   15
and closer; there's nothing literally to say thank you for. Like many rituals typical of women's conversation, it depends on the goodwill of the
other to restore the balance. When the other speaker doesn't reciprocate, a woman may feel like someone on a seesaw whose partner aban-

doned his end. Instead of balancing in the air, she has plopped to the ground, wondering how she got there.

4. Fighting

Many men expect the discussion of ideas to be a ritual fight— explored through verbal opposition. They state their ideas in the strongest possible terms, thinking that if there are weaknesses someone will point them out, and by trying to argue against those objections, they will see how well their ideas hold up.

Those who expect their own ideas to be challenged will respond to another's ideas by trying to poke holes and find weak links—as a way of *helping*. The logic is that when you are challenged you will rise to the occasion: Adrenaline makes your mind sharper; you get ideas and insights you would not have thought of without the spur of battle.

But many women take this approach as a personal attack. Worse, they find it impossible to do their best work in such a contentious environment. If you're not used to ritual fighting, you begin to hear criticism of your ideas as soon as they are formed. Rather than making you think more clearly, it makes you doubt what you know. When you state your ideas, you hedge in order to fend off potential attacks. Ironically, this is more likely to *invite* attack because it makes you look weak.

Although you may never enjoy verbal sparring, some women find it helpful to learn how to do it. An engineer who was the only woman among four men in a small company found that as soon as she learned to argue she was accepted and taken seriously. A doctor attending a hospital staff meeting made a similar discovery. She was becoming more and more angry with a male colleague who'd loudly disagreed with a point she'd made. Her better judgment told her to hold her tongue, to avoid making an enemy of this powerful senior colleague. But finally she couldn't hold it in any longer, and she rose to her feet and delivered an impassioned attack on his position. She sat down in a panic, certain she had permanently damaged her relationship with him. To her amazement, he came up to her afterward and said, "That was a great rebuttal. I'm really impressed. Let's go out for a beer after work and hash out our approaches to this problem."

5. Praise

A manager I'll call Lester had been on his new job six months when he heard that the women reporting to him were deeply dissatisfied. When he talked to them about it, their feelings erupted; two said they were on the verge of quitting because he didn't appreciate their work, and they didn't want to wait to be fired. Lester was dumbfounded:

He believed they were doing a fine job. Surely, he thought, he had said nothing to give them the impression he didn't like their work. And indeed he hadn't. That was the problem. He had said *nothing*—and the women assumed he was following the adage "If you can't say something nice, don't say anything." He thought he was showing confidence in them by leaving them alone.

Men and women have different habits in regard to giving praise. 21 For example, Deirdre and her colleague William both gave presentations at a conference. Afterward, Deirdre told William, "That was a great talk!" He thanked her. Then she asked, "What did you think of mine?" and he gave her a lengthy and detailed critique. She found it uncomfortable to listen to his comments. But she assured herself that he meant well, and that his honesty was a signal that she, too, should be honest when he asked for a critique of his performance. As a matter of fact, she had noticed quite a few ways in which he could have improved his presentation. But she never got a chance to tell him because he never asked—and she felt put down. The worst part was that it seemed she had only herself to blame, since she *had* asked what he thought of her talk.

But had she really asked for his critique? The truth is, when she 22 asked for his opinion, she was expecting a compliment, which she felt was more or less required following anyone's talk. When he responded with criticism, she figured, "Oh, he's playing 'Let's critique each other'"—not a game she'd initiated, but one which she was willing to play. Had she realized he was going to criticize her and not ask her to reciprocate, she would never have asked in the first place.

It would be easy to assume that Deirdre was insecure, whether she 23 was fishing for a compliment or soliciting a critique. But she was simply talking automatically, performing one of the many conversational rituals that allow us to get through the day. William may have sincerely misunderstood Deirdre's intention—or may have been unable to pass up a chance to one-up her when given the opportunity.

6. Complaints

"Troubles talk" can be a way to establish rapport with a colleague. 24 You complain about a problem (which shows that you are just folks) and the other person responds with a similar problem (which puts you on equal footing). But while such commiserating is common among women, men are likely to hear it as a request to *solve* the problem.

One woman told me she would frequently initiate what she 25 thought would be pleasant complaint-airing sessions at work. She'd talk about situations that bothered her just to talk about them, maybe to understand them better. But her male office mate would quickly tell her how she could improve the situation. This left her feeling conde-scended to and frustrated. She was delighted to see this very impasse in a section in my book *You Just Don't Understand*, and showed it to him. "Oh," he said, "I see the problem. How can we solve it?" Then they both laughed, because it had happened again: He short-circuited the detailed discussion she'd hoped for and cut to the chase of finding a so-lution.

Sometimes the consequences of complaining are more serious: A　26 man might take a woman's lighthearted griping literally, and she can get a reputation as a chronic malcontent. Furthermore, she may be seen as not up to solving the problems that arise on the job.

7. Jokes

I heard a man call in to a talk show and say, "I've worked for two　27 women and neither one had a sense of humor. You know, when you work with men, there's a lot of joking and teasing." The show's host and the guest (both women) took his comment at face value and as-sumed the women this man worked for were humorless. The guest said, "Isn't it sad that women don't feel comfortable enough with authority to see the humor?" The host said, "Maybe when more women are in au-thority roles, they'll be more comfortable with power." But although the women this man worked for *may* have taken themselves too seri-ously, it's just as likely that they each had a terrific sense of humor, but maybe the humor wasn't the type he was used to. They may have been like the woman who wrote to me: "When I'm with men, my wit or clev-erness seems inappropriate (or lost!) so I don't bother. When I'm with my women friends, however, there's no hold on puns or cracks and my humor is fully appreciated."

The types of humor women and men tend to prefer differ. Research　28 has shown that the most common form of humor among men is razzing, teasing, and mock-hostile attacks, while among women it's self-mocking. Women often mistake men's teasing as genuinely hostile. Men often mistake women's mock self-deprecation as truly putting themselves down.

Women have told me they were taken more seriously when they　29 learned to joke the way the guys did. For example, a teacher who went to a national conference with seven other teachers (mostly women) and a group of administrators (mostly men) was annoyed that the ad-ministrators always found reasons to leave boring seminars, while the teachers felt they had to stay and take notes. One evening, when the group met at a bar in the hotel, the principal asked her how one such seminar had turned out. She retorted, "As soon as you left, it got much better." He laughed out loud at her response. The playful insult appealed to the men—but there was a trade-off. The women seemed to back off from her after this. (Perhaps they were put off by her using joking to align herself with the bosses.)

There is no "right" way to talk. When problems arise, the culprit 30 may be style differences—and *all* styles will at times fail with others who don't share or understand them, just as English won't do you much good if you try to speak to someone who knows only French. If you want to get your message across, it's not a question of being "right"; it's a question of using language that's shared—or at least understood.

QUESTIONS ON MEANING

1. What is Tannen's PURPOSE in writing this essay? What does she hope it will accomplish?
2. What does Tannen mean when she writes, "Conversation is a ritual" (para. 1)?
3. What does Tannen see as the fundamental difference between men's and women's conversational strategies?
4. Why is "You're welcome" not always an appropriate response to "Thank you"?

QUESTIONS ON WRITING STRATEGY

1. This essay has a large cast of characters: twenty-three to be exact. What function do these characters serve? How does Tannen introduce them to the reader? Does she describe them in sufficient detail?
2. How does Tannen's DESCRIPTION of a columnist as "well-known" (para. 4) contribute to the effectiveness of her EXAMPLE?
3. Whom does Tannen see as her primary AUDIENCE? ANALYZE her use of the pronoun *you* in paragraphs 9 and 19. Whom does she seem to be addressing here? Why?
4. **OTHER METHODS.** For each of her seven areas of miscommunication, Tannen COMPARES AND CONTRASTS male and female communication styles and strategies. SUMMARIZE the main source of misunderstanding in each area.

QUESTIONS ON LANGUAGE

1. What is the EFFECT of "I put her out of her misery" (para. 11)? What does this phrase usually mean?
2. What does Tannen mean by a "right-between-the-eyes style" (para. 12)? What is the FIGURE OF SPEECH involved here?
3. What is the effect of Tannen's use of figurative verbs, such as "barking" (para. 11) and "erupted" (20)? Find at least one other example of the use of a verb in a nonliteral sense.

4. Look up any of the following words whose meanings you are unsure of: synonymous, self-deprecating (para. 4); lucid, tentativeness (11); intrinsically (12); reciprocate (14); adrenaline, spur (17); contentious, hedge (18); sparring, rebuttal (19); adage (20); soliciting (23); commiserating (24); initiate, condescended, impasse (25); chronic, malcontent (26); razzing (28); retorted (29).

SUGGESTIONS FOR WRITING

1. **JOURNAL WRITING.** Tannen's ANECDOTE about the newspaper columnist (para. 4) illustrates that much of what we say is purely automatic. Do you excuse yourself when you bump into inanimate objects? When someone says, "Have a good trip," do you answer, "You too," even if the other person isn't going anywhere? Do you find yourself overusing certain words or phrases such as "like" or "you know"? Pay close attention to these kinds of verbal tics in your own and others' speech. Over the course of a few days, note as many of them as you can in your journal.

   FROM JOURNAL TO ESSAY. Write an essay classifying the examples from your journal into categories of your own devising. You might sort out the examples by context ("phone blunders," "faulty farewells"), by purpose ("nervous tics," "space fillers"), or by some other principle of classification. Given your subject matter, you might want to adopt a humorous TONE.

2. How well does your style of communication conform to that of your gender as described by Tannen? Write a short essay about a specific communication problem or misunderstanding you have had with someone of the opposite sex (sibling, friend, parent, significant other). How well does Tannen's differentiation of male and female communication styles account for your particular problem?

3. How true do you find Tannen's assessment of miscommunication between the sexes? Consider the conflicts you have observed between your parents, among fellow students or coworkers, in fictional portrayals in books and movies. Are Tannen's conclusions confirmed or called into question by your own observations and experiences? Write an essay confirming or questioning Tannen's GENERALIZATIONS, using your own examples.

4. **CRITICAL WRITING.** Tannen insists that "neither [communication] style is intrinsically better" (para. 12), that "There is no 'right' way to talk" (30). What do you make of this refusal to take sides in the battle of the sexes? Is Tannen always successful? Is absolute neutrality possible, or even desirable, when it comes to such divisive issues?

5. **CONNECTIONS.** What pictures of men and women emerge from Tannen's essay and from Dave Barry's "Batting Clean-Up and Striking Out" (p. 191)? In an essay, DEFINE each sex as portrayed by these two authors, and then agree or disagree with the definitions. Support your opinions with examples from your own observations and experience.

DEBORAH TANNEN ON WRITING

Though Deborah Tannen's "But What Do You Mean?" is written for a general audience, Tannen is a linguistics scholar who does considerable academic writing. One debate among scholarly writers is whether it is appropriate to incorporate one's experiences and biases into academic writing, especially given the goal of objectivity in conducting and reporting research. The October 1996 *PMLA* (*Publications of the Modern Language Association of America*) printed a discussion of the academic uses of the personal, with contributions from more than two dozen scholars. Tannen's comments, excerpted here, focused on the first-person *I*.

When I write academic prose, I use the first person, and I instruct my students to do the same. The principle that researchers should acknowledge their participation in their work is an outgrowth of a humanistic approach to linguistic analysis.... Understanding discourse is not a passive act of decoding but a creative act of imagining a scene (composed of people engaged in culturally recognizable activities) within which the ideas being talked about have meaning. The listener's active participation in sense making both results from and creates interpersonal involvement. For researchers to deny their involvement in their interpreting of discourse would be a logical and ethical violation of this framework....

[O]bjectivity in the analysis of interactions is impossible anyway. Whether they took part in the interaction or not, researchers identify with one or another speaker, are put off or charmed by the styles of participants. This one reminds you of a cousin you adore; that one sounds like a neighbor you despise. Researchers are human beings, not atomic particles or chemical elements....

Another danger of claiming objectivity rather than acknowledging and correcting for subjectivity is that scholars who don't reveal their participation in interactions they analyze risk the appearance of hiding it. "Following is an exchange that occurred between a professor and a student," I have read in articles in my field. The speakers are identified as "A" and "B." The reader is not told that the professor, A (of course the professor is A and the student B), is the author. Yet that knowledge is crucial to contextualizing the author's interpretation. Furthermore, the impersonal designations A and B are another means of constructing a false objectivity. They obscure the fact that human interaction is being analyzed, and they interfere with the reader's understanding. The letters replace what in the author's mind are names and voices and personas that are the basis for understanding the discourse. Readers, given only initials, are left to scramble for understanding by imagining people in place of letters.

Avoiding self-reference by using the third person also results in the depersonalization of knowledge. Knowledge and understanding do not occur in abstract isolation. They always and only occur among people.... [D]enying that scholarship is a personal endeavor entails a failure to understand and correct for the inevitable bias that human beings bring to all their enterprises.

FOR DISCUSSION

1. In arguing for the use of the first-person *I* in academic prose, Tannen is speaking primarily about its use in her own field, linguistics. From your experience with academic writing, is Tannen's argument applicable to other disciplines as well, such as history, biology, psychology, or government? Why, or why not? What have your teachers in various courses advised you about writing in the first person?
2. Try this experiment on the effects of the first person and third person (*he, she, they*): Write a passage of academic prose in one person or the other. (Tannen's example of professor A and student B can perhaps suggest a direction for your passage, or you may have one already written in a paper you've submitted.) Rewrite the passage in the other person, and ANALYZE the two versions. Does one sound more academic than the other? What are the advantages and disadvantages of each one?

STEPHANIE ERICSSON

STEPHANIE ERICSSON is an insightful and frank writer who composes out of her own life. Her book on loss, *Companion Through the Darkness: Inner Dialogues on Grief* (1993), grew out of journal entries and extensive research into the grieving process following the sudden death of her husband while she was pregnant. Ericsson was born in 1953, grew up in San Francisco, and began writing at the age of fifteen. After studying filmmaking in college, she became a screenwriter's assistant and later a writer of situation comedies and advertising. During these years she struggled with substance abuse; after her recovery in 1980 she published *Shamefaced* and *Women of AA: Recovering Together* (both 1985). *Companion into the Dawn: Inner Dialogues on Loving* (1994) is Ericsson's most recent book. She lives in Saint Paul, Minnesota, with her two children.

The Ways We Lie

Ericsson wrote this essay from notes for *Companion into the Dawn,* and it was published in the *Utne Reader* for November/December 1992. With classification, Ericsson identifies the kinds of lies we all tell at one time or another. Lying, she finds, may be unavoidable and even sometimes beneficial. But then how do we know when to stop?

William Lutz's "The World of Doublespeak," the essay following Ericsson's, also uses classification to examine types of lies, specifically the verbal substitutions that make "the bad seem good, the negative appear positive."

The bank called today and I told them my deposit was in the mail, even though I hadn't written a check yet. It'd been a rough day. The baby I'm pregnant with decided to do aerobics on my lungs for two hours, our three-year-old daughter painted the living-room couch with lipstick, the IRS put me on hold for an hour, and I was late to a business meeting because I was tired.

I told my client that traffic had been bad. When my partner came home, his haggard face told me his day hadn't gone any better than mine, so when he asked, "How was your day?" I said, "Oh, fine," knowing that one more straw might break his back. A friend called and wanted to take me to lunch. I said I was busy. Four lies in the course of a day, none of which I felt the least bit guilty about.

We lie. We all do. We exaggerate, we minimize, we avoid confrontation, we spare people's feelings, we conveniently forget, we keep secrets, we justify lying to the big-guy institutions. Like most people, I indulge in small falsehoods and still think of myself as an honest person. Sure I lie, but it doesn't hurt anything. Or does it?

I once tried going a whole week without telling a lie, and it was paralyzing. I discovered that telling the truth all the time is nearly impossible. It means living with some serious consequences: The bank charges me $60 in overdraft fees, my partner keels over when I tell him about my travails, my client fires me for telling her I didn't feel like being on time, and my friend takes it personally when I say I'm not hungry. There must be some merit to lying.

But if I justify lying, what makes me any different from slick politicians or the corporate robbers who raided the S&L industry? Saying it's okay to lie one way and not another is hedging. I cannot seem to escape the voice deep inside me that tells me: When someone lies, someone loses.

What far-reaching consequences will I, or others, pay as a result of my lie? Will someone's trust be destroyed? Will someone else pay *my* penance because I ducked out? We must consider the *meaning of our actions*. Deception, lies, capital crimes, and misdemeanors all carry meanings. *Webster's* definition of *lie* is specific:

> 1: a false statement or action especially made with the intent to deceive; 2: anything that gives or is meant to give a false impression.

A definition like this implies that there are many, many ways to tell a lie. Here are just a few.

The White Lie

A man who won't lie to a woman has very little consideration for her feelings.
—Bergen Evans

The white lie assumes that the truth will cause more damage than a simple, harmless untruth. Telling a friend he looks great when he looks like hell can be based on a decision that the friend needs a compliment more than a frank opinion. But, in effect, it is the liar deciding what is best for the lied to. Ultimately, it is a vote of no confidence. It is an act of subtle arrogance for anyone to decide what is best for someone else.

Yet not all circumstances are quite so cut-and-dried. Take, for instance, the sergeant in Vietnam who knew one of his men was killed in action but listed him as missing so that the man's family would receive indefinite compensation instead of the lump-sum pittance the military gives widows and children. His intent was honorable. Yet for twenty years this family kept their hopes alive, unable to move on to a new life.

Façades

Et tu, Brute?
—Caesar

We all put up façades to one degree or another. When I put on a   10
suit to go to see a client, I feel as though I am putting on another face,
obeying the expectation that serious businesspeople wear suits rather
than sweatpants. But I'm a writer. Normally, I get up, get the kid off to
school, and sit at my computer in my pajamas until four in the afternoon. When I answer the phone, the caller thinks I'm wearing a suit
(though the UPS man knows better).

But façades can be destructive because they are used to seduce others   11
into an illusion. For instance, I recently realized that a former friend was
a liar. He presented himself with all the right looks and the right words
and offered lots of new consciousness theories, fabulous books to read,
and fascinating insights. Then I did some business with him, and the
time came for him to pay me. He turned out to be all talk and no walk. I
heard a plethora of reasonable excuses, including in-depth descriptions
of the big break around the corner. In six months of work, I saw less than
a hundred bucks. When I confronted him, he raised both eyebrows and
tried to convince me that I'd heard him wrong, that he'd made no commitment to me. A simple investigation into his past revealed a crowded
graveyard of disenchanted former friends.

Ignoring the Plain Facts

Well, you must understand that Father Porter is only human. . . .
—A Massachusetts priest

In the '60s, the Catholic Church in Massachusetts began hear-   12
ing complaints that Father James Porter was sexually molesting
children. Rather than relieving him of his duties, the ecclesiastical
authorities simply moved him from one parish to another between
1960 and 1967, actually providing him with a fresh supply of unsuspecting families and innocent children to abuse. After treatment in
1967 for pedophilia, he went back to work, this time in Minnesota.
The new diocese was aware of Father Porter's obsession with children,
but they needed priests and recklessly believed treatment had cured
him. More children were abused until he was relieved of his duties a
year later. By his own admission, Porter may have abused as many as a
hundred children.

Ignoring the facts may not in and of itself be a form of lying, but   13
consider the context of this situation. If a lie is *a false action done with
the intent to deceive,* then the Catholic Church's conscious covering for

Porter created irreparable consequences. The church became a co-perpetrator with Porter.

Deflecting

When you have no basis for an argument, abuse the plaintiff.
—Cicero

I've discovered that I can keep anyone from seeing the true me by   14
being selectively blatant. I set a precedent of being up-front about intimate issues, but I never bring up the things I truly want to hide; I
just let people assume I'm revealing everything. It's an effective way of
hiding.

Any good liar knows that the way to perpetuate an untruth is to de-   15
flect attention from it. When Clarence Thomas exploded with accusations that the Senate hearings were a "high-tech lynching," he simply
switched the focus from a highly charged subject to a radioactive subject.[1] Rather than defending himself, he took the offensive and accused
the country of racism. It was a brilliant maneuver. Racism is now politically incorrect in official circles—unlike sexual harassment, which
still rewards those who can get away with it.

Some of the most skilled deflectors are passive-aggressive people   16
who, when accused of inappropriate behavior, refuse to respond to the
accusations. This you-don't-exist stance infuriates the accuser, who,
understandably, screams something obscene out of frustration. The trap
is sprung and the act of deflection successful, because now the passive-
aggressive person can indignantly say, "Who can talk to someone as unreasonable as you?" The real issue is forgotten and the sins of the
original victim become the focus. Feeling guilty of name-calling, the
victim is fully tamed and crawls into a hole, ashamed. I have watched
this fighting technique work thousands of times in disputes between
men and women, and what I've learned is that the real culprit is not
necessarily the one who swears the loudest.

Omission

The cruelest lies are often told in silence.
—R. L. Stevenson

Omission involves telling most of the truth minus one or two key   17
facts whose absence changes the story completely. You break a pair of
glasses that are guaranteed under normal use and get a new pair, without

---

[1] Ericsson refers to the 1991 hearings to confirm Thomas for the Supreme Court, at which Thomas was accused by Anita Hill of sexual harassment.—EDS.

mentioning that the first pair broke during a rowdy game of basketball. Who hasn't tried something like that? But what about omission of information that could make a difference in how a person lives his or her life?

For instance, one day I found out that rabbinical legends tell of another woman in the Garden of Eden before Eve. I was stunned. The omission of the Sumerian goddess Lilith from Genesis—as well as her demonization by ancient misogynists as an embodiment of female evil—felt like spiritual robbery. I felt like I'd just found out my mother was really my stepmother. To take seriously the tradition that Adam was created out of the same mud as his equal counterpart, Lilith, redefines all of Judeo-Christian history.

Some renegade Catholic feminists introduced me to a view of Lilith that had been suppressed during the many centuries when this strong goddess was seen only as a spirit of evil. Lilith was a proud goddess who defied Adam's need to control her, attempted negotiations, and when this failed, said adios and left the Garden of Eden.

This omission of Lilith from the Bible was a patriarchal strategy to keep women weak. Omitting the strong-woman archetype of Lilith from Western religions and starting the story with Eve the Rib has helped keep Christian and Jewish women believing they were the lesser sex for thousands of years.

Stereotypes and Clichés

Where opinion does not exist, the status quo becomes stereotyped and all originality is discouraged. —Bertrand Russell

Stereotype and cliché serve a purpose as a form of shorthand. Our need for vast amounts of information in nanoseconds has made the stereotype vital to modern communication. Unfortunately, it often shuts down original thinking, giving those hungry for the truth a candy bar of misinformation instead of a balanced meal. The stereotype explains a situation with just enough truth to seem unquestionable.

All the "isms"—racism, sexism, ageism, et al.—are founded on and fueled by the stereotype and the cliché, which are lies of exaggeration, omission, and ignorance. They are always dangerous. They take a single tree and make it a landscape. They destroy curiosity. They close minds and separate people. The single mother on welfare is assumed to be cheating. Any black male could tell you how much of his identity is obliterated daily by stereotypes. Fat people, ugly people, beautiful people, old people, large-breasted women, short men, the mentally ill, and the homeless all could tell you how much more they are like us than we want to think. I once admitted to a group of people that I had a mouth like a truck driver. Much to my surprise, a man stood up and said, "I'm a truck driver, and I never cuss." Needless to say, I was humbled.

Groupthink

Who is more foolish, the child afraid of the dark, or the man afraid of the light?
                                                                —Maurice Freehill

Irving Janis, in *Victims of Group Think*, defines this sort of lie as a   23
psychological phenomenon within decision-making groups in which loyalty to the group has become more important than any other value, with the result that dissent and the appraisal of alternatives are suppressed. If you've ever worked on a committee or in a corporation, you've encountered groupthink. It requires a combination of other forms of lying—ignoring facts, selective memory, omission, and denial, to name a few.

The textbook example of groupthink came on December 7, 1941.   24
From as early as the fall of 1941, the warnings came in, one after another, that Japan was preparing for a massive military operation. The Navy command in Hawaii assumed Pearl Harbor was invulnerable—the Japanese weren't stupid enough to attack the United States' most important base. On the other hand, racist stereotypes said the Japanese weren't smart enough to invent a torpedo effective in less than 60 feet of water (the fleet was docked in 30 feet); after all, U.S. technology hadn't been able to do it.

On Friday, December 5, normal weekend leave was granted to all   25
the commanders at Pearl Harbor, even though the Japanese consulate in Hawaii was busy burning papers. Within the tight, good-ole-boy cohesiveness of the U.S. command in Hawaii, the myth of invulnerability stayed well entrenched. No one in the group considered the alternatives. The rest is history.

Out-and-Out Lies

The only form of lying that is beyond reproach is lying for its own sake.
                                                                —Oscar Wilde

Of all the ways to lie, I like this one the best, probably because I get   26
tired of trying to figure out the real meanings behind things. At least I can trust the bald-faced lie. I once asked my five-year-old nephew, "Who broke the fence?" (I had seen him do it.) He answered, "The murderers." Who could argue?

At least when this sort of lie is told it can be easily confronted.   27
As the person who is lied to, I know where I stand. The bald-faced lie doesn't toy with my perceptions—it argues with them. It doesn't try to

refashion reality, it tries to refute it. *Read my lips*...No sleight of hand. No guessing. If this were the only form of lying, there would be no such things as floating anxiety or the adult-children-of-alcoholics movement.

Dismissal

Pay no attention to that man behind the curtain! I am the Great Oz!
        — The Wizard of Oz

Dismissal is perhaps the slipperiest of all lies. Dismissing feelings, 28 perceptions, or even the raw facts of a situation ranks as a kind of lie that can do as much damage to a person as any other kind of lie.

The roots of many mental disorders can be traced back to the dis- 29 missal of reality. Imagine that a person is told from the time she is a tot that her perceptions are inaccurate. "Mommy, I'm scared." "No you're not, darling." "*I don't like that man next door, he makes me feel icky.*" "Johnny, that's a terrible thing to say, of course you like him. You go over there right now and be nice to him."

I've often mused over the idea that madness is actually a sane re- 30 action to an insane world. Psychologist R. D. Laing supports this hypothesis in *Sanity, Madness and the Family*, an account of his investigation into the families of schizophrenics. The common thread that ran through all of the families he studied was a deliberate, staunch dismissal of the patient's perceptions from a very early age. Each of the patients started out with an accurate grasp of reality, which, through meticulous and methodical dismissal, was demolished until the only reality the patient could trust was catatonia.

Dismissal runs the gamut. Mild dismissal can be quite handy for 31 forgiving the foibles of others in our day-to-day lives. Toddlers who have just learned to manipulate their parents' attention sometimes are dismissed out of necessity. Absolute attention from the parents would require so much energy that no one would get to eat dinner. But we must be careful and attentive about how far we take our "necessary" dismissals. Dismissal is a dangerous tool, because it's nothing less than a lie.

Delusion

We lie loudest when we lie to ourselves.
        — Eric Hoffer

I could write the book on this one. Delusion, a cousin of dismissal, 32 is the tendency to see excuses as facts. It's a powerful lying tool because it filters out information that contradicts what we want to believe. Alcoholics who believe that the problems in their lives are legitimate reasons for drinking rather than results of the drinking offer the classic example of deluded thinking. Delusion uses the mind's ability to see things in myriad ways to support what it wants to be the truth.

But delusion is also a survival mechanism we all use. If we were 33 to fully contemplate the consequences of our stockpiles of nuclear weapons or global warming, we could hardly function on a day-to-day level. We don't want to incorporate that much reality into our lives because to do so would be paralyzing.

Delusion acts as an adhesive to keep the status quo intact. It 34 shamelessly employs dismissal, omission, and amnesia, among other sorts of lies. Its most cunning defense is that it cannot see itself.

•   •   •

The liar's punishment . . . is that he cannot believe anyone else.
            —George Bernard Shaw

These are only a few of the ways we lie. Or are lied to. As I said ear- 35 lier, it's not easy to entirely eliminate lies from our lives. No matter how pious we may try to be, we will still embellish, hedge, and omit to lubricate the daily machinery of living. But there is a world of difference between telling functional lies and living a lie. Martin Buber once said, "The lie is the spirit committing treason against itself." Our acceptance of lies becomes a cultural cancer that eventually shrouds and reorders reality until moral garbage becomes as invisible to us as water is to a fish.

How much do we tolerate before we become sick and tired of being 36 sick and tired? When will we stand up and declare our *right* to trust? When do we stop accepting that the real truth is in the fine print? Whose lips do we read this year when we vote for president? When will we stop being so reticent about making judgments? When do we stop turning over our personal power and responsibility to liars?

Maybe if I don't tell the bank the check's in the mail I'll be less tol- 37 erant of the lies told me every day. A country song I once heard said it all for me: "You've got to stand for something or you'll fall for anything."

QUESTIONS ON MEANING

1. What is Ericsson's THESIS?
2. Does Ericsson think it's possible to eliminate lies from our lives? What EV-IDENCE does she offer?
3. If it were possible to eliminate lies from our lives, why would that be desirable?
4. What is this essay's PURPOSE?

QUESTIONS ON WRITING STRATEGY

1. Ericsson starts out by recounting her own four-lie day (paras. 1–2). What is the EFFECT of this INTRODUCTION?
2. At the beginning of each kind of lie, Ericsson provides an epigraph, a short quotation that forecasts a theme. Which of these epigraphs work best, do you think? What are your criteria for judgment?
3. What is the message of Ericsson's CONCLUSION? Does the conclusion work well? Why, or why not?
4. **OTHER METHODS.** Examine the way Ericsson uses DEFINITION and EXAMPLE to support her classification. Which definitions are clearest? Which examples are the most effective? Why?

QUESTIONS ON LANGUAGE

1. In paragraph 35, Ericsson writes, "Our acceptance of lies becomes a cultural cancer that eventually shrouds and reorders reality until moral garbage becomes as invisible to us as water is to a fish." How do the two FIGURES OF SPEECH in this sentence—cancer and garbage—relate to each other?
2. Occasionally Ericsson's anger shows through, as in paragraphs 12–13 and 18–20. Is the TONE appropriate in these cases? Why, or why not?
3. Look up any of these words you do not know: haggard (para. 2); travails (4); façades (10); plethora (11); ecclesiastical, pedophilia (12); irreparable, co-perpetrator (13); patriarchal, archetype (20); gamut (31); myriad (32); reticent (36).
4. Ericsson uses several words and phrases from the fields of psychology and sociology. Define: passive-aggressive (para. 16); floating anxiety, adult-children-of-alcoholics movement (27); schizophrenics, catatonia (30).

SUGGESTIONS FOR WRITING

1. **JOURNAL WRITING.** Ericsson says, "We lie. We all do" (para. 3), and that must mean you, too. Write about some of the lies you have told. Why did you lie? What were the consequences?
   FROM JOURNAL TO ESSAY. Develop one or more of the lies you've recalled into an essay. You may choose to elaborate on your lies by classifying according to some principle or by NARRATING the story of a particular lie and its outcome. Try to give your reader a sense of your motivation for lying in the first place.
2. Ericsson writes, "All the 'isms'—racism, sexism, ageism, et al.—are founded on and fueled by the stereotype and the cliché, which are lies of exaggeration, omission, and ignorance. They are always dangerous. They take a single tree and make it a landscape" (para. 22). Write an essay discussing stereotypes and how they work to encourage prejudice. Use Ericsson's definition as a base, and expand it to include stereotypes you find particularly injurious. How do these stereotypes oversimplify? How are they "dangerous"?
3. **CRITICAL WRITING.** EVALUATE the success of Ericsson's essay, considering especially how effectively her evidence supports her GENERALIZATIONS. Are

there important categories she overlooks, exceptions she neglects to account for, gaps in definitions or examples? Offer specific evidence for your own view, whether positive or negative.

4. **CONNECTIONS.** Ericsson begins her essay by acknowledging her own lies, and she often uses the first-person *I* or *we* in explaining her categories. In contrast, the author of the following essay, William Lutz, takes a more distant approach in classifying the dishonest language called *doublespeak*. Which of these two approaches, confessional or more distant, do you find more effective, and why? When, in your view, is it appropriate to inject yourself into your writing, and when is it not?

STEPHANIE ERICSSON ON WRITING

In a recent interview on the Amazon.com Web site, Stephanie Ericsson discussed when and why she began writing. At first, she said, she did not write to communicate but to find and express herself.

I was fifteen in the year 1968, in the heart of hippie-saturated San Francisco, and like the world, I, too, underwent a major transformation. These spiritual awakenings tend to sound lofty, but the truth is that they are always messy. I began writing regularly then, when I lost my family. There was no one to tell my feelings to, so I turned to the blank white page. The page will never contradict you, never ignore you, and never judge you. I could put the chaos outside of me, and move on. It was a survival tool that I became attached to.

FOR DISCUSSION

1. Do you agree with Ericsson's assessment of the "blank white page" as benevolent and nonjudgmental?
2. In the passage above, Ericsson is talking about writing for oneself. Is it merely the absence of an audience that makes such writing potentially therapeutic? Why does articulating her thoughts — if only for herself — help Ericsson "move on"?

WILLIAM LUTZ

William Lutz was born in 1940 in Racine, Wisconsin. He received a
B.A. from Dominican College, an M.A. from Marquette University,
a Ph.D. from the University of Nevada at Reno, and a J.D. from Rutgers School of Law. Since 1971, Lutz has taught at Rutgers University
in Camden, New Jersey. For much of his career, Lutz's interest in
words and composition has made him an active campaigner against
misleading and irresponsible language. He is the author of the best-
seller *Doublespeak: From Revenue Enhancement to Terminal Living*
(1989) and its sequel, *The New Doublespeak: Why No One Knows
What Anyone's Saying Anymore* (1996). For fourteen years, he edited
the *Quarterly Review of Doublespeak*. He has written, cowritten, or
edited numerous other books, including *The Cambridge Thesaurus of
American English* and *Webster's New World Thesaurus*. In 1996, he received the George Orwell Award for Distinguished Contribution to
Honesty and Clarity in Public Language.

The World of Doublespeak

In the previous essay, Stephanie Ericsson examines the damage
caused by the outright lies we tell each other every day. But what if
our language doesn't lie, exactly, and instead just obscures meanings
we'd rather not admit to? Such intentional fudging, or *doublespeak*, is
the sort of language Lutz specializes in, and here he uses classification
to expose its many guises. "The World of Doublespeak" abridges the
first chapter in Lutz's book *Doublespeak*; the essay's title is the chapter's subtitle.

There are no potholes in the streets of Tucson, Arizona, just "pave-   1
ment deficiencies." The Reagan Administration didn't propose any
new taxes, just "revenue enhancement" through new "user's fees."
Those aren't bums on the street, just "non-goal oriented members of society." There are no more poor people, just "fiscal underachievers."
There was no robbery of an automatic teller machine, just an "unau-
thorized withdrawal." The patient didn't die because of medical mal-
practice, it was just a "diagnostic misadventure of a high magnitude."
The U.S. Army doesn't kill the enemy anymore, it just "services the
target." And the doublespeak goes on.

Doublespeak is language that pretends to communicate but really   2
doesn't. It is language that makes the bad seem good, the negative appear positive, the unpleasant appear attractive or at least tolerable.
Doublespeak is language that avoids or shifts responsibility, language
that is at variance with its real or purported meaning. It is language

that conceals or prevents thought; rather than extending thought, doublespeak limits it.

Doublespeak is not a matter of subjects and verbs agreeing; it is a matter of words and facts agreeing. Basic to doublespeak is incongruity, the incongruity between what is said or left unsaid, and what really is. It is the incongruity between the word and the referent, between seem and be, between the essential function of language—communication—and what doublespeak does—mislead, distort, deceive, inflate, circumvent, obfuscate.

How to Spot Doublespeak

How can you spot doublespeak? Most of the time you will recognize doublespeak when you see or hear it. But, if you have any doubts, you can identify doublespeak just by answering these questions: Who is saying what to whom, under what conditions and circumstances, with what intent, and with what results? Answering these questions will usually help you identify as doublespeak language that appears to be legitimate or that at first glance doesn't even appear to be doublespeak.

First Kind of Doublespeak

There are at least four kinds of doublespeak. The first is the euphemism, an inoffensive or positive word or phrase used to avoid a harsh, unpleasant, or distasteful reality. But a euphemism can also be a tactful word or phrase which avoids directly mentioning a painful reality, or it can be an expression used out of concern for the feelings of someone else, or to avoid directly discussing a topic subject to a social or cultural taboo.

When you use a euphemism because of your sensitivity for someone's feelings or out of concern for a recognized social or cultural taboo, it is not doublespeak. For example, you express your condolences that someone has "passed away" because you do not want to say to a grieving person, "I'm sorry your father is dead." When you use the euphemism "passed away," no one is misled. Moreover, the euphemism functions here not just to protect the feelings of another person, but to communicate also your concern for that person's feelings during a period of mourning. When you excuse yourself to go to the "restroom," or you mention that someone is "sleeping with" or "involved with" someone else, you do not mislead anyone about your meaning, but you do respect the social taboos about discussing bodily functions and sex in direct terms. You also indicate your sensitivity to the feelings of your audience, which is usually considered a mark of courtesy and good manners.

However, when a euphemism is used to mislead or deceive, it be- 7
comes doublespeak. For example, in 1984 the U.S. State Department
announced that it would no longer use the word "killing" in its annual
report on the status of human rights in countries around the world. Instead, it would use the phrase "unlawful or arbitrary deprivation of life,"
which the department claimed was more accurate. Its real purpose for
using this phrase was simply to avoid discussing the embarrassing situation of government-sanctioned killings in countries that are supported by the United States and have been certified by the United
States as respecting the human rights of their citizens. This use of a euphemism constitutes doublespeak, since it is designed to mislead, to
cover up the unpleasant. Its real intent is at variance with its apparent
intent. It is language designed to alter our perception of reality.

The Pentagon, too, avoids discussing unpleasant realities when it 8
refers to bombs and artillery shells that fall on civilian targets as "in-
continent ordnance." And in 1977 the Pentagon tried to slip funding
for the neutron bomb unnoticed into an appropriations bill by calling
it a "radiation enhancement device."

Second Kind of Doublespeak

A second kind of doublespeak is jargon, the specialized language of a 9
trade, profession, or similar group, such as that used by doctors, lawyers,
engineers, educators, or car mechanics. Jargon can serve an important
and useful function. Within a group, jargon functions as a kind of verbal
shorthand that allows members of the group to communicate with each
other clearly, efficiently, and quickly. Indeed, it is a mark of membership
in the group to be able to use and understand the group's jargon.

But jargon, like the euphemism, can also be doublespeak. It can 10
be—and often is—pretentious, obscure, and esoteric terminology used
to give an air of profundity, authority, and prestige to speakers and their
subject matter. Jargon as doublespeak often makes the simple appear
complex, the ordinary profound, the obvious insightful. In this sense it is
used not to express but impress. With such doublespeak, the act of
smelling something becomes "organoleptic analysis," glass becomes
"fused silicate," a crack in a metal support beam becomes a "discontinu-
ity," conservative economic policies become "distributionally conservative notions."

Lawyers, for example, speak of an "involuntary conversion" of prop- 11
erty when discussing the loss or destruction of property through theft, accident, or condemnation. If your house burns down or if your car is
stolen, you have suffered an involuntary conversion of your property.
When used by lawyers in a legal situation, such jargon is a legitimate use
of language, since lawyers can be expected to understand the term.

However, when a member of a specialized group uses its jargon to   12
communicate with a person outside the group, and uses it knowing that
the nonmember does not understand such language, then there is
doublespeak. For example, on May 9, 1978, a National Airlines 727
airplane crashed while attempting to land at the Pensacola, Florida, airport. Three of the fifty-two passengers aboard the airplane were killed.
As a result of the crash, National made an after-tax insurance benefit of
$1.7 million, or an extra 18¢ a share dividend for its stockholders. Now
National Airlines had two problems: It did not want to talk about one
of its airplanes crashing, and it had to account for the $1.7 million
when it issued its annual report to its stockholders. National solved the
problem by inserting a footnote in its annual report which explained
that the $1.7 million income was due to "the involuntary conversion of
a 727." National thus acknowledged the crash of its airplane and the
subsequent profit it made from the crash, without once mentioning the
accident or the deaths. However, because airline officials knew that
most stockholders in the company, and indeed most of the general public, were not familiar with legal jargon, the use of such jargon consti-
tuted doublespeak.

Third Kind of Doublespeak

A third kind of doublespeak is gobbledygook or bureaucratese. Ba-   13
sically, such doublespeak is simply a matter of piling on words, of overwhelming the audience with words, the bigger the words and the
longer the sentences the better. Alan Greenspan, then chair of President Nixon's Council of Economic Advisors, was quoted in *The
Philadelphia Inquirer* in 1974 as having testified before a Senate committee that "It is a tricky problem to find the particular calibration in
timing that would be appropriate to stem the acceleration in risk premiums created by falling incomes without prematurely aborting the decline in the inflation-generated risk premiums."

Nor has Mr. Greenspan's language changed since then. Speaking   14
to the meeting of the Economic Club of New York in 1988, Mr.
Greenspan, now Federal Reserve chair, said, "I guess I should warn you,
if I turn out to be particularly clear, you've probably misunderstood
what I've said." Mr. Greenspan's doublespeak doesn't seem to have held
back his career.

Sometimes gobbledygook may sound impressive, but when the   15
quote is later examined in print it doesn't even make sense. During the
1988 presidential campaign, vice-presidential candidate Senator Dan
Quayle explained the need for a strategic-defense initiative by saying,
"Why wouldn't an enhanced deterrent, a more stable peace, a better
prospect to denying the ones who enter conflict in the first place to

have a reduction of offensive systems and an introduction to defense capability? I believe this is the route the country will eventually go."

The investigation into the Challenger disaster in 1986 revealed   16
the doublespeak of gobbledygook and bureaucratese used by too many involved in the shuttle program. When Jesse Moore, NASA's associate administrator, was asked if the performance of the shuttle program had improved with each launch or if it had remained the same, he answered, "I think our performance in terms of the liftoff performance and in terms of the orbital performance, we knew more about the envelope we were operating under, and we have been pretty accurately staying in that. And so I would say the performance has not by design drastically improved. I think we have been able to characterize the performance more as a function of our launch experience as opposed to it improving as a function of time." While this language may appear to be jargon, a close look will reveal that it is really just gobbledygook laced with jargon. But you really have to wonder if Mr. Moore had any idea what he was saying.

Fourth Kind of Doublespeak

The fourth kind of doublespeak is inflated language that is designed   17
to make the ordinary seem extraordinary; to make everyday things seem impressive; to give an air of importance to people, situations, or things that would not normally be considered important; to make the simple seem complex. Often this kind of doublespeak isn't hard to spot, and it is usually pretty funny. While car mechanics may be called "automotive internists," elevator operators members of the "vertical transportation corps," used cars "pre-owned" or "experienced cars," and black-and-white television sets described as having "non-multicolor capability," you really aren't misled all that much by such language.

However, you may have trouble figuring out that, when Chrysler   18
"initiates a career alternative enhancement program," it is really laying off five thousand workers; or that "negative patient-care outcome" means the patient died; or that "rapid oxidation" means a fire in a nuclear power plant.

The doublespeak of inflated language can have serious conse-   19
quences. In Pentagon doublespeak, "pre-emptive counterattack" means that American forces attacked first; "engaged the enemy on all sides" means American troops were ambushed; "backloading of augmentation personnel" means a retreat by American troops. In the doublespeak of the military, the 1983 invasion of Grenada was conducted not by the U.S. Army, Navy, Air Force, and Marines, but by the "Caribbean Peace Keeping Forces." But then, according to the Pentagon, it wasn't an invasion, it was a "predawn vertical insertion." ...

The Dangers of Doublespeak

Doublespeak is not the product of carelessness or sloppy thinking.   20
Indeed, most doublespeak is the product of clear thinking and is carefully designed and constructed to appear to communicate when in fact
it doesn't. It is language designed not to lead but mislead. It is language
designed to distort reality and corrupt thought.... In the world created
by doublespeak, if it's not a tax increase, but rather "revenue enhancement" or "tax base broadening," how can you complain about higher
taxes? If it's not acid rain, but rather "poorly buffered precipitation,"
how can you worry about all those dead trees? If that isn't the Mafia in
Atlantic City, but just "members of a career-offender cartel," why worry
about the influence of organized crime in the city? If Supreme Court
Justice William Rehnquist wasn't addicted to the pain-killing drug his
doctor prescribed, but instead it was just that the drug had "established
an interrelationship with the body, such that if the drug is removed precipitously, there is a reaction," you needn't question that his decisions
might have been influenced by his drug addiction. If it's not a Titan II
nuclear-armed intercontinental ballistic missile with a warhead 630
times more powerful than the atomic bomb dropped on Hiroshima, but
instead, according to Air Force Colonel Frank Horton, it's just a "very
large, potentially disruptive reentry system," why be concerned about
the threat of nuclear destruction? Why worry about the neutron bomb
escalating the arms race if it's just a "radiation enhancement weapon"?
If it's not an invasion, but a "rescue mission" or a "predawn vertical insertion," you won't need to think about any violations of U.S. or international law.

Doublespeak has become so common in everyday living that many   21
people fail to notice it. Even worse, when they do notice doublespeak
being used on them, they don't react, they don't protest. Do you protest
when you are asked to check your packages at the desk "for your convenience," when it's not for your convenience at all but for someone
else's? You see advertisements for "genuine imitation leather," "virgin
vinyl," or "real counterfeit diamonds," but do you question the language or the supposed quality of the product? Do you question politicians who don't speak of slums or ghettos but of the "inner city" or
"substandard housing" where the "disadvantaged" live and thus avoid
talking about the poor who have to live in filthy, poorly heated, ramshackle apartments or houses? Aren't you amazed that patients don't
die in the hospital anymore, it's just "negative patient-care outcome"?

Doublespeak such as that noted earlier that defines cab drivers as   22
"urban transportation specialists," elevator operators as members of the
"vertical transportation corps," and automobile mechanics as "automotive internists" can be considered humorous and relatively harmless.

However, when a fire in a nuclear reactor building is called "rapid oxidation," an explosion in a nuclear power plant is called an 'energetic disassembly," the illegal overthrow of a legitimate government is termed "destabilizing a government," and lies are seen as "inoperative statements," we are hearing doublespeak that attempts to avoid responsibility and make the bad seem good, the negative appear positive, something unpleasant appear attractive; and which seems to communicate but doesn't. It is language designed to alter our perception of reality and corrupt our thinking. Such language does not provide us with the tools we need to develop, advance, and preserve our culture and our civilization. Such language breeds suspicion, cynicism, distrust, and, ultimately, hostility.

Doublespeak is insidious because it can infect and eventually destroy the function of language, which is communication between people and social groups. This corruption of the function of language can have serious and far-reaching consequences. We live in a country that depends upon an informed electorate to make decisions in selecting candidates for office and deciding issues of public policy. The use of doublespeak can become so pervasive that it becomes the coin of the political realm, with speakers and listeners convinced that they really understand such language. After a while we may really believe that politicians don't lie but only "misspeak," that illegal acts are merely "inappropriate actions," that fraud and criminal conspiracy are just "miscertification." President Jimmy Carter in April of 1980 could call the aborted raid to free the American hostages in Teheran an "incomplete success" and really believe that he had made a statement that clearly communicated with the American public. So, too, could President Ronald Reagan say in 1985 that "ultimately our security and our hopes for success at the arms reduction talks hinge on the determination that we show here to continue our program to rebuild and refortify our defenses" and really believe that greatly increasing the amount of money spent building new weapons would lead to a reduction in the number of weapons in the world. If we really believe that we understand such language and that such language communicates and promotes clear thought, then the world of 1984,[1] with its control of reality through language, is upon us.

[1]In a section omitted from this abridgement of his chapter, Lutz discusses 1984, the 1949 novel by George Orwell in which a frightening totalitarian state devises a language, called newspeak, to shape and control thought in politically acceptable forms. (For an example of Orwell's writing, see p. 596). —Eds.

QUESTIONS ON MEANING

1. What is Lutz's THESIS? Where does he state it?
2. According to Lutz, four questions can help us identify doublespeak. What are they? How can they help us distinguish between truthful language and doublespeak?
3. What, according to Lutz, are "the dangers of doublespeak"?
4. What ASSUMPTIONS does the author make about his readers' educational backgrounds and familiarity with his subject?

QUESTIONS ON WRITING STRATEGY

1. What principle does Lutz use for creating his four kinds of doublespeak — that is, what mainly distinguishes the groups?
2. Lutz quotes Alan Greenspan twice in paragraphs 13–14. What is surprising about the comment in paragraph 14? Why does Lutz include this second quotation?
3. Lutz uses many quotations that were quite current when he first published this piece in 1989 but that now may seem dated — for instance, references to Presidents Carter and Reagan or to the nuclear arms race. Do these EXAMPLES undermine Lutz's essay in any way? Is his discussion of doublespeak still valid today? Explain your answers.
4. **OTHER METHODS.** Lutz's essay is not only a classification but also a DEFINITION of *doublespeak* and an examination of CAUSE AND EFFECT. Where are these other methods used most prominently? What do they contribute to the essay?

QUESTIONS ON LANGUAGE

1. How does Lutz's own language compare with the language he quotes as doublespeak? Do you find his language clear and easy to understand?
2. ANALYZE Lutz's language in paragraphs 22 and 23. How do the CONNOTATIONS of words such as "corrupt," "hostility," "insidious," and "control" strengthen the author's message?
3. The following list of possibly unfamiliar words includes only those found in Lutz's own sentences, not those in the doublespeak he quotes. Be sure you can define variance (para. 2); incongruity, referent (3); taboo (5); condolences (6); esoteric, profundity (10); condemnation (11); ramshackle (21); cynicism (22); insidious (23).

SUGGESTIONS FOR WRITING

1. **JOURNAL WRITING.** Search for examples of doublespeak in what you read and hear — on the evening news or in newspapers, in your lease, on medical forms, in advertising for food or medications or cars, in overheard conversations. In the course of two or three days, write down all the examples you find.

FROM JOURNAL TO ESSAY. Choose at least one of the examples of doublespeak noted in your journal, and write an essay explaining why it qualifies as doublespeak. Which of Lutz's categories does it fit under? How did you recognize it? Can you understand what it means?

2. Just about all of us have resorted to doublespeak at one time or another—when making an excuse, when trying to conceal the fact that we're unprepared for an exam, when trying to impress a supervisor or potential employer. Write a NARRATIVE about a time you used deliberately unclear language, perhaps language that you yourself didn't understand. What were the circumstances? Did you consciously decide to use unclear language, or did it just leak out? How did others react to your use of this language?

3. CRITICAL WRITING. Can you determine from his essay who Lutz believes is responsible for the proliferation of doublespeak? Whose responsibility is it to curtail the use of doublespeak: just those who use it? the schools? the government? the media? we who hear it? Write an essay that considers these questions, citing specific passages from the essay and incorporating your own ideas.

4. CONNECTIONS. Read Stephanie Ericsson's "The Ways We Lie" (p. 340), which classifies the lies we tell in our daily lives. In what way, if any, do doublespeakers also lie? How, if at all, do the intentions of Ericsson's liars and Lutz's doublespeakers differ? How, if at all, are their intentions the same? Are the results of lying and doublespeak, according to each author, different or the same? Write an essay that answers these questions and that points out any other similarities or differences you notice between liars and doublespeakers. Use EVIDENCE from the two essays or from your own experience to support your thesis.

WILLIAM LUTZ ON WRITING

In 1989, C-SPAN aired an interview between Brian Lamb and William Lutz. Lamb asked Lutz about his writing process. "I have a rule about writing," Lutz answered, "which I discovered when I wrote my dissertation: You never write a book, you write three pages, or you write five pages. I put off writing my dissertation for a year, because I could not think of writing this whole thing.... I had put off doing this book [*Doublespeak*] for quite a while, and my wife said, 'You've got to do the book.' And I said, 'Yes, I am going to, just as soon as I...,' and, of course, I did every other thing I could possibly think of before that, and then I realized one day that she was right, I had to start writing.... So one day, I sit down and say, 'I am going to write five pages—that's all—and when I am done with five pages, I'll reward myself.' So I do the five pages, or the next time I will do ten pages or whatever number of pages, but I set a number of pages."

Perhaps wondering just how high Lutz's daily page count might go, Lamb asked Lutz how much he wrote at one time. "It depends," Lutz admitted. "I always begin a writing session by sitting down and rewriting what I wrote the previous day—and that is the first thing, and it does two things. First of all, it makes your writing a little bit better, because rewriting is the essential part of writing. And the second thing is to get you flowing again, get back into the mainstream. Truman Capote[1] once gave the best piece of advice for writers ever given. He said, 'Never pump the well dry; always leave a bucket there.' So, I never stop writing when I run out of ideas. I always stop when I have something more to write about, and write a note to myself, 'This is what I am going to do next,' and then I stop. The worst feeling in the world is to have written yourself dry and have to come back the next day, knowing that you are dry and not knowing where you are going to pick up at this point."

FOR DISCUSSION

1. Though his work is devoted to words and writing, William Lutz once spent a great deal of time avoiding writing. What finally got him to stop procrastinating? When you are avoiding a writing assignment, is it the length of the project or something else that prevents you from getting to work?
2. Lutz always rewrites before he starts producing new material on the idea that he didn't develop on the previous day. How come? Do you think Lutz's strategy is a good one?

---

[1]Truman Capote (1924–84) was an American journalist and fiction writer. —EDS.

ADDITIONAL WRITING TOPICS

Classification

Write an essay by the method of classification, in which you sort one of the following subjects into categories of your own. Make clear your PURPOSE in classifying and the basis of your classification. Explain each class with DEFINITIONS and EXAMPLES (you may find it helpful to make up a name for each group). Check your classes to be sure they neither gap nor overlap.

1. Commuters, or people who use public transportation
2. Environmental problems
3. Environmental solutions
4. Vegetarians
5. Talk shows
6. The ills or benefits of city life
7. The recordings you own
8. Families
9. Stand-up comedians
10. Present-day styles of marriage
11. Vacations
12. College students today
13. Movies for teenagers or men or women
14. Waiters you'd never tip
15. Comic strips
16. Movie monsters
17. Sports announcers
18. Inconsiderate people
19. Radio stations
20. Mall millers (people who mill around malls)

8

CAUSE AND EFFECT
Asking Why

THE METHOD

Press the button of a doorbell and, inside the house or apartment, chimes sound. Why? Because the touch of your finger on the button closed an electrical circuit. But why did you ring the doorbell? Because you were sent by your dispatcher: You are a bill collector calling on a customer whose payments are three months overdue.

The touch of your finger on the button is the *immediate cause* of the chimes: the event that precipitates another. That you were ordered by your dispatcher to go ring the doorbell is a *remote cause*: an underlying, more basic reason for the event, not apparent to an observer. Probably, ringing the doorbell will lead to some results: The door will open, and you may be given a check—or a kick in the teeth.

To figure out reasons and results is to use the method of CAUSE AND EFFECT. Either to explain events or to argue for one version of them, you try to answer the question "Why did something happen?" or "What were the consequences?" or "What might be the consequences?" As part of answering such a question, you use DIVISION or ANALYSIS (Chap. 6) to separate the flow of events into causes.

Seeking causes, you can ask, for example, "Why did Yugoslavia break apart?" "For what reason or reasons do birds migrate?" "What has caused sales of Detroit-made cars to pick up (or decline) lately?" Looking for effects, you can ask "What have been the effects of the birth-control pill on the typical American family?" "What impact has the personal computer had on the nursing profession?" You can look to a possible future and ask "Of what use might a course in psychology be to me if I become an office manager?" "Suppose an asteroid the size of a sofa were to strike Philadelphia — what would be the probable consequences?" Essay exams in history and economics courses tend often to ask for either causes or effects: "What were the principal causes of America's involvement in the war in Vietnam?" "What were the immediate effects on the world monetary system of Franklin D. Roosevelt's removing the United States from the gold standard?"

Don't, by the way, confuse cause and effect with the method of PROCESS ANALYSIS (Chap. 5). Some process analysis essays, too, deal with happenings; but they focus more on repeatable events (rather than unique ones) and they explain *how* (rather than why) something happened. If you were explaining the process by which the doorbell rings, you might break the happening into stages — (1) the finger presses the button; (2) the circuit closes; (3) the current travels the wire; (4) the chimes make music — and you'd set forth the process in detail. But why did the finger press the button? What happened because the doorbell rang? To answer those questions, you need cause and effect.

In trying to explain why things happen, you can expect to find a whole array of causes — interconnected, perhaps, like the strands of a spiderweb. You'll want to do an honest job of unraveling, and this may take time. For a jury to acquit or convict an accused slayer, weeks of testimony from witnesses, detectives, and psychiatrists may be required, then days of deliberation. It took a great historian, Jakob Burckhardt, most of his lifetime to set forth a few reasons for the dawn of the Italian Renaissance. To be sure, juries must take great care when a life hangs in the balance; and Burckhardt, after all, was writing an immense book. To produce a college essay, you don't have forty years; but before you start to write, you will need to devote extra time and thought to seeing which facts are the causes, and which matter most.

To answer the questions "Why?" and "What followed as a result?" may sometimes be hard, but it can be satisfying — even illuminating. Indeed, to seek causes and effects is one way for the mind to discover order in a reality that otherwise might seem (as life came to seem to Macbeth) "a tale told by an idiot, full of sound and fury, signifying nothing."

THE PROCESS

Subjects and Purposes

The method of cause and effect tends to suggest itself: If you have a subject and soon start thinking "Why?" or "What results?" or "What if?" then you are on the way to analyzing causation. Your subject may be impersonal—like a political victory or a sports defeat—or it may be quite personal. Indeed, an excellent cause-and-effect paper may be written on a subject very near to you. You can ask yourself why you behaved in a certain way at a certain moment. You can examine the reasons for your current beliefs and attitudes. Writing such a paper, you might happen upon a truth you hadn't realized before.

Whether your subject is personal or impersonal, make sure it is manageable: You should be able to get to the bottom of it, given the time and information available. For a 500-word essay due Thursday, the causes of teenage rebellion would be a less feasible topic than why a certain thirteen-year-old you know ran away from home.

Before rushing to list causes or effects, stop a moment to consider what your PURPOSE might be in writing. Much of the time you'll seek simply to explain what did or might occur, discovering and laying out the connections as clearly and accurately as you can. But when reasonable people could disagree over causes or effects, you may want to go further, arguing for one interpretation over others. You'll still need to be clear and accurate in presenting your interpretation, but you'll also need to treat the others fairly. (See Chap. 10 on argument and persuasion.)

Causal Relations

Your toughest job in writing a cause-and-effect essay may be figuring out what caused what. Sometimes one event will appear to trigger another, and it in turn will trigger yet another, and another still, in an order we call a *causal chain*. A classic example of such a chain is set forth in a Mother Goose rhyme:

> For want of a nail the shoe was lost,
> For want of a shoe the horse was lost,
> For want of a horse the rider was lost,
> For want of a rider the battle was lost,
> For want of a battle the kingdom was lost—
> And all for the want of a nail.

In reality, causes are seldom so easy to find as that missing nail: They tend to be many and complicated. A battle may be lost for more than one reason. Perhaps the losing general had fewer soldiers and had a blinding hangover the morning he mapped out his battle strategy. Perhaps winter set in, expected reinforcements failed to arrive, and a Joan of Arc inspired the winning army. The downfall of a kingdom is not to be explained as though it were the toppling of the last domino in a file. Still, one event precedes another in time, and in discerning causes you don't ignore chronological order; you pay attention to it.

When you can see a number of apparent causes, weigh them and assign each a relative importance. Which do you find matter most? Often, you will see that causes are more important or less so: major or minor. If Judd acquires a heavy drug habit and also takes up residence in a video arcade, and as a result finds himself penniless, it is probably safe to assume that the drug habit is the major cause of his going broke and his addiction to video games a minor one. If you were writing about his sad case, you'd probably emphasize the drug habit by giving it most of your space, perhaps touching on video games briefly.

When seeking remote causes, look only as far back as necessary. Explaining why a small town has fallen on hard times, you might confine yourself to the immediate cause of the hardship: the closing of a factory. You might explain what caused the shutdown: a dispute between union and management. You might even go back to the cause of the dispute (announced firings) and the cause of the firings (loss of sales to a competitor). For a short essay, that might be far enough back in time to go; but if you were writing a whole book (*Pottsville: Its Glorious Past and Its Present Agony*), you might look to causes still more remote. You could trace the beginning of the decline of Pottsville back to the invention, in 1845, of a better carrot grater. A manageable short paper showing effects might work in the other direction, moving from the factory closing to its impact on the town: unemployment, the closing of stores and the only movie house, people packing up and moving away.

Two cautions about causal relations are in order here. One is to beware of confusing coincidence with cause. In the logical FALLACY called *post hoc* (short for Latin *post hoc, ergo propter hoc*, "after this, therefore because of this"), one assumes, erroneously, that because A happened before B, A must have caused B. This is the error of the superstitious man who decides that he lost his job because a black cat walked in front of him. Another error is to oversimplify causes by failing to recognize their full number and complexity—claiming, say, that violent crime is simply a result of "all those gangster shows on TV." Avoid such wrong turns in reasoning by patiently looking for evidence before you write, and by giving it careful thought. (For a fuller list of such fallacies, or errors in reasoning, see pp. 461–63.)

Discovery of Causes

To help find causes of actions and events, you can ask yourself a few searching questions. These have been suggested by the work of the literary critic Kenneth Burke:

1. *What act am I trying to explain?*
2. *What is the character, personality, or mental state of whoever acted?*
3. *In what scene or location did the act take place, and in what circumstances?*
4. *What instruments or means did the person use?*
5. *For what purpose did the person act?*

Burke calls these elements a *pentad* (or set of five): the *act*, the *actor*, the *scene*, the *agency*, and the *purpose*. If you are trying to explain, for instance, why a person burned down a liquor shop, it will be revealing to ask about his character and mental state. Was the act committed by the shop's worried, debt-ridden owner? a mentally disturbed anti-alcohol crusader? a drunk who had been denied a purchase? The scene of the burning, too, might tell you something. Was the shop near a church, a mental hospital, or a fireworks factory? And what was the agency (or means of the act): a flaming torch or a flipped-away cigarette butt? To learn the purpose might be illuminating, whether it was to collect insurance on the shop, to get revenge, or to work what the actor believed to be the will of the Lord. You can further deepen your inquiry by seeing relationships between the terms of the pentad. Ask, for instance, what does the actor have to do with this scene? (Is he or she the neighbor across the street, who has been staring at the liquor shop resentfully for the past twenty years?)[1]

You can use Burke's pentad to help explain the acts of groups as well as those of individuals. Why, for instance, did the sophomore class revel degenerate into a brawl? Here are some possible answers:

1. *Act:* the brawl
2. *Actors:* the sophs were letting off steam after exams, and a mean, tense spirit prevailed
3. *Scene:* a keg-beer party outdoors in the quad at midnight on a sticky and hot May night
4. *Agencies:* fists and sticks

---

[1] If you are interested and care to explore the possibilities of Burke's pentad, you can pair up its five terms in ten different ways: act to actor, actor to scene, actor to agency, actor to purpose, act to scene, act to agency, act to purpose, scene to agency, scene to purpose, agency to purpose. This approach can go profoundly deep. We suggest you try writing ten questions (one for each pair) in the form "What does act have to do with actor?" Ask them of some act you'd like to explain.

5. *Purpose:* the brawlers were seeking to punish whoever kicked over the keg

Don't worry if not all the questions apply, if not all the answers are immediately forthcoming. Bring the pentad to bear on the sad case of Judd, the drug addict, and probably only the question about his character and mental state would help you much. Even a single hint, though, can help you write. Burke's pentad isn't meant to be a grim rigmarole; it is a means of discovery, to generate a lot of possible material for you—insights, observations, hunches to pursue. It won't solve each and every human mystery, but sometimes it will helpfully deepen your thought.

Purpose and Thesis

Your cause-and-effect writing may have started with a question, but you don't want your essay to leave your readers asking their own question: "Why did this writer bother to analyze causes and effects?" Forestall such a question by *telling* why: Assert your main idea in a THE-SIS SENTENCE or sentences.

The essays in this chapter provide good examples of thesis sentences that put across, concisely, what the subject is and why the author is bothering to analyze causes or effects. Here are a few examples:

It is possible to stop most drug addiction in the United States within a very short time. Simply make all drugs available and sell them at cost. (Gore Vidal, "Drugs")

My suspicion is, in fact, that very few of us...have really responded to the AIDS crisis the way the Federal Government and educators would like us to believe. My guess is that we're all but ignoring it and that almost anyone who claims otherwise is lying. (Meghan Daum, "Safe-Sex Lies")

There are voices enough, both inner and outer, urging us to deal with difficulties by pulling up stakes and heading for new territory....I wish to raise here a contrary voice, to say a few words on behalf of staying put, learning the ground, going deeper. (Scott Russell Sanders, "Homeplace")

Final Word

In stating what you believe to be causes and effects, don't be afraid to voice a well-considered hunch. Your instructor doesn't expect you to write, in a short time, a definitive account of the causes of an event or a belief or a phenomenon—only to write a coherent and reasonable one. To discern all causes—including remote ones—and all effects is beyond the power of any one human mind. Still, admirable and well-informed writers on matters such as politics, economics, and world and national affairs are often canny guessers and brave drawers of inferences. At times, even the most cautious and responsible writer has to leap boldly over a void to strike firm ground on the far side. Consider your evidence. Focus your thinking. Look well before leaping. Then take off.

CHECKLIST FOR REVISING A CAUSE-AND-EFFECT ESSAY

✔ **SUBJECT.** Have you been able to cover your subject adequately in the time and space available? Should you perhaps narrow the subject so that you can fairly address the important causes and/or effects?

✔ **COMPLETENESS.** Have you included all relevant causes or effects? Does your analysis reach back for remote causes or forward for remote effects?

✔ **CAUSAL RELATIONS.** Have you presented a clear pattern of causes or effects? Have you distinguished the remote from the immediate, the major from the minor?

✔ **ACCURACY AND FAIRNESS.** Have you avoided the *post hoc* fallacy, assuming that A caused B just because it preceded B? Have you also avoided oversimplifying and instead covered causes or effects in all their complexity?

✔ **FOCUS.** For your readers' benefit, have you focused your analysis by stating your main idea succinctly in a thesis sentence or sentences?

CAUSE AND EFFECT IN A PARAGRAPH: TWO ILLUSTRATIONS

Using Cause and Effect to Write About Television

In the following paragraph, the writer poses and concisely answers a question about soccer's near-absence from American TV. The paragraph was written especially for *The Bedford Reader*, but it could serve as a component of a full essay, perhaps one analyzing how television affects sports in general.

Why is it that, despite a growing interest in soccer among American athletes, and despite its ranking as the most popular sport in the world, commercial television all but ignores it? Granted, soccer sometimes makes it to cable, as during the World Cup, but mostly it's shut out. The reason stems partly from the basic nature of commercial television, which

Topic sentence: question to be answered

Analysis of causes

exists not to inform and entertain but to sell. During most major sporting events on television—football, baseball, basketball, boxing—producers can take advantage of natural interruptions in the action to broadcast sales pitches; or, if the natural breaks occur too infrequently, the producers can contrive time-outs for the sole purpose of airing lucrative commercials. But soccer is played in two solid halves of forty-five minutes each; not even injury to a player is cause for a time-out. How, then, to insert the requisite number of commercial breaks without resorting to false fouls or other questionable tactics? After CBS aired a soccer match, on May 27, 1967, players reported, according to Stanley Frank, that before the game the referee had instructed them "to stay down every nine minutes." The resulting hue and cry rose all the way to the House Communications Subcommittee. From that day to this, no one has been able to figure out how to screen advertising jingles during a televised soccer game. The result is that commercial television has treated soccer almost as if it didn't exist.

Commercial TV requires commercial breaks

Soccer is played with only one break

Example of failed attempt to adapt soccer to TV

Result: little soccer on TV

Using Cause and Effect in an Academic Discipline

This paragraph from a textbook on American history explains the causes of a "fateful decision" in the 1960s—fateful because, as the authors' text goes on to explain, the decision had grave and far-reaching consequences for the United States.

Many factors played a role in [President Lyndon] Johnson's fateful decision [to escalate the Vietnam War]. But the most obvious explanation is that the new president faced many pressures to expand the American involvement and only a very few to limit it. As the untested successor to a revered and martyred president, he felt obliged to prove his worthiness for the office by continuing the policies of his predecessor. Aid to South Vietnam had been one of the most prominent of those policies. Johnson also felt it necessary to retain in his administration many of the important figures of the Kennedy years. In doing so, he surrounded himself with a group of foreign policy advisers—Secretary of State Dean Rusk, Secretary of Defense Robert McNamara, National Security Adviser McGeorge Bundy—who strongly believed not only that the United States had an important obligation to resist communism in Vietnam, but that it possessed the ability and resources to make that resistance successful. As a result, Johnson seldom had access to information making clear how difficult the new commitment might become. A

Topic sentence: summary of causes to be discussed

Causes:

Need to prove worthiness

Advisers urging involvement and shutting off alternative views

compliant Congress raised little protest to, and indeed at one point openly endorsed, Johnson's use of executive powers to lead the nation into war. And for several years at least, public opinion remained firmly behind him—in part because Barry Goldwater's bellicose remarks about the war during the 1964 campaign made Johnson seem by comparison to be a moderate on the issue. Above all, intervention in South Vietnam was fully consistent with nearly twenty years of American foreign policy. An anticommunist ally was appealing to the United States for assistance; all the assumptions of the containment doctrine seemed to require the nation to oblige. Johnson seemed unconcerned that the government of South Vietnam existed only because the United States had put it there, and that the regime had never succeeded in acquiring the loyalty of its people. Vietnam, he believed, provided a test of American willingness to fight communist aggression, a test he was determined not to fail.

—Richard N. Current et al., *American History: A Survey*

Congressional cooperation

Support of public opinion

Consistency with American foreign policy against communism

CAUSE AND EFFECT ELSEWHERE IN *THE BEDFORD READER*

Reasoning from causes to effects is such a basic and powerful pattern of thought that the method serves most of the authors in this book, not just those in this chapter. The essays listed below rely heavily on cause and effect, while developing ideas with other methods as well.

PART ONE

Ralph Ellison, "On Being the Target of Discrimination"
Barbara Huttmann, "A Crime of Compassion"
Brad Manning, "Arm Wrestling with My Father"
Itabari Njeri, "When Morpheus Held Him"
Barbara Lazear Ascher, "On Compassion"
Brent Staples, "Black Men and Public Space"
Bruce Catton, "Grant and Lee: A Study in Contrasts"
Nancy Mairs, "Disability"
Jeff Greenfield, "The Black and White Truth About Basketball"
Linnea Saukko, "How to Poison the Earth"
Phillip Lopate, "Confessions of a Shusher"
Gail Sheehy, "Predictable Crises of Adulthood"
Deborah Tannen, "But What Do You Mean?"
Stephanie Ericsson, "The Ways We Lie"
William Lutz, "The World of Doublespeak"
Gloria Naylor, "The Meanings of a Word"

CASE STUDY
Using Cause and Effect

An ardent supporter of her school's track team, Kate Krueger was a sophomore during the team's first winning season in many years. At the end of the season, the student newspaper published a letter to the editor saying that the successes were due to a new coach. Krueger found this explanation inadequate and decided to say so in her own letter. The cause-and-effect analysis below appeared in the newspaper the following week.

Between the first draft and the final version of her letter, Krueger made one significant addition. At first, she ignored any contributions of the new coach, thinking that the original letter writer had more than covered them. But since Krueger actually agreed that the coach had helped the team, her first draft did what she accused the letter of doing: It oversimplified. In her revision, Krueger acknowledged the coach's contributions while also detailing the other causes she saw at work.

May 2, 1999

To the Editor:

I take issue with Tom Boatz's letter that was printed in the April 30 *Weekly*. Boatz attributes the success of this year's track team solely to the new coach, John Barak. I have several close friends who are athletes on the track team, so as an interested observer and fan I believe that Boatz oversimplified the causes of the team's recent success.

To be sure, Coach Barak did improve the training regimen and overall morale, and these have certainly contributed to the winning season. Both Coach Barak and the team members themselves can share credit for an impressive work ethic and a sense of camaraderie unequaled in previous years. However, several factors outside Coach Barak's control may have been even more influential.

This year's team gained several phenomenal freshman athletes, such as Kristin Hall, who anchored the 4x400 and 4x800 relays and played an integral part in setting several school records, and Eric Asper, who was undefeated in the shot put.

Even more important, and also unmentioned by Tom Boatz, is the college's increased funding for the track program. Last year the school allotted 50 percent more for equipment, and the results have been dramatic. For example, the new vaulting poles are now the correct length and correspond to the weights of the individual athletes, giving them more power and height. Some vaulters have been able to vault as much as a foot higher than their previous records. Similarly, new starting blocks have allowed the team's sprinters to drop valuable seconds off their times.

I agree with Tom Boatz that Coach Barak deserves much credit for the track team's successes. But the athletes do, too, and so does the college for at last supporting its track program.

—KATE KRUEGER '01

GORE VIDAL

GORE VIDAL was born in 1925 at the U.S. Military Academy at West Point, where his father was an instructor. At the age of nineteen, he wrote his first novel, *Williwaw* (1946), while serving as a warrant officer aboard an army supply ship. Twenty-one other novels followed, including *Burr* (1973), *Duluth* (1983), *Lincoln* (1984), *Empire* (1987), and *Hollywood* (1989). He has also written mysteries under the pen name Edgar Box. As a playwright, he is best known for *Visit to a Small Planet* (1957), which was made into a film. The grandson of Senator T. P. Gore, who represented Oklahoma for thirty years, Vidal twice ran unsuccessfully for Congress, and in 1992 he portrayed a senator in the movie *Bob Roberts*. A provocative and perceptive literary and social critic, Vidal is a frequent contributor to *The New York Review of Books* and other magazines, and he has published more than a dozen collections of essays, most recently *The Essential Gore Vidal* (1999). His latest books also include a memoir, *Palimpsest* (1995); a history, *The American Presidency* (1998); and a novel, *The Smithsonian Institution* (1998). Vidal divides his time between Italy and America.

Drugs

Vidal first published "Drugs" in 1970 on the *New York Times*'s op-ed page and then included the essay in *Homage to Daniel Shays: Collected Essays 1952–1972*. In just twelve short paragraphs, Vidal analyzes several sets of cause and effect: why making drugs illegal does not work to stop drug addiction and trafficking, why legalizing drugs would work, and why nonetheless legalization is unlikely to occur. "Drugs" is dated in some ways, but the problem it addresses has only worsened. Lately, an increasing number of social scientists, medical professionals, and politicians have urged that we consider just such a radical solution as Vidal proposes.

It is possible to stop most drug addiction in the United States within 1 a very short time. Simply make all drugs available and sell them at cost. Label each drug with a precise description of what effect—good and bad—the drug will have on the taker. This will require heroic honesty. Don't say that marijuana is addictive or dangerous when it is neither, as millions of people know—unlike "speed," which kills most unpleasantly, or heroin, which is addictive and difficult to kick.

For the record, I have tried—once—almost every drug and liked 2 none, disproving the popular Fu Manchu theory that a single whiff of opium will enslave the mind. Nevertheless many drugs are bad for certain people to take and they should be told why in a sensible way.

Along with exhortation and warning, it might be good for our cit-   3
izens to recall (or learn for the first time) that the United States was the
creation of men who believed that each man has the right to do what
he wants with his own life as long as he does not interfere with his
neighbor's pursuit of happiness. (That his neighbor's idea of happiness
is persecuting others does confuse matters a bit.)

This is a startling notion to the current generation of Americans.   4
They reflect a system of public education which has made the Bill of
Rights, literally, unacceptable to a majority of high school graduates
(see the annual Purdue reports) who now form the "silent majority"—
a phrase which that underestimated wit Richard Nixon took from
Homer, who used it to describe the dead.

Now one can hear the warning rumble begin: If everyone is al-   5
lowed to take drugs everyone will and the GNP will decrease, the Com-
mies will stop us from making everyone free, and we shall end up a race
of zombies, passively murmuring "groovy" to one another. Alarming
thought. Yet it seems most unlikely that any reasonably sane person
will become a drug addict if he knows in advance what addiction is going to be like.

Is everyone reasonably sane? No. Some people will always become   6
drug addicts just as some people will always become alcoholics, and it is
just too bad. Every man, however, has the power (and should have the
legal right) to kill himself if he chooses. But since most men don't, they
won't be mainliners either. Nevertheless, forbidding people things they
like or think they might enjoy only makes them want those things all
the more. This psychological insight is, for some mysterious reason,
perennially denied our governors.

It is a lucky thing for the American moralist that our country has   7
always existed in a kind of time-vacuum: We have no public memory of
anything that happened before last Tuesday. No one in Washington today recalls what happened during the years alcohol was forbidden to
the people by a Congress that thought it had a divine mission to stamp
out Demon Rum—launching, in the process, the greatest crime wave
in the country's history, causing thousands of deaths from bad alcohol,
and creating a general (and persisting) contempt among the citizenry
for the laws of the United States.

The same thing is happening today. But the government has   8
learned nothing from past attempts at prohibition, not to mention re-
pression.

Last year when the supply of Mexican marijuana was slightly   9
curtailed by the Feds, the pushers got the kids hooked on heroin
and deaths increased dramatically, particularly in New York. Whose
fault? Evil men like the Mafiosi? Permissive Dr. Spock? Wild-eyed Dr.
Leary? No.

The government of the United States was responsible for those 10 deaths. The bureaucratic machine has a vested interest in playing cops and robbers. Both the Bureau of Narcotics and the Mafia want strong laws against the sale and use of drugs because if drugs are sold at cost there would be no money in it for anyone.

If there was no money in it for the Mafia, there would be no 11 friendly playground pushers, and addicts would not commit crimes to pay for the next fix. Finally, if there was no money in it, the Bureau of Narcotics would wither away, something they are not about to do without a struggle.

Will anything sensible be done? Of course not. The American 12 people are as devoted to the idea of sin and its punishment as they are to making money—and fighting drugs is nearly as big a business as pushing them. Since the combination of sin and money is irresistible (particularly to the professional politician), the situation will only grow worse.

QUESTIONS ON MEANING

1. What do you take to be Vidal's main PURPOSE in writing this essay? How well does he accomplish it?
2. For what reasons, according to Vidal, is it unlikely that our drug laws will be eased? Can you suggest other possible reasons why the Bureau of Narcotics favors strict drug laws?
3. Vidal's essay was first published three decades ago. Do you find the views expressed in it still timely, or out of date?

QUESTIONS ON WRITING STRATEGY

1. How would you characterize Vidal's humor? Find some examples of it.
2. Where in the essay does Vidal appear to anticipate the response of his AUDIENCE? How can you tell?
3. What function do the essay's RHETORICAL QUESTIONS perform?
4. **OTHER METHODS.** Study Vidal's use of EXAMPLE in paragraphs 8–10. Does the example of the U.S. government's role in heroin deaths effectively support Vidal's point that restricting drug use does not work? Is Vidal guilty here of oversimplification (p. 364)?

QUESTIONS ON LANGUAGE

1. Know the definitions of the following terms: exhortation (para. 3); GNP (5); mainliners, perennially (6); curtailed (9).
2. How do you interpret Vidal's use of the phrase "underestimated wit" to describe Richard Nixon?

SUGGESTIONS FOR WRITING

1. **JOURNAL WRITING.** Vidal is convinced that the best way to combat the drug problem in this country is to "make all drugs available and sell them at cost." Does this seem like a good idea to you? What do you think would be the practical effects—positive or negative—of legalizing drugs?

   FROM JOURNAL TO ESSAY. Now that you have considered the effects of legalizing drugs, look back at Vidal's explanations for why they have *not* been legalized. In an essay, explain why you think the United States resists legalizing drugs. You may support Vidal's moral and economic arguments, you may oppose one or several of his claims, or you may propose new reasons of your own. In any case, be sure to make clear, as Vidal does, the connection between the foreseeable effects of legalization and the reasoning that keeps drugs illegal.

2. Research the situation reported by Vidal in paragraphs 9 and 10. (Begin with the *New York Times Index* for the years 1969 and 1970.) Write an essay that clearly and objectively analyzes the causes of the situation.

3. **CRITICAL WRITING.** How readily do you accept Vidal's statement that "each man has the right to do what he wants with his own life"—including, presumably, to be a drug addict—"as long as he does not interfere with his neighbor's pursuit of happiness" (para. 3)? Do you accept Vidal's implicit ASSUMPTION that people with easy access to drugs are not necessarily threats to their neighbors? Back up your answers with EVIDENCE from your experience and reading.

4. **CONNECTIONS.** Like Vidal, Meghan Daum, in "Safe-Sex Lies" (p. 384), takes a controversial view. Write an essay that COMPARES AND CONTRASTS the ways these two authors present their views. Consider in your essay how each author establishes his or her authority and credibility; uses evidence such as personal experience, facts, and examples; anticipates readers' responses; and addresses readers through TONE.

GORE VIDAL ON WRITING

"Do you find writing easy?" Gerald Clark asked Gore Vidal for the *Paris Review*. "Do you enjoy it?"

Oh, yes, of course I enjoy it. I wouldn't do it if I didn't. Whenever I get up in the morning, I write for about three hours. I write novels in longhand on yellow pads, exactly like the First Criminal Nixon. For some reason I write plays and essays on the typewriter. The first draft usually comes rather fast. One oddity: I never reread a text until I have finished the first draft. Otherwise it's too discouraging. Also, when you have the whole thing in front of you for the first time, you've forgotten most of it and see it fresh. Rewriting, however, is a slow, grinding business.

When I first started writing, I used to plan everything in advance, not only chapter to chapter but page to page. Terribly constricting—

like doing a film from someone else's meticulous treatment. About the time of *The Judgment of Paris* [a novel published in 1952] I started improvising. I began with a mood. A sentence. The first sentence is all-important. [My novel] *Washington, D.C.* began with a dream, a summer storm at night in a garden above the Potomac—that was Merrywood, where I grew up.

The most interesting thing about writing is the way that it obliterates time. Three hours seem like three minutes. Then there is the business of surprise. I never know what is coming next. The phrase that sounds in the head changes when it appears on the page. Then I start probing it with a pen, finding new meanings. Sometimes I burst out laughing at what is happening as I twist and turn sentences. Strange business, all in all. One never gets to the end of it. That's why I go on, I suppose. To see what the next sentences I write will be.

FOR DISCUSSION

1. What is it that Vidal seems to enjoy most about writing?
2. What advantage does he find in not planning every page in advance?

K. C. COLE

K. C. COLE is a journalist and essayist who writes mainly about science and women's issues. She was born in 1946 in Detroit, Michigan, and received a B.A. in 1968 from Columbia University. She began her journalism career as a specialist in Eastern European affairs, working as a reporter in Hungary and the former Czechoslovakia and Soviet Union. In the early 1970s, back in the United States, she began writing about science for the Exploratorium, a science museum in San Francisco. She has published several books with the Exploratorium, including *Facets of Light: Colors and Images and Things That Glow in the Dark* (1980). Cole has published articles on education, science, and women in *Saturday Review*, *Newsday*, the *New York Times*, and other periodicals. She is currently a science writer for the *Los Angeles Times*. Other books include *Between the Lines* (1982), a collection of her essays on women and women's issues; *Order in the Universe: The Shape of Relative Motion* (1986); *The Universe and the Teacup: The Mathematics of Truth and Beauty* (1998); and *First You Build a Cloud: And Other Reflections on Physics as a Way of Life* (1999). In 1995 Cole received the American Institute of Physics award for best science writer.

The Arrow of Time

One of Cole's great talents is translating complex scientific concepts so that nonscientists find them not only clear but downright interesting. In "The Arrow of Time" (editors' title), she shows how a law of nature affects our everyday lives. The essay first appeared in the *New York Times* in 1982.

It was about two months ago when I realized that entropy was getting the better of me. On the same day my car broke down (again), my refrigerator conked out and I learned that I needed root-canal work in my right rear tooth. The windows in the bedroom were still leaking every time it rained and my son's baby sitter was still failing to show up every time I really needed her. My hair was turning gray and my typewriter was wearing out. The house needed paint and I needed glasses. My son's sneakers were developing holes and I was developing a deep sense of futility.

After all, what was the point of spending half of Saturday at the Laundromat if the clothes were dirty all over again the following Friday?

Disorder, alas, is the natural order of things in the universe. There is even a precise measure of the amount of disorder, called entropy. Unlike almost every other physical property (motion, gravity, energy), entropy does not work both ways. It can only increase. Once it's created it can never be destroyed. The road to disorder is a one-way street.

Because of its unnerving irreversibility, entropy has been called the   4 arrow of time. We all understand this instinctively. Children's rooms, left on their own, tend to get messy, not neat. Wood rots, metal rusts, people wrinkle and flowers wither. Even mountains wear down; even the nuclei of atoms decay. In the city we see entropy in the rundown subways and worn-out sidewalks and torn-down buildings, in the increasing disorder of our lives. We know, without asking, what is old. If we were suddenly to see the paint jump back on an old building, we would know that something was wrong. If we saw an egg unscramble itself and jump back into its shell, we would laugh in the same way we laugh at a movie run backward.

Entropy is no laughing matter, however, because with every increase   5 in entropy energy is wasted and opportunity is lost. Water flowing down a mountainside can be made to do some useful work on its way. But once all the water is at the same level it can work no more. That is entropy. When my refrigerator was working, it kept all the cold air ordered in one part of the kitchen and warmer air in another. Once it broke down the warm and cold mixed into a lukewarm mess that allowed my butter to melt, my milk to rot and my frozen vegetables to decay.

Of course the energy is not really lost, but it has diffused and dissi-   6 pated into a chaotic caldron of randomness that can do us no possible good. Entropy is chaos. It is loss of purpose.

People are often upset by the entropy they seem to see in the hap-   7 hazardness of their own lives. Buffeted about like so many molecules in my tepid kitchen, they feel that they have lost their sense of direction, that they are wasting youth and opportunity at every turn. It is easy to see entropy in marriages, when the partners are too preoccupied to patch small things up, almost guaranteeing that they will fall apart. There is much entropy in the state of our country, in the relationships between nations — lost opportunities to stop the avalanche of disorders that seems ready to swallow us all.

Entropy is not inevitable everywhere, however. Crystals and   8 snowflakes and galaxies are islands of incredibly ordered beauty in the midst of random events. If it was not for exceptions to entropy, the sky would be black and we would be able to see where the stars spend their days; it is only because air molecules in the atmosphere cluster in ordered groups that the sky is blue.

The most profound exception to entropy is the creation of life. A   9 seed soaks up some soil and some carbon and some sunshine and some water and arranges it into a rose. A seed in the womb takes some oxygen and pizza and milk and transforms it into a baby.

The catch is that it takes a lot of energy to produce a baby. It also   10
takes energy to make a tree. The road to disorder is all downhill but the
road to creation takes work. Though combating entropy is possible, it
also has its price. That's why it seems so hard to get ourselves together,
so easy to let ourselves fall apart.

Worse, creating order in one corner of the universe always creates   11
more disorder somewhere else. We create ordered energy from oil and
coal at the price of the entropy of smog.

I recently took up playing the flute again after an absence of several   12
months. As the uneven vibrations screeched through the house, my
son covered his ears and said, "Mom, what's wrong with your flute?"
Nothing was wrong with my flute, of course. It was my ability to play
it that had atrophied, or entropied, as the case may be. The only way
to stop that process was to practice every day, and sure enough my
tone improved, though only at the price of constant work. Like anything else, abilities deteriorate when we stop applying our energies
to them.

That's why entropy is depressing. It seems as if just breaking even is   13
an uphill fight. There's a good reason that this should be so. The mechanics of entropy are a matter of chance. Take any ice-cold air mole-
cule milling around my kitchen. The chances that it will wander in the
direction of my refrigerator at any point are exactly 50-50. The chances
that it will wander away from my refrigerator are also 50-50. But take
billions of warm and cold molecules mixed together, and the chances
that all the cold ones will wander toward the refrigerator and all the
warm ones will wander away from it are virtually nil.

Entropy wins not because order is impossible but because there are   14
always so many more paths toward disorder than toward order. There
are so many more different ways to do a sloppy job than a good one, so
many more ways to make a mess than to clean it up. The obstacles and
accidents in our lives almost guarantee that constant collisions will
bounce us on to random paths, get us off the track. Disorder is the path
of least resistance, the easy but not the inevitable road.

Like so many others, I am distressed by the entropy I see around me   15
today. I am afraid of the randomness of international events, of the lack
of common purpose in the world; I am terrified that it will lead into the
ultimate entropy of nuclear war. I am upset that I could not in the city
where I live send my child to a public school; that people are unemployed and inflation is out of control; that tensions between sexes and
races seem to be increasing again; that relationships everywhere seem
to be falling apart.

Social institutions—like atoms and stars—decay if energy is not   16
added to keep them ordered. Friendships and families and economies
all fall apart unless we constantly make an effort to keep them working

and well oiled. And far too few people, it seems to me, are willing to contribute consistently to those efforts.

Of course, the more complex things are, the harder it is. If there   17
were only a dozen or so air molecules in my kitchen, it would be likely—if I waited a year or so—that at some point the six coldest ones would congregate inside the freezer. But the more factors in the equation—the more players in the game—the less likely it is that their paths will coincide in an orderly way. The more pieces in the puzzle, the harder it is to put back together once order is disturbed. "Irreversibility," said a physicist, "is the price we pay for complexity."

QUESTIONS ON MEANING

1. How does entropy differ from most other properties of the physical world? How are the IMAGES "one-way street" (para. 3) and "arrow of time" (4) helpful in establishing the difference?
2. Why is the creation of life an exception to entropy (para. 9)? What is the relationship between entropy and energy?
3. Why does Cole find the law of entropy depressing? Do you agree with her? Why, or why not?
4. What is this essay's THESIS? What seems to be Cole's PURPOSE?

QUESTIONS ON WRITING STRATEGY

1. How does paragraph 14 link the science of entropy to the human consequences that Cole goes on to discuss?
2. Examine Cole's INTRODUCTION. Where does it end and the body of the essay begin? How effective is the introduction, and why?
3. What ASSUMPTIONS does Cole seem to make about her readers' background in science? Support your answer by referring to passages in the essay.
4. **OTHER METHODS.** How does Cole's EXAMPLE of her refrigerator (paras. 5, 13) help to explain how entropy works? In your own words, explain why the broken refrigerator won't stay cold.

QUESTIONS ON LANGUAGE

1. "The obstacles and accidents in our lives almost guarantee that constant collisions will bounce us on to random paths," Cole says in paragraph 14. How does this metaphor link the workings of entropy to human relations? (See "Figures of speech" in Useful Terms if you need a definition of *metaphor.*)
2. In discussing the effects of entropy, Cole uses words such as "futility" (para. 1), "chaos" (6), "avalanche of disorders" (7), and "decay" (16). How do the CONNOTATIONS of these words serve Cole's purpose?

3. Give definitions of the following words: nuclei, atoms (para. 4); caldron (6); haphazardness, buffeted, molecules (7); atrophied (12); nil (13).

SUGGESTIONS FOR WRITING

1. **JOURNAL WRITING.** Look around you for examples of entropy in the physical world, using as a guide the examples Cole gives in paragraphs 1, 4, and 5. In your journal, write down at least five examples.
   FROM JOURNAL TO ESSAY. Write a brief essay explaining how each example from your journal illustrates entropy. Quote or PARAPHRASE passages from Cole's essay to support your explanation.
2. Think of a two-person relationship you're familiar with, either because you're involved in it or because you are close to someone involved. In an essay, explain how entropy could affect—or is affecting—the relationship. (Cole suggests such an effect in paras. 7 and 16.) What can either or both persons in the relationship do to prevent the tendency of things to "fall apart"?
3. **CRITICAL WRITING.** Cole extends the physical law of entropy to human interaction, asserting that, unchallenged, it causes "the haphazardness" (para. 7) of life as well as social problems and international tensions (15–16). Do you agree or disagree with her view? To what extent does life seem disorderly to you? Who or what is responsible for disorder? Who or what can or should control it? Respond to Cole in an essay of your own, considering these questions and others that Cole's essay may have raised for you.
4. **CONNECTIONS.** Read "I Have a Dream," by Martin Luther King, Jr. (p. 567). How might King's "dream" and the actions he proposes to achieve it relate to Cole's view of our role in counteracting entropy? Write an essay in which you explore not only King's vision but also the visions of people you admire today (politicians, religious leaders, teachers, and so on) for solving social problems by stemming disorder.

K. C. COLE ON WRITING

When you write a paper, you may need to say far less than you know. Good writing demands not only a respect for your information but also an awareness of the reader's needs for that information. Facts may be interesting but unnecessary for your larger purpose or wrong for your audience. In this 1997 essay from the *Los Angeles Times*, K. C. Cole explains the choices she must make in writing about science.

You always have to lie a little to tell the truth. A first-rate popularizer of science, MIT physicist Victor Weisskopf, once told me that was the secret to explaining science in nontechnical terms. He should know. His enchanting book *Knowledge and Wonder* has been seducing laypeople into the world of science for decades.

And so I confess: Week after week, I tell what I hope are well-considered lies. I write about electric currents that "flow" through wires like rivers—even though I know they do no such thing. I talk about elementary "particles" and "forces" even though physicists have only the foggiest notion what those terms mean. I toss off words such as "time" and "gravity," knowing that to some extent, their very existence is illusionary.

The lies are simplifications that ease the way to the central point. The art is knowing the difference between acceptable—even necessary—lies and oversimplifications that slide into mistakes. Sometimes, it's hard to tell which is which, and even scientists frequently don't agree.

I vividly remember the first deliberate lie I told in a science essay. I was writing in Time Inc.'s *Discover* magazine about the ways seemingly small differences can sometimes produce enormous effects.

The elements neon and sodium, for example, have starkly contrasting characters. Neon is what chemists call a noble gas. It is so self-contained and standoffish that it won't react with anything. Sodium, on the other hand, is a highly reactive metal.

And yet, the only difference between the two, I wrote, is one lousy extra electron in sodium's outer shell. Neon has ten electrons to sodium's eleven.

To be honest, I stole the example from Weisskopf.... And strictly speaking, it is wrong. There's something else different about neon and sodium: Sodium also has an extra proton in its nucleus. However, atomic nuclei don't affect an element's chemical character. And as the mathematicians like to say, a difference is a difference only if it makes a difference.

Was pushing that proton under the rug an acceptable lie? Or a misleading representation?

FOR DISCUSSION

1. Is Cole's slighting of the truth justifiable? Why, or why not? Do her thoughts about truth and clarity affect your reading of her essay "The Arrow of Time"?

2. Is the problem of honestly representing reality limited to those with specialized knowledge, like scientists? With what other subjects might writers encounter the challenges Cole faces as she tries to help readers understand complex ideas?

3. Have you ever experienced problems in doing justice to your experience or to your knowledge when you wrote an essay or research paper? How would you explain the difficulty of accurately representing the truth?

MEGHAN DAUM

Born in 1970 in Palo Alto, California, MEGHAN DAUM is a writer who specializes in the communications media. Daum graduated from Vassar College with a B.A. in English (1992) and from Columbia University with an M.A. in writing (1996). She worked on the staffs of *Allure* magazine and Columbia University Press. Now writing full-time, Daum contributes a monthly column to *Self* magazine and has published articles in the *New York Times Book Review*, *GQ*, and *New York* magazine. She lives in New York City.

Safe-Sex Lies

This essay from the *New York Times Magazine* caused a stir when it was first published in January 1996. Daum deftly analyzes several damaging effects of the media's coverage of AIDS, especially the anxiety, shame, mistrust, and dishonesty that she and others of her generation experience.

I have been tested for HIV three times. I've gone to clinics and stuck my arm out for those disposable needles, each time forgetting the fear and nausea that descend upon me before the results come back, those minutes spent in a publicly financed waiting room staring at a video loop about "living with" this thing that kills you. These tests have taken place over five years, and the results have always been negative—not surprisingly in retrospect, since I am not a member of a "high-risk group," don't sleep around and don't take pity on heroin-addicted bass players by going to bed with them in the hopes of being thanked in the liner notes of their first major independent release. Still, getting tested always seemed like the thing to do. Despite my demographic profile, despite the fact that I grew up middle class, attended an elite college and do not personally know any women or straight men within that demographic profile who have the AIDS virus, I am terrified of this disease. I went to a college where condoms and dental dams lay in baskets in dormitory lobbies, where it seemed incumbent on health service counselors to give us the straight talk, to tell us never, ever to have sex without condoms unless we wanted to die; that's right, *die*, shrivel overnight, vomit up our futures, pose a threat to others. (And they'd seen it happen, oh, yes, they had.) They gave us pamphlets, didn't quite explain how to use dental dams, told us where we could get tested, threw us more fistfuls of condoms (even some glow-in-the-dark brands, just for variety). This can actually be fun, they said, if only we'd adopt a better attitude.

1

We're told we can get this disease and we believe it and vow to pro-	2
tect ourselves, and intend (really, truly) to stick by this rule, until we
don't because we just can't, because it's just not fair, because our sense
of entitlement exceeds our sense of vulnerability. So we blow off precaution again and again, and then we get scared and get tested, and
when it comes out O.K., we run out of the clinic, pamphlets in hand,
eyes cast upward, promising ourselves we'll never be stupid again. But
of course we are stupid, again and again. And the testing is always for
the same reasons and with the same results, and soon it becomes more
like fibbing about SAT scores ten years after the fact than lying about
whether we practice unsafe sex, a lie that sounds like such a breach of
contract with ourselves that we might as well be talking about putting
a loaded gun under our pillow every night.

Still, I've gone into more than a few relationships with the safest of	3
intentions and discarded them after the fourth or fifth encounter. Perhaps this is a shocking admission, but my hunch is that I'm not the only
one doing it. My suspicion is, in fact, that very few of us — "us" being
the demographic profile frequently charged with thinking we're immortal, the population accused of being cynical and lazy and weak —
have really responded to the AIDS crisis the way the Federal Government and educators would like us to believe. My guess is that we're all
but ignoring it and that almost anyone who claims otherwise is lying.

It seems there is a lot of lying going around. One of the main tenets	4
of the safe-sex message is that ageless mantra "you don't know where he's
been," meaning that everyone is a potential threat, that we're all either
scoundrels or ignoramuses. "He didn't tell me he was shooting drugs,"
says an HIV-positive woman on a public-service advertisement. Safe-sex
"documentaries" on MTV and call-in radio shows on pop stations give us
woman after woman whose boyfriend "claimed he loved me but was
sleeping around." The message we receive is that trusting anyone is itself
an irresponsible act, that having faith in an intimate partner, particularly
women in relation to men, is a symptom of such profound naïveté that
we're obviously not mature enough to be having sex anyway.

I find this reasoning almost more troubling than the disease itself.	5
It flies in the face of the social order from which I, as someone born in
1970, was supposed to benefit. That this reasoning runs counter to almost any feminist ideology — the ideology that proclaimed, at least
back in the seventies, that women should feel free to ask men on dates
and wear jeans and have orgasms — is an admission that no AIDS-
concerned citizen is willing to make. Two decades after *The Joy of Sex*
made sexual pleasure permissible for both sexes and three decades after
the pill put a government-approved stamp on premarital sex, we're still
told not to trust each other. We've entered a period where mistrust
equals responsibility, where fear signifies health.

Since I spent all of the seventies under the age of ten, I've never   6
known a significantly different sexual and social climate. Supposedly
this makes it easier to live with the AIDS crisis. Health educators and
AIDS activists like to think that people of my generation can be made
to unlearn what we never knew, to break the reckless habits we didn't
actually form. But what we have learned thoroughly is how not to enjoy ourselves. Just like our mothers, whose adolescences were haunted
by the abstract taboo against being "bad" girls, my contemporaries and
I are discouraged from doing what feels good. As it did with our mothers, the onus falls largely on the women. We know that it's much easier
for women to contract HIV from a man than the other way around. We
know that an "unsafe" man generally means someone who has shot
drugs or slept with other men, or possibly slept with prostitutes. We
find ourselves wondering about these things over dinner dates. We look
for any hints of homosexual tendencies, any references to a hypodermic
moment. We try to catch him in the lie we've been told he'll tell.

What could be sadder? We're not allowed to believe anyone any-   7
more. And the reason we're not isn't so much because of AIDS but because of the anxiety that ripples around the disease. The information
about AIDS that is supposed to produce "awareness" has been subsumed into the aura of style. AIDS awareness has become so much a
part of the pop culture that not only is it barely noticeable, it is largely
ineffectual. MTV runs programs about safe sex that are barely distin-
guishable from documentaries about Madonna. A print advertisement
for Benetton features a collage of hundreds of tiny photographs of
young people, some of whom are shaded with the word AIDS written
across their faces. Many are white and blond and have the tousled,
moneyed look common to more traditional fashion spreads or even
yearbooks from colleges like the one I attended. There is no text other
than the company's slogan. There is no explanation of how these faces
were chosen, no public statement of whether these people actually
have the disease or not. I called Benetton for clarification and was told
that the photographs were supposed to represent people from all over
the world and that no one was known to be HIV-positive—just as I
suspected. The advertisement was a work of art, which meant I could
interpret the image any way I liked. This is how the deliverers of the
safe-sex message shoot themselves in the foot. Confronted with arty effects instead of actual information, people like me are going to believe
what we want to believe, which, of course, is whatever isn't too scary.
So we turn the page.

Since I am pretty sure I do not sleep with bisexual men or IV drug   8
users, my main personal concern about AIDS is that men can get the
virus from women and subsequently pass it on to other women. According to the Centers for Disease Control's National AIDS Clearing-

house surveillance report, less than three-quarters of 1 percent of white non-Hispanic men with HIV infection contracted the virus through heterosexual sex with a non–IV drug–using woman. (Interestingly, the CDC labels this category as "risk not specified.") But this statistic seems too dry for MTV and campus health brochures, whose eye-catching "sex kills" rhetoric tells us nothing other than to ignore what we don't feel like thinking about. Obviously, there are still too many cases of HIV; there is a deadly risk in certain kinds of sexual behavior and therefore reason to take precautions. But until more people appear on television, look into the camera and tell me that they contracted HIV through heterosexual sex with someone who had no risk factors, I will continue to disregard the message.

Besides, the very sophistication that allows people like me to filter out much of the hype behind music videos, fashion magazines and television talk shows is what we use to block out the safe-sex message. We are not a population that makes personal decisions based on the public service work of a rock star. We're not going to sacrifice the thing we believe we deserve, the experiences we waited for, because Levi Strauss is a major sponsor of MTV's coverage of World AIDS Day. 9

So the inconsistent behavior continues, as do the confessions among friends and the lies to health care providers during routine exams, because we just can't bear the terrifying lectures that ensue when we confess to not always protecting ourselves. Life in your twenties is fraught not only with financial and professional uncertainty, but also with a specter of death that floats above the pursuit of a sex life. And there is no solution, only the conclusion that invariably finishes the hushed conversations: the whole thing simply "sucks." It's a bummer on a grand scale. 10

Heterosexuals are receiving vague signals. We're told that if we are sufficiently vigilant, we will probably be all right. We're being told to assume the worst and to not invite disaster by hoping for the best. We're being encouraged to keep our fantasies on a tight rein, otherwise we'll lose control of the whole buggy, and no one can say we weren't warned. So for us AIDS remains a private hell, smoldering beneath intimate conversations among friends and surfacing on those occasional sleepless nights when it occurs to us to wonder about it, upon which that dark hysteria sets in, and those catalogues of whom we've done it with and whom they might have done it with and oh-my-God-I'll-surely-die seem to project themselves onto the ceiling, the way fanged monsters did when we were children. But we fall asleep and then we wake up. And nothing has changed except our willingness to forget about it, which has become the ultimate survival mechanism. What my peers and I are left with is a generalized anxiety, a low-grade fear and anger that resides at the core of everything we do. Our attitudes 11 have been affected by the disease by leaving us scared, but our behavior has stayed largely the same. One result is a corrosion of the soul, a chronic dishonesty and fear that will most likely damage us more than the disease itself. In this world, peace of mind is a utopian concept.

QUESTIONS ON MEANING

1. What is Daum's PURPOSE in writing this essay? On whom, or what, is she placing blame? Does she offer any solutions in the essay, or is she merely outlining a problem previously unacknowledged?
2. What is Daum's THESIS? Where is it stated?
3. What does Daum mean when she says, "Our sense of entitlement exceeds our sense of vulnerability" (para. 2)?
4. Explain how AIDS awareness has become "part of the pop culture" (para. 7).
5. Explain the title's double meaning: What are the two kinds of "Safe-Sex Lies" discussed in the essay?

QUESTIONS ON WRITING STRATEGY

1. Daum asserts that the media exaggerate the prevalence of AIDS among heterosexuals who are not IV drug users. Explain the chain of causes and effects that she sees as leading from this exaggeration.
2. What is the TONE of the essay?
3. What is the EFFECT of Daum's confession in the second paragraph?
4. What AUDIENCE do you think Daum had in mind when she was writing this essay? Is she targeting all readers of the New York Times or a more specific subset of them?
5. **OTHER METHODS.** In paragraph 7 Daum uses an extended EXAMPLE of a Benetton ad to support her assertion that "[t]he information about AIDS that is supposed to produce 'awareness' has been subsumed into the aura of style." Why does it make a difference to Daum that the people represented in the Benetton ad are not known to be HIV-positive?

QUESTIONS ON LANGUAGE

1. Look up any of the following words you don't already know: retrospect, demographic, incumbent (para. 1); entitlement, breach (2); cynical (3); mantra, scoundrels, ignoramuses, naïveté (4); ideology (5); abstract, contemporaries, onus (6); subsumed, aura, tousled (7); surveillance (8); fraught, specter (10); vigilant, smoldering (11).
2. What is the effect of the word *those* in "those disposable needles" and "those minutes spent in a publicly financed waiting room" (para. 1)?
3. Daum's language is often quite informal, as in conversation—for instance, "unless we wanted to die; that's right, *die*" and "they'd seen it happen, oh,

yes, they had" (para. 1); "It seems there is a lot of lying going around" (4); or "It's a bummer on a grand scale" (10). What is the effect of this language? Is it appropriate to Daum's subject and purpose? Why, or why not?

SUGGESTIONS FOR WRITING

1. **JOURNAL WRITING.** Daum wrote "Safe-Sex Lies" when she was twenty-six, in transition from adolescence to mature adulthood. What do you think are the characteristics of this age group? (It may help to read Gail Sheehy on "Pulling Up Roots" and "The Trying Twenties," pp. 295–97.) **FROM JOURNAL TO ESSAY.** Write an essay DEFINING the age group roughly from eighteen to thirty, drawing on your journal entry, Daum's essay, and any other sources that offer ideas. Keep in mind that characterization of such a large and diverse group will require GENERALIZATION on your part. How does your definition compare with other definitions you have heard in the media? Does any attempt to characterize an age group necessarily oversimplify? Do you find some value or interest in the exercise?

2. Write an essay about how AIDS has (or hasn't) changed your life, considering the following questions: Is AIDS something you think about often, or is it something "out there" that happens to other people? How do the media influence your attitudes toward the disease? If a cure for AIDS were discovered tomorrow, would your approach to sexuality and relationships change, or has AIDS permanently affected your attitudes?

3. **CRITICAL WRITING.** Analyze how Daum's "demographic profile" (para. 1) determines her perspective on AIDS. Do you find this limited perspective appropriate, or do you think Daum should have mentioned other views as well—perhaps of those who urge sexual abstinence or who care for AIDS patients or who have AIDS themselves? To what extent does Daum's limited perspective weaken or strengthen her essay?

4. **CONNECTIONS.** Daum and Armin A. Brott, in "Not All Men Are Sly Foxes" (p. 279), are both concerned about the subtle effects of words and pictures on an audience: Daum is interested in the way safe sex is marketed, the face advertising puts on AIDS; Brott is troubled by the negative stereotyping of fathers in books for children. Write an essay criticizing what you consider to be inaccurate or inappropriate media representation of a given group (for example, single mothers, gays and lesbians, lawyers, football players, fashion models). What message do these portrayals send to members of that group and to those outside the group? How might the portrayals be improved?

SCOTT RUSSELL SANDERS

SCOTT RUSSELL SANDERS writes stories, novels, and essays about plain people who, in his words, "are neither literary nor intellectual." He was born in 1945 in Memphis, Tennessee, and reports a somewhat nomadic childhood. He attended Brown University (B.A., 1967) and Cambridge University (Ph.D., 1971) and for three decades has taught English at Indiana University in Bloomington. His books include stories for children, such as *Aurora Means Dawn* (1989) and *Meeting Trees* (1996); novels for adults, such as *Terrarium* (1985) and *The Invisible Company* (1989); collections of short stories, such as *Fetching the Dead* (1984) and *Hear the Wind Blow* (1985); and collections of essays, such as *Secrets of the Universe* (1991), *Staying Put: Making a Home in a Restless World* (1993), and *Writing from the Center* (1995). His latest book is *Hunting for Hope: A Father's Journey* (1998), about "the powers in nature, in culture, in community, in my depths and in yours, that nourish and heal."

Homeplace

A 1993 issue of the *Utne Reader* printed this essay by Sanders along with the following essay, Richard Ford's "I Must Be Going." The two selections take opposing views of why we do or don't find satisfaction in staying put in one place, and of the consequences of our choices to remain or to go. Sanders favors staying put. His essay was first published in *Orion* magazine in 1992.

As a boy in Ohio, I knew a farm family, the Millers, who suffered 1 from three tornadoes. The father, mother, and two sons were pulling into their driveway after church when the first tornado hoisted up their mobile home, spun it around, and carried it off. With the insurance money, they built a small frame house on the same spot.

Several years later, a second tornado peeled off the roof, splintered 2 the garage, and rustled two cows. The Millers rebuilt again, raising a new garage on the old foundation and adding another story to the house. That upper floor was reduced to kindling by a third tornado, which also pulled out half the apple trees and slurped water from the stock pond. Soon after that I left Ohio, snatched away by college as forcefully as by any cyclone. Last thing I heard, the family was preparing to rebuild yet again.

Why did the Millers refuse to move? I knew them well enough to 3 say they were neither stupid nor crazy. Plain stubbornness was a factor. These were people who, once settled, might have remained at the foot of a volcano or on the bank of a flood-prone river or beside an earthquake fault. They had relatives nearby, helpful neighbors, jobs and stores and schools within a short drive, and those were all good reasons to stay. But the main reason, I believe, was that the Millers had invested so much of their lives in the land, planting orchards and gardens, spreading manure on the fields, digging ponds, building sheds, seeding pastures. Out back of the house were groves of walnuts, hickories, and oaks, all started by hand from acorns and nuts. April through October, perennial flowers in the yard pumped out a fountain of blossoms. This farm was not just so many acres of dirt, easily exchanged for an equal amount elsewhere; it was a particular place, intimately known, worked on, dreamed over, cherished.

Psychologists tell us that we answer trouble with one of two impulses, either fight or flight. I believe that the Millers exhibited a third instinct, that of staying put. They knew better than to fight a tornado, and they chose not to flee. Their commitment to the place may have been foolhardy, but it was also grand. I suspect that most human achievements worth admiring are the result of such devotion.   4

The Millers dramatize a choice we are faced with constantly: whether to go or stay, whether to move to a situation that is safer, richer, easier, more attractive, or to stick where we are and make what we can of it. If the shine goes off our marriage, our house, our car, do we trade it for a new one? If the fertility leaches out of our soil, the creativity out of our job, the money out of our pocket, do we start over somewhere else? There are voices enough, both inner and outer, urging us to deal with difficulties by pulling up stakes and heading for new territory. I know them well, for they have been calling to me all my days. I wish to raise here a contrary voice, to say a few words on behalf of staying put, learning the ground, going deeper.   5

Claims for the virtues of moving on are familiar and seductive to Americans, this nation founded by immigrants and shaped by restless seekers. From the beginning, our heroes have been sailors, explorers, cowboys, prospectors, speculators, backwoods ramblers, rainbow chasers, vagabonds of every stripe. Our Promised Land has always been over the next ridge or at the end of the trail, never under our feet. In our national mythology, the worst fate is to be trapped on a farm, in a village, in the sticks, in some dead-end job or unglamorous marriage or played-out game.   6

Stand still, we are warned, and you die. Americans have dug the most canals, laid the most rails, built the most roads and airports of any nation. In a newspaper I read that, even though our sprawling system of interstate highways is crumbling, politicians think we should triple its size. Only a populace drunk on driving, a populace infatuated with the myth of the open road, could hear such a proposal without hooting.   7

Novelist Salman Rushdie chose to leave his native India for Eng-   8
land, where he has written a series of brilliant books from the perspective of a cultural immigrant. In his book of essays *Imaginary Homelands*
he celebrates the migrant sensibility: "The effect of mass migrations has
been the creation of radically new types of human being: people who
root themselves in ideas rather than places, in memories as much as in
material things." He goes on to say that "to be a migrant is, perhaps, to
be the only species of human being free of the shackles of nationalism
(to say nothing of its ugly sister, patriotism)." Lord knows we could do
with less nationalism (to say nothing of its ugly siblings, racism, religious sectarianism, and class snobbery). But who would pretend that a
history of migration has immunized the United States against bigotry?
And even if, by uprooting ourselves, we shed our chauvinism, is that all
we lose?

In this hemisphere, many of the worst abuses — of land, forests, an-   9
imals, and communities — have been carried out by "people who root
themselves in ideas rather than places." Migrants often pack up their
visions and values with the rest of their baggage and carry them along.
The Spaniards devastated Central and South America by imposing on
this New World the religion, economics, and politics of the Old.
Colonists brought slavery with them to North America, along with
smallpox and Norway rats. The Dust Bowl of the 1930s was caused not
by drought but by the transfer onto the Great Plains of farming methods that were suitable to wetter regions. The habit of our industry and
commerce has been to force identical schemes onto differing locales, as
though the mind were a cookie cutter and the land were dough.

I quarrel with Rushdie because he articulates as eloquently as any-   10
one the orthodoxy that I wish to counter: the belief that movement is
inherently good, staying put is bad; that uprooting brings tolerance,
while rootedness breeds intolerance; that to be modern, enlightened,
fully of our time is to be displaced. Wholesale displacement may be
inevitable in today's world; but we should not suppose that it occurs
without disastrous consequences for the earth and for ourselves. People
who root themselves in places are likelier to know and care for those
places than are people who root themselves in ideas. When we cease to
be migrants and become inhabitants, we might begin to pay enough
heed and respect to where we are. By settling in, we have a chance of
making a durable home for ourselves, our fellow creatures, and our descendants.

The poet Gary Snyder writes frequently about our need to "in-   11
habit" a place. One of the key problems in American society now, he
points out, is people's lack of commitment to any given place:

Neighborhoods are allowed to deteriorate, landscapes are allowed to be strip-mined, because there is nobody who will live there and take responsibility; they'll just move on. The reconstruction of a people and of a life in the United States depends in part on people, neighborhood by neighborhood, county by county, deciding to stick it out and make it work where they are, rather than flee.

But if you stick in one place, won't you become a stick-in-the-mud? 12 If you stay put, won't you be narrow, backward, dull? You might. I have met ignorant people who never moved; and I have also met ignorant people who never stood still. Committing yourself to a place does not guarantee that you will become wise, but neither does it guarantee that you will become parochial.

To become intimate with your home region, to know the territory 13 as well as you can, to understand your life as woven into the local life does not prevent you from recognizing and honoring the diversity of other places, cultures, ways. On the contrary, how can you value other places if you do not have one of your own? If you are not yourself *placed*, then you wander the world like a sightseer, a collector of sensations, with no gauge for measuring what you see. Local knowledge is the grounding for global knowledge. Those who care about nothing beyond the confines of their parish are in truth parochial, and are at least mildly dangerous to their parish; on the other hand, those who *have* no parish, those who navigate ceaselessly among postal zones and area codes, those for whom the world is only a smear of highways and bank accounts and stores, are a danger not just to their parish but to the planet.

Since birth, my children have regularly seen images of the earth as 14 viewed from space, images that I first encountered when I was in my twenties. Those photographs show vividly what in our sanest moments we have always known — that the earth is a closed circle, lovely and rare. On the wall beside me as I write there is a poster of the big blue marble encased in its white swirl of clouds. That is one pole of my awareness; but the other pole is what I see through my window. I try to keep both in sight at once.

For all my convictions, I still have to wrestle with the fear — in my- 15 self, in my children, and even in some of my neighbors — that our place is too remote from the action. This fear drives many people to pack their bags and move to some resort or burg they have seen on television, leaving behind what they learn to think of as the boondocks. I deal with my own unease by asking just what action I am remote *from* — a stock market? a debating chamber? a drive-in mortuary? The action that matters, the work of nature and community, goes on everywhere.

Since Copernicus,[1] we have known better than to see the earth as 16 the center of the universe. Since Einstein,[2] we have learned that there is no center; or alternatively, that any point is as good as any other for observing the world. I find a kindred lesson in the words of the Zen master Thich Nhat Hanh: "This spot where you sit is your own spot. It is on this very spot and in this very moment that you can become enlightened. You don't have to sit beneath a special tree in a distant land." If you stay put, your place may become a holy center, not because it gives you special access to the divine, but because in your stillness you hear what might be heard anywhere.

I think of my home ground as a series of nested rings, with house 17 and family and marriage at the center, surrounded by the wider and wider hoops of neighborhood and community, the bioregion within walking distance of my door, the wooded and rocky hills of southern Indiana, the watershed of the Ohio Valley, and soon outward—and inward—to the ultimate source.

The longing to become an inhabitant rather than a drifter sets me 18 against the current of my culture, which nudges everyone into motion. Newton taught us that a body at rest tends to stay at rest, unless it is acted on by an outside force. We are acted on ceaselessly by outside forces—advertising, movies, magazines, speeches—and also by the inner force of biology. I am not immune to their pressure. Before settling in my present home, I lived in seven states and two countries, tugged from place to place in childhood by my father's work and in early adulthood by my own. This itinerant life is so common among the people I know that I have been slow to conceive of an alternative. Only by knocking against the golden calf of mobility, which looms so large and shines so brightly, have I come to realize that it is hollow. Like all idols, it distracts us from what is truly divine.

I am encouraged by the words of a Crow elder,[3] quoted by Gary 19 Snyder in *The Practice of the Wild:*

> You know, I think if people stay somewhere long enough—even white people—the spirits will begin to speak to them. It's the power of the spirits coming up from the land. The spirits and the old powers aren't lost, they just need people to be around long enough and the spirits will begin to influence them.

---

[1]Nicolaus Copernicus (1473–1543), considered the founder of modern astronomy, established that the planets revolve around the sun.—Eds.

[2]Albert Einstein (1879–1955), a physicist, developed the theory of relativity, showing that space and time are not independent but form a space-time continuum.—Eds.

[3]The Crow are a Native American people that originally lived in the Great Plains.—Eds.

As I write this, I hear the snarl of earth movers and chain saws a   20
mile away destroying a farm to make way for another shopping strip. I
would rather hear a tornado, whose damage can be undone. The elderly
woman who owned the farm had it listed in the National Register, then
willed it to her daughters on condition they preserve it. After her
death, the daughters, who live out of state, had the will broken, so the
land could be turned over to the chain saws and earthmovers. The machines work around the clock. Their noise wakes me at midnight, at
three in the morning, at dawn. The roaring abrades my dreams. The
sound is a reminder that we are living in the midst of a holocaust. I do
not use the word lightly. The earth is being pillaged, and every one of
us, willingly or grudgingly, is taking part. We ask how sensible, educated, supposedly moral people could have tolerated slavery or the
slaughter of Jews. Similar questions will be asked about us by our descendants, to whom we bequeath an impoverished planet. They will
demand to know how we could have been party to such waste and ruin.

What does it mean to be alive in an era when the earth is being de-   21
voured, and in a country that has set the pattern for that devouring?
What are we called to do? I think we are called to the work of healing,
both inner and outer: healing of the mind through a change in consciousness, healing of the earth through a change in our lives. We can
begin that work by learning how to inhabit a place.

"The man who is often thinking that it is better to be somewhere   22
else than where he is excommunicates himself," we are cautioned by
Thoreau,[4] that notorious stay-at-home. The metaphor is religious: To
withhold yourself from where you are is to be cut off from communion
with the source. It has taken me half a lifetime of searching to realize
that the likeliest path to the ultimate ground leads through my local
ground. I mean the land itself, with its creeks and rivers, its weather,
seasons, stone outcroppings, and all the plants and animals that share
it. I cannot have a spiritual center without having a geographical one;
I cannot live a grounded life without being grounded in a *place*.

In belonging to a landscape, one feels a rightness, an at-homeness,   23
a knitting of self and world. This condition of clarity and focus, this being fully present, is akin to what the Buddhists call mindfulness, what
Christian contemplatives refer to as recollection, what Quakers call
centering down. I am suspicious of any philosophy that would separate
this-worldly from other-worldly commitment. There is only one world,
and we participate in it here and now, in our flesh and our place.

---

[4]Henry David Thoreau (1817–62) was an American essayist, poet, and philosopher. His *Walden* (1854) recorded his years living a simple, self-sufficient life at Walden
Pond in Massachusetts. —Eds.

QUESTIONS ON MEANING

1. What is this essay's THESIS? Where does Sanders state it concisely and clearly?
2. Sanders writes, "In our national mythology, the worst fate is to be trapped on a farm, in a village, in the sticks, in some dead-end job or unglamorous marriage or played-out game" (para. 6). What does the author mean by "our national mythology"?
3. "The action that matters, the work of nature and community, goes on everywhere" (para. 15). What do you think Sanders means here by "action that matters"?

QUESTIONS ON WRITING STRATEGY

1. What causes does Sanders identify for our tendency to move? What are the effects?
2. What does Sanders achieve by including the EXAMPLE of the Millers (paras. 1–5)?
3. What fundamental ASSUMPTION does Sanders seem to make about his audience?
4. **OTHER METHODS.** How is Sanders's cause-and-effect essay also a CLASSIFICATION? What groups does he identify? Which one do you belong to?

QUESTIONS ON LANGUAGE

1. What does Sanders mean when he says that "we are living in the midst of a holocaust" (para. 20)? What is a *holocaust*?
2. What does Sanders's ALLUSION to "the golden calf of mobility" (para. 18) refer to? What does "golden calf" mean in this context?
3. Give definitions of the following words: rustled (para. 2); perennial (3); foolhardy (4); leaches (5); vagabonds (6); shackles (8); orthodoxy, inherently (10); parochial (12); parish (13); boondocks (15); bioregion (17); itinerant (18); abrades, pillaged (20).

SUGGESTIONS FOR WRITING

1. **JOURNAL WRITING.** In your life, have you been a mover or a stayer? Has your degree of motion agreed with you, or have you wished for more or less? How do you see your future in this regard: Do you think you'll likely move as the need (or urge) arises, or will you likely stay put? Sketch out answers to these questions in your journal.
   FROM JOURNAL TO ESSAY. From your journal entry, write an essay that places you in one of Sanders's two categories, people who stay put or people who move. Explain and defend your preference with specific quotations and PARAPHRASES from Sanders's essay and with details from your own experience.

2. Consider what you know of your family's history over the past hundred or so years. Is it a story of moving from place to place (perhaps as "immigrants" or "restless seekers," para. 6)? Or is it a story of rootedness to a particular place? Write a NARRATIVE of the major moves your family has made, in as much detail as you can. Has the family benefited or lost something as a result of its decisions to move or stay put?

3. **CRITICAL WRITING.** In the course of his essay, Sanders cites Salman Rushdie (para. 8), Gary Snyder (11), Nicolaus Copernicus, Albert Einstein, and Thich Nhat Hanh (16), a Crow elder (19), and Henry David Thoreau (22). Write an essay ANALYZING what each of these citations contributes to Sanders's ideas. How does he use each one? What does his essay gain from any and all of the citations?

4. **CONNECTIONS.** Read the following essay, Richard Ford's "I Must Be Going" (p. 399). Then write an essay of your own COMPARING AND CONTRASTING Sanders's and Ford's views. Try to go beyond the obvious main difference between the authors' opinions to consider the scope of their essays—for instance, how personal their approaches are, how much they rely on GENERALIZATION, how concerned they are with the implications of their ideas. Support your comparison with EVIDENCE from both essays.

SCOTT RUSSELL SANDERS ON WRITING

In exchanges with *Contemporary Authors* over the years, Scott Russell Sanders has connected writing and community in a way that extends the ideas of "Homeplace."

I do not much value experimentation in form and style, if it is not engendered by new insights into human experience. I do value clarity of language and vision.... I believe that a writer should be a servant of language, community, and nature. Language is the creation and sustenance of community; and any community, if it is to be healthy and durable, must be respectful of the natural order which makes life possible. Because there is no true human existence apart from family and community, I feel a deep commitment to my region, to the land, to the people and all other living things with which I share this place. My writing is driven by a deep regard for particular places and voices, persons and tools, plants and animals, for human skills and stories, for the small change of daily life—a regard compounded of grief and curiosity and love. If my writing does not help my neighbors to live more alertly, pleasurably, or wisely, then it is worth little.

FOR DISCUSSION

1. What does Sanders mean by "Language is the creation and sustenance of community"? What does language do for a community? Could a community exist without some form of language?
2. Do you think "Homeplace" achieves the goal Sanders states in his last sentence: Will he help *you* "live more alertly, pleasurably, or wisely"? Why, or why not?

RICHARD FORD

Often called one of the best fiction writers of his generation, Richard Ford was born in Jackson, Mississippi, in 1954. He has lived in fourteen states and currently splits his time between Montana, Mississippi, and New Orleans, with an occasional stay in Paris. He received a B.A. from Michigan State University in 1966, briefly attended law school, and then received an M.F.A. in 1970 from the University of California at Irvine. His novels include *A Piece of My Heart* (1976), *The Ultimate Good Luck* (1981), *The Sportswriter* (1986), and *Wildlife* (1990). In 1996, his novel *Independence Day*—a sequel to *The Sportswriter*—became the first book to win both the PEN/Faulkner Award and the Pulitzer Prize. Ford's short-story collections are *Rock Springs* (1987), set primarily in Montana, and *Women with Men: Three Stories* (1997). Ford has also taught fiction writing, worked as a sportswriter, and written essays for *Harper's* and other periodicals.

I Must Be Going

Like Scott Russell Sanders in the previous selection, Richard Ford here considers the causes and effects of moving on; but, as his title indicates, Ford takes quite a different perspective from Sanders. "I Must Be Going" first appeared in *Harper's* magazine in 1992 and then was reprinted, with Sanders's "Homeplace," in the *Utne Reader*.

I've read someplace that in our descending order of mighty and important human anxieties, Americans suffer the death of a spouse, the loss of a house by fire, and moving to be the worst three things that can happen to us.

So far, I've missed the worst of these—the first, unspeakable, and my house up in flames. Though, like most of us, I've contemplated burning my house *myself*—prior to the spring fix-up season or during those grinding "on-the-market" periods when prices sag and interest rates "skyrocket" and I brood over the sign on my lawn bitterly demanding "make offer."

But moving. Moving's another matter. Moving's not so bad. I've done it a lot.

Twenty times, probably, in twenty years (I'm sure I've forgotten a move or two). And always for excellent reasons. St. Louis to New York, New York to California, California to Chicago, Chicago to Michigan, Michigan to New Jersey, New Jersey to Vermont, Vermont to Montana, Montana to Mississippi, Mississippi to Montana, Montana to Montana to here—New Orleans, land of dreamy dreams, where I doubt I'll stay much longer.

To speed the getaways I've sacrificed valuable mortgage points, 5
valuable rent deposits, valuable realtors' commissions, valuable capital
gains write-offs. I've blown off exterminator contracts, forsaken new
paint jobs, abandoned antique mirrors, oil paintings, ten-speeds, ar-
moires, wedding presents, snow chains, and—unintentionally—my
grandfather's gold-handled cane engraved with his name.

What are my excellent reasons? No different from the usual, I 6
imagine. I've just put more of mine into motion. My wife got a better
job, I got a better job, I needed to leave a bad job. I began to hate the
suburbs and longed for the country, I began to hate New York and
longed for the Berkshires, I got frightened of becoming a Californian
and longed for the Middle West, I longed to live again in the place
where I was born, then later I couldn't stand to live in the place where
I was born. I missed the West. I missed the South. I missed the East
Coast. I missed my pals. I got sick of their company.

Longing's at the heart of it, I guess. Longing that overtakes me like 7
a fast car on the freeway and makes me willing to withstand a feeling of
personal temporariness. Maybe, on a decidedly reduced scale, it's what
a rock star feels, or a chewing-gum heiress, celebs who keep houses all
over the globe, visit them often, but never fully live in any: a sense that
life's short and profuse and mustn't be missed.

In the past, when people have asked me why I've moved so often, 8
I've answered that if you were born in Mississippi you either believed
you lived in the vivid center of a sunny universe, or you believed as I
did that the world outside of there was the more magical, exotic place
and *that*'s what you needed to see. Or else I've said it was because my father was a traveling salesman, and every Monday morning I would hear
him whistling as he got ready to leave again: a happy weekend at home
with his bag packed in the bedroom, then a happy workweek traveling,
never seeming to suffer the wrench-pang of departure, never seeming
to think life was disrupted or lonely.

I doubt now if either of those reasons is satisfactory. And, indeed, 9
I'm suspicious of explanations that argue that any of us does anything
because of a single reason, or two, or three.

Place, that old thorny-bush in our mind's backyard, is supposed to 10
be important to us Southerners. It's supposed to hold us. But where I
grew up was a bland, unadhesive place—Jackson, Mississippi—a city
in love with the suburban Zeitgeist, a city whose inert character I could
never much get interested in. I just never seemed like enough of a native, and Jackson just never meant as much to me as it did to others.
Other places just interested me more.

My most enduring memories of childhood are mental snapshots 11
not of my hometown streets or its summery lawns but of roads leading
out of town. Highway 51 to New Orleans. Highway 49 to the delta and

the coast. Highway 80 to Vicksburg and darkest Alabama. These were my father's customary routes, along which I was often his invited companion — I and my mother together.

Why these should be what I now recollect most vividly, instead of, say, an odor of verbena or watermelons in a tub on the Fourth of July, I don't know, other than to conjecture that we were on the move a lot, and that it mattered to me that my parents were my parents and that they loved me, more than *where* they loved me.

Home — real home — the important place that holds you, always meant that: affection, love.

Once my wife and I were stranded with car trouble in the town of Kearney, Nebraska, on a blurry, hot midsummer day late in the '70s. And when we'd eaten our dinner in a little, home-cook place at the edge of town not far from the interstate, we walked out into the breezy, warm air and stood and watched the sun go down beyond the ocean of cornfields and the shining Platte River. And as the shadows widened on, my wife said to me, drowsily, "I've just gotten so sleepy now. I've got to go home and go to sleep." "Home?" I said. "How far is that from here?" "Oh, you know," she said and shook her head and laughed at the absurdity of that idea. "Just back to the motel. Where else?"

Oh, I've stayed places, plenty of times. I've owned "homes," three or four, with likable landscapes, pleasant prospects, safe streets, folksy friends nearby. I've held down jobs, paid millages, served on juries, voted for mayors. As with all of us, some part of me is a stayer. *Transient* is a word of reproach; *impermanence* bears a taint, a suspicion that the gentleman in question isn't quite... well... solid, lacks a certain depth, can't be fully *known*, possibly has messy business left on the trail somewhere — another county, something hushed up.

Other people's permanences are certainly in our faces all the time; their lengthy lengths-of-stay at one address, their many-layered senses of place, their store of lorish, insider blab. Their commitment. Yet I don't for a minute concede their establishment to be any more established than mine, or their self-worth richer, or their savvy regarding risk management and reality any more meticulous. They don't know any more than I do. In fact, given where they've been and haven't been, they probably know less.

"But you," they might say, "you only get a superficial view of life living this way, skimming the top layer off things the way you do." And my answer is: Memory always needs replenishing, and anyway you misunderstand imagination and how it thrives in us by extending partial knowledge to complete any illusion of reality. "We live amid surfaces, and the true art of life is to skate well on them," Emerson[1] wrote.

---

[1]Ralph Waldo Emerson (1803–82) was an American essayist and philosopher. —Eds.

One never moves without an uneasiness that staying is the norm   18
and that what you're after is something not just elusive but desperate,
and that eventually you'll fail and have to stop. But those who'll tell
you what you *have to do* say so only because that's what they've done
and are glad about it—or worse, are not so glad. Finally, I'll be the
judge. It'll be on my bill, not theirs.

On the first night I ever spent in the first house I ever owned, I said   19
to my wife as we were going to sleep on a mattress on the bedroom floor
amid boxes and paper and disheveled furniture, "Owning feels a lot like
renting, doesn't it? You just can't leave when you want to." This was in
New Jersey, fifteen years ago—a nice, brown three-story stucco of a
vaguely Flemish vernacular, on a prizable double lot on a prizable oak-
lined street named for President Jefferson—a home that cost $117,500,
and that now probably runs above a half million if you could buy it,
which you can't. This was a house I eventually grew to feel so trapped in
that one night I got stirringly drunk, roared downstairs with a can of
white paint, and flung paint on everything—all over the living room,
the rugs, the furniture, the walls, my wife, even all over our novelist
friend who was visiting and who hasn't been back since. I wanted, I
think, to desanctify "the home," get the *joujou* out of permanence.
And, in fact, in two months' time we were gone from there, for good.

Today, when people ask me, people who banked their fires and   20
their equity, "Don't you wish you'd hung onto that house on Jefferson?
You'd have it half paid for now. You'd be rich!" my answer is, "Holy Jesus no! Don't you realize I'd have had to live in that house all this time?
Life's too short." It's an odd thing to ask a man like me.

It may simply and finally be that the way most people feel when   21
they're settled is the way I feel when I move: safe and in possession of
myself. So much so that when I'm driving along some ribbony highway
over a distant and heat-miraged American landscape, and happen to
spy, far across the median strip, a U-Haul van humping its cargo toward
some pay dirt far away, its beetle-browed driver alone in the buzzing
capsule of his own fears and hopes and silent explanations of the future,
who I think of is…me. He's me. And my heart goes out to him. It's
never a wasted effort to realize that what we do is what anybody does,
all of us clinging to our little singularities, making it in the slow lane toward someplace we badly need to go.

QUESTIONS ON MEANING

1. What is this essay's THESIS?
2. What is the point of the ANECDOTE in paragraph 14? What does it illustrate?
3. Why does Ford use quotation marks around "homes" in paragraph 15 but not around "home" in paragraph 14?
4. What is Ford's attitude toward his native Mississippi? How can you tell?

QUESTIONS ON WRITING STRATEGY

1. Where does Ford explicitly resist oversimplifying the causes of his frequent moving? What causes does he identify for his actions?
2. What is the EFFECT of Ford's INTRODUCTION (paras. 1–3), which details "the worst things that can happen to us" and the author's experiences with them?
3. What is Ford's TONE: casual? serious? hostile? defensive? humorous? something else? Cite passages from the essay to support your answer.
4. **OTHER METHODS.** How does Ford use EXAMPLES in his essay? What do the most extended ones illustrate?

QUESTIONS ON LANGUAGE

1. Ford writes, "I brood over the sign on my lawn bitterly demanding 'make offer'" (para. 2). What are the effects of the words "brood" and "bitterly demanding"?
2. Ford examines words associated with movers: "*Transient* is a word of reproach; *impermanence* bears a taint, a suspicion..." (para. 15). Is he offering the words' DENOTATIONS or CONNOTATIONS?
3. What does Ford mean by "lorish, insider blab" (para. 16)? (Look up the word *lore*, the origin of Ford's invented "lorish.") Why do you think Ford objects to this aspect of "[o]ther people's permanences"?
4. Give definitions of the following words: profuse (para. 7); Zeitgeist, inert (10); conjecture (12); millages, taint (15); savvy, meticulous (16); desanctify, *joujou* (some dictionaries may list *juju*, an alternate spelling) (19).

SUGGESTIONS FOR WRITING

1. **JOURNAL WRITING.** In paragraph 6, Ford gives many immediate reasons for moving. What would prompt you to move — or, if you have moved recently, why did you? Write a journal entry on the reasons you might move or have moved.
   FROM JOURNAL TO ESSAY. Write an essay weighing the reasons you would or did move against the probable or actual costs of the move, not only financial but emotional. What might or did you gain by moving? What would or did you sacrifice? Which are more compelling to you, the gains or the sacrifices? Why?

2. Why would moving be one of the "worst three things that can happen to us," up there with the death of a spouse and the burning of a house? What is stressful about moving? Does it have to be stressful? Write an essay about a move you've made, even if just to a new dwelling in the same town. How stressful was it? Were there compensations for the stress? In the end, was the move a positive or a negative event for you?

3. **CRITICAL WRITING.** In a brief essay, ANALYZE Ford's tone in paragraphs 16–17, considering what the author's words and sentence structures convey about his attitudes toward those who don't move. What do these paragraphs contribute to the essay? Do they undermine it in any way? Support your ideas with quotations from the essay.

4. **CONNECTIONS.** In paragraph 17, Ford refutes the assertion that in moving "you only get a superficial view of life…, skimming the top layer off things…." The assertion refuted by Ford echoes the contention of Scott Russell Sanders in "Homeplace" that without a place "you wander the world like a sightseer, a collector of sensations, with no gauge for measuring what you see" (para. 13, p. 393). Closely read Ford's paragraphs 15–17 and Sanders's paragraph 13, which in essence present two opposed views of what nourishes us and how we should live. In an essay, discuss the differences in the authors' views and then weigh in with your own opinion. Do you side with one author or the other? Do they both have a point? Does either miss something you believe to be true? Explain your own opinion with EVIDENCE from your reading and experiences.

RICHARD FORD ON WRITING

In an interview published in 1987 in *The Missouri Review*, Kay Bonetti asked Richard Ford, "Do you enjoy writing?" Ford answered, "I would never use that word, no. Writing's what I felt early in my life I might be best suited to do, and I didn't mind doing it. Even as a sort of untaught fellow in Mississippi, I always thought writers were people who had a high calling. My mother used to take me over to Jackson and she would say to me, 'That's Eudora Welty,'[1] and I would say, 'Who's she?' And my mother would say, 'She's a writer.' I could tell in her voice that was something other than the ordinary."

Bonetti persisted, commenting, "Many writers will say outright that it's painful to write." Ford replied, "Well, that sounds too much like a complaint to me, and I don't like complaining in public. A lot of things you like might be painful. It just doesn't seem to be an adequate way of talking about that thing that you do all your life. To say that it was painful would be really perverse. Being a novelist, being a story

---

[1]Eudora Welty (born 1909) is an American fiction writer who is generally revered for her precise and hopeful stories of small-town life. With Michael Kreyling, Ford has edited two collections of Welty's work. —EDS.

writer, being an essayist, there's nothing perverse about it at all. Most of the time it's really quite interesting. And sometimes quite exhilarating."

FOR DISCUSSION

1. Why do you think Ford denies that he enjoys writing when he also says he sometimes finds it exhilarating?
2. If you were being interviewed by Kay Bonetti, how would you respond to the question "Do you enjoy writing?" What parts of the writing process do you like? What parts do you not like? Why?

ADDITIONAL WRITING TOPICS
Cause and Effect

1. In a short essay, explain *either* the causes *or* the effects of a situation that concerns you. Narrow your topic enough to treat it in some detail, and provide more than a mere list of causes or effects. If seeking causes, you will have to decide carefully how far back to go in your search for remote causes. If stating effects, fill your essay with examples. Here are some topics to consider:

    Labor strikes in professional sports
    Children searching for pornography on the Internet
    State laws mandating the use of seat belts in cars (or the wearing of helmets on motorcycles)
    Friction between two roommates, or two friends
    The pressure on students to get good grades
    Some quirk in your personality, or a friend's
    The increasing need for more than one breadwinner per family
    The temptation to do something dishonest to get ahead
    The popularity of a particular television program, comic strip, rock group, or pop singer
    The steady increase in college costs
    The scarcity of people in training for employment as skilled workers: plumbers, tool and die makers, electricians, masons, carpenters, to name a few
    A decision to enter the ministry or a religious order
    The fact that cigarette advertising is banned from television
    The absence of a peacetime draft
    The fact that more couples are choosing to have only one child, or none
    The growing popularity of private elementary and high schools
    The fact that most Americans can communicate in no language other than English
    Being "born again"
    The fact that women increasingly get jobs formerly regarded as being for men only
    The pressure on young people to conform to the standards of their peers
    The emphasis on competitive sports in high school and college

2. In *Blue Highways* (1982), an account of his rambles around America, William Least Heat Moon explains why Americans, and not the British, settled the vast tract of northern land that lies between the Mississippi and the Rockies. He traces what he believes to be the major cause in this paragraph:

    > Were it not for a web-footed rodent and a haberdashery fad in eighteenth-century Europe, Minnesota might be a Canadian province today. The beaver, almost as much as the horse, helped shape the course of early American history. Some *Mayflower*

colonists paid their passage with beaver pelts; and a good fur could bring an Indian three steel knives or a five-foot stack could bring a musket. But even more influential were the trappers and fur traders penetrating the great Northern wilderness between the Mississippi River and the Rocky Mountains, since it was their presence that helped hold the Near West against British expansion from the north; and it was their explorations that opened the heart of the nation to white settlement. These men, by making pelts the currency of the wilds, laid the base for a new economy that quickly overwhelmed the old. And all because European men of mode simply had to wear a beaver hat.

In a Least Heat Moon–like paragraph of your own, explain how a small cause produced a large effect. You might generate ideas by browsing in a history book—where you might find, for instance, that a cow belonging to Mrs. Patrick O'Leary is believed to have started the Great Chicago Fire of 1871 by kicking over a lighted lantern—or in a collection of *Ripley's Believe It or Not*. If some small event in your life has had large consequences, you might care to write instead from personal experience.

9

DEFINITION
Tracing a Boundary

THE METHOD

As a rule, when we hear the word DEFINITION, we immediately think of a dictionary. In that helpful storehouse—a writer's best friend—we find the literal and specific meaning (or meanings) of a word. The dictionary supplies this information concisely: in a sentence, in a phrase, or even in a *synonym*—a single word that means the same thing ("**narrative** [năr-e-tĭv] *n.* **1**: story...").

Stating such a definition is often a good way to begin an essay when basic terms may be in doubt. A short definition can clarify your subject to your reader, and perhaps help you to limit what you have to say. If, for instance, you are going to discuss a demolition derby, explaining such a spectacle to readers who may never have seen one, you might offer at the outset a short definition of *demolition derby*, your subject and your key term.

In constructing a short definition, the usual procedure is to state the general class to which the subject belongs and then add any particular features that distinguish it. You could say: "A demolition derby is a contest"—that is its general class—"in which drivers ram old cars into one another until only one car is left running." Short definitions may

be useful at *any* moment in an essay, whenever you introduce a technical term that readers may not know.

When a term is really central to your essay and likely to be misunderstood, a *stipulative definition* may be helpful. This fuller explanation
stipulates, or specifies, the particular way you are using a term. The paragraph on page 415, defining *TV addiction*, could be a stipulative definition in an essay on the causes and cures of the addiction.

In this chapter, we are mainly concerned with *extended definition*, a
kind of expository writing that relies on a variety of other methods.
Suppose you wanted to write an essay to make clear what *poetry* means.
You would specify its elements—rhythm, IMAGES, and so on—by using
DIVISION or ANALYSIS. You'd probably provide EXAMPLES of each element.
You might COMPARE AND CONTRAST poetry with prose. You might discuss
the EFFECT of poetry on the reader. (Emily Dickinson, a poet herself,
once stated the effect that reading a poem had on her: "I feel as if the
top of my head were taken off.") In fact, extended definition, unlike
other methods of writing discussed in this book, is perhaps less a
method in itself than the application of a variety of methods to clarify
a purpose. Like DESCRIPTION, extended definition tries to *show* a reader its
subject. It does so by establishing boundaries, for its writer tries to differentiate a subject from anything that might be confused with it.

When Gloria Naylor, in her essay in this chapter, seeks to define
the freighted word *nigger*, she recalls her experiences of the word as an
African American, recounting exactly what she heard in varying situations. Extended definition examines the nature of the subject, carefully summing up its chief characteristics and drawing boundaries
around it, striving to answer the question "What makes this what it is,
not something else?"

An extended definition can define a word (like *nigger*), a thing (a
laser beam), a concept (TV addiction), or a general phenomenon (the
popularity of the demolition derby). Unlike a sentence definition, or any
you would find in a standard dictionary, an extended definition takes
room: at least a paragraph, often an entire essay. In having many methods
of writing at your disposal, you have ample freedom and wide latitude.

Outside an English course, how is this method of writing used? In a
newspaper feature, a sportswriter defines what makes a *great team* great.
In a journal article, a physician defines the nature of a previously unknown syndrome or disease. In a written opinion, a judge defines not
only a word but a concept, *obscenity*. In a book review, a critic defines a
newly prevalent kind of poem. In a letter to a younger brother or sister
contemplating college, a student might define a *gut course* and how to
recognize one.

Unlike a definition in a dictionary that sets forth the literal meaning of a word in an unimpassioned manner, some definitions imply

biases. In defining *patron* to the earl of Chesterfield, who had tried to befriend him after ignoring his petitions for aid during his years of grinding poverty, Samuel Johnson wrote scornfully: "Is not a Patron, my Lord, one who looks with unconcern on a man struggling for life in the water, and, when he has reached the ground, encumbers him with help?" IRONY, a FIGURE OF SPEECH (metaphor), and a short definition have rarely been wielded with such crushing power. (*Encumbers*, by the way, is a wonderfully physical word in its context: It means "to burden with dead weight.")

THE PROCESS

Discovery of Meanings

The purpose of almost any extended definition is to explore a topic in its full complexity, to explain its meaning or sometimes to argue for (or against) a particular meaning. To discover this complexity, you may find it useful to ask yourself a series of questions. These questions may be applied both to individual subjects, such as a basketball superstar or a comet, and to collective subjects: institutions (like the American family, a typical savings bank, a university, the Church of Jesus Christ of Latter-Day Saints) and organizations (IBM, the Mafia, a heavy-metal band, a Little League baseball team). To illustrate how the questions might work, at least in one instance, let's say you plan to write a paper defining *sexism*.[1]

1. *Is this subject unique, or are there others of its kind? If it resembles others, in what ways? How is it different?* As you can see, these last two questions invite you to compare and contrast. Applied to the concept of sexism, these questions might prompt you to compare sexism with one or two other -isms, such as racism or ageism. Or they might remind you that sexists can be both women and men, leading you to note the differences.

2. *In what different forms does it occur, while keeping its own identity?* Specific examples might occur to you: your Uncle George, who won't hire any "damned females" in his auto repair shop, or a girlfriend who is nastily suspicious of all men. Each form—Uncle George and the girlfriend—might rate a description.

---

[1] The six questions that follow are freely adapted from those first stated by Richard E. Young, Alton L. Becker, and Kenneth L. Pike, who have applied insights from psychology and linguistics to the writing process. Their procedure for generating ideas and discovering information is called *tagmemics*. To investigate subjects in greater depth, their own six questions may be used in nine possible combinations, as they explain in detail in *Rhetoric: Discovery and Change* (New York: Harcourt, 1970).

3. *When and where do we find it? Under what circumstances and in what situations?* Well, where have you been lately? At any parties where sexism reared its ugly head? In any classroom discussions? Consider other areas of your experience: Did you encounter any sexists while holding a part-time summer job?

4. *What is it at the present moment?* Perhaps you might make the point that sexism was once considered an exclusively male preserve but is now an attribute of women as well. Or you could observe that many men have gone underground with their sexism, refraining from expressing it blatantly while still harboring negative attitudes about women. In either case, you might care to draw examples from life.

5. *What does it do? What are its functions and activities?* Sexists stereotype and sometimes act to exclude or oppress people of the opposite sex. These questions might also invite you to reply with a PROCESS ANALYSIS: You might show, for instance, how a sexist man you know, a personnel director who determines pay scales, systematically eliminates women from better-paying jobs.

6. *How is it put together? What parts make it up? What holds these parts together?* You could apply analysis to the various beliefs and assumptions that, all together, make up sexism. This question might work well in writing about an organization: the personnel director's company, for instance, with its unfair hiring and promotion policies.

Not all these questions will fit every subject under the sun, and some may lead nowhere, but you will usually find them well worth asking. They can make you aware of points to notice, remind you of facts you already know. They can also suggest interesting points you need to find out more about.

Methods of Development

The preceding questions will give you a good start on using whatever method or methods of writing can best answer the overall question "What is the nature of this subject?" You will probably find yourself making use of much that you have learned earlier from this book. A short definition like the one for *demolition derby* on page 409 may be a good start for your essay, especially if you think your readers need a quick grounding in the subject or in your view of it. (But feel no duty to place a dictionaryish definition in the INTRODUCTION of every essay you write: The device is overused.) In explaining a demolition derby, if your readers already have at least a vague idea of the meaning of the term and need no short, formal definition of it, you could open your extended definition by

NARRATING the events at a typical demolition derby, starting with a description of the lineup of old beat-up vehicles:

> One hundred worthless cars—everything from a 1960 Cadillac to a Dodge Dart to a recently wrecked Thunderbird, their glass removed, their radiators leaking—assemble on a racetrack or an open field. Their drivers, wearing crash helmets, buckle themselves into their seats, some pulling at beer cans to soften the blows to come.

You could proceed by example, listing demolition derbies you have known ("The great destruction of 184 vehicles took place at the Orleans County Fair in Barton, Vermont, in the summer of '97..."). If you have enough examples, you could CLASSIFY them; or perhaps you could analyze a demolition derby, dividing it into its components of cars, drivers, judges, first-aid squad, and spectators, and discussing each. You could compare and contrast a demolition derby with that amusement park ride known as Bumper Cars or Dodge-'ems, in which small cars with rubber bumpers bash one another head-on, but (unlike cars in the derby) harmlessly. A process analysis of a demolition derby might help your readers understand the nature of the spectacle: how in round after round, cars are eliminated until one remains. You could ask "What causes the owners of old cars to want to smash them?" or "What causes people to watch the destruction?" or "What are the consequences?" To answer such questions in an essay, you would apply the method of CAUSE AND EFFECT.

Thesis

Opening up your subject with questions and developing it with various methods are good ways to see what your subject has to offer, but they can also leave you with a welter of ideas and a blurred focus. As in description, when all your details build to a dominant impression, so in definition you want to center all your thoughts and evidence about the subject on a single controlling idea, a THESIS. It's not essential to state this idea in a THESIS SENTENCE, although doing so can be a service to your readers. What is essential is that the idea govern.

Here, from the essays in this chapter, are two thesis sentences. Notice how each focuses the broad subject to an assertion about the subject, and how we can detect the author's bias toward the subject.

> The word *chink* may have been created to harm, ridicule, and humiliate, but for us [Chinese Americans] it may have done the exact opposite. (Christine Leong, "Being a Chink")

> We should give [the murder of the Jews] its true designation and not hide it behind polite, erudite terms [such as *holocaust*] created out of classical words. (Bruno Bettelheim, "The Holocaust")

Evidence

Writing an extended definition, you are like a mapmaker charting a territory, taking in some of what lies within the boundaries and ignoring what lies outside. The boundaries, of course, may be wide; and for this reason, the writing of an extended definition sometimes tempts a writer to sweep across a continent airily and to soar off into abstract clouds. Like any other method of expository writing, though, definition will work only for the writer who remembers the world of the senses and supports every generalization with concrete evidence.

There may be no finer illustration of the perils of definition than the scene, in Charles Dickens's novel *Hard Times*, of the grim schoolroom of a teacher named Gradgrind, who insists on facts but who completely ignores living realities. When a girl whose father is a horse trainer is unable to define a horse, Gradgrind blames her for not knowing what a horse is; and he praises the definition of a horse supplied by a pet pupil: "Quadruped. Graminivorous. Forty teeth, namely twenty-four grinders, four eye-teeth, and twelve incisive. Sheds coat in the spring; in marshy countries, sheds hoofs, too. Hoofs hard, but requiring to be shod with iron. Age known by marks in mouth." To anyone who didn't already know what a horse is, this enumeration of facts would prove of little help. In writing an extended definition, never lose sight of the reality you are attempting to bound, even if its frontiers are as inclusive as those of *psychological burnout* or *human rights*. Give your reader examples, narrate an illustrative story, bring in specific description — in whatever method you use, keep coming down to earth. Without your eyes on the world, you will define no reality. You might define *animal husbandry* till the cows come home and never make clear what it means.

CHECKLIST FOR REVISING A DEFINITION

✔ **MEANINGS.** Have you explored your subject fully, turning up both its obvious and its not-so-obvious meanings?

✔ **METHODS OF DEVELOPMENT.** Have you used an appropriate range of other methods to develop your subject?

✔ **THESIS.** Have you focused your definition and kept within that focus, drawing clear boundaries around your subject?

✔ **EVIDENCE.** Is your definition specific? Do examples, anecdotes, and concrete details both pin the subject down and make it vivid for readers?

DEFINITION IN A PARAGRAPH:
TWO ILLUSTRATIONS

Using Definition to Write About Television

The paragraph below SUMMARIZES the definition of *TV addiction* given in Marie Winn's essay on pages 431–33. The paragraph was written for *The Bedford Reader* as an example of definition, but its opening question suggests a broader use than just illustration: In a full essay on the causes and cures of the addiction, the paragraph could serve as a stipulative definition of the essay's key term.

Who is addicted to TV? According to Marie Winn, author of *The Plug-in Drug: Television, Children, and the Family*, TV addicts are similar to drug or alcohol addicts: They seek a more pleasurable experience than they can get from normal life; they depend on the source of this pleasure; and their lives are damaged by their dependency. TV addicts, says Winn, use TV to screen out the real world of feelings, worries, demands. They watch compulsively—four, five, even six hours on a work day. And they reject (usually passively, sometimes actively) interaction with family or friends, diverting or productive work at hobbies or chores, and chances for change and growth.

Definition of TV addiction

Comparison with drug or alcohol addiction

Analysis is of TV addicts' characteristics

Using Definition in an Academic Discipline

This paragraph from a biology textbook defines a term, *homology*, that is useful in explaining the evolution of different species from a common ancestor (the topic at this point in the textbook). The paragraph provides a brief definition, a more extensive one, and finally examples of the concept.

When the character traits found in any two species owe their resemblance to a common ancestry, taxonomists say the states are *homologous*, or are *homologues* of each other. *Homology* is defined as correspondence between two structures due to inheritance from a common ancestor. Homologous structures can be identical in appearance and can even be based on identical genes. However, such structures can diverge until they become very different in both appearance and function. Nevertheless, homologous structures usually retain certain basic features that betray a common ancestry. Consider the forelimbs of vertebrates. It is easy to make a detailed, bone-by-bone, muscle-by-muscle comparison of the forearm of a person and a monkey and to conclude that the forearms, as well as the various parts of the forearm, are

Definition of homology *and related words*

Short definition

Refined definition

Examples:
   Similar appearance, function, and structure

homologous. The forelimb of a dog, however, shows marked differences from those of primates in both appearance and function. The forelimb is used for locomotion by dogs but for grasping and manipulation by people and monkeys. Even so, all of the bones can still be matched. The wing of a bird and the flipper of a seal are even more different from each other or from the human forearm, yet they too are constructed around bones that can be matched on a nearly perfect one-to-one basis.

Dissimilar appearance and function, but similar structure

—William K. Purves and Gordon H. Orians,
Life: The Science of Biology

DEFINITION ELSEWHERE IN *THE BEDFORD READER*

Many of the essays in this book include at least a short definition of some key term. In the selections listed below, the authors mix extended definition with the other methods they use to achieve their purposes.

PART ONE

Barbara Lazear Ascher, "On Compassion"
Anna Quindlen, "Homeless"
Nancy Mairs, "Disability"
Judy Brady, "I Want a Wife"
Jamaica Kincaid, "Girl"
Marion Winik, "What Are Friends For?"
William Lutz, "The World of Doublespeak"
K. C. Cole, "The Arrow of Time"
Scott Russell Sanders, "Homeplace"

PART TWO

Stephen L. Carter, "The Insufficiency of Honesty"
Joan Didion, "In Bed"
Martin Luther King, Jr., "I Have a Dream"
Tom Wolfe, "Pornoviolence"

CASE STUDY
Using Definition

Susan Iessi was a freshman at the State University of New York at New Paltz when she volunteered to become a member of Hall Government, a dormitory association dedicated to student support. Discovering that many dorm residents, especially other freshmen, were unclear about the work of Hall Government, Iessi wrote the following statement.

Iessi's main goal of specifying Hall Government's purposes and responsibilities drew her into defining the mission of the association. After she drafted the statement, she showed it to other members. When one reader suggested that she explain the connections between Hall Government and other campus organizations, Iessi agreed: The change would clarify the boundaries of Hall Government. Iessi's final draft appears below.

The Mission of Hall Government

Hall Government consists of students who volunteer to provide the residents of their dormitory with social and emotional support. Hall Government creates opportunities for residents to meet other residents and build a network of friends through structured discussions, social events, and educational programs. It also mediates in situations such as conflicts between students and teachers or between roommates. The members of Hall Government believe that their support will encourage residents to provide support for each other as well, building a community in which students may learn and thrive during their college years.

Each dormitory's Hall Government functions independently. The groups have no formal relationship with the campus-wide elected student government but are sponsored and funded by the Residence Hall Student Association.

GLORIA NAYLOR

GLORIA NAYLOR describes herself as "just a girl from Queens who can
turn a sentence," but she is well known for bringing African American women vividly within the fold of American literature. She was
born in 1950 in New York City and served for some years as a missionary for the Jehovah's Witnesses, working "for better world conditions." While in college, she made her living as a telephone operator.
She graduated from Brooklyn College in 1981 and received an M.A. in
African American literature from Yale University in 1983. While
teaching at several universities and publishing numerous stories and essays, Naylor has written five interconnected novels: *The Women of
Brewster Place* (1982), *Linden Hills* (1985), *Mama Day* (1988), *Bailey's
Cafe* (1992), and *The Men of Brewster Place* (1998). *The Women of
Brewster Place* won the American Book Award for best first novel, and
Naylor has also received fellowships from the National Endowment for
the Arts and the Guggenheim Foundation. She lives in New York City.

The Meanings of a Word

When she was in third grade, Naylor was stung by a word that seemed
new. Only later did she realize that she'd been hearing the word all
her life, but in an entirely different context. In "The Meanings of a
Word," she uses definition to explore the varying meanings that context creates. The essay first appeared in the *New York Times* in 1986.

The essay following this one, Christine Leong's "Being a Chink,"
responds directly to Naylor and extends her point about context and
meaning.

Language is the subject. It is the written form with which I've   1
managed to keep the wolf away from the door and, in diaries, to keep
my sanity. In spite of this, I consider the written word inferior to the
spoken, and much of the frustration experienced by novelists is the
awareness that whatever we manage to capture in even the most transcendent passages falls far short of the richness of life. Dialogue
achieves its power in the dynamics of a fleeting moment of sight,
sound, smell, and touch.

I'm not going to enter the debate here about whether it is language   2
that shapes reality or vice versa. That battle is doomed to be waged
whenever we seek intermittent reprieve from the chicken and egg dispute. I will simply take the position that the spoken word, like the written word, amounts to a nonsensical arrangement of sounds or letters
without a consensus that assigns "meaning." And building from the

meanings of what we hear, we order reality. Words themselves are in-nocuous; it is the consensus that gives them true power.

I remember the first time I heard the word *nigger*. In my third-grade   3
class, our math tests were being passed down the rows, and as I handed the papers to a little boy in back of me, I remarked that once again he had received a much lower mark than I did. He snatched his test from me and spit out that word. Had he called me a nymphomaniac or a necrophiliac, I couldn't have been more puzzled. I didn't know what a nigger was, but I knew that whatever it meant, it was something he shouldn't have called me. This was verified when I raised my hand, and in a loud voice re-peated what he had said and watched the teacher scold him for using a "bad" word. I was later to go home and ask the inevitable question that every black parent must face—"Mommy, what does *nigger* mean?"

And what exactly did it mean? Thinking back, I realize that this   4
could not have been the first time the word was used in my presence. I was part of a large extended family that had migrated from the rural South after World War II and formed a close-knit network that gravi-tated around my maternal grandparents. Their ground-floor apartment in one of the buildings they owned in Harlem was a weekend mecca for my immediate family, along with countless aunts, uncles, and cousins who brought along assorted friends. It was a bustling and open house with assorted neighbors and tenants popping in and out to exchange bits of gossip, pick up an old quarrel, or referee the ongoing checkers game in which my grandmother cheated shamelessly. They were all there to let down their hair and put up their feet after a week of labor in the factories, laundries, and shipyards of New York.

Amid the clamor, which could reach deafening proportions—two   5
or three conversations going on simultaneously, punctuated by the sound of a baby's crying somewhere in the back rooms or out on the street—there was still a rigid set of rules about what was said and how. Older children were sent out of the living room when it was time to get into the juicy details about "you-know-who" up on the third floor who had gone and gotten herself "p-r-e-g-n-a-n-t!" But my parents, know-ing that I could spell well beyond my years, always demanded that I fol-low the others out to play. Beyond sexual misconduct and death, ev-erything else was considered harmless for our young ears. And so among the anecdotes of the triumphs and disappointments in the vari-ous workings of their lives, the word *nigger* was used in my presence, but it was set within contexts and inflections that caused it to register in my mind as something else.

In the singular, the word was always applied to a man who had dis-   6
tinguished himself in some situation that brought their approval for his strength, intelligence, or drive:

"Did Johnny *really* do that?" 7

"I'm telling you, that nigger pulled in $6,000 of overtime last year. 8
Said he got enough for a down payment on a house."

When used with a possessive adjective by a woman—"my nig- 9
ger"—it became a term of endearment for her husband or boyfriend.
But it could be more than just a term applied to a man. In their mouths
it became the pure essence of manhood—a disembodied force that
channeled their past history of struggle and present survival against the
odds into a victorious statement of being: "Yeah, that old foreman
found out quick enough—you don't mess with a nigger."

In the plural, it became a description of some group within the 10
community that had overstepped the bounds of decency as my family
defined it. Parents who neglected their children, a drunken couple who
fought in public, people who simply refused to look for work, those
with excessively dirty mouths or unkempt households were all "trifling
niggers." This particular circle could forgive hard times, unemployment, the occasional bout of depression—they had gone through all of
that themselves—but the unforgivable sin was a lack of self-respect.

A woman could never be a "nigger" in the singular, with its con- 11
notation of confirming worth. The noun *girl* was its closest equivalent
in that sense, but only when used in direct address and regardless of the
gender doing the addressing. *Girl* was a token of respect for a woman.
The one-syllable word was drawn out to sound like three in recognition
of the extra ounce of wit, nerve, or daring that the woman had shown
in the situation under discussion.

"G-i-r-l, stop. You mean you said that to his face?" 12

But if the word was used in a third-person reference or shortened so 13
that it almost snapped out of the mouth, it always involved some element of communal disapproval. And age became an important factor
in these exchanges. It was only between individuals of the same generation, or from any older person to a younger (but never the other way
around), that *girl* would be considered a compliment.

I don't agree with the argument that use of the word *nigger* at this 14
social stratum of the black community was an internalization of racism.
The dynamics were the exact opposite: the people in my grandmother's
living room took a word that whites used to signify worthlessness or
degradation and rendered it impotent. Gathering there together, they
transformed *nigger* to signify the varied and complex human beings
they knew themselves to be. If the word was to disappear totally from
the mouths of even the most liberal of white society, no one in that
room was naive enough to believe it would disappear from white
minds. Meeting the word head-on, they proved it had absolutely nothing to do with the way they were determined to live their lives.

So there must have been dozens of times that *nigger* was spoken in   15
front of me before I reached the third grade. But I didn't "hear" it until
it was said by a small pair of lips that had already learned it could be a
way to humiliate me. That was the word I went home and asked my
mother about. And since she knew that I had to grow up in America,
she took me in her lap and explained.

QUESTIONS ON MEANING

1. Why does Naylor think that written language is inferior to spoken language (para. 1)?
2. In paragraph 15, Naylor says that although the word *nigger* had been used in her presence many times, she didn't really "hear" the word until a mean little boy said it. How do you explain this contradiction?
3. Naylor says that "the people in my grandmother's living room...transformed *nigger*" (para. 14). How?
4. What is Naylor's primary PURPOSE in this essay?

QUESTIONS ON WRITING STRATEGY

1. In her first two paragraphs, Naylor discusses language in the ABSTRACT. How are these paragraphs connected to her stories about the word *nigger*? Why do you think she begins the essay this way? Is this INTRODUCTION effective or not? Why?
2. Look back at the last two sentences of Naylor's essay. What is the EFFECT of ending on this idea?
3. Go through Naylor's essay and note which paragraphs discuss the racist uses of *nigger* and which discuss the nonracist uses. How do Naylor's organization and the space she devotes to each use help Naylor make her point?
4. **OTHER METHODS.** After each DEFINITION of the words *nigger* and *girl*, Naylor gives an EXAMPLE in the form of a quotation. These examples are in paragraphs 7–10 (for instance, "'Yeah, that old foreman found out quick enough—you don't mess with a nigger'" [9]) and paragraph 12 ("'G-i-r-l, stop. You mean you said that to his face?'"). What do such examples add to Naylor's definitions?

QUESTIONS ON LANGUAGE

1. What is "the chicken and egg dispute" (para. 2)? What does this dispute say about the relationship between language and reality?
2. What do the words *nymphomaniac* and *necrophiliac* CONNOTE in paragraph 3?
3. If you don't know the meanings of the following words, look them up in a dictionary: transcendent, dynamics (para. 1); intermittent, reprieve, consensus, innocuous (2); verified (3); gravitated, mecca (4); clamor, inflections

(5); endearment, disembodied (9); unkempt, trifling (10); communal (13); stratum, internalization, degradation, rendered, impotent, naive (14).

SUGGESTIONS FOR WRITING

1. **JOURNAL WRITING.** As Naylor shows, the language of stereotypes can be powerful and painful to encounter. Have you ever experienced or witnessed this kind of labeling? What were your reactions? (Keep in mind that race is but one object of stereotypes. Consider income, marital status, sexual preference, weight, height, education, and neighborhood, for just a few other characteristics.)

   FROM JOURNAL TO ESSAY. Using your own experiences as examples, write an essay modeled on Naylor's in which you define "the meanings of a word" (or words). Do you find, too, that meaning varies with context? If so, make the variations clear.

2. Can you think of other labels that may be defined in more than one way? (These might include *smart, childish, old-fashioned, artistic, proud, attractive, heroic*, and so on.) Choose one such label, and write one paragraph for each possible definition. Be sure to explain the contexts for each definition and to give enough examples so that the meanings are clear.

3. **CRITICAL WRITING.** Naylor claims that words are "nonsensical...without a consensus that assigns 'meaning'" (para. 2). If so, how do we understand the meaning of a word like *nigger*, when Naylor has shown us that there is more than one consensus about its meaning? Does Naylor contradict herself? Write an essay that either supports or refutes Naylor's claim about meaning and context. You will need to consider how she and you define *consensus*.

4. **CONNECTIONS.** The next essay, Christine Leong's "Being a Chink," identifies a moment when Leong was first struck by the negative power of racist language. Write an essay that COMPARES AND CONTRASTS these two women's reactions to a derogatory label. How did the context help shape their reactions?

GLORIA NAYLOR ON WRITING

Studying literature in college was somewhat disappointing for Gloria Naylor. "What I wanted to see," she told William Goldstein of *Publishers Weekly*, "were reflections of me and my existence and experience." Then, reading African American literature in graduate school, she discovered that "blacks have been writing in this country since this country has been writing and have a literary heritage of their own. Unfortunately, they haven't had encouragement or recognition for their efforts....What had happened was that when black people wrote, it wasn't quite [considered] serious work—it was race work or protest work."

For Naylor this discovery was a turning point. "I wanted to become a writer because I felt that my presence as a black woman and my perspective as a woman in general had been underrepresented." Her work tries to "articulate experiences that want articulating—for those readers who reflect the subject matter, black readers, and for those who don't, basically white middle-class readers."

FOR DISCUSSION

1. What does Naylor mean when she says that she tries to "articulate experiences that want articulating"?
2. Naylor is motivated to write by a consciousness of herself as an African American and a woman. How do you see this motivation driving her essay "The Meanings of a Word"?

CHRISTINE LEONG

CHRISTINE LEONG was born in New York City in 1976 and attended Stuyvesant High School there, graduating in 1994. At the Stern School of Business at New York University, she majored in finance and information systems and interned at an investment firm. After graduating with a B.S. in 1998, she took a job as a consultant at J. P. Morgan in New York. In her free time, Leong writes, reads, takes pictures, and participates in outdoor activities. "The one thing I couldn't live without," she says, "is music."

Being a Chink

Leong wrote this essay for her freshman composition class at NYU, and it was published in Mercer Street, 1995–96, a collection of NYU students' essays. As you'll see, Leong was inspired by Gloria Naylor's "The Meanings of a Word" (p. 418) to report her own experiences and to define a word that can be either hurtful or warm, depending on the speaker.

The power of language is something that people often underestimate. It is the one thing that allows people to communicate with each other, to be understood, to be heard. It gives us identity, personality, social status, and it also creates communities, defining both insiders and outsiders. Language has the ability to heal or to harm, to praise or belittle, to promote peace or even to glorify hate. But perhaps most important, language is the tool used to define us and differentiate us from the next person. Names and labels are what separate us from each other. Sometimes these things are innocuous, depending on the particular word and the context in which it is used. Often they serve to ridicule and humiliate.

I remember the first time I saw the word *chink*. I used to work over the summers at my father's Chinese restaurant, the Oriental, to earn a few extra dollars of spending money. It was a warm, sunny Friday morning, and I was busy performing my weekly task of cleaning out the storage area under the cash register at the front of the store. Armed with a large can of Pledge furniture polish and an old cloth, I started attacking the old oak shelves, sorting through junk mail that had accumulated over the last week, separating the bills and other important things that had to be set aside for later, before wiping each wooden panel clean. It was a pretty uneventful chore, that is, until I got to the bottom shelf, the last of three. I always hated cleaning this particular shelf because it required me to get down on my hands and knees behind the counter and reach all the way back into the compartment to dig out all the stuff that managed to get wedged against the wall.

After bending to scoop all the papers out of that third cubicle, I be-   3
gan to sort through them haphazardly. A few old menus, a gum wrapper (I always wondered how little things like that got stuffed in there), some promotional flyers, two capless pens, a dusty scratch pad, and something that appeared to be a little white envelope. Nothing seemed unusual until I examined that last item more closely. It was an old MidLantic envelope from the bank across the street. I was just about to crumple it up and throw it into the trash can when I decided to check if there was any money left in it. Too lazy to deal with the actual "chore" of opening the envelope, I held it up to the light.

As the faint yellow glow from the antique light fixture above me   4
shone through the envelope, turning it transparent, my suspicion that it was empty was confirmed. However, what I found was more shocking than anything I could have imagined. There, outlined by the light, was the word *chink* written backwards. I quickly lowered my arm onto the cool, smooth surface of the counter and flipped the envelope onto its other side, refusing to believe what I had just read. On the back, in dark blue ink with a large circle drawn around it, was the word CHINK written in my father's handwriting.

Up until that moment, I hadn't known that my father knew such   5
words, and thinking again, perhaps he didn't know this one either. Af-ter all, it was a habit of his to write down English words he did not know when he heard them and look them up in the dictionary later that day, learning them and adding them to his vocabulary. My mind began spinning with all the possible reasons he had written this partic-ular word down. I wondered if an angry patron who had come in earlier had called him that.

I was shocked at that possibility, but I was not surprised. Being one   6
of only two Asian families living and running a business in a small suburban town predominately inhabited by old Caucasian people was bound to breed some kind of discrimination, if not hatred. I know that my father might not have known exactly what the word *chink* meant, but he must have had a good idea, because he never came to ask me about it as he did with all the other slang words that couldn't be found in the dictionary. It's funny, though, I do not remember the first time I was called a *chink*. I only remember the pain and outrage I felt the first time I saw it in writing, perhaps the first time I discovered that some-one had used that hateful word to degrade my father.

In her essay "The Meanings of a Word," Gloria Naylor examines   7
the various meanings of the word *nigger*, definitions that have consen-sual meanings throughout society and others that vary according to how and when the word is used. In this piece, Naylor uses personal

examples to describe how "the people in [her] grandmother's living room took a word that whites used to signify worthlessness or degradation and rendered it impotent," by transforming *nigger* into a word signifying "the varied and complex human beings that they knew themselves to be." Naylor goes on to add that although none of these people were foolish enough to believe that the word *nigger* would magically be erased from the minds of all humankind, they were convinced that their "head-on" approach of dealing with the label that society had put on them "proved that it had absolutely nothing to do with the way they were determined to live their lives."

It has been nearly eight years since that day I stumbled across the bank envelope. Since then we have moved from that suburb in New Jersey to New York City, where the Asian population is much larger, and the word *chink*, although still heard, is either heard less frequently or in a rather "harmless" manner between myself and fellow Chinese (Asian) teenage friends. I do not remember how it happened exactly. I just know that we have been calling each other *chink* for quite a long while now. The word has never been used to belittle or degrade, but rather as a term of endearment, a loving insult between friends, almost but not quite exactly the way *nigger* is sometimes used among black people. It is a practice that we still engage in today, and although we know that there are times when the use of the word *chink* is very inappropriate, it is an accepted term within our circle.

Do not misunderstand us, we are all intelligent Asian youths, all graduating from New York City's top high school, all college students, and we know what the word *chink* truly means. We know, because over the years we have heard it countless times, from strangers on the streets and in stores, from fellow students and peers, and in some instances even from teachers, although it might not have been meant for us to hear.

So you see, even though we may use the term *chink* rather casually, it is only used that way amongst ourselves because we know that when we say it to each other it is truly without malice or harmful intent. I do not think that any of us knows exactly why we do it, but perhaps it is our own way, like the characters in Naylor's piece, of dealing with a label that can never be removed. It is not determined by who we are on the inside, or what we are capable of accomplishing, but instead by what we look like—the shape of our eyes, the color of our skin, the texture of our hair, and our delicate features. Perhaps we intentionally misuse the word as a symbol of our overcoming the stereotypes that American society has imposed upon us, a way of showing that although others have tried to make us feel small, weak, and insignificant, we are the opposite. We are strong, we are determined, we are the voices of the future, and we refuse to let a simple word paralyze us, belittle us, or control us.

The word *chink* may have been created to harm, ridicule, and humiliate, but for us it may have done the exact opposite. In some ways it has helped us find a certain comfort in each other, each of us knowing what the other has gone through, a common thread of racism binding us all together, a strange union born from the word *chink* that was used against us, and a shared goal of perseverance. 11

QUESTIONS ON MEANING

1. In paragraph 9 Leong says that she and her friends "know what the word *chink* truly means." Where in her essay does she explain this "true" meaning?
2. What has the word *chink* come to mean when Leong and her friends use it? Where in the essay does Leong explain this?
3. One might argue that the THESIS of Leong's essay is that language is not absolute. Is her PURPOSE, then, to propose a new DEFINITION for a word, to teach the reader something about how labels work, or to explain how adapting a racist term can be a form of gaining power? How do you know?

QUESTIONS ON WRITING STRATEGY

1. Look carefully at Gloria Naylor's essay "The Meanings of a Word" (p. 418). What structural similarities do you notice between it and Leong's? Why do you think Leong adapts these features of Naylor's essay?
2. In paragraph 3, Leong details all the forgotten items she finds under the counter. What is the EFFECT of ending with the "old MidLantic envelope from the bank across the street"?
3. What is the main purpose of the extended example from Naylor's essay in paragraph 7?
4. Why is Leong so careful to explain that she and her friends are all intelligent and educated (para. 9)?
5. **OTHER METHODS.** Leong suggests CAUSE AND EFFECT when she expresses "outrage" at seeing the word *chink* in writing (para. 4). Why does Leong react so strongly to the writing on the envelope?

QUESTIONS ON LANGUAGE

1. In paragraph 10 Leong explains that she and her friends are "dealing with a label that can never be removed." What other words does she use in this paragraph to suggest the potential helplessness of being permanently labeled?
2. What do the CONNOTATIONS of "term of endearment" (para. 8) indicate about the way Leong and her friends have redefined *chink*?

3. Make sure you know the meanings of the following words: status, belittle, innocuous (para. 1); cubicle, haphazardly (3); Caucasian, degrade (6); consensual (7); malice (10); perseverance (11).

SUGGESTIONS FOR WRITING

1. **JOURNAL WRITING.** Although children often assume they will be protected by their parents, Leong presents a situation in which she wanted to protect her father. Have you ever felt particularly angry or defensive on behalf of a parent? Why? What did you do about it?

   FROM JOURNAL TO ESSAY. Write an essay that explores why and how children might feel compelled to act like parents toward their own parents. Is this a shift that comes with age? with specific circumstances? out of the blue? Make some GENERALIZATIONS about this process, using the personal recollections from your journal entry as EVIDENCE.

2. As Leong explains in her INTRODUCTION, not all labels are intended to be hurtful. Often they are shorthand ways for our families and friends to identify us, perhaps reflecting something about our appearance ("Red," "Slim") or our interests ("Sport," "Chef"). What do your family or friends call you? Write several paragraphs giving a careful definition of this label. Where did it come from? Why is it appropriate (or not)?

3. **CRITICAL WRITING.** In her opening paragraph Leong says that "language is the tool used to define us." But she goes on to explain how she and her friends *refuse* to be defined by racist language. Does this apparent contradiction weaken her essay? Why, or why not? (To answer this question, consider the purpose of Leong's essay; see "Meaning" question 3.)

4. **CONNECTIONS.** Both Leong and Gloria Naylor, in "The Meanings of a Word" (p. 418), show that racist language can be taken over by those against whom it is directed. They also show that for groups or communities to redefine, and thus to own, these racist slurs can be empowering. Do you find their ARGUMENTS convincing, or do these redefinitions reveal what Naylor denies—namely, "an internalization of racism" (para. 14)? In an essay, explain your opinion on this issue, using as evidence passages from Naylor's and Leong's essays as well as insights and EXAMPLES from your own observations and experience.

CHRISTINE LEONG ON WRITING

For *The Bedford Reader*, Christine Leong commented on the difficulties of writing and the rewards that can ensue.

Writing is something that comes easily for many people, but unfortunately I am not one of them. For me the writing process is one of the hardest and quite possibly is *the* most nerve wracking thing that I have ever experienced. I can't even begin to count all the hours I have spent throughout the course of my life staring at a blank computer screen, trying desperately to come up with the right combination of words to express my thoughts and feelings, and although after many hours of frustration I eventually end up with something, I am never happy with it because I am undoubtedly my own worst critic. Perhaps my mentality of "it's not good enough yet" stems from my belief that writing can never really be completed; to me it has no beginning and no end but is rather a small representation of who I am at a given moment in time, and I believe that the more things I experience in life, the more I am able to contribute to my writing. Thus, whatever I write always has the potential of being better; there's always room for improvement via more revisions, greater insight, and about a hundred more drafts.

I used to believe that writing always had to make sense, but since then I have learned that there are many things in this life that do not adhere to this "rule." I now realize that writing doesn't necessarily have to be grammatically correct or even sensible, and the only thing that really matters is that whatever is written is truly inspired. Passion comes through very clearly in a writer's words, and the more emotion that goes into a piece, the more impact it will ultimately have on the reader. In recent years I have learned that there are no real writing guidelines, and that writing is much like any other art form: It can be abstract or it can follow more traditional "themes." However, in order for a piece of writing to be effective, in the sense that it can differentiate itself from any other writing sample and hopefully have some significance to the reader, I believe that it has to come from within.

The majority of what I write about, and that which I feel is worth reading, is inspired by actual experiences that I have had. For example, "Being a Chink" began as an assignment in a freshman writing workshop class in college. When first presented with the task of writing it, I was at a complete loss for words and had absolutely no clue where to start. However, after reading Gloria Naylor's "The Meanings of a Word," I was reminded of one of the most traumatic and memorable events in my life. The piece triggered a very strong memory, and before long I found myself writing down anything that came into my head, letting my thoughts and emotions flow freely in the form of words without thinking about whether or not they made any kind of sense. Many hours later I discovered that I had written the basic structure of what would eventually be my final product. I must honestly say that I can't really recall the actual process of writing "Being a Chink"; it was just an essay that seemed to take on a life and form of its own. Perhaps that, along with its universal theme, is what makes it such a strong piece. It not only is a recollection from my adolescence but is something that defines the very essence of the person that I have become since then.

In retrospect, I now realize that writing "Being a Chink" was not only about completing an essay and fulfilling a writing requirement; it was also about the acknowledgment of my own growth as a person. In many ways, without my initially being aware of it, the piece has helped me come to terms with one of the most controversial issues that I have ever been faced with.

FOR DISCUSSION

1. Does Leong's characterization of writing as "nerve-wracking" ring bells with you? How do you overcome writer's block?
2. What do you think about Leong's statement that "writing doesn't necessarily have to be grammatically correct or even sensible, and the only thing that really matters is that whatever is written is truly inspired"? In your experience with writing, what are the roles of correctness, sense, and inspiration? What matters most to you? What matters most to readers?

MARIE WINN

MARIE WINN was born in Czechoslovakia in 1936. As a child she immigrated with her family to New York City, where she attended the public schools. She graduated from Radcliffe College and went on to Columbia University for further study. She has contributed articles to the *New York Times Magazine*, the *New York Times Book Review*, *Smithsonian*, and the *Wall Street Journal*, where she now writes a column on nature and bird watching. She is also the author of eleven books for both adults and children, including *The Fireside Book of Fun and Game Songs* (1974). Three of her books for adults raise difficult issues of child rearing and have attracted much attention: *The Plug-In Drug: Television, Children, and the Family* (1977, revised 1985), *Children Without Childhood* (1983), and *Unplugging the Plug-In Drug* (1987). Winn's latest book, *Red-Tails in Love: A Wildlife Drama in Central Park* (1998), tells the story of a pair of red-tailed hawks that nested on a New York highrise, and the community of people who observed them.

TV Addiction

Do you know someone who can't stop watching television? In this excerpt from *The Plug-In Drug*, Winn defines the troubling malady named in the title. The essay actually performs double duty as a definition, first explaining *addiction*, then *TV addiction*.

The word "addiction" is often used loosely and wryly in conversation. People will refer to themselves as "mystery book addicts" or "cookie addicts." E. B. White[1] writes of his annual surge of interest in gardening: "We are hooked and are making an attempt to kick the habit." Yet nobody really believes that reading mysteries or ordering seeds by catalogue is serious enough to be compared with addictions to heroin or alcohol. The word "addiction" is here used jokingly to denote a tendency to overindulge in some pleasurable activity. 1

People often refer to being "hooked on TV." Does this, too, fall into the lighthearted category of cookie eating and other pleasures that people pursue with unusual intensity, or is there a kind of television viewing that falls into the more serious category of destructive addiction? 2

When we think about addiction to drugs or alcohol, we frequently focus on negative aspects, ignoring the pleasures that accompany 3

[1] See page 644. —EDS.

drinking or drug-taking. And yet the essence of any serious addiction is a pursuit of pleasure, a search for a "high" that normal life does not supply. It is only the inability to function without the addictive substance that is dismaying, the dependence of the organism upon a certain experience and an increasing inability to function normally without it. Thus a person will take two or three drinks at the end of the day not merely for the pleasure drinking provides, but also because he "doesn't feel normal" without them.

An addict does not merely pursue a pleasurable experience and need to experience it in order to function normally. He needs to *repeat* it again and again. Something about that particular experience makes life without it less than complete. Other potentially pleasurable experiences are no longer possible, for under the spell of the addictive experience, his life is peculiarly distorted. The addict craves an experience and yet he is never really satisfied. The organism may be temporarily sated, but soon it begins to crave again. 4

Finally, a serious addiction is distinguished from a harmless pursuit of pleasure by its distinctly destructive elements. A heroin addict, for instance, leads a damaged life: His increasing need for heroin in increasing doses prevents him from working, from maintaining relationships, from developing in human ways. Similarly an alcoholic's life is narrowed and dehumanized by his dependence on alcohol. 5

Let us consider television viewing in the light of the conditions that define serious addictions. 6

Not unlike drugs or alcohol, the television experience allows the participant to blot out the real world and enter into a pleasurable and passive mental state. The worries and anxieties of reality are as effectively deferred by becoming absorbed in a television program as by going on a "trip" induced by drugs or alcohol. And just as alcoholics are only inchoately aware of their addiction, feeling that they control their drinking more than they really do ("I can cut it out any time I want — I just like to have three or four drinks before dinner"), people similarly overestimate their control over television watching. Even as they put off other activities to spend hour after hour watching television, they feel they could easily resume living in a different, less passive style. But somehow or other while the television set is present in their homes, the click doesn't sound. With television pleasures available, those other experiences seem less attractive, more difficult somehow. 7

A heavy viewer (a college English instructor) observes: "I find television almost irresistible. When the set is on, I cannot ignore it. I can't turn it off. I feel sapped, will-less, enervated. As I reach out to turn off the set, the strength goes out of my arms. So I sit there for hours and hours." 8

The self-confessed television addict often feels he "ought" to do other things — but the fact that he doesn't read and doesn't plant his 9 garden or sew or crochet or play games or have conversations means that those activities are no longer as desirable as television viewing. In a way a heavy viewer's life is as imbalanced by his television "habit" as a drug addict's or an alcoholic's. He is living in a holding pattern, as it were, passing up the activities that lead to growth or development or a sense of accomplishment. This is one reason people talk about their television viewing so ruefully, so apologetically. They are aware that it is an unproductive experience, that almost any other endeavor is more worthwhile by any human measure.

Finally, it is the adverse effect of television viewing on the lives of   10 so many people that defines it as a serious addiction. The television habit distorts the sense of time. It renders other experiences vague and curiously unreal while taking on a greater reality for itself. It weakens relationships by reducing and sometimes eliminating normal opportunities for talking, for communicating.

And yet television does not satisfy, else why would the viewer con-   11 tinue to watch hour after hour, day after day? "The measure of health," writes Lawrence Kubie, "is flexibility...and especially the freedom to cease when sated." But the television viewer can never be sated with his television experiences—they do not provide the true nourishment that satiation requires—and thus he finds that he cannot stop watching.

QUESTIONS ON MEANING

1. What distinction does Winn make between the "harmless pursuit of pleasure" and addiction?
2. In paragraph 2, Winn poses the question that leads to her THESIS. What is the answer to this question? Do you find it explicitly stated anywhere?
3. What does Winn think are the main problems caused by excessive TV viewing?
4. Does Winn think there can be anything good about watching television? How do you know?

QUESTIONS ON WRITING STRATEGY

1. Why does Winn take such care to define *addiction* (paras. 3–5)? What does this stipulative definition do for the essay?
2. Winn does not answer her thesis question immediately after she asks it (para. 2). Why, do you think? What is the EFFECT of this delay?
3. Throughout her essay, Winn puts a number of words and phrases in quotation marks—for example, "hooked on TV" (para. 2), "high" (3), "trip" (7), "ought" (9). What does this punctuation contribute to Winn's essay?

4. **OTHER METHODS.** Study Winn's COMPARISON between drug or alcohol addiction and TV addiction. How are the two similar? Are they different in any way?

QUESTIONS ON LANGUAGE

1. Especially in paragraphs 4 and 11, Winn uses several metaphors of eating to explain addiction. (See "Figures of speech" in Useful Terms if you need a definition of *metaphor*.) If you do not know the meanings of *craves, sated, nourishment,* and *satiated,* look them up in a dictionary. What is the effect of using such terms to define addiction?
2. What does Winn mean when she describes addiction as "living in a holding pattern" (para. 9)?
3. Consult a dictionary if you don't know the meanings of any of the following words: wryly, denote (para. 1); dismaying, organism (3); dehumanized (5); inchoately (7); sapped, enervated (8); ruefully, apologetically, endeavor (9); adverse, renders, vague (10).

SUGGESTIONS FOR WRITING

1. **JOURNAL WRITING.** If you like to watch television, Winn's essay may seem exaggerated. After all, isn't turning on the TV a great way to unwind or to be entertained? Write about your own relationship to television. How often do you watch? Does TV viewing interfere with your life, or do you have it under control? What does TV viewing do for (or to) you? If you don't watch TV at all, write instead about why you don't.

   FROM JOURNAL TO ESSAY. If you are a TV watcher, write an essay that compares and contrasts your relationship with TV and Winn's definition of *TV addiction:* Would Winn consider you a television addict? Do you consider yourself one? Is it possible to watch a lot of television without being an addict? If you are not a TV watcher, write an essay that compares and contrasts your life with that of a frequent watcher (not necessarily an addict): How do you benefit? What might you be missing?
2. As Winn's opening paragraph points out, people often claim to be "addicted" to all kinds of things. From your experience, you probably know that such addictions can include everything from spy novels to Snickers candy bars to driving dangerously. Write an essay defining an addiction (but not to cigarettes, drugs, alcohol, or television). Your essay's TONE may be serious or humorous, but you should give your readers a sense of the addiction's CAUSES AND EFFECTS as well as EXAMPLES of its sufferers.
3. **CRITICAL WRITING.** "Finally, it is the adverse effect of television viewing on the lives of so many people that defines it as a serious addiction" (para. 10). Do you agree with this statement? Does the number of people affected define an addiction as "serious"? If fewer people suffered the "adverse effect" of TV viewing, would it not be a serious addiction? Or, in contrast, do the huge numbers of TV viewers remove the behavior from addicted to normal? Write an essay that either confirms or refutes Winn's assertion, using examples to support your opinion.

4. **CONNECTIONS.** Gore Vidal's "Drugs" (p. 373) proposes legalizing drugs as a solution to the problem of drug addiction and its effects on our society. Following Vidal's model (though not his precise recommendations, of course, since television is already legal), propose a solution to the problem of TV addiction. Your solution may be serious or humorous, and it may approach the problem at the level of the individual addict or at the level of society as a whole.

MARIE WINN ON WRITING

For Marie Winn, the most enjoyable part of writing is making improvements. "I love spending an hour or two with a dictionary and a thesaurus looking for a more nearly perfect word," she declares in an account of her working habits written for *The Bedford Reader.* "Or taking my pen and ruthlessly pruning all the unnecessary adjectives (a practice I can wholeheartedly recommend to you), or fooling around with the rhythm of a sentence or a paragraph by changing a verb into a participle, or making any number of little changes that a magazine editor I work with ruefully calls 'mouse milking.'"

But the proportion of time Winn spends at this "delightful occupation" is small. "For me, the pleasure and pain of writing go on simultaneously. Once I have finally forced myself to bite the bullet and get to work, as soon as the flow of writing stops—after a few sentences or paragraphs or, if I am extraordinarily lucky, a few pages—then, as a little reward for having actually written something and also as a procrastinating measure to delay the painful necessity of having to write something again, I play with the words and sentences on the page.

"That's the trouble, of course: There have to be words and sentences on the page before I can enjoy the pleasure of playing with them. Somehow I have to transform the vague and confused tangle of ideas in my head into an orderly and logical sequence on a blank piece of paper. That's the real hell of writing: the inescapable need to think clearly.... You have to figure it out, make it all hang together, consider the implications, the alternatives, eliminate the contradictions, the extraneous thoughts, the illogical conclusions. I *hate* that part of writing and I have a feeling you know perfectly well what I'm talking about."

FOR DISCUSSION

1. For Winn, what is the most difficult part of the writing process? What part does she most enjoy?
2. What does the author see as the role that thinking plays in writing?

BRUNO BETTELHEIM

Described in his *New York Times* obituary as "a psychoanalyst of great impact" and "a gifted writer∴.. with a great literary and moral sensibility," BRUNO BETTELHEIM was born in Austria in 1903 and died in the United States in 1990. Growing up in the Vienna of Sigmund Freud, Bettelheim became interested in psychoanalysis as a young teenager and trained as a psychologist at the University of Vienna. He had already earned a wide reputation when he was imprisoned by the Nazis in the Buchenwald and Dachau concentration camps. When released because of American intervention in 1939, Bettelheim emigrated to Chicago. After several research and teaching positions, in 1944 he began teaching at the University of Chicago and continued there until his retirement in 1973. Bettelheim's work concentrated on children with severe emotional disorders such as autism and psychosis, and many of his theories were provocative and controversial. Some of his well-known books, all on children, are *Love Is Not Enough* (1950), *Truants from Life* (1955), *The Children of the Dream* (1969), and *The Uses of Enchantment* (1976).

The Holocaust

In two books, *The Informed Heart* (1960) and *Surviving, and Other Essays* (1979), Bettelheim probed his and others' experiences in the Nazis' concentration camps. What follows is a freestanding slice of a much longer essay, "The Holocaust—One Generation After," from *Surviving*. With cool passion, Bettelheim uses definition to set the record straight on a loaded word.

To begin with, it was not the hapless victims of the Nazis who 1
named their incomprehensible and totally unmasterable fate the "holocaust." It was the Americans who applied this artificial and highly technical term to the Nazi extermination of the European Jews. But while the event when named as mass murder most foul evokes the most immediate, most powerful revulsion, when it is designated by a rare technical term, we must first in our minds translate it back into emotionally meaningful language. Using technical or specially created terms instead of words from our common vocabulary is one of the best-known and most widely used distancing devices, separating the intellectual from the emotional experience. Talking about "the holocaust" permits us to manage it intellectually where the raw facts, when given their ordinary names, would overwhelm us emotionally—because it was catastrophe beyond comprehension, beyond the limits of our imag-

ination, unless we force ourselves against our desire to extend it to encompass these terrible events.

This linguistic circumlocution began while it all was only in the 2 planning stage. Even the Nazis—usually given to grossness in language and action—shied away from facing openly what they were up to and called this vile mass murder "the final solution of the Jewish problem." After all, solving a problem can be made to appear like an honorable enterprise, as long as we are not forced to recognize that the solution we are about to embark on consists of the completely unprovoked, vicious murder of millions of helpless men, women, and children. The Nuremberg judges of these Nazi criminals followed their example of circumlocution by coining a neologism out of one Greek and one Latin root: genocide. These artificially created technical terms fail to connect with our strongest feelings. The horror of murder is part of our most common human heritage. From earliest infancy on, it arouses violent abhorrence in us. Therefore in whatever form it appears we should give such an act its true designation and not hide it behind polite, erudite terms created out of classical words.

To call this vile mass murder "the holocaust" is not to give it a spe- 3 cial name emphasizing its uniqueness which would permit, over time, the word becoming invested with feelings germane to the event it refers to. The correct definition of *holocaust* is "burnt offering." As such, it is part of the language of the psalmist, a meaningful word to all who have some acquaintance with the Bible, full of the richest emotional connotations. By using the term "holocaust," entirely false associations are established through conscious and unconscious connotations between the most vicious of mass murders and ancient rituals of a deeply religious nature.

Using a word with such strong unconscious religious connotations 4 when speaking of the murder of millions of Jews robs the victims of this abominable mass murder of the only thing left to them: their uniqueness. Calling the most callous, most brutal, most horrid, most heinous mass murder a burnt offering is a sacrilege, a profanation of God and man.

Martyrdom is part of our religious heritage. A martyr, burned at the 5 stake, is a burnt offering to his god. And it is true that after the Jews were asphyxiated, the victims' corpses were burned. But I believe we fool ourselves if we think we are honoring the victims of systematic murder by using this term, which has the highest moral connotations. By doing so, we connect for our own psychological reasons what happened in the extermination camps with historical events we deeply regret, but also greatly admire. We do so because this makes it easier for us to cope; only in doing so we cope with our distorted image of what happened, not with the events the way they did happen.

By calling the victims of the Nazis martyrs, we falsify their fate.   6
The true meaning of *martyr* is: "One who voluntarily undergoes the penalty of death for refusing to renounce his faith" (*Oxford English Dictionary*). The Nazis made sure that nobody could mistakenly think that their victims were murdered for their religious beliefs. Renouncing their faith would have saved none of them. Those who had converted to Christianity were gassed, as were those who were atheists, and those who were deeply religious Jews. They did not die for any conviction, and certainly not out of choice.

Millions of Jews were systematically slaughtered, as were untold   7
other "undesirables," not for any convictions of theirs, but only because they stood in the way of the realization of an illusion. They neither died for their convictions, nor were they slaughtered because of their convictions, but only in consequence of the Nazis' delusional belief about what was required to protect the purity of their assumed superior racial endowment, and what they thought necessary to guarantee them the living space they believed they needed and were entitled to. Thus while these millions were slaughtered for an idea, they did not die for one.

Millions—men, women, and children—were processed after they   8
had been utterly brutalized, their humanity destroyed, their clothes torn from their bodies. Naked, they were sorted into those who were destined to be murdered immediately, and those others who had a short-term usefulness as slave labor. But after a brief interval they, too, were to be herded into the same gas chambers into which the others were immediately piled, there to be asphyxiated so that, in their last moments, they could not prevent themselves from fighting each other in vain for a last breath of air.

To call these most wretched victims of a murderous delusion, of de-   9
structive drives run rampant, martyrs or a burnt offering is a distortion invented for our comfort, small as it may be. It pretends that this most vicious of mass murders had some deeper meaning; that in some fashion the victims either offered themselves or at least became sacrifices to a higher cause. It robs them of the last recognition which could be theirs, denies them the last dignity we could accord them: to face and accept what their death was all about, not embellishing it for the small psychological relief this may give us.

We could feel so much better if the victims had acted out of choice.   10
For our emotional relief, therefore, we dwell on the tiny minority who did exercise some choice: the resistance fighters of the Warsaw ghetto, for example, and others like them. We are ready to overlook the fact that these people fought back only at a time when everything was lost, when the overwhelming majority of those who had been forced into the ghettos had already been exterminated without resisting. Certainly those few who finally fought for their survival and their convictions,

risking and losing their lives in doing so, deserve our admiration; their deeds give us a moral lift. But the more we dwell on these few, the more unfair are we to the memory of the millions who were slaughtered—who gave in, did not fight back—because we deny them the only thing which up to the very end remained uniquely their own: their fate.

QUESTIONS ON MEANING

1. Why does Bettelheim believe that *holocaust* is an inappropriate term for the mass murder of Jews during World War II? Why does he say this sort of "linguistic circumlocution" is used? (What is a "linguistic circumlocution"?)
2. What is Bettelheim's PURPOSE here?
3. According to Bettelheim, what do we do besides using unemotional terms to distance ourselves from the murder of the Jews?
4. Does Bettelheim suggest an alternative term for *holocaust?*

QUESTIONS ON WRITING STRATEGY

1. Where does Bettelheim stress etymologies, or word histories, and dictionary definitions? What is their EFFECT?
2. What does Bettelheim accomplish with paragraph 8? Why is this paragraph essential?
3. How would you characterize Bettelheim's TONE? What creates it? Is it appropriate, do you think?
4. In several places Bettelheim repeats or restates passages—for instance, "By doing so...We do so...only in doing so" (para. 5), or "stood in the way of the realization of an illusion...in consequence of the Nazis' delusional belief...slaughtered for an idea" (7). Do you think such repetition and restatement is deliberate on Bettelheim's part? Why, or why not?
5. **OTHER METHODS.** Bettelheim's definition is an ARGUMENT. What is the THESIS of his argument? What EVIDENCE supports the thesis?

QUESTIONS ON LANGUAGE

1. ANALYZE the words Bettelheim uses to refer to the murder of the Jews. How do the words support his argument?
2. What is the effect of Bettelheim's use of *we*—for instance, in paragraphs 5 and 10?
3. Look up any unfamiliar words: hapless (para. 1); neologism, abhorrence, erudite (2); germane, psalmist (3); abominable, callous, heinous, sacrilege, profanation (4); asphyxiated (5); delusional, endowment (7); rampant, embellishing (9).

SUGGESTIONS FOR WRITING

1. **JOURNAL WRITING.** Sports, dance, music, business, medicine, cooking, auto mechanics, and parenting—these are just a few activities with languages of "technical or specially created terms" (para. 1) that work often like shorthand for insiders and sound like code to outsiders. In an activity or field you know well, how did you move from outsider to insider? Where, when, and how did you learn the meanings of specialized terms? **FROM JOURNAL TO ESSAY.** Write an essay in which you define and discuss the specialized terms in the activity or field you wrote of in your journal. What are the most important and common terms? What do they mean? How did you learn their meanings? What purpose do these terms serve— or what problems do they cause?

2. Although Bettelheim does not use the term, he is objecting to the use of a EUPHEMISM, or inoffensive word, in place of a word that might wound or offend. Euphemisms abound in the speech of politicians: The economy undergoes a "slowdown" or a "downturn"; people who are laid off are "downsized"; lying is "misspeaking." Drawing on Bettelheim's arguments as you see fit, write an essay about one or more euphemisms appearing in a daily newspaper. What do the euphemisms accomplish, and for whom? What do they conceal, and who is hurt? (For further insight into this topic, see William Lutz's "The World of Doublespeak" on p. 350).

3. **CRITICAL WRITING.** Research the word *holocaust* in a dictionary of word histories (an etymological dictionary) and an interpretation of the Bible. (A librarian can direct you to these sources.) On the basis of your research, do you agree or disagree with Bettelheim's rejection of the word? (In your answer, consider whether the word's wide use for the Nazi murders has provided it with new meanings.)

4. **CONNECTIONS.** Read "I Have a Dream," by Martin Luther King, Jr. (p. 567). COMPARE it with Bettelheim's essay on the purposeful use of repetition and restatement. How does each author use this device? For what aim? What is the EFFECT? If you like, you can narrow your comparison to one representative passage of each essay. Just be sure to use quotations to support your comparison.

BARBARA KINGSOLVER

A writer of fiction, poetry, and nonfiction and a self-described "human rights activist," BARBARA KINGSOLVER was born in Annapolis, Maryland, in 1955 and grew up in eastern Kentucky. She studied biology at DePauw University (B.A., 1977) and the University of Arizona (M.S., 1981) and worked in the field as a researcher and technical writer. A full-time writer since 1985, Kingsolver has published the novels *The Bean Trees* (1988), *Animal Dreams* (1990), *Pigs in Heaven* (1993), and *The Poisonwood Bible* (1998); a story collection, *Homeland and Other Stories* (1989); a poetry collection, *Another America* (1990); and an essay collection, *High Tide in Tucson* (1995). She lives in Tucson, a desert setting that she prefers because it "makes you pay attention to color and contrast and hard edges, in terms of both physical landscape and human landscape."

Stone Soup

Taking issue with the traditional definition of *family* — "Dad, Mom, Sis, Junior" — Kingsolver seeks another definition that embraces today's equally nurturing variations. The essay relies in part on Kingsolver's own experiences because, she says, "You can't just put the ideas there. You have to put clothes on them and make them walk around." "Stone Soup" originally appeared in 1995 in *Parenting* magazine and then in Kingsolver's collection *High Tide in Tucson*.

In the catalog of family values, where do we rank an occasion like this? A curly-haired boy who wanted to run before he walked, age seven now, a soccer player scoring a winning goal. He turns to the bleachers with his fists in the air and a smile wide as a gap-toothed galaxy. His own cheering section of grown-ups and kids all leap to their feet and hug each other, delirious with love for this boy. He's Andy, my best friend's son. The cheering section includes his mother and her friends, his brother, his father and stepmother, a stepbrother and stepsister, and a grandparent. Lucky is the child with this many relatives on hand to hail a proud accomplishment. I'm there too, witnessing a family fortune. But in spite of myself, defensive words take shape in my head. I am thinking: I dare *anybody* to call this a broken home. 1

Families change, and remain the same. Why are our names for home so slow to catch up to the truth of where we live? 2

When I was a child, I had two parents who loved me without cease. One of them attended every excuse for attention I ever contrived, and the other made it to the ones with higher production values, like piano recitals and appendicitis. So I was a lucky child too. I played with a set 3 of paper dolls called "The Family of Dolls," four in number, who came with the factory-assigned names of Dad, Mom, Sis, and Junior. I think you know what they looked like, at least before I loved them to death and their heads fell off.

Now I've replaced the dolls with a life. I knit my days around my   4 daughter's survival and happiness, and am proud to say her head is still on. But we aren't the Family of Dolls. Maybe you're not, either. And if not, even though you are statistically no oddity, it's probably been suggested to you in a hundred ways that yours isn't exactly a real family, but an impostor family, a harbinger of cultural ruin, a slapdash substitute—something like counterfeit money. Here at the tail end of our century, most of us are up to our ears in the noisy business of trying to support and love a thing called family. But there's a current in the air with ferocious moral force that finds its way even into political campaigns, claiming there is only one right way to do it, the Way It Has Always Been.

In the face of a thriving, particolored world, this narrow view is so   5 pickled and absurd I'm astonished that it gets airplay. And I'm astonished that it still stings.

Every parent has endured the arrogance of a child-unfriendly   6 grump sitting in judgment, explaining what those kids of ours really need (for example, "a good licking"). If we're polite, we move our crew to another bench in the park. If we're forthright (as I am in my mind, only, for the rest of the day), we fix them with a sweet imperious stare and say, "Come back and let's talk about it after you've changed a thousand diapers."

But it's harder somehow to shrug off the Family-of-Dolls Family   7 Values crew when they judge (from their safe distance) that divorced people, blended families, gay families, and single parents are failures. That our children are at risk, and the whole arrangement is messy and embarrassing. A marriage that ends is not called "finished," it's called *failed.* The children of this family may have been born to a happy union, but now they are called *the children of divorce.*

I had no idea how thoroughly these assumptions overlaid my cul-   8 ture until I went through divorce myself. I wrote to a friend: "This might be worse than being widowed. Overnight I've suffered the same losses—companionship, financial and practical support, my identity as a wife and partner, the future I'd taken for granted. I am lonely, grieving, and hard-pressed to take care of my household alone. But instead of bringing casseroles, people are acting like I had a fit and broke up the family china."

Once upon a time I held these beliefs about divorce: That everyone   9 who does it could have chosen not to do it. That it's a lazy way out of marital problems. That it selfishly puts personal happiness ahead of family integrity. Now I tremble for my ignorance. It's easy, in fortunate times, to forget about the ambush that could leave your head reeling: serious mental or physical illness, death in the family, abandonment, financial calamity, humiliation, violence, despair.

I started out like any child, intent on being the Family of Dolls. I 10 set upon young womanhood believing in most of the doctrines of my generation: I wore my skirts four inches above the knee. I had that Barbie with her zebra-striped swimsuit and a figure unlike anything found in nature. And I understood the Prince Charming Theory of Marriage, a quest for Mr. Right that ends smack dab where you find him. I did not completely understand that another whole story *begins* there, and no fairy tale prepared me for the combination of bad luck and persistent hope that would interrupt my dream and lead me to other arrangements. Like a cancer diagnosis, a dying marriage is a thing to fight, to deny, and finally, when there's no choice left, to dig in and survive. Casseroles would help. Likewise, I imagine it must be a painful reckoning in adolescence (or later on) to realize one's own true love will never look like the soft-focus fragrance ads because Prince Charming (surprise!) is a princess. Or vice versa. Or has skin the color your parents didn't want you messing with, except in the Crayola box.

It's awfully easy to hold in contempt the straw broken home, and 11 that mythical category of persons who toss away nuclear family for the sheer fun of it. Even the legal terms we use have a suggestion of caprice. I resent the phrase "irreconcilable differences," which suggests a stubborn refusal to accept a spouse's little quirks. This is specious. Every happily married couple I know has loads of irreconcilable differences. Negotiating where to set the thermostat is not the point. A nonfunctioning marriage is a slow asphyxiation. It is waking up despised each morning, listening to the pulse of your own loneliness before the radio begins to blare its raucous gospel that you're nothing if you aren't loved. It is sharing your airless house with the threat of suicide or other kinds of violence, while the ghost that whispers, "Leave here and destroy your children," has passed over every door and nailed it shut. Disassembling a marriage in these circumstances is as much *fun* as amputating your own gangrenous leg. You do it, if you can, to save a life — or two, or more.

I know of no one who really went looking to hoe the harder row, 12 especially the daunting one of single parenthood. Yet it seems to be the most American of customs to blame the burdened for their destiny. We'd like so desperately to believe in freedom and justice for all, we can hardly name that rogue bad luck, even when he's a close enough snake to bite us. In the wake of my divorce, some friends (even a few close ones) chose to vanish, rather than linger within striking distance of misfortune.

But most stuck around, bless their hearts, and if I'm any the wiser 13 for my trials, it's from having learned the worth of steadfast friendship. And also, what not to say. The least helpful question is: "Did you want the divorce, or didn't you?" Did I want to keep that gangrenous leg, or not? How to explain, in a culture that venerates choice: Two terrifying options are much worse than none at all. Give me any day the quick hand of cruel fate that will leave me scarred but blameless. As it was, I kept thinking of that wicked third-grade joke in which some boy comes up behind you and grabs your ear, starts in with a prolonged tug, and asks, "Do you want this ear any longer?"

Still, the friend who holds your hand and says the wrong thing is 14 made of dearer stuff than the one who stays away. And generally, through all of it, you live. My favorite fictional character, Kate Vaiden (in the novel by Reynolds Price), advises: "Strength just comes in one brand — you stand up at sunrise and meet what they send you and keep your hair combed."

Once you've weathered the straits, you get to cross the tricky junc- 15 ture from casualty to survivor. If you're on your feet at the end of a year or two, and have begun putting together a happy new existence, those friends who were kind enough to feel sorry for you when you needed it must now accept you back to the ranks of the living. If you're truly blessed, they will dance at your second wedding. Everybody else, for heaven's sake, should stop throwing stones.

Arguing about whether nontraditional families deserve pity or tol- 16 erance is a little like the medieval debate about left-handedness as a mark of the devil. Divorce, remarriage, single parenthood, gay parents, and blended families simply are. They're facts of our time. Some of the reasons listed by sociologists for these family reconstructions are: the idea of marriage as a romantic partnership rather than a pragmatic one; a shift in women's expectations, from servility to self-respect and inde- pendence; and longevity (prior to antibiotics no marriage was expected to last many decades — in Colonial days the average couple lived to be married less than twelve years). Add to all this our growing sense of entitlement to happiness and safety from abuse. Most would agree these are all good things. Yet their result — a culture in which serial monogamy and the consequent reshaping of families are the norm — gets diagnosed as "failing."

For many of us, once we have put ourselves Humpty-Dumpty-wise 17 back together again, the main problem with our reorganized family is that other people think we have a problem. My daughter tells me the only time she's uncomfortable about being the child of divorced parents is when her friends say they feel sorry for her. It's a bizarre sympathy, given that half the kids in her school and nation are in the same boat, pursuing childish happiness with the same energy as their married-parent peers. When anyone asks how *she* feels about it, she spontaneously lists the benefits: Our house is in the country and we have a dog, but she can go to her dad's neighborhood for the urban thrills of a pool and sidewalks for roller-skating. What's more, she has three sets of grandparents!

Why is it surprising that a child would revel in a widened family 18 and the right to feel at home in more than one house? Isn't it the opposite that should worry us — a child with no home at all, or too few resources to feel safe? The child at risk is the one whose parents are too immature themselves to guide wisely; too diminished by poverty to nurture; too far from opportunity to offer hope. The number of children in the U.S. living in poverty at this moment is almost unfathomably large: 20 percent. There are families among us that need help all right, and by no means are they new on the landscape. The rate at which teenage girls had babies in 1957 (ninety-six per thousand) was twice what it is now. That remarkable statistic is ignored by the religious right — probably because the teen birth rate was cut in half mainly by legalized abortion. In fact, the policy gatekeepers who coined the phrase "family values" have steadfastly ignored the desperation of too-small families, and since 1979 have steadily reduced the amount of financial support available to a single parent. But this camp's most outspoken attacks seem aimed at the notion of families getting too complex, with add-ons and extras such as a gay parent's partner, or a remarried mother's new husband and his children.

To judge a family's value by its tidy symmetry is to purchase a book 19 for its cover. There's no moral authority there. The famous family comprised of Dad, Mom, Sis, and Junior living as an isolated economic unit is not built on historical bedrock. In *The Way We Never Were*, Stephanie Coontz writes, "Whenever people propose that we go back to the traditional family, I always suggest that they pick a ballpark date for the family they have in mind." Colonial families were tidily disciplined, but their members (meaning everyone but infants) labored incessantly and died young. Then the Victorian family adopted a new division of labor, in which women's role was domestic and children were allowed time for study and play, but this was an upper-class construct supported by myriad slaves. Coontz writes, "For every nineteenth-century middle-class family that protected its wife and child within the family circle, there was an Irish or German girl scrubbing floors...a Welsh boy mining coal to keep the home-baked goodies warm, a black girl doing the family laundry, a black mother and child picking cotton to be made into clothes for the family, and a Jewish or an Italian daughter in a sweatshop making 'ladies' dresses or artificial flowers for the family to purchase."

The abolition of slavery brought slightly more democratic arrange- 20
ments, in which extended families were harnessed together in cottage
industries; at the turn of the century came a steep rise in child labor in
mines and sweatshops. Twenty percent of American children lived in
orphanages at the time; their parents were not necessarily dead, but
couldn't afford to keep them.

During the Depression and up to the end of World War II, many 21
millions of U.S. households were more multigenerational than nuclear.
Women my grandmother's age were likely to live with a fluid assort-
ment of elderly relatives, in-laws, siblings, and children. In many cases
they spent virtually every waking hour working in the company of
other women—a companionable scenario in which it would be easier,
I imagine, to tolerate an estranged or difficult spouse. I'm reluctant to
idealize a life of so much hard work and so little spousal intimacy, but
its advantage may have been resilience. A family so large and varied
would not easily be brought down by a single blow: It could absorb a
death, long illness, an abandonment here or there, and any number of
irreconcilable differences.

The Family of Dolls came along midcentury as a great American 22
experiment. A booming economy required a mobile labor force and demanded that women surrender jobs to returning soldiers. Families came
to be defined by a single breadwinner. They struck out for single-family
homes at an earlier age than ever before, and in unprecedented numbers they raised children in suburban isolation. The nuclear family was
launched to sink or swim.

More than a few sank. Social historians corroborate that the sub- 23
urban family of the postwar economic boom, which we have recently
selected as our definition of "traditional," was no panacea. Twenty-five
percent of Americans were poor in the mid-1950s, and as yet there
were no food stamps. Sixty percent of the elderly lived on less than
$1,000 a year, and most had no medical insurance. In the sequestered
suburbs, alcoholism and sexual abuse of children were far more widespread than anyone imagined.

Expectations soared, and the economy sagged. It's hard to depend 24
on one other adult for everything, come what may. In the last three
decades, that amorphous, adaptable structure we call "family" has been
reshaped once more by economic tides. Compared with fifties families,
mothers are far more likely now to be employed. We are statistically
more likely to divorce, and to live in blended families or other extranuclear arrangements. We are also more likely to plan and space our
children, and to rate our marriages as "happy." We are less likely to suffer abuse without recourse, or to stare out at our lives through a glaze of
prescription tranquilizers. Our aged parents are less likely to be destitute, and we're half as likely to have a teenage daughter turn up a

mother herself. All in all, I would say that if "intact" in modern family-values jargon means living quietly desperate in the bell jar,[1] then hip-hip-hooray for "broken." A neat family model constructed to service the Baby Boom economy seems to be returning gradually to a grand, lumpy shape that human families apparently have tended toward since they first took root in the Olduvai Gorge.[2] We're social animals, deeply fond of companionship, and children love best to run in packs. If there is a *normal* for humans, at all, I expect it looks like two or three Families of Dolls, connected variously by kinship and passion, shuffled like cards and strewn over several shoeboxes.

The sooner we can let go the fairy tale of families functioning per- 25
fectly in isolation, the better we might embrace the relief of community. Even the admirable parents who've stayed married through thick and thin are very likely, at present, to incorporate other adults into their families—household help and baby-sitters if they can afford them, or neighbors and grandparents if they can't. For single parents, this support is the rock-bottom definition of family. And most parents who have split apart, however painfully, still manage to maintain family continuity for their children, creating in many cases a boisterous phenomenon that Constance Ahrons in her book *The Good Divorce* calls the "binuclear family." Call it what you will—when ex-spouses beat swords into plowshares and jump up and down at a soccer game together, it makes for happy kids.

Cinderella, look, who needs her? All those evil stepsisters? That 26
story always seemed like too much cotton-picking fuss over clothes. A childhood tale that fascinated me more was the one called "Stone Soup," and the gist of it is this: Once upon a time, a pair of beleaguered soldiers straggled home to a village empty-handed, in a land ruined by war. They were famished, but the villagers had so little they shouted evil words and slammed their doors. So the soldiers dragged out a big kettle, filled it with water, and put it on a fire to boil. They rolled a clean round stone into the pot, while the villagers peered through their curtains in amazement.

"What kind of soup is that?" they hooted. 27

"Stone soup," the soldiers replied. "Everybody can have some when 28
it's done."

"Well, thanks," one matron grumbled, coming out with a shriveled 29
carrot. "But it'd be better if you threw this in."

---

[1] A glass vessel shaped like a bell, used to contain a delicate object or a controlled experiment.—EDS.

[2] A site in Tanzania, East Africa, where remains of some of the earliest human ancestors have been discovered.—EDS.

And so on, of course, a vegetable at a time, until the whole suspi-   30
cious village managed to feed itself grandly.

Any family is a big empty pot, save for what gets thrown in. Each   31
stew turns out different. Generosity, a resolve to turn bad luck into
good, and respect for variety—these things will nourish a nation of
children. Name-calling and suspicion will not. My soup contains a rock
or two of hard times, and maybe yours does too. I expect it's a heck of a
bouillabaisse.

──────────

QUESTIONS ON MEANING

1. Kingsolver uses the phrase "family values" in her first line and refers to the
   idea many times throughout. What are the CONNOTATIONS of this phrase?
   What is the connection between this phrase and Kingsolver's PURPOSE?
2. What is Kingsolver trying to suggest with the RHETORICAL QUESTION in paragraph 2: "Why are our names for home so slow to catch up with the truth
   of where we live?"
3. Kingsolver claims that "the Way It Has Always Been" has a "ferocious
   moral force," but then immediately labels this a "narrow...pickled" view
   of the world (paras. 4–5). What does each interpretation mean? What
   does this contrast suggest?
4. What is the ALLUSION in the line "Everybody else, for heaven's sake, should
   stop throwing stones" (para. 15)?
5. Kingsolver writes, "All in all, I would say that if 'intact' in modern family-
   values jargon means living quietly desperate in the bell jar, then hip-hip-
   hooray for 'broken'" (para. 24). How does her contrast of "intact" with
   "broken" reveal the THESIS of her essay?

QUESTIONS ON WRITING STRATEGY

1. Kingsolver tells us that we know what the Family of Dolls looks like (para.
   3). Can you describe it? Why does she ASSUME we know this?
2. Why does Kingsolver present us with a "revised" arrangement of the Family of Dolls (para. 24)? How does the advice about strength given by Kingsolver's favorite fictional character (14) serve a similar purpose?
3. What conclusions are we supposed to draw from Kingsolver's statistics
   in paragraph 18 and her suggestions about the children who are "at
   risk"?
4. **OTHER METHODS.** In paragraphs 19–24, Kingsolver uses CAUSE AND EFFECT
   to outline the history of the American family. What key changes does
   Kingsolver identify? Why does she provide this history? Why does she
   bring up the Olduvai Gorge at the end of this discussion?

QUESTIONS ON LANGUAGE

1. Kingsolver contrasts the "nuclear" family with the "blended" family that may have "extranuclear arrangements" (para. 24). What are the meanings of each of these terms?
2. In paragraph 4 Kingsolver uses a string of negative terms ("impostor," "harbinger of cultural ruin," "slapdash," "counterfeit") to describe how the nontraditional family "isn't exactly a real family." Look up any of these words you don't know. How do they support Kingsolver's idea that the real problem divorced families face is that others think there is a problem (para. 17)?
3. In paragraph 8, Kingsolver contrasts two possible reactions to news of a divorce. What do the IMAGES of bringing over a casserole versus acting like she's broken up the family china suggest?
4. If any of the following words are unfamiliar, look them up in a dictionary: delirious (para. 1); particolored (5); imperious (6); integrity, calamity (9); doctrines, reckoning (10); caprice, irreconcilable, specious, asphyxiation, raucous, disassembling, gangrenous (11); daunting, rogue (12); venerates (13); straits, casualty (15); pragmatic, longevity, entitlement (16); revel, unfathomably (18); symmetry, bedrock, incessantly, myriad (19); abolition (20); companionable, scenario, spousal, resilience (21); unprecedented (22); corroborate, panacea, sequestered (23); amorphous, recourse, destitute (24); boisterous (25); beleaguered (26); bouillabaisse (31).

SUGGESTIONS FOR WRITING

1. **JOURNAL WRITING.** In Kingsolver's terms, what kind of family did you grow up in, traditional or not? What experiences or events from your childhood highlight that family structure? (Examples: differences in your mother's and father's styles of discipline; taking on extra chores when one of your parents moved out; watching your parents argue; getting along with a stepsibling.)
   FROM JOURNAL TO ESSAY. Based on some of the experiences you recalled in your journal, what conclusions can you draw about the "healthiness" of your family structure versus another one? What are the advantages and disadvantages of making GENERALIZATIONS about "nuclear" and "blended" families?
2. Analyze Kingsolver's uses of the tales "Cinderella" (paras. 10, 26) and "Stone Soup" (paras. 26–30). What is the EFFECT of these tales? What does Kingsolver gain by merely ALLUDING to "Cinderella" rather than spelling out the tale? How do the details of both stories (whether repeated or not) add to Kingsolver's argument?
3. **CRITICAL WRITING.** Kingsolver contrasts the independent, isolated family (which she calls a "fairy tale") with the support network of an extended family (para. 25). Do you agree with her preference for the second kind? Is it any more realistic than the first? Write an essay supporting or refuting Kingsolver's views of family, drawing on your own experiences and observations.
4. **CONNECTIONS.** Kingsolver claims that it "seems to be the most American of customs to blame the burdened for their destiny" (para. 12). Maxine

Hong Kingston's "No Name Woman" (p. 573) shows how Chinese villagers punished a whole family for one member's mistakes. Write an essay COMPARING these two selections' ideas on the justice of blame and punishment endured by families. Are the families at fault? What role do traditional values play in each situation?

BARBARA KINGSOLVER ON WRITING

"People think it's sort of funny," Barbara Kingsolver says, "that I went to graduate school as a biologist and then became a writer." In a 1996 interview with Robin Epstein of *The Progressive* magazine, Kingsolver explains that the processes of science and writing are very similar. "What I learned [in science] is how to formulate or identify a new question that hasn't been asked before, and then to set about solving it, to do original research to find the way to an answer. And that's what I do when I write a book."

Asked if she ever has doubts about her "abilities as a writer," Kingsolver replies, "I still have them. Beginning a book is really hard. I'm trying to begin one now and I just keep throwing stuff away and thinking, 'Can I do this? I don't think I'm smart enough.' You have to have a reverence for the undertaking. And I think reverence implies a certain lack of self-esteem.... You feel daunted and unworthy. But in this age of glorifying the individual and self-esteem, I think there's something healthy about being daunted. Cockiness doesn't lend itself to good writing. It really doesn't."

FOR DISCUSSION

1. Kingsolver sees parallels between scientific inquiry and writing. What are they? How might Kingsolver's insights about writing be potentially helpful to nonscientists?
2. Many writers, including experienced ones, often feel hampered by a lack of confidence in their abilities. How then could an excess of confidence harm a writer's work?

ADDITIONAL WRITING TOPICS

Definition

1. Write an essay in which you define an institution, trend, phenomenon, or abstraction as specifically and concretely as possible. Following are some suggestions designed to stimulate ideas. Before you begin, limit your subject.

   Responsibility
   Fun
   Sorrow
   Unethical behavior
   The environment
   Education
   Progress
   Advertising
   Happiness
   Fads
   Feminism
   Marriage
   Sportsmanship
   Leadership
   Leisure
   Originality
   Character
   Imagination
   Democracy
   A smile
   A classic (of music, literature, art, or film)
   Dieting
   Meditation
   Friendship

2. In a brief essay, define one of the following. In each instance, you have a choice of something good or something bad to talk about.

   A good or bad boss
   A good or bad parent
   A good or bad host
   A good or bad TV newscaster
   A good or bad physician
   A good or bad nurse
   A good or bad minister, priest, or rabbi
   A good or bad roommate
   A good or bad driver
   A good or bad disk jockey

3. In a paragraph, define one of the following slang expressions for someone who has never heard the term: *dis, wigged out, dweeb, awesome, fool around, wimp, druggie, snob, freak, loser, loner, freeloader, burnout, soul, quack,* "chill," *pig-out, gross out, winging it,* "bad," "sweet."

10

ARGUMENT AND PERSUASION
Stating Opinions and Proposals

THE METHOD

Practically every day, we try to persuade ourselves or someone else. We usually attempt such persuasion without being aware that we follow any special method at all. Often, we'll state an *opinion*: We'll tell someone our own way of viewing things. We say to a friend, "I'm starting to like Senator Clark. Look at all she's done to help people with disabilities. Look at her voting record on toxic waste." And, having stated these opinions, we might go on to make a *proposal*, to recommend that some action be taken. Addressing our friend, we might suggest, "Hey, Senator Clark is talking on campus at four-thirty. Want to come with me and listen to her?"

Sometimes you try to convince yourself that a certain way of interpreting things is right. You even set forth an opinion in writing—as in a letter to a friend who has asked, "Now that you're at New Age College, how do you like the place?" You may write a letter of protest to a landlord who wants to raise your rent, pointing out that the bathroom hot water faucet doesn't work. As a concerned citizen, you may wish to speak your mind in an occasional letter to a newspaper or to your elected representatives.

If you should enter certain professions, you will be expected to persuade people in writing. Before arguing a case in court, a lawyer prepares briefs setting forth all the points in favor of his or her side. Business executives regularly put in writing their ideas for new products and ventures, for improvements in cost control and job efficiency. Researchers write proposals for grants to obtain money to support their work. Scientists write and publish papers to persuade the scientific community that their findings are valid, often stating hypotheses, or tentative opinions.

Even if you never produce a single persuasive work (which is very unlikely), you will certainly encounter such works directed at you. In truth, we live our lives under a steady rain of opinions and proposals. Organizations that work for causes campaign with posters and direct mail, all hoping that we will see things their way. Moreover, we are bombarded with proposals from people who wish us to act. Religious leaders urge us to lead more virtuous lives. Advertisers urge us to rush right out and buy the large economy size.

Small wonder, then, that argument and persuasion—and CRITICAL READING of argument and persuasion—may be among the most useful skills a college student can acquire. Time and again, your instructors will ask you to criticize or to state opinions, either in class or in writing. You may be asked to state your view of anything from the electoral college to animal experimentation. You may be asked to judge the desirability or undesirability of compulsory testing for AIDS or the revision of existing immigration laws. On an examination in, say, sociology, you may be asked, "Suggest three practical approaches to the most pressing needs of disadvantaged people in urban areas." Critically reading other people's arguments and composing your own, you will find, helps you discover what you think, refine it, and share what you believe.

Is there a difference between argument and persuasion? It is, admittedly, not always clear. Strictly speaking, PERSUASION aims to influence readers' actions, or their support for an action, by engaging their beliefs and feelings, while ARGUMENT aims to win readers' agreement with an assertion or claim by engaging their powers of reasoning. But most effective persuasion or argument contains elements of both methods; hence the confusion. In this book we tend to use the terms interchangeably. And one other point: We tend to talk here about *writing* argument and persuasion, but most of what we say has to do with *reading* them as well. When we discuss your need, as a writer, to support your assertions, we are also discussing your need, as a reader, to question the support other authors provide for their assertions. In reading arguments critically, you apply the critical reading skills we discussed in the book's Introduction—ANALYSIS, INFERENCE, SYNTHESIS, EVALUATION—to a particular kind of writing.

Basic Considerations

Transaction Between Writer and Reader

Unlike some television advertisers, responsible writers of argument and persuasion do not try to storm people's minds. In writing a paper for a course, you persuade by gentler means: by sharing your view with a reader willing to consider it. You'll want to learn how to express your view clearly and vigorously. But to be fair and persuasive, it is important to understand your reader's view as well.

In stating your opinion, you present the truth as you see it: "The immigration laws discourage employers from hiring nonnative workers" or "The immigration laws protect legal aliens." To persuade your readers that your view makes sense, you need not begin by proclaiming that, by Heaven, your view is absolutely right and should prevail. Instead, you might begin by trying to state what your reader probably thinks, as best you can infer it. You don't consider views that differ from your own merely to flatter your reader. You do so to correct your own view and make it more accurate. Regarded in this light, argument and persuasion aren't cynical ways to pull other people's strings. Writer and reader become two sensible people trying to find a common ground. This view will relieve you, whenever you have to state your opinions in writing, of the terrible obligation to be 100 percent right at all times.

Thesis Sentence

In an argument you champion or defend your opinion about something. This opinion is the THESIS, or *claim*, of your argument, and it will probably appear in your essay as your THESIS SENTENCE or sentences. Usually, but not always, you'll state your thesis sentence at the beginning of your essay, making a play for readers' attention and clueing them in to your purpose. But if you think readers may have difficulty accepting your thesis until they've heard some or all of your argument, then you might save the thesis sentence for the middle or end.

The essays in this chapter provide a variety of thesis sentences as models. Here are three examples:

> For crimes involving the deliberate and inexcusable taking of human life, by men openly defiant of all civilized order—for such crimes [the death penalty] seems...a just and proper punishment. (H. L. Mencken, "The Penalty of Death")

> I think the observable reluctance of the majority of Americans to assert themselves in minor matters is related to our increased sense of helplessness in an age of technology and centralized political and economic power. (William F. Buckley, Jr., "Why Don't We Complain?")

A bill [that forbids importing goods from factories that use forced
child labor]... is of no use unless it goes hand in hand with programs
that will offer a new life to these newly released children. (Chitra Divakaruni, "Live Free and Starve")

Evidence and Appeals

To support the thesis of your argument, you need EVIDENCE—anything that demonstrates what you're claiming. Evidence may include
facts, statistics (facts expressed in numbers), expert opinions, examples,
reported experience. Chitra Divakaruni, for example, supports the thesis quoted above with DESCRIPTIONS of the lives of child laborers, a statistic about the number of child laborers, and most notably an extended
example of a child laborer CONTRASTED with other children who have no
resources at all.

Like other writers of argument, Divakaruni also appeals to readers'
intelligence and to their feelings. In appealing to reason—a RATIONAL
APPEAL—she relies on conventional methods of reasoning (see the facing page) and supplies the evidence cited above. In appealing to feelings—an EMOTIONAL APPEAL—she acknowledges her American readers'
probable sympathy for child laborers, tries to broaden that sympathy,
and reminds readers of their own relative privilege. Editorials in publications for special audiences (such as members of religious denomina-
tions, or people whose political views are far to the left or right) tend to
contain few factual surprises for their subscribers, who presumably read
to have their views reinforced. In spoken discourse, you can hear emotional appeals in a commencement day speech or a Fourth of July ora-
tion. An impressive example of emotional appeal is included in Part
Two (p. 567): the speech by Martin Luther King, Jr., "I Have a Dream."
Dr. King's speech did not tell its audience anything new to them, for
the listeners were mostly African Americans disappointed in the
American Dream. The speaker appeals primarily not to reason but to
feelings—and to the willingness of his listeners to be inspired.

Emotional argument, to be sure, can sometimes be cynical manipulation. It can mean selling a sucker a bill of shoddy goods by appealing to pride or shame—"Do you really want to deprive your children of
what's best for them?" But emotional argument can also stir readers to
constructive action by fair means. It recognizes that we are not intellectual robots but creatures with feelings. Indeed, in any effective argument, a writer had better engage the feelings of readers or they may
reply, "True enough, but who cares?" Argument, to succeed in persuading, makes us feel that a writer's views are close to our own.

Yet another resource in argument is ETHICAL APPEAL: impressing your
reader that you are a well-informed person of good will, good sense, and
good moral character—and, therefore, to be believed. You make such an

appeal by reasoning carefully, writing well, and collecting ample evidence. You can also cite or quote respected authorities. If you don't know whether an authority is respected, you can ask a reference librarian for tips on finding out, or talk to an instructor who is a specialist in that field.

In arguing, you don't prove your assertion in the same irrefutable way in which a chemist demonstrates that hydrogen will burn. If you say, "Health coverage for the uninsured should be given top priority in Congress," that kind of claim isn't clearly either true or false. Argument takes place in areas that invite more than one opinion. In writing an argument, you help your reader see and understand just one open-eyed, open-minded view of reality.

Reasoning

When we argue rationally, we reason—that is, we make statements that lead to a conclusion. From the time of the ancient Greeks down to our own day, distinctly different methods of proceeding from statements to conclusions have been devised. This section will tell you of a recent, informal method of reasoning and also of two traditional methods. Understanding these methods, knowing how to use them, and being able to recognize when they are misused will make you a better writer *and* reader.

The Toulmin Method

Data, claim, and warrant.   In recent decades, a simple, practical method of reasoning has been devised by the British philosopher Stephen Toulmin.[1] Helpfully, Toulmin has divided a typical argument into three parts:

1. The DATA: *the evidence to prove something*
2. The CLAIM: *what you are proving with the data*
3. The WARRANT: *the assumption or principle that connects the data to the claim*

Any clear, explicit argument has to have all three parts. Toulmin's own example of such an argument is this:

Harry was born in Bermuda ——————— Harry is a British subject
          (Data)   (Claim)
                         Since a man born in Bermuda
                           will be a British subject
                                 (Warrant)

---

[1] *The Uses of Argument* (1969) sets forth Toulmin's system in detail. His views are further explained and applied by Douglas Ehninger and Wayne Brockriede in *Decision by Debate* (2nd ed., 1978) and by Toulmin himself, with Richard Rieke and Allan Janik, in *An Introduction to Reasoning* (2nd ed., 1984).

Of course, the data for a larger, more controversial claim will be more extensive. Here are some claims that would call for many more data, perhaps thousands of words.

> The war on drugs is not winnable.

> The United States must help to destroy drug production in South America.

> Drug addiction is a personal matter.

The warrant at the center.   The warrant, that middle term, is often crucially important. It is usually an ASSUMPTION or a GENERALIZATION that explains *why* the claim follows from the data. Often a writer won't bother to state a warrant because it is obvious: "In his bid for reelection, Mayor Perkins failed miserably. Out of 5,000 votes cast for both candidates, he received only 200." The warrant might be stated, "To make what I would consider a strong showing, he would have had to receive 2,000 votes or more," but it is clear that 200 out of 5,000 is a small minority, and no further explanation seems necessary.

A flaw in many arguments, though, is that the warrant is not clear. A clear warrant is essential. To be persuaded, a reader needs to understand your assumptions and the thinking that follows from them. If you were to argue, "Drug abuse is a serious problem in the United States. Therefore, the United States must help to destroy drug production in Latin America," then your reader might well be left wondering why the second statement follows from the first. But if you were to add, between the statements, "As long as drugs are manufactured in Latin America, they will be smuggled into the United States, and drug abuse will continue," then you supply a warrant. You show why your claim follows from your data—which, of course, you must also supply to make your case.

The unstated warrant can pitch an argument into trouble—whether your own or another writer's. Since warrants are usually assumptions or generalizations, rather than assertions of fact, they are valid only if readers accept or agree that they are valid. With stated warrants, any weaknesses are more likely to show. Suppose someone asserts that a certain woman should not be elected mayor because women cannot form ideas independently of their husbands and this woman's husband has bad ideas on how to run the city. At least the warrant—that women cannot form ideas independently of their husbands—is out there on the table, exposed for all to inspect. But unstated warrants can be just as absurd, or even just doubtful, and pass unnoticed because they are not exposed. Here's the same argument without its warrant: "She shouldn't be elected mayor because her husband has bad ideas on how to run the city."

Here's another argument with an unstated warrant, this one adapted from a magazine advertisement: "Scientists have no proof, just statistical correlations, linking smoking and heart disease, so you needn't worry about the connection." Now, the fact that this ad was placed by a cigarette manufacturer would tip off any reasonably alert reader to beware of bias in the claim. To discover the slant, we need to examine the unstated warrant, which runs something like this: "Since they are not proof, statistical correlations are worthless as guides to behavior." It is true that statistical correlations are not scientific proof, by which we generally mean repeated results obtained under controlled laboratory conditions—the kind of conditions to which human beings cannot ethically be subjected. But statistical correlations *can* establish connections and in fact inform much of our healthful behavior, such as getting physical exercise, avoiding fatty foods, brushing our teeth, and not driving while intoxicated. The advertiser's unstated warrant isn't valid, so neither is the argument.

Example of a Toulmin argument. Let's look at how the data-claim-warrant scheme can work in constructing an argument. In an assignment for her course in English composition, Maire Flynn was asked to produce a condensed argument in three short paragraphs. The first paragraph was to set forth some data; the second, a claim; and the third, a warrant. The result became a kind of outline that the writer could then expand into a whole essay. Here is Flynn's argument.

DATA

Over the past five years, assistance in the form of food stamps has had the effect of increasing the number of people on welfare instead of reducing it. Despite this help, 95 percent of long-term recipients remain below the poverty line today.

CLAIM

The present system of distributing food stamps is a dismal failure, a less effective way to help the needy than other possible ways.

WARRANT

No one is happy to receive charity. We need to encourage people to quit the welfare rolls; we need to make sure that government aid goes only to the deserving. More effective than giving out food stamps would be to help untrained young people learn job skills; to help single mothers with small children to obtain child care, freeing them for the job market; and to enlarge and improve our state employment counseling and job-placement services. The problem of poverty will be helped only if more people will find jobs and become self-sufficient.

In her warrant paragraph, Flynn spells out her reasons for holding her opinion—the one she states in her claim. "The warrant," she found, "was the hardest part to write," but hers turned out to be clear. Like any good warrant, hers expresses those thoughts that her data set in motion. Another way of looking at the warrant: It is the thinking that led the writer on to the opinion she holds. In this statement of her warrant, Flynn makes clear her assumptions: that people who can support themselves don't deserve food stamps and that a person is better off (and happier) holding a job than receiving charity. By generating more ideas and evidence, she was easily able to expand both the data paragraph and the warrant paragraph, and the result was a coherent essay of seven hundred words.

How, by the way, would someone who didn't accept Flynn's warrant argue with her? What about old, infirm, or disabled persons who cannot work? What quite different assumptions about poverty might be possible?

Deductive and Inductive Reasoning

Stephen Toulmin's method of argument is a fairly recent—and very helpful—way to analyze and construct arguments. Two other reliable methods date back to the Greek philosopher Aristotle, who identified the complementary processes of INDUCTIVE REASONING (induction) and DEDUCTIVE REASONING (deduction). In *Zen and the Art of Motorcycle Maintenance*, Robert M. Pirsig gives examples of deductive and inductive reasoning:

> If the cycle goes over a bump and the engine misfires, and then goes over another bump and the engine misfires, and then goes over another bump and the engine misfires, and then goes over a long smooth stretch of road and there is no misfiring, and then goes over a fourth bump and the engine misfires again, one can logically conclude that the misfiring is caused by the bumps. That is induction: reasoning from particular experiences to general truths.
>
> Deductive inferences do the reverse. They start with general knowledge and predict a specific observation. For example if, from reading the hierarchy of facts about the machine, the mechanic knows the horn of the cycle is powered exclusively by electricity from the battery, then he can logically infer that if the battery is dead the horn will not work. That is deduction.

In inductive reasoning, the method of the sciences, we collect bits of evidence on which to base generalizations. From interviews with a hundred self-identified conservative Republicans (the evidence), you might conclude that conservative Republicans favor less government regulation of business (the generalization). The more evidence you have, the more trustworthy your generalization is, but it would never be airtight unless you talked to every conservative Republican in the country. Since such thoroughness is impractical if not impossible, inductive reasoning involves making an *inductive leap* from the evidence to the conclusion. The smaller the leap—the more evidence you have—the better.

Deductive reasoning works the other way, from a general statement to particular cases. The basis of deduction is the SYLLOGISM, a three-step form of reasoning practiced by Aristotle:

> All men are mortal.
> Socrates is a man.
> Therefore, Socrates is mortal.

The first statement (the major premise) is a generalization about a large group: It is the result of inductive reasoning. The second statement (the minor premise) says something about a particular member of that large group. The third statement (the conclusion) follows inevitably from the premises and applies the generalization to the particular: If the premises are true, then the conclusion must be true. Here is another syllogism:

> MAJOR PREMISE: Conservative Republicans favor less government regulation of business.
>
> MINOR PREMISE: William F. Buckley, Jr., is a conservative Republican.
>
> CONCLUSION: Therefore, William F. Buckley, Jr., favors less government regulation of business.

Problems with deductive reasoning start in the premises. In 1633, Scipio Chiaramonti, professor of philosophy at the University of Pisa, came up with this untrustworthy syllogism: "Animals, which move, have limbs and muscles. The earth has no limbs and muscles. Hence, the earth does not move." This is bad deductive reasoning, and its flaw is to assume that all things need limbs and muscles to move—ignoring raindrops, rivers, and many other moving things. In the next pages, we'll look at some of the things that can go wrong with any kind of reasoning.

Logical Fallacies

In arguments we read and hear, we often meet logical FALLACIES: errors in reasoning that lead to wrong conclusions. From the time when you start thinking about your proposition or claim and planning your paper, you'll need to watch out for them. To help you recognize logical fallacies when you see them or hear them, and so guard against them when you write, here is a list of the most common.

- *Non sequitur* (from the Latin, "it does not follow"): stating a conclusion that doesn't follow from the first premise or premises. "I've lived in this town a long time—why, my grandfather was the first mayor—so I'm against putting fluoride in the drinking water."

- *Oversimplification:* supplying neat and easy explanations for large and complicated phenomena. "No wonder drug abuse is out of control. Look at how the courts have hobbled police officers." Oversimplified solutions are also popular: "All these teenage kids that get in trouble with the law—why, they ought to ship 'em over to China. That would straighten 'em out!" (See also p. 364.)
- *Hasty generalization:* leaping to a generalization from inadequate or faulty evidence. The most familiar hasty generalization is the stereotype: "Men aren't sensitive enough to be day-care providers." "Women are too emotional to fight in combat."
- *Either/or reasoning:* assuming that a reality may be divided into only two parts or extremes; assuming that a given problem has only one of two possible solutions. "What's to be done about the trade imbalance with Asia? Either we ban all Asian imports, or American industry will collapse." Obviously, either/or reasoning is a kind of extreme oversimplification.
- *Argument from doubtful or unidentified authority:* "We ought to castrate all sex offenders; Uncle Oswald says we should." Or: "According to reliable sources, my opponent is lying."
- *Argument ad hominem* (from the Latin, "to the man"): attacking a person's views by attacking his or her character. "Mayor Burns is divorced and estranged from his family. How can we listen to his pleas for a city nursing home?"
- *Begging the question:* taking for granted from the start what you set out to demonstrate. When you reason in a *logical* way, you state that because something is true, then, as a result, some other truth follows. When you beg the question, however, you repeat that what is true is true. If you argue, for instance, that dogs are a menace to people because they are dangerous, you don't prove a thing, since the idea that dogs are dangerous is already assumed in the statement that they are a menace. Beggars of questions often just repeat what they already believe, only in different words. This fallacy sometimes takes the form of arguing in a circle, or demonstrating a premise by a conclusion and a conclusion by a premise: "I am in college because that is the right thing to do. Going to college is the right thing to do because it is expected of me."
- *Post hoc, ergo propter hoc* (from the Latin, "after this, therefore because of this"), or *post hoc* for short: assuming that because B follows A, B was caused by A. "Ever since the city suspended height restrictions on skyscrapers, the city budget has been balanced." (See also p. 364.)
- *False analogy:* the claim of persuasive likeness when no significant likeness exists. An ANALOGY asserts that because two things are comparable in some respects, they are comparable in other respects as

well. Analogies cannot serve as evidence in a rational argument because the differences always outweigh the similarities; but analogies can reinforce such arguments *if* the subjects are indeed similar in some ways. If they aren't, the analogy is false. Many observers see the "war on drugs" as a false and damaging analogy because warfare aims for clear victory over a specific, organized enemy, whereas the complete eradication of illegal drugs is probably unrealistic and, in any event, the "enemy" isn't well defined: the drugs themselves? users? sellers? producers? the producing nations? (These critics urge approaching drugs as a social problem to be skillfully managed and reduced.)

THE PROCESS

In stating an opinion, you set forth and support a claim—a truth you believe. You may find such a truth by thinking and feeling, by reading, by talking to your instructors or fellow students, by listening to a discussion of some problem or controversy.

In stating a proposal, you already have an opinion in mind, and from there, you go on to urge an action or a solution to a problem. Usually, these two statements will take place within the same piece of writing: A writer will first set forth a view ("Compact discs are grossly overpriced") and then go right on to a proposal ("Compact discs should be discounted in the college store").

Whether your essay states an opinion, a proposal, or both, it is likely to contain similar ingredients. One essential is your thesis—the proposition or claim you are going to defend. As we noted earlier (p. 455), the likeliest spot for your thesis statement is near the start of your essay, where you might also explain why you think the thesis worth upholding, perhaps showing how it concerns your readers. If you plan to include both an opinion and a proposal in your essay, you may wish to set forth your opinion first, saving your proposal for later, perhaps for your conclusion.

Your thesis stated, introduce your least important point first. Then build in a crescendo to the strongest point you have. This structure will lend emphasis to your essay and perhaps make your chain of ideas more persuasive as the reader continues to follow it.

For every point, give evidence: facts, figures, examples, expert opinions. If you introduce statistics, make sure that they are up to date and fairly represented. In an essay advocating a law against smoking, it would be unfair to declare that "in Pottsville, Illinois, last year, 50 percent of all deaths were caused by lung cancer" if only two people died in Pottsville last year—one of them struck by a car.

If you are arguing fairly, you should be able to face potential criticisms fairly, and give your critics due credit, by recognizing the objections you expect your assertion will meet. This is the strategy H. L. Mencken uses in "The Penalty of Death" in this chapter, and he introduces it in his essay right at the beginning. (You might also tackle the opposition at the end of your essay or at relevant points throughout.) Notice that Mencken takes pains to dispense with his opponents: He doesn't just dismiss them; he reasons with them.

In your conclusion, briefly restate your claim, if possible in a fresh, pointed way. (For example, see the concluding sentence in the essay by William F. Buckley, Jr., in this chapter.) In an essay with a strong emotional component, you may want to end with an appeal to feelings. (See "Live Free and Starve" by Chitra Divakaruni.)

Finally, don't forget the power of humor in argument. You don't have to crack gratuitous jokes, but there is often an advantage in having a reader or listener who laughs on your side. When Abraham Lincoln debated Stephen Douglas, he triumphed in his reply to Douglas's snide remark that Lincoln had once been a bartender. "I have long since quit my side of the bar," Lincoln declared, "while Mr. Douglas clings to his as tenaciously as ever."

In arguing—doing everything you can to bring your reader around to your view—you can draw on any method of writing discussed in this book. Arguing for or against further reductions in welfare funding, you might give EXAMPLES of wasteful spending, or of neighborhoods where welfare funds are still needed. You might analyze the CAUSES of social problems that call for welfare funds, or foresee the likely EFFECTS of cutting welfare programs or of keeping them. You might COMPARE AND CONTRAST the idea of slashing welfare funds with the idea of increasing them. You could use NARRATION to tell a pointed story; you could use DESCRIPTION to portray certain welfare recipients and their neighborhoods. If it suited your purposes, you could employ several of these methods in writing a single argument.

You will rarely find, when you begin to write a persuasive paper, that you have too much evidence to support your claim. But unless you're writing a term paper and have months to spend on it, you're limited in how much evidence you can gather. Begin by stating your claim. Make it narrow enough to support in the time you have available. For a paper due a week from now, the opinion that "our city's downtown area has a serious litter problem" can probably be backed up in part by your own eyewitness reports. But to support the claim "Litter is one of the worst environmental problems of North American cities," you would surely need to spend time in a library.

In rewriting, you may find yourself tempted to keep all the evidence you have collected with such effort. Of course, some of it may not support your claim; some may seem likely to persuade the reader only to go to sleep. If so, throw it out. A stronger argument will remain.

CHECKLIST FOR REVISING ARGUMENT OR PERSUASION

✔ **AUDIENCE.** Have you taken account of your readers' probable views? Have you reasoned with readers, not attacked them? Are your emotional appeals appropriate to readers' likely feelings? Do you acknowledge opposing views?

✔ **THESIS.** Does your argument have a thesis, a claim about how your subject is or should be? Is the thesis narrow enough to argue convincingly in the space and time available? Is it stated clearly? Is it reasonable?

✔ **EVIDENCE.** Is your thesis well supported with facts, statistics, expert opinions, and examples? Is your evidence recent and fair?

✔ **WARRANT.** Have you made sound connections between your evidence and your thesis or claim?

✔ **LOGICAL FALLACIES.** Have you avoided common errors in reasoning, such as oversimplifying or begging the question? (See pp. 461–63 for a list of fallacies.)

✔ **STRUCTURE.** Does your organization lead readers through your argument step by step, building to your strongest ideas and frequently connecting your evidence to your central claim?

ARGUMENT AND PERSUASION IN A PARAGRAPH: TWO ILLUSTRATIONS

Arguing About Television

This self-contained paragraph, written for *The Bedford Reader*, argues that TV news aims for entertainment at the expense of serious coverage of events and issues. The argument here could serve a number of different purposes in full essays: For instance, in a paper claiming that television is our least reliable source of news, the paragraph would give one cause of unreliability; or in an essay analyzing television news, the paragraph would examine one element.

Television news has a serious failing: It's show business. *Topic sentence: the claim* Unlike a newspaper, its every image has to entertain the average beer drinker. To score high ratings and win advertisers, the visual medium favors the spectacular: riots, tornados, air

crashes. Now that satellite transmission invites live coverage, newscasters go for the fast-breaking story at the expense
of thoughtful analysis. "The more you can get data out instantly," says media critic Jeff Greenfield, "the more you rely
on instant data to define the news." TV zooms in on people
who make news, but, to avoid boredom, won't let them argue or explain. (How can they, in speeches limited to fifteen
seconds?) In 1996, as American missiles bombed military
sites in Iraq, President Clinton held a press conference to
explain the action. His lengthy remarks were clipped to
twenty seconds on one news broadcast, and then an anchor-
woman digested the opposition to a single line: "Republicans tonight were critical of the president's actions." During
the 1996 presidential election, both candidates sometimes
deliberately packaged bad news so that it could not be dis-
tilled to a sound bite on the evening news—and thus would
not make the evening news at all. Americans who rely on
television for their news (two-thirds, according to recent
polls) exist on a starvation diet.

Evidence:

Expert opinion

Facts and examples

Statistic

Arguing in an Academic Discipline

Taken from a textbook on public relations, the following paragraph
argues that lobbyists (who work to persuade public officials in behalf of
a cause) are not slick manipulators but something else. The paragraph
falls in the textbook's section on lobbying as a form of public relations,
and its purpose is to correct a mistaken definition.

Although the public stereotypes a lobbyist as a fast-
talking person twisting an elected official's arm to get special
concessions, the reality is quite different. Today's lobbyist, who
may be fully employed by one industry or represent a variety of
clients, is often a quiet-spoken, well-educated man or woman
armed with statistics and research reports. Robert Gray, former head of Hill and Knowlton's Washington office and a
public affairs expert for thirty years, adds, "Lobbying is no
longer a booze and buddies business. It's presenting honest
facts and convincing Congress that your side has more merit
than the other." He rejects lobbying as being simply "influence peddling and button-holing" top administration officials.
Although the public has the perception that lobbying is done
only by big business, Gray correctly points out that a variety
of special interests also do it. These may include such groups
as the Sierra Club, Mothers Against Drunk Driving, the National Association of Social Workers, the American Civil
Liberties Union, and the American Federation of Labor.
Even the American Society of Plastic and Reconstructive
Surgeons hired a Washington public relations firm in their

Topic sentence: the claim

Evidence:

Expert opinion

Facts and examples

battle against restrictions on breast implants. Lobbying, quite literally, is an activity in which widely diverse groups and organizations engage as an exercise of free speech and representation in the marketplace of ideas. Lobbyists often balance each other and work toward legislative compromises that not only benefit their self-interests but society as a whole.
—Dennis L. Wilcox, Phillip H. Ault, and Warren K. Agee, *Public Relations: Strategies and Tactics*

ARGUMENT AND PERSUASION ELSEWHERE IN *THE BEDFORD READER*

The essays below, each illustrating some other method or methods of development, also argue in support of a claim.

PART ONE

Barbara Huttmann, "A Crime of Compassion"
Anna Quindlen, "Homeless"
Nancy Mairs, "Disability"
Linnea Saukko, "How to Poison the Earth"
Judy Brady, "I Want a Wife"
Armin A. Brott, "Not All Men Are Sly Foxes"
Barbara Ehrenreich, "In Defense of Talk Shows"
William Lutz, "The World of Doublespeak"
Gore Vidal, "Drugs"
Meghan Daum, "Safe-Sex Lies"
Scott Russell Sanders, "Homeplace"
Marie Winn, "TV Addiction"
Bruno Bettelheim, "The Holocaust"
Barbara Kingsolver, "Stone Soup"

PART TWO

Stephen L. Carter, "The Insufficiency of Honesty"
Stephen Jay Gould, "Sex, Drugs, Disasters, and the Extinction of Dinosaurs"
Martin Luther King, Jr., "I Have a Dream"
Richard Rodriguez, "Aria: A Memoir of a Bilingual Childhood"
Jonathan Swift, "A Modest Proposal"

CASE STUDY
Using Argument and Persuasion

As a college freshman, Kristen Corcoran commuted to school at night. In the following letter, she appealed to her college's president to have a parking ticket canceled because legal parking was unavailable.

Corcoran's letter is a model of argument for a specific purpose, but it didn't start out that way. In her much longer first draft, she let her anger push her into detailing every one of her five previous parking difficulties and criticizing the president personally for not solving the problem. She did not get to her request to have the ticket canceled until the very end.

Reviewing her draft, Corcoran realized that she was trying to negotiate with the president, not tell her off, and for that a more direct, conciliatory approach was needed. In the revision you see here, Corcoran focuses immediately on her purpose for writing, summarizes her problems with parking, and takes the tack of informing, rather than criticizing, the president.

```
                              1073 Dogwood Terrace
                              North Andover, MA 01845
                              May 2, 1999
```

```
President Delores Reed
North State College
755 Little Road
Danvers, MA 01923
```

Dear President Reed:

I write to ask you to rescind a ten-dollar citation I received on April 4 for parking in North State's Lot E. I know that this lot is reserved for faculty use, but flooding in three of the four commuter lots left me with no reasonable parking alternatives. The campus police have not been able to help me, so I turn to you.

As you know, flooding is a recurring problem at North State, but perhaps you don't know how it affects commuting students. April 4 was one of six evenings this semester when I arrived to find Lots A, C, and D overrun by nearby marshes. On the other nights, Lot B filled quickly with cars and I was forced on two occasions to hunt for parking in the crowded residential areas off-campus. On April 4, I chose not to spend a half-hour finding a space and parked in Lot E. Many of its spaces are vacant at night when there are fewer classes and most campus offices are closed.

I understand from the campus police that North State has no plan for solving this seasonal problem. I, like hundreds of other commuter students, paid fifty dollars for a parking permit in the beginning of the semester and should be able to expect convenient parking like that described in North State's brochures. The parking problem is a serious one that affects not only commuters, who make up more than half of the student body, but also North State's neighbors, who are inconvenienced by crowds of cars monopolizing their streets each spring.

Please rescind my ticket and try to create some solutions to this problem. As a first step, may I suggest amending the school's parking policy to allow commuter use of Lot E in emergencies?

Sincerely,

Kristen Corcoran

Kristen Corcoran

H. L. MENCKEN

HENRY LOUIS MENCKEN (1880–1956) was a native of Baltimore, where for four decades he worked as newspaper reporter, editor, and columnist. In the 1920s, his boisterous, cynical observations on American life, appearing regularly in *The Smart Set* and later in *The American Mercury* (which he founded and edited), made him probably the most widely quoted writer in the country. As an editor and literary critic, Mencken championed Sinclair Lewis, Theodore Dreiser, and other realistic writers. As a social critic, he leveled blasts at pomp, hypocrisy, and the middle classes (whom he labeled "the booboisie"). (The publication of *The Diary of H. L. Mencken* in 1989 revealed more of its author's outspoken opinions and touched off a controversy: Was Mencken a bigot? The debate goes on.) In 1933, when Mencken's attempts to laugh off the Depression began to ring hollow, his magazine died. He then devoted himself to revising and supplementing *The American Language* (4th ed., 1948), his learned and highly entertaining survey of a nation's speech habits and vocabulary. Two dozen of Mencken's books are now in print, including *A Mencken Chrestomathy* (1949), a representative selection of his best writings of various kinds; and *A Choice of Days* (1980), a selection from his memoirs.

The Penalty of Death

Above all, Mencken was a humorist whose thought had a serious core. He argues by first making the reader's jaw drop, then inducing a laugh, and finally causing the reader to ponder, "Hmmmm—what if he's right?" The following still-controversial essay, from *Prejudices, Fifth Series* (1926), shows Mencken the persuader in top form as he argues in favor of capital punishment. In the essay following Mencken's, Michael Kroll takes a very different approach to arguing about the same issue.

Of the arguments against capital punishment that issue from up-   1
lifters, two are commonly heard most often, to wit:

1. That hanging a man (or frying him or gassing him) is a dreadful business, degrading to those who have to do it and revolting to those who have to witness it.
2. That it is useless, for it does not deter others from the same crime.

The first of these arguments, it seems to me, is plainly too weak to   2
need serious refutation. All it says, in brief, is that the work of the hangman is unpleasant. Granted. But suppose it is? It may be quite necessary to society for all that. There are, indeed, many other jobs that

are unpleasant, and yet no one thinks of abolishing them—that of the plumber, that of the soldier, that of the garbageman, that of the priest hearing confessions, that of the sandhog, and so on. Moreover, what evidence is there that any actual hangman complains of his work? I have heard none. On the contrary, I have known many who delighted in their ancient art, and practiced it proudly.

In the second argument of the abolitionists there is rather more   3
force, but even here, I believe, the ground under them is shaky. Their fundamental error consists in assuming that the whole aim of punishing criminals is to deter other (potential) criminals—that we hang or electrocute A simply in order to so alarm B that he will not kill C. This, I believe, is an assumption which confuses a part with the whole. Deterrence, obviously, is *one* of the aims of punishment, but it is surely not the only one. On the contrary, there are at least a half dozen, and some are probably quite as important. At least one of them, practically considered, is *more* important. Commonly, it is described as revenge, but revenge is really not the word for it. I borrow a better term from the late Aristotle: *katharsis*. *Katharsis*, so used, means a salubrious discharge of emotions, a healthy letting off of steam. A schoolboy, disliking his teacher, deposits a tack upon the pedagogical chair; the teacher jumps and the boy laughs. This is *katharsis*. What I contend is that one of the prime objects of all judicial punishments is to afford the same grateful relief (*a*) to the immediate victims of the criminal punished, and (*b*) to the general body of moral and timorous men.

These persons, and particularly the first group, are concerned only   4
indirectly with deterring other criminals. The thing they crave primarily is the satisfaction of seeing the criminal actually before them suffer as he made them suffer. What they want is the peace of mind that goes with the feeling that accounts are squared. Until they get that satisfaction they are in a state of emotional tension, and hence unhappy. The instant they get it they are comfortable. I do not argue that this yearning is noble; I simply argue that it is almost universal among human beings. In the face of injuries that are unimportant and can be borne without damage it may yield to higher impulses; that is to say, it may yield to what is called Christian charity. But when the injury is serious Christianity is adjourned, and even saints reach for their sidearms. It is plainly asking too much of human nature to expect it to conquer so natural an impulse. A keeps a store and has a bookkeeper, B. B steals $700, employs it in playing at dice or bingo, and is cleaned out. What is A to do? Let B go? If he does so he will be unable to sleep at night. The sense of injury, of injustice, of frustration will haunt him like pruritus. So he turns B over to the police, and they hustle B to prison. Thereafter A can sleep. More, he has pleasant dreams. He pictures B chained to the wall of a dungeon a hundred feet underground, devoured by rats and

scorpions. It is so agreeable that it makes him forget his $700. He has got his *katharsis*.

The same thing precisely takes place on a larger scale when there is   5
a crime which destroys a whole community's sense of security. Every law-abiding citizen feels menaced and frustrated until the criminals have been struck down — until the communal capacity to get even with them, and more than even, has been dramatically demonstrated. Here, manifestly, the business of deterring others is no more than an afterthought. The main thing is to destroy the concrete scoundrels whose act has alarmed everyone, and thus made everyone unhappy. Until they are brought to book that unhappiness continues; when the law has been executed upon them there is a sigh of relief. In other words, there is *katharsis*.

I know of no public demand for the death penalty for ordinary   6
crimes, even for ordinary homicides. Its infliction would shock all men of normal decency of feeling. But for crimes involving the deliberate and inexcusable taking of human life, by men openly defiant of all civilized order — for such crimes it seems, to nine men out of ten, a just and proper punishment. Any lesser penalty leaves them feeling that the criminal has got the better of society — that he is free to add insult to injury by laughing. That feeling can be dissipated only by a recourse to *katharsis*, the invention of the aforesaid Aristotle. It is more effectively and economically achieved, as human nature now is, by wafting the criminal to realms of bliss.

The real objection to capital punishment doesn't lie against the actual extermination of the condemned, but against our brutal American   7
habit of putting it off so long. After all, every one of us must die soon or late, and a murderer, it must be assumed, is one who makes that sad fact the cornerstone of his metaphysic. But it is one thing to die, and quite another thing to lie for long months and even years under the shadow of death. No sane man would choose such a finish. All of us, despite the Prayer Book, long for a swift and unexpected end. Unhappily, a murderer, under the irrational American system, is tortured for what, to him, must seem a whole series of eternities. For months on end he sits in prison while his lawyers carry on their idiotic buffoonery with writs, injunctions, mandamuses, and appeals. In order to get his money (or that of his friends) they have to feed him with hope. Now and then, by the imbecility of a judge or some trick of juridic science, they actually justify it. But let us say that, his money all gone, they finally throw up their hands. Their client is now ready for the rope or the chair. But he must still wait for months before it fetches him.

That wait, I believe, is horribly cruel. I have seen more than one   8
man sitting in the death-house, and I don't want to see any more. Worse, it is wholly useless. Why should he wait at all? Why not hang

him the day after the last court dissipates his last hope? Why torture him as not even cannibals would torture their victims? The common answer is that he must have time to make his peace with God. But how long does that take? It may be accomplished, I believe, in two hours quite as comfortably as in two years. There are, indeed, no temporal limitations upon God. He could forgive a whole herd of murderers in a millionth of a second. More, it has been done.

QUESTIONS ON MEANING

1. Identify Mencken's main reasons for his support of capital punishment. What is his THESIS?
2. In paragraph 3, Mencken asserts that there are at least half a dozen reasons for punishing offenders. In his essay, he mentions two, deterrence and revenge. What others can you supply?
3. For which class of offenders does Mencken advocate the death penalty?
4. What is Mencken's "real objection" to capital punishment?

QUESTIONS ON WRITING STRATEGY

1. How would you characterize Mencken's humor? Point to examples of it. In light of the grim subject, do you find the humor funny?
2. In his first paragraph, Mencken pares his subject down to manageable size. What techniques does he employ for this purpose?
3. At the start of paragraph 7, Mencken shifts his stance from concern for the victims of crime to concern for prisoners awaiting execution. Does the shift help or weaken the effectiveness of his earlier justification for capital punishment?
4. Do you think the author expects his AUDIENCE to agree with him? At what points does he seem to recognize the fact that some readers may see things differently?
5. In paragraphs 2 and 3, Mencken uses ANALOGIES in an apparent attempt to strengthen his argument. What are the analogies? Do they seem false to you? (See pp. 462–63 for a discussion of false analogy.) Do you think Mencken would agree with your judgment?
6. **OTHER METHODS.** To explain what he sees as the most important aim of capital punishment, Mencken uses DEFINITION. What does he define, and what techniques does he use to make the definition clear?

QUESTIONS ON LANGUAGE

1. Mencken opens his argument by referring to those who reject capital punishment as "uplifters." What CONNOTATIONS does this word have for you? Does the use of this "loaded" word strengthen or weaken Mencken's position? Explain.

2. Be sure you know the meanings of the following words: refutation, sandhog (para. 2); salubrious, pedagogical, timorous (3); pruritus (4); wafting (6); mandamuses, juridic (7).
3. What emotional overtones can you detect in Mencken's reference to the hangman's job as an "ancient art" (para. 2)?
4. Writing at a time when there was no debate over the usage, Mencken often uses "man" and "he" for examples that could be either a man or a woman (such as A in para. 4) and uses "men" to mean people in general ("all men of normal decency of feeling," para. 6). Does this usage weaken the essay? Why, or why not?

SUGGESTIONS FOR WRITING

1. JOURNAL WRITING. Although Mencken supports capital punishment, he condemns "our brutal American habit" of delaying executions for court appeals (paras. 7–8). What do you think of our methods of trying, sentencing, or appealing the sentences of criminals in this country? Does our system seem just to you?

   FROM JOURNAL TO ESSAY. Develop a focused and persuasive thesis from the opinions you expressed in your journal entry, and support it with EVIDENCE from your reading and observations. (You may also wish to do research among the many books and articles written on the criminal justice system.) Rather than take on the entire administration of justice, follow Mencken's model and narrow your thesis to one aspect of the system.
2. In a brief essay, argue for or against humor as a technique of argument or persuasion. Use examples from Mencken's essay as EVIDENCE.
3. CRITICAL WRITING. Write an essay refuting Mencken's argument; or take Mencken's side but supply any additional reasons you can think of. In either case, begin your argument with an ANALYSIS of Mencken's argument, and use examples (real or hypothetical) to support your view.
4. CONNECTIONS. Compare this essay with the following one by Michael Kroll, "The Unquiet Death of Robert Harris." Imagine a debate between the two writers. How would Kroll respond to Mencken's argument that fallible human beings can't do without *katharsis*? How would Mencken answer Kroll's charge that turning death into a public spectacle is barbarous? On what point do they agree?

H. L. MENCKEN ON WRITING

"All my work hangs together," wrote H. L. Mencken in a piece called "Addendum on Aims," "once the main ideas under it are discerned. Those ideas are chiefly of a skeptical character. I believe that nothing is unconditionally true, and hence I am opposed to every statement of positive truth and to every man who states it. Such men seem to me to be either idiots or scoundrels. To one category or the other belong all theologians, professors, editorial writers, right-thinkers, etc...."

Whether [my work] appears to be burlesque, or serious criticism, or mere casual controversy, it is always directed against one thing: unwarranted pretension."

Mencken cheerfully acknowledged his debts to his teachers: mostly writers he read as a young man and newspaper editors he worked under. "My style of writing is chiefly grounded upon an early enthusiasm for Huxley,[1] the greatest of all masters of orderly exposition. He taught me the importance of giving to every argument a simple structure. As for the fancy work on the surface, it comes chiefly from an anonymous editorial writer in the *New York Sun*, circa 1900. He taught me the value of apt phrases. My vocabulary is pretty large; it probably runs to 25,000 words. It represents much labor. I am constantly expanding it. I believe that a good phrase is better than a Great Truth—which is usually buncombe. I delight in argument, not because I want to convince, but because argument itself is an end."

In another essay, "The Fringes of Lovely Letters," Mencken wrote that "what is in the head infallibly oozes out of the nub of the pen. If it is sparkling Burgundy the writing is full of life and charm. If it is mush the writing is mush too." He recalls the example of President Warren G. Harding, who once sent a message to Congress that was quite incomprehensible. "Why? Simply because Dr. Harding's thoughts, on the high and grave subjects he discussed, were so muddled that he couldn't understand them himself. But on matters within his range of customary meditation he was clear and even charming, as all of us are....Style cannot go beyond the ideas which lie at the heart of it. If they are clear, it too will be clear. If they are held passionately, it will be eloquent."

FOR DISCUSSION

1. According to Mencken, what PURPOSE animates his writing?
2. What relationship does Mencken see between a writer's thought and his or her STYLE?
3. Where in his views on writing does Mencken use FIGURES OF SPEECH to advantage?

---

[1] Thomas Henry Huxley (1825–95), English biologist and educator, who wrote many essays popularizing science. In Victorian England, Huxley was the leading exponent and defender of Charles Darwin's theory of evolution.—EDS.

MICHAEL KROLL

MICHAEL KROLL is a writer and investigator specializing in the criminal justice system. Born in 1943 and raised in rural California, Kroll graduated in 1965 from the University of California at Berkeley with a B.A. in political science. For almost two decades he has been a journalist and editor with the Pacific News Service, writing about juvenile justice, capital punishment, and prisons. His articles have appeared in periodicals such as the *Los Angeles Times*, the *New York Times*, *California Lawyer*, and *The Progressive*, and he has been a guest on talk shows. With a special interest in capital punishment, Kroll also founded the Death Penalty Information Center in Washington, D.C., and he conducts investigations on behalf of prisoners who are condemned to death.

The Unquiet Death of Robert Harris

Kroll met Robert Alton Harris in 1984, when Harris was awaiting execution for the 1978 murders of two teenagers. The two men became friends, giving Kroll a uniquely personal view of Harris's long journey to the gas chamber and to death on April 21, 1992. In this narrative of the journey's end, published in *The Nation* a few months afterward, Kroll makes an argument against what he witnessed. Contrast this essay with the previous one, H. L. Mencken's "The Penalty of Death."

"Ladies and gentlemen. Please stay in your places until your escort   1
comes for you. Follow your escort, as instructed. Thank you."

The words were spoken in the manner of the operator of the   2
Jungle Cruise at Disneyland: well-rehearsed and "professional." They
were spoken by the public information officer of California's San Quentin penitentiary, Vernell Crittendon, as we waited to be ushered out of
the gas chamber where my friend Robert Harris was slumped over, dead,
in Chair B.

When not conveying us to and from the gas chamber, our "escorts"   3
guarded us in a small, tidy office with barred windows facing the east
gate, where a circus of media lights lit up the night sky, letting us see silhouettes in the darkness. There were two desks, the exact number of
straight-backed chairs needed to accommodate us, some nineteen-cent
bags of potato chips, a couple of apples and bananas, and bad coffee.

We—a psychologist and lawyer who knew Robert Harris professionally, his brother Randy, whom he had designated to witness the   4
gassing, and I, a close friend for nearly a decade—had entered at the
west gate at 10 P.M. as instructed to present our credentials (a written
invitation from Warden Daniel Vasquez himself) and submit to a thor-

ough pat-down search and a metal detector. Our escorts took us in a prison van to the front of the old fortress and escorted us up a few steps into the office of one G. Mosqueda, program administrator. Then we began what we thought at the time would be a short vigil. It turned out to be eight hours.

We'd been there only a few minutes when another staff person arrived wearing a civilian suit and a name tag that identified him as Martinez. He walked up to Randy, pointed his finger, and said, "Randall Harris. Come with me!" Randy smiled, got up, and followed him out. (Randy thought they were taking him for counseling. It was a fair assumption; counselors had been provided to advise members of the victims' families who had come to witness the execution. This was to insure, Warden Vasquez told them, that "there is only one casualty in that room.")   5

When they brought him back, he told his own horror story. He had been ordered to submit to a full body-cavity search. "We have learned from a reliable source that you are planning something," Martinez had said. Randy was ordered to open his mouth for inspection, take his clothes off, bend over, lift his testicles, pull back his foreskin. "If you try anything," Martinez had threatened, "you'll be sorry, and so will your brother."   6

His brother was waiting just a few feet from the gas chamber.   7

After Randy rejoined us, shaken and humiliated, our escort gave us our marching orders. "When the phone rings and I get the order to go, stand and follow me quickly." The phone, which had the kind of clanging ring that scares you to death even when you are not already scared to death, rang many times that night, and each time our hearts stopped. But *the* call did not come at midnight. It did not come for a long time. With no television to inform us, we waited, hour after hour, wondering what was happening, drinking bad coffee and asking to be escorted to the bathroom.   8

Later, we learned that in those hours the U.S. Court of Appeals for the Ninth Circuit had granted three stays of execution. One concerned newly discovered evidence that Robert's brother Danny, who had participated in the crime but served fewer than four years in exchange for his testimony against Robert, had actually fired the first shot. The two other stays—including one signed by ten judges—were based on the pending suit challenging the constitutionality of cyanide gas as a method of execution. Each of the three stays was dissolved by the U.S. Supreme Court.   9

Finally, a little after three o'clock, the call came and Mendez said, "Now."   10

We followed him into the freezing, brilliant night, but Mendez stopped us just short of the entrance to the gas chamber. Shivering, we   11 watched the other witnesses being led out of the cold — the media into one building opposite the gas chamber and the victims' family members into the East Block visiting room just beyond it. After a while, responding to words coming over his walkie-talkie that I could not hear, Mendez led us into the main visiting room to our immediate right. I had been in this room many times, but never at night, and never, as now, was it deserted of staff and inmates.

Finally the wait was over. Mendez spoke into his walkie-talkie.   12
"Okay," he said, and then turned his attention to us. "Let's go."

We, the family and friends of the condemned, were led to risers   13
along a wall behind and to the left of the chamber. Three burly guards brought Robert in and strapped him quickly to Chair B. His back was to us. He could see us only by craning his neck and peering over his left shoulder. From behind him, I looked over his right shoulder into the unblinking red eye of the video camera that was trained on his face in order to assist U.S. District Judge Marilyn Patel in determining whether death by lethal gas is cruel and unusual punishment. He peered around the room, making eye contact, smiling and nodding at people he knew. I held my breath. A guard's digital watch started beeping. She smiled sheepishly and covered it with her sleeve.

Minutes passed. Some people whispered. Some smiled. And then   14
the phone rang. The phone to the gas chamber rings for only one reason: A stay of execution has been granted. But nothing happened. Nobody moved — nobody except Robert, that is, who twisted and turned trying to figure out what was happening. He peered down between his legs to see if he could see the vat of acid beneath him. He sniffed the air and mouthed the words, "Pull it." More minutes passed. He peered over his left shoulder where I was just out his line of vision. "Where's Mike?" he mouthed.

I jumped down to the lower riser and walked over to the window.   15
A female guard ordered me back to my place, but not before Robert saw me, smiled, and settled down.

Ten minutes after the phone rang, the gas chamber door was   16
opened and the three guards unfastened Robert and took him from the chamber. Nothing like that had ever happened in the history of the gas chamber. (I later learned that during that eternity, California's attorney general, Dan Lungren, had been on the phone to the clerk of the U.S. Supreme Court informing him that Robert was in the chamber. Lungren begged the justices to overturn the stay. But the court wanted to read what circuit court Judge Harry Pregerson had written in the fourth and last stay of execution, so Lungren was told to take Robert from the chamber.)

We were escorted back to Mosqueda's office to continue waiting. I   17
shook uncontrollably for a long time, and cried openly. My escort sug-

gested I needed medical attention, hinting I might have to leave. I forced back my tears and pulled myself together, although I could not stop trembling.

We resumed the grim vigil, cut off from the outside world. Just af- 18 ter six in the morning, I saw the witnesses from the victims' families being led past our window toward the chamber. Some were laughing. As honored guests, they had been playing video games, napping in the warden's home, and eating specially prepared food. My heart stopped. Something was happening. Karen, the lawyer with us, called the office where lawyers who supported Harris had gathered, and was told the stay of execution was still in place. But, as with the aborted execution attempt, they were the last to know.

Within fifteen seconds, the phone clattered to life, and Mendez 19 told us the stay had been dissolved. (He did not tell us the Supreme Court had ordered all federal courts to enter no more stays of execution regardless of the issues.) We were going again.

Quickly we moved through the chill dawn air toward the chamber. 20 Randy whispered in my ear, "Slow down." Near the entrance, Vernell Crittendon stood watching the procession move smoothly into the chamber. He pumped his upturned fist three times, the way football players do when their team has scored.

When they brought Robert in, he was grim-faced, tired and ashen. 21 Beyond the horror of having stood at the brink of the abyss just two and a half hours before, he had been up for several days and nights. He was under horrific pressure. Again, he nodded to acquaintances. He did not smile. He faced to his right and said "I'm sorry" to the father of murder victim Michael Baker. He craned his neck left once more and nodded quickly toward us. "It's all right," he reassured us. After about two minutes, he sniffed the air, then breathed deeply several times.

His head began to roll and his eyes closed, then opened again. His 22 head dropped, then came up with an abrupt jerk, and rolled some more. It was grotesque and hideous, and I looked away. When I looked back, his head came up again, and I covered my mouth. Randy was whimpering in pain next to me, and we clutched each other. The lawyer, sobbing audibly, put her arms around us and tried to comfort us. I could not stop shivering. Reverend Harris, Robert's second cousin and spiritual adviser, who had been with Robert in the holding cell almost until the moment they took him away, whispered, "He's ready. He was tired. It's all right. His punishment is over."

He writhed for seven minutes, his head falling on his chest, saliva 23 drooling from his open mouth. He lifted his head again and again. Seven minutes. A lifetime. Nine more minutes passed with his head slumped on his chest. His heart, a survivor's heart, had kept pumping for nine more minutes, while we held each other. Some of the witnesses laughed. I thought of the label "Laughing Killer," affixed to Robert by the media, and knew these good people would never be described as laughing killers.

We were in the middle of something indescribably ugly. Not just   24
the cold-blooded killing of a human being, and not even the fact that we happened to love him—but the ritual of it, the participation of us, the witnesses, the witnessing itself of this most private and personal act. It was nakedly barbaric. Nobody could say this had anything to do with justice, I thought. Yet this medieval torture chamber is what a large majority of my fellow Californians, including most in the room with me, believe in. The implications of this filled me with fear—fear for myself and for all of us, a fear I am ashamed to confess—while my friend was being strangled slowly to death in front me.

Some witnesses began shuffling nervously. People looked at their   25
watches. Then a guard stepped forward and announced that Robert Alton Harris, C.D.C. Prisoner B-66883, had expired in the gas chamber at 6:21 A.M., sixteen minutes after the cyanide had been gently lowered into the sulfuric acid.

It was the moment Crittendon had been waiting for. He stepped   26
into the middle of the quiet room, his Jheri-Kurls reflecting the eerie green light from the gas chamber where my friend lay dead, slumped forward against the straps in Chair B.

"Ladies and gentlemen. Please stay in your places until your escort   27
comes for you. Follow your escort, as instructed. Thank you."

Our guard came and we followed him out. The eighteen media wit-   28
nesses, who had stood against the wall opposite us scribbling on paper provided by the prison, preceded us out of the room. As they had been for weeks, they were desperate for a Harris family member to say something to them. "Is this a Harris? Is this a Harris?" a reporter standing just outside the door shouted, pointing at each of us as we emerged into the first light of morning over San Francisco Bay.

My god, it was a beautiful day.   29

QUESTIONS ON MEANING

1. Is Kroll's PURPOSE merely to serve as a witness to his friend's execution, or is there an unstated proposal in the essay? If so, what is it?
2. Why did the execution take so long? What was taking place behind the scenes?
3. What can you INFER about Kroll's opinion of the Supreme Court's decision to dissolve all three of the Court of Appeals' stays of execution (para. 9)? How does he indirectly make this opinion known?
4. How do you read the last sentence of the essay? Is it merely IRONIC?

5. Do you think Kroll is against the death penalty, or merely against the way it was carried out in this case?

QUESTIONS ON WRITING STRATEGY

1. At what three points does Kroll pause in the story of the execution? What does he accomplish each time?
2. What is the TONE of the essay? How does it contribute to Kroll's ETHICAL APPEAL (see pp. 456–57)?
3. Is Kroll's approach generally based on a RATIONAL or an EMOTIONAL APPEAL (see p. 456)?
4. What is the EFFECT of Kroll's DESCRIPTION of the victims' families in paragraphs 18 and 23? How does Kroll's POINT OF VIEW shape this description?
5. Why does Kroll describe Harris's death in such detail (paras. 22–23)?
6. **OTHER METHODS.** This essay is an example of NARRATION being used in the service of an argument. What advantage does Kroll gain by presenting his argument in the form of a personal account?

QUESTIONS ON LANGUAGE

1. Make sure you know the meanings of the following words: silhouettes (para. 3); vigil (4); stays (9); burly (13); ashen, abyss (21); grotesque (22); barbaric (24).
2. What is Kroll's objection to Vernell Crittendon's tone (paras. 1–2)? What do you make of his job title: "public information officer"?
3. What is the tone of the phrase "a written invitation from Warden Daniel Vasquez himself" (para. 4)?
4. How does Kroll's use of reported speech contribute to his portrait of the prison officials?

SUGGESTIONS FOR WRITING

1. **JOURNAL WRITING.** What do you think of the death penalty? Write down as many reasons both for and against it as you can. Your reasons may be moral, emotional, or purely pragmatic. You may know of statistics or historical precedents that support the existence or abolition of the death penalty. Write down whatever comes to mind.
   FROM JOURNAL TO ESSAY. Write an essay in which you argue either for or against the death penalty. Support your argument with the EVIDENCE in favor of your position that you developed in your journal writing. As for the evidence that contradicts your opinion, use it to try to anticipate, and respond to, readers' likely objections to your view.
2. What is your opinion on televising public executions? How would a televised account of an execution differ from the kind of written narrative Kroll provides? What are the advantages of each method of narration, visual and written?
3. **CRITICAL WRITING.** Kroll's THESIS about the barbarity of staging executions as public spectacle comes nearly at the end of the essay (para. 24), yet he

hints throughout the essay that this is the aspect of his friend's execution that disturbs him the most. How does Kroll prepare the reader for his statement of thesis? What details emphasize the packaging of the execution as public entertainment?

4. **CONNECTIONS.** In "The Penalty of Death" (p. 470), H. L. Mencken approaches the death penalty quite differently from Kroll. Not only do their opinions differ fundamentally, but Mencken's view is broad and ABSTRACT, while Kroll's is intensely personal; and Mencken's appeal is largely rational, while Kroll's is largely emotional. In an essay, discuss the effectiveness of these two essays apart from the opinions they support—that is, focus on the authors' strategies of argument rather than on the arguments themselves. What are the advantages and disadvantages of each strategy?

ESTHER DYSON

ESTHER DYSON, born in 1951, is a prominent spokesperson for the information superhighway. In 1972 she received a B.A. in economics from Harvard University, where she wrote for the *Harvard Crimson*. After college she reported for *Forbes* magazine and then worked as a securities analyst. She now serves as chair of EDventure Holdings, a company specializing in information technology. Dyson has written for the *Harvard Business Review*, the *New York Times*, and *Wired* magazine, among other periodicals, and she has published two books: *Release 2.0: A Design for Living in the Digital Age* (1997) and its upgrade, *Release 2.1* (1998). She lectures widely and serves on the boards of international corporations and networks. In 1998 *Fortune* magazine named her one of the fifty most powerful women in American business.

Cyberspace for All

Debates about legislation to regulate the Internet, especially to restrict or ban "indecent" material, prompted Dyson to write "Cyberspace for All" (editors' title). She defends cyberspace from what she sees as intrusive and damaging regulation, predicting a future of individual choice and affiliation, free of the constraints of geography and government. For a different view of the cyberfuture, see the essay following Dyson's, "Welcome to Cyberbia" by Heidi Pollock.

Something in the American psyche loves new frontiers. We hanker 1
after wide-open spaces; we like to explore; we like to make rules instead of follow them. But in this age of political correctness and other intrusions on our national cult of independence, it's hard to find a place where you can go and be yourself without worrying about the neighbors.

There is such a place: cyberspace. Lost in the furor over porn on 2
the Net is the exhilarating sense of freedom that this new frontier once promised—and still does in some quarters. Formerly a playground for computer nerds and techies, cyberspace now embraces every conceivable constituency: schoolchildren, flirtatious singles, Hungarian-Americans, accountants—along with pederasts and porn fans. Can they all get along? Or will our fear of kids surfing for cyberporn behind their bedroom doors provoke a crackdown?

The first order of business is to grasp what cyberspace *is*. It might 3
help to leave behind metaphors of highways and frontiers and to think instead of real estate. Real estate, remember, is an intellectual, legal, artificial environment constructed *on top of* land. Real estate recognizes the difference between parkland and shopping mall, between red-light zone and school district, between church, state and drugstore.

In the same way, you could think of cyberspace as a giant and un- 4
bounded world of virtual real estate. Some property is privately owned
and rented out; other property is common land; some places are suitable for children, and others are best avoided by all but the kinkiest
citizens. Unfortunately, it's those places that are now capturing the
popular imagination: places that offer bomb-making instructions,
pornography, advice on how to procure stolen credit cards. They make
cyberspace sound like a nasty place. Good citizens jump to a conclusion: better regulate it. . . .

Regardless of how many laws or lawsuits are launched, regulation 5
won't work.

Aside from being unconstitutional, using censorship to counter in- 6
decency and other troubling "speech" fundamentally misinterprets the
nature of cyberspace. Cyberspace isn't a frontier where wicked people
can grab unsuspecting children, nor is it a giant television system that
can beam offensive messages at unwilling viewers. In this kind of real
estate, users have to *choose* where they visit, what they see, what they
do. It's optional, and it's much easier to bypass a place on the Net than
it is to avoid walking past an unsavory block of stores on the way to
your local 7-11.

Put plainly, cyberspace is a voluntary destination — in reality, 7
many destinations. You don't just get "onto the Net"; you have to go
someplace in particular. That means that people can choose where to
go and what to see. Yes, community standards should be enforced, but
those standards should be set by cyberspace communities themselves,
not by the courts or by politicians in Washington. What we need isn't
Government control over all these electronic communities: We need
self-rule.

What makes cyberspace so alluring is precisely the way in which 8
it's *different* from shopping malls, television, highways and other terrestrial jurisdictions. But let's define the territory:

First, there are private e-mail conversations, akin to the conversa- 9
tions you have over the telephone or voice mail. These are private and
consensual and require no regulation at all.

Second, there are information and entertainment services, where 10
people can download anything from legal texts and lists of "great new
restaurants" to game software or dirty pictures. These places are like
bookstores, malls and movie houses — places where you go to buy
something. The customer needs to request an item or sign up for a sub-
scription; stuff (especially pornography) is not sent out to people who
don't ask for it. Some of these services are free or included as part of a
broad service like Compuserve or America Online; others charge and
may bill their customers directly.

Third, there are "real" communities—groups of people who com- 11
municate among themselves. In real-estate terms, they're like bars or
restaurants or bathhouses. Each active participant contributes to a general conversation, generally through posted messages. Other participants may simply listen or watch. Some are supervised by a moderator;
others are more like bulletin boards—anyone is free to post anything.
Many of these services started out unmoderated but are now imposing
rules to keep out unwanted advertising, extraneous discussions or increasingly rude participants. Without a moderator, the decibel level often gets too high.

Ultimately, it's the rules that determine the success of such places. 12
Some of the rules are determined by the supplier of content; some of
the rules concern prices and membership fees. The rules may be simple:
"Only high-quality content about oil-industry liability and pollution
legislation: $120 an hour." Or: "This forum is unmoderated, and re-
stricted to information about copyright issues. People who insist on
posting advertising or unrelated material will be asked to desist (and
may eventually be barred)." Or: "Only children 8 to 12, on school-
related topics and only clean words. The moderator will decide what's
acceptable."

Cyberspace communities evolve just the way terrestrial communi- 13
ties do: People with like-minded interests band together. Every cyberspace community has its own character. Overall, the communities on
Compuserve tend to be more techy or professional; those on America
Online, affluent young singles; Prodigy, family oriented. Then there are
independents like Echo, a hip, downtown New York service, or Women's Wire, targeted to women who want to avoid the male culture
prevalent elsewhere on the Net. There's SurfWatch, a new program allowing access only to locations deemed suitable for children. On the
Internet itself, there are lots of passionate noncommercial discussion
groups on topics ranging from Hungarian politics (Hungary-Online) to
copyright law.

And yes, there are also porn-oriented services, where people share 14
dirty pictures and communicate with one another about all kinds of
practices, often anonymously. Whether these services encourage the
fantasies they depict is subject to debate—the same debate that has
raged about pornography in other media. But the point is that no one
is forcing this stuff on anybody.

What's unique about cyberspace is that it liberates us from the 15
tyranny of government, where everyone lives by the rule of the majority. In a democracy, minority groups and minority preferences tend to
get squeezed out, whether they are minorities of race and culture or minorities of individual taste. Cyberspace allows communities of any size
and kind to flourish; in cyberspace, communities are chosen by the

users, not forced on them by accidents of geography. This freedom gives the rules that preside in cyberspace a moral authority that rules in terrestrial environments don't have. Most people are stuck in the country of their birth, but if you don't like the rules of a cyberspace community, you can just sign off. Love it or leave it. Likewise, if parents don't like the rules of a given cyberspace community, they can restrict their children's access to it.

What's likely to happen in cyberspace is the formation of new communities, free of the constraints that cause conflict on earth. Instead of a global village, which is a nice dream but impossible to manage, we'll have invented another world of self-contained communities that cater to their own members' inclinations without interfering with anyone else's. The possibility of a real market-style evolution of governance is at hand. In cyberspace, we'll be able to test and evolve rules governing what needs to be governed—intellectual property, content and access control, rules about privacy and free speech. Some communities will allow anyone in; others will restrict access to members who qualify on one basis or another. Those communities that prove self-sustaining will prosper (and perhaps grow and split into subsets with ever-more-particular interests and identities). Those that can't survive—either because people lose interest or get scared off—will simply wither away.

In the near future, explorers in cyberspace will need to get better at defining and identifying their communities. They will need to put in place—and accept—their own local governments, just as the owners of expensive real estate often prefer to have their own security guards rather than call in the police. But they will rarely need help from any terrestrial government.

Of course, terrestrial governments may not agree. What to do, for instance, about pornography? The answer is labeling—not banning—questionable material. In order to avoid censorship and lower the political temperature, it makes sense for cyberspace participants themselves to agree on a scheme for questionable items, so that people or automatic filters can avoid them. In other words, posting pornography in "alt.sex.bestiality" would be O.K.; it's easy enough for software manufacturers to build an automatic filter that would prevent you—or your child—from ever seeing that item on a menu. (It's as if all the items were wrapped, with labels on the wrapper.) Someone who posted the same material under the title "Kid-Fun" could be sued for mislabeling.

Without a lot of fanfare, private enterprises and local groups are already producing a variety of labeling and ranking services, along with kid-oriented sites like Kidlink, EdWeb and Kids' Space. People differ in their tastes and values and can find services or reviewers on the Net that suit them in the same way they select books and magazines. Or they can wander freely if they prefer, making up their own itinerary.

In the end, our society needs to grow up. Growing up means un-   20
derstanding that there are no perfect answers, no all-purpose solutions, no government-sanctioned safe havens. We haven't created a perfect society on earth and we won't have one in cyberspace either. But at least we can have individual choice—and individual responsibility.

QUESTIONS ON MEANING

1. What are the two main reasons Dyson gives for saying that "regulation [of cyberspace] won't work"?
2. Is Dyson opposed to any kind of regulation, or just censorship? How do you know?
3. Why does Dyson reject censorship of cyberspace? What is her solution to "indecency and other 'troubling' speech" in cyberspace?
4. In your own words, state the THESIS of Dyson's essay.

QUESTIONS ON WRITING STRATEGY

1. Dyson frequently acknowledges that there is objectionable content on the Internet—in paragraphs 2, 4, 10, 14, and 18. Do these admissions undermine her ARGUMENT against censorship? Why, or why not?
2. What is the main similarity between cybercommunities and terrestrial (or earthbound) communities? What is the main difference? Why is this contrast important to Dyson's thesis?
3. Dyson introduces the traditional IMAGE of cyberspace as a frontier (para. 2), only to discard it in the next paragraph. Why does Dyson prefer the image of real estate for cyberspace?
4. **OTHER METHODS.** Dyson CLASSIFIES the sites available on the Internet and COMPARES each group to something familiar (paras. 9–15). What groups does she identify? What important attributes of cyberspace emerge from this comparison?

QUESTIONS ON LANGUAGE

1. How does Dyson's DEFINITION of *democracy* (para. 15) refine our usual sense of this term?
2. Dyson assumes that her AUDIENCE is familiar with the vocabulary of computers. Although she clearly defines *cyberspace*, she leaves other terms undefined. If any of the following are unfamiliar to you, find out what they mean in a book such as *The Internet for Dummies* or *Student's Guide to the Internet*: surfing (para. 2); virtual (4); e-mail (9); download, software (10); posted, bulletin boards (11); sign off (15).

3. Why does Dyson describe the many Internet sites available in terms of their "constituencies"? How do the CONNOTATIONS of that word help Dyson make her point about self-rule?

4. If you need help with the meanings of any of the following words, look them up in the dictionary: psyche (para. 1); exhilarating, pederasts (2); procure (4); unsavory (6); alluring (8); akin, consensual (9); extraneous, decibel (11); liability, forum, desist (12); terrestrial, prevalent (13); cater (16); itinerary (19); sanctioned, havens (20).

SUGGESTIONS FOR WRITING

1. **JOURNAL WRITING.** What is your personal experience of the Internet? What kind of role does it play in your life? How might censorship of the Internet affect you or the quality or quantity of the information you receive? **FROM JOURNAL TO ESSAY.** Do you agree with Dyson's argument that censorship of the Internet will cause more harm than good? Write a brief essay that explains why or why not, using your own experience as EVIDENCE. Or, if you are not an Internet user, write a brief essay that explains how you think censorship might affect your ability to become one.

2. Dyson says that "our society needs to grow up" (para. 20). What does she mean by this? In an essay, explain another problem or issue in our society that you think might be solved if we just "grew up." Be sure to spell out not just the details of the problem but also how "growing up" would help solve it.

3. **CRITICAL WRITING.** Dyson's solution to the problem of potentially offensive material in cyberspace is to advocate user responsibility and mandatory classification and labeling of sites. Are you convinced that her solution would work? Is it practical to implement? Write an essay in which you argue either for or against self-government as a solution to this Internet problem. Consider how responsible users could or would really be, who would make decisions about labeling, and how rule-breakers would be discovered and stopped.

4. **CONNECTIONS.** Dyson's view of the Internet's future is mostly optimistic, while Heidi Pollock, in "Welcome to Cyberbia" (p. 491), takes a much dimmer view. Write an essay that compares and contrasts these two authors' attitudes toward the Internet. What is the substance of each author's argument? What does each base her opinion on? Use evidence from both essays to support your comparison.

ESTHER DYSON ON WRITING

We asked Esther Dyson to tell us about her writing process. She responded by telling us how she wrote "Esther Dyson on Writing."

How did I write this essay? (And how do I write most things?) First of all, I *avoided* writing it for weeks, while I thought about it from time to time. "How do I write?" That's an easy topic: All I have to do is describe my actual experience—with a little overview of tactics, strategy, psychological motivation.

When I finally resolved to do it, I thought about it at length in the swimming pool—which is where I spend an hour thinking every day. Thinking in the pool is effective. When I'm actually writing, it's hard to think broadly; instead I move from sentence to sentence, detail to detail, nits of grammar and clever transitions. But in the pool, with no way to write things down (other than jumping out of the pool for a particularly felicitous phrase), I can think about structure, basic points, what I'm trying to accomplish with a particular piece of work.

It's easier to produce the words once I've got the broad idea.

Writing a 500-word essay, of course, is different from writing a 20,000-word newsletter or the ultimate challenge—a book. It's a question of scale, yes, but a newsletter is not simply 40 essays strung together, nor is a book just a series of essays. You have to construct any piece of writing as a coherent work, with sequence, cross-references, a flow of arguments, and a conclusion that draws everything together...ideally.

In fact, the writing often starts with paragraphs. Just get the thoughts out, and then you can organize them later. (I believe that word-processing has been a huge boon to writing—although it has probably encouraged a lot of redundant prose.) You can start work without starting The Work: You can begin in the middle, so that you don't face the fear of starting wrong. Often, I leave the beginning until the end; the process of writing helps me figure out what I was saying and how to present it. In the case of this essay, however, I began with the beginning, partly because it is so short. I wanted to write something clever, an example of itself.

Often, I've written so much material that by the time I actually "start," most of the writing is already done. The task is to organize all the material, provide the links, and often get rid of redundancies. One of the toughest parts of editing is when you've said the same thing twice, both times very elegantly, and have to decide which to sacrifice.

I faced this challenge once as a high-school student, when I was doing an assigned paper explaining the theory of relativity. I wrote it in the form of a two-person play, a cocktail-party conversation between a Sweet Young Thing and an elderly professor who was delighted to explain it to her over and over. Yes, it was an outrageous set of stereotypes. The young lady was a bit dim, so the professor got to explain things several times, each time with wit and elegance. I don't remember what grade I got, but I do remember I had a wonderful time writing it. (There—that was a colorful, embellishing anecdote.)

Now, how to end this? What did I really say? I always have the most trouble with endings...

FOR DISCUSSION

1. What is the advantage for Dyson of thinking about writing while she is swimming? How do you think best about a writing project—while occupied with something else or with pencil or keyboard at hand?
2. How do you get started on a writing project? Have you ever tried skipping the beginning and starting in the middle instead?

HEIDI POLLOCK

A self-described "cyberjunkie," HEIDI POLLOCK is a computer consultant and a writer on computing technology and trends. She attended
the University of California at Berkeley, graduating in 1991 with a
degree in religious studies and philosophy. She has worked as a systems administrator and content manager for businesses and is a senior
editor at *h2so4*, a magazine on political and cultural issues. As a journalist writing under both her real name and the pen name M. Kadi,
Pollock has published in many periodicals, including *h2so4*, the *Utne
Reader*, *Smug*, *bOING bOING*, *Might*, and *Temp Slave*. Her essays
have also appeared in nearly a dozen anthologies.

Welcome to Cyberbia

With her work and, she says, all her hobbies centering on computers,
Pollock is well positioned to probe the pluses and minuses of the latest technology. This essay first appeared in *h2so4* and then in a 1995
Utne Reader, and it has been updated for *The Bedford Reader*. In arguing against the Internet's promises of a "fabulous, wonderful, limitless
world of communication," Pollock takes quite a different view from
Esther Dyson's in the previous essay.

*Computer networking offers the soundest basis for world peace that has yet
been presented. Peace must be created on the bulwark of understanding.
International computer networks will knit together the peoples of the world
in bonds of mutual respect; its possibilities are vast, indeed.*
— *Scientific American*, June 1994

Computer bulletin board services offer up the glories of e-mail, the 1
thought provocation of newsgroups, the sharing of ideas implicit in
public posting, and the interaction of real-time chats. The fabulous,
wonderful, limitless world of communication is just waiting for you to
log on. Sure. Yeah. Right. What this whole delirious, interconnected,
global community of a world needs is a little reality check.

Let's face facts. The U.S. government by and large foots the bill for 2
the Internet, through maintaining the structural (hardware) backbone,
including, among other things, funding to major universities. As surely
as the Department of Defense started this whole thing, AT&T or Ted
Turner[1] is going to end up running it, so I don't think it's too unrealistic to take a look at the Net as it exists in its commercial form in order

---

[1] Ted Turner owned a conglomerate of media companies that is now part of Time
Warner, where he is an executive. — EDS.

to expose some of the realities lurking behind the regurgitated media rhetoric and the religious fanaticism of Net junkies.

Let's pretend that you have as much time and as much money to spend online as you damn well want. What do you actually do online? 3

Well, you download some cool shareware, you post technical questions in the computer user group forums, you check your stocks, you read the news and maybe some reviews. And, of course, since computer networks are supposed to make it easy to reach out and touch strangers who share a particular obsession or concern, you are also participating in the online forums, discussion groups, and conferences. 4

Let's review the structure of forums. For the purposes of this essay, we will examine the largest of the major user-friendly commercial services—America Online (AOL). There is no precise statistic available (at least none that the company will reveal—you have to do the research by HAND!!!) on exactly how many subject-specific discussion areas (folders) exist on America Online. Any online service is going to have zillions of posts—contributions from users—pertaining to computer usage (the computer games area of America Online, for example, breaks into 500 separate topics with over 100,000 individual posts), so let's look at a less popular area: the "Lifestyles and Interests" department. 5

For starters, as I write this, there are 57 initial categories within the Lifestyles and Interests area. One of these categories is Ham Radio. Ham Radio? How can there possibly be 5,909 separate, individual posts about Ham Radio? There are 5,865 postings in the Biking (and that's just bicycles, not motorcycles) category. Genealogy—22,525 posts. The Gay and Lesbian category is slightly more substantial—36,333 posts. There are five separate categories for political and issue discussion. The big catchall topic area, the Exchange, has over 100,000 posts. Servicewide, there are over a million posts. 6

You may want to join the online revolution, but obviously you can't wade through everything that's being discussed—you need to decide which topics interest you, which folders to browse. Within the Exchange alone (one of 57 subdivisions within one of another 50 higher divisions) there are 1,492 separate topic-specific folders—each containing a rough average of 50 posts, but many containing closer to 400. (Note: America Online automatically empties folders when their post totals reach 400, so total post numbers do not reflect the overall historical totals for a given topic. Sometimes the posting is so frequent that the "shelf life" of a given post is no more than four weeks.) 7

So, there you are, J. Individual, ready to start interacting with folks, sharing stories and communicating. You have narrowed yourself into a single folder, three tiers down in the America Online hierarchy, and now 8 you must choose between nearly 1,500 folders. Of course, once you choose a few of these folders, you will then have to read all the posts in order to catch up, be current, and not merely repeat a previous post.

A polite post is no more than two paragraphs long (a screenful of   9
text, which obviously has a number of intellectually negative implications). Let's say you choose 10 folders (out of 1,500). Each folder contains an average of 50 posts. Five hundred posts, at, say, one paragraph each, and you're now looking at the equivalent of a 200-page book.

Enough with the stats. Let me back up a minute and present you   10
with some very disturbing, but rational, assumptions. J. Individual wants to join the online revolution, to connect and communicate. But J. is not going to read all one million posts on AOL. (After all, J. has a second online service.) Exercising choice is J. Individual's God-given right as an American, and, by gosh, J. Individual is going to make some decisions. So J. is going to ignore all the support groups — after all, J. is a normal, well-adjusted person, and all of J.'s friends are normal, well-adjusted people; what does J. need to know about alcoholism or incest victims? J. Individual is white. So J. Individual is going to ignore all the multicultural folders. J. couldn't give a hoot about gender issues and does not want to discuss religion or philosophy. Ultimately, J. Individual does not engage in topics that do not interest J. Individual. So who is J. meeting? Why, people who are *just like* J.

J. Individual has now joined the electronic community. Surfed the   11
Net. Found some friends. *Tuned in, turned on, and geeked out.* Traveled the Information Highway and, just a few miles down that great democratic expressway, J. Individual has settled into an electronic suburb.

Are any of us so very different? It's my time and my money and I am   12
not going to waste any of it reading posts by disgruntled Robert-Bly drum-beating men's-movement boys who think that they should have some say over, for instance, whether or not I choose to carry a child to term simply because a condom broke. I know where I stand. I'm an adult. I know what's up and I am not going to waste my money arguing with a bunch of Neanderthals.

Oh yeah; I am so connected, so enlightened, so open to the oppos-   13
ing viewpoint. I'm out there, meeting all kinds of people from different economic backgrounds (who have about $20 a month to burn), from all religions (yeah, right, like anyone actually discusses religion anymore from a user standpoint), from all kinds of different ethnic backgrounds and with all kinds of sexual orientations (as if any of this ever comes up outside of the appropriate topic folder).

People are drawn to topics and folders that interest them and   14
therefore people will only meet people who are interested in the same topics in the same folders. Rarely does anyone venture into a random folder just to see what others (the Other?) are talking about.

Basically, with the sheer number of topics and individual posts, the   15
great Information Highway is not a place where you will enter an
"amazing web of new people, places, and ideas." One does not encounter people from "all walks of life" because there are too many people and too many folders. Diversity might be out there (and personally
I don't think it is), but the simple fact is that the average person will
not encounter it because with one brain, one job, one partner, one family, and one life, no one has the time!

Just in case these arguments based on time aren't completely con-   16
vincing, let me bring up a historical reference. Please take another look
at the opening quote of this essay, from *Scientific American*. It was featured in their "50 Years Ago Today" column. Where you read "computer networking," the quote originally contained the word *television*.
Amusing, isn't it?

QUESTIONS ON MEANING

1. What does "Cyberbia" in Pollock's title refer to? How does this word capture Pollock's main idea?
2. What is Pollock's THESIS? Where does she state it?
3. Why does Pollock say that the Internet community needs "a little reality
   check" (para. 1)?
4. What does Pollock mean to imply by mentioning the Department of Defense, AT&T, and Ted Turner in paragraph 2?

QUESTIONS ON WRITING STRATEGY

1. What is the TONE of this essay? Is it effective, do you think?
2. What is the PURPOSE of Pollock's detailed calculations of volume (paras.
   4–9)?
3. What does Pollock's last paragraph add to your understanding of her AR-
   GUMENT? What is her purpose in using and manipulating the quotation
   from *Scientific American*?
4. **OTHER METHODS.** Pollock offers a detailed PROCESS ANALYSIS as an EXAMPLE
   of how the Internet works to limit a user's experience of diversity. Is this
   example effective as support for Pollock's argument, or should she have
   provided more or different kinds of EVIDENCE? Explain your answer.

QUESTIONS ON LANGUAGE

1. Pollock accuses heavy Internet users of "religious fanaticism" (para. 2).
   Why does she use this phrase? What does it imply more generally about
   those who advocate the Internet?

2. What are the "intellectually negative implications" of writing and receiving only two paragraphs of text at once (para. 9)? Is Pollock being SARCASTIC?

3. Although Pollock defines *folders* and *posts*, she leaves a number of computer terms undefined. Refer to a book such as *The Internet for Dummies* or *Student's Guide to the Internet* for the meanings of any of these terms: bulletin board, e-mail, newsgroups, log on (para. 1); hardware (2); download, shareware, forums, discussion groups (4).

4. Make sure you know the meanings of the following words from earth-bound language: provocation, implicit, delirious (para. 1); regurgitated, rhetoric (2); genealogy (6); tiers, hierarchy (8); disgruntled, Neanderthals (12); venture (14).

SUGGESTIONS FOR WRITING

1. **JOURNAL WRITING.** What do you think of this essay? Consider its examples, tone, overall argument—whatever strikes you.
   FROM JOURNAL TO ESSAY. Expand and refine your gut reaction to Pollock's essay. Do you like it? Is your liking or not liking based more on Pollock's argument or on her tone? Write an ANALYSIS and EVALUATION of this essay that makes clear what the essay's main elements are and what you think of them.

2. Pollock mentions "the Other" in paragraph 14, using a term that, when capitalized, refers to those who are different from ourselves in socioeconomic class, race, religion, or other fundamental ways and are thus unknown to us. In a brief essay, explain how "the Other" figures in Pollock's essay, perhaps more significantly than its appearance in parentheses would otherwise imply.

3. **CRITICAL WRITING.** What's wrong with the suburbs? Pollock clearly considers them unpleasant, or worse, but do you? Are people really all the same in a suburb, as Pollock implies? And what's wrong with sameness, anyway? Why shouldn't people seek out and associate with others like themselves? What's so valuable about diversity? Consider these questions in evaluating Pollock's metaphor of "cyberbia." (See "Figures of speech" in Useful Terms for a definition of *metaphor*.)

4. **CONNECTIONS.** Esther Dyson, in "Cyberspace for All" (p. 483), and Pollock have similar but also widely dissimilar visions of cyberspace. Write an essay that COMPARES their visions. Consider who they think participates, what the responsibilities of the participants are, what the consequences are of being free to roam the Internet, what the limitations of the Internet are, and who does or should control the Internet.

WILLIAM F. BUCKLEY, JR.

Born in New York in 1925, WILLIAM FRANK BUCKLEY, JR., is one of the most articulate proponents of American conservatism. Shortly after his graduation from Yale, he published *God and Man at Yale* (1951), a memoir espousing conservative political values and traditional Christian principles. Since then, he has written more than twenty works on politics and government, published a syndicated newspaper column, and founded and edited *The National Review*, a magazine of conservative opinion. His most recent nonfiction book is *Nearer My God: An Autobiography of Faith* (1997), but he has also written several books on sailing and many novels. In 1991 Buckley was awarded the Presidential Medal of Freedom. With all his publications and honors, however, Buckley has probably been best known for *Firing Line*, his weekly television debate program that ran from 1966 to 1999. As the program's several million viewers learned, he is a man of wry charm. When he was half-seriously running for mayor of New York City in 1965, someone asked him what he would do if elected. "Demand a recount," he replied.

Why Don't We Complain?

Most people riding in an overheated commuter train would perspire quietly. For Buckley, this excess of warmth sparks an indignant essay, first published in *Esquire* in 1961, in which he takes to task both himself and his fellow Americans. Does the essay appeal mainly to reason or to emotion? And what would happen if everyone were to do as Buckley urges?

It was the very last coach and the only empty seat on the entire train, so there was no turning back. The problem was to breathe. Outside, the temperature was below freezing. Inside the railroad car the temperature must have been about 85 degrees. I took off my overcoat, and a few minutes later my jacket, and noticed that the car was flecked with the white shirts of the passengers. I soon found my hand moving to loosen my tie. From one end of the car to the other, as we rattled through Westchester County, we sweated; but we did not moan.

I watched the train conductor appear at the head of the car. "Tickets, all tickets, please!" In a more virile age, I thought, the passengers would seize the conductor and strap him down on a seat over the radiator to share the fate of his patrons. He shuffled down the aisle, picking up tickets, punching commutation cards. *No one addressed a word to him*. He approached my seat, and I drew a deep breath of resolution. "Conductor," I began with a considerable edge to my voice....In-

1

2

stantly the doleful eyes of my seatmate turned tiredly from his newspaper to fix me with a resentful stare: What question could be so important as to justify my sibilant intrusion into his stupor? I was shaken by those eyes. I am incapable of making a discreet fuss, so I mumbled a question about what time we were due in Stamford (I didn't even ask whether it would be before or after dehydration could be expected to set in), got my reply, and went back to my newspaper and to wiping my brow.

The conductor had nonchalantly walked down the gauntlet of   3
eighty sweating American freemen, and not one of them had asked him to explain why the passengers in that car had been consigned to suffer. There is nothing to be done when the temperature *outdoors* is 85 degrees, and indoors the air conditioner has broken down; obviously when that happens there is nothing to do, except perhaps curse the day that one was born. But when the temperature outdoors is below freezing, it takes a positive act of will on somebody's part to set the temperature *indoors* at 85. Somewhere a valve was turned too far, a furnace overstocked, a thermostat maladjusted: something that could easily be remedied by turning off the heat and allowing the great outdoors to come indoors. All this is so obvious. What is not obvious is what has happened to the American people.

It isn't just the commuters, whom we have come to visualize as a   4
supine breed who have got on to the trick of suspending their sensory faculties twice a day while they submit to the creeping dissolution of the railroad industry. It isn't just they who have given up trying to rectify irrational vexations. It is the American people everywhere.

A few weeks ago at a large movie theater I turned to my wife and   5
said, "The picture is out of focus." "Be quiet," she answered. I obeyed. But a few minutes later I raised the point again, with mounting impatience. "It will be all right in a minute," she said apprehensively. (She would rather lose her eyesight than be around when I make one of my infrequent scenes.) I waited. It was *just* out of focus—not glaringly out, but out. My vision is 20-20, and I assume that is the vision, adjusted, for most people in the movie house. So, after hectoring my wife throughout the first reel, I finally prevailed upon her to admit that it *was* off, and very annoying. We then settled down, coming to rest on the presumption that: a) someone connected with the management of the theater must soon notice the blur and make the correction; or b) that someone seated near the rear of the house would make the complaint in behalf of those of us up front; or c) that—any minute now—the entire house would explode into catcalls and foot stamping, calling dramatic attention to the irksome distortion.

What happened was nothing. The movie ended, as it had begun,   6
just out of focus, and as we trooped out, we stretched our faces in a variety of contortions to accustom the eye to the shock of normal focus.

I think it is safe to say that everybody suffered on that occasion.   7
And I think it is safe to assume that everyone was expecting someone
else to take the initiative in going back to speak to the manager. And
it is probably true even that if we had supposed the movie would run
right through the blurred image, someone surely would have summoned up the purposive indignation to get up out of his seat and file his
complaint.

But notice that no one did. And the reason no one did is because   8
we are all increasingly anxious in America to be unobtrusive, we are reluctant to make our voices heard, hesitant about claiming our rights;
we are afraid that our cause is unjust, or that if it is not unjust, that it is
ambiguous; or if not even that, that it is too trivial to justify the horrors
of a confrontation with Authority; we will sit in an oven or endure a
racking headache before undertaking a head-on, I'm-here-to-tell-you
complaint. That tendency to passive compliance, to a heedless endurance, is something to keep one's eyes on — in sharp focus.

I myself can occasionally summon the courage to complain, but I   9
cannot, as I have intimated, complain softly. My own instinct is so
strong to let the thing ride, to forget about it — to expect that someone
will take the matter up, when the grievance is collective, in my
behalf — that it is only when the provocation is at a very special key,
whose vibrations touch simultaneously a complexus of nerves, aller-
gies, and passions, that I catch fire and find the reserves of courage and
assertiveness to speak up. When that happens, I get quite carried away.
My blood gets hot, my brow wet, I become unbearably and unconscionably sarcastic and bellicose; I am girded for a total showdown.

Why should that be? Why could not I (or anyone else) on that rail-   10
road coach have said simply to the conductor, "Sir" — I take that back:
that sounds sarcastic — "Conductor, would you be good enough to turn
down the heat? I am extremely hot. In fact, I tend to get hot every time
the temperature reaches 85 degr — ." Strike that last sentence. Just end
it with the simple statement that you are extremely hot, and let the
conductor infer the cause.

Every New Year's Eve I resolve to do something about the Milque-   11
toast in me and vow to speak up, calmly, for my rights, and for the bet-
terment of our society, on every appropriate occasion. Entering last
New Year's Eve I was fortified in my resolve because that morning at
breakfast I had had to ask the waitress three times for a glass of milk.
She finally brought it — after I had finished my eggs, which is when I
don't want it anymore. I did not have the manliness to order her to take
the milk back, but settled instead for a cowardly sulk, and ostentatiously refused to drink the milk — though I later paid for it — rather
than state plainly to the hostess, as I should have, why I had not drunk
it, and would not pay for it.

So by the time the New Year ushered out the Old, riding in on my   12
morning's indignation and stimulated by the gastric juices of resolution
that flow so faithfully on New Year's Eve, I rendered my vow. Hence-
forward I would conquer my shyness, my despicable disposition to
supineness. I would speak out like a man against the unnecessary an-
noyances of our time.

Forty-eight hours later, I was standing in line at the ski repair store   13
in Pico Peak, Vermont. All I needed, to get on with my skiing, was the
loan, for one minute, of a small screwdriver, to tighten a loose binding.
Behind the counter in the workshop were two men. One was industri-
ously engaged in servicing the complicated requirements of a young
lady at the head of the line, and obviously he would be tied up for quite
a while. The other — "Jiggs," his workmate called him — was a middle-
aged man, who sat in a chair puffing a pipe, exchanging small talk with
his working partner. My pulse began its telltale acceleration. The minutes ticked on. I stared at the idle shopkeeper, hoping to shame him
into action, but he was impervious to my telepathic reproof and continued his small talk with his friend, brazenly insensitive to the nervous
demands of six good men who were raring to ski.

Suddenly my New Year's Eve resolution struck me. It was now or   14
never. I broke from my place in line and marched to the counter. I was
going to control myself. I dug my nails into my palms. My effort was
only partially successful.

"If you are not too busy," I said icily, "would you mind handing me   15
a screwdriver?"

Work stopped and everyone turned his eyes on me, and I experi-   16
enced that mortification I always feel when I am the center of centripetal shafts of curiosity, resentment, perplexity.

But the worst was yet to come. "I am sorry, sir," said Jiggs deferen-   17
tially, moving the pipe from his mouth. "I am not supposed to move. I
have just had a heart attack." That was the signal for a great whirring
noise that descended from heaven. We looked, stricken, out the window, and it appeared as though a cyclone had suddenly focused on the
snowy courtyard between the shop and the ski lift. Suddenly a gigantic
army helicopter materialized, and hovered down to a landing. Two men
jumped out of the plane carrying a stretcher, tore into the ski shop, and
lifted the shopkeeper onto the stretcher. Jiggs bade his companion
good-bye and was whisked out the door, into the plane, up to the heav-
ens, down — we learned — to a nearby army hospital. I looked up man-
fully — into a score of man-eating eyes. I put the experience down as a
reversal.

As I write this, on an airplane, I have run out of paper and need to   18
reach into my briefcase under my legs for more. I cannot do this until
my empty lunch tray is removed from my lap. I arrested the stewardess

as she passed empty-handed down the aisle on the way to the kitchen to fetch the lunch trays for the passengers up forward who haven't been served yet. "Would you please take my tray?" "Just a *moment*, sir!" she said, and marched on sternly. Shall I tell her that since she is headed for the kitchen *anyway*, it could not delay the feeding of the other passengers by more than two seconds necessary to stash away my empty tray? Or remind her that not fifteen minutes ago she spoke unctuously into the loudspeaker the words undoubtedly devised by the airline's highly paid public relations counselor: "If there is anything I or Miss French can do for you to make your trip more enjoyable, *please* let us—" I have run out of paper.

I think the observable reluctance of the majority of Americans to 19 assert themselves in minor matters is related to our increased sense of helplessness in an age of technology and centralized political and economic power. For generations, Americans who were too hot, or too cold, got up and did something about it. Now we call the plumber, or the electrician, or the furnace man. The habit of looking after our own needs obviously had something to do with the assertiveness that characterized the American family familiar to readers of American literature. With the technification of life goes our direct responsibility for our material environment, and we are conditioned to adopt a position of helplessness not only as regards the broken air conditioner, but as regards the overheated train. It takes an expert to fix the former, but not the latter; yet these distinctions, as we withdraw into helplessness, tend to fade away.

Our notorious political apathy is a related phenomenon. Every 20 year, whether the Republican or the Democratic Party is in office, more and more power drains away from the individual to feed vast reservoirs in far-off places; and we have less and less say about the shape of events which shape our future. From this alienation of personal power comes the sense of resignation with which we accept the political dispensations of a powerful government whose hold upon us continues to increase.

An editor of a national weekly news magazine told me a few years 21 ago that as few as a dozen letters of protest against an editorial stance of his magazine was enough to convene a plenipotentiary meeting of the board of editors to review policy. "So few people complain, or make their voices heard," he explained to me, "that we assume a dozen letters represent the inarticulate views of thousands of readers." In the past ten years, he said, the volume of mail has noticeably decreased, even though the circulation of his magazine has risen.

When our voices are finally mute, when we have finally suppressed 22 the natural instinct to complain, whether the vexation is trivial or grave, we shall have become automatons, incapable of feeling. When Premier Khrushchev[1] first came to this country late in 1959 he was primed, we are informed, to experience the bitter resentment of the American people against his tyranny, against his persecutions, against the movement which is responsible for the great number of American deaths in Korea, for billions in taxes every year, and for life everlasting on the brink of disaster; but Khrushchev was pleasantly surprised, and reported back to the Russian people that he had been met with overwhelming cordiality (read: apathy), except, to be sure, for "a few fascists who followed me around with their wretched posters, and should be horsewhipped."

I may be crazy, but I say there would have been lots more posters in   23
a society where train temperatures in the dead of winter are not allowed to climb to 85 degrees without complaint.

———————

QUESTIONS ON MEANING

1. How does Buckley account for his failure to complain to the train conductor? What reasons does he give for not taking action when he notices that the movie he is watching is out of focus?
2. Where does Buckley finally place the blame for the average American's reluctance to try to "rectify irrational vexations"?
3. By what means does the author bring his argument around to the subject of political apathy?
4. What THESIS does Buckley attempt to support? What is his PURPOSE?

QUESTIONS ON WRITING STRATEGY

1. In taking to task not only his fellow Americans but also himself, does Buckley strengthen or weaken his charge that, as a people, Americans do not complain enough?
2. Judging from the vocabulary displayed in this essay, would you say that Buckley is writing for a highly specialized AUDIENCE or an educated but nonspecialized general audience?
3. As a whole, is Buckley's essay an example of appeal to emotion or reasoned argument or both? Give EVIDENCE for your answer.
4. **OTHER METHODS.** Buckley includes as evidence four NARRATIVES of his personal experiences. What is the point of the narrative about Jiggs (paras. 13–17)?

[1]Nikita Khrushchev (1894–1971) was premier of the former Soviet Union from 1958 to 1964. —EDS.

QUESTIONS ON LANGUAGE

1. Define the following words: virile, doleful, sibilant (para. 2); supine (4); hectoring (5); unobtrusive, ambiguous (8); intimated, unconscionably, bellicose (9); ostentatiously (11); despicable (12); impervious (13); mortification, centripetal (16); deferentially (17); unctuously (18); notorious, dispensations (20); plenipotentiary, inarticulated (21); automatons (22).
2. What does Buckley's use of the capital A in *Authority* (para. 8) contribute to the sentence in which he uses it?
3. What is Buckley talking about when he alludes to "the Milquetoast in me" (para. 11)? (Notice how well the ALLUSION fits into the paragraph, with its emphasis on breakfast and a glass of milk.)

SUGGESTIONS FOR WRITING

1. **JOURNAL WRITING.** One reason we don't complain, Buckley says, is that we expect someone else to. Do you ever "take the initiative" (para. 7) to complain about big or little hassles, or do you, too, sit in silent annoyance? Why?
   FROM JOURNAL TO ESSAY. Write an essay about one moment when you either spoke up against an annoyance or didn't complain when you should have. Narrate this incident, also using the information from your journal entry to help explain why you did or did not act.
2. Think of some disturbing incident you have witnessed, or some annoying treatment you have received in a store or other public place, and write a letter of complaint to whomever you believe responsible. Be specific in your evidence, be temperate in your language, make clear what you would like to come of your complaint (your proposal), and be sure to put your letter in the mail.
3. **CRITICAL WRITING.** Write a paper in which you ANALYZE and EVALUATE any one of Buckley's ideas. For instance: Do we feel as helpless as Buckley says (para. 19)? Are we politically apathetic, and if so should the government be blamed (para. 20)? For that matter, do we not complain? Support your view with evidence from your experience, observation, or reading.
4. **CONNECTIONS.** Both Buckley and Barbara Huttmann, in "A Crime of Compassion" (p. 76), make a strong ETHICAL APPEAL (see pp. 456–57), going out of their way to convince readers of their goodwill, reasonableness, and authority. Write an essay in which you analyze the ethical appeal of both authors, using quotations and PARAPHRASES from both essays to support your analysis.

WILLIAM F. BUCKLEY, JR., ON WRITING

In the autobiographical *Overdrive*, Buckley recalls a conversation with a friend and fellow columnist: "George Will once told me how deeply he loves to write. 'I wake in the morning,' he explained to me, 'and I ask myself: Is this one of the days I have to write a column? And if the answer is yes, I rise a happy man.' I, on the other hand, wake neither particularly happy nor unhappy, but to the extent that my mood is affected by the question whether I need to write a column that morning, the impact of Monday-Wednesday-Friday"—the days when he must write a newspaper column—"is definitely negative. Because I do not like to write, for the simple reason that writing is extremely hard work, and I do not 'like' extremely hard work."

Still, in the course of a "typical year," Buckley estimates that he produces not only 150 newspaper columns, but also a dozen longer articles, eight or ten speeches, fifty introductions for his television program, various editorial pieces for the magazine he edits, *The National Review*, and a book or two. "Why do I do so much?... It is easier to stay up late working for hours than to take one tenth the time to inquire into the question whether the work is worth performing."

In the introduction to another book, *A Hymnal: The Controversial Arts*, Buckley states an attitude toward writing that most other writers would not share. "I have discovered, in sixteen years of writing columns," he declares, "that there is no observable difference in the quality of that which is written at very great speed (twenty minutes, say), and that which takes three or four times as long.... Pieces that take longer to write sometimes, on revisiting them, move along grumpily."

FOR DISCUSSION

1. Given that he so dislikes writing, why does Buckley do it?
2. Buckley's attitude toward giving time to writing is unusual. What is the more usual view of writing?

CHITRA DIVAKARUNI

Born in 1956 in Calcutta, India, CHITRA BANERJEE DIVAKARUNI spent nineteen years in her homeland before immigrating to the United States. She holds an M.A. from Wright State University and a Ph.D. from the University of California at Berkeley. Her books, often addressing the immigrant experience in America, include the novels *The Mistress of Spice* (1997) and *Sister of My Heart* (1999), the collection of stories *Arranged Marriage* (1995), and the collection of poems *Leaving Yuba City* (1997). A teacher of creative writing at Foothill College in California, Divakaruni has received a number of awards for her work, including the Before Columbus Foundation's 1996 American Book Award. Since 1991, Divakaruni has been the president of MAITRI, a San Francisco–based, nonprofit organization that helps South Asian victims of domestic abuse.

Live Free and Starve

Some of the consumer goods sold in the United States—shoes, clothing, toys, rugs—are made in countries whose labor practices do not meet U.S. standards for safety and fairness. As these practices have gained wide publicity in recent years, Americans have been horrified at tales of children put to work by force or under contracts (called *indentures*) with the children's parents. Shouldn't the United States use its power to stop such practices? In this essay, Divakaruni argues that efforts to do so, though certainly well intentioned, are nonetheless misguided. The essay first appeared in the online magazine *Salon* in October 1997.

Some days back, the House passed a bill that stated that the United States would no longer permit the import of goods from factories where forced or indentured child labor was used.[1] My liberal friends applauded the bill. It was a triumphant advance in the field of human rights. Now children in Third World countries wouldn't have to spend their days chained to their posts in factories manufacturing goods for other people to enjoy while their childhoods slipped by them. They could be free and happy, like American children.

I am not so sure.

It is true that child labor is a terrible thing, especially for those children who are sold to employers by their parents at the age of five or six

---

[1]At the time *The Bedford Reader* was published, the House bill Divakaruni refers to had not made it out of Congress. Similar bills were still under consideration by committees of the House and the Senate. —EDS.

and have no way to protect themselves from abuse. In many cases it will be decades—perhaps a lifetime, due to the fines heaped upon them whenever they make mistakes—before they can buy back their freedom. Meanwhile these children, mostly employed by rug-makers, spend their days in dark, ill-ventilated rooms doing work that damages their eyes and lungs. They aren't even allowed to stand up and stretch. Each time they go to the bathroom, they suffer a pay cut.

But is this bill, which, if it passes the Senate and is signed by President Clinton, will lead to the unemployment of almost a million children, the answer? If the children themselves were asked whether they would rather work under such harsh conditions or enjoy a leisure that comes without the benefit of food or clothing or shelter, I wonder what their response would be. 4

It is easy for us in America to make the error of evaluating situations in the rest of the world as though they were happening in this country and propose solutions that make excellent sense—in the context of our society. Even we immigrants, who should know better, have wiped from our minds the memory of what it is to live under the kind of desperate conditions that force a parent to sell his or her child. Looking down from the heights of Maslow's pyramid,[2] it seems inconceivable to us that someone could actually prefer bread to freedom. 5

When I was growing up in Calcutta, there was a boy who used to work in our house. His name was Nimai, and when he came to us, he must have been about ten or so, just a little older than my brother and I. He'd been brought to our home by his uncle, who lived in our ancestral village and was a field laborer for my grandfather. The uncle explained to my mother that Nimai's parents were too poor to feed their several children, and while his older brothers were already working in the fields and earning their keep, Nimai was too frail to do so. My mother was reluctant to take on a sickly child who might prove more of a burden than a help, but finally she agreed, and Nimai lived and worked in our home for six or seven years. My mother was a good employer—Nimai ate the same food that we children did and was given new clothes during Indian New Year, just as we were. In the time between his chores—dusting and sweeping and pumping water from the tube-well and running to the market—my mother encouraged him to learn to read and write. Still, I would not disagree with anyone who says that it was hardly a desirable existence for a child. 6

But what would life have been like for Nimai if an anti–child-labor law had prohibited my mother from hiring him? Every year, when we 7

[2]The psychologist Abraham Maslow (1908–70) proposed a "hierarchy of needs" in the shape of a five-level pyramid with survival needs at the bottom and "self-actualization" and "self-transcendence" at the top. According to Maslow, one must satisfy the needs at each level before moving up to the next. —Eds.

went to visit our grandfather in the village, we were struck by the many children we saw by the mud roads, their ribs sticking out through the rags they wore. They trailed after us, begging for a few paise.[3] When the hunger was too much to bear, they stole into the neighbors' fields and ate whatever they could find—raw potatoes, cauliflower, green sugar cane and corn torn from the stalk—even though they knew they'd be beaten for it. Whenever Nimai passed these children, he always walked a little taller. And when he handed the bulk of his earnings over to his father, there was a certain pride in his eye. Exploitation, you might be thinking. But he thought he was a responsible member of his family.

A bill like the one we've just passed is of no use unless it goes hand in hand with programs that will offer a new life to these newly released children. But where are the schools in which they are to be educated? Where is the money to buy them food and clothing and medication, so that they don't return home to become the extra weight that capsizes the already shaky raft of their family's finances? Their own governments, mired in countless other problems, seem incapable of bringing these services to them. Are we in America who, with one blithe stroke of our congressional pen, rendered these children jobless, willing to shoulder that burden? And when many of these children turn to the streets, to survival through thievery and violence and begging and prostitution—as surely in the absence of other options they must— are we willing to shoulder that responsibility?

8

QUESTIONS ON MEANING

1. What do you take to be Divakaruni's PURPOSE in this essay? At what point did it become clear?
2. What are "Third World countries" (para. 1)?
3. From the further information given in the footnote on page 505, what does it mean to be "[l]ooking down from the heights of Maslow's pyramid" (para. 5)? What point is Divakaruni making here?
4. In paragraph 8, Divakaruni suggests some of the reasons that children in other countries may be forced or sold into labor. What are they?

QUESTIONS ON WRITING STRATEGY

1. Where in her argument does Divakaruni specifically acknowledge her audience's likely views?

---

[3]*Paise* are the smallest unit of Indian currency, worth a fraction of an American penny. —EDS.

2. What is the EFFECT of Divakaruni's final paragraph? Does it strengthen her argument? Why, or why not?

3. **OTHER METHODS.** What does the extended EXAMPLE of Nimai (paras. 6–7) contribute to Divakaruni's argument? What, if anything, does it add to Divakaruni's authority? What does it tell us about child labor abroad?

QUESTIONS ON LANGUAGE

1. Divakaruni says that laboring children could otherwise be "the extra weight that capsizes the already shaky raft of their family's finances" (para. 8). How does this metaphor capture the problem of children in poor families? (See "Figures of speech" in Useful Terms for a definition of *metaphor*.)

2. What do the words in paragraph 7 tell you about Divakaruni's attitude toward the village children? Is it disdain? pity? compassion? horror?

3. Consult a dictionary if you need help in defining the following: indentured (para. 1); inconceivable (5); exploitation (7); mired, blithe (8).

SUGGESTIONS FOR WRITING

1. **JOURNAL WRITING.** Write a response to Divakaruni's argument against legislation that would ban goods produced by forced or indentured child laborers. Do you basically agree or disagree with the author? Why?

   FROM JOURNAL TO ESSAY. As this book went to press, the kind of legislation Divakaruni takes issue with was still pending in both the House and the Senate of the U.S. Congress. Starting from your journal entry, write a letter to your representative or one of your senators taking a position for or against such legislation. You can use quotations from Divakaruni's essay if they serve your purpose, but the letter should center on your own views of the issue. When you've finished your letter, send it. (You can find your representative's and your senators' names and addresses on the Web at *http://www.fedgate.org*.)

2. When, if ever, do you think child labor can be justified? Like most people, you probably believe that forced or indentured child labor is unacceptable for any reason, but what about other situations—for instance, children working in their family's business? What kind of paid work, for how many hours a week, is appropriate for, say, a ten- or twelve-year-old child? Where do you draw the line between occasional babysitting or lawn mowing and full-time factory work?

3. **CRITICAL WRITING.** Divakaruni's argument depends significantly on appeals to readers' emotions (see p. 456). Locate one emotional appeal that either helps to convince you of the author's point or, in your mind, weakens the argument. What does the appeal ASSUME about the reader's (your) feelings or values? Why are the assumptions correct or incorrect in your case? How, specifically, does the appeal strengthen or undermine Divakaruni's argument?

4. **CONNECTIONS.** Chitra Divakaruni in this essay and Michael Kroll in "The Unquiet Death of Robert Harris" (p. 476) both project something of themselves in their arguments—in other words, both make ethical appeals (see pp. 456–57). In an essay, COMPARE AND CONTRAST the ethical appeals of

these two writers. What can we INFER about each one? Which ethical appeal is the stronger in your view, and why? Cite specific passages from
each essay to support your comparison.

CHITRA DIVAKARUNI ON WRITING

Chitra Divakaruni is both a writer and a community worker, reaching
out to refugees and other disadvantaged people through organizations
such as MAITRI, which she helped found. In a 1998 interview in *Atlantic Unbound* (the online version of *The Atlantic Monthly*), Katie
Bolick asked Divakaruni how her activism and writing affected one
another. Here is Divakaruni's response.

Being helpful where I can has always been an important value for
me. I did community work in India, and I continue to do it in America,
because being involved in my community is something I feel I need to
do. Activism has given me enormous satisfaction—not just as a person, but also as a writer. The lives of people I would have only known
from the outside, or had stereotyped notions of, have been opened up
to me. My hotline work with MAITRI has certainly influenced both
my life and my writing immensely. Overall, I have a great deal of sensitivity that I did not have before, and a lot of my preconceptions have
changed. I hope that translates into my writing and reaches my readers.

FOR DISCUSSION

1. What evidence does "Live Free and Starve" give to support Divakaruni's
    statement about how her activist work has affected her writing?
2. What does Divakaruni mean when she speaks of lives that she "would
    have only known from the outside"? Of what use is "insider's" knowledge
    to an activist? to a writer?
3. Do you have a project or activity—comparable to Divakaruni's activism—
    that you believe positively affects your writing? What is it? How does it
    help you as you write?

CURTIS CHANG

A 1990 graduate of Harvard University, CURTIS CHANG majored in government. He was born in Taiwan and immigrated to the United States in 1971 with his family. He attended public school near Chicago. At Harvard, Chang helped found the Minority Student Alliance, belonged to the debating society, wrote for the *Harvard Political Review*, and was a leader of the Harvard-Radcliffe Christian Fellowship. Winner of the Michael C. Rockefeller Fellowship for Travel Abroad, Chang spent 1992 in Soweto, South Africa. He was a teaching fellow in Harvard's government department and is now area director with the Intervarsity Christian Fellowship of Boston. Chang's book, *Taking Every Thought Captive: A Postmodern Correspondence with Augustine and Aquinas*, is due to be published in 2000.

Streets of Gold:
The Myth of the Model Minority

This essay, like Brad Manning's (p. 100) and Linnea Saukko's (p. 228), won a Bedford Prize in Student Writing and was published in *Student Writers at Work*. Written when Chang was a freshman at Harvard, the essay grew out of his friendships with African American students, his increasing interest in issues of racial identity, and his realization that Asian Americans had at best an ambiguous position in American society. "Streets of Gold" states and supports an opinion forcefully and, we think, convincingly. And it has something else to recommend it as well: It provides a model of research writing and documentation. The documentation style is that of the Modern Language Association, explained on pages 672–82.

Over one hundred years ago, an American myth misled many of   1
my ancestors. Seeking cheap labor, railroad companies convinced numerous Chinese that American streets were paved with gold. Today, the media portray Asian-Americans as finally mining those golden streets. Major publications like *Time, Newsweek, U.S. News & World Report, Fortune, The New Republic*, the *Wall Street Journal*, and the *New York Times Magazine* have all recently published congratulatory "Model Minority" headline stories with such titles as

America's Super Minority
An American Success Story
A "Model Minority"
Why They Succeed
The Ultimate Assimilation
The Triumph of Asian-Americans.

But the Model Minority is another "Streets of Gold" tale. It distorts 2
Asian-Americans' true status and ignores our racial handicaps. And
the Model Minority's ideology is even worse than its mythology. It attempts to justify the existing system of racial inequality by blaming the
victims rather than the system itself.

The Model Minority myth introduces us as an ethnic minority that 3
is finally "making it in America," as stated in *Time* (Doerner 42). The
media consistently define "making it" as achieving material wealth,
wealth that flows from our successes in the workplace and the schoolroom. This economic achievement allegedly proves a minority can, as
Fortune says, "lay claim to the American dream" (Ramirez 149).

Trying to show how "Asian-Americans present a picture of afflu- 4
ence and economic success," as the *New York Times Magazine* puts it
(Oxnam 72), nine out of ten of the major Model Minority stories of the
last four years relied heavily on one statistic: the family median income. The median Asian-American family income, according to the
U.S. Census Survey of Income and Education data, is $22,713 com-
pared to $20,800 for white Americans. Armed with that figure, na-
tional magazines such as *Newsweek* have trumpeted our "remarkable,
ever-mounting achievements" (Kasindorf et al. 51).

Such assertions demonstrate the truth of the aphorism "Statistics 5
are like a bikini. What they reveal is suggestive, but what they conceal
is vital." The family median income statistic conceals the fact that
Asian-American families generally (1) have more children and live-in
relatives and thus have more mouths to feed; (2) are often forced by necessity to have everyone in the family work, averaging *more* than two
family income earners (whites only have 1.6) (Cabezas 402); and (3)
live disproportionately in high cost of living areas (i.e., New York,
Chicago, Los Angeles, and Honolulu) which artificially inflate income
figures. Dr. Robert S. Mariano, professor of economics at the University
of Pennsylvania, has calculated that

> when such appropriate adjustments and comparisons are made, a dif-
> ferent and rather disturbing picture emerges, showing indeed a
> clearly disadvantaged group.... Filipino and Chinese men *are no bet-
> ter off than black men with regard to median incomes.* (55)[1]

Along with other racial minorities, Asian-Americans are still scraping
for the crumbs of the economic pie.

Throughout their distortion of our status, the media propagate two 6
crucial assumptions. First, they lump all Asian-Americans into one

---

[1] The picture becomes even more disturbing when one realizes the higher income
figures do not necessarily equal higher quality of life. For instance, in New York Chi-
natown, more than 1 out of 5 work more than 57 hours per week, almost 1 out of 10 elderly must labor more than 55 hours per week (Nishi 503).

monolithic, homogeneous, yellow-skinned mass. Such a view ignores the existence of an incredibly disadvantaged Asian-American underclass. Asians work in low-income and low-status jobs two to three times more than whites (Cabezas 438). Recent Vietnamese refugees in California are living like the Appalachian poor. While going to his Manhattan office, multimillionaire architect I. M. Pei's car passes Chinese restaurants and laundries where 72% of all New York Chinese men still work (U.S. Bureau of the Census qtd. in Cabezas 443).

But the media make an even more dangerous assumption. They   7
suggest that (alleged) material success is the same thing as basic racial equality. Citing that venerable family median income figure, magazines claim Asian-Americans are "obviously nondisadvantaged folks," as stated in *Fortune* (Seligman 64). Yet a 1979 United States Equal Employment Opportunity Commission study on Asian-Americans discovered widespread anti-Asian hiring and promotion practices. Asian-Americans "in the professional, technical, and managerial occupations" often face "modern racism—the subtle, sophisticated, systemic patterns and practices...which function to effect and to obscure the discriminatory outcomes" (Nishi 398). One myth simply does not prove another: Neither our "astonishing economic prosperity" (Ramirez 152) nor a racially equal America exist.

An emphasis on material success also pervades the media's stress on   8
Asian-Americans' educational status at "the top of the class" ("Asian Americans" 4). Our "march into the ranks of the educational elite," as *U.S. News & World Report* puts it (McBee et al. 41), is significant, according to *Fortune*, because "all that education is paying off spectacularly" (Ramirez 149). Once again, the same fallacious assumptions plague this "whiz kids" image of Asian-Americans.

The media again ignore the fact that class division accounts for   9
much of the publicized success. Until 1976, the U.S. Immigration Department only admitted Asian immigrants that were termed "skilled" workers. "Skilled" generally meant college educated, usually in the sciences since poor English would not be a handicap. The result was that the vast majority of pre-1976 Asian immigrants came from already well-educated, upper-class backgrounds—the classic "brain drain" syndrome (Hirschman and Wong 507–10).

The post-1976 immigrants, however, come generally from the   10
lower, less educated classes (Kim 24). A study by Professor Elizabeth Ahn Toupin of Tufts University matched similar Asian and non-Asian students *along class lines* and found that Asian-Americans "did not perform at a superior academic level to non-Asian students. Asian-Americans were more likely to be placed on academic probation than their white counterparts.... Twice as many Asian-American students withdrew from the university" (12).

Thus, it is doubtful whether the perceived widespread educational   11
success will continue as the Asian-American population eventually bal-
ances out along class lines. When 16.2% of all Chinese have less than
four years of schooling (*four times* the percentage of whites) (Azores 73),
it seems many future Asian-Americans will worry more about being able
to read a newspaper rather than a Harvard acceptance letter.

Most important, the media assume once again that achieving a cer-   12
tain level of material or educational success means achieving real
equality. People easily forget that to begin with, Asians invest heavily
in education since other means of upward mobility are barred to them
by race. Until recently, for instance, Asian-Americans were barred
from unions and traditional lines of credit (Yun 23–24).[2] Other "white"
avenues to success, such as the "old-boy network," are still closed to
Asian-Americans.

When *Time* claims "as a result of their academic achievement   13
Asians are climbing the economic ladder with remarkable speed," it
glosses over an inescapable fact: There is a white ladder and then there
is a yellow one. Almost all of the academic studies on the *actual returns
Asians receive* from their education point to prevalent discrimination.
A striking example of this was found in a City University of New York
research project which constructed résumés with equivalent educational backgrounds. Applications were then sent to employers, one
group under an Asian name and a similar group under a Caucasian
name. Whites received interviews five times more than Asians (Nishi
399). The media never headline even more shocking data that can be
easily found in the U.S. Census. For instance, Chinese and Filipino
males only earned respectively 74% and 52% as much as their *equally
educated* white counterparts. Asian females fared even worse. Their
salaries were only 44% to 54% as large as equivalent white males' paychecks (Cabezas 391). Blacks suffer from this same statistical disparity.
We Asian-Americans are indeed a Model Minority—a perfect model
of racial discrimination in America.

Yet this media myth encourages neglect of our pressing needs.   14
"Clearly, many Asian-Americans and Pacific peoples are invisible to
the governmental agencies," reported the California State Advisory
Committee to the U.S. Commission on Civil Rights. "Discrimination
against Asian-Americans and Pacific peoples is as much the result of
omission as commission" (qtd. in Chun 7). In 1979, while the president praised Asian-Americans' "successful integration into American
society," his administration revoked Asian-Americans' eligibility for

---

[2] For further analysis on the role racism plays in Asian-Americans' stress on education and certain technical and scientific fields, see Suzuki (44).

minority small business loans, devastating thousands of struggling, newly arrived small businessmen. Hosts of other minority issues, ranging from reparations for the Japanese-American internment to the ominous rise of anti-Asian violence, are widely ignored by the general public.

The media, in fact, insist to the general populace that we are not a true racial minority. In an attack on affirmative action, the *Boston Globe* pointed out that universities, like many people, "obviously feel that Asian-Americans, especially those of Chinese and Japanese descent, are brilliant, privileged, and wrongly classified as minorities" ("Affirmative Non-actions" 10). Harvard Dean Henry Rosovsky remarked in the same article that "It does not seem to me that as a group, they are disadvantaged.... Asian-Americans appear to be in an odd category among other protected minorities." [15]

The image that we Asians aren't like "other minorities" is fundamental to the Model Minority ideology. Any elementary-school student knows that the teacher designates one student the model, the "teacher's pet," in order to set an example for others to follow. One only sets up a "model minority" in order to communicate to the other "students," the blacks and Hispanics, "Why can't you be like that?" The media, in fact, almost admit to "grading" minorities as they headline Model Minority stories "Asian-Americans: Are They Making the Grade?" (McBee et al.). And Asians have earned the highest grade by fulfilling one important assignment: identifying with the white majority, with its values and wishes. [16]

Unlike blacks, for instance, we Asian-Americans have not vigorously asserted our ethnic identity (a.k.a. Black Power). And the American public has historically demanded assimilation over racial pluralism.[3] Over the years, *Newsweek* has published titles from "Success Story: Outwhiting the Whites" to "The Ultimate Assimilation," which lauded the increasing number of Asian-white marriages as evidence of Asian-Americans' "acceptance into American society" (Kantrowitz et al. 80). [17]

Even more significant is the public's approval of how we have succeeded in the "American tradition" (Ramirez 164). Unlike the blacks and Hispanics, we "Puritan-like" Asians (Oxnam 72) disdain governmental assistance. A *New Republic* piece, "The Triumph of Asian-Americans," similarly applauded how "Asian-Americans pose no [18]

---

[3] A full discussion of racial pluralism versus assimilation is impossible here. But suffice it to say that pluralism accepts ethnic cultures as equally different; assimilation asks for a "melting" into the majority. An example of the assimilation philosophy is the massive "Americanization" programs of the late 1880s, which successfully erased Eastern European immigrants' customs in favor of Anglo-Saxon ones.

problems at all" (Bell 30). The media consistently compare the crime-ridden image of other minorities with the picture of law-abiding Asian parents whose "well-behaved kids" hit books and not the streets ("Asian Americans" 4).

Some insist there is nothing terrible about whites conjuring up our   19
"tremendous" success, divining from it model American traits, then preaching, "Why can't you blacks and Hispanics be like that?" After all, one might argue, aren't those traits desirable?

Such a view, as mentioned, neglects Asian-Americans' true and   20
pressing needs. Moreover, this view completely misses the Model Minority image's fundamental ideology, an ideology meant to falsely grant America absolution from its racial barriers.

David O. Sears and Donald R. Kinder, two social scientists, have   21
recently published significant empirical studies on the underpinnings of American racial attitudes. They consistently discovered that Americans' stress on "values, such as 'individualism and self-reliance, the work ethic, obedience, and discipline'... can be invoked, however perversely, to feed racist appetites" (qtd. in Kennedy 88). In other words, the Model Minority image lets Americans' consciences rest easy. They can think: "It's not our fault those blacks and Hispanics can't make it. They're just too lazy. After all, look at the Asians."[4] Consequently, American society never confronts the systemic racial and economic factors underlying such inequality. The victims instead bear the blame.

This ideology behind the Model Minority image is best seen when   22
we examine one of the first Model Minority stories, which suddenly appeared in the mid-1960s. It is important to note that the period was marked by newfound, strident black demands for equality and power.

> At a time when it is being proposed that hundreds of billions be spent to uplift Negroes and other minorities, the nation's 300,000 Chinese-Americans are moving ahead on their own—with no help from anyone else....Few Chinese-Americans are getting welfare handouts—or even want them....They don't sit around moaning. ("Success Story of One Minority Group" 73)

The same article then concludes that the Chinese-American history and accomplishment "would shock those now complaining about the hardships endured by today's Negroes."

---

[4]This phenomenon of blaming the victim for racial inequality is as old as America itself. For instance, southerners once eased their consciences over slavery by labeling blacks as animals lacking humanity. Today, America does it by labeling them as inferior people lacking "desirable" traits. For an excellent further analysis of this ideology, actually widespread among American intellectuals, see *Iron Cages: Race and Culture in 19th-Century America* by Ronald T. Takaki.

Not surprisingly, the dunce-capped blacks and Hispanics resent us   23
apple-polishing, "well-behaved" teacher's pets. Black comedian Richard
Pryor performs a revealing routine in which new Asian immigrants learn
from whites their first English word: "Nigger." And Asian-Americans
themselves succumb to the Model Minority's deceptive mythology and
racist ideology.[5] "I made it without help," one often hears among Asian
circles; "why can't they?" In a 1986 nationwide poll, only 27% of Asian-
American students rated "racial understanding" as "essential." The figure
plunged 9% in the last year alone (a year marked by a torrent of Model
Minority stories) (Hune). We "whitewashed" Asians have simply lost
our identity as a fellow, disadvantaged minority.

But we don't even need to look beyond the Model Minority stories   24
themselves to realize that whites see us as "whiter" than blacks—but not
quite white enough. For instance, citing that familiar median family income figure, *Fortune* magazine of 17 May 1982 complained that the
Asian-American community is in fact "getting *more* than its share of the
pie" (Seligman 64). For decades, when white Americans were leading
the nation in every single economic measure, editorials arguing that
whites were getting more than *their* share of the pie were rather rare.

No matter how "well-behaved" we are, Asian-Americans are still   25
excluded from the real pie, the "positions of institutional power and
political power" (Kuo 289). Professor Harry Kitano of UCLA has written extensively on the plight of Asian-Americans as the "middle-man
minority," a minority supposedly satisfied materially but forever racially
barred from a true, *significant* role in society. Empirical studies indicate
that Asian-Americans "have been channeled into lower-echelon
white-collar jobs having little or no decision making authority"
(Suzuki 38). For example, in *Fortune's* 1,000 largest companies, Asian-
American nameplates rest on a mere half of one percent of all officers'
and directors' desks (a statistical disparity worsened by the fact that
most of the Asians founded their companies) (Ramirez 152). While the
education of the upper-class Asians may save them from the bread
lines, their race still keeps them from the boardroom.

Our docile acceptance of such exclusion is actually one of our   26
"model" traits. When Asian-Americans in San Francisco showed their
first hint of political activism and protested Asian exclusion from city
boards, the *Washington Monthly* warned in a long Asian-American article, "Watch out, here comes another group to pander to" ("The

[5] America has a long history of playing off one minority against the other. During the
early 1900s, for instance, mining companies in the west often hired Asians solely as scabs
against striking black miners. Black versus Asian hostility and violence usually followed.
This pattern was repeated in numerous industries. In a larger historical sense, almost every
immigrant group has assimilated, to some degree, the culture of antiblack racism.

Wrong Way" 21). *The New Republic* praised Asian-American political movements because

> Unlike blacks or Hispanics, Asian-American politicians have the luxury of not having to devote the bulk of their time to an "Asian-American agenda," and thus escape becoming prisoners of such an agenda.... The most important thing for Asian-Americans... is simply "being part of the process." (Bell 31)

This is strikingly reminiscent of another of the first Model Minor- 27
ity stories:

> As the Black and Brown communities push for changes in the present system, the Oriental is set forth as an example to be followed—a minority group that has achieved success through adaptation rather than confrontation. (*Gidra* qtd. in Chun 7)

But it is precisely this "present system," this system of subtle, persis- 28
tent racism that we all must confront, not adapt to. For example, we Asians gained our right to vote from the 1964 Civil Rights Act that blacks marched, bled, died, and, in the words of that original Model Minority story, "sat around moaning for." Unless we assert our true identity as a minority and challenge racial misconceptions and inequalities, we will be nothing more than techno-coolies—collecting our wages but silently enduring basic political and economic inequality.

This country perpetuated a myth once. Today, no one can afford to 29
dreamily chase after that gold in the streets, oblivious to the genuine treasure of racial equality. When racism persists, can one really call any minority a "model"?

Works Cited

"Affirmative Non-actions." Op-ed. *Boston Globe* 14 Jan. 1985: 10.

"Asian Americans, The Drive to Excel." *Newsweek on Campus* April 1984: 4–13.

Asian American Studies: Contemporary Issues. Proc. from East Coast Asian American Scholars Conf. 1986.

Azores, Fortunata M. "Census Methodology and the Development of Social Indicators for Asian and Pacific Americans." United States Commission on Civil Rights 70–79.

Bell, David A. "The Triumph of Asian-Americans." *New Republic* 15 & 22 July 1985: 24–31.

Cabezas, Armado. "Employment Issues of Asian Americans." United States Commission on Civil Rights.

Chun, Ki-Taek. "The Myth of Asian American Success and Its Educational Ramifications." *IRCD Bulletin* Winter/Spring 1980.

Doerner, William R. "To America with Skills." *Time* 8 July 1985: 42–44.

Dutta, Manoranjan. "Asian/Pacific American Employment Profile: Myth and Reality—Issues and Answers." United States Commission on Civil Rights 445–89.

Hirschman, Charles, and Morrison G. Wong. "Trends in Socioeconomic Achievement Among Immigrants and Native-Born Asian-Americans, 1960–1976." *Sociological Quarterly* 22.4 (1981): 495–513.

Hune, Shirley. Keynote address. East Coast Asian Student Union Conference. Boston University. 14 Feb. 1987.

Kahng, Anthony. "Employment Issues." United States Commission on Civil Rights 1980.

Kantrowitz, Barbara, et al. "The Ultimate Assimilation." *Newsweek* 24 Nov. 1986: 80.

Kasindorf, Martin, et al. "Asian-Americans: A 'Model Minority.'" *Newsweek* 6 Dec. 1982: 39–51.

Kennedy, David M. "The Making of a Classic. Gunnar Myrdal and Black-White Relations: The Use and Abuse of *An American Dilemma*." *Atlantic* May 1987: 86–89.

Kiang, Peter. Personal interview. 1 May 1987.

Kim, Illsoo. "Class Division Among Asian Immigrants: Its Implications for Social Welfare Policy." *Asian American Studies* 24–25.

Kuo, Wen H. "On the Study of Asian-Americans: Its Current State and Agenda." *Sociological Quarterly* 20.2 (1979): 279–90.

Mariano, Robert S. "Census Issues." United States Commission on Civil Rights 54–59.

McBee, Susanna, et al. "Asian-Americans: Are They Making the Grade?" *U.S. News & World Report* 2 Apr. 1984: 41–47.

Nishi, Setsuko Matsunaga. "Asian American Employment Issues: Myths and Realities." United States Commission on Civil Rights 397–99, 495–507.

Oxnam, Robert B. "Why Asians Succeed Here." *New York Times Magazine* 30 Nov. 1986: 72+.

Ramirez, Anthony. "America's Super Minority." *Fortune* 24 Nov. 1986: 148–49.

Seligman, Daniel. "Keeping Up: Working Smarter." *Fortune* 17 May 1982: 64.

"Success Story of One Minority Group in the U.S." *U.S. News & World Report* 26 Dec. 1966: 73–76.

"Success Story: Outwhiting the Whites." *Newsweek* 21 June 1971: 24–25.

Sung, Betty Lee. *A Survey of Chinese American Manpower and Employment*. New York: Praeger, 1976.

Suzuki, Bob H. "Education and the Socialization of Asian Americans: A Revisionist Analysis of the 'Model Minority' Thesis." *Amerasia Journal* 4.2 (1977): 23–51.

Toupin, Elizabeth Ahn. "A Model University for a Model Minority." *Asian American Studies* 10–12.

United States Commission on Civil Rights. *Civil Rights Issues of Asian and Pacific Americans: Myths and Realities.* 1980.

"The Wrong Way to Court Ethnics." *Washington Monthly* May 1986: 21–26.

Yun, Grace. "Notes from Discussions on Asian American Education." *Asian American Studies* 20–24.

QUESTIONS ON MEANING

1. What is Chang's THESIS? Why does he introduce it where he does?
2. What "two crucial assumptions" do the media mistakenly propagate about Asian Americans?
3. What exactly does Chang mean by the "pressing needs" of Asian Americans?
4. SUMMARIZE Chang's ideas about the "Model Minority ideology" (beginning in para. 16). What is an *ideology*? What does this one do?

QUESTIONS ON WRITING STRATEGY

1. Is Chang's argument based more on EMOTIONAL APPEAL or on RATIONAL APPEAL? Why do you say so?
2. Try to summarize Chang's argument in a SYLLOGISM (as demonstrated on p. 461). What part of the syllogism corresponds to Chang's thesis?
3. What types of EVIDENCE does Chang base his argument on? Is the evidence adequate?
4. ANALYZE Chang's POINT OF VIEW. With whom does he ally himself? How does his position affect the essay?
5. Where does Chang acknowledge and address possible objections to his argument?
6. **OTHER METHODS.** How does Chang use DIVISION or ANALYSIS to develop his argument?

QUESTIONS ON LANGUAGE

1. What is the "old-boy network" (para. 12)? What are the implications of this phrase?

2. In paragraph 28, Chang uses the term "techno-coolies." What ALLUSION is he making? Why is it especially suitable at this point in the essay?
3. Chang refers in paragraphs 5, 24, and 25 to an "economic pie." What images does this metaphor evoke? (See "Figures of speech" in Useful Terms for a definition of *metaphor*.)
4. Consult your dictionary if any of the following words are unfamiliar: allegedly (para. 3); median (4); aphorism (5); propagate, monolithic (6); venerable, systemic (7); fallacious (8); prevalent, disparity (13); reparations, internment (14); assimilation, lauded (17); absolution (20); empirical (21); succumb, torrent (23); lower-echelon (25); docile, pander (26); perpetuated (29).

SUGGESTIONS FOR WRITING

1. **JOURNAL WRITING.** Chang's essay suggests how important it is to view newspapers, television, and other media critically. Can you think of a time when the media distorted or omitted facts you were familiar with? The subject may be as local or as national as you like: a neighborhood fire, a demonstration, an arrest, student attitudes, a legislative debate, anything. Write about the distortion in your journal.

    FROM JOURNAL TO ESSAY. Write an essay in which you analyze and correct the media record of the subject you wrote of in your journal. To convince your readers of how and why the media record was inaccurate, you'll need to provide lots of details comparing what you know and what the media reported.

2. Take Chang's essay further: Write a concrete proposal for correcting the situation he describes.

3. **CRITICAL WRITING.** Number 4 under "Questions on Meaning" asked you to summarize Chang's assertions about the "Model Minority ideology" (paras. 16–29). In an essay, analyze and EVALUATE these assertions. What ASSUMPTIONS is Chang making — for instance, about the existence or denial of racial barriers in the United States? Do you agree or disagree with Chang's assumptions and with his argument about the Model Minority ideology? Why?

4. **CONNECTIONS.** A number of the authors in *The Bedford Reader* belong to a racial or ethnic minority — not only Chang but Maya Angelou (p. 52), Amy Tan (p. 57), Ralph Ellison (p. 67), Itabari Njeri (p. 108), Brent Staples (p. 168), Gloria Naylor (p. 418), Christine Leong (p. 424), Chitra Divakaruni (p. 504), Sandra Cisneros (p. 533), Martin Luther King, Jr. (p. 567), Maxine Hong Kingston (p. 573), N. Scott Momaday (p. 587), Richard Rodriguez (p. 606), and Alice Walker (p. 632). Consider the essays by Chang and two of the other authors listed. How central is each author's racial or ethnic identity to his or her PURPOSE and thesis? To what extent does each author claim to represent his or her group? Does each author's stance in relation to his or her group work for or against the essay, in your mind? Why? Answer these questions in an essay. (You may want to draw on "N. Scott Momaday on Writing," p. 595, which addresses the question about representing the group.)

CURTIS CHANG ON WRITING

For Curtis Chang, a word processor is an "essential" writing tool. Once he completes and outlines his research, he explains in *Student Writers at Work,* "I must see my thoughts on the computer screen. I find it difficult to manipulate thoughts unless I can physically manipulate the words that represent them."

But the word processor can be a mixed blessing, for it supports Chang's "urge to perfect each sentence as I am writing. One is especially vulnerable when working on a word processor. I often have to force myself to continue getting the basic facts out first." Once he does have his thoughts on screen, Chang turns to global revision, an important part of his writing process. Although he strives for perfect sentences, Chang thinks of revision as "more than just the usual forms of correcting grammar and spelling and using one adjective instead of another." For Chang, "Revising means acting as devil's advocate and trying to pick apart my paper's argument. Then I have to answer to those criticisms."

Like many writers, Chang is rarely satisfied with his work. For each paper, he reports, "I average about three drafts, but it is usually determined by time constraints. I never really finish an essay; I just tire of tinkering with it."

FOR DISCUSSION

1. Why does Chang try not to perfect his sentences until the entire essay is written? What is the advantage of "getting the basic facts out first"?
2. Chang considers the word processor essential for writing. Would his extensive revisions be possible without one?

ADDITIONAL WRITING TOPICS

Argument and Persuasion

1. Write a persuasive essay in which you express a deeply felt opinion. In it, address a particular person or audience. For instance, you might direct your essay

   To a friend unwilling to attend a ballet performance (or a wrestling match) with you on the grounds that such an event is a waste of time

   To a teacher who asserts that more term papers, and longer ones, are necessary for students to master academic writing

   To a state trooper who intends to give you a ticket for speeding

   To a male employer skeptical of hiring women

   To a developer who plans to tear down a historic house

   To someone who sees no purpose in studying a foreign language

   To a high-school class whose members don't want to go to college

   To an older generation skeptical of the value of "all that noise" (meaning current popular music)

   To an atheist who asserts that religion just distracts us from the here and now

   To the members of a library board who want to ban a certain book

2. Write a letter to your campus newspaper, or to a city newspaper, in which you argue for or against a certain cause or view. You may wish to object to a particular feature, column, or editorial in the paper. Send your letter and see if it is published.

3. Write a short letter to your congressional or state representative, arguing in favor of (or against) the passage of some pending legislation. See a news magazine or a newspaper for a worthwhile bill to write about. Or else write in favor of some continuing cause: for instance, requiring (or not requiring) cars to reduce exhaust emissions, reducing (or increasing) military spending, providing (or reducing) aid to the arts, expanding (or reducing) government loans to college students.

4. Write an essay arguing that something you feel strongly about should be changed, removed, abolished, enforced, repeated, revised, reinstated, or reconsidered. Be sure to propose some plan for carrying out whatever suggestions you make. Possible topics, listed to start you thinking, are these:

   Gun laws
   Low-income housing
   Graduation requirements
   The mandatory retirement age
   ROTC programs in schools and colleges
   Movie ratings (G, PG, PG-13, R, NC-17, X)
   School prayer
   Fraternities and sororities

Dress codes in primary and secondary schools
TV advertising

5. On the model of Maire Flynn's three-part condensed argument on pages 459–60, write a condensed argument in three paragraphs demonstrating data, claim, and warrant. For a topic, consider any of the preceding ideas or any problem or controversy in this morning's newspaper.

MIXING THE METHODS

Everywhere in this book, we have tried to prove how flexible the methods of development are. All the preceding essays offer superb examples of DESCRIPTION or CLASSIFICATION or DEFINITION or ARGUMENT, but every one also illustrates other methods, too—description in PROCESS ANALYSIS, ANALYSIS and NARRATION in COMPARISON, EXAMPLES and CAUSE AND EFFECT in argument.

In this part of the book, we take this point even further by abandoning the individual methods. Instead, we offer a collection of fifteen essays, many of them considered classics, all of them by well-known writers. The essays range widely in their subjects and approaches, but they share a significant feature: All the authors draw on whatever methods of development, at whatever length, will help them achieve their PURPOSES with readers. (To show how the writers combine methods, we have highlighted the most significant ones in the note preceding each essay.)

You have already begun to attain this command of the methods by focusing on them individually, making each a part of your kit of writing tools. Now, when you face a writing assignment, you can consider whether and how each method may help you sharpen your focus, develop your ideas, and achieve your aim. Indeed, as we noted in this book's Introduction, one way to approach a subject is to apply each method to it, one by one. The following list distills the discussion on pages 25–26 to a set of questions that you can ask about any subject:

1. *Narration:* Can you tell a story about the subject?
2. *Description:* Can you use your senses to illuminate the subject?
3. *Example:* Can you point to instances that will make the subject concrete and specific?
4. *Comparison and contrast:* Will setting the subject alongside another generate useful information?
5. *Process analysis:* Will a step-by-step explanation of how the subject works add to the reader's understanding?
6. *Division or analysis:* Can slicing the subject into its parts produce a clearer vision of it?
7. *Classification:* Is it worthwhile to sort the subject into kinds or groups?
8. *Cause and effect:* Does it add to the subject to ask why it happened or what its results are?
9. *Definition:* Can you trace a boundary that will clarify the subject's meaning?
10. *Argument and persuasion:* Can you state an opinion or make a proposal about the subject?

Rarely will every one of these questions produce fruit for a given essay, but inevitably two or three or four will. Try the whole list when you're stuck at the beginning of an assignment or when you're snagged in the middle of a draft. You'll find the questions are as good at removing obstacles as they are at generating ideas.

STEPHEN L. CARTER

A writer on race, religion, and law, STEPHEN L. CARTER is currently William Nelson Cromwell Professor of Law at Yale University Law School. He was born in Harlem in 1954 and received a B.A. from Stanford University in 1976 and a J.D. from Yale Law School in 1979. He clerked for Supreme Court Justice Thurgood Marshall for a year and worked at a law firm in Washington, D.C., before returning to Yale to teach in 1982. Though Carter has benefited personally from affirmative action, his first book—*Reflections of an Affirmative Action Baby* (1991)—considers the potential racism of affirmative action programs. Carter's subsequent books have taken issue with "the project of liberal constitutionalism," which Carter understands as an "effort to knit the nation into a single community sharing a single normative vision of the world." In *The Culture of Disbelief: How American Law and Politics Trivialize Religious Devotion* (1993), Carter—a devout Episcopalian—holds mainstream political parties accountable for their wariness of religion and religiously derived values. His other nonfiction books include *The Confirmation Mess* (1994), *The Dissent of the Governed* (1998), and *Civility* (1998).

The Insufficiency of Honesty

A writing textbook once gave *honesty and integrity* as an example of a redundant phrase, one in which the words repeat each other with no gain in meaning. But according to Stephen Carter, there is no redundancy in the phrase, for *honesty* and *integrity* in fact have quite different meanings. "The Insufficiency of Honesty" first appeared in the February 1996 *Atlantic Monthly*.

Carter's essay is mainly a work of definition and argument developed by several other methods as well:

Narration (Chap. 1): paragraphs 1, 7–9, 13–15, 21
Example (Chap. 3): paragraphs 7–9, 13–15, 17, 21
Comparison and contrast (Chap. 4): paragraphs 3, 5–6, 11–12, 20, 22
Cause and effect (Chap. 8): paragraphs 8–9, 11, 12–16, 20, 23
Definition (Chap. 9): throughout
Argument and persuasion (Chap. 10): throughout

A couple of years ago I began a university commencement address 1
by telling the audience that I was going to talk about integrity. The crowd broke into applause. Applause! Just because they had heard the word "integrity": that's how starved for it they were. They had no idea how I was using the word, or what I was going to say about integrity, or, indeed, whether I was for it or against it. But they knew they liked the idea of talking about it.

Very well, let us consider this word "integrity." Integrity is like the weather: Everybody talks about it but nobody knows what to do about it. Integrity is that stuff that we always want more of. Some say that we need to return to the good old days when we had a lot more of it. Others say that we as a nation have never really had enough of it. Hardly anybody stops to explain exactly what we mean by it, or how we know it is a good thing, or why everybody needs to have the same amount of it. Indeed, the only trouble with integrity is that everybody who uses the word seems to mean something slightly different. ⟨2⟩

For instance, when I refer to integrity, do I mean simply "honesty"? The answer is no; although honesty is a virtue of importance, it is a different virtue from integrity. Let us, for simplicity, think of honesty as not lying; and let us further accept Sissela Bok's definition of a lie: "any intentionally deceptive message which is *stated*." Plainly, one cannot have integrity without being honest (although, as we shall see, the matter gets complicated), but one can certainly be honest and yet have little integrity. ⟨3⟩

When I refer to integrity, I have something very specific in mind. Integrity, as I will use the term, requires three steps: discerning what is right and what is wrong; acting on what you have discerned, even at personal cost; and saying openly that you are acting on your understanding of right and wrong. The first criterion captures the idea that integrity requires a degree of moral reflectiveness. The second brings in the ideal of a person of integrity as steadfast, a quality that includes keeping one's commitments. The third reminds us that a person of integrity can be trusted. ⟨4⟩

The first point to understand about the difference between honesty and integrity is that a person may be entirely honest without ever engaging in the hard work of discernment that integrity requires: She may tell us quite truthfully what she believes without ever taking the time to figure out whether what she believes is good and right and true. The problem may be as simple as someone's foolishly saying something that hurts a friend's feelings; a few moments of thought would have revealed the likelihood of the hurt and the lack of necessity for the comment. Or the problem may be more complex, as when a man who was raised from birth in a society that preaches racism states his belief in one race's inferiority as a fact, without ever really considering that perhaps this deeply held view is wrong. Certainly the racist is being honest—he is telling us what he actually thinks—but his honesty does not add up to integrity. ⟨5⟩

Telling Everything You Know

A wonderful epigram sometimes attributed to the filmmaker Sam Goldwyn goes like this: "The most important thing in acting is hon- ⟨6⟩

esty; once you learn to fake that, you're in." The point is that honesty can be something one *seems* to have. Without integrity, what passes for honesty often is nothing of the kind; it is fake honesty—or it is honest but irrelevant and perhaps even immoral.

Consider an example. A man who has been married for fifty years   7
confesses to his wife on his deathbed that he was unfaithful thirty-five years earlier. The dishonesty was killing his spirit, he says. Now he has cleared his conscience and is able to die in peace.

The husband has been honest—sort of. He has certainly unbur-   8
dened himself. And he has probably made his wife (soon to be his widow) quite miserable in the process, because even if she forgives him, she will not be able to remember him with quite the vivid image of love and loyalty that she had hoped for. Arranging his own emotional affairs to ease his transition to death, he has shifted to his wife the burden of confusion and pain, perhaps for the rest of her life. Moreover, he has attempted his honesty at the one time in his life when it carries no risk; acting in accordance with what you think is right and risking no loss in the process is a rather thin and unadmirable form of honesty.

Besides, even though the husband has been honest in a sense, he   9
has now twice been unfaithful to his wife: once thirty-five years ago, when he had his affair, and again when, nearing death, he decided that his own peace of mind was more important than hers. In trying to be honest he has violated his marriage vow by acting toward his wife not with love but with naked and perhaps even cruel self-interest.

As my mother used to say, you don't have to tell people everything   10
you know. Lying and nondisclosure, as the law often recognizes, are not the same thing. Sometimes it is actually illegal to tell what you know, as, for example, in the disclosure of certain financial information by market insiders. Or it may be unethical, as when a lawyer reveals a confidence entrusted to her by a client. It may be simple bad manners, as in the case of a gratuitous comment to a colleague on his or her attire. And it may be subject to religious punishment, as when a Roman Catholic priest breaks the seal of the confessional—an offense that carries automatic excommunication.

In all the cases just mentioned, the problem with telling every-   11
thing you know is that somebody else is harmed. Harm may not be the intention, but it is certainly the effect. Honesty is most laudable when we risk harm to ourselves; it becomes a good deal less so if we instead risk harm to others when there is no gain to anyone other than ourselves. Integrity may counsel keeping our secrets in order to spare the feelings of others. Sometimes, as in the example of the wayward husband, the reason we want to tell what we know is precisely to shift our pain onto somebody else—a course of action dictated less by integrity than by self-interest. Fortunately, integrity and self-interest

often coincide, as when a politician of integrity is rewarded with our votes. But often they do not, and it is at those moments that our integrity is truly tested.

Error

Another reason that honesty alone is no substitute for integrity is   12
that if forthrightness is not preceded by discernment, it may result in the expression of an incorrect moral judgment. In other words, I may be honest about what I believe, but if I have never tested my beliefs, I may be wrong. And here I mean "wrong" in a particular sense: The proposition in question is wrong if I would change my mind about it after hard moral reflection.

Consider this example. Having been taught all his life that women   13
are not as smart as men, a manager gives the women on his staff less-challenging assignments than he gives the men. He does this, he believes, for their own benefit: He does not want them to fail, and he believes that they will if he gives them tougher assignments. Moreover, when one of the women on his staff does poor work, he does not berate her as harshly as he would a man, because he expects nothing more. And he claims to be acting with integrity because he is acting according to his own deepest beliefs.

The manager fails the most basic test of integrity. The question is not   14
whether his actions are consistent with what he most deeply believes but whether he has done the hard work of discerning whether what he most deeply believes is right. The manager has not taken this harder step.

Moreover, even within the universe that the manager has con-   15
structed for himself, he is not acting with integrity. Although he is obviously wrong to think that the women on his staff are not as good as the men, even were he right, that would not justify applying different standards to their work. By so doing he betrays both his obligation to the institution that employs him and his duty as a manager to evaluate his employees.

The problem that the manager faces is an enormous one in our   16
practical politics, where having the dialogue that makes democracy work can seem impossible because of our tendency to cling to our views even when we have not examined them. As Jean Bethke Elshtain has said, borrowing from John Courtney Murray, our politics are so fractured and contentious that we often cannot even reach *disagreement*. Our refusal to look closely at our own most cherished principles is surely a large part of the reason. Socrates thought the unexamined life not worth living. But the unhappy truth is that few of us actually have the time for constant reflection on our views—on public or private

morality. Examine them we must, however, or we will never know whether we might be wrong.

None of this should be taken to mean that integrity as I have described it presupposes a single correct truth. If, for example, your integrity-guided search tells you that affirmative action is wrong, and my integrity-guided search tells me that affirmative action is right, we need not conclude that one of us lacks integrity. As it happens, I believe—both as a Christian and as a secular citizen who struggles toward moral understanding—that we *can* find true and sound answers to our moral questions. But I do not pretend to have found very many of them, nor is an exposition of them my purpose here.   17

It is the case not that there aren't any right answers but that, given human fallibility, we need to be careful in assuming that we have found them. However, today's political talk about how it is wrong for the government to impose one person's morality on somebody else is just mindless chatter. *Every* law imposes one person's morality on somebody else, because law has only two functions: to tell people to do what they would rather not or to forbid them to do what they would.   18

And if the surveys can be believed, there is far more moral agreement in America than we sometimes allow ourselves to think. One of the reasons that character education for young people makes so much sense to so many people is precisely that there seems to be a core set of moral understandings—we might call them the American Core—that most of us accept. Some of the virtues in this American Core are, one hopes, relatively noncontroversial. About 500 American communities have signed on to Michael Josephson's program to emphasize the "six pillars" of good character: trustworthiness, respect, responsibility, caring, fairness, and citizenship. These virtues might lead to a similarly noncontroversial set of political values: having an honest regard for ourselves and others, protecting freedom of thought and religious belief, and refusing to steal or murder.   19

Honesty and Competing Responsibilities

A further problem with too great an exaltation of honesty is that it may allow us to escape responsibilities that morality bids us bear. If honesty is substituted for integrity, one might think that if I say I am not planning to fulfill a duty, I need not fulfill it. But it would be a peculiar morality indeed that granted us the right to avoid our moral responsibilities simply by stating our intention to ignore them. Integrity does not permit such an easy escape.   20

Consider an example. Before engaging in sex with a woman, her lover tells her that if she gets pregnant, it is her problem, not his. She   21 says that she understands. In due course she does wind up pregnant. If we believe, as I hope we do, that the man would ordinarily have a moral responsibility toward both the child he will have helped to bring into the world and the child's mother, then his honest statement of what he intends does not spare him that responsibility.

This vision of responsibility assumes that not all moral obligations   22 stem from consent or from a stated intention. The linking of obligations to promises is a rather modern and perhaps uniquely Western way of looking at life, and perhaps a luxury that only the well-to-do can afford. As Fred and Shulamit Korn (a philosopher and an anthropologist) have pointed out, "If one looks at ethnographic accounts of other societies, one finds that, while obligations everywhere play a crucial role in social life, promising is not preeminent among the sources of obligation and is not even mentioned by most anthropologists." The Korns have made a study of Tonga, where promises are virtually unknown but the social order is remarkably stable. If life without any promises seems extreme, we Americans sometimes go too far the other way, parsing not only our contracts but even our marriage vows in order to discover the absolute minimum obligation that we have to others as a result of our promises.

That some societies in the world have worked out evidently func-   23 tional structures of obligation without the need for promise or consent does not tell us what *we* should do. But it serves as a reminder of the basic proposition that our existence in civil society creates a set of mutual responsibilities that philosophers used to capture in the fiction of the social contract. Nowadays, here in America, people seem to spend their time thinking of even cleverer ways to avoid their obligations, instead of doing what integrity commands and fulfilling them. And all too often honesty is their excuse.

QUESTIONS ON MEANING

1. What is Carter's PURPOSE in this essay? How does he intend the essay to affect readers?
2. Where does Carter state his THESIS? What is it?
3. What does Carter mean by "hard moral reflection" (para. 12)?
4. What ASSUMPTIONS does the author seem to make about his readers' interest in and knowledge about integrity? What values does he seem to assume?

QUESTIONS ON WRITING STRATEGY

1. How does each subheaded section of the essay ("Telling Everything You Know," "Error," "Honesty and Competing Responsibilities") relate to Carter's thesis?

2. How would you characterize Carter's TONE? How does his use of *we* and *our* contribute to the tone? How would it be different if he had used *you* and *your*?

3. **MIXED METHODS.** Carter uses DEFINITION to explain his use of the word *integrity*, establishing three steps that integrity requires. How do these three steps remain central to the rest of the essay? What does Carter refer to when he mentions "the most basic test of integrity" in paragraph 14?

4. **MIXED METHODS.** Carter expands his distinction between integrity and honesty through EXAMPLES. How does each of his extended examples (paras. 7–9, 13–15, 21) illustrate a distinction? Which of these examples did you find most informative, and why?

QUESTIONS ON LANGUAGE

1. What is the EFFECT of the one-word sentence "Applause!" in paragraph 1?

2. What does Carter mean by "moral agreement" (para. 19)?

3. Give definitions of the following words: discerning, criterion, reflectiveness (para. 4); epigram (6); gratuitous, excommunication (10); laudable (11); berate (13); contentious (16); presupposes (17); fallibility (18); exaltation (20); ethnographic, parsing (22).

SUGGESTIONS FOR WRITING

1. **JOURNAL WRITING.** When have you felt your integrity was tested? Write about one such situation and your response to it.

   FROM JOURNAL TO ESSAY. Write a NARRATIVE about a time when you showed, or perhaps didn't show, integrity. What was the moral issue? Do you believe you were morally right? What, if anything, did your actions cost you? Were others helped or hurt in any way?

2. Write an essay that explains how someone you know well demonstrates integrity as Carter defines it—or, alternatively, how someone you know has failed to demonstrate integrity. Draw on quotations and PARAPHRASES from Carter's essay to establish the definition, and provide detailed examples of the person's behavior to illustrate.

3. **CRITICAL WRITING.** ANALYZE and EVALUATE one of Carter's extended examples (paras. 7–9, 13–15, 21). How helpful is it in clarifying Carter's point? What assumptions does Carter make in presenting and discussing the example, and do you think they are valid? Do you agree or disagree with Carter's conclusions about his example?

4. **CONNECTIONS.** Both Carter's essay and Stephanie Ericsson's "The Ways We Lie" (p. 340) discuss motives for honesty and for lying. Which, if any,

of Ericsson's types of lies might Carter accept in the interest of integrity? Why? Would Ericsson agree? Why, or why not? Write an essay that examines the two authors' perspectives on honesty, supporting your ideas with quotations or paraphrases from both.

5. **CONNECTIONS.** Read George Orwell's "Shooting an Elephant" (p. 596) alongside Carter's "The Insufficiency of Honesty." To what extent did Orwell display honesty or integrity, as Carter defines both, in shooting the elephant and in his reflections on the incident? Write a brief essay explaining your answer to this question.

SANDRA CISNEROS

Born in 1954 in Chicago, SANDRA CISNEROS attended Loyola University, where she received a B.A. in 1976. Two years later, she earned an M.F.A. from the University of Iowa Writers' Workshop. While at Iowa, she embraced her Chicano heritage in her writing, turning to her childhood for inspiration. Most of her published work deals explicitly with issues of ethnic heritage, poverty, and personal identity. She is the author of two short-story collections—*The House on Mango Street* (1984) and *Woman Hollering Creek* (1991)—and several books of poems, including *My Wicked, Wicked Ways* (1987). Cisneros has received numerous awards, including two from the National Endowment for the Arts and the Lannan Foundation Literary Award. In 1995 she was named a MacArthur fellow.

Only Daughter

How could a man who had little interest in reading, whose only ambition for his daughter was marriage, prove to be the main reason that daughter became a writer? In this essay from a 1990 *Glamour* magazine, Cisneros explains.

"Only Daughter" mixes several methods of development to show the difficult yet fruitful bond between daughter and father:

Narration (Chap. 1): paragraphs 9–12, 15–22
Description (Chap. 2): paragraphs 7, 13, 16–21
Cause and effect (Chap. 8): paragraphs 3, 5, 7, 8
Definition (Chap. 9): paragraphs 1–2

Once, several years ago, when I was just starting out my writing career, I was asked to write my own contributor's note for an anthology I was part of. I wrote: "I am the only daughter in a family of six sons. *That* explains everything."

Well, I've thought about that ever since, and yes, it explains a lot to me, but for the reader's sake I should have written: "I am the only daughter in a *Mexican* family of six sons." Or even: "I am the only daughter of a Mexican father and a Mexican-American mother." Or: "I am the only daughter of a working-class family of nine." All of these had everything to do with who I am today.

I was/am the only daughter and *only* a daughter. Being an only daughter in a family of six sons forced me by circumstance to spend a lot of time by myself because my brothers felt it beneath them to play with a *girl* in public. But that aloneness, that loneliness, was good for a would-be writer—it allowed me time to think and think, to imagine, to read and prepare myself.

Being only a daughter for my father meant my destiny would lead   4
me to become someone's wife. That's what he believed. But when I was
in fifth grade and shared my plans for college with him, I was sure he
understood. I remember my father saying, *"Que bueno, mi'ja,* that's
good." That meant a lot to me, especially since my brothers thought
the idea hilarious. What I didn't realize was that my father thought college was good for girls—for finding a husband. After four years in college and two more in graduate school, and still no husband, my father
shakes his head even now and says I wasted all that education.

In retrospect, I'm lucky my father believed daughters were meant   5
for husbands. It meant it didn't matter if I majored in something silly
like English. After all, I'd find a nice professional eventually, right?
This allowed me the liberty to putter about embroidering my little poems and stories without my father interrupting with so much as a
"What's that you're writing?"

But the truth is, I wanted him to interrupt. I wanted my father to   6
understand what it was I was scribbling, to introduce me as "My only
daughter, the writer." Not as "This is my only daughter. She teaches."
El maestra—teacher. Not even *profesora.*

In a sense, everything I have ever written has been for him, to win   7
his approval even though I know my father can't read English words,
even though my father's only reading includes the brown-ink *Esto*
sports magazines from Mexico City and the bloody *¡Alarma!* magazines
that feature yet another sighting of *La Virgen de Guadalupe* on a tortilla
or a wife's revenge on her philandering husband by bashing his skull in
with a *molcajete* (a kitchen mortar made of volcanic rock). Or the
fotonovelas, the little picture paperbacks with tragedy and trauma
erupting from the characters' mouths in bubbles.

My father represents, then, the public majority. A public who is   8
uninterested in reading, and yet one whom I am writing about and for,
and privately trying to woo.

When we were growing up in Chicago, we moved a lot because of my   9
father. He suffered periodic bouts of nostalgia. Then we'd have to let go
our flat, store the furniture with mother's relatives, load the station wagon
with baggage and bologna sandwiches, and head south. To Mexico City.

We came back, of course. To yet another Chicago flat, another   10
Chicago neighborhood, another Catholic school. Each time, my father
would seek out the parish priest in order to get a tuition break, and
complain or boast: "I have seven sons."

He meant *siete hijos,* seven children, but he translated it as "sons."   11
"I have seven sons." To anyone who would listen. The Sears Roebuck
employee who sold us the washing machine. The short-order cook
where my father ate his ham-and-eggs breakfasts. "I have seven sons."
As if he deserved a medal from the state.

My papa. He didn't mean anything by that mistranslation, I'm sure. 12
But somehow I could feel myself being erased. I'd tug my father's sleeve
and whisper: "Not seven sons. Six! and *one daughter*."

When my oldest brother graduated from medical school, he ful- 13
filled my father's dream that we study hard and use this — our heads, instead of this — our hands. Even now my father's hands are thick and
yellow, stubbed by a history of hammer and nails and twine and coils
and springs. "Use this," my father said, tapping his head, "and not this,"
showing us those hands. He always looked tired when he said it.

Wasn't college an investment? And hadn't I spent all those years in 14
college? And if I didn't marry, what was it all for? Why would anyone
go to college and then choose to be poor? Especially someone who had
always been poor.

Last year, after ten years of writing professionally, the financial re- 15
wards started to trickle in. My second National Endowment for the
Arts Fellowship. A guest professorship at the University of California,
Berkeley. My book, which sold to a major New York publishing house.

At Christmas, I flew home to Chicago. The house was throbbing, 16
same as always; hot *tamales* and sweet *tamales* hissing in my mother's
pressure cooker, and everybody — mother, six brothers, wives, babies,
aunts, cousins — talking too loud and at the same time, like in a Fellini[1]
film, because that's just how we are.

I went upstairs to my father's room. One of my stories had just been 17
translated into Spanish and published in an anthology of Chicano
writing, and I wanted to show it to him. Ever since he recovered from
a stroke two years ago, my father likes to spend his leisure hours hori-
zontally. And that's how I found him, watching a Pedro Infante movie
on Galavision and eating rice pudding.

There was a glass filmed with milk on the bedside table. There were 18
several vials of pills and balled Kleenex. And on the floor, one black sock
and a plastic urinal that I didn't want to look at but looked at anyway. Pedro Infante was about to burst into song, and my father was laughing.

I'm not sure if it was because my story was translated into Spanish, or 19
because it was published in Mexico, or perhaps because the story dealt
with Tepeyac, the *colonia* my father was raised in, but at any rate, my father punched the mute button on his remote control and read my story.

I sat on the bed next to my father and waited. He read it very 20
slowly. As if he were reading each line over and over. He laughed at all
the right places and read lines he liked out loud. He pointed and asked
questions: "Is this So-and-so?" "Yes," I said. He kept reading.

---

[1]Federico Fellini (1920–93), an Italian, directed *La Strada, La Dolce Vita, Satyri-
con*, and other movies. — EDS.

When he was finally finished, after what seemed like hours, my fa- 21
ther looked up and asked: "Where can we get more copies of this for
the relatives?"

Of all the wonderful things that happened to me last year, that was 22
the most wonderful.

QUESTIONS ON MEANING

1. What do you take to be Cisneros's main PURPOSE in this essay?
2. Cisneros writes, "I am the only daughter in a family of six sons. *That ex-*
   plains everything" (para. 1). What does it explain in this essay?
3. What are some of the parallels Cisneros draws between her father and
   "the public majority" (para. 8)?
4. Why do you think her father's appreciation of her story was, for Cisneros,
   "the most wonderful" thing that happened to her in a year that was already good?

QUESTIONS ON WRITING STRATEGY

1. Does Cisneros seem to be writing mainly for other Mexican Americans or
   for a wider AUDIENCE? Cite passages from the essay to support your answer.
2. What can you INFER about Cisneros's stories and poems from the information about her education (para. 4), the details about her father's reading
   (7–8), and the list of her successes (15)?
3. **MIXED METHODS.** Cisneros's INTRODUCTION (paras. 1–2) gives a DEFINITION
   of the author. How effective is this introduction for setting up the essay
   that follows?
4. **MIXED METHODS.** Perhaps a third of Cisneros's essay is devoted to a NAR-
   RATIVE and DESCRIPTION of a Christmas visit home (paras. 16–22). Why do
   you think Cisneros relates this incident in so much detail? What do we
   gain from knowing what was cooking, what her father was watching on
   TV, or what questions he asked as he read Cisneros's story?

QUESTIONS ON LANGUAGE

1. What are the contrasting ideas in Cisneros's paired phrases "the only
   daughter and *only* a daughter" (para. 3)?
2. How do Cisneros's words convey her feeling about her father's translation
   of *siete hijos* as "seven sons" (paras. 11–12)?
3. Consult a dictionary if you need help in defining the following: retrospect, putter (para. 5); philandering, mortar (7); woo (8).

SUGGESTIONS FOR WRITING

1. **JOURNAL WRITING.** In your journal, consider the meaning of *success*. To
   begin, think of the attributes of successful people you know or know of.

Then try to answer these questions: How do you define *success* for yourself? Where do your ideas of success come from—your friends? your parents? your religious views? the media?

FROM JOURNAL TO ESSAY. Write an extended definition of *success* that also examines the sources of your definition. (The sources could be negative as well as positive—that is, your own ideas may have formed in reaction *against* others' ideas as well as in agreement *with* them.) Be sure your essay has a clear THESIS and plenty of EXAMPLES to make your definition precise.

2. Cisneros writes of differences from her father that frustrated her but that also motivated her to achieve. In a narrative and descriptive essay, relate some aspect of a relationship with a parent or other figure of authority that you found troubling or even maddening at the time but that now seems to have shaped you in positive ways. Did a parent (or someone else) push you to study when you wanted to play sports or hang out with your friends? make you attend religious services when they seemed unimportant? refuse to acknowledge accomplishments you were proud of? try to direct you onto a path you didn't care to take?

3. **CRITICAL WRITING.** Cisneros attributes many of her father's attitudes to his Mexican heritage. As an extension of the previous assignment, consider whether Cisneros's experiences are particular to Mexican American families or are common in all families, whatever their ethnicity. Are conflicts between children and their parents inevitable, do you think? Why, or why not?

4. **CONNECTIONS.** Both Cisneros's "Only Daughter" and John McPhee's "Silk Parachute" (p. 155) examine a relationship with a parent. How are the two authors' parents different? How are the authors' feelings about their parents similar and different? Write an essay of COMPARISON AND CONTRAST that quotes or PARAPHRASES passages from both essays as EVIDENCE.

5. **CONNECTIONS.** Several authors in this book recall interaction with a parent and use dialogue to make the interaction vivid. Examples include M. F. K. Fisher's "The Broken Chain" (p. 9), Amy Tan's "Fish Cheeks" (p. 57), Brad Manning's "Arm Wrestling with My Father" (p. 100), Itabari Njeri's "When Morpheus Held Him" (p. 108), and John McPhee's "Silk Parachute" (p. 155). Try your hand at using dialogue in a brief narrative that recalls a significant incident between yourself and a parent. Then write briefly about your experience using dialogue: How easy or difficult was it to remember who said what? How easy or difficult was it to make the speakers sound like themselves?

SANDRA CISNEROS ON WRITING

A bilingual author, Sandra Cisneros writes primarily in English. Yet Spanish influences her English sentences, and she frequently uses Spanish words in her prose. She spoke with Feroza Jussawalla and Reed Way Dasenbrock about how Spanish affects her writing:

"What it does is change the rhythm of my writing. I think that incorporating the Spanish, for me, allows me to create new expressions in

English—to say things that have never been said before. And I get to do that by translating literally. I love calling stories by Spanish expressions. I have this story called 'Salvador, Late or Early.' It's a nice title. It means 'sooner or later,' *tarde o temprano*, which literally translates as 'late or early.' All of a sudden something happens to the English, something really new is happening, a new spice is added to the English language."

In some of her work, Cisneros uses Spanish and then offers a translation for English readers. At other times, she thinks complete translation is unnecessary: "See, sometimes, you don't have to say the whole thing. Now I'm learning how you can say something in English so that you know the person is saying it in Spanish. I like that. You can say a phrase in Spanish, and you can choose not to translate it, but you can make it understood through the context. 'And then my *abuelita* called me a *sin verguenza* and cried because I am without shame,' you see? Just in the sentence you can weave it in. To me it's really fun to be doing that; to me it's like I've uncovered this whole motherlode that I haven't tapped into. All the *expresiones* in Spanish when translated make English wonderful."

That said, Cisneros believes that "[t]he readers who are going to like my stories the best and catch all the subtexts and all the subtleties, that even my editor can't catch, are Chicanas. When there are Chicanas in the audience, and they laugh, they are laughing at stuff that we talk about among ourselves. And there's no way that my editor at Random House is ever going to get those jokes." This seems particularly true, she finds, when she's making use of Mexican and Southwestern myths and legends about which the general public might not be aware. "That's why I say the real ones who are going to get it are the Latinos, the Chicanos. They're going to get it in that they're going to understand the myth and how I've revised it. When I talked to someone at *Interview* magazine, I had to explain to him what I was doing with *la llorona*, *La Malinche*, and the Virgin of Guadalupe in the story ['Woman Hollering Creek']. But he said, 'Hey, I didn't know that, but I still got the story.' You can get it at some other level. He reminded me, 'Sandra, if you're from Ireland, you're going to get a lot more out of Joyce than if you're not, but just because you're not Irish doesn't mean you're not going to get it at another level.'"

FOR DISCUSSION

1. In the passages quoted here, Sandra Cisneros is talking about her fiction writing. Do her thoughts about Spanish apply to the kind of English she uses when she writes a nonfiction piece like "Only Daughter"?

2. In "Only Daughter," Sandra Cisneros writes of her father: "In a sense, everything I have ever written has been for him, to win his approval, even though I know my father can't read English words...." How does this square with her claim that Chicana readers are her best readers?
3. Who is the reader who would best understand your essays?

JOAN DIDION

A writer whose fame is fourfold — as novelist, essayist, journalist, and screenwriter — JOAN DIDION was born in 1934 in California, where her family has lived for five generations. After graduation from the University of California, Berkeley, she spent a few years in New York, working as a feature editor for *Vogue*, a fashion magazine. In 1964 she returned to California, where she worked as a freelance journalist, compiled two esteemed essay collections (*Slouching Towards Bethlehem*, 1969; *The White Album*, 1979), and wrote four much-discussed novels (*River Run*, 1963; *Play It as It Lays*, 1971; *A Book of Common Prayer*, 1977; and *Democracy*, 1984). *Salvador* (1983), her book-length essay based on a visit to war-torn El Salvador, and *Miami* (1987), a study of Cuban exiles in Florida, also received wide attention. With her husband, John Gregory Dunne, Didion has coauthored screenplays, notably for *A Star Is Born* (1976), *True Confessions* (1981), and, most recently, *Up Close and Personal* (1996). Didion's latest books are *After Henry* (1992), a collection of essays, and *The Last Thing He Wanted* (1996), a novel. She contributes regularly to *The New York Review of Books*.

In Bed

In this essay from *The White Album*, Didion explains migraine headaches in general and her own in particular. Any migraine sufferer will recognize the pain and debility she describes. Even nonsufferers are likely to wince under the spell of Didion's vivid, sensuous prose.

Didion draws on half a dozen methods of development to give a full picture of migraine:

Narration (Chap. 1): paragraphs 1–2, 7–8
Description (Chap. 2): paragraphs 1–2, 5, 7–8
Example (Chap. 3): paragraphs 2–3, 5, 7
Process analysis (Chap. 5): paragraphs 3–5, 7–8
Cause and effect (Chap. 8): paragraph 6
Definition (Chap. 9): paragraph 3

Three, four, sometimes five times a month, I spend the day in bed with a migraine headache, insensible to the world around me. Almost every day of every month, between these attacks, I feel the sudden irrational irritation and flush of blood into the cerebral arteries which tell me that migraine is on its way, and I take certain drugs to avert its arrival. If I did not take the drugs, I would be able to function perhaps one day in four. The physiological error called migraine is, in brief, central to the given of my life. When I was fifteen, sixteen, even twenty-five, I used to think that I could rid myself of this error by simply denying it, character over chemistry. "Do you have headaches *sometimes? frequently? never?*" the application forms would demand. "Check one." Wary of the trap, wanting whatever it was that the successful circumnavigation of that particular form could bring (a job, a scholarship, the respect of mankind and the grace of God), I would check one. "*Sometimes*," I would lie. That in fact I spent one or two days a week almost unconscious with pain seemed a shameful secret, evidence not merely of some chemical inferiority but of all my bad attitudes, unpleasant tempers, wrongthink.

For I had no brain tumor, no eyestrain, no high blood pressure, nothing wrong with me at all: I simply had migraine headaches, and migraine headaches were, as everyone who did not have them knew, imaginary. I fought migraine then, ignored the warnings sent, went to school and later to work in spite of it, sat through lectures in Middle English and presentations to advertisers with involuntary tears running down the right side of my face, threw up in washrooms, stumbled home by instinct, emptied ice trays onto my bed and tried to freeze the pain in my right temple, wished only for a neurosurgeon who would do a lobotomy on house call, and cursed my imagination.

It was a long time before I began thinking mechanistically enough to accept migraine for what it was: something with which I would be living, the way some people live with diabetes. Migraine is something more than the fancy of a neurotic imagination. It is an essentially hereditary complex of symptoms, the most frequently noted but by no means the most unpleasant of which is a vascular headache of blinding severity, suffered by a surprising number of women, a fair number of men (Thomas Jefferson had migraine, and so did Ulysses S. Grant, the day he accepted Lee's surrender), and by some unfortunate children as young as two years old. (I had my first when I was eight. It came on during a fire drill at the Columbia School in Colorado Springs, Colorado. I was taken first home and then to the infirmary at Peterson Field, where my father was stationed. The Air Corps doctor prescribed an enema.) Almost anything can trigger a specific attack of migraine: stress, allergy, fatigue, an abrupt change in barometric pressure, a contretemps over a parking ticket. A flashing light. A fire drill. One inherits, of course, only the predisposition. In other words I spent yesterday in bed with a headache not merely because of my bad attitudes, unpleasant tempers and wrongthink, but because both my grandmothers had migraine, my father has migraine and my mother has migraine.

No one knows precisely what it is that is inherited. The chemistry of migraine, however, seems to have some connection with the nerve hormone named serotonin, which is naturally present in the brain. The amount of serotonin in the blood falls sharply at the onset of migraine, and one migraine drug, Methysergide, or Sansert, seems to have some effect on serotonin. Methysergide is a derivative of lysergic acid (in fact Sandoz Pharmaceuticals first synthesized LSD-25 while looking for a migraine cure), and its use is hemmed about with so many contraindications and side effects that most doctors prescribe it only in the most incapacitating cases. Methysergide, when it is prescribed, is taken daily, as a preventive; another preventive which works for some people is old-fashioned ergotamine tartrate, which helps to constrict the swelling blood vessels during the "aura," the period which in most cases precedes the actual headache.

Once an attack is under way, however, no drug touches it. Migraine   5 gives some people mild hallucinations, temporarily blinds others, shows up not only as a headache but as a gastrointestinal disturbance, a painful sensitivity to all sensory stimuli, an abrupt overpowering fatigue, a strokelike aphasia, and a crippling inability to make even the most routine connections. When I am in a migraine aura (for some people the aura lasts fifteen minutes, for others several hours), I will drive through red lights, lose the house keys, spill whatever I am holding, lose the ability to focus my eyes or frame coherent sentences, and generally give the appearance of being on drugs, or drunk. The actual headache, when it comes, brings with it chills, sweating, nausea, a debility that seems to stretch the very limits of endurance. That no one dies of migraine seems, to someone deep into an attack, an ambiguous blessing.

My husband also has migraine, which is unfortunate for him but   6 fortunate for me: Perhaps nothing so tends to prolong an attack as the accusing eye of someone who has never had a headache. "Why not take a couple of aspirin," the unafflicted will say from the doorway, or "I'd have a headache, too, spending a beautiful day like this inside with all the shades drawn." All of us who have migraine suffer not only from the attacks themselves but from this common conviction that we are perversely refusing to cure ourselves by taking a couple of aspirin, that we are making ourselves sick, that we "bring it on ourselves." And in the most immediate sense, the sense of why we have a headache this Tuesday and not last Thursday, of course we often do. There certainly is what doctors call a "migraine personality," and that personality tends to be ambitious, inward, intolerant of error, rather rigidly organized, perfectionist. "You don't look like a migraine personality," a doctor once said to me. "Your hair's messy. But I suppose you're a compulsive housekeeper." Actually my house is kept even more negligently than my hair, but the doctor was right nonetheless: Perfectionism can also take the form of spending most of a week writing and rewriting and not writing a single paragraph.

But not all perfectionists have migraine, and not all migrainous   7 people have migraine personalities. We do not escape heredity. I have tried in most of the available ways to escape my own migrainous heredity (at one point I learned to give myself two daily injections of histamine with a hypodermic needle, even though the needle so frightened me that I had to close my eyes when I did it), but I still have migraine. And I have learned now to live with it, learned when to expect it, how to outwit it, even how to regard it, when it does come, as more friend than lodger. We have reached a certain understanding, my migraine and I. It never comes when I am in real trouble. Tell me that my house is burned down, my husband has left me, that there is gunfighting in the streets and panic in the banks, and I will not respond by getting a headache. It comes instead when I am fighting not an open but a guerrilla war with my own life, during weeks of small household confusions, lost laundry, unhappy help, canceled appointments, on days when the telephone rings too much and I get no work done and the wind is coming up. On days like that my friend comes uninvited.

And once it comes, now that I am wise in its ways, I no longer fight it. I lie down and let it happen. At first every small apprehension is magnified, every anxiety a pounding terror. Then the pain comes, and I concentrate only on that. Right there is the usefulness of migraine, there in that imposed yoga, the concentration on the pain. For when the pain recedes, ten or twelve hours later, everything goes with it, all the hidden resentments, all the vain anxieties. The migraine has acted as a circuit breaker, and the fuses have emerged intact. There is a pleasant convalescent euphoria. I open the windows and feel the air, eat gratefully, sleep well. I notice the particular nature of a flower in a glass on the stair landing. I count my blessings.

8

QUESTIONS ON MEANING

1. According to the author, how do migraines differ from ordinary headaches? What are their distinctive traits?
2. What once made Didion ashamed to admit that she suffered from migraines?
3. While imparting facts about migraine, what does Didion simultaneously reveal about her own personality?
4. Sum up in your own words the tremendous experience that Didion describes in the final paragraph.

QUESTIONS ON WRITING STRATEGY

1. Didion's essay mixes SUBJECTIVE DESCRIPTION based on personal experience with OBJECTIVE information based on medical knowledge. How does she

signal her TRANSITIONS from subjective to objective and from objective back to subjective?

2. Point to a few examples of sensuous detail in Didion's writing. What do such IMAGES contribute to her essay's EFFECT?

3. In paragraph 2, Didion declares that she "wished only for a neurosurgeon who would do a lobotomy on house call." Do you take her literally? What do you make of her remark in paragraph 5: "That no one dies of migraine seems, to someone deep into an attack, an ambiguous blessing"? (See *hyperbole* under "Figures of speech" in Useful Terms.)

4. **MIXED METHODS.** In paragraph 5, the author uses strings of EXAMPLES. What is the effect of these examples? What GENERALIZATION do they support?

5. **MIXED METHODS.** What do Didion's two uses of PROCESS ANALYSIS (paras. 3–5 and 7–8) contribute to her essay?

QUESTIONS ON LANGUAGE

1. How would you characterize Didion's word choice: colorful, utilitarian, flowery, careless, or lyrical? Support your answer with examples.

2. In the title of Didion's essay, what arrests you? Is this title a teaser, having little to do with the essay, or does it fit?

3. Speaking in paragraph 1 of the "circumnavigation" of an application form, Didion employs a metaphor. In paragraph 7 she introduces another—"a guerrilla war." In paragraph 8 she uses a simile—"The migraine has acted as a circuit breaker." Comment on the aptness of these FIGURES OF SPEECH.

4. Consult a dictionary if you need help in defining the following: vascular, contretemps, predisposition (para. 3); synthesized, contraindications, aura (4); aphasia (5).

SUGGESTIONS FOR WRITING

1. **JOURNAL WRITING.** Write a passage of objective description about an illness you know intimately, even a cold. Or, if you prefer, pick an unwelcome mood you know: the blues, for instance, or an irresistible desire to giggle during a solemn ceremony. Then, on the same subject, write a second passage—this time, a subjective description of the same malady or mood.
   FROM JOURNAL TO ESSAY. Write a full descriptive essay, blending objective and subjective description as you see fit to explain your illness or mood, to convey the way it makes you feel, and to show how it affects your life.

2. Didion mentions "the accusing eye" (para. 6) she endures from those who don't suffer migraine. Write an essay in which you express and defend something about yourself that other people don't seem to understand. It could be a disability, a need for solitude, a habit, a hobby or interest that others find odd or dull. Explain the reactions you receive and how you respond to and cope with them.

3. **CRITICAL WRITING.** Write an essay examining Didion's TONE. Are there passages in which she seems self-pitying? courageous? determined? resigned? triumphant? What is the overall tone of the essay? Is it effective? Why?

4. **CONNECTIONS.** COMPARE Didion's essay to Nancy Mairs's "Disability" (p. 203). Mairs and Didion describe how multiple sclerosis and migraine,

respectively, affect their lives. What is the PURPOSE of each essay? What do Mairs and Didion want us to understand about them and their lives? How does each want us to respond?

5. **CONNECTIONS.** Both Joan Didion's "In Bed" and Annie Dillard's "Lenses" (p. 547) offer close, detailed study of particular experiences. Write a description of something small—not breakfast, but an egg; not going to bed, but closing your eyes. Focus on minute details to convey the object or experience to readers.

JOAN DIDION ON WRITING

In "Why I Write," an essay published by the *New York Times Book Review*, adapted from her Regents' Lecture at the University of California at Berkeley, Joan Didion writes, "Of course I stole the title for this talk, from George Orwell [excerpts of his essay appear on pages 604–05]. One reason I stole it was that I like the sound of the words: Why I Write. There you have three short unambiguous words that share a sound, and the sound they share is this:

I

I

I

In many ways writing is the act of saying *I*, of imposing oneself upon other people, of saying *listen to me, see it my way, change your mind....*"

Didion's "way," though, comes not from notions of how the world works or should work but from its observable details. She writes, "I am not in the least an intellectual, which is not to say that when I hear the word 'intellectual' I reach for my gun, but only to say that I do not think in abstracts. During the years when I was an undergraduate at Berkeley I tried, with a kind of hopeless late-adolescent energy, to buy some temporary visa into the world of ideas, to forge for myself a mind that could deal with the abstract.... In short, I tried to think. I failed. My attention veered inexorably back to the specific, to the tangible, to what was generally considered, by everyone I knew then and for that matter have known since, the peripheral. I would try to contemplate the Hegelian dialectic and would find myself concentrating instead on the flowering pear tree outside my window and the particular way the petals fell on my floor."

Later in the essay, Didion writes, "During those years I was traveling on what I knew to be a very shaky passport, forged papers: I knew that I was no legitimate resident in any world of ideas. I knew I couldn't think. All I knew then was what I wasn't, and it took me some years to discover what I was.

"Which was a writer.

"By which I mean not a 'good' writer or a 'bad' writer but simply a writer, a person whose most absorbed and passionate hours are spent arranging words on pieces of paper. Had my credentials been in order I would never have become a writer. Had I been blessed with even limited access to my own mind there would have been no reason to write. I write entirely to find out what I'm thinking, what I'm looking at, what I see, and what it means. What I want and what I fear.... *What is going on in these pictures in my mind?*"

In the essay, Didion emphasizes that these mental pictures have a grammar. "Grammar is a piano I play by ear, since I seem to have been out of school the year the rules were mentioned. All I know about grammar is its infinite power. To shift the structure of a sentence alters the meaning of that sentence, as definitely and inflexibly as the position of a camera alters the meaning of the object photographed. Many people know about camera angles now, but not so many know about sentences. The arrangement of the words matters, and the arrangement you want can be found in the picture in your mind. The picture dictates the arrangement. The picture dictates whether this will be a sentence with or without clauses, a sentence that ends hard or a dying-fall sentence, long or short, active or passive. The picture tells you how to arrange the words and the arrangement of the words tells you, or tells me, what's going on in the picture."

FOR DISCUSSION

1. What is Didion's definition of *thinking*? Do you agree with it?
2. To what extent does Didion's writing support her remarks about how and why she writes?
3. What does Didion mean when she says that grammar has "infinite power"? Power to do what?

ANNIE DILLARD

ANNIE DILLARD is accomplished as a prose writer, poet, and literary critic. Born in 1945, she earned a B.A. (1967) and an M.A. (1968) from Hollins College in Virginia. She now teaches writing at Wesleyan University in Connecticut. Dillard's first published prose, *Pilgrim at Tinker Creek* (1974), is a work alive with close, intense, and poetic descriptions of the natural world. It won her a Pulitzer Prize and comparison with Thoreau. Since then, Dillard's entranced and entrancing writing has appeared regularly in *Harper's, American Scholar, The Atlantic Monthly,* and other magazines and in her books: *Tickets for a Prayer Wheel* (1975), poems; *Holy the Firm* (1978), a prose poem; *Living by Fiction* (1982), literary criticism; *Teaching a Stone to Talk* (1982), nonfiction; *Encounters with Chinese Writers* (1984), an account of a trip to China; *An American Childhood* (1987), an autobiography; *The Writing Life* (1989), anecdotes and metaphors about writing; *The Living* (1992), a historical novel set in the Pacific Northwest; *Mornings Like This: Found Poems* (1995); and *For the Time Being* (1999), an exploration of how God and evil can coexist.

Lenses

Looking at pond life through a microscope and observing a pair of swans through binoculars may seem to be unrelated pursuits, but, as Dillard discovered, they are surprisingly alike. The author included this essay in *Teaching a Stone to Talk.*

"Lenses" is mainly a work of description and narration, but it also significantly features two other methods of development:

Narration (Chap. 1): paragraphs 5–15
Description (Chap. 2): throughout
Comparison and contrast (Chap. 4): paragraphs 1–2, 15
Process analysis (Chap. 5): paragraphs 1–3

You get used to looking through lenses; it is an acquired skill. 1
When you first look through binoculars, for instance, you can't see a thing. You look at the inside of the barrel; you blink and watch your eyelashes; you play with the focus knob till one eye is purblind.

The microscope is even worse. You are supposed to keep both eyes 2
open as you look through its single eyepiece. I spent my childhood in Pittsburgh trying to master this trick: seeing through one eye, with both eyes open. The microscope also teaches you to move your hands wrong, to shove the glass slide to the right if you are following a creature who is swimming off to the left—as if you were operating a tiller, or backing a trailer, or performing any other of those paradoxical maneuvers which

require either sure instincts or a grasp of elementary physics, neither of which I possess.

A child's microscope set comes with a little five-watt lamp. You place 3 this dim light in front of the microscope's mirror; the mirror bounces the light up through the slide, through the magnifying lenses, and into your eye. The only reason you do not see everything in silhouette is that microscopic things are so small they are translucent. The animals and plants in a drop of pond water pass light like pale stained glass; they seem so soaked in water and light that their opacity has leached away.

The translucent strands of algae you see under a microscope— 4 Spirogyra, Oscillatoria, Cladophora—move of their own accord, no one knows how or why. You watch these swaying yellow, green, and brown strands of algae half mesmerized; you sink into the microscope's field forgetful, oblivious, as if it were all a dream of your deepest brain. Occasionally a zippy rotifer comes barreling through, black and white, and in a tremendous hurry.

My rotifers and daphniae and amoebae were in an especially 5 tremendous hurry because they were drying up. I burnt out or broke my little five-watt bulb right away. To replace it, I rigged an old table lamp laid on its side; the table lamp carried a seventy-five-watt bulb. I was about twelve, immortal and invulnerable, and did not know what I was doing; neither did anyone else. My parents let me set up my laboratory in the basement, where they wouldn't have to smell the urine I collected in test tubes and kept in the vain hope it would grow something horrible. So in full, solitary ignorance I spent evenings in the basement staring into a seventy-five-watt bulb magnified three hundred times and focused into my eye. It is a wonder I can see at all. My eyeball itself would start drying up; I blinked and blinked.

But the pond water creatures fared worse. I dropped them on a slide, 6 floated a cover slip over them, and laid the slide on the microscope's stage, which the seventy-five-watt bulb had heated like a grill. At once the drop of pond water started to evaporate. Its edges shrank. The creatures swam among algae in a diminishing pool. I liked this part. The heat worked for me as a centrifuge, to concentrate the biomass. I had about five minutes to watch the members of a very dense population, excited by the heat, go about their business until—as I fancied sadly—they all caught on to their situation and started making out wills.

I was, then, not only watching the much-vaunted wonders in a 7 drop of pond water; I was also, with mingled sadism and sympathy, setting up a limitless series of apocalypses. I set up and staged hundreds of ends-of-the world and watched, enthralled, as they played themselves out. Over and over again, the last trump sounded, the final scroll unrolled, and the known world drained, dried, and vanished. When all the creatures lay motionless, boiled and fried in the positions they had when the last of their water dried completely, I washed the slide in the sink and started over with a fresh drop. How I loved that deep, wet world where the colored algae waved in the water and the rotifers swam!

But oddly, this is a story about swans. It is not even a story; it is a 8 description of swans. This description of swans includes the sky over a pond, a pair of binoculars, and a mortal adult who had long since moved out of the Pittsburgh basement.

In the Roanoke valley of Virginia, rimmed by the Blue Ridge 9 Mountains to the east and the Allegheny Mountains to the west, is a little semi-agricultural area called Daleville. In Daleville, set among fallow fields and wooded ridges, is Daleville Pond. It is a big pond, maybe ten acres; it holds a lot of sky. I used to haunt the place because I loved it; I still do. In winter it had that airy scruffiness of deciduous lands; you greet the daylight and the open space, and spend the evening picking burrs out of your pants.

One Valentine's Day, in the afternoon, I was crouched among dried 10 reeds at the edge of Daleville Pond. Across the pond from where I crouched was a low forested mountain ridge. In every other direction I saw only sky, sky crossed by the reeds which blew before my face whichever way I turned.

I was looking through binoculars at a pair of whistling swans! It is 11 impossible to say how excited I was to see whistling swans in Daleville, Virginia. The two were a pair, mated for life, migrating north and west from the Atlantic coast to the high arctic. They had paused to feed at Daleville Pond. I had flushed them, and now they were flying and cir-cling the pond. I crouched in the reeds so they would not be afraid to come back to the water.

Through binoculars I followed the swans, swinging where they 12 flew. All their feathers were white; their eyes were black. Their wingspan was six feet; they were bigger than I was. They flew in unison, one behind the other; they made pass after pass at the pond. I watched them change from white swans in front of the mountain to black swans in front of the sky. In clockwise ellipses they flew, necks long and re-laxed, alternately beating their wide wings and gliding.

As I rotated on my heels to keep the black frame of the lenses 13 around them, I lost all sense of space. If I lowered the binoculars I was always amazed to learn in which direction I faced—dazed, the way you emerge awed from a movie and try to reconstruct, bit by bit, a real world, in order to discover where in it you might have parked the car.

I lived in that circle of light, in great speed and utter silence. When 14 the swans passed before the sun they were distant—two black threads, two live stitches. But they kept coming, smoothly, and the sky deepened to blue behind them and they took on light. They gathered dimension as they neared, and I could see their ardent, straining eyes. Then I could hear the brittle blur of their wings, the blur which faded as they circled on, and the sky brightened to yellow behind them and the swans flattened and darkened and diminished as they flew. Once I lost them behind the mountain ridge; when they emerged they were flying suddenly very high, and it was like music changing key.

I was lost. The reeds in front of me, swaying and out of focus in the   15
binoculars' circular field, were translucent. The reeds were strands of color passing light like cells in water. They were those yellow and green and brown strands of pond algae I had watched so long in a light-soaked field. My eyes burned; I was watching algae wave in a shrinking drop; they crossed each other and parted wetly. And suddenly into the field swam two whistling swans, two tiny whistling swans. They swam as fast as rotifers: two whistling swans, infinitesimal, beating their tiny wet wings, perfectly formed.

QUESTIONS ON MEANING

1. What does Dillard's title have to do with her essay's PURPOSE? What further information concerning her purpose does Dillard supply in "Annie Dillard on Writing" (p. 552)?
2. What difficulties did Dillard, as a child, encounter when she tried to look through a microscope? What is the author's point in mentioning them?
3. Exactly what connection did the author find between watching swans through binoculars and studying pond water under a microscope? At what points in her essay does she emphasize the connection?
4. What does Dillard mean, in her final paragraph, when she says, "I was lost"?

QUESTIONS ON WRITING STRATEGY

1. How much knowledge of science and nature does Dillard expect of her AUDIENCE? How much did Dillard herself need in order to write "Lenses"?
2. By what means does the author make her TRANSITIONS from pond life to swans and then back again? Do you find the transitions effective, or too abrupt?
3. With what sensuous details does Dillard indicate that the swans are near to her and far away?
4. Where, in Dillard's essay, do you find touches of humor?
5. **MIXED METHODS.** Where and why does Dillard use COMPARISON AND CONTRAST? What do the comparisons show?

6. **MIXED METHODS.** Reread the first three paragraphs of Dillard's essay, which explain the PROCESS of looking through a microscope. What is the EFFECT of the second-person *you* in these paragraphs?

QUESTIONS ON LANGUAGE

1. If necessary, look up the following words in your dictionary: purblind (para. 1); paradoxical (2); translucent, opacity, leached (3); mesmerized, rotifer (4); daphniae, amoebae, invulnerable (5); centrifuge, biomass (6); apocalypses (7); fallow, deciduous (9); flushed (11); ellipses (12); ardent (14); infinitesimal (15).
2. How could the swans Dillard describes "change from white swans in front of the mountain to black swans in front of the sky" (para. 12)? How could they have "tiny wet wings" (15)?
3. Point to passages in which the author makes effective use of FIGURES OF SPEECH such as similes and metaphors.
4. What do the IMAGES in paragraph 14 contribute to Dillard's description?

SUGGESTIONS FOR WRITING

1. **JOURNAL WRITING.** Write at least five vivid images to describe something in the natural world, such as a cat, a turtle, a butterfly, a goldfish, a flower, a sunrise or sunset. Try to make at least one or two images similes or metaphors (see "Figures of speech" in Useful Terms).
   FROM JOURNAL TO ESSAY. Develop your journal writing into a detailed paragraph or two that DESCRIBES your subject. You may want to take Dillard's cue and draw out more detail by comparing your subject to something unexpected.
2. In an essay, detail your struggles with some instrument or gadget you had to use before you understood fully how it worked: a telescope, a household appliance, a pinball machine, a chain saw, a lawn mower, a computer, a video game, a pitching machine, a bicycle pump, a self-service gasoline pump. Your TONE need not be serious.
3. **CRITICAL WRITING.** EVALUATE the effectiveness of Dillard's transition in paragraph 8 between her use of a microscope in childhood and her use of binoculars in adulthood. Does the shift — "But oddly, this is a story about swans" — work to draw you in, startle you, or put you off? Does Dillard's CONCLUSION work, or not, to explain or justify the shift?
4. **CONNECTIONS.** Both Dillard and Calvin Trillin, in "Spelling Yiffniff" (p. 62), tell humorous stories about childhood and learning. With humor of your own, write an essay about learning something when you were young, such as tying your shoes, riding a bike, handwriting, whistling, using fractions.
5. **CONNECTIONS.** Dillard's "Lenses" bears comparison with E. B. White's "Once More to the Lake" (p. 644) for the ways the two authors describe the distortions they experience as they shuttle between past and present. In an essay, ANALYZE the images each author uses to capture a sense of distortion or disorientation.

ANNIE DILLARD ON WRITING

We asked Annie Dillard to tell us about the writing of "Lenses." Her wonderfully detailed response tells much about journal keeping, revising, and editing.

I wrote "Lenses" to see if I could evoke in the reader the same switcheroo that caught me when, looking through binoculars, I seemed suddenly to be looking through a microscope. I wrote it a few years after the event, working from a journal entry.

The key passage in the journal entry reads:

> And the weeds in front of me, as I faced the light, were translucent, out-of-focus, crossed and waving; they looked in the circle of light through the binoculars just like algae strands in pond water, and it was very easy to see the field of vision as pond water, algae strands, flat on a microscope's stage—and in it, among the strands, two tiny flying whistling swans.

The rest of the journal entry was full of details I could use. The swans changed like Escher birds from white in front of the mountain to black in front of the sky. (I disliked invoking Escher, who isn't much of an artist, but I thought the simile would communicate quickly the effect I wanted.) The swans flew in unison, clockwise, in ellipses; I lost all sense of space; the swans were like stitches; I lived in that circle of light; I could hear their wings; the sky changed color behind them; when I lost them behind a ridge and they emerged flying high, it was like music changing key.

In order to work this enthusiastic, personal description into what I hoped would be an interesting essay, everything had to push towards a punch line, towards the moment when the binoculars' field turns into a microscope's field, and the swans appear as small as rotifers. In order for *that* to work, I'd have to lay in a lot of background about looking at pond water through a microscope—so the microscope would be in the reader's "experience," as it were, just as it had been in my experience when the swans came along.

So I began a draft of roughly the same form as the final essay. It started with a long-winded, generalized description (or complaint) about looking at things through lenses, and continued with a description of children's microscope kits, and of my childhood forays with the microscope, looking at pond water. In writing this draft I indulged in some perhaps extraneous reminiscing: Because my makeshift light was so strong, my specimens dried up as I watched. I hoped this would be amusing enough and self-deprecating enough to justify its inclusion. By the end of the draft I had hopes of returning to this drying-up business to suggest a general apocalypse—to suggest that the big, real world might be somebody's overheated drop, or to suggest, at any rate, a feeling of mortality and immanent loss. (Alas, I had to abandon this; a friend convinced me it was phony.) To return the reader to the subject at hand, and to get off the joking tone (the creatures lay boiled and fried), I added a sentence at the end of the microscope section: "How I loved that deep, wet world where the colored algae waved in the water and the rotifers swam!" I was distant enough from that feeling to state it badly, I hoped; the point of the sentence was not the feeling—my love for the wet world—but a restatement of the image I wanted the reader to bear in mind—the waving algaes and swimming rotifers.

Then I had a nasty problem. How could I change the subject? How could I change the subject, and with it the setting in both time and space? I was so afraid that readers would feel they'd been had that in the first draft I addressed them directly: "Perhaps I should break it to you gently that this is a story about swans. It is not even a story; it is a description of swans. Like the creatures in pond water, you have been heartlessly set up for an unsuspected end." Later I thought that this frontal assault would only reinforce the readers' sense of being had. I tried instead to brazen it out, with as much authority and as little fear as I could muster, throwing only to readers the sympathetic word "oddly" [see para. 8].

And so I plowed through the first draft, leaning heavily on the journal entry for data. I took pains to lay in the Virginia setting, so the reader would have time to catch his breath and accustom himself to the new time and place. I tried to keep the swans visible and the verbs interesting and matter-of-fact.

I had a devil of a time with the paragraph about losing a sense of space [13]—where should it go? Logically it didn't fit anywhere; it was loose. Therefore, I should take it out. But I left it in, hoping its bringing up my dazedness would prepare for the perceptual switch at the essay's end. Really I left it in because I was ridiculously fond of the simile about emerging from a movie. "Lenses" is, I think, a slight essay; I collected it in a book only because I still liked that bit about coming out of a movie and trying to reconstruct, bit by bit, a real world, in order to discover where in it you might have parked the car.

The first draft ended:

> And suddenly into the field swam two whistling swans, two tiny whistling swans. They swam as fast as rotifers: two whistling swans, infinitesimal, beating their tiny wet wings, perfectly formed.
> How much time, I wondered, do we have?

In a subsequent draft I tried, very delicately, to expand this last notion. In one phrase, and one phrase only, I described a shrinking sky. I wanted some idea of mortality. The joking of the first part, when the microscopic creatures' drop shrank, would now become quickly serious. It would stun, I fondly hoped, the reader with a rushing sense of death, a sense of the beauty of human life and its swift loss. It would be a premonition, a pang; the essay would contract to that moment and expand to that meaning. I myself had lost those days—both my innocent childhood days at the microscope, and those grand days in my twenties on Daleville Pond. Now Daleville Pond was drained and developed, and I no longer lived in Virginia.

But I couldn't do it. Every six months or so I looked at the "finished" piece. The ending always seemed forced; my friend had been right. (She's my best critic.) I'd write another version, look at it again later, and write yet another version. Finally after several years I decided to cut my losses and give up what had been my brightest hopes for the piece. Even now, after the piece has been published several times, I can't help but think: Couldn't I still do it? The groundwork's all there. Just a few strong sentences, right at the end, could mean so much, and make it all so much more interesting.

There were, of course, many more changes from the first draft to the published version. I was happy to have so many things to look up. Whenever you get to look something up, you find all sorts of information you can use to give your writing substance. As I write, I mark queries in the page's margin: Check plural *daphnia*. Do swans pair for life? Migrating from where to where? Don't they fly at night?

I looked up all the algae, to check color and spelling; I looked up whistling swans and learned where they were going and the span of their wings (six feet). I called Virginia to learn the size of Daleville Pond (ten acres).

Rewriting, I also condensed, of course. Of the heated drop, I'd said, "Its contours pulled together." Waking up to the tortured abstraction of the phrase, I changed it to "Its edges shrank." I like short sentences. They're forceful, and they can get you out of big trouble. I changed the order of some paragraphs, sentences, and phrases. I had, for instance, a seventy-five-watt bulb focused into my eye and magnified three hundred times; I changed it to "magnified three hundred times and focused into my eye." I took out many self-indulgent references to myself and my feelings.

I condensed the opening a lot. I always have to condense or toss openings; I suspect most writers do. When you begin something, you're so grateful to have begun you'll write down anything, just to prolong the sensation. Later, when you've learned what the writing is really about, you go back and throw away the beginning and start over.

"Lenses" was easy to write; it had only six or seven versions, and most of those were fiddlings with the last few paragraphs. I sent the book version to the publisher seven years after the journal entry. I'm not entirely sure I'm done with it yet. It was easy only because I abandoned my far-fetched ambition for it, and settled for pure description. Description's not too hard if you mind your active verbs, keep ticking off as many sense impressions as you can, and omit feelings.

FOR DISCUSSION

1. How was Dillard's journal entry the starting point for her essay? Why did she have to add considerable material about looking through a microscope?
2. What does Dillard reveal about the drafting and revising process in her discussion of having to condense her essay's opening (second-to-last paragraph)?
3. Look at Dillard's last sentence about writing "pure description." In what way does the author "omit feelings" from "Lenses"—which, after all, conveys her responses to her observations?

STEPHEN JAY GOULD

A paleontologist and collector of snails, STEPHEN JAY GOULD was born in New York City in 1941, went to Antioch College, and took a doctorate from Columbia University. Since the age of twenty-five, Gould has taught biology, geology, and the history of science at Harvard, where his courses are among the most popular. Although he has written for specialists (*Ontogeny and Phylogeny*, 1977), Gould is best known for essays that explore science in prose a layperson can enjoy. He writes a monthly column for *Natural History* magazine, and these and other essays have been collected in many books, including *The Panda's Thumb* (1980), *Hens' Teeth and Horses' Toes* (1983), *Eight Little Piggies* (1993), *Dinosaur in a Haystack* (1995), and *Leonardo's Mountain of Clams and the Diet of Worms* (1998). His latest book is *Rocks of Ages* (1999), which attempts to heal the rift between science and religion. In 1981, Gould received $200,000 (popularly called a "genius grant") from the MacArthur Foundation, which subsidizes the work of original artists and thinkers. In 1999, he became president of the American Association for the Advancement of Science.

Sex, Drugs, Disasters, and the Extinction of Dinosaurs

In this essay, Stephen Jay Gould tackles one of the greatest mysteries in the evolution of life on this planet: the extinction of dinosaurs. Employing both scholarship and wit, Gould works backward from a specific effect (the fact that dinosaurs are extinct) to ask "Why?" The essay originally appeared in a 1984 *Discover* magazine and then in Gould's fourth essay collection, *The Flamingo's Smile*.

Though Gould relies most notably on cause and effect (examining several possible causes), he also makes extensive use of several other methods to answer his central question:

Comparison and contrast (Chap. 4): paragraphs 4–5, 18–24
Process analysis (Chap. 5): paragraphs 4–5, 9–12, 14, 16
Division or analysis (Chap. 6): paragraphs 18–22
Cause and effect (Chap. 8): throughout
Argument and persuasion (Chap. 10): paragraphs 18–25

Science, in its most fundamental definition, is a fruitful mode of inquiry, not a list of enticing conclusions. The conclusions are the consequence, not the essence.

My greatest unhappiness with most popular presentations of science concerns their failure to separate fascinating claims from the methods that scientists use to establish the facts of nature. Journalists, and the public, thrive on controversial and stunning statements. But science is, basically, a way of knowing—in P. B. Medawar's apt words, "the art of the soluble." If the growing corps of popular science writers would focus on *how* scientists develop and defend those fascinating claims, they would make their greatest possible contribution to public understanding.

Consider three ideas, proposed in perfect seriousness to explain that   3 greatest of all titillating puzzles—the extinction of dinosaurs. Since these three notions invoke the primally fascinating themes of our culture—sex, drugs, and violence—they surely reside in the category of fascinating claims. I want to show why two of them rank as silly speculation, while the other represents science at its grandest and most useful.

Science works with testable proposals. If, after much compilation   4 and scrutiny of data, new information continues to affirm a hypothesis, we may accept it provisionally and gain confidence as further evidence mounts. We can never be completely sure that a hypothesis is right, though we may be able to show with confidence that it is wrong. The best scientific hypotheses are also generous and expansive: They suggest extensions and implications that enlighten related, and even far distant, subjects. Simply consider how the idea of evolution has influenced virtually every intellectual field.

Useless speculation, on the other hand, is restrictive. It generates   5 no testable hypothesis, and offers no way to obtain potentially refuting evidence. Please note that I am not speaking of truth or falsity. The speculation may well be true; still, if it provides, in principle, no material for affirmation or rejection, we can make nothing of it. It must simply stand forever as an intriguing idea. Useless speculation turns in on itself and leads nowhere; good science, containing both seeds for its potential refutation and implications for more and different testable knowledge, reaches out. But, enough preaching. Let's move on to dinosaurs, and the three proposals for their extinction.

1. *Sex.*   Testes function only in a narrow range of temperature (those of mammals hang externally in a scrotal sac because internal body temperatures are too high for their proper function). A worldwide rise in temperature at the close of the Cretaceous period caused the testes of dinosaurs to stop functioning and led to their extinction by sterilization of males.

2. *Drugs.*   Angiosperms (flowering plants) first evolved toward the end of the dinosaurs' reign. Many of these plants contain psychoactive agents, avoided by mammals today as a result of their bitter taste. Dinosaurs had neither means to taste the bitterness nor livers effective enough to detoxify the substances. They died of massive overdoses.

3. *Disasters.*   A large comet or asteroid struck the earth some 65 mil-

lion years ago, lofting a cloud of dust into the sky and blocking sunlight, thereby suppressing photosynthesis and so drastically lowering world temperatures that dinosaurs and hosts of other creatures
became extinct.

Before analyzing these three tantalizing statements, we must establish a
basic ground rule often violated in proposals for the dinosaurs' demise.
There is no separate problem of the extinction of dinosaurs. Too often we divorce specific events from their wider contexts and systems of cause
and effect. The fundamental fact of dinosaur extinction is its synchrony with the demise of so many other groups across a wide range of
habitats, from terrestrial to marine.

The history of life has been punctuated by brief episodes of mass   6
extinction. A recent analysis by University of Chicago paleontologists
Jack Sepkoski and Dave Raup, based on the best and most exhaustive
tabulation of data ever assembled, shows clearly that five episodes of
mass dying stand well above the "background" extinctions of normal
times (when we consider all mass extinctions, large and small, they
seem to fall in a regular 26-million-year cycle). The Cretaceous debacle, occurring 65 million years ago and separating the Mesozoic and
Cenozoic eras of our geological time scale, ranks prominently among
the five. Nearly all the marine plankton (single-celled floating creatures) died with geological suddenness; among marine invertebrates,
nearly 15 percent of all families perished, including many previously
dominant groups, especially the ammonites (relatives of squids in
coiled shells). On land, the dinosaurs disappeared after more than 100
million years of unchallenged domination.

In this context, speculations limited to dinosaurs alone ignore the   7
larger phenomenon. We need a coordinated explanation for a system of
events that includes the extinction of dinosaurs as one component.
Thus it makes little sense, though it may fuel our desire to view mammals as inevitable inheritors of the earth, to guess that dinosaurs died
because small mammals ate their eggs (a perennial favorite among
untestable speculations). It seems most unlikely that some disaster peculiar to dinosaurs befell these massive beasts—and that the debacle
happened to strike just when one of history's five great dyings had enveloped the earth for completely different reasons.

The testicular theory, an old favorite from the 1940s, had its root   8
in an interesting and thoroughly respectable study of temperature tolerances in the American alligator, published in the staid *Bulletin of the
American Museum of Natural History* in 1946 by three experts on living
and fossil reptiles—E. H. Colbert, my own first teacher in paleontology; R. B. Cowles; and C. M. Bogert.

The first sentence of their summary reveals a purpose beyond alli-   9
gators: "This report describes an attempt to infer the reactions of extinct reptiles, especially the dinosaurs, to high temperatures as based
upon reactions observed in the modern alligator." They studied, by rec-
tal thermometry, the body temperatures of alligators under changing
conditions of heating and cooling. (Well, let's face it, you wouldn't
want to try sticking a thermometer under a 'gator's tongue.) The pre-
dictions under test go way back to an old theory first stated by Galileo
in the 1630s—the unequal scaling of surfaces and volumes. As an animal, or any object, grows (provided its shape doesn't change), surface
areas must increase more slowly than volumes—since surfaces get
larger as length squared, while volumes increase much more rapidly, as
length cubed. Therefore, small animals have high ratios of surface
to volume, while large animals cover themselves with relatively little
surface.

Among cold-blooded animals lacking any physiological mecha-   10
nism for keeping their temperatures constant, small creatures have a
hell of a time keeping warm—because they lose so much heat through
their relatively large surfaces. On the other hand, large animals, with
their relatively small surfaces, may lose heat so slowly that, once warm,
they may maintain effectively constant temperatures against ordinary
fluctuations of climate. (In fact, the resolution of the "hot-blooded
dinosaur" controversy that burned so brightly a few years back may simply be that, while large dinosaurs possessed no physiological mechanism for constant temperature, and were not therefore warm-blooded
in the technical sense, their large size and relatively small surface area
kept them warm.)

Colbert, Cowles, and Bogert compared the warming rates of small   11
and large alligators. As predicted, the small fellows heated up (and
cooled down) more quickly. When exposed to a warm sun, a tiny 50-
gram (1.76-ounce) alligator heated up one degree Celsius every minute
and a half, while a large alligator, 260 times bigger at 13,000 grams
(28.7 pounds), took seven and a half minutes to gain a degree. Extrapolating up to an adult 10-ton dinosaur, they concluded that a one-
degree rise in body temperature would take eighty-six hours. If large
animals absorb heat so slowly (through their relatively small surfaces),
they will also be unable to shed any excess heat gained when temperatures rise above a favorable level.

The authors then guessed that large dinosaurs lived at or near their   12
optimum temperatures; Cowles suggested that a rise in global temperatures just before the Cretaceous extinction caused the dinosaurs to
heat up beyond their optimal tolerance—and, being so large, they
couldn't shed the unwanted heat. (In a most unusual statement within
a scientific paper, Colbert and Bogert then explicitly disavowed this

speculative extension of their empirical work on alligators.) Cowles conceded that this excess heat probably wasn't enough to kill or even to enervate the great beasts, but since testes often function only within a narrow range of temperature, he proposed that this global rise might have sterilized all the males, causing extinction by natural contraception.

The overdose theory has recently been supported by UCLA psy-   13 chiatrist Ronald K. Siegel. Siegel has gathered, he claims, more than 2,000 records of animals who, when given access, administer various drugs to themselves—from a mere swig of alcohol to massive doses of the big H. Elephants will swill the equivalent of twenty beers at a time, but do not like alcohol in concentrations greater than 7 percent. In a silly bit of anthropocentric speculation, Siegel states that "elephants drink, perhaps, to forget... the anxiety produced by shrinking range-land and the competition for food."

Since fertile imaginations can apply almost any hot idea to the ex-   14 tinction of dinosaurs, Siegel found a way. Flowering plants did not evolve until late in the dinosaurs' reign. These plants also produced an array of aromatic, amino-acid-based alkaloids—the major group of psychoactive agents. Most mammals are "smart" enough to avoid these potential poisons. The alkaloids simply don't taste good (they are bitter); in any case, we mammals have livers happily supplied with the capacity to detoxify them. But, Siegel speculates, perhaps dinosaurs could neither taste the bitterness nor detoxify the substances once ingested. He recently told members of the American Psychological Association: "I'm not suggesting that all dinosaurs OD'd on plant drugs, but it certainly was a factor." He also argued that death by overdose may help explain why so many dinosaur fossils are found in contorted positions. (Do not go gently into that good night.)

Extraterrestrial catastrophes have long pedigrees in the popular lit-   15 erature of extinction, but the subject exploded again in 1979, after a long lull, when the father-son, physicist-geologist team of Luis and Walter Alvarez proposed that an asteroid, some 10 km in diameter, struck the earth 65 million years ago. (Comets, rather than asteroids, have since gained favor. Good science is self-corrective.)

The force of such a collision would be immense, greater by far than   16 the megatonnage of all the world's nuclear weapons. In trying to reconstruct a scenario that would explain the simultaneous dying of dinosaurs on land and so many creatures in the sea, the Alvarezes proposed that a gigantic dust cloud, generated by particles blown aloft in the impact, would so darken the earth that photosynthesis would cease and temperatures drop precipitously. (Rage, rage against the dying of the light.) The single-celled photosynthetic oceanic plankton, with life cycles measured in weeks, would perish outright, but land plants might survive through the dormancy of their seeds (land plants were not much affected by the Cretaceous extinction, and any adequate theory must account for the curious pattern of differential survival). Dinosaurs would die by starvation and freezing; small, warm-blooded mammals, with more modest requirements for food and better regulation of body temperature, would squeak through. "Let the bastards freeze in the dark," as bumper stickers of our chauvinistic neighbors in sunbelt states proclaimed several years ago during the Northeast's winter oil crisis.

All three theories, testicular malfunction, psychoactive overdos-   17
ing, and asteroidal zapping, grab our attention mightily. As pure phenomenology, they rank about equally high on any hit parade of primal fascination. Yet one represents expansive science, the others restrictive and untestable speculation. The proper criterion lies in evidence and methodology; we must probe behind the superficial fascination of particular claims.

How could we possibly decide whether the hypothesis of testicular   18
frying is right or wrong? We would have to know things that the fossil record cannot provide. What temperatures were optimal for dinosaurs? Could they avoid the absorption of excess heat by staying in the shade, or in caves? At what temperatures did their testicles cease to function? Were late Cretaceous climates ever warm enough to drive the internal temperatures of dinosaurs close to this ceiling? Testicles simply don't fossilize, and how could we infer their temperature tolerances even if they did? In short, Cowles's hypothesis is only an intriguing speculation leading nowhere. The most damning statement against it appeared right in the conclusion of Colbert, Cowles, and Bogert's paper, when they admitted: "It is difficult to advance any definite arguments against this hypothesis." My statement may seem paradoxical — isn't a hypothesis really good if you can't devise any arguments against it? Quite the contrary. It is simply untestable and unusable.

Siegel's overdosing has even less going for it. At least Cowles ex-   19
trapolated his conclusion from some good data on alligators. And he didn't completely violate the primary guideline of siting dinosaur extinction in the context of a general mass dying — for rise in temperature could be the root cause of a general catastrophe, zapping dinosaurs by testicular malfunction and different groups for other reasons. But Siegel's speculation cannot touch the extinction of ammonites or oceanic plankton (diatoms make their own food with good sweet sunlight; they don't OD on the chemicals of terrestrial plants). It is simply a gratuitous, attention-grabbing guess. It cannot be tested, for how can we know what dinosaurs tasted and what their livers could do? Livers don't fossilize any better than testicles.

The hypothesis doesn't even make any sense in its own context.   20
Angiosperms were in full flower ten million years before dinosaurs went
the way of all flesh. Why did it take so long? As for the pains of a chemical death recorded in contortions of fossils, I regret to say (or rather I'm
pleased to note for the dinosaurs' sake) that Siegel's knowledge of geology must be a bit deficient: Muscles contract after death and geological
strata rise and fall with motions of the earth's crust after burial —more
than enough reason to distort a fossil's pristine appearance.

The impact story, on the other hand, has a sound basis in evidence.   21
It can be tested, extended, refined, and, if wrong, disproved. The
Alvarezes did not just construct an arresting guess for public consumption. They proposed their hypothesis after laborious geochemical studies with Frank Asaro and Helen Michael had revealed a massive
increase of iridium in rocks deposited right at the time of extinction.
Iridium, a rare metal of the platinum group, is virtually absent from in-
digenous rocks of the earth's crust; most of our iridium arrives on extraterrestrial objects that strike the earth.

The Alvarez hypothesis bore immediate fruit. Based originally on ev-   22
idence from two European localities, it led geochemists throughout the
world to examine other sediments of the same age. They found abnor-
mally high amounts of iridium everywhere—from continental rocks of
the western United States to deep sea cores from the South Atlantic.

Cowles proposed his testicular hypothesis in the mid-1940s. Where   23
has it gone since then? Absolutely nowhere, because scientists can do
nothing with it. The hypothesis must stand as a curious appendage to
a solid study of alligators. Siegel's overdose scenario will also win a
few press notices and fade into oblivion. The Alvarezes' asteroid falls
into a different category altogether, and much of the popular commentary has missed this essential distinction by focusing on the impact
and its attendant results, and forgetting what really matters to a scientist—the iridium. If you talk just about asteroids, dust, and darkness, you
tell stories no better and no more entertaining than fried testicles or
terminal trips. It is the iridium—the source of testable evidence—
that counts and forges the crucial distinction between speculation and
science.

The proof, to twist a phrase, lies in the doing. Cowles's hypothesis   24
has generated nothing in thirty-five years. Since its proposal in 1979,
the Alvarez hypothesis has spawned hundreds of studies, a major conference, and attendant publications. Geologists are fired up. They are
looking for iridium at all other extinction boundaries. Every week exposes a new wrinkle in the scientific press. Further evidence that the
Cretaceous iridium represents extraterrestrial impact and not indige-
nous volcanism continues to accumulate. As I revise this essay in November 1984 (this paragraph will be out of date when [it] is published),

new data include chemical "signatures" of other isotopes indicating unearthly provenance, glass spherules of a size and sort produced by impact and not by volcanic eruptions, and high-pressure varieties of silica formed (so far as we know) only under the tremendous shock of impact.

My point is simply this: Whatever the eventual outcome (I suspect   25
it will be positive), the Alvarez hypothesis is exciting, fruitful science because it generates tests, provides us with things to do, and expands outward. We are having fun, battling back and forth, moving toward a resolution, and extending the hypothesis beyond its original scope.

As just one example of the unexpected, distant cross-fertilization   26
that good science engenders, the Alvarez hypothesis made a major contribution to a theme that has riveted public attention in the past few months—so-called nuclear winter. In a speech delivered in April 1982, Luis Alvarez calculated the energy that a ten-kilometer asteroid would release on impact. He compared such an explosion with a full nuclear exchange and implied that all-out atomic war might unleash similar consequences.

This theme of impact leading to massive dust clouds and falling   27
temperatures formed an important input to the decision of Carl Sagan and a group of colleagues to model the climatic consequences of nuclear holocaust. Full nuclear exchange would probably generate the same kind of dust cloud and darkening that may have wiped out the dinosaurs. Temperatures would drop precipitously and agriculture might become impossible. Avoidance of nuclear war is fundamentally an ethical and political imperative, but we must know the factual consequences to make firm judgments. I am heartened by a final link across disciplines and deep concerns—another criterion, by the way, of science at its best: A recognition of the very phenomenon that made our evolution possible by exterminating the previously dominant dinosaurs and clearing a way for the evolution of large mammals, including us, might actually help to save us from joining those magnificent beasts in contorted poses among the strata of the earth.

QUESTIONS ON MEANING

1. According to Gould, what constitutes a scientific hypothesis? What constitutes useless speculation? Where in the essay do you find his DEFINITIONS of these terms?
2. State, in your own words, the THESIS of this essay.
3. What does Gould perceive to be the major flaws in the testicular malfunction and drug overdose theories about the extinction of dinosaurs? Cite his specific reasons for discrediting each theory.

4. What is the connection between nuclear holocaust and the extinction of dinosaurs? (See the essay's last paragraph.)

QUESTIONS ON WRITING STRATEGY

1. How do you understand the phrases "hit parade of primal fascination" (para. 17) and "the hypothesis of testicular frying" (18)? Is the TONE here somber, silly, whimsical, ironic, or what?
2. Paragraphs 14 and 16 both contain references to Dylan Thomas's poem "Do Not Go Gentle into That Good Night." (The poem's title is used in para. 14; "Rage, rage against the dying of the light," one of the poem's refrains, appears in para. 16.) If you are not familiar with the poem, look it up. Is it necessary to know the poem to understand Gould's use of these lines? What is the EFFECT of these ALLUSIONS?
3. **MIXED METHODS.** In explaining the Alvarezes' hypothesis about the CAUSES of the dinosaurs' extinction, Gould outlines a causal chain. Draw a diagram to illustrate this chain.
4. **MIXED METHODS.** How does the PROCESS ANALYSIS in paragraphs 4–5, 9–12, 14, and 16 help Gould analyze the possible causes of dinosaur extinction? What would the essay lack without these paragraphs?

QUESTIONS ON LANGUAGE

1. What do you take the sentence "There is no separate problem of the extinction of dinosaurs" (para. 5) to mean? Separate from what? According to Gould, then, what *is* the problem being discussed?
2. Be sure you can define the following words: enticing (para. 1); hypothesis (4); psychoactive, photosynthesis, synchrony (5); paleontology (8); extrapolating (11); empirical (12); gratuitous (19).

SUGGESTIONS FOR WRITING

1. **JOURNAL WRITING.** Gould's essay is interesting partly because he proposes several possible causes for the same effect. We all do the same thing daily (if more informally) when we try to solve puzzles like "Why is my bike tire flat?" (it was slashed; I rode over glass; I haven't ridden the bike in weeks) or "Why do little siblings ask so many questions?" (to annoy us; because they're curious; because someone puts them up to it). In your journal, try to work out the probable cause(s) of a situation in which you are directly involved—working in the school cafeteria, taking a psychology course offered only on Wednesday evenings, riding to school with a person you detest, dating your former best friend, whatever. What are all the causes you can think of—both immediate and remote? (See pp. 361 and 364 for a discussion of kinds of causes.)
   FROM JOURNAL TO ESSAY. Once you have a number of ideas about the causes of your situation, write a formal essay that explains the causes in detail. Make sure to give your AUDIENCE a clear sense of the situation. You may want to rely on NARRATION, telling the story of the circumstances.

2. As Gould himself predicts (para. 24), his summary of the research into the Alvarez hypothesis is now dated: More data have accumulated; the hypothesis has been challenged, tested, revised. Consult the *Readers' Guide to Periodical Literature* or *InfoTrac* for the past several years to find articles on the extinction of the dinosaurs. Write an essay updating Gould's in which you summarize the significant EVIDENCE for and against the Alvarez hypothesis.

3. **CRITICAL WRITING.** Apply Gould's distinction between hypothesis and speculation (paras. 4–5) in an area you know well—for instance, Civil War battles, dance, basketball, waste recycling, carpentry, nursing. What, in your area, is the equivalent of the useful hypothesis? What is the equivalent of the useless speculation? Be as specific as possible so that a reader outside the field can understand you.

4. **CONNECTIONS.** Gould's is one of several essays in this book written by specialists for an audience of nonspecialists; others include Bruce Catton's "Grant and Lee" (p. 196), Linnea Saukko's "How to Poison the Earth" (p. 228), Deborah Tannen's "But What Do You Mean?" (p. 330), and William Lutz's "The World of Doublespeak" (p. 350). In an essay, compare Gould's essay with one of the others listed in terms of complexity of material, use and explanation of specialized vocabulary, and clarity of explanation. Overall, which essay do you find most effective in explaining a specialized subject for nonspecialists?

5. **CONNECTIONS.** COMPARE AND CONTRAST Gould's essay with K. C. Cole's "The Arrow of Time" (p. 378), taking as your main point of comparison each author's attitudes toward the science he or she discusses and toward its implications. To gauge attitudes, look not only at what the authors say but also at their TONES.

STEPHEN JAY GOULD ON WRITING

In his prologue to *The Flamingo's Smile*, Stephen Jay Gould positions himself in a long and respectable tradition of writers who communicate scientific ideas to a general audience. To popularize, he says, does not mean to trivialize, cheapen, or adulterate. "I follow one cardinal rule in writing these essays," he insists. "No compromises. I will make language accessible by defining or eliminating jargon; I will not simplify concepts. I can state all sorts of highfalutin, moral justifications for this approach (and I do believe in them), but the basic reason is simple and personal. I write these essays primarily to aid my own quest to learn and understand as much as possible about nature in the short time allotted."

In his own view, Gould is lucky: He is a writer carried along by a single, fascinating theme. "If my volumes work at all, they owe their reputation to coherence supplied by the common theme of evolutionary theory. I have a wonderful advantage among essayists because no other theme so beautifully encompasses both the particulars that fascinate and the generalities that instruct....Each essay is both a single long argument and a welding together of particulars."

FOR DISCUSSION

1. What differences would occur naturally between the work of a scientist writing for other scientists and the work of Gould, who writes about science for a general AUDIENCE?
2. How does the author defend himself against the possible charge that, as a popularizer of science, he trivializes his subject?

MARTIN LUTHER KING, JR.

MARTIN LUTHER KING, JR. (1929–68), was born in Atlanta, the son of a Baptist minister, and was himself ordained in the same denomination. Stepping to the forefront of the civil rights movement in 1955, King led African Americans in a boycott of segregated city buses in Montgomery, Alabama; became first president of the Southern Christian Leadership Conference; and staged sit-ins and mass marches that helped bring about the Civil Rights Act passed by Congress in 1964 and the Voting Rights Act of 1965. He received the Nobel Peace Prize in 1964. While King preached "nonviolent resistance," he was himself the target of violence. He was stabbed in New York, pelted with stones in Chicago; his home in Montgomery was bombed; and finally in Memphis he was assassinated by a sniper. On his tombstone near Atlanta's Ebenezer Baptist Church are these words from the spiritual he quotes at the conclusion of "I Have a Dream": "Free at last, free at last, thank God almighty, I'm free at last." Martin Luther King's birthday, January 15, is now a national holiday.

I Have a Dream

In Washington, D.C., on August 28, 1963, King's campaign of nonviolent resistance reached its historic climax. On that date, commemorating the centennial of Lincoln's Emancipation Proclamation freeing the slaves, King led a march of 200,000 persons, black and white, from the Washington Monument to the Lincoln Memorial. Before this throng, and to millions who watched on television, he delivered this unforgettable speech.

Intended to inspire and motivate its audience, King's speech is a model of a certain kind of persuasion. To make his point, King draws on a number of methods:

Narration (Chap. 1): paragraphs 1–2
Description (Chap. 2): paragraphs 2, 4
Example (Chap. 3): paragraphs 6–9, 12–16, 21–22
Comparison and contrast (Chap. 4): paragraphs 3–4, 6
Cause and effect (Chap. 8): paragraphs 5, 7, 19
Argument and persuasion (Chap. 10): throughout

Five score years ago, a great American, in whose symbolic shadow 1 we stand, signed the Emancipation Proclamation. This momentous decree came as a great beacon light of hope to millions of Negro slaves who had been seared in the flames of withering injustice. It came as a joyous daybreak to end the long night of captivity.

But one hundred years later, we must face the tragic fact that the 2 Negro is still not free. One hundred years later, the life of the Negro is still sadly crippled by the manacles of segregation and the chains of discrimination. One hundred years later, the Negro lives on a lonely island of poverty in the midst of a vast ocean of material prosperity. One hundred years later, the Negro is still languishing in the corners of American society and finds himself in exile in his own land. So we have come here today to dramatize an appalling condition.

In a sense we have come to our nation's capital to cash a check.   3
When the architects of our republic wrote the magnificent words of the Constitution and the Declaration of Independence, they were signing a promissory note to which every American was to fall heir. This note was a promise that all men would be guaranteed the unalienable rights of life, liberty, and the pursuit of happiness.

It is obvious today that America has defaulted on this promissory   4
note insofar as her citizens of color are concerned. Instead of honoring this sacred obligation, America has given the Negro people a bad check; a check which has come back marked "insufficient funds." But we refuse to believe that the bank of justice is bankrupt. We refuse to believe that there are insufficient funds in the great vaults of opportunity of this nation. So we have come to cash this check—a check that will give us upon demand the riches of freedom and the security of justice. We have also come to this hallowed spot to remind America of the fierce urgency of *now*. This is no time to engage in the luxury of cooling off or to take the tranquilizing drugs of gradualism. *Now* is the time to make real the promises of Democracy. *Now* is the time to rise from the dark and desolate valley of segregation to the sunlit path of racial justice. *Now* is the time to open the doors of opportunity to all of God's children. *Now* is the time to lift our nation from the quicksands of racial injustice to the solid rock of brotherhood.

It would be fatal for the nation to overlook the urgency of the mo-   5
ment and to underestimate the determination of the Negro. This sweltering summer of the Negro's legitimate discontent will not pass until there is an invigorating autumn of freedom and equality; 1963 is not an end, but a beginning. Those who hope that the Negro needed to blow off steam and will now be content will have a rude awakening if the nation returns to business as usual. There will be neither rest nor tranquillity in America until the Negro is granted his citizenship rights. The whirlwinds of revolt will continue to shake the foundations of our nation until the bright day of justice emerges.

But there is something that I must say to my people who stand   6
on the warm threshold which leads into the palace of justice. In the process of gaining our rightful place we must not be guilty of wrongful deeds. Let us not seek to satisfy our thirst for freedom by drinking from the cup of bitterness and hatred. We must forever conduct our struggle

on the high plane of dignity and discipline. We must not allow our creative protest to degenerate into physical violence. Again and again we must rise to the majestic heights of meeting physical force with soul force. The marvelous new militancy which has engulfed the Negro community must not lead us to a distrust of all white people, for many of our white brothers, as evidenced by their presence here today, have come to realize that their destiny is tied up with our destiny and their freedom is inextricably bound to our freedom. We cannot walk alone.

And as we walk, we must make the pledge that we shall march 7 ahead. We cannot turn back. There are those who are asking the devotees of civil rights, "When will you be satisfied?" We can never be satisfied as long as the Negro is the victim of the unspeakable horrors of police brutality. We can never be satisfied as long as our bodies, heavy with the fatigue of travel, cannot gain lodging in the motels of the highways and the hotels of the cities. We cannot be satisfied as long as the Negro's basic mobility is from a smaller ghetto to a larger one. We can never be satisfied as long as a Negro in Mississippi cannot vote and a Negro in New York believes he has nothing for which to vote. No, no, we are not satisfied, and we will not be satisfied until justice rolls down like waters and righteousness like a mighty stream.

I am not unmindful that some of you have come here out of great 8 trials and tribulations. Some of you have come fresh from narrow jail cells. Some of you have come from areas where your quest for freedom left you battered by the storms of persecution and staggered by the winds of police brutality. You have been the veterans of creative suffering. Continue to work with the faith that unearned suffering is redemptive.

Go back to Mississippi, go back to Alabama, go back to South Car- 9 olina, go back to Georgia, go back to Louisiana, go back to the slums and ghettos of our northern cities, knowing that somehow this situation can and will be changed. Let us not wallow in the valley of despair.

I say to you today, my friends, that in spite of the difficulties and 10 frustrations of the moment I still have a dream. It is a dream deeply rooted in the American dream.

I have a dream that one day this nation will rise up and live out the 11 true meaning of its creed: "We hold these truths to be self-evident; that all men are created equal."

I have a dream that one day on the red hills of Georgia the sons of 12 former slaves and the sons of former slaveowners will be able to sit down together at the table of brotherhood.

I have a dream that one day even the state of Mississippi, a desert 13 state sweltering with the heat of injustice and oppression, will be transformed into an oasis of freedom and justice.

I have a dream that my four little children will one day live in a na- 14
tion where they will not be judged by the color of their skin but by the
content of their character.

I have a dream today. 15

I have a dream that one day the state of Alabama, whose governor's 16
lips are presently dripping with the words of interposition and nullification, will be transformed into a situation where little black boys and
black girls will be able to join hands with little white boys and white
girls and walk together as sisters and brothers.

I have a dream today. 17

I have a dream that one day every valley shall be exalted, every hill 18
and mountain shall be made low, the rough places will be made plain,
and the crooked places will be made straight, and the glory of the Lord
shall be revealed, and all flesh shall see it together.

This is our hope. This is the faith with which I return to the South. 19
With this faith we will be able to hew out of the mountain of despair a
stone of hope. With this faith we will be able to transform the jangling
discords of our nation into a beautiful symphony of brotherhood. With
this faith we will be able to work together, to pray together, to struggle
together, to go to jail together, to stand up for freedom together, knowing that we will be free one day.

This will be the day when all of God's children will be able to sing 20
with new meaning

> My country, 'tis of thee,
> Sweet land of liberty,
>   Of thee I sing:
> Land where my fathers died,
> Land of the pilgrims' pride,
>   From every mountainside
>   Let freedom ring.

And if America is to be a great nation this must become true. So let 21
freedom ring from the prodigious hilltops of New Hampshire. Let freedom ring from the mighty mountains of New York. Let freedom ring
from the heightening Alleghenies of Pennsylvania!

Let freedom ring from the snowcapped Rockies of Colorado! 22

Let freedom ring from the curvaceous peaks of California! 23

But not only that; let freedom ring from Stone Mountain of Georgia! 24

Let freedom ring from Lookout Mountain of Tennessee! 25

Let freedom ring from every hill and molehill of Mississippi. From 26
every mountainside, let freedom ring.

When we let freedom ring, when we let it ring from every village 27
and every hamlet, from every state and every city, we will be able to
speed up that day when all of God's children, black men and white

men, Jews and Gentiles, Protestants and Catholics, will be able to join hands and sing in the words of the old Negro spiritual, "Free at last! free at last! thank God almighty, we are free at last!"

QUESTIONS ON MEANING

1. What is the apparent PURPOSE of this speech?
2. What THESIS does King develop in his first four paragraphs?
3. What does King mean by the "marvelous new militancy which has engulfed the Negro community" (para. 6)? Does this contradict King's nonviolent philosophy?
4. In what passages of his speech does King notice events of history? Where does he acknowledge the historic occasion on which he is speaking?

QUESTIONS ON WRITING STRATEGY

1. What indicates that King's words were meant primarily for an AUDIENCE of listeners, and only secondarily for a reading audience? To hear these indications, try reading the speech aloud. What uses of PARALLELISM do you notice?
2. Where in the speech does King acknowledge that not all of his listeners are African American?
3. How much EMPHASIS does King place on the past? How much does he place on the future?
4. **MIXED METHODS.** Analyze the ETHICAL APPEAL of King's ARGUMENT (see pp. 456–57). Where in the speech, for instance, does he present himself as reasonable despite his passion? To what extent does his personal authority lend power to his words?
5. **MIXED METHODS.** The DESCRIPTION in paragraphs 2 and 4 depends on metaphor, a FIGURE OF SPEECH in which one thing is said to be another thing. How do the metaphors in these paragraphs work for King's purpose?

QUESTIONS ON LANGUAGE

1. In general, is the language of King's speech ABSTRACT or CONCRETE? How is this level appropriate to the speaker's message and to the span of history with which he deals?
2. Point to memorable figures of speech besides those examined in the "Mixed Methods" question above.
3. Define momentous (para. 1); manacles, languishing (2); promissory note, unalienable (3); defaulted, hallowed, gradualism (4); inextricably (6); mobility, ghetto (7); tribulations, redemptive (8); interposition, nullification (16); prodigious (21); curvaceous (23); hamlet (27).

SUGGESTIONS FOR WRITING

1. **JOURNAL WRITING.** Do you think we have moved closer to fulfilling King's dream in the decades since he gave this famous speech? Why, or why not? **FROM JOURNAL TO ESSAY.** Write an essay that explains your sense of how well the United States has progressed toward realizing King's dream. You may choose to focus on America as a whole or on your particular community, but you should use specific EVIDENCE to support your opinion.

2. Propose some course of action in a situation that you consider an injustice. Racial injustice is one possible area, or unfairness to any minority, or to women, children, the elderly, ex-convicts, the disabled, the poor. If possible, narrow your subject to a particular incident or a local situation on which you can write knowledgeably.

3. **CRITICAL WRITING.** What can you INFER from this speech about King's own attitudes toward oppression and injustice? Does he follow his own injunction not "to satisfy our thirst for freedom by drinking from the cup of bitterness and hatred" (para. 6)? Explain your answer, using evidence from the speech.

4. **CONNECTIONS.** King's "I Have a Dream" and H. L. Mencken's "The Penalty of Death" (p. 470) both seek to influence readers, either to cause them to act or to change their views. Yet the two authors take very different approaches to achieve their purposes. COMPARE AND CONTRAST the authors' persuasive strategies, considering especially their effectiveness for the situation each writes about and the audience each addresses.

5. **CONNECTIONS.** King's speech was delivered in 1963. Brent Staples's essay "Black Men and Public Space" (p. 168) was first published in 1986. In an essay, explore the changes, if any, that are evident in the ASSUMPTIONS the authors make about their audiences' attitudes, about race in general, and about racism.

MAXINE HONG KINGSTON

MAXINE HONG KINGSTON grew up caught between two complex and very different cultures: the China of her parents and the America of her surroundings. In her first two books, *The Woman Warrior: Memoirs of a Girlhood Among Ghosts* (1979) and *China Men* (1980), Kingston combines Chinese myth and history with family tales to create a dreamlike world that shifts between reality and fantasy. Born in 1940 in Stockton, California, Kingston was the first American-born child of a scholar and a medical practitioner who became laundry workers in this country. After graduating from the University of California at Berkeley (B.A., 1962), Kingston taught English at California and Hawaii high schools and at the University of Hawaii. She now teaches at U.C. Berkeley, where she is Chancellor's Distinguished Professor. Kingston has contributed essays, poems, and stories to *The New Yorker*, the *New York Times Magazine*, *Ms.*, and other periodicals. Her most recent books are the novel *Tripmaster Monkey: His Fake Book* (1989) and a collection of essays, *Hawai'i One Summer* (1998). In 1997 she was awarded the National Humanities Medal.

No Name Woman

"No Name Woman" is part of *The Woman Warrior*. Like much of Kingston's writing, it blends the "talk-stories" of Kingston's elders, her own vivid imaginings, and the reality of her experience—this time to discover why her Chinese aunt drowned herself in the family well.

Kingston develops "No Name Woman" with four main methods, all intertwined: In the context of narrating her own experiences, she seeks the causes of her aunt's suicide by comparing various narratives of it, and she employs description to make the narratives concrete and vivid. The main uses of these methods appear below:

Narration (Chap. 1): paragraphs 1–8, 14, 16–20, 23, 28–30, 34–35, 37–46

Description (Chap. 2): paragraphs 4–8, 21, 23–27, 31, 37, 40–46

Comparison and contrast (Chap. 4): paragraphs 15–18, 20–24, 27–28, 31

Cause and effect (Chap. 8): paragraphs 10–11, 15–18, 21–25, 29–31, 33–39, 44–48

"You must not tell anyone," my mother said, "what I am about to tell you. In China your father had a sister who killed herself. She jumped into the family well. We say that your father has all brothers because it is as if she had never been born.

"In 1924 just a few days after our village celebrated seventeen hurry-up weddings—to make sure that every young man who went 'out on the road' would responsibly come home—your father and his brothers and your grandfather and his brothers and your aunt's new husband sailed for America, the Gold Mountain. It was your grandfather's last trip. Those lucky enough to get contracts waved good-bye from the decks. They fed and guarded the stowaways and helped them off in Cuba, New York, Bali, Hawaii. 'We'll meet in California next year,' they said. All of them sent money home.

"I remember looking at your aunt one day when she and I were   3 dressing; I had not noticed before that she had such a protruding melon of a stomach. But I did not think, 'She's pregnant,' until she began to look like other pregnant women, her shirt pulling and the white tops of her black pants showing. She could not have been pregnant, you see, because her husband had been gone for years. No one said anything. We did not discuss it. In early summer she was ready to have the child, long after the time when it could have been possible.

"The village had also been counting. On the night the baby was to   4 be born the villagers raided our house. Some were crying. Like a great saw, teeth strung with lights, files of people walked zigzag across our land, tearing the rice. Their lanterns doubled in the disturbed black water, which drained away through the broken bunds. As the villagers closed in, we could see that some of them, probably men and women we knew well, wore white masks. The people with long hair hung it over their faces. Women with short hair made it stand up on end. Some had tied white bands around their foreheads, arms, and legs.

"At first they threw mud and rocks at the house. Then they threw   5 eggs and began slaughtering our stock. We could hear the animals scream their deaths—the roosters, the pigs, a last great roar from the ox. Familiar wild heads flared in our night windows; the villagers encircled us. Some of the faces stopped to peer at us, their eyes rushing like searchlights. The hands flattened against the panes, framed heads, and left red prints.

"The villagers broke in the front and the back doors at the same   6 time, even though we had not locked the doors against them. Their knives dripped with the blood of our animals. They smeared blood on the doors and walls. One woman swung a chicken, whose throat she had slit, splattering blood in red arcs about her. We stood together in the middle of our house, in the family hall with the pictures and tables of the ancestors around us, and looked straight ahead.

"At that time the house had only two wings. When the men came   7 back, we would build two more to enclose our courtyard and a third one to begin a second courtyard. The villagers pushed through both wings, even your grandparents' rooms, to find your aunt's, which was also mine until the men returned. From this room a new wing for one of the younger families would grow. They ripped up her clothes and shoes and broke her combs, grinding them underfoot. They tore her work from the loom. They scattered the cooking fire and rolled the new weaving in it. We could hear them in the kitchen breaking our bowls and banging the pots. They overturned the great waist-high earthenware jugs; duck eggs, pickled fruits, vegetables burst out and mixed in acrid torrents. The old woman from the next field swept a broom through the air and loosed the spirits-of-the-broom over our heads. 'Pig.' 'Ghost.' 'Pig,' they sobbed and scolded while they ruined our house.

"When they left, they took sugar and oranges to bless themselves. They cut pieces from the dead animals. Some of them took bowls that were not broken and clothes that were not torn. Afterward we swept up the rice and sewed it back up into sacks. But the smells from the spilled preserves lasted. Your aunt gave birth in the pigsty that night. The next morning when I went up for the water, I found her and the baby plugging up the family well.   8

"Don't let your father know that I told you. He denies her. Now that you have started to menstruate, what happened to her could happen to you. Don't humiliate us. You wouldn't like to be forgotten as if you had never been born. The villagers are watchful."   9

Whenever she had to warn us about life, my mother told stories that ran like this one, a story to grow up on. She tested our strength to establish realities. Those in the emigrant generations who could not reassert brute survival died young and far from home. Those of us in the first American generations have had to figure out how the invisible world the emigrants built around our childhoods fit in solid America.   10

The emigrants confused the gods by diverting their curses, misleading them with crooked streets and false names. They must try to confuse their offspring as well, who, I suppose, threaten them in similar ways — always trying to get things straight, always trying to name the unspeakable. The Chinese I know hide their names; sojourners take new names when their lives change and guard their real names with silence.   11

Chinese-Americans, when you try to understand what things in you are Chinese, how do you separate what is peculiar to childhood, to poverty, insanities, one family, your mother who marked your growing with stories, from what is Chinese? What is Chinese tradition and what is the movies?   12

If I want to learn what clothes my aunt wore, whether flashy or ordinary, I would have to begin, "Remember Father's drowned-in-the-well sister?" I cannot ask that. My mother has told me once and for all the useful parts. She will add nothing unless powered by Necessity, a riverbank that guides her life. She plants vegetable gardens rather than lawns; she carries the odd-shaped tomatoes home from the fields and eats food left for the gods.   13

Whenever we did frivolous things, we used up energy; we flew high   14
kites. We children came up off the ground over the melting cones our
parents brought home from work and the American movie on New
Year's Day—*Oh, You Beautiful Doll* with Betty Grable one year, and *She
Wore a Yellow Ribbon* with John Wayne another year. After the one carnival ride each, we paid in guilt; our tired father counted his change on
the dark walk home.

Adultery is extravagance. Could people who hatch their own   15
chicks and eat the embryos and the heads for delicacies and boil the
feet in vinegar for party food, leaving only the gravel, eating even the
gizzard lining—could such people engender a prodigal aunt? To be a
woman, to have a daughter in starvation time was a waste enough. My
aunt could not have been the lone romantic who gave up everything
for sex. Women in the old China did not choose. Some man had com-
manded her to lie with him and be his secret evil. I wonder whether he
masked himself when he joined the raid on her family.

Perhaps she encountered him in the fields or on the mountain   16
where the daughters-in-law collected fuel. Or perhaps he first noticed
her in the marketplace. He was not a stranger because the village
housed no strangers. She had to have dealings with him other than sex.
Perhaps he worked an adjoining field, or he sold her the cloth for the
dress she sewed and wore. His demand must have surprised, then terrified her. She obeyed him; she always did as she was told.

When the family found a young man in the next village to be her   17
husband, she stood tractably beside the best rooster, his proxy, and
promised before they met that she would be his forever. She was lucky
that he was her age and she would be the first wife, an advantage secure
now. The night she first saw him, he had sex with her. Then he left for
America. She had almost forgotten what he looked like. When she
tried to envision him, she only saw the black and white face in the
group photograph the men had had taken before leaving.

The other man was not, after all, much different from her husband.   18
They both gave orders: she followed. "If you tell your family, I'll beat
you. I'll kill you. Be here again next week." No one talked sex, ever.
And she might have separated the rapes from the rest of living if only
she did not have to buy her oil from him or gather wood in the same
forest. I want her fear to have lasted just as long as rape lasted so that
the fear could have been contained. No drawn-out fear. But women at
sex hazarded birth and hence lifetimes. The fear did not stop but permeated everywhere. She told the man, "I think I'm pregnant." He organized the raid against her.

On nights when my mother and father talked about their life back   19
home, sometimes they mentioned an "outcast table" whose business
they still seemed to be settling, their voices tight. In a commensal tra-

dition, where food is precious, the powerful older people made wrong-
doers eat alone. Instead of letting them start separate new lives like the
Japanese, who could become samurais and geishas, the Chinese family,
faces averted but eyes glowering sideways, hung on to the offenders and
fed them leftovers. My aunt must have lived in the same house as my
parents and eaten at an outcast table. My mother spoke about the raid
as if she had seen it, when she and my aunt, a daughter-in-law to a
different household, should not have been living together at all.
Daughters-in-law lived with their husbands' parents, not their own; a
synonym for marriage in Chinese is "taking a daughter-in-law." Her
husband's parents could have sold her, mortgaged her, stoned her. But
they had sent her back to her own mother and father, a mysterious act
hinting at disgraces not told me. Perhaps they had thrown her out to
deflect the avengers.

She was the only daughter; her four brothers went with her father, 20
husband, and uncles "out on the road" and for some years became western men. When the goods were divided among the family, three of the
brothers took land, and the youngest, my father, chose an education.
After my grandparents gave their daughter away to her husband's family, they had dispensed all the adventure and all the property. They expected her alone to keep the traditional ways, which her brothers, now
among the barbarians, could fumble without detection. The heavy,
deep-rooted women were to maintain the past against the flood, safe for
returning. But the rare urge west had fixed upon our family, and so my
aunt crossed boundaries not delineated in space.

The work of preservation demands that the feelings playing about in 21
one's guts not be turned into action. Just watch their passing like cherry
blossoms. But perhaps my aunt, my forerunner, caught in a slow life, let
dreams grow and fade and after some months or years went toward what
persisted. Fear at the enormities of the forbidden kept her desires delicate, wire and bone. She looked at a man because she liked the way the
hair was tucked behind his ears, or she liked the question-mark line of a
long torso curving at the shoulder and straight at the hip. For warm eyes
or a soft voice or a slow walk—that's all—a few hairs, a line, a brightness, a sound, a pace, she gave up family. She offered us up for a charm
that vanished with tiredness, a pigtail that didn't toss when the wind
died. Why, the wrong lighting could erase the dearest thing about him.

It could very well have been, however, that my aunt did not take 22
subtle enjoyment of her friend, but, a wild woman, kept rollicking company. Imagining her free with sex doesn't fit, though. I don't know any
women like that, or men either. Unless I see her life branching into
mine, she gives me no ancestral help.

To sustain her being in love, she often worked at herself in the mir- 23
ror, guessing at the colors and shapes that would interest him, changing

them frequently in order to hit on the right combination. She wanted him to look back.

On a farm near the sea, a woman who tended her appearance 24 reaped a reputation for eccentricity. All the married women blunt-cut their hair in flaps about their ears or pulled it back in tight buns. No nonsense. Neither style blew easily into heart-catching tangles. And at their weddings they displayed themselves in their long hair for the last time. "It brushed the backs of my knees," my mother tells me. "It was braided, and even so, it brushed the backs of my knees."

At the mirror my aunt combed individuality into her bob. A bun 25 could have been contrived to escape into black streamers blowing in the wind or in quiet wisps about her face, but only the older women in our picture album wear buns. She brushed her hair back from her forehead, tucking the flaps behind her ears. She looped a piece of thread, knotted into a circle between her index fingers and thumbs, and ran the double strand across her forehead. When she closed her fingers as if she were making a pair of shadow geese bite, the string twisted together catching the little hairs. Then she pulled the thread away from her skin, ripping the hairs out neatly, her eyes watering from the needles of pain. Opening her fingers, she cleaned the thread, then rolled it along her hairline and the tops of her eyebrows. My mother did the same to me and my sisters and herself. I used to believe that the expression "caught by the short hairs" meant a captive held with a depilatory string. It especially hurt at the temples, but my mother said we were lucky we didn't have to have our feet bound when we were seven. Sisters used to sit on their beds and cry together, she said, as their mothers or their slave removed the bandages for a few minutes each night and let the blood gush back into their veins. I hope that the man my aunt loved appreciated a smooth brow, that he wasn't just a tits-and-ass man.

Once my aunt found a freckle on her chin, at a spot that the al- 26 manac said predestined her for unhappiness. She dug it out with a hot needle and washed the wound with peroxide.

More attention to her looks than these pullings of hairs and pick- 27 ings at spots would have caused gossip among the villagers. They owned work clothes and good clothes, and they wore good clothes for feasting the new seasons. But since a woman combing her hair hexes beginnings, my aunt rarely found an occasion to look her best. Women looked like great sea snails—the corded wood, babies, and laundry they carried were the whorls on their backs. The Chinese did not admire a bent back; goddesses and warriors stood straight. Still there must have been a marvelous freeing of beauty when a worker laid down her burden and stretched and arched.

Such commonplace loveliness, however, was not enough for my aunt. 28 She dreamed of a lover for the fifteen days of New Year's, the time for families to exchange visits, money, and food. She plied her secret comb. And sure enough she cursed the year, the family, the village, and herself.

Even as her hair lured her imminent lover, many other men looked 29 at her. Uncles, cousins, nephews, brothers would have looked, too, had they been home between journeys. Perhaps they had already been restraining their curiosity, and they left, fearful that their glances, like a field of nesting birds, might be startled and caught. Poverty hurt, and that was their first reason for leaving. But another, final reason for leaving the crowded house was the never-said.

She may have been unusually beloved, the precious only daughter, 30 spoiled and mirror gazing because of the affection the family lavished on her. When her husband left, they welcomed the chance to take her back from the in-laws; she could live like the little daughter for just a while longer. There are stories that my grandfather was different from other people, "crazy ever since the little Jap bayoneted him in the head." He used to put his naked penis on the dinner table, laughing. And one day he brought home a baby girl, wrapped up inside his brown western-style greatcoat. He had traded one of his sons, probably my father, the youngest, for her. My grandmother made him trade back. When he finally got a daughter of his own, he doted on her. They must have all loved her, except perhaps my father, the only brother who never went back to China, having once been traded for a girl.

Brothers and sisters, newly men and women, had to efface their 31 sexual color and present plain miens. Disturbing hair and eyes, a smile like no other, threatened the ideal of five generations living under one roof. To focus blurs, people shouted face to face and yelled from room to room. The immigrants I know have loud voices, unmodulated to American tones even after years away from the village where they called their friendships out across the fields. I have not been able to stop my mother's screams in public libraries or over telephones. Walking erect (knees straight, toes pointed forward, not pigeon-toed, which is Chinese-feminine) and speaking in an inaudible voice, I have tried to turn myself American-feminine. Chinese communication was loud, public. Only sick people had to whisper. But at the dinner table, where the family members came nearest one another, no one could talk, not the outcasts nor any eaters. Every word that falls from the mouth is a coin lost. Silently they gave and accepted food with both hands. A preoccupied child who took his bowl with one hand got a sideways glare. A complete moment of total attention is due everyone alike. Children and lovers have no singularity here, but my aunt used a secret voice, a separate attentiveness.

She kept the man's name to herself throughout her labor and dy- 32 ing; she did not accuse him that he be punished with her. To save her inseminator's name she gave silent birth.

He may have been somebody in her own household, but inter- 33
course with a man outside the family would have been no less abhorrent. All the village were kinsmen, and the titles shouted in loud
country voices never let kinship be forgotten. Any man within visiting
distance would have been neutralized as a lover—"brother," "younger
brother," "older brother"—one hundred and fifteen relationship titles.
Parents researched birth charts probably not so much to assure good
fortune as to circumvent incest in a population that has but one hundred surnames. Everybody has eight million relatives. How useless then
sexual mannerisms, how dangerous.

As if it came from an atavism deeper than fear, I used to add 34
"brother" silently to boys' names. It hexed the boys, who would or
would not ask me to dance, and made them less scary and as familiar
and deserving of benevolence as girls.

But, of course, I hexed myself also—no dates. I should have stood 35
up, both arms waving, and shouted out across libraries, "Hey, you! Love
me back." I had no idea, though, how to make attraction selective, how
to control its direction and magnitude. If I made myself American-
pretty so that the five or six Chinese boys in the class fell in love with
me, everyone else—the Caucasian, Negro, and Japanese boys—would
too. Sisterliness, dignified and honorable, made much more sense.

Attraction eludes control so stubbornly that whole societies de- 36
signed to organize relationships among people cannot keep order, not
even when they bind people to one another from childhood and raise
them together. Among the very poor and the wealthy, brothers married
their adopted sisters, like doves. Our family allowed some romance,
paying adult brides' prices and providing dowries so that their sons and
daughters could marry strangers. Marriage promises to turn strangers
into friendly relatives—a nation of siblings.

In the village structure, spirits shimmered among the live crea- 37
tures, balanced and held in equilibrium by time and land. But one human being flaring up into violence could open up a black hole, a
maelstrom that pulled in the sky. The frightened villagers, who depended on one another to maintain the real, went to my aunt to show
her a personal, physical representation of the break she made in the
"roundness." Misallying couples snapped off the future, which was to be
embodied in true offspring. The villagers punished her for acting as if
she could have a private life, secret and apart from them.

If my aunt had betrayed the family at a time of large grain yields 38
and peace, when many boys were born, and wings were being built on
many houses, perhaps she might have escaped such severe punishment.
But the men—hungry, greedy, tired of planting in dry soil, cuckolded—
had been forced to leave the village in order to send food-money home.

There were ghost plagues, bandit plagues, wars with the Japanese, floods. My Chinese brother and sister had died of an unknown sickness. Adultery, perhaps only a mistake during good times, became a crime when the village needed food.

The round moon cakes and round doorways, the round tables of 39 graduated size that fit one roundness inside another, round windows and rice bowls—these talismans had lost their power to warn this family of the law: A family must be whole, faithfully keeping the descent line by having sons to feed the old and the dead who in turn look after the family. The villagers came to show my aunt and lover-in-hiding a broken house. The villagers were speeding up the circling of events because she was too shortsighted to see that her infidelity had already harmed the village, that waves of consequences would return unpredictably, sometimes in disguise, as now, to hurt her. This roundness had to be made coin-sized so that she would see its circumference: punish her at the birth of her baby. Awaken her to the inexorable. People who refused fatalism because they could invent small resources insisted on culpability. Deny accidents and wrest fault from the stars.

After the villagers left, their lanterns now scattering in various di- 40 rections toward home, the family broke their silence and cursed her. "Aiaa, we're going to die. Death is coming. Death is coming. Look what you've done. You've killed us. Ghost! Dead Ghost! Ghost! You've never been born." She ran out into the fields, far enough from the house so that she could no longer hear their voices, and pressed herself against the earth, her own land no more. When she felt the birth coming, she thought that she had been hurt. Her body seized together. "They've hurt me too much," she thought. "This is gall, and it will kill me." With forehead and knees against the earth, her body convulsed and then relaxed. She turned on her back, lay on the ground. The black well of sky and stars went out and out and out forever; her body and her complexity seemed to disappear. She was one of the stars, a bright dot in blackness, without home, without a companion, in eternal cold and silence. An agoraphobia rose in her, speeding higher and higher, bigger and bigger; she would not be able to contain it; there would be no end to fear.

Flayed, unprotected against space, she felt pain return, focusing her 41 body. This pain chilled her—a cold, steady kind of surface pain. Inside, spasmodically, the other pain, the pain of the child, heated her. For hours she lay on the ground, alternately body and space. Sometimes a vision of normal comfort obliterated reality: she saw the family in the evening gambling at the dinner table, the young people massaging their elders' backs. She saw them congratulating one another, high joy on the mornings the rice shoots came up. When these pictures burst, the stars drew out further apart. Black space opened.

She got to her feet to fight better and remembered that old- 42
fashioned women gave birth in their pigsties to fool the jealous, pain-
dealing gods, who do not snatch piglets. Before the next spasms could
stop her, she ran to the pigsty, each step a rushing out into emptiness.
She climbed over the fence and knelt in the dirt. It was good to have a
fence enclosing her, a tribal person alone.

Laboring, this woman who had carried her child as a foreign growth 43
that sickened her every day, expelled it at last. She reached down to
touch the hot, wet, moving mass, surely smaller than anything human,
and could feel that it was human after all—fingers, toes, nails, nose. She
pulled it up on to her belly, and it lay curled there, butt in the air, feet
precisely tucked one under the other. She opened her loose shirt and but-
toned the child inside. After resting, it squirmed and thrashed and she
pushed it up to her breast. It turned its head this way and that until it
found her nipple. There, it made little snuffling noises. She clenched
her teeth at its preciousness, lovely as a young calf, a piglet, a little dog.

She may have gone to the pigsty as a last act of responsibility: she 44
would protect this child as she had protected its father. It would look
after her soul, leaving supplies on her grave. But how would this tiny
child without family find her grave when there would be no marker for
her anywhere, neither in the earth nor the family hall? No one would
give her a family hall name. She had taken the child with her into the
wastes. At its birth the two of them had felt the same raw pain of separation, a wound that only the family pressing tight could close. A child
with no descent line would not soften her life but only trail after her,
ghost-like, begging her to give it purpose. At dawn the villagers on
their way to the fields would stand around the fence and look.

Full of milk, the little ghost slept. When it awoke, she hardened 45
her breasts against the milk that crying loosens. Toward morning she
picked up the baby and walked to the well.

Carrying the baby to the well shows loving. Otherwise abandon it. 46
Turn its face into the mud. Mothers who love their children take them
along. It was probably a girl; there is some hope of forgiveness for boys.

"Don't tell anyone you had an aunt. Your father does not want to 47
hear her name. She has never been born." I have believed that sex was
unspeakable and words so strong and fathers so frail that "aunt" would
do my father mysterious harm. I have thought that my family, having
settled among immigrants who had also been their neighbors in the ancestral land, needed to clean their name, and a wrong word would in-
cite the kinspeople even here. But there is more to this silence: they
want me to participate in her punishment. And I have.

In the twenty years since I heard this story I have not asked for de- 48
tails nor said my aunt's name; I do not know it. People who comfort the

dead can also chase after them to hurt them further—a reverse ancestor worship. The real punishment was not the raid swiftly inflicted by the villagers, but the family's deliberately forgetting her. Her betrayal so maddened them, they saw to it that she would suffer forever, even after death. Always hungry, always needing, she would have to beg food from other ghosts, snatch and steal it from those whose living descendants give them gifts. She would have to fight the ghosts massed at crossroads for the buns a few thoughtful citizens leave to decoy her away from village and home so that the ancestral spirits could feast unharassed. At peace, they could act like gods, not ghosts, their descent lines providing them with paper suits and dresses, spirit money, paper houses, paper automobiles, chicken, meat, and rice into eternity—essences delivered up in smoke and flames, steam and incense rising from each rice bowl. In an attempt to make the Chinese care for people outside the family, Chairman Mao encourages us now to give our paper replicas to the spirits of outstanding soldiers and workers, no matter whose ancestors they may be. My aunt remains forever hungry. Goods are not distributed evenly among the dead.

My aunt haunts me—her ghost drawn to me because now, after 49 fifty years of neglect, I alone devote pages of paper to her, though not origamied into houses and clothes. I do not think she always means me well. I am telling on her, and she was a spite suicide, drowning herself in the drinking water. The Chinese are always very frightened of the drowned one, whose weeping ghost, wet hair hanging and skin bloated, waits silently by the water to pull down a substitute.

QUESTIONS ON MEANING

1. What PURPOSE does Kingston have in telling her aunt's story? How does this differ from her mother's purpose in relating the tale?
2. According to Kingston, who could have been the father of her aunt's child? Who could not?
3. Kingston says that her mother told stories "to warn us about life." What warning does this story provide?
4. Why is Kingston so fascinated by her aunt's life and death?

QUESTIONS ON WRITING STRATEGY

1. Whom does Kingston seem to include in her AUDIENCE: her family and other older Chinese? second-generation Chinese Americans like herself? other Americans? How might she expect each of these groups to respond to her essay?

2. Why is Kingston's opening line—her mother's "You must not tell any-one"—especially fitting for this essay? What secrets are being told? Why does Kingston divulge them?

3. As Kingston tells her tale of her aunt, some events are based on her mother's story or her knowledge of Chinese customs, and some are wholly imaginary. What is the EFFECT of blending these several threads of reality, perception, and imagination?

4. **MIXED METHODS.** Examine the details in the two contrasting NARRATIVES of how Kingston's aunt became pregnant: one in paragraphs 15–18 and the other in paragraphs 21–28. How do the details create different realities? Which version does Kingston seem more committed to? Why?

5. **MIXED METHODS.** Kingston COMPARES AND CONTRASTS various versions of her aunt's story, trying to find the CAUSES that led her aunt to drown in the well. In the end, what causes does Kingston seem to accept?

QUESTIONS ON LANGUAGE

1. How does Kingston's language—lyrical, poetic, full of FIGURES OF SPEECH and other IMAGES—reveal her relationship to her Chinese heritage? Find phrases that are especially striking.

2. Look up any of these words you do not know: bunds (para. 4); acrid (7); frivolous (14); tractably, proxy (17); hazarded (18); commensal (19); delineated (20); depilatory (25); plied (28); miens (31); abhorrent, circumvent (33); atavism (34); maelstrom (37); talismans, inexorable, fatalism, culpability (39); gall, agoraphobia (40); spasmodically (41).

3. Sometimes Kingston indicates that she is reconstructing or imagining events through verbs like "would have" and words like "maybe" and "perhaps" ("Perhaps she encountered him in the fields," para. 16). Other times she presents obviously imaginary events as if they actually happened ("Once my aunt found a freckle on her chin," 26). What effect does Kingston achieve with these apparent inconsistencies?

SUGGESTIONS FOR WRITING

1. **JOURNAL WRITING.** Most of us have heard family stories that left lasting impressions—ghost stories like Kingston's, or superstitions, traditions, biographies of ancestors, and so on. What family stories do you remember vividly from your childhood?
FROM JOURNAL TO ESSAY. Develop one of your family stories in a narrative essay. Build in the context of the story as well: Who told it to you? What purpose did he or she have in telling it to you? How does it illustrate your family's beliefs and values?

2. Write an essay explaining the role of ancestors in Chinese family and religious life, supplementing what Kingston says with research in the library or (if you are Chinese American) drawing on your own experiences.

3. **CRITICAL WRITING.** ANALYZE the ideas about gender roles revealed in "No Name Woman," both in China and in the Chinese American culture Kingston grew up in. How have these ideas affected Kingston? Do you perceive any semblance of them in contemporary American culture?

4. **CONNECTIONS.** Both Kingston and Gloria Naylor, in "The Meanings of a Word" (p. 418), examine communication within their families. Relate an incident or incidents from your own childhood that portray something about the communication within your family. You might want to focus on the language of communication, such as the words used to discuss (or not discuss) a taboo topic, the special family meanings for familiar words, a misunderstanding between you and an adult about something the adult said. Use dialogue and as much concrete detail as you can to clarify your experience and its significance.

5. **CONNECTIONS.** Richard Rodriguez's "Aria" (p. 606) and Kingston's "No Name Woman" both address the conflicts between traditions and change in terms of language: what can and cannot be spoken about, who can speak, what language is used when. However, the two authors come to different conclusions about the relevance of such traditions to today's world. Write an essay detailing the similarities and differences between their views of tradition and change.

MAXINE HONG KINGSTON ON WRITING

In an interview with Jean W. Ross published in *Contemporary Authors* in 1984, Maxine Hong Kingston discusses the writing and revising of *The Woman Warrior*. Ross asks Kingston to clarify an earlier statement that she had "no idea how people who don't write endure their lives." Kingston replies: "When I said that, I was thinking about how words and stories create order. Some of the things that happen to us in life seem to have no meaning, but when you write them down you find the meanings for them; or, as you translate life into words, you force a meaning. Meaning is intrinsic in words and stories."

Ross then asks if Kingston used an outline and planned to blend fact with legend in *The Woman Warrior*. "Oh no, no," Kingston answers. "What I have at the beginning of a book is not an outline. I have no idea of how stories will end or where the beginning will lead. Sometimes I draw pictures. I draw a blob and then I have a little arrow and it goes to this other blob, if you want to call that an outline. It's hardly even words; it's like a doodle. Then when it turns into words, I find the words lead me to various scenes and stories which I don't know about until I get there. I don't see the order until very late in the writing and sometimes the ending just comes. I just run up against it. All of a sudden the book's over and I didn't know it would be over."

A question from Ross about whether her emotions enter her writing leads Kingston to talk about revision. "Well, when I first set something down I feel the emotions I write about. But when I do a second draft, third draft, ninth draft, then I don't feel very emotional. The rewriting is very intellectual; all my education and reading and intellect are involved.

The mechanics of sentences, how one phrase or word goes with an-other one—all that happens in later drafts. There's a very emotional first draft and a very technical last draft."

FOR DISCUSSION

1. Do you agree with Kingston that when you write things down you find their meaning? Give examples of when the writing process has or hasn't clarified an experience for you.
2. Kingston doodles as a way to discover her material. How do you discover what you have to say?
3. What does Kingston mean by "the mechanics of sentences"? Do you con-sider this element as you revise?

N. SCOTT MOMADAY

NAVARRE SCOTT MOMADAY was born in 1934 on the Kiowa Indian reservation in Oklahoma and grew up there and on other reservations in the Southwest. His father was a Kiowa, his mother a descendant of white pioneers, and their fusion of Native and European American cultures permeates Momaday's work. He has always pursued an academic career, earning a B.A. in 1958 from the University of New Mexico and a Ph.D. in 1963 from Stanford University, teaching at several American universities, and writing on American poetry. At the same time he has been one of the country's foremost interpreters of Native Americans' history, myths, and landscapes. His novel *House Made of Dawn* won the Pulitzer Prize in 1969, and he has published many other books as well, including *The Names* (memoir, 1976), *In the Presence of the Sun* (stories and poems, 1992), *The Man Made of Words* (stories and essays), and *In the Bear's House* (poems, essays, and artwork, 1999). Momaday is also a playwright and a painter. In the position of Regents Professor, he teaches English at the University of Arizona.

The Way to Rainy Mountain

"The Way to Rainy Mountain" is the introduction to a book of that title, published in 1969, in which Momaday tells Kiowa myths and history and his own story of discovering his heritage. Writing on the occasion of his grandmother's death, Momaday begins and ends this essay in the same place, the Oklahoma plain where the Kiowa tribe was brought down by the U.S. government. In between he visits the sites where the Kiowas had formed the powerful, noble society from which his grandmother sprang.

To develop "The Way to Rainy Mountain," Momaday draws mainly on five methods:

Narration (Chap. 1): paragraphs 2–5, 7–10, 12–15
Description (Chap. 2): throughout
Example (Chap. 3): paragraphs 1, 6–8, 10, 12–13
Comparison and contrast (Chap. 4): paragraphs 3–4, 12–14
Cause and effect (Chap. 8): paragraphs 3–4, 9

A single knoll rises out of the plain in Oklahoma, north and west 1 of the Wichita Range.[1] For my people, the Kiowas, it is an old landmark, and they gave it the name Rainy Mountain. The hardest weather in the world is there. Winter brings blizzards, hot tornadic winds arise in the spring, and in summer the prairie is an anvil's edge. The grass

---

[1] The Wichita Mountains are southwest of Oklahoma City. —EDS.

turns brittle and brown, and it cracks beneath your feet. There are green belts along the rivers and creeks, linear groves of hickory and pecan, willow and witch hazel. At a distance in July or August the steaming foliage seems almost to writhe in fire. Great green and yellow grasshoppers are everywhere in the tall grass, popping up like corn to sting the flesh, and tortoises crawl about on the red earth, going nowhere in the plenty of time. Loneliness is an aspect of the land. All things in the plain are isolate; there is no confusion of objects in the eye, but *one* hill or *one* tree or *one* man. To look upon that landscape in the early morning, with the sun at your back, is to lose the sense of proportion. Your imagination comes to life, and this, you think, is where Creation was begun.

I returned to Rainy Mountain in July. My grandmother had died in   2
the spring, and I wanted to be at her grave. She had lived to be very old and at last infirm. Her only living daughter was with her when she died, and I was told that in death her face was that of a child.

I like to think of her as a child. When she was born, the Kiowas   3
were living that last great moment of their history. For more than a hundred years they had controlled the open range from the Smoky Hill River to the Red, from the headwaters of the Canadian to the fork of the Arkansas and Cimarron.[2] In alliance with the Comanches, they had ruled the whole of the southern plains. War was their sacred business, and they were among the finest horsemen the world has ever known. But warfare for the Kiowas was preeminently a matter of disposition rather than of survival, and they never understood the grim, unrelenting advance of the U.S. Cavalry. When at last, divided and ill-provisioned, they were driven onto the Staked Plains in the cold rains of autumn, they fell into panic. In Palo Duro Canyon they abandoned their crucial stores to pillage and had nothing then but their lives. In order to save themselves, they surrendered to the soldiers at Fort Sill and were imprisoned in the old stone corral that now stands as a military museum. My grandmother was spared the humiliation of those high gray walls by eight or ten years, but she must have known from birth the affliction of defeat, the dark brooding of old warriors.

Her name was Aho, and she belonged to the last culture to evolve   4
in North America. Her forebears came down from the high country in western Montana nearly three centuries ago. They were a mountain people, a mysterious tribe of hunters whose language has never been positively classified in any major group. In the late seventeenth century they began a long migration to the south and east. It was a journey to-

---

[2] Momaday describes an area covering much of present-day Kansas and Oklahoma as well as the Texas Panhandle and parts of Colorado and New Mexico. Later in this paragraph, Palo Duro Canyon is south of Amarillo, Texas, and Fort Sill is southwest of Oklahoma City, near the Wichita Mountains. —Eds.

ward the dawn, and it led to a golden age. Along the way the Kiowas were befriended by the Crows, who gave them the culture and religion of the Plains. They acquired horses, and their ancient nomadic spirit was suddenly free of the ground. They acquired Tai-me, the sacred Sun Dance doll, from that moment the object and symbol of their worship, and so shared in the divinity of the sun. Not least, they acquired the sense of destiny, therefore courage and pride. When they entered upon the southern Plains they had been transformed. No longer were they slaves to the simple necessity of survival; they were a lordly and dangerous society of fighters and thieves, hunters and priests of the sun. According to their origin myth, they entered the world through a hollow log. From one point of view, their migration was the fruit of an old prophecy, for indeed they emerged from a sunless world.

Although my grandmother lived out her long life in the shadow of   5
Rainy Mountain, the immense landscape of the continental interior lay like memory in her blood. She could tell of the Crows, whom she had never seen, and of the Black Hills,[3] where she had never been. I wanted to see in reality what she had seen more perfectly in the mind's eye, and traveled fifteen hundred miles to begin my pilgrimage.

Yellowstone, it seemed to me, was the top of the world, a region of   6
deep lakes and dark timber, canyons and waterfalls. But, beautiful as it is, one might have the sense of confinement there. The skyline in all directions is close at hand, the high wall of the woods and deep cleavages of shade. There is a perfect freedom in the mountains, but it belongs to the eagle and the elk, the badger and the bear. The Kiowas reckoned their stature by the distance they could see, and they were bent and blind in the wilderness.

Descending eastward, the highland meadows are a stairway to the   7
plain. In July the inland slope of the Rockies is luxuriant with flax and buckwheat, stonecrop and larkspur. The earth unfolds and the limit of the land recedes. Clusters of trees, and animals grazing far in the distance, cause the vision to reach away and wonder to build upon the mind. The sun follows a longer course in the day, and the sky is immense beyond all comparison. The great billowing clouds that sail upon it are shadows that move upon the grain like water, dividing light. Farther down, in the land of the Crows and Blackfeet, the plain is yellow. Sweet clover takes hold of the hills and bends upon itself to cover and seal the soil. There the Kiowas paused on their way; they had come to the place where they must change their lives. The sun is at home on the plains. Precisely there does it have the certain character of a god.

---

[3] The Black Hills are in western South Dakota. Yellowstone (next paragraph) is in northwestern Wyoming. In paragraphs 7–8, Momaday describes movement eastward across the top of Wyoming. —EDS.

When the Kiowas came to the land of the Crows, they could see the dark lees of the hills at dawn across the Bighorn River, the profusion of light on the grain shelves, the oldest deity ranging after the solstices. Not yet would they veer southward to the caldron of the land that lay below; they must wean their blood from the northern winter and hold the mountains a while longer in their view. They bore Tai-me in procession to the east.

A dark mist lay over the Black Hills, and the land was like iron. At the top of a ridge I caught sight of Devil's Tower[4] upthrust against the gray sky as if in the birth of time the core of the earth had broken through its crust and the motion of the world was begun. There are things in nature that engender an awful quiet in the heart of man; Devil's Tower is one of them. Two centuries ago, because they could not do otherwise, the Kiowas made a legend at the base of the rock. My grandmother said: 8

> Eight children were there at play, seven sisters and their brother. Suddenly the boy was struck dumb; he trembled and began to run upon his hands and feet. His fingers became claws, and his body was covered with fur. Directly there was a bear where the boy had been. The sisters were terrified; they ran, and the bear after them. They came to the stump of a great tree, and the tree spoke to them. It bade them climb upon it, and as they did so it began to rise into the air. The bear came to kill them, but they were just beyond its reach. It reared against the tree and scored the bark all around with its claws. The seven sisters were borne into the sky, and they became the stars of the Big Dipper.

From that moment, and so long as the legend lives, the Kiowas have kinsmen in the night sky. Whatever they were in the mountains, they could be no more. However tenuous their well-being, however much they had suffered and would suffer again, they had found a way out of the wilderness.

My grandmother had a reverence for the sun, a holy regard that now is all but gone out of mankind. There was a wariness in her, and an ancient awe. She was a Christian in her later years, but she had come a long way about, and she never forgot her birthright. As a child she had been to the Sun Dances; she had taken part in those annual rites, and by them she had learned the restoration of her people in the presence of Tai-me. She was about seven when the last Kiowa Sun Dance was held in 1887 on the Washita River above Rainy Mountain Creek.[5] The 9

---

[4] An 865-foot stone outcropping in northeastern Wyoming, now a national monument. —EDS.

[5] The Washita runs halfway between Oklahoma City and the Wichita Mountains. —EDS.

buffalo were gone. In order to consummate the ancient sacrifice—to impale the head of a buffalo bull upon the medicine tree—a delegation of old men journeyed into Texas, there to beg and barter for an animal from the Goodnight herd. She was ten when the Kiowas came together for the last time as a living Sun Dance culture. They could find no buffalo; they had to hang an old hide from the sacred tree. Before the dance could begin, a company of soldiers rode out from Fort Sill under orders to disperse the tribe. Forbidden without cause the essential act of their faith, having seen the wild herds slaughtered and left to rot upon the ground, the Kiowas backed away forever from the medicine tree. That was July 20, 1890, at the great bend of the Washita. My grandmother was there. Without bitterness, and for as long as she lived, she bore a vision of deicide.[6]

Now that I can have her only in memory, I see my grandmother in   10 the several postures that were peculiar to her: standing at the wood stove on a winter morning and turning meat in a great iron skillet; sitting at the south window, bent above her beadwork, and afterwards, when her vision failed, looking down for a long time into the fold of her hands; going out upon a cane, very slowly as she did when the weight of age came upon her; praying. I remember her most often at prayer. She made long, rambling prayers out of suffering and hope, having seen many things. I was never sure that I had the right to hear, so exclusive were they of all mere custom and company. The last time I saw her she prayed standing by the side of her bed at night, naked to the waist, the light of a kerosene lamp moving upon her dark skin. Her long, black hair, always drawn and braided in the day, lay upon her shoulders and against her breasts like a shawl. I do not speak Kiowa, and I never understood her prayers, but there was something inherently sad in the sound, some merest hesitation upon the syllables of sorrow. She began in a high and descending pitch, exhausting her breath to silence; then again and again—and always the same intensity of effort, of something that is, and is not, like urgency in the human voice. Transported so in the dancing light among the shadows of her room, she seemed beyond the reach of time. But that was illusion; I think I knew then that I should not see her again.

Houses are like sentinels in the plain, old keepers of the weather   11 watch. There, in a very little while, wood takes on the appearance of great age. All colors wear soon away in the wind and rain, and then the wood is burned gray and the grain appears and the nails turn red with rust. The windowpanes are black and opaque; you imagine there is nothing within, and indeed there are many ghosts, bones given up to

---

[6] The killing of a divine being or beings (from Latin words meaning "god" and "kill").—EDS.

the land. They stand here and there against the sky, and you approach them for a longer time than you expect. They belong in the distance; it is their domain.

Once there was a lot of sound in my grandmother's house, a lot of   12
coming and going, feasting and talk. The summers there were full of excitement and reunion. The Kiowas are a summer people; they abide the cold and keep to themselves, but when the season turns and the land becomes warm and vital they cannot hold still; an old love of going returns upon them. The aged visitors who came to my grandmother's house when I was a child were made of lean and leather, and they bore themselves upright. They wore great black hats and bright ample shirts that shook in the wind. They rubbed fat upon their hair and wound their braids with strips of colored cloth. Some of them painted their faces and carried the scars of old and cherished enmities. They were an old council of warlords, come to remind and be reminded of who they were. Their wives and daughters served them well. The women might indulge themselves; gossip was at once the mark and compensation of their servitude. They made loud and elaborate talk among themselves, full of jest and gesture, fright and false alarm. They went abroad in fringed and flowered shawls, bright beadwork and German silver. They were at home in the kitchen, and they prepared meals that were banquets.

There were frequent prayer meetings, and great nocturnal feasts.   13
When I was a child I played with my cousins outside, where the lamplight fell upon the ground and the singing of the old people rose up around us and carried away into the darkness. There were a lot of good things to eat, a lot of laughter and surprise. And afterwards, when the quiet returned, I lay down with my grandmother and could hear the frogs away by the river and feel the motion of the air.

Now there is a funeral silence in the rooms, the endless wake of   14
some final word. The walls have closed in upon my grandmother's house. When I returned to it in mourning, I saw for the first time in my life how small it was. It was late at night, and there was a white moon, nearly full. I sat for a long time on the stone steps by the kitchen door. From there I could see out across the land; I could see the long row of trees by the creek, the low light upon the rolling plains, and the stars of the Big Dipper. Once I looked at the moon and caught sight of a strange thing. A cricket had perched upon the handrail, only a few inches away from me. My line of vision was such that the creature filled the moon like a fossil. It had gone there, I thought, to live and die, for there, of all places, was its small definition made whole and eternal. A warm wind rose up and purled like the longing within me.

The next morning I awoke at dawn and went out on the dirt road   15
to Rainy Mountain. It was already hot, and the grasshoppers began to fill the air. Still, it was early in the morning, and the birds sang out of

the shadows. The long yellow grass on the mountain shone in the bright light, and a scissortail hied above the land. There, where it ought to be, at the end of a long and legendary way, was my grandmother's grave. Here and there on the dark stones were ancestral names. Looking back once, I saw the mountain and came away.

QUESTIONS ON MEANING

1. What is the significance of Momaday's statement that the Kiowas "reckoned their stature by the distance they could see" (para. 6)? How does this statement relate to the ultimate fate of the Kiowas?
2. Remembering his grandmother, Momaday writes, "She made long, rambling prayers out of suffering and hope, having seen many things" (para. 10). What is the key point here, and how does the concept of prayer connect with the essay as a whole?
3. What do you think Momaday's main idea is? What thread links all the essay's parts?
4. What seems to be Momaday's PURPOSE in writing this essay? Can we read this as more than a personal story about a visit to his grandmother's grave?
5. Who is Momaday's AUDIENCE? Do you think he is writing for other Kiowa descendants? for non-Indians? for others who have lost an older relative?

QUESTIONS ON WRITING STRATEGY

1. "Loneliness is an aspect of the land," Momaday writes (para. 1). To what extent do you think this sentence captures the DOMINANT IMPRESSION of the essay? If you perceive a different impression, what is it?
2. How does Momaday organize his essay? (It may help to plot the structure by preparing a rough outline.) How effective do you find this organization, and why?
3. **MIXED METHODS.** Momaday's essay is significantly a work of DESCRIPTION. Would you characterize this description as SUBJECTIVE or OBJECTIVE? What about his use of language suggests one over the other?
4. **MIXED METHODS.** Besides description, Momaday relies on other methods as well, such as NARRATION, EXAMPLE, COMPARISON AND CONTRAST, and CAUSE AND EFFECT. What is the purpose of the comparison in paragraphs 12–14?

QUESTIONS ON LANGUAGE

1. If you do not know the meanings of the following words, look them up in a dictionary: anvil (para. 1); infirm (2); preeminently, pillage, affliction (3); nomadic (4); cleavages (6); lees, profusion, deity, caldron (7); engender, tenuous (8); reverence, consummate (9); inherently (10); purled (14); hied (15).

2. Momaday uses many vivid FIGURES OF SPEECH. Locate at least one use each of metaphor, simile, and hyperbole (review these terms in Useful Terms if necessary). What does each of these figures convey?

3. Momaday's first and last paragraphs present contrasting images of Rainy Mountain and the surrounding plain: At first, "the prairie is an anvil's edge" and the "grass turns brittle and brown"; in the end, "the birds sang out of the shadows" and the "long yellow grass on the mountain shone in the bright light." How does this contrast serve Momaday's purpose?

4. Notice Momaday's use of PARALLELISM in describing the visitors to his grandmother's house (para. 12)—for instance, "They wore....They rubbed....They made...." What does the parallelism convey about the people being described?

SUGGESTIONS FOR WRITING

1. **JOURNAL WRITING.** "The Way to Rainy Mountain" is about Momaday's associations between his grandmother and Rainy Mountain. Think of somebody special to you and a specific place that you associate with this person. Jot down as many details about the person and place as you can. **FROM JOURNAL TO ESSAY.** Develop your journal entry into an essay that describes both the person and the place, using concrete and specific details to make the connection between them clear to your readers.

2. Momaday writes about his ancestors and a way of life very different from that of the present. For this assignment you may need to investigate your family's history. Write an essay that describes your ancestors' way of life. (Your ancestors may be as recent as your grandparents or as distant as your research allows.) Who were these people? How did they live? How does that way of life differ from the way you and your family live now? Be specific in your description and comparison, providing concrete details and examples for clarity.

3. **CRITICAL WRITING.** In an essay, ANALYZE Momaday's attitudes toward the Kiowas as revealed in the language he uses to describe them. Support your THESIS (your idea about Momaday's attitudes) with specific quotations from the essay.

4. **CONNECTIONS.** Scott Russell Sanders, in "Homeplace" (p. 390), expresses a belief in the importance of place, of "staying put." He writes, "I cannot have a spiritual center without having a geographic one." Momaday conveys a similar conviction through his detailed description of Rainy Mountain. Write an essay describing a place that functions as your own geographic center. Remember to include lots of vivid details to take your reader to this place. Comment on how the place has changed you or how it supports you even when you are away from it.

5. **CONNECTIONS.** Both Momaday and E. B. White, in "Once More to the Lake" (p. 644), write about places that tie them to their families. Write an essay that contrasts the sense of continuity in White's essay with the sense of loss and change in Momaday's. Are there also similarities in their relations with their families and these places?

N. SCOTT MOMADAY ON WRITING

In an interview in *Sequoia* magazine in 1975, N. Scott Momaday was asked by William T. Morgan, Jr., whether he saw himself as a "spokesman" for Native Americans.

No, and it's something I don't think about very often. I don't identify with any group of writers, and I don't think of myself as being a spokesman for the Indian people. That would be presumptuous, it seems to me.... When I write I find it a very private kind of thing, and I like to keep it that way. You know, I would be uncomfortable I think if I were trying to express the views of other people. When I write I write out of my own experience, and out of my own ideas of that experience, and I'm not concerned to write the history of a people except as that history bears upon me directly. When I was writing *The Way to Rainy Mountain*, for example, I was dealing with something that belongs to the Indian world, and the Kiowa people as a whole, but I wasn't concerned with that so much as I was concerned with the fact that it meant this to me—this is how I as a person felt about it. And I want my writing to reflect myself in certain ways—that is my first concern.

FOR DISCUSSION

1. Why does Momaday say it would be "presumptuous" to write as a spokesperson for Native Americans?
2. How does the essay "The Way to Rainy Mountain" demonstrate Momaday's concern with showing how the history he treats affects himself? Do you think the author succeeds in writing about "the history of a people... as that history bears upon me directly"? Why, or why not?

GEORGE ORWELL

GEORGE ORWELL was the pen name of Eric Blair (1903–50), born in Bengal, India, the son of an English civil servant. After attending Eton on a scholarship, he joined the British police in Burma, where he acquired a distrust for the methods of the empire. Then followed years of tramping, odd jobs, and near-starvation—recalled in *Down and Out in Paris and London* (1933). From living on the fringe of society and from his reportorial writing about English miners and factory workers, Orwell deepened his sympathy with underdogs. Severely wounded while fighting in the Spanish Civil War, he wrote a memoir, *Homage to Catalonia* (1938), voicing disillusionment with Loyalists who, he claimed, sought not to free Spain but to exterminate their political enemies. A socialist by conviction, Orwell kept pointing to the dangers of a collective state run by totalitarians. In *Animal Farm* (1945), he satirized Soviet bureaucracy; and in his famous novel *1984* (1949), he foresaw a regimented England whose government perverts truth and spies on citizens by two-way television. (The motto of the state and its leader: Big Brother Is Watching You.)

Shooting an Elephant

Orwell wrote compellingly of his experiences as a police officer in Burma. In this selection from *Shooting an Elephant and Other Essays* (1950), he combines personal experience and piercing insight to expose both an oppressive government and himself as the government's hireling.

"Shooting an Elephant" is foremost a narrative, but Orwell uses description, example, and cause and effect as well to develop and give significance to his tale.

Narration (Chap. 1): throughout
Description (Chap. 2): paragraphs 2, 4–12
Example (Chap. 3): paragraphs 1–2, 4, 14
Cause and effect (Chap. 8): paragraphs 1–2, 6–7

In Moulmein, in Lower Burma, I was hated by large numbers of 1
people—the only time in my life that I have been important enough
for this to happen to me. I was subdivisional police officer of the town,
and in an aimless, petty kind of way anti-European feeling was very bitter. No one had the guts to raise a riot, but if a European woman went
through the bazaars alone somebody would probably spit betel juice
over her dress. As a police officer I was an obvious target and was baited
whenever it seemed safe to do so. When a nimble Burman tripped me
up on the football field and the referee (another Burman) looked the

other way, the crowd yelled with hideous laughter. This happened more than once. In the end the sneering yellow faces of young men that met me everywhere, the insults hooted after me when I was at a safe distance, got badly on my nerves. The young Buddhist priests were the worst of all. There were several thousands of them in the town and none of them seemed to have anything to do except stand on street corners and jeer at Europeans.

All this was perplexing and upsetting. For at that time I had already made up my mind that imperialism was an evil thing and the sooner I chucked up my job and got out of it the better. Theoretically—and secretly, of course—I was all for the Burmese and all against the oppressors, the British. As for the job I was doing, I hated it more bitterly than I can perhaps make clear. In a job like that you see the dirty work of Empire at close quarters. The wretched prisoners huddling in the stinking cages of the lockups, the grey, cowed faces of the long-term convicts, the scarred buttocks of the men who had been flogged with bamboos— all these oppressed me with an intolerable sense of guilt. But I could get nothing into perspective. I was young and ill-educated and I had had to think out my problems in the utter silence that is imposed on every Englishman in the East. I did not even know that the British Empire is dying, still less did I know that it is a great deal better than the younger empires that are going to supplant it. All I knew was that I was stuck between my hatred of the empire I served and my rage against the evil-spirited little beasts who tried to make my job impossible. With one part of my mind I thought of the British Raj[1] as an unbreakable tyranny, as something clamped down, in *saecula saeculorum*,[2] upon the will of prostrate peoples; with another part I thought that the greatest joy in the world would be to drive a bayonet into a Buddhist priest's guts. Feelings like these are the normal by-products of imperialism; ask any Anglo-Indian official, if you can catch him off duty.

One day something happened which in a roundabout way was enlightening. It was a tiny incident in itself, but it gave me a better glimpse than I had had before of the real nature of imperialism—the real motives for which despotic governments act. Early one morning the subinspector at a police station the other end of town rang me up on the phone and said that an elephant was ravaging the bazaar. Would I please come and do something about it? I did not know what I could do, but I wanted to see what was happening and I got on to a pony and started out. I took my rifle, an old .44 Winchester and much too small

---

[1] British imperial government. *Raj* in Hindi means "reign," a word similar to *rajah*, "ruler."—Eds.

[2] Latin, "world without end."—Eds.

to kill an elephant, but I thought the noise might be useful *in terrorem.*[3] Various Burmans stopped me on the way and told me about the elephant's doings. It was not, of course, a wild elephant, but a tame one which had gone "must." It had been chained up, as tame elephants always are when their attack of "must" is due, but on the previous night it had broken its chain and escaped. Its mahout,[4] the only person who could manage it when it was in that state, had set out in pursuit, but had taken the wrong direction and was now twelve hours' journey away, and in the morning the elephant had suddenly reappeared in the town. The Burmese population had no weapons and were quite helpless against it. It had already destroyed somebody's bamboo hut, killed a cow and raided some fruit stalls and devoured the stock; also it had met the municipal rubbish van and, when the driver jumped out and took to his heels, had turned the van over and inflicted violences upon it.

The Burmese subinspector and some Indian constables were waiting for me in the quarter where the elephant had been seen. It was a very poor quarter, a labyrinth of squalid bamboo huts, thatched with palmleaf, winding all over a steep hillside. I remember that it was a cloudy, stuffy morning at the beginning of the rains. We began questioning the people as to where the elephant had gone and, as usual, failed to get any definite information. That is invariably the case in the East; a story always sounds clear enough at a distance, but the nearer you get to the scene of events the vaguer it becomes. Some of the people said that the elephant had gone in one direction, some said that he had gone in another, some professed not even to have heard of any elephant. I had almost made up my mind that the whole story was a pack of lies, when we heard yells a little distance away. There was a loud, scandalized cry of "Go away, child! Go away this instant!" and an old woman with a switch in her hand came round the corner of a hut, violently shooing away a crowd of naked children. Some more women followed, clicking their tongues and exclaiming; evidently there was something that the children ought not to have seen. I rounded the hut and saw a man's dead body sprawling in the mud. He was an Indian, a black Dravidian coolie, almost naked, and he could not have been dead many minutes. The people said that the elephant had come suddenly upon him round the corner of the hut, caught him with its trunk, put its foot on his back and ground him into the earth. This was the rainy season and the ground was soft, and his face had scored a trench a foot deep and a couple of yards long. He was lying on his belly with arms crucified and head sharply twisted to one side. His face was coated with mud, the eyes wide open, the teeth bared and grinning with an expres-

---

[3] Latin, "to give warning."—EDS.
[4] Keeper or groom, a servant of the elephant's owner.—EDS.

sion of unendurable agony. (Never tell me, by the way, that the dead look peaceful. Most of the corpses I have seen looked devilish.) The friction of the great beast's foot had stripped the skin from his back as neatly as one skins a rabbit. As soon as I saw the dead man I sent an orderly to a friend's house nearby to borrow an elephant rifle. I had already sent back the pony, not wanting it to go mad with fright and throw me if it smelled the elephant.

The orderly came back in a few minutes with a rifle and five cartridges, and meanwhile some Burmans had arrived and told us that the elephant was in the paddy fields below, only a few hundred yards away. As I started forward practically the whole population of the quarter flocked out of the houses and followed me. They had seen the rifle and were all shouting excitedly that I was going to shoot the elephant. They had not shown much interest in the elephant when he was merely ravaging their homes, but it was different now that he was going to be shot. It was a bit of fun to them, as it would be to an English crowd; besides they wanted the meat. It made me vaguely uneasy. I had no intention of shooting the elephant—I had merely sent for the rifle to defend myself if necessary—and it is always unnerving to have a crowd following you. I marched down the hill, looking and feeling a fool, with the rifle over my shoulder and an ever-growing army of people jostling at my heels. At the bottom, when you got away from the huts, there was a metalled road and beyond that a miry waste of paddy fields a thousand yards across, not yet ploughed but soggy from the first rains and dotted with coarse grass. The elephant was standing eight yards from the road, his left side towards us. He took not the slightest notice of the crowd's approach. He was tearing up bunches of grass, beating them against his knees to clean them and stuffing them into his mouth.

I had halted on the road. As soon as I saw the elephant I knew with perfect certainty that I ought not to shoot him. It is a serious matter to shoot a working elephant—it is comparable to destroying a huge and costly piece of machinery—and obviously one ought not to do it if it can possibly be avoided. And at that distance, peacefully eating, the elephant looked no more dangerous than a cow. I thought then and I think now that his attack of "must" was already passing off; in which case he would merely wander harmlessly about until the mahout came back and caught him. Moreover, I did not in the least want to shoot him. I decided that I would watch him for a little while to make sure that he did not turn savage again, and then go home.

But at that moment, I glanced round at the crowd that had followed me. It was an immense crowd, two thousand at the least and growing every minute. It blocked the road for a long distance on either side. I looked at the sea of yellow faces above the garish clothes—faces all happy and excited over this bit of fun, all certain that the elephant was going to be shot. They were watching me as they would watch a conjuror about to perform a trick. They did not like me, but with the magical rifle in my hands I was momentarily worth watching. And suddenly I realized that I should have to shoot the elephant after all. The people expected it of me and I had got to do it; I could feel their two thousand wills pressing me forward, irresistibly. And it was at this moment, as I stood there with the rifle in my hands, that I first grasped the hollowness, the futility of the white man's dominion in the East. Here was I, the white man with his gun, standing in front of the unarmed native crowd—seemingly the leading actor of the piece; but in reality I was only an absurd puppet pushed to and fro by the will of those yellow faces behind. I perceived in this moment that when the white man turns tyrant it is his own freedom that he destroys. He becomes a sort of hollow, posing dummy, the conventionalized figure of a sahib. For it is the condition of his rule that he shall spend his life in trying to impress the "natives," and so in every crisis he has got to do what the "natives" expect of him. He wears a mask, and his face grows to fit it. I had got to shoot the elephant. I had committed myself to doing it when I sent for the rifle. A sahib has got to act like a sahib; he has got to appear resolute, to know his own mind and do definite things. To come all that way, rifle in hand, with two thousand people marching at my heels, and then to trail feebly away, having done nothing—no, that was impossible. The crowd would laugh at me. And my whole life, every white man's life in the East, was one long struggle not to be laughed at.

But I did not want to shoot the elephant. I watched him beating   8
his bunch of grass against his knees, with that preoccupied grandmotherly air that elephants have. It seemed to me that it would be murder to shoot him. At that age I was not squeamish about killing animals, but I had never shot an elephant and never wanted to. (Somehow it always seems worse to kill a *large* animal.) Besides, there was the beast's owner to be considered. Alive, the elephant was worth at least a hundred pounds; dead, he would only be worth the value of his tusks, five pounds, possibly. But I had got to act quickly. I turned to some experienced-looking Burmans who had been there when we arrived, and asked them how the elephant had been behaving. They all said the same thing: He took no notice of you if you left him alone, but he might charge if you went too close to him.

It was perfectly clear to me what I ought to do. I ought to walk up   9
to within, say, twenty-five yards of the elephant and test his behavior. If he charged, I could shoot; if he took no notice of me, it would be safe to leave him until the mahout came back. But also I knew that I was going to do no such thing. I was a poor shot with a rifle and the ground was soft mud into which one would sink at every step. If the elephant

charged and I missed him, I should have about as much chance as a toad under a steamroller. But even then I was not thinking particularly of my own skin, only of the watchful yellow faces behind. For at that moment, with the crowd watching me, I was not afraid in the ordinary sense, as I would have been if I had been alone. A white man mustn't be frightened in front of "natives"; and so, in general, he isn't frightened. The sole thought in my mind was that if anything went wrong those two thousand Burmans would see me pursued, caught, trampled on, and reduced to a grinning corpse like that Indian up the hill. And if that happened it was quite probable that some of them would laugh. That would never do. There was only one alternative. I shoved the cartridges into the magazine and lay down on the road to get a better aim.

The crowd grew very still, and a deep, low, happy sigh, as of people who see the theater curtain go up at last, breathed from innumerable throats. They were going to have their bit of fun after all. The rifle was a beautiful German thing with cross-hair sights. I did not then know that in shooting an elephant one would shoot to cut an imaginary bar running from ear-hole to ear-hole. I ought, therefore, as the elephant was sideways on, to have aimed straight at his ear-hole; actually I aimed several inches in front of this, thinking the brain would be further forward. 10

When I pulled the trigger I did not hear the bang or feel the kick—one never does when a shot goes home—but I heard the devilish roar of glee that went up from the crowd. In that instant, in too short a time, one would have thought, even for the bullet to get there, a mysterious, terrible change had come over the elephant. He neither stirred nor fell, but every line of his body had altered. He looked suddenly stricken, shrunken, immensely old, as though the frightful impact of the bullet had paralyzed him without knocking him down. At last, after what seemed a long time—it might have been five seconds, I dare say—he sagged flabbily to his knees. His mouth slobbered. An enormous senility seemed to have settled upon him. One could have imagined him thousands of years old. I fired again into the same spot. At the second shot he did not collapse but climbed with desperate slowness to his feet and stood weakly upright, with legs sagging and head drooping. I fired a third time. That was the shot that did for him. You could see the agony of it jolt his whole body and knock the last remnant of strength from his legs. But in falling he seemed for a moment to rise, for as his hind legs collapsed beneath him he seemed to tower upward like a huge rock toppling, his trunk reaching skywards like a tree. He trumpeted, for the first and only time. And then down he came, his belly towards me, with a crash that seemed to shake the ground even where I lay. 11

I got up. The Burmans were already racing past me across the mud. It was obvious that the elephant would never rise again, but he was not dead. He was breathing very rhythmically with long rattling gasps, his 12 great mound of a side painfully rising and falling. His mouth was wide open. I could see far down into caverns of pale pink throat. I waited a long time for him to die, but his breathing did not weaken. Finally I fired my two remaining shots into the spot where I thought his heart must be. The thick blood welled out of him like red velvet, but still he did not die. His body did not even jerk when the shots hit him, the tortured breathing continued without a pause. He was dying, very slowly and in great agony, but in some world remote from me where not even a bullet could damage him further. I felt I had got to put an end to that dreadful noise. It seemed dreadful to see the great beast lying there, powerless to move and yet powerless to die, and not even to be able to finish him. I sent back for my small rifle and poured shot after shot into his heart and down his throat. They seemed to make no impression. The tortured gasps continued as steadily as the ticking of a clock.

In the end I could not stand it any longer and went away. I heard   13
later that it took him half an hour to die. Burmans were bringing dahs and baskets even before I left, and I was told they had stripped his body almost to the bones by the afternoon.

Afterwards, of course, there were endless discussions about the   14
shooting of the elephant. The owner was furious, but he was only an Indian and could do nothing. Besides, legally I had done the right thing, for a mad elephant has to be killed, like a mad dog, if its owner fails to control it. Among the Europeans opinion was divided. The older men said I was right, the younger men said it was a damn shame to shoot an elephant for killing a coolie, because the elephant was worth more than any damn Coringhee coolie. And afterwards I was very glad that the coolie had been killed; it put me legally in the right and it gave me sufficient pretext for shooting the elephant. I often wondered whether any of the others grasped that I had done it solely to avoid looking a fool.

QUESTIONS ON MEANING

1. How would you answer the exasperated student who, after reading this essay, exploded, "Why didn't Orwell just leave his gun at home?"
2. Why did Orwell shoot the elephant?
3. Describe the epiphany that Orwell experiences in the course of the event he writes about. (An *epiphany* is a sudden realization of a truth.)
4. In the last paragraph of his essay, Orwell says he was "glad that the coolie had been killed." How do you account for this remark?
5. What is the PURPOSE of this essay?

QUESTIONS ON WRITING STRATEGY

1. In addition to serving as an INTRODUCTION to Orwell's essay, what function is performed by paragraphs 1 and 2?
2. From what circumstances does the IRONY of Orwell's essay spring?
3. What does "Shooting an Elephant" gain from having been written years after the events it recounts?
4. **MIXED METHODS.** Look at paragraphs 11–12. What does the blend of NARRATION and DESCRIPTION here contribute to the story? How does it further Orwell's purpose?
5. **MIXED METHODS.** How do the EXAMPLES in paragraphs 1 and 2 illustrate Orwell's conflict about his work as a police officer in Burma?

QUESTIONS ON LANGUAGE

1. What do you understand by Orwell's statement that the elephant had "gone 'must'" (para. 3)? Look up *must* or its variant *musth* in your dictionary.
2. What examples of English (as opposed to American) usage do you find in Orwell's essay?
3. Define, if necessary, bazaars, betel (para. 1); intolerable, supplant, prostrate (2); despotic (3); labyrinth, squalid, invariably (4); dominion, sahib (7); magazine (9); innumerable (10); senility (11).

SUGGESTIONS FOR WRITING

1. **JOURNAL WRITING.** Recall a time when you acted against your better judgment to save face. Write as honestly as you can about what motivated you and what mistakes you made.
   FROM JOURNAL TO ESSAY. Write a narrative essay from your journal entry. Tell the story of your action, and consider what the results were, what you might have done differently, and what you learned from the experience.
2. With what examples of governmental face saving are you familiar? If none leaps to mind, read a newspaper or watch the news on television to catch public officials in the act of covering themselves. (Not only national government but local or student government may provide examples.) In an essay, ANALYZE two or three examples: What do you think was really going on that needed covering? Did the officials succeed in saving face, or did their efforts fail? Were the efforts harmful in any way?
3. **CRITICAL WRITING.** Orwell is honest with himself and his readers in acknowledging his mistakes as a government official. Write an essay that examines the degree to which confession may, or may not, erase blameworthiness for misdeeds. Does Orwell remain just as guilty as he would have been if he had not taken responsibility for his actions? Why, or why not? Feel free to supplement your analysis of Orwell's case with examples from your own life or from the news.
4. **CONNECTIONS.** Read William Lutz's "The World of Doublespeak" (p. 350), which CLASSIFIES language that deliberately conceals or misleads. In an essay, examine which of Lutz's categories of doublespeak seem to

arise from the motives Orwell describes in paragraph 7: the need "to impress," to do what is expected of one, "to appear resolute," "not to be laughed at." Use specific examples from Lutz's essay—or from your own experience—to support your ideas.

5. **CONNECTIONS.** Like "Shooting an Elephant," Virginia Woolf's "The Death of the Moth" (p. 663) also blends narration and description. COMPARE AND CONTRAST the two essays, not on their purposes, which are vastly different, but on this blending. What senses do the authors rely on? How do they keep their narratives moving? How much of themselves do they inject into their essays?

GEORGE ORWELL ON WRITING

George Orwell explains the motives for his own writing in the essay "Why I Write" (1946), from which we reprint the following excerpts.

What I have most wanted to do throughout the past ten years is to make political writing into an art. My starting point is always a feeling of partisanship, a sense of injustice. When I sit down to write a book, I do not say to myself, "I am going to produce a work of art." I write it because there is some lie that I want to expose, some fact to which I want to draw attention, and my initial concern is to get a hearing. But I could not do the work of writing a book, or even a long magazine article, if it were not also an esthetic experience. Anyone who cares to examine my work will see that even when it is downright propaganda it contains much that a full-time politician would consider irrelevant. I am not able, and I do not want, completely to abandon the worldview that I acquired in childhood. So long as I remain alive and well I shall continue to feel strongly about prose style, to love the surface of the earth, and to take a pleasure in solid objects and scraps of useless information. It is no use trying to suppress that side of myself. The job is to reconcile my ingrained likes and dislikes with the essentially public, nonindividual activities that this age forces on all of us.

It is not easy. It raises problems of construction and of language, and it raises in a new way the problem of truthfulness. Let me give just one example of the cruder kind of difficulty that arises. My book about the Spanish civil war, *Homage to Catalonia,* is, of course, a frankly political book, but in the main it is written with a certain detachment and regard for form. I did try very hard in it to tell the whole truth without violating my literary instincts. But among other things it contains a long chapter, full of newspaper quotations and the like, defending the Trotskyists who were accused of plotting with Franco. Clearly such a chapter, which after a year or two would lose its interest for any ordi-

nary reader, must ruin the book. A critic whom I respect read me a lecture about it. "Why did you put in all that stuff?" he said. "You've turned
what might have been a good book into journalism." What he said was
true, but I could not have done otherwise. I happened to know, what
very few people in England had been allowed to know, that innocent
men were being falsely accused. If I had not been angry about that I
should never have written the book.

In one form or another this problem comes up again. The problem
of language is subtler and would take too long to discuss. I will only say
that of late years I have tried to write less picturesquely and more exactly. In any case I find that by the time you have perfected any style of
writing, you have always outgrown it. *Animal Farm* was the first book in
which I tried, with full consciousness of what I was doing, to fuse political purpose and artistic purpose into the whole....

Looking back through the last page or two, I see that I have made
it appear as though my motives in writing were wholly public-spirited.
I don't want to leave that as the final impression. All writers are vain,
selfish, and lazy, and at the very bottom of their motives there lies a
mystery. Writing a book is a horrible, exhausting struggle, like a long
bout of some painful illness. One would never undertake such a thing
if one were not driven on by some demon whom one can neither resist
nor understand. For all one knows that demon is simply the same instinct that makes a baby squall for attention. And yet it is also true that
one can write nothing readable unless one constantly struggles to efface one's own personality. Good prose is like a windowpane. I cannot
say with certainty which of my motives are the strongest, but I know
which of them deserve to be followed. And looking back through my
work, I see that it is invariably where I lacked a *political* purpose that I
wrote lifeless books and was betrayed into purple passages, sentences
without meaning, decorative adjectives, and humbug generally.

FOR DISCUSSION

1. What does Orwell mean by his "political purpose" in writing? by his "artistic purpose"? How did he sometimes find it hard to fulfill both purposes?
2. Think about Orwell's remark that "one can write nothing readable unless
   one constantly struggles to efface one's own personality." From your own
   experience, have you found any truth in this observation, or any reason to
   think otherwise?

RICHARD RODRIGUEZ

The son of Spanish-speaking Mexican Americans, RICHARD RODRIGUEZ was born in 1944 in San Francisco. After graduation from Stanford in 1967, he earned an M.A. from Columbia, studied at the Warburg Institute in London, and received a Ph.D. in English literature from the University of California at Berkeley. He once taught but now devotes himself to writing and lecturing. Rodriguez's essays have appeared in *The American Scholar, Change,* and many other magazines. He is an editor at Pacific News Service and a contributing editor for *U.S. News & World Report, Harper's,* and the *Los Angeles Times.* His on-air essays for PBS's *Newshour with Jim Lehrer* won him the George Foster Peabody Award in 1997. In 1982 he published *Hunger of Memory,* a widely discussed book of autobiographical essays. *Mexico's Children* (1991) is a study of Mexicans in America, and *Days of Obligation: An Argument with My Mexican Father* (1992) is also a memoir. *Brown,* due in 2000, explores color and race in American society.

Aria: A Memoir of a Bilingual Childhood

"Aria: A Memoir of a Bilingual Childhood" is taken from *Hunger of Memory.* First published in *The American Scholar* in 1981, this poignant memoir sets forth the author's views of bilingual education. To the child Rodriguez, Spanish was a private language, English a public one. Would the boy have learned faster and better if his teachers had allowed him the use of his native language in school?

In this essay, four main methods of development serve a fifth, argument. The argument is pervasive but most explicit in the paragraphs listed below.

Narration (Chap. 1): paragraphs 1–3, 5–9, 13, 16–18, 21, 23–37
Description (Chap. 2): paragraphs 7–11, 13, 16–18, 21, 23–29
Comparison and contrast (Chap. 4): paragraphs 10–11, 14, 22, 29–30, 33–35, 38–40
Cause and effect (Chap. 8): paragraphs 12, 15, 18–20, 28–32, 36, 38–40
Argument and persuasion (Chap. 10): paragraphs 4, 19–20, 38–39

I remember, to start with, that day in Sacramento, in a California now nearly thirty years past, when I first entered a classroom—able to understand about fifty stray English words. The third of four children, I had been preceded by my older brother and sister to a neighborhood Roman Catholic school. But neither of them had revealed very much about their classroom experiences. They left each morning and returned each afternoon, always together, speaking Spanish as they climbed the five steps to the porch. And their mysterious books, wrapped in brown shopping-bag paper, remained on the table next to the door, closed firmly behind them.

An accident of geography sent me to a school where all my classmates were white and many were the children of doctors and lawyers and business executives. On that first day of school, my classmates must certainly have been uneasy to find themselves apart from their families, in the first institution of their lives. But I was astonished. I was fated to be the "problem student" in class.

The nun said, in a friendly but oddly impersonal voice: "Boys and girls, this is Richard Rodriguez." (I heard her sound it out: *Rich-heard Road-ree-guess.*) It was the first time I had heard anyone say my name in English. "Richard," the nun repeated more slowly, writing my name down in her book. Quickly I turned to see my mother's face dissolve in a watery blur behind the pebbled-glass door.

Now, many years later, I hear of something called "bilingual education"—a scheme proposed in the late 1960s by Hispanic-American social activists, later endorsed by a congressional vote. It is a program that seeks to permit non–English-speaking children (many from lower class homes) to use their "family language" as the language of school. Such, at least, is the aim its supporters announce. I hear them, and am forced to say no: It is not possible for a child, any child, ever to use his family's language in school. Not to understand this is to misunderstand the public uses of schooling and to trivialize the nature of intimate life.

Memory teaches me what I know of these matters. The boy reminds the adult. I was a bilingual child, but of a certain kind: "socially disadvantaged," the son of working-class parents, both Mexican immigrants.

In the early years of my boyhood, my parents coped very well in America. My father had steady work. My mother managed at home. They were nobody's victims. When we moved to a house many blocks from the Mexican-American section of town, they were not intimidated by those two or three neighbors who initially tried to make us unwelcome. ("Keep your brats away from my sidewalk!") But despite all they achieved, or perhaps because they had so much to achieve, they lacked any deep feeling of ease, of belonging in public. They regarded the people at work or in crowds as being very distant from us. Those were the others, *los gringos*. That term was interchangeable in their speech with another, even more telling: *los americanos.*

I grew up in a house where the only regular guests were my relations. On a certain day, enormous families of relatives would visit us, and there would be so many people that the noise and the bodies would spill out to the backyard and onto the front porch. Then for weeks no one would come. (If the doorbell rang, it was usually a salesman.) Our house stood apart—gaudy yellow in a row of white bungalows. We were the people with the noisy dog, the people who raised chickens. We were the foreigners on the block. A few neighbors would smile and wave at us. We waved back. But until I was seven years old, I did not know the name of the old couple living next door or the names of the kids living across the street.

In public, my father and mother spoke a hesitant, accented, and not always grammatical English. And then they would have to strain, their bodies tense, to catch the sense of what was rapidly said by *los gringos*. At home, they returned to Spanish. The language of their Mexican past sounded in counterpoint to the English spoken in public. The words would come quickly, with ease. Conveyed through those sounds was the pleasing, soothing, consoling reminder that one was at home. 8

During those years when I was first learning to speak, my mother and father addressed me only in Spanish; in Spanish I learned to reply. By contrast, English (*inglés*) was the language I came to associate with gringos, rarely heard in the house. I learned my first words of English overhearing my parents speaking to strangers. At six years of age, I knew just enough words for my mother to trust me on errands to stores one block away—but no more. 9

I was then a listening child, careful to hear the very different sounds of Spanish and English. Wide-eyed with hearing, I'd listen to sounds more than to words. First, there were English (gringo) sounds. So many words still were unknown to me that when the butcher or the lady at the drugstore said something, exotic polysyllabic sounds would bloom in the midst of their sentences. Often the speech of people in public seemed to me very loud, booming with confidence. The man behind the counter would literally ask, "What can I do for you?" But by being so firm and clear, the sound of his voice said that he was a gringo; he belonged in public society. There were also the high, nasal notes of middle-class American speech—which I rarely am conscious of hearing today because I hear them so often, but could not stop hearing when I was a boy. Crowds at Safeway or at bus stops were noisy with the birdlike sounds of *los gringos*. I'd move away from them all—all the chirping chatter above me. 10

My own sounds I was unable to hear, but I knew that I spoke English poorly. My words could not extend to form complete thoughts. And the words I did speak I didn't know well enough to make distinct sounds. (Listeners would usually lower their heads to hear better what I was trying to say.) But it was one thing for *me* to speak English with difficulty; it was more troubling to hear my parents speaking in public: their high-whining vowels and guttural consonants; their sentences that got stuck with "eh" and "ah" sounds; the confused syntax; the hesitant rhythm of sounds so different from the way gringos spoke. I'd no- 11

tice, moreover, that my parents' voices were softer than those of gringos we would meet.

I am tempted to say now that none of this mattered. (In adulthood 12
I am embarrassed by childhood fears.) And, in a way, it didn't matter
very much that my parents could not speak English with ease. Their
linguistic difficulties had no serious consequences. My mother and father made themselves understood at the county hospital clinic and at
government offices. And yet, in another way, it mattered very much. It
was unsettling to hear my parents struggle with English. Hearing them,
I'd grow nervous, and my clutching trust in their protection and power
would be weakened.

There were many times like the night at a brightly lit gasoline sta- 13
tion (a blaring white memory) when I stood uneasily hearing my father
talk to a teenage attendant. I do not recall what they were saying, but I
cannot forget the sounds my father made as he spoke. At one point his
words slid together to form one long word—sounds as confused as the
threads of blue and green oil in the puddle next to my shoes. His voice
rushed through what he had left to say. Toward the end, he reached
falsetto notes, appealing to his listener's understanding. I looked away
at the lights of passing automobiles. I tried not to hear any more. But I
heard only too well the attendant's reply, his calm, easy tones. Shortly
afterward, headed for home, I shivered when my father put his hand on
my shoulder. The very first chance that I got, I evaded his grasp and ran
on ahead into the dark, skipping with feigned boyish exuberance.

But then there was Spanish: *español*, the language rarely heard 14
away from the house; *español*, the language which seemed to me therefore a private language, my family's language. To hear its sounds was to
feel myself specially recognized as one of the family, apart from *los otros*.
A simple remark, an inconsequential comment could convey that assurance. My parents would say something to me and I would feel embraced by the sounds of their words. Those sounds said: *I am speaking
with ease in Spanish. I am addressing you in words I never use with los gringos. I recognize you as someone special, close, like no one outside. You belong with us. In the family. Ricardo.*

At the age of six, well past the time when most middle-class chil- 15
dren no longer notice the difference between sounds uttered at home
and words spoken in public, I had a different experience. I lived in a
world compounded of sounds. I was a child longer than most. I lived in
a magical world, surrounded by sounds both pleasing and fearful. I
shared with my family a language enchantingly private—different
from that used in the city around us.

Just opening or closing the screen door behind me was an impor- 16
tant experience. I'd rarely leave home all alone or without feeling reluctance. Walking down the sidewalk, under the canopy of tall trees,

I'd warily notice the (suddenly) silent neighborhood kids who stood warily watching me. Nervously, I'd arrive at the grocery store to hear there the sounds of the gringo, reminding me that in this so-big world I was a foreigner. But if leaving home was never routine, neither was coming back. Walking toward our house, climbing the steps from the sidewalk, in summer when the front door was open, I'd hear voices beyond the screen door talking in Spanish. For a second or two I'd stay, linger there listening. Smiling, I'd hear my mother call out, saying in Spanish, "Is that you, Richard?" Those were her words, but all the while her sounds would assure me: *You are home now. Come close inside. With us.* "*Sí*," I'd reply.

Once more inside the house, I would resume my place in the family. The sounds would grow harder to hear. Once more at home, I would grow less conscious of them. It required, however, no more than the blurt of the doorbell to alert me all over again to listen to sounds. The house would turn instantly quiet while my mother went to the door. I'd hear her hard English sounds. I'd wait to hear her voice turn to soft-sounding Spanish, which assured me, as surely as did the clicking tongue of the lock on the door, that the stranger was gone. 17

Plainly it is not healthy to hear such sounds so often. It is not healthy to distinguish public from private sounds so easily. I remained cloistered by sounds, timid and shy in public, too dependent on the voices at home. I remember many nights when my father would come back from work, and I'd hear him call out to my mother in Spanish, sounding relieved. In Spanish, his voice would sound the light and free notes that he never could manage in English. Some nights I'd jump up just hearing his voice. My brother and I would come running into the room where he was with our mother. Our laughing (so deep was the pleasure!) became screaming. Like others who feel the pain of public alienation, we transformed the knowledge of our public separateness into a consoling reminder of our intimacy. Excited, our voices joined in a celebration of sounds. *We are speaking now the way we never speak out in public—we are together*, the sounds told me. Some nights no one seemed willing to loosen the hold that sounds had on us. At dinner we invented new words that sounded Spanish, but made sense only to us. We pieced together new words by taking, say, an English verb and giving it Spanish endings. My mother's instructions at bedtime would be lacquered with mock-urgent tones. Or a word like *sí*, sounded in several notes, would convey added measures of feeling. Tongues lingered around the edges of words, especially fat vowels, and we happily sounded that military drum roll, the twirling roar of the Spanish *r*. Family language, my family's sounds: the voices of my parents and sisters and brother. Their voices insisting: *You belong here. We are family members. Related. Special to one another. Listen!* Voices singing and sigh- 18 ing, rising and straining, then surging, teeming with pleasure which burst syllables into fragments of laughter. At times it seemed there was steady quiet only when, from another room, the rustling whispers of my parents faded and I edged closer to sleep.

Supporters of bilingual education imply today that students like me   19
miss a great deal by not being taught in their family's language. What they seem not to recognize is that, as a socially disadvantaged child, I regarded Spanish as a private language. It was a ghetto language that deepened and strengthened my feeling of separateness. What I needed to learn in school was that I had the right, and the obligation, to speak the public language. The odd truth is that my first-grade classmates could have become bilingual, in the conventional sense of the word, more easily than I. Had they been taught early (as upper-middle-class children often are taught) a "second language" like Spanish or French, they could have regarded it simply as another public language. In my case, such bilingualism could not have been so quickly achieved. What I did not believe was that I could speak a single public language.

Without question, it would have pleased me to have heard my teach-   20
ers address me in Spanish when I entered the classroom. I would have felt much less afraid. I would have imagined that my instructors were some-how "related" to me; I would indeed have heard their Spanish as my fam-ily's language. I would have trusted them and responded with ease. But I would have delayed—postponed for how long?—having to learn the language of public society. I would have evaded—and for how long?— learning the great lesson of school: that I had a public identity.

Fortunately, my teachers were unsentimental about their responsi-   21
bility. What they understood was that I needed to speak public English. So their voices would search me out, asking me questions. Each time I heard them I'd look up in surprise to see a nun's face frowning at me. I'd mumble, not really meaning to answer. The nun would persist. "Richard, stand up. Don't look at the floor. Speak up. Speak to the en-tire class, not just to me!" But I couldn't believe English could be my language to use. (In part, I did not want to believe it.) I continued to mumble. I resisted the teacher's demands. (Did I somehow suspect that once I learned this public language my family life would be changed?) Silent, waiting for the bell to sound, I remained dazed, diffident, afraid.

Because I wrongly imagined that English was intrinsically a public   22
language and Spanish was intrinsically private, I easily noted the dif-ference between classroom language and the language at home. At school, words were directed to a general audience of listeners. ("Boys and girls...") Words were meaningfully ordered. And the point was not self-expression alone, but to make oneself understood by many others. The teacher quizzed: "Boys and girls, why do we use that word in this

sentence? Could we think of a better word to use there? Would the sentence change its meaning if the words were differently arranged? Isn't there a better way of saying much the same thing?" (I couldn't say. I wouldn't try to say.)

Three months passed. Five. A half year. Unsmiling, ever watchful,   23 my teachers noted my silence. They began to connect my behavior with the slow progress my brother and sisters were making. Until, one Saturday morning, three nuns arrived at the house to talk to our parents. Stiffly they sat on the blue living-room sofa. From the doorway of another room, spying on the visitors, I noted the incongruity, the clash of two worlds, the faces and voices of school intruding upon the familiar setting of home. I overheard one voice gently wondering, "Do your children speak only Spanish at home, Mrs. Rodriguez?" While another voice added, "That Richard especially seems so timid and shy."

That Rich-heard!   24

With great tact, the visitors continued, "Is it possible for you and   25 your husband to encourage your children to practice their English when they are home?" Of course my parents complied. What would they not do for their children's well-being? And how could they question the Church's authority which those women represented? In an instant they agreed to give up the language (the sounds) which had revealed and accentuated our family's closeness. The moment after the visitors left, the change was observed. "*Ahora,* speak to us only *en inglés,*" my father and mother told us.

At first, it seemed a kind of game. After dinner each night, the fam-   26 ily gathered together to practice "our" English. It was still then *inglés,* a language foreign to us, so we felt drawn to it as strangers. Laughing, we would try to define words we could not pronounce. We played with strange English sounds, often overanglicizing our pronunciations. And we filled the smiling gaps of our sentences with familiar Spanish sounds. But that was cheating, somebody shouted, and everyone laughed.

In school, meanwhile, like my brother and sisters, I was required to   27 attend a daily tutoring session. I needed a full year of this special work. I also needed my teachers to keep my attention from straying in class by calling out, "*Rich-heard*"—their English voices slowly loosening the ties to my other name, with its three notes, *Ri-car-do.* Most of all, I needed to hear my mother and father speak to me in a moment of seriousness in "broken"—suddenly heartbreaking—English. This scene was inevitable. One Saturday morning I entered the kitchen where my parents were talking, but I did not realize that they were talking in Spanish until, the moment they saw me, their voices changed and they began speaking English. The gringo sounds they uttered startled me. Pushed me away. In that moment of trivial misunderstanding and profound insight, I felt my throat twisted by unsounded grief. I simply turned and left the room. But I had no place to escape to where I could grieve in Spanish. My brother and sisters were speaking English in another part of the house.

Again and again in the days following, as I grew increasingly angry, 28 I was obliged to hear my mother and father encouraging me: "Speak to us *en inglés*." Only then did I determine to learn classroom English. Thus, sometime afterward it happened: One day in school, I raised my hand to volunteer an answer to a question. I spoke out in a loud voice and I did not think it remarkable when the entire class understood. That day I moved very far from being the disadvantaged child I had been only days earlier. Taken hold at last was the belief, the calming assurance, that I *belonged* in public.

Shortly after, I stopped hearing the high, troubling sounds of *los* 29 *gringos*. A more and more confident speaker of English, I didn't listen to how strangers sounded when they talked to me. With so many English-speaking people around me, I no longer heard American accents. Conversations quickened. Listening to persons whose voices sounded eccentrically pitched, I might note their sounds for a few seconds, but then I'd concentrate on what they were saying. Now when I heard someone's tone of voice—angry or questioning or sarcastic or happy or sad—I didn't distinguish it from the words it expressed. Sound and word were thus tightly wedded. At the end of each day I was often bemused, and always relieved, to realize how "soundless," though crowded with words, my day in public had been. An eight-year-old boy, I finally came to accept what had been technically true since my birth: I was an American citizen.

But diminished by then was the special feeling of closeness at home. 30 Gone was the desperate, urgent, intense feeling of being at home among those with whom I felt intimate. Our family remained a loving family, but one greatly changed. We were no longer so close, no longer bound tightly together by the knowledge of our separateness from *los gringos*. Neither my older brother nor my sisters rushed home after school anymore. Nor did I. When I arrived home, often there would be neighborhood kids in the house. Or the house would be empty of sounds.

Following the dramatic Americanization of their children, even 31 my parents grew more publicly confident—especially my mother. First she learned the names of all the people on the block. Then she decided we needed to have a telephone in our house. My father, for his part, continued to use the word gringo, but it was no longer charged with bitterness or distrust. Stripped of any emotional content, the word simply became a name for those Americans not of Hispanic descent. Hearing him, sometimes, I wasn't sure if he was pronouncing the Spanish word *gringo*, or saying gringo in English.

There was a new silence at home. As we children learned more and more English, we shared fewer and fewer words with our parents. Sentences needed to be spoken slowly when one of us addressed our mother or father. Often the parent wouldn't understand. The child would need to repeat himself. Still the parent misunderstood. The young voice, frustrated, would end up saying, "Never mind"—the subject was closed. Dinners would be noisy with the clinking of knives and forks against dishes. My mother would smile softly between her remarks; my father, at the other end of the table, would chew and chew his food while he stared over the heads of his children.   32

My mother! My father! After English became my primary language, I no longer knew what words to use in addressing my parents. The old Spanish words (those tender accents of sound) I had earlier used—*mamá* and *papá*—I couldn't use anymore. They would have been all-too-painful reminders of how much had changed in my life. On the other hand, the words I heard neighborhood kids call their parents seemed equally unsatisfactory. "Mother" and "father," "ma," "pa," "dad," "pop" (how I hated the all-American sound of that last word)— all these I felt were unsuitable terms of address for *my* parents. As a result, I never used them at home. Whenever I'd speak to my parents, I would try to get their attention by looking at them. In public conversations, I'd refer to them as my "parents" or my "mother" and "father."   33

My mother and father, for their part, responded differently, as their children spoke to them less. My mother grew restless, seemed troubled and anxious at the scarceness of words exchanged in the house. She would question me about my day when I came home from school. She smiled at my small talk. She pried at the edges of my sentences to get me to say something more. ("What...?") She'd join conversations she overheard, but her intrusions often stopped her children's talking. By contrast, my father seemed to grow reconciled to the new quiet. Though his English somewhat improved, he tended more and more to retire into silence. At dinner he spoke very little. One night his children and even his wife helplessly giggled at his garbled English pronunciation of the Catholic "Grace Before Meals." Thereafter he made his wife recite the prayer at the start of each meal, even on formal occasions when there were guests in the house.   34

Hers became the public voice of the family. On official business it was she, not my father, who would usually talk to strangers on the phone or in stores. We children grew so accustomed to his silence that years later we would routinely refer to his "shyness." (My mother often   35 tried to explain: Both of his parents died when he was eight. He was raised by an uncle who treated him as little more than a menial servant. He was never encouraged to speak. He grew up alone—a man of few words.) But I realized my father was not shy whenever I'd watch him speaking Spanish with relatives. Using Spanish, he was quickly effusive. Especially when talking with other men, his voice would spark, flicker, flare alive with varied sounds. In Spanish he expressed ideas and feelings he rarely revealed when speaking English. With firm Spanish sounds he conveyed a confidence and authority that English would never allow him.

The silence at home, however, was not simply the result of fewer 36 words passing between parents and children. More profound for me was the silence created by my inattention to sounds. At about the time I no longer bothered to listen with care to the sounds of English in public, I grew careless about listening to the sounds made by the family when they spoke. Most of the time I would hear someone speaking at home and didn't distinguish his sounds from the words people uttered in public. I didn't even pay much attention to my parents' accented and ungrammatical speech—at least not at home. Only when I was with them in public would I become alert to their accents. But even then their sounds caused me less and less concern. For I was growing increasingly confident of my own public identity.

I would have been happier about my public success had I not re- 37 called, sometimes, what it had been like earlier, when my family conveyed its intimacy through a set of conveniently private sounds. Sometimes in public, hearing a stranger, I'd hark back to my lost past. A Mexican farm worker approached me one day downtown. He wanted directions to some place. "*Hijito,*..." he said. And his voice stirred old longings. Another time I was standing beside my mother in the visiting room of a Carmelite convent, before the dense screen which rendered the nuns shadowy figures. I heard several of them speaking Spanish in their busy, singsong, overlapping voices, assuring my mother that, yes, yes, we were remembered, all our family was remembered, in their prayers. Those voices echoed faraway family sounds. Another day a dark-faced old woman touched my shoulder lightly to steady herself as she boarded a bus. She murmured something to me I couldn't quite comprehend. Her Spanish voice came near, like the face of a never-before-seen relative in the instant before I was kissed. That voice, like so many of the Spanish voices I'd hear in public, recalled the golden age of my childhood.

Bilingual educators say today that children lose a degree of "indi- 38 viduality" by becoming assimilated into public society. (Bilingual schooling is a program popularized in the seventies, that decade when middle-class "ethnics" began to resist the process of assimilation—the "American melting pot.") But the bilingualists oversimplify when they scorn the value and necessity of assimilation. They do not seem to realize that a person is individualized in two ways. So they do not realize that, while one suffers a diminished sense of *private* individuality by being assimilated into public society, such assimilation makes possible the achievement of *public* individuality.

Simplistically again, the bilingualists insist that a student should be   39
reminded of his difference from others in mass society, of his "heritage." But they equate mere separateness with individuality. The fact is that only in private—with intimates—is separateness from the crowd a prerequisite for individuality; an intimate "tells" me that I am unique, unlike all others, apart from the crowd. In public, by contrast, full individuality is achieved, paradoxically, by those who are able to consider themselves members of the crowd. Thus it happened for me. Only when I was able to think of myself as an American, no longer an alien in gringo society, could I seek the rights and opportunities necessary for full public individuality. The social and political advantages I enjoy as a man began on the day I came to believe that my name is indeed *Rich-heard Road-ree-guess*. It is true that my public society today is often impersonal; in fact, my public society is usually mass society. But despite the anonymity of the crowd, and despite the fact that the individuality I achieve in public is often tenuous—because it depends on my being one in a crowd—I celebrate the day I acquired my new name. Those middle-class ethnics who scorn assimilation seem to me filled with decadent self-pity, obsessed by the burden of public life. Dangerously, they romanticize public separateness and trivialize the dilemma of those who are truly socially disadvantaged.

If I rehearse here the changes in my private life after my Ameri-   40
canization, it is finally to emphasize a public gain. The loss implies the gain. The house I returned to each afternoon was quiet. Intimate sounds no longer greeted me at the door. Inside there were other noises. The telephone rang. Neighborhood kids ran past the door of the bedroom where I was reading my schoolbooks—covered with brown shopping-bag paper. Once I learned the public language, it would never again be easy for me to hear intimate family voices. More and more of my day was spent hearing words, not sounds. But that may only be a way of saying that on the day I raised my hand in class and spoke loudly to an entire roomful of faces, my childhood started to end.

QUESTIONS ON MEANING

1. Rodriguez's essay is both memoir and ARGUMENT. What is the thrust of the author's argument?
2. How did the child Rodriguez react when, in his presence, his parents had to struggle to make themselves understood by "*los gringos*"?
3. What does the author mean when he says, "I was a child longer than most" (para. 15)?
4. According to the author, what impact did the Rodriguez children's use of English have on relationships within the family?
5. Contrast the child Rodriguez's view of the nuns who insisted he speak English with his adult view.

QUESTIONS ON WRITING STRATEGY

1. How effective an INTRODUCTION is Rodriguez's first paragraph?
2. Several times in his essay Rodriguez shifts from memoir to argument and back again. What is the overall EFFECT of these shifts? Do they strengthen or weaken the author's stance against bilingual education?
3. Twice in his essay (in paras. 1 and 40) the author mentions schoolbooks wrapped in shopping-bag paper. How does the use of this detail enhance his argument?
4. What AUDIENCE probably would not like this essay? Why would they not like it?
5. **MIXED METHODS.** Examine how Rodriguez uses DESCRIPTION to COMPARE AND CONTRAST the sounds of Spanish and English (paras. 10, 11, 13, 14, 18, 33, 37). What sounds does he evoke? What are the differences among them?
6. **MIXED METHODS.** Rodriguez's essay is an argument supported mainly by personal NARRATIVE—Rodriguez's own experience. What kind of ETHICAL APPEAL (pp. 456–57) does the narrative make? What can we INFER about Rodriguez's personality, intellect, fairness, and trustworthiness?

QUESTIONS ON LANGUAGE

1. Consult the dictionary if you need help defining these words: counterpoint (para. 8); polysyllabic (10); guttural, syntax (11); falsetto, exuberance (13); inconsequential (14); cloistered, lacquered (18); diffident (21); intrinsically (22); incongruity (23); bemused (29); effusive (35); assimilated (38); paradoxically, tenuous, decadent (39).
2. In Rodriguez's essay, how do the words *public* and *private* relate to the issue of bilingual education? What important distinction does the author make between *individuality* and *separateness* (para. 39)?
3. What exactly does the author mean when he says, "More and more of my day was spent hearing words, not sounds" (para. 40)?

SUGGESTIONS FOR WRITING

1. **JOURNAL WRITING.** Rodriguez remembers thinking as a child, "We are speaking now the way we never speak out in public—we are together" (para. 18). Was there language in your childhood home that was similarly private? Did you and your family speak a language other than the dominant one, or did you share tones of voice, slang words, ALLUSIONS, inside jokes, or other kinds of language that were different from what you heard in public?

    FROM JOURNAL TO ESSAY. Write an essay DEFINING the distinctive quality of the language spoken in your home when you were a child. What effect, if any, did this language have on you when you went out into public? Does it influence your memories of childhood? Do you revert to this private language when you are with your family?

2. Bilingual education is a controversial issue with EVIDENCE and strong feelings on both sides. In a page or so of preliminary writing, respond to Rodriguez's essay with your own gut feelings on the issue. Then do some library research to extend, support, or refute your views. (Consult the *Readers' Guide to Periodical Literature* or *InfoTrac* as a first step.) In a well-reasoned and well-supported essay, give your opinion on whether or not public schools should teach children in their "family language."

3. **CRITICAL WRITING.** In his argument against bilingual education, Rodriguez offers no data from studies, no testimony from education experts, indeed no evidence at all except his personal experience. In an essay, ANALYZE and EVALUATE this evidence: How convincing do you find it? Is it adequate to support the argument? (In your essay consider Rodriguez's ethical appeal, the topic of the sixth question on writing strategy, previous page.)

4. **CONNECTIONS.** Rodriguez's mother and father seem to have had a definite idea of their parental obligations to their children. Look at Jamaica Kincaid's story "Girl" (p. 304) and write a COMPARISON between that mother's sense of parental obligations and the Rodriguezes'. What, for example, is the connection between good parenting and teaching one's child to conform? In both cases, you will have to infer the parents' values from their actions and words. Use evidence from both works to support your inferences.

5. **CONNECTIONS.** Though it apparently included relatives outside the nucleus of parents and children, Rodriguez's family seems to have been quite isolated by culture and language from the rest of American society. In "Stone Soup" (p. 441), Barbara Kingsolver also explores the isolation of the independent nuclear family, but she does not focus on culture and language as much as on physical and emotional separation from others, including extended family. Write an essay about the differences between these two kinds of isolation. What are their possible disadvantages? possible advantages? Which might be more harmful to family members? For evidence, draw on Rodriguez's and Kingsolver's essays and your own experiences.

RICHARD RODRIGUEZ ON WRITING

For *The Bedford Reader,* Richard Rodriguez described the writing of "Aria."

From grammar school to college, my teachers offered perennial encouragement: "Write about what you know." Every year I would respond with the student's complaint: "I have nothing to write about ... I haven't done anything." (Writers, real writers, I thought, lived in New York or Paris; they smoked on the back jackets of library books, their chores done.)

Stories die for not being told. My story got told because I had received an education; my teachers had given me the skill of stringing words together in a coherent line. But it was not until I was a man that I felt any need to write my story. A few years ago I left graduate school, quit teaching for political reasons (to protest affirmative action). But after leaving the classroom, as the months passed, I grew desperate to talk to serious people about serious things. In the great journals of the world, I noticed, there was conversation of a sort, glamorous company of a sort, and I determined to join it. I began writing to stay alive — not as a job, but to stay alive.

Even as you see my essay now, in cool printer's type, I look at some pages and cannot remember having written them. Or else I can remember earlier versions — unused incident, character, description (rooms, faces) — crumbled and discarded. Flung from possibility. They hit the wastebasket, those pages, and yet, defying gravity with a scratchy, starchy resilience, tried to reopen themselves. Then they fell silent. I read certain other sentences now and they recall the very day they were composed — the afternoon of rain or the telephone call that was to come a few moments after, the house, the room where these sentences were composed, the pattern of the rug, the wastebasket. (In all there were about thirty or forty versions that preceded this final "Aria.") I tried to describe my experiences exactly, at once to discover myself and to reveal myself. Always I had to write against the fear I felt that no one would be able to understand what I was saying.

As a reader, I have been struck by the way those novels and essays that are most particular, most particularly about one other life and time (Hannibal, Missouri; one summer; a slave; the loveliness of a muddy river) most fully achieve universality and call to be cherished. It is a paradox apparently: The more a writer unearths the detail that makes a life singular, the more a reader is led to feel a kind of sharing. Perhaps the reason we are able to respond to the life that is so different is because we all, each of us, think privately that we are different from one another.

And the more closely we examine another life in its misery or wisdom or foolishness, the more it seems we take some version of ourselves.

It is, in any case, finally you that I end up having to trust not to laugh, not to snicker. Even as you regard me in these lines, I try to imagine your face as you read. You who read "Aria," especially those of you with your theme-divining yellow felt pen poised in your hand, you for whom this essay is yet another assignment, please do not forget that it is my life I am handing you in these pages—memories that are as personal for me as family photographs in an old cigar box.

FOR DISCUSSION

1. What seems to be Rodriguez's attitude toward his AUDIENCE when he writes? Do you think he writes chiefly for his readers, or for himself? Defend your answer.
2. Rodriguez tells us what he said when, as a student, he was told, "Write about what you know." What do you think he would say now?

JONATHAN SWIFT

JONATHAN SWIFT (1667–1745), the son of English parents who had set-tled in Ireland, divided his energies among literature, politics, and the Church of England. Dissatisfied with the quiet life of an Anglican parish priest, Swift spent much of his time in London hobnobbing with writers and producing pamphlets in support of the Tory Party. In 1713 Queen Anne rewarded his political services with an assign-ment the London-loving Swift didn't want: to supervise St. Patrick's Cathedral in Dublin. There, as Dean Swift, he ended his days— beloved by the Irish, whose interests he defended against the English government. Although Swift's chief works include the remarkable satires *The Battle of the Books* and *A Tale of a Tub* (both 1704) and scores of fine poems, he is best remembered for *Gulliver's Travels* (1726), an account of four imaginary voyages. This classic is always abridged when it is given to children because of its frank descriptions of human filth and viciousness. In *Gulliver's Travels*, Swift pays tribute to the reasoning portion of "that animal called man," and delivers a stinging rebuke to the rest of him.

A Modest Proposal

Three consecutive years of drought and sparse crops had worked hardship upon the Irish when Swift wrote this ferocious essay in the summer of 1729. At the time, there were said to be thirty-five thou-sand wandering beggars in the country: Whole families had quit their farms and had taken to the roads. Large landowners, of English an-cestry, preferred to ignore their tenants' sufferings and lived abroad to dodge taxes and payment of church duties. Swift had no special fond-ness for the Irish, but he hated the inhumanity he witnessed.

Although printed as a pamphlet in Dublin, Swift's essay is clearly meant for English readers as well as Irish ones. When circulated, the pamphlet caused a sensation in both Ireland and England and had to be reprinted seven times in the same year. Swift is an expert with plain, vigorous English prose, and "A Modest Proposal" is a master-piece of SATIRE and IRONY. (If you are uncertain what Swift argues for, see the discussion of these devices in Useful Terms.)

"A Modest Proposal" is an argument developed chiefly by process analysis and cause and effect. These two methods mix with notable uses of description, example, and comparison and contrast.

Description (Chap. 2): paragraphs 1–2, 19
Example (Chap. 3): paragraphs 1–2, 6, 10, 14, 18, 32
Comparison and contrast (Chap. 4): paragraph 17
Process analysis (Chap. 5): paragraphs 4, 6–7, 10–17
Cause and effect (Chap. 8): paragraphs 4–5, 13, 21–29, 31, 33
Argument and persuasion (Chap. 10): throughout

*For Preventing the Children of Poor People in Ireland
from Being a Burden to Their Parents or Country,
and for Making Them Beneficial to the Public*

It is a melancholy object to those who walk through this great   1
town[1] or travel in the country, when they see the streets, the roads, and
cabin doors, crowded with beggars of the female sex, followed by three,
four, or six children, all in rags and importuning every passenger for an
alms. These mothers, instead of being able to work for their honest
livelihood, are forced to employ all their time in strolling to beg sustenance for their helpless infants, who, as they grow up, either turn
thieves for want of work, or leave their dear native country to fight for
the Pretender in Spain, or sell themselves to the Barbados.[2]

I think it is agreed by all parties that this prodigious number of chil-   2
dren in the arms, or on the backs, or at the heels of their mothers, and
frequently of their fathers, is in the present deplorable state of the kingdom a very great additional grievance; and therefore whoever could
find out a fair, cheap, and easy method of making these children sound,
useful members of the commonwealth would deserve so well of the
public as to have his statue set up for a preserver of the nation.

But my intention is very far from being confined to provide only for   3
the children of professed beggars; it is of a much greater extent, and
shall take in the whole number of infants at a certain age who are born
of parents in effect as little able to support them as those who demand
our charity in the streets.

As to my own part, having turned my thoughts for many years   4
upon this important subject, and maturely weighed the several schemes
of other projectors,[3] I have always found them grossly mistaken in their
computation. It is true, a child just dropped from its dam may be supported by her milk for a solar year, with little other nourishment; at
most not above the value of two shillings, which the mother may certainly get, or the value in scraps, by her lawful occupation of begging;
and it is exactly at one year that I propose to provide for them in such
a manner as instead of being a charge upon their parents or the parish,
or wanting food and raiment for the rest of their lives, they shall on the
contrary contribute to the feeding, and partly to the clothing, of many
thousands.

[1] Dublin. —Eds.
[2] The Pretender was James Stuart, exiled in Spain; in 1718 many Irishmen had
joined an army seeking to restore him to the English throne. Others wishing to emi-
grate had signed papers as indentured servants, agreeing to work for a number of years
in the Barbados or other British colonies in exchange for their ocean passage. —Eds.
[3] Planners. —Eds.

There is likewise another great advantage in my scheme, that it will prevent those voluntary abortions, and that horrid practice of women murdering their bastard children, alas, too frequent among us, sacrificing the poor innocent babes, I doubt, more to avoid the expense than the shame, which would move tears and pity in the most savage and inhuman breast.

The number of souls in this kingdom being usually reckoned one million and a half, of these I calculate there may be about two hundred thousand couples whose wives are breeders; from which number I subtract thirty thousand couples who are able to maintain their own children, although I apprehend there cannot be so many under the present distress of the kingdom; but this being granted, there will remain an hundred and seventy thousand breeders. I again subtract fifty thousand for those women who miscarry, or whose children die by accident or disease within the year. There only remain an hundred and twenty thousand children of poor parents annually born. The question therefore is, how this number shall be reared and provided for, which, as I have already said, under the present situation of affairs, is utterly impossible by all the methods hitherto proposed. For we can neither employ them in handicraft or agriculture; we neither build houses (I mean in the country) nor cultivate land. They can very seldom pick up a livelihood stealing till they arrive at six years old, except where they are of towardly parts;[4] although I confess they learn the rudiments much earlier, during which time they can however be looked upon only as probationers, as I have been informed by a principal gentleman in the country of Cavan, who protested to me that he never knew above one or two instances under the age of six, even in a part of the kingdom so renowned for the quickest proficiency in that art.

I am assured by our merchants that a boy or a girl before twelve years old is no salable commodity; and even when they come to this age they will not yield above three pounds, or three pounds and half a crown at most on the Exchange; which cannot turn to account either to the parents or the kingdom, the charge of nutriment and rags having been at least four times that value.

I shall now therefore humbly propose my own thoughts, which I hope will not be liable to the least objection.

I have been assured by a very knowing American of my acquaintance in London, that a young healthy child well nursed is at a year old a most delicious, nourishing, and wholesome food, whether stewed, roasted, baked, or boiled; and I make no doubt that it will equally serve in a fricassee or a ragout.[5]

---

[4] Teachable wits, innate abilities. — Eds.
[5] Stew. — Eds.

I do therefore humbly offer it to public consideration that of the 10 hundred and twenty thousand children, already computed, twenty thousand may be reserved for breed, whereof only one fourth part to be males, which is more than we allow to sheep, black cattle, or swine; and my reason is that these children are seldom the fruits of marriage, a circumstance not much regarded by our savages, therefore one male will be sufficient to serve four females. That the remaining hundred thousand may at a year old be offered in sale to the persons of quality and fortune through the kingdom, always advising the mother to let them suck plentifully in the last month, so as to render them plump and fat for a good table. A child will make two dishes at an entertainment for friends; and when the family dines alone, the fore or hind quarter will make a reasonable dish, and seasoned with a little pepper or salt will be very good boiled on the fourth day, especially in winter.

I have reckoned upon a medium that a child just born will weigh 11 twelve pounds, and in a solar year it tolerably nursed increaseth to twenty-eight pounds.

I grant this food will be somewhat dear, and therefore very proper 12 for landlords, who, as they have already devoured most of the parents, seem to have the best title to the children.

Infant's flesh will be in season throughout the year, but more plen- 13 tiful in March, and a little before and after. For we are told by a grave author, an eminent French physician,[6] that fish being a prolific diet, there are more children born in Roman Catholic countries about nine months after Lent than at any other season; therefore, reckoning a year after Lent, the markets will be more glutted than usual, because the number of popish infants is at least three to one in this kingdom; and therefore it will have one other collateral advantage, by lessening the number of Papists among us.

I have already computed the charge of nursing a beggar's child (in 14 which list I reckon all cottagers, laborers, and four-fifths of the farmers) to be about two shillings per annum, rags included; and I believe no gentleman would repine to give ten shillings for the carcass of a good fat child, which, as I have said, will make four dishes of excellent nutritive meat, when he hath only some particular friend or his own family to dine with him. Thus the squire will learn to be a good landlord, and grow people among the tenants; the mother will have eight shillings net profit, and be fit for work till she produces another child.

Those who are more thrifty (as I must confess the times require) 15 may flay the carcass; the skin of which artificially[7] dressed will make admirable gloves for ladies, and summer boots for fine gentlemen.

---

[6] Swift's favorite French writer, François Rabelais, sixteenth-century author; not "grave" at all, but a broad humorist. —EDS.

[7] With art or craft. —EDS.

As to our city of Dublin, shambles[8] may be appointed for this pur-   16
pose in the most convenient parts of it, and butchers we may be assured
will not be wanting; although I rather recommend buying the children
alive, and dressing them hot from the knife as we do roasting pigs.

A very worthy person, a true lover of his country, and whose virtues   17
I highly esteem, was lately pleased in discoursing on this matter to offer a refinement upon my scheme. He said that many gentlemen of his
kingdom, having of late destroyed their deer, he conceived that the
want of venison might be well supplied by the bodies of young lads and
maidens, not exceeding fourteen years of age nor under twelve, so great
a number of both sexes in every county being now ready to starve for
want of work and service; and these to be disposed of by their parents,
if alive, or otherwise by their nearest relations. But with due deference
to so excellent a friend and so deserving a patriot, I cannot be altogether in his sentiments; for as to the males, my American acquaintance assured me from frequent experience that their flesh was
generally tough and lean, like that of our schoolboys, by continual exercise, and their taste disagreeable; and to fatten them would not answer the charge. Then as to the females, it would, I think with humble
submission, be a loss to the public, because they soon would become
breeders themselves; and besides, it is not improbable that some
scrupulous people might be apt to censure such a practice (although indeed very unjustly) as a little bordering upon cruelty; which, I confess,
hath always been with me the strongest objection against any project,
how well soever intended.

But in order to justify my friend, he confessed that this expedient   18
was put into his head by the famous Psalmanazar,[9] a native of the island
Formosa, who came from thence to London above twenty years ago,
and in conversation told my friend that in his country when any young
person happened to be put to death, the executioner sold the carcass to
persons of quality as a prime dainty; and that in his time the body of a
plump girl of fifteen, who was crucified for an attempt to poison the emperor, was sold to his Imperial Majesty's prime minister of state, and
other great mandarins of the court, in joints from the gibbet, at four
hundred crowns. Neither indeed can I deny that if the same use were
made of several plump young girls in this town, who without one single
groat to their fortunes cannot stir abroad without a chair, and appear at
the playhouse and assemblies in foreign fineries which they never will
pay for, the kingdom would not be the worse.

Some persons of a desponding spirit are in great concern about that   19

---

[8] Butcher shops or slaughterhouses. —EDS.
[9] Georges Psalmanazar, a Frenchman who pretended to be Japanese, author of a
completely imaginary *Description of the Isle Formosa* (1705), had become a well-known
figure in gullible London society. —EDS.

vast number of poor people who are aged, diseased, or maimed, and I have been desired to employ my thoughts what course may be taken to ease the nation of so grievous an encumbrance. But I am not in the least pain upon that matter, because it is very well known that they are every day dying and rotting by cold and famine, and filth and vermin, as fast as can be reasonably expected. And as to the younger laborers, they are now in almost as hopeful a condition. They cannot get work, and consequently pine away for want of nourishment to a degree that if any time they are accidentally hired to common labor, they have not strength to perform it; and thus the country and themselves are happily delivered from the evils to come.

I have too long digressed, and therefore shall return to my subject. 20 I think the advantages by the proposal which I have made are obvious and many, as well as of the highest importance.

For first, as I have already observed, it would greatly lessen the 21 number of Papists, with whom we are yearly overrun, being the principal breeders of the nation as well as our most dangerous enemies; and who stay at home on purpose to deliver the kingdom to the Pretender, hoping to take their advantage by the absence of so many good Protestants, who have chosen rather to leave their country than to stay at home and pay tithes against their conscience to an Episcopal curate.

Secondly, the poorer tenants will have something valuable of their 22 own, which by law may be made liable to distress,[10] and help to pay their landlord's rent, their corn and cattle being already seized and money a thing unknown.

Thirdly, whereas the maintenance of an hundred thousand children, 23 from two years old and upwards, cannot be computed at less than ten shillings a piece per annum, the nation's stock will be thereby increased fifty thousand pounds per annum, besides the profit of a new dish introduced to the tables of all gentlemen of fortune in the kingdom who have any refinement in taste. And the money will circulate among ourselves, the goods being entirely of our own growth and manufacture.

Fourthly, the constant breeders, besides the gain of eight shillings 24 sterling per annum by the sale of their children, will be rid of the charge of maintaining them after the first year.

Fifthly, this food would likewise bring great custom to taverns, 25 where the vintners will certainly be so prudent as to procure the best receipts for dressing it to perfection, and consequently have their houses frequented by all the fine gentlemen, who justly value themselves upon their knowledge in good eating; and a skillful cook, who understands how to oblige his guests, will contrive to make it as expensive as they please.

[10] Subject to seizure by creditors. —EDS.

Sixthly, this would be a great inducement to marriage, which all   26
wise nations have either encouraged by rewards or enforced by laws and
penalties. It would increase the care and tenderness of mothers toward
their children, when they were sure of a settlement for life to the poor
babes, provided in some sort by the public, to their annual profit instead of expense. We should see an honest emulation among the married women, which of them could bring the fattest child to the market.
Men would become as fond of their wives during the time of their pregnancy as they are now of their mares in foal, their cows in calf, or sows
when they are ready to farrow; nor offer to beat or kick them (as is too
frequent a practice) for fear of a miscarriage.

Many other advantages might be enumerated. For instance, the ad-   27
dition of some thousand carcasses in our exportation of barreled beef, the
propagation of swine's flesh, and improvements in the art of making good
bacon, so much wanted among us by the great destruction of pigs, too frequent at our tables, which are no way comparable in taste or magnifi-
cence to a well-grown, fat, yearling child, which roasted whole will make
a considerable figure at a lord mayor's feast or any other public entertainment. But this and many others I omit, being studious of brevity.

Supposing that one thousand families in this city would be con-   28
stant customers for infants' flesh, besides others who might have it at
merry meetings, particularly weddings and christenings, I compute that
Dublin would take off annually about twenty thousand carcasses, and
the rest of the kingdom (where probably they will be sold somewhat
cheaper) the remaining eighty thousand.

I can think of no one objection that will possibly be raised against   29
this proposal, unless it should be urged that the number of people will
be thereby much lessened in the kingdom. This I freely own, and it was
indeed one principal design in offering it to the world. I desire the
reader will observe, that I calculate my remedy for this one individual
kingdom of Ireland and for no other that ever was, is, or I think ever
can be upon earth. Therefore let no man talk to me of other expedients: of taxing our absentees at five shillings a pound: of using neither
clothes nor household furniture except what is of our own growth and
manufacture: of utterly rejecting the materials and instruments that
promote foreign luxury: of curing the expensiveness of pride, vanity,
idleness, and gaming in our women: of introducing a vein of parsimony,
prudence, and temperance: of learning to love our country, in the want
of which we differ even from Laplanders and the inhabitants of Top-
inamboo:[11] of quitting our animosities and factions, nor acting any
longer like the Jews, who were murdering one another at the very mo-

---

[11] A district of Brazil. —EDS.

ment their city was taken:[12] of being a little cautious not to sell our country and conscience for nothing: of teaching landlords to have at least one degree of mercy toward their tenants: lastly, of putting a spirit of honesty, industry, and skill into our shopkeepers; who, if a resolution could now be taken to buy only our native goods, would immediately unite to cheat and exact upon us in the price, the measure, and the goodness, nor could ever yet be brought to make one fair proposal of just dealing, though often and earnestly invited to it.

Therefore I repeat, let no man talk to me of these and the like expedients, till he hath at least some glimpse of hope that there will ever be some hearty and sincere attempt to put them in practice.   30

But as to myself, having been wearied out for many years with offering vain, idle, visionary thoughts, and at length utterly despairing of success, I fortunately fell upon this proposal, which, as it is wholly new, so it hath something solid and real, of no expense and little trouble, full in our own power, and whereby we can incur no danger in disobliging England. For this kind of commodity will not bear exportation, the flesh being of too tender a consistence to admit a long continuance in salt, although perhaps I could name a country which would be glad to eat up our whole nation without it.   31

After all, I am not so violently bent upon my own opinion as to reject any offer proposed by wise men, which shall be found equally innocent, cheap, easy, and effectual. But before something of that kind shall be advanced in contradiction to my scheme, and offering a better, I desire the author or authors will be pleased maturely to consider two points. First, as things now stand, how they will be able to find food and raiment for an hundred thousand useless mouths and backs. And secondly, there being a round million of creatures in human figure throughout this kingdom, whose sole subsistence put into a common stock would leave them in debt two millions of pounds sterling, adding those who are beggars by profession to the bulk of farmers, cottagers, and laborers, with their wives and children who are beggars in effect; I desire those politicians who dislike my overture, and may perhaps be so bold to attempt an answer, that they will first ask the parents of these mortals whether they would not at this day think it a great happiness to have been sold for food at a year old in this manner I prescribe, and thereby have avoided such a perpetual scene of misfortunes as they have since gone through by the oppression of landlords, the impossibility of paying rent without money or trade, the want of common sustenance, with neither house nor clothes to cover them from the   32

---

[12] During the Roman siege of Jerusalem (A.D. 70), prominent Jews were executed on the charge of being in league with the enemy. — EDS.

inclemencies of the weather, and the most inevitable prospect of entailing the like or greater miseries upon their breed forever.

I profess, in the sincerity of my heart, that I have not the least personal interest in endeavoring to promote this necessary work, having no other motive than the public good of my country, by advancing our trade, providing for infants, relieving the poor, and giving some pleasure to the rich. I have no children by which I can propose to get a single penny; the youngest being nine years old, and my wife past childbearing. 33

QUESTIONS ON MEANING

1. On the surface, what is Swift proposing?
2. Beneath his IRONY, what is Swift's argument?
3. What do you take to be the PURPOSE of Swift's essay?
4. How does the introductory paragraph serve Swift's purpose?
5. Comment on the statement "I can think of no one objection that will possibly be raised against this proposal" (para. 29). What objections can you think of?

QUESTIONS ON WRITING STRATEGY

1. Describe the mask of the personage through whom Swift writes.
2. By what means does the writer attest to his reasonableness?
3. At what point in the essay did it become clear to you that the proposal isn't modest but horrible?
4. **MIXED METHODS.** As an essay of ARGUMENT, does "A Modest Proposal" appeal primarily to reason or to emotion? (See p. 456 for a discussion of the distinction.)
5. **MIXED METHODS.** What does Swift's argument gain by his careful attention to PROCESS ANALYSIS and to CAUSE AND EFFECT?

QUESTIONS ON LANGUAGE

1. How does Swift's choice of words enforce the monstrousness of his proposal? Note especially words from the vocabulary of breeding and butchery.
2. Consult your dictionary for the meanings of any of the following words not yet in your vocabulary: importuning, sustenance (para. 1); prodigious, commonwealth (2); computation, raiment (4); apprehend, rudiments, probationers (6); nutriment (7); fricassee (9); repine (14); flay (15); scrupulous, censure (17); mandarins (18); desponding, encumbrance (19); per annum (23); vintners (25); emulation, foal, farrow (26); expedients, parsimony, animosities (29); disobliging, consistence (31); overture, inclemencies (32).

SUGGESTIONS FOR WRITING

1. **JOURNAL WRITING.** Swift's proposal is aimed at a serious social problem of his day. What problems can you think of today that—like the poverty and starvation Swift describes—seem to require drastic action? You might consider groups of people whom you regard as mistreated or victimized. Look at the newspaper if nothing leaps to mind.

   FROM JOURNAL TO ESSAY. Write an essay in which you propose a solution to one of the problems raised in your journal. Your essay may be either of the following:

   a. A straight argument, giving EVIDENCE, in which you set forth possible solutions to the problem.

   b. An ironic proposal in the manner of Swift. If you do this one, find a device other than cannibalism to eliminate the victims or their problems. You don't want to imitate Swift too closely; he is probably inimitable.

2. In an encyclopedia, look into what has happened in Ireland since Swift wrote. Choose a specific contemporary aspect of Irish-English relations, research it in books and periodicals, and write a report on it.

3. **CRITICAL WRITING.** Choose several examples of irony in "A Modest Proposal" that you find particularly effective. In a brief essay, ANALYZE Swift's use of irony. Do your examples of irony depend on understating, overstating, or saying the opposite of what is meant? How do they improve on literal statements? What is the value of irony in argument?

4. **CONNECTIONS.** Read H. L. Mencken's "The Penalty of Death" (p. 470) alongside "A Modest Proposal," and ANALYZE the use of irony and humor in these two essays. How heavily does each author depend on irony and humor to make his argument? Do these elements strengthen both authors' arguments? What EVIDENCE does each offer that would also work in a more straightforward argument?

5. **CONNECTIONS.** Analyze the ways Swift and Martin Luther King, Jr., in "I Have a Dream" (p. 567), create sympathy for the oppressed groups they are concerned about. Concentrate not only on what they say but on the words they use and their TONE. Then write a process analysis explaining techniques for portraying oppression so as to win the reader's sympathy. Use quotations or PARAPHRASES from Swift's and King's essays as examples. If you can think of other techniques that neither author uses, by all means include and illustrate them as well.

JONATHAN SWIFT ON WRITING

Although surely one of the most inventive writers in English literature, Swift voiced his contempt for writers of his day who bragged of their newness and originality. In *The Battle of the Books*, he compares such a self-professed original to a spider who "spins and spits wholly from himself, and scorns to own any obligation or assistance from without." Swift has the fable-writer Aesop praise that writer who, like a bee gathering nectar, draws from many sources.

> Erect your schemes with as much method and skill as you please; yet if the materials be nothing but dirt, spun out of your own entrails (the guts of modern brains), the edifice will conclude at last in a cobweb.... As for us Ancients, we are content, with the bee, to pretend to nothing of our own beyond our wings and our voice, that is to say, our flights and our language. For the rest, whatever we have got has been by infinite labor and search and ranging through every corner of nature; the difference is, that, instead of dirt and poison, we have rather chosen to fill our hives with honey and wax, thus furnishing mankind with the two noblest of things, which are sweetness and light.

Swift's advice for a writer would seem to be: Don't just invent things out of thin air; read the best writers of the past. Observe and converse. Do legwork.

Interestingly, when in *Gulliver's Travels* Swift portrays his ideal beings, the Houyhnhnms, a race of noble and intelligent horses, he includes no writers at all in their society. "The Houyhnhnms have no letters," Gulliver observes, "and consequently their knowledge is all traditional." Still, "in poetry they must be allowed to excel all other mortals; wherein the justness of their description are indeed inimitable." (Those very traits—striking comparisons and detailed descriptions—make much of Swift's own writing memorable.)

In his great book, in "A Modest Proposal," and in virtually all he wrote, Swift's purpose was forthright and evident. He declared in "Verses on the Death of Dr. Swift,"

> As with a moral view designed
> To cure the vices of mankind:...
> Yet malice never was his aim;
> He lashed the vice but spared the name.
> No individual could resent,
> Where thousands equally were meant.
> His satire points at no defect
> But what all mortals may correct.

FOR DISCUSSION

1. Try applying Swift's parable of the spider and the bee to our own day. How much truth is left in it?
2. Reread thoughtfully the quotation from Swift's poem. According to the poet, what faults or abuses can a satiric writer fall into? How may these be avoided?
3. What do you take to be Swift's main PURPOSE as a writer? In your own words, SUMMARIZE it.

ALICE WALKER

ALICE WALKER is best known for her novel *The Color Purple* (1982), which won both a Pulitzer Prize and an American Book Award and was made into a movie by Steven Spielberg. Born into a sharecropping family in Eatonton, Georgia, in 1944, Walker is the youngest of eight children. She spent two years at Spelman College in Atlanta before transferring to Sarah Lawrence College. Upon graduation in 1965, Walker became active in the civil rights movement, helping to register voters in Georgia by day and pursuing her writing by night. She has won fellowships from the Radcliffe Institute, the Guggenheim Foundation, and the National Endowment for the Arts. In addition to *The Color Purple*, Walker's novels include *The Third Life of Grange Copeland* (1970) and *The Temple of My Familiar* (1989). She has also written several volumes of poetry; two short-story collections; a biography of Langston Hughes; an anthology of the work of Zora Neale Hurston; and the essays in the collections *In Search of Our Mothers' Gardens* (1983) and *Living by the Word* (1988). Walker has taught at numerous colleges and universities, including Wellesley, Yale, Brandeis, and the University of California at Berkeley.

In Search of
Our Mothers' Gardens

"In Search of Our Mothers' Gardens," the title essay in Alice Walker's book of the same name, was originally published in Ms. magazine in 1974. The essay is based on her childhood belief "that there was nothing, literally nothing, [her] mother couldn't do." Walker explores how that belief shaped her own writing and, as you will discover, gives us much more than an autobiography. Notice how she moves beyond her personal experience to state a truth about other African American women.

Walker's essay uses narrative, description, and example to explore causes and effects. These methods develop the following paragraphs:

Narration (Chap. 1): paragraphs 20–23, 29–31, 40–45
Description (Chap. 2): paragraphs 1, 4–5, 8–11, 20–23, 29–31, 34, 40–46, 48
Example (Chap. 3): paragraphs 12, 15–25, 29–32, 34–35, 38–45, 49–50
Cause and effect (Chap. 8): paragraphs 1, 4, 6–12, 15–26, 37–38, 44–45, 48–50

I described her own nature and temperament. Told how they needed a larger life for their expression. . . . I pointed out that in lieu of proper channels, her emotions had overflowed into paths that dissipated them. I talked, beautifully I thought, about an art that would be born, an art that would open the way for women the likes of her. I asked her to hope, and build up an inner life against the coming of that day.... I sang, with a strange quiver in my voice, a promise song.

—"Avey," Jean Toomer, *Cane*[1]
The poet speaking to a prostitute who falls asleep while he's talking.

When the poet Jean Toomer walked through the South in the early   1
twenties, he discovered a curious thing: black women whose spirituality was so intense, so deep, so *unconscious*, they were themselves unaware of the richness they held. They stumbled blindly through their lives: creatures so abused and mutilated in body, so dimmed and confused by pain, that they considered themselves unworthy even of hope. In the selfless abstractions their bodies became to the men who used them, they became more than "sexual objects," more even than mere women: They became "Saints." Instead of being perceived as whole persons, their bodies became shrines: What was thought to be their minds became temples suitable for worship. These crazy Saints stared out at the world, wildly, like lunatics—or quietly, like suicides; and the "God" that was in their gaze was as mute as a great stone.

Who were these Saints? These crazy, loony, pitiful women?   2

Some of them, without a doubt, were our mothers and grandmothers.   3

In the still heat of the post-Reconstruction South, this is how they   4
seemed to Jean Toomer: exquisite butterflies trapped in an evil honey, toiling away their lives in an era, a century, that did not acknowledge them, except as "the *mule* of the world." They dreamed dreams that no one knew—not even themselves, in any coherent fashion—and saw visions no one could understand. They wandered or sat about the countryside crooning lullabies to ghosts, and drawing the mother of Christ in charcoal on courthouse walls.

They forced their minds to desert their bodies and their striving   5
spirits sought to rise, like frail whirlwinds from the hard red clay. And when those frail whirlwinds fell, in scattered particles, upon the ground, no one mourned. Instead, men lit candles to celebrate the emptiness that remained, as people do who enter a beautiful but vacant space to resurrect a God.

Our mothers and grandmothers, some of them: moving to music   6
not yet written. And they waited.

They waited for a day when the unknown thing that was in them   7
would be made known; but guessed, somehow in their darkness, that on

---

[1] Jean Toomer (1894–1967) was an African American poet and novelist. *Cane*, his best-known work, is a novel about the African American experience. —EDS.

the day of their revelation they would be long dead. Therefore to Toomer they walked, and even ran, in slow motion. For they were going nowhere immediate, and the future was not yet within their grasp. And men took our mothers and grandmothers, "but got no pleasure from it." So complex was their passion and their calm.

To Toomer, they lay vacant and fallow as autumn fields, with har-   8 vest time never in sight: and he saw them enter loveless marriages, without joy; and become prostitutes, without resistance; and become mothers of children, without fulfillment.

For these grandmothers and mothers of ours were not Saints, but   9 Artists; driven to a numb and bleeding madness by the springs of creativity in them for which there was no release. They were Creators, who lived lives of spiritual waste, because they were so rich in spirituality—which is the basis of Art—that the strain of enduring their unused and unwanted talent drove them insane. Throwing away this spirituality was their pathetic attempt to lighten the soul to a weight their work-worn, sexually abused bodies could bear.

What did it mean for a black woman to be an artist in our grand-   10 mothers' time? In our great-grandmothers' day? It is a question with an answer cruel enough to stop the blood.

Did you have a genius of a great-great-grandmother who died under   11 some ignorant and depraved white overseer's lash? Or was she required to bake biscuits for a lazy backwater tramp, when she cried out in her soul to paint watercolors of sunsets, or the rain falling on the green and peaceful pasturelands? Or was her body broken and forced to bear children (who were more often than not sold away from her)—eight, ten, fifteen, twenty children—when her one joy was the thought of modeling heroic figures of rebellion, in stone or clay?

How was the creativity of the black woman kept alive, year after   12 year and century after century, when for most of the years black people have been in America, it was a punishable crime for a black person to read or write? And the freedom to paint, to sculpt, to expand the mind with action did not exist. Consider, if you can bear to imagine it, what might have been the result if singing, too, had been forbidden by law. Listen to the voices of Bessie Smith, Billie Holiday, Nina Simone, Roberta Flack, and Aretha Franklin, among others, and imagine those voices muzzled for life. Then you may begin to comprehend the lives of our "crazy," "Sainted" mothers and grandmothers. The agony of the lives of women who might have been Poets, Novelists, Essayists, and Short-Story Writers (over a period of centuries), who died with their real gifts stifled within them.

And, if this were the end of the story, we would have cause to cry   13 out in my paraphrase of Okot p´Bitek's great poem:

O, my clanswomen
Let us all cry together!
Come,
Let us mourn the death of our mother,
The death of a Queen
The ash that was produced
By a great fire!
O, this homestead is utterly dead
Close the gates
With *lacari* thorns,
For our mother
The creator of the Stool is lost!
And all the young men
Have perished in the wilderness!

But this is not the end of the story, for all the young women—our   14
mothers and grandmothers, *ourselves*—have not perished in the wilderness. And if we ask ourselves why, and search for and find the answer,
we will know beyond all efforts to erase it from our minds, just exactly
who, and of what, we black American women are.

One example, perhaps the most pathetic, most misunderstood one,   15
can provide a backdrop for our mothers' work: Phillis Wheatley, a slave
in the 1700s.

Virginia Woolf,[2] in her book *A Room of One's Own*, wrote that in   16
order for a woman to write fiction she must have two things, certainly:
a room of her own (with key and lock) and enough money to support
herself.

What then are we to make of Phillis Wheatley, a slave, who owned   17
not even herself? This sickly, frail black girl who required a servant of
her own at times—her health was so precarious—and who, had she
been white, would have been easily considered the intellectual superior
of all the women and most of the men in the society of her day.

Virginia Woolf wrote further, speaking of course not of our Phillis,   18
that "any woman born with a great gift in the sixteenth century [insert
"eighteenth century," insert "black woman," insert "born or made a
slave"] would certainly have gone crazed, shot herself, or ended her
days in some lonely cottage outside the village, half witch, half wizard
[insert "Saint"], feared and mocked at. For it needs little skill and psychology to be sure that a highly gifted girl who had tried to use her gift
of poetry would have been so thwarted and hindered by contrary instincts [add "chains, guns, the lash, the ownership of one's body by
someone else, submission to an alien religion"], that she must have lost
her health and sanity to a certainty."

[2] See page 663.—EDS.

The key words, as they relate to Phillis, are "contrary instincts." For   19
when we read the poetry of Phillis Wheatley—as when we read the
novels of Nella Larsen or the oddly false-sounding autobiography of that
freest of all black women writers, Zora Hurston—evidence of "contrary instincts" is everywhere. Her loyalties were completely divided, as
was, without question, her mind.

But how could this be otherwise? Captured at seven, a slave of   20
wealthy, doting whites who instilled in her the "savagery" of the Africa
they "rescued" her from . . . one wonders if she was even able to remember her homeland as she had known it, or as it really was.

Yet, because she did try to use her gift for poetry in a world that   21
made her a slave, she was "so thwarted and hindered by . . . contrary instincts, that she . . . lost her health. . . ." In the last years of her brief life,
burdened not only with the need to express her gift but also with a penniless, friendless "freedom" and several small children for whom she
was forced to do strenuous work to feed, she lost her health, certainly.
Suffering from malnutrition and neglect and who knows what mental
agonies, Phillis Wheatley died.

So torn by "contrary instincts" was black, kidnapped, enslaved   22
Phillis that her description of "the Goddess"—as she poetically called
the Liberty she did not have—is ironically, cruelly humorous. And, in
fact, has held Phillis up to ridicule for more than a century. It is usually
read prior to hanging Phillis's memory as that of a fool. She wrote:

> The Goddess comes, she moves divinely fair,
> Olive and laurel binds her *golden* hair.
> Wherever shines this native of the skies,
> Unnumber'd charms and recent graces rise. [My italics]

It is obvious that Phillis, the slave, combed the "Goddess's" hair   23
every morning; prior, perhaps, to bringing in the milk, or fixing her
mistress's lunch. She took her imagery from the one thing she saw ele-
vated above all others.

With the benefit of hindsight we ask, "How could she?"   24

But at last, Phillis, we understand. No more snickering when your   25
stiff, struggling, ambivalent lines are forced on us. We know now that
you were not an idiot or a traitor; only a sickly little black girl, snatched
from your home and country and made a slave; a woman who still
struggled to sing the song that was your gift, although in a land of barbarians who praised you for your bewildered tongue. It is not so much
what you sang, as that you kept alive, in so many of our ancestors, *the
notion of song.*

Black women are called, in the folklore that so aptly identified   26
one's status in society, "the *mule* of the world," because we have been

handed the burdens that everyone else—*everyone* else—refused to carry. We have also been called "Matriarchs," "Superwomen," and "Mean and Evil Bitches." Not to mention "Castraters" and "Sapphire's Mama." When we have pleaded for understanding, our character has been distorted; when we have asked for simple caring, we have been handed empty inspirational appellations, then stuck in the farthest corner. When we have asked for love, we have been given children. In short, even our plainer gifts, our labors of fidelity and love, have been knocked down our throats. To be an artist and a black woman, even today, lowers our status in many respects, rather than raises it: And yet, artists we will be.

Therefore we must fearlessly pull out of ourselves and look at 27 and identify with our lives the living creativity some of our great-grandmothers were not allowed to know. I stress *some* of them because it is well known that the majority of our great-grandmothers knew, even without "knowing" it, the reality of their spirituality, even if they didn't recognize it beyond what happened in the singing at church— and they never had any intention of giving it up.

How they did it—those millions of black women who were not 28 Phillis Wheatley, or Lucy Terry or Frances Harper or Zora Hurston or Nella Larsen or Bessie Smith; or Elizabeth Catlett, or Katherine Dunham, either—brings me to the title of this essay, "In Search of Our Mothers' Gardens," which is a personal account that is yet shared, in its theme and its meaning, by all of us. I found, while thinking about the far-reaching world of the creative black woman, that often the truest answer to a question that really matters can be found very close.

In the late 1920s my mother ran away from home to marry my fa- 29 ther. Marriage, if not running away, was expected of seventeen-year-old girls. By the time she was twenty, she had two children and was pregnant with a third. Five children later, I was born. And this is how I came to know my mother: She seemed a large, soft, loving-eyed woman who was rarely impatient in our home. Her quick, violent temper was on view only a few times a year, when she battled with the white landlord who had the misfortune to suggest to her that her children did not need to go to school.

She made all the clothes we wore, even my brothers' overalls. She 30 made all the towels and sheets we used. She spent the summers canning vegetables and fruits. She spent the winter evenings making quilts enough to cover our beds.

During the "working" day, she labored beside—not behind—my fa- 31 ther in the fields. Her day began before sunup, and did not end until late at night. There was never a moment for her to sit down, undisturbed, to unravel her own private thoughts; never a time free from interruption—by work or the noisy inquiries of her many children. And yet, it is to my mother—and all our mothers who were not famous—that I went in search of the secret of what has fed that muzzled and often mutilated, but vibrant, creative spirit that the black woman has inherited, and that pops out in wild and unlikely places to this day.

But when, you will ask, did my overworked mother have time to   32
know or care about feeding the creative spirit?

The answer is so simple that many of us have spent years discover-   33
ing it. We have constantly looked high, when we should have looked high—and low.

For example: In the Smithsonian Institution in Washington, D.C.,   34
there hangs a quilt unlike any other in the world. In fanciful, inspired, and yet simple and identifiable figures, it portrays the story of the Crucifixion. It is considered rare, beyond price. Though it follows no known pattern of quilt-making, and though it is made of bits and pieces of worthless rags, it is obviously the work of a person of powerful imagination and deep spiritual feeling. Below this quilt I saw a note that says it was made by "an anonymous Black woman in Alabama, a hundred years ago."

If we could locate this "anonymous" black woman from Alabama,   35
she would turn out to be one of our grandmothers—an artist who left her mark in the only materials she could afford, and in the only medium her position in society allowed her to use.

As Virginia Woolf wrote further, in *A Room of One's Own*:   36

> Yet genius of a sort must have existed among women as it must have existed among the working class. [Change this to "slaves" and "the wives and daughters of sharecroppers."] Now and again an Emily Brontë or a Robert Burns [change this to "a Zora Hurston or a Richard Wright"] blazes out and proves its presence. But certainly it never got itself on paper. When, however, one reads of a witch being ducked, of a woman possessed by devils [or "Sainthood"], of a wise woman selling herbs [our root workers], or even a very remarkable man who had a mother, then I think we are on the track of a lost novelist, a suppressed poet, or some mute and inglorious Jane Austen.... Indeed, I would venture to guess that Anon, who wrote so many poems without signing them, was often a woman....

And so our mothers and grandmothers have, more often than not   37
anonymously, handed on the creative spark, the seed of the flower they themselves never hoped to see: or like a sealed letter they could not plainly read.

And so it is, certainly, with my own mother. Unlike "Ma" Rainey's   38
songs, which retained their creator's name even while blasting forth from Bessie Smith's mouth, no song or poem will bear my mother's

name. Yet so many of the stories that I write, that we all write, are my mother's stories. Only recently did I fully realize this: that through years of listening to my mother's stories of her life, I have absorbed not only the stories themselves, but something of the manner in which she spoke, something of the urgency that involves the knowledge that her stories—like her life—must be recorded. It is probably for this reason that so much of what I have written is about characters whose counterparts in real life are so much older than I am.

But the telling of these stories, which came from my mother's lips   39
as naturally as breathing, was not the only way my mother showed herself as an artist. For stories, too, were subject to being distracted, to dying without conclusion. Dinners must be started, and cotton must be gathered before the big rains. The artist that was and is my mother showed itself to me only after many years. This is what I finally noticed:

Like Mem, a character in *The Third Life of Grange Copeland*, my   40
mother adorned with flowers whatever shabby house we were forced to live in. And not just your typical straggly country stand of zinnias, either. She planted ambitious gardens—and still does—with over fifty different varieties of plants that bloom profusely from early March until late November. Before she left home for the fields, she watered her flowers, chopped up the grass, and laid out new beds. When she returned from the fields, she might divide clumps of bulbs, dig a cold pit, uproot and replant roses, or prune branches from her taller bushes or trees—until night came and it was too dark to see.

Whatever she planted grew as if by magic, and her fame as a grower   41
of flowers spread over three counties. Because of her creativity with her flowers, even my memories of poverty are seen through a screen of blooms—sunflowers, petunias, roses, dahlias, forsythia, spirea, delphiniums, verbena...and on and on.

And I remember people coming to my mother's yard to be given   42
cuttings from her flowers; I hear again the praise showered on her because whatever rocky soil She landed on, she turned into a garden. A garden so brilliant with colors, so original in its design, so magnificent with life and creativity, that to this day people drive by our house in Georgia—perfect strangers and imperfect strangers—and ask to stand or walk among my mother's art.

I notice that it is only when my mother is working in her flowers   43
that she is radiant, almost to the point of being invisible—except as Creator: hand and eye. She is involved in work her soul must have. Ordering the universe in the image of her personal conception of Beauty.

Her face, as she prepares the Art that is her gift, is a legacy of respect   44
she leaves to me, for all that illuminates and cherishes life. She has handed down respect for the possibilities—and the will to grasp them.

For her, so hindered and intruded upon in so many ways, being an   45
artist has still been a daily part of her life. This ability to hold on, even
in very simple ways, is work black women have done for a very long
time.

This poem is not enough, but it is something, for the woman who   46
literally covered the holes in our walls with sunflowers:

> They were women then
> My mama's generation
> Husky of voice — Stout of
> Step
> With fists as well as
> Hands
> How they battered down
> Doors
> And ironed
> Starched white
> Shirts
> How they led
> Armies
> Headragged Generals
> Across mined
> Fields
> Booby-trapped
> Kitchens
> To discover books
> Desks
> A place for us
> How they knew what we
> *Must* know
> Without knowing a page
> Of it
> Themselves

Guided by my heritage of a love of beauty and a respect for   47
strength — in search of my mother's garden, I found my own.

And perhaps in Africa over two hundred years ago, there was just   48
such a mother; perhaps she painted vivid and daring decorations in oranges and yellows and greens on the walls of her hut; perhaps she sang —
in a voice like Roberta Flack's — *sweetly* over the compounds of her village; perhaps she wove the most stunning mats or told the most ingenious
stories of all the village storytellers. Perhaps she was herself a poet —
though only her daughter's name is signed to the poems that we know.

Perhaps Phillis Wheatley's mother was also an artist.   49

Perhaps in more than Phillis Wheatley's biological life is her   50
mother's signature made clear.

QUESTIONS ON MEANING

1. What does the essay's title mean? Is the phrase "our mothers' gardens" to be taken literally? What other meanings might it suggest?
2. Why does Walker label early twentieth-century black women "Saints" (para. 1)? How does she define *saint*? What is the connection between saints and artists?
3. What is the point of the story about Phillis Wheatley (paras. 17–25)? What does Walker mean by applying Virginia Woolf's phrase "contrary instincts" to Wheatley? If Wheatley's loyalties and mind were divided, what is it that divided them? Why does Walker believe Wheatley is not to blame for depicting Liberty as white in her poem? Why, according to Walker, does Wheatley deserve praise?
4. When *did* Alice Walker's mother "have time to know or care about feeding the creative spirit" (para. 32)? Walker claims the answer is "simple." What is it?

QUESTIONS ON WRITING STRATEGY

1. Review the organization of this essay. How does the author's focus shift in paragraphs 1–14, 15–25, 26–28, and 29–47? How effective are these shifts, do you think?
2. How do the quotations from Jean Toomer and Virginia Woolf strengthen this essay?
3. The author makes bracketed additions to Woolf's statements in paragraphs 18 and 36. Are these additions fair? That is, do they follow Woolf's meaning, or do they change the meaning?
4. **MIXED METHODS.** To illustrate the main ideas of her essay, Walker uses two extended EXAMPLES — Phillis Wheatley and Walker's mother. What do these women have in common, and how do they differ? What kind of knowledge does Walker have about her mother? Compared to that knowledge, how would you characterize Walker's knowledge of Phillis Wheatley? How are these two examples different from the examples given (in the form of a list of singers) in paragraph 12?
5. **MIXED METHODS.** Walker's essay draws on CAUSE AND EFFECT to explain the circumstances of African American women in the 1920s. SUMMARIZE the causes and effects given in paragraphs 1–11.

QUESTIONS ON LANGUAGE

1. Look at the simile in paragraph 5: "They forced their minds to desert their bodies and their striving spirits sought to rise, like frail whirlwinds from the hard red clay." Find other FIGURES OF SPEECH in the essay, especially those involving the land and nature. How do these figures connect with each other and with the essay's title?

2. Where does the author use CONCRETE language? Where is the language more ABSTRACT? What relationship do you sense between the kind of language being used and the kind of example being presented?

3. Give definitions of the following words: lieu, dissipated (opening quotation); abstractions (para. 1); fallow (8); ambivalent (25); matriarchs, appellations (26); inglorious (quotation in 36); profusely (40); legacy (44); ingenious (48).

SUGGESTIONS FOR WRITING

1. **JOURNAL WRITING.** Consider your routine and daily chores (such as brushing your teeth, washing the dishes, doing the laundry, mowing the lawn) or the uninteresting, even oppressive, jobs you may have held (working the counter in a fast-food restaurant, typing or filing, handing out leaflets on a crowded street corner). In your journal, make a list of all you can think of in five minutes.

   FROM JOURNAL TO ESSAY. Choose one of the chores or jobs you listed in your journal. How could you make this activity an art rather than a boring or unpleasant task? Imagining yourself as a skilled artist, write an essay describing yourself at work. If you prefer, you may cast this essay in the third PERSON, imagining someone else at work.

2. In paragraph 14, Walker writes that "all the young women...have not perished in the wilderness. And if we ask ourselves why, and search for and find the answer, we will know...just exactly who, and of what, we black American women are." Using examples, write an essay explaining Walker's view of who and what African American women are. Keep in mind the author's concepts of saints, spirituality, creativity, and art.

3. **CRITICAL WRITING.** In her examination of the spiritual and artistic lives of African American women, Walker draws on her own experience and imagination, passages by Jean Toomer and Virginia Woolf, and examples of singers, writers, and her mother. Is this evidence sufficient to support Walker's THESIS that for the African American woman, "hindered and intruded upon in so many ways, being an artist has still been a daily part of life. This ability to hold on, even in very simple ways, is work black women have done for a very long time" (para. 45)? In an essay, ANALYZE and EVALUATE the evidence: Which do you find most convincing? Which, if any, is unconvincing? Why?

4. **CONNECTIONS.** Look at Walker's essay alongside John McPhee's "Silk Parachute" (p. 155). Both authors DESCRIBE their mothers through examples. In an essay, COMPARE AND CONTRAST the feelings about their mothers that emerge from the examples. Use quotations and PARAPHRASES from both essays to support your ideas.

5. **CONNECTIONS.** Both Alice Walker and Maxine Hong Kingston, in "No Name Woman" (p. 573), explore the lives of their female relatives by mingling imagined events with what they have heard or read. In what ways, according to these essays, were the circumstances of a 1920s African American woman and a 1920s Chinese woman similar? In what ways were they different? Write an essay of your own comparing and contrasting the two authors' visions.

ALICE WALKER ON WRITING

In an interview with David Bradley in the *New York Times Magazine*, Alice Walker described her method of writing as waiting for friendly spirits to visit her. Usually, she doesn't outline or devote much time to preliminary organization. She plunges in with a passion, and she sees a definite purpose in most of her work: to correct injustices. "I was brought up to try to see what was wrong, and right it. Since I am a writer, writing is how I right it. I was brought up to look at things that are out of joint, out of balance, and to try to bring them into balance. And as a writer that's what I do."

An articulate feminist, Walker has written in support of greater rights for women, including African American women. If most of her works are short—stories, essays, and poems—there is a reason: She sees thick, long-winded volumes as alien to a female sensibility. "The books women write can be more like us—much thinner, much leaner, much cleaner."

Much of Alice Walker's writing has emerged from painful experience: She has written of her impoverished early days on a Georgia sharecropper's farm, a childhood accident with a BB gun that cost her the sight of one eye, a traumatic abortion, years as a civil rights worker in Mississippi. "I think," she says, "writing really helps you heal yourself. I think if you write long enough, you will be a healthy person. That is, if you write what you need to write, as opposed to what will make money or what will make fame."

FOR DISCUSSION

1. What does the author mean when she speaks of the importance of writing "what you need to write"?
2. What writers can you think of whose work has helped to right the world's wrongs?
3. Can you cite any exceptions to Walker's generalization that long books are alien to women's sensibilities?

E. B. WHITE

ELWYN BROOKS WHITE (1899–1985) for half a century was a regular
contributor to *The New Yorker,* and his essays, editorials, anonymous
features for "The Talk of the Town," and fillers helped build the magazine a reputation for wit and good writing. If as a child you read
Charlotte's Web (1952), you have met E. B. White before. The book
reflects some of his own life on a farm in North Brooklin, Maine. His
Letters were collected in 1976, his *Essays* in 1977, and his *Poems and
Sketches* in 1981. On July 4, 1963, President Kennedy named White
in the first group of Americans to receive the Presidential Medal of
Freedom, with a citation that called him "an essayist whose concise
comment...has revealed to yet another age the vigor of the English
sentence."

Once More to the Lake

"Once More to the Lake" first appeared in *Harper's* magazine in 1941.
Perhaps if a duller writer had written the essay, or an essay with the
same title, we wouldn't much care about it, for at first its subject
seems as personal and ordinary as a letter home. White's loving and
exact portrayal, however, brings this lakeside camp to life for us. In
the end, the writer arrives at an awareness that shocks him—shocks
us, too, with a familiar sensory detail.

"Once More to the Lake" is a stunning mixture of description
and narration, but it is also more. To make his observations and emotions clear and immediate, White relies extensively on several other
methods of development as well.

Narration (Chap. 1): throughout
Description (Chap. 2): throughout
Example (Chap. 3): paragraphs 2, 7–8, 11, 12
Comparison and contrast (Chap. 4): 4–7, 9–10, 11–12
Process analysis (Chap. 5): paragraphs 9, 10, 12

August 1941

One summer, along about 1904, my father rented a camp on a lake   1
in Maine and took us all there for the month of August. We all got
ringworm from some kittens and had to rub Pond's Extract on our arms
and legs night and morning, and my father rolled over in a canoe with
all his clothes on; but outside of that the vacation was a success and
from then on none of us ever thought there was any place in the world
like that lake in Maine. We returned summer after summer—always
on August 1 for one month. I have since become a salt-water man, but
sometimes in summer there are days when the restlessness of the tides

and the fearful cold of the sea water and the incessant wind that blows across the afternoon and into the evening make me wish for the placidity of a lake in the woods. A few weeks ago this feeling got so strong I bought myself a couple of bass hooks and a spinner and returned to the lake where we used to go, for a week's fishing and to revisit old haunts.

I took along my son, who had never had any fresh water up his nose and who had seen lily pads only from train windows. On the journey over to the lake I began to wonder what it would be like. I wondered how time would have marred this unique, this holy spot—the coves and streams, the hills that the sun set behind, the camps and the paths behind the camps. I was sure that the tarred road would have found it out, and I wondered in what other ways it would be desolated. It is strange how much you can remember about places like that once you allow your mind to return into the grooves that lead back. You remember one thing, and that suddenly reminds you of another thing. I guess I remembered clearest of all the early mornings, when the lake was cool and motionless, remembered how the bedroom smelled of the lumber it was made of and of the wet woods whose scent entered through the screen. The partitions in the camp were thin and did not extend clear to the top of the rooms, and as I was always the first up I would dress softly so as not to wake the others, and sneak out into the sweet outdoors and start out in the canoe, keeping close along the shore in the long shadows of the pines. I remembered being very careful never to rub my paddle against the gunwale for fear of disturbing the stillness of the cathedral.

The lake had never been what you would call a wild lake. There were cottages sprinkled around the shores, and it was in farming country although the shores of the lake were quite heavily wooded. Some of the cottages were owned by nearby farmers, and you would live at the shore and eat your meals at the farmhouse. That's what our family did. But although it wasn't wild, it was a fairly large and undisturbed lake and there were places in it that, to a child at least, seemed infinitely remote and primeval.

I was right about the tar: It led to within half a mile of the shore. But when I got back there, with my boy, and we settled into a camp near a farmhouse and into the kind of summertime I had known, I could tell that it was going to be pretty much the same as it had been before—I knew it, lying in bed the first morning smelling the bedroom and hearing the boy sneak quietly out and go off along the shore in a boat. I began to sustain the illusion that he was I, and therefore, by simple transposition, that I was my father. This sensation persisted, kept cropping up all the time we were there. It was not an entirely new feeling, but in this setting it grew much stronger. I seemed to be living a dual existence. I would be in the middle of some simple act, I would be

picking up a bait box or laying down a table fork, or I would be saying
something and suddenly it would be not I but my father who was saying the words or making the gesture. It gave me a creepy sensation.

We went fishing the first morning. I felt the same damp moss cov-   5
ering the worms in the bait can, and saw the dragonfly alight on the tip
of my rod as it hovered a few inches from the surface of the water. It was
the arrival of this fly that convinced me beyond any doubt that everything was as it always had been, that the years were a mirage and that
there had been no years. The small waves were the same, chucking the
rowboat under the chin as we fished at anchor, and the boat was the
same boat, the same color green and the ribs broken in the same places,
and under the floorboards the same fresh water leavings and debris—
the dead hellgrammite, the wisps of moss, the rusty discarded fishhook,
the dried blood from yesterday's catch. We stared silently at the tips of
our rods, at the dragonflies that came and went. I lowered the tip of
mine into the water, tentatively, pensively dislodging the fly, which
darted two feet away, poised, darted two feet back, and came to rest
again a little farther up the rod. There had been no years between the
ducking of this dragonfly and the other one—the one that was part of
memory. I looked at the boy, who was silently watching his fly, and it
was my hands that held his rod, my eyes watching. I felt dizzy and didn't
know which rod I was at the end of.

We caught two bass, hauling them in briskly as though they were   6
mackerel, pulling them over the side of the boat in a businesslike manner without any landing net, and stunning them with a blow on the
back of the head. When we got back for a swim before lunch, the lake
was exactly where we had left it, the same number of inches from the
dock, and there was only the merest suggestion of a breeze. This seemed
an utterly enchanted sea, this lake you could leave to its own devices
for a few hours and come back to, and find that it had not stirred, this
constant and trustworthy body of water. In the shallows, the dark,
water-soaked sticks and twigs, smooth and old, were undulating in clusters on the bottom against the clean ribbed sand, and the track of the
mussel was plain. A school of minnows swam by, each minnow with its
small individual shadow, doubling the attendance, so clear and sharp in
the sunlight. Some of the other campers were in swimming, along the
shore, one of them with a cake of soap, and the water felt thin and clear
and unsubstantial. Over the years there had been this person with the
cake of soap, this cultist, and here he was. There had been no years.

Up to the farmhouse to dinner through the teeming dusty field, the   7
road under our sneakers was only a two-track road. The middle track
was missing, the one with the marks of the hooves and the splotches of
dried, flaky manure. There had always been three tracks to choose from

in choosing which track to walk in; now the choice was narrowed down to two. For a moment I missed terribly the middle alternative. But the way led past the tennis court, and something about the way it lay there in the sun reassured me; the tape had loosened along the backline, the alleys were green with plantains and other weeds, and the net (installed in June and removed in September) sagged in the dry noon, and the whole place steamed with midday heat and hunger and emptiness. There was a choice of pie for dessert, and one was blueberry and one was apple, and the waitresses were the same country girls, there having been no passage of time, only the illusion of it as in a dropped curtain—the waitresses were still fifteen; their hair had been washed, that was the only difference—they had been to the movies and seen the pretty girls with the clean hair.

Summertime, oh, summertime, pattern of life indelible, the fade-proof lake, the woods unshatterable, the pasture with the sweetfern and the juniper forever and ever, summer without end; this was the background, and the life along the shore was the design, the cottages with their innocent and tranquil design, their tiny docks with the flagpole and the American flag floating against the white clouds in the blue sky, the little paths over the roots of the trees leading from camp to camp and the paths leading back to the outhouses and the can of lime for sprinkling, and at the souvenir counters at the store the miniature birchbark canoes and the postcards that showed things looking a little better than they looked. This was the American family at play, escaping the city heat, wondering whether the newcomers in the camp at the head of the cove were "common" or "nice," wondering whether it was true that the people who drove up for Sunday dinner at the farmhouse were turned away because there wasn't enough chicken.

It seemed to me, as I kept remembering all this, that those times and those summers had been infinitely precious and worth saving. There had been jollity and peace and goodness. The arriving (at the beginning of August) had been so big a business in itself, at the railway station the farm wagon drawn up, the first smell of the pine-laden air, the first glimpse of the smiling farmer, and the great importance of the trunks and your father's enormous authority in such matters, and the feel of the wagon under you for the long ten-mile haul, and at the top of the last long hill catching the first view of the lake after eleven months of not seeing this cherished body of water. The shouts and cries of the other campers when they saw you, and the trunks to be unpacked, to give up their rich burden. (Arriving was less exciting nowadays, when you sneaked up in your car and parked it under a tree near the camp and took out the bags and in five minutes it was all over, no fuss, no loud wonderful fuss about trunks.)

Peace and goodness and jollity. The only thing that was wrong   10
now, really, was the sound of the place, an unfamiliar nervous sound of
the outboard motors. This was the note that jarred, the one thing that
would sometimes break the illusion and set the years moving. In those
other summertimes all motors were inboard; and when they were at a
little distance, the noise they made was a sedative, an ingredient of
summer sleep. They were one-cylinder and two-cylinder engines, and
some were make-and-break and some were jump-spark, but they all
made a sleepy sound across the lake. The one-lungers throbbed and
fluttered, and the twin-cylinder ones purred and purred, and that was a
quiet sound, too. But now the campers all had outboards. In the daytime, in the hot mornings, these motors made a petulant irritable
sound; at night in the still evening when the afterglow lit the water,
they whined about one's ears like mosquitoes. My boy loved our rented
outboard, and his great desire was to achieve single-handed mastery
over it, and authority, and he soon learned the trick of choking it a little (but not too much), and the adjustment of the needle valve.
Watching him I would remember the things you could do with the old
one-cylinder engine with the heavy flywheel, how you could have it
eating out of your hand if you got really close to it spiritually. Motor-
boats in those days didn't have clutches, and you would make a landing
by shutting off the motor at the proper time and coasting in with a dead
rudder. But there was a way of reversing them, if you learned the trick,
by cutting the switch and putting it on again exactly on the final dying
revolution of the flywheel, so that it would kick back against compres-
sion and begin reversing. Approaching a dock in a strong following
breeze, it was difficult to slow up sufficiently by the ordinary coasting
method, and if a boy felt he had complete mastery over his motor, he
was tempted to keep it running beyond its time and then reverse it a
few feet from the dock. It took a cool nerve, because if you threw the
switch a twentieth of a second too soon you would catch the flywheel
when it still had speed enough to go up past center, and the boat would
leap ahead, charging bull-fashion at the dock.

    We had a good week at the camp. The bass were biting well and the   11
sun shone endlessly, day after day. We would be tired at night and lie
down in the accumulated heat of the little bedrooms after the long hot
day and the breeze would stir almost imperceptibly outside and the
smell of the swamp drift in through the rusty screens. Sleep would come
easily and in the morning the red squirrel would be on the roof, tapping
out his gay routine. I kept remembering everything, lying in bed in the
mornings—the small steamboat that had a long rounded stern like the
lip of a Ubangi, and how quietly she ran on the moonlight sails, when
the older boys played their mandolins and the girls sang and we ate

doughnuts dipped in sugar, and how sweet the music was on the water in the shining night, and what it had felt like to think about girls then. After breakfast we would go up to the store and the things were in the same place—the minnows in a bottle, the plugs and spinners disarranged and pawed over by the youngsters from the boys' camp, the Fig Newtons and the Beeman's gum. Outside, the road was tarred and cars stood in front of the store. Inside, all was just as it had always been, except there was more Coca-Cola and not so much Moxie and root beer and birch beer and sarsaparilla. We would walk out with a bottle of pop apiece and sometimes the pop would backfire up our noses and hurt. We explored the streams, quietly, where the turtles slid off the sunny logs and dug their way into the soft bottom; and we lay on the town wharf and fed worms to the tame bass. Everywhere we went I had trouble making out which was I, the one walking at my side, the one walking in my pants.

One afternoon while we were at the lake a thunderstorm came up.   12
It was like the revival of an old melodrama that I had seen long ago with childish awe. The second-act climax of the drama of the electrical disturbance over a lake in America had not changed in any important respect. This was the big scene, still the big scene. The whole thing was so familiar, the first feeling of oppression and heat and a general air around camp of not wanting to go very far away. In midafternoon (it was all the same) a curious darkening of the sky, and a lull in everything that had made life tick; and then the way the boats suddenly swung the other way at their moorings with the coming of a breeze out of the new quarter, and the premonitory rumble. Then the kettle drum, then the snare, then the bass drum and cymbals, then crackling light against the dark, and the gods grinning and licking their chops in the hills. Afterward the calm, the rain steadily rustling in the calm lake, the return of light and hope and spirits, and the campers running out in joy and relief to go swimming in the rain, their bright cries perpetuating the deathless joke about how they were getting simply drenched, and the children screaming with delight at the new sensation of bathing in the rain, and the joke about getting drenched linking the generations in a strong indestructible chain. And the comedian who waded in carrying an umbrella.

When the others went swimming my son said he was going in, too.   13
He pulled his dripping trunks from the line where they had hung all through the shower and wrung them out. Languidly, and with no thought of going in, I watched him, his hard little body, skinny and bare, saw him wince slightly as he pulled up around his vitals the small, soggy, icy garment. As he buckled the swollen belt, suddenly my groin felt the chill of death.

QUESTIONS ON MEANING

1. How do you account for the distortions that creep into the author's sense of time?
2. What does the discussion of inboard and outboard motors (para. 10) have to do with the author's divided sense of time?
3. To what degree does White make us aware of his son's impression of this trip to the lake?
4. What do you take to be White's main PURPOSE in the essay? At what point do you become aware of it?

QUESTIONS ON WRITING STRATEGY

1. In paragraph 4 the author first introduces his confused feeling that he has gone back in time to his own childhood, an idea that he repeats and expands throughout his account. What is the function of these repetitions?
2. Try to describe the impact of the essay's final paragraph. By what means is it achieved?
3. To what extent is this essay written to appeal to any but middle-aged readers? Is it comprehensible to anyone whose vacations were never spent at a Maine summer cottage?
4. What is the TONE of White's essay?
5. **MIXED METHODS.** White's description depends on many IMAGES that are not FIGURES OF SPEECH but literal translations of sensory impressions. Locate four such images.
6. **MIXED METHODS.** Within White's description and NARRATION of his visit to the lake, what purpose is served by the COMPARISON AND CONTRAST between the lake now and when he was a boy?

QUESTIONS ON LANGUAGE

1. Be sure you know the meanings of the following words: incessant, placidity (para. 1); gunwale (2); primeval (3); transposition (4); hellgrammite (5); undulating, cultist (6); indelible, tranquil (8); petulant (10); imperceptibly (11); premonitory (12); languidly (13).
2. Comment on White's DICTION in his reference to the lake as "this unique, this holy spot" (para. 2).
3. Explain what White is describing in the sentence that begins, "Then the kettle drum…" (para. 12). Where else does the author use figures of speech?

SUGGESTIONS FOR WRITING

1. **JOURNAL WRITING.** What place or places were most important to you as a child? What was important about them?

FROM JOURNAL TO ESSAY. Choose one of the places suggested by your journal entry, and write an essay describing the place now, revisiting it as an adult. (If you haven't visited the place since childhood, you can imagine what seeing it now would be like.) Your description should draw on your childhood memories, making them as vivid as possible for the reader, but you should also consider how your POINT OF VIEW toward the place differs now.

2. In a descriptive paragraph about a real or imagined place, try to appeal to each of your reader's five senses.

3. **CRITICAL WRITING.** While on the vacation he describes, White wrote to his wife, Katharine, "This place is as American as a drink of Coca Cola. The white collar family having its annual liberty." Obviously, not everyone has a chance at the lakeside summers White enjoyed. To what extent, if at all, does White's privileged point of view deprive his essay of universal meaning and significance? Write an essay answering this question. Back up your ideas with EVIDENCE from White's essay.

4. **CONNECTIONS.** In White's "Once More to the Lake" and Brad Manning's "Arm Wrestling with My Father" (p. 100), the writers reveal a changing sense of what it means to be a father. Write an essay that examines the similarities and differences in their definitions of fatherhood. How does a changing idea of what it means to be a son connect with this redefinition of fatherhood?

5. **CONNECTIONS.** White's essay is full of images that place his audience in a setting important to him in childhood. Judith Ortiz Cofer, in "Silent Dancing" (p. 122), also uses vivid images to evoke childhood. After reading these two essays, write an essay of your own ANALYZING four or five images from each that strike you as especially evocative. What sense impression does each image draw on? What does each one tell you about the author's feelings?

E. B. WHITE ON WRITING

"You asked me about writing—how I did it," E. B. White replied to a seventeen-year-old who had written to him, wanting to become a professional writer but feeling discouraged. "There is no trick to it. If you like to write and want to write, you write, no matter where you are or what else you are doing or whether anyone pays any heed. I must have written half a million words (mostly in my journal) before I had anything published, save for a couple of short items in St. Nicholas.[1] If you want to write about feelings, about the end of the summer, about growing, write about it. A great deal of writing is not 'plotted'—most of my essays have no plot structure, they are a ramble in the woods, or a ramble in the basement of my mind. You ask, 'Who cares?' Everybody cares. You say, 'It's been written before.' Everything has been written

---

[1] A magazine for children, popular early in the century. —EDS.

before.....Henry Thoreau, who wrote *Walden*, said, 'I learned this at least by my experiment: that if one advances confidently in the direction of his dreams and endeavors to live the life which he has imagined, he will meet with a success unexpected in common hours.' The sentence, after more than a hundred years, is still alive. So, advance confidently."

In trying to characterize his own writing, White was modest in his claims. To his brother Stanley Hart White, he once remarked, "I discovered a long time ago that writing of the small things of the day, the trivial matters of the heart, the inconsequential but near things of this living, was the only kind of creative work which I could accomplish with any sincerity or grace. As a reporter, I was a flop, because I always came back laden not with facts about the case, but with a mind full of the little difficulties and amusements I had encountered in my travels. Not till *The New Yorker* came along did I ever find any means of expressing those impertinences and irrelevancies. Thus yesterday, setting out to get a story on how police horses are trained, I ended by writing a story entitled "How Police Horses Are Trained" which never even mentions a police horse, but has to do entirely with my own absurd adventures at police headquarters. The rewards of such endeavor are not that I have acquired an audience or a following, as you suggest (fame of any kind being a Pyrrhic victory), but that sometimes in writing of myself—which is the only subject anyone knows intimately—I have occasionally had the exquisite thrill of putting my finger on a little capsule of truth, and heard it give the faint squeak of mortality under my pressure, an antic sound."

FOR DISCUSSION

1. Sometimes young writers are counseled to study the market and then try to write something that will sell. How would you expect E. B. White to have reacted to such advice?
2. What, exactly, does White mean when he says, "Everything has been written before"? How might an aspiring writer take this remark as encouragement?
3. What interesting distinction does White make between reporting and essay writing?

TOM WOLFE

TOM WOLFE, author, journalist, and cartoonist, was born in 1931 in Richmond, Virginia, and went to Washington and Lee University. After taking a Ph.D. in American Studies at Yale, he decided against an academic career and instead worked as a reporter for the *Springfield Union* and the *Washington Post*. Early in the 1960s, Wolfe began writing his electrifying, satiric articles on the American scene (with special, mocking attention to subcultures and trendsetters), which have enlivened *New York, Esquire, Rolling Stone, Harper's,* and other magazines. Among his books are *The Electric Kool-Aid Acid Test* (1965), a memoir of LSD-spaced-out hippies; *The Pump House Gang* (1968), a study of California surfers; *The Right Stuff* (1979), a chronicle of America's first astronauts, which won the American Book Award and was made into a movie; and *From Bauhaus to Our House* (1981), a complaint against modern architecture. Wolfe's two novels, *The Bonfire of the Vanities* (1987) and *A Man in Full* (1998), have been both controversial and hugely popular.

Pornoviolence

This essay, from a collection raking over the 1970s, *Mauve Gloves & Madmen, Clutter & Vine* (1976), is vintage Tom Wolfe. He played a large part in the invention of "the new journalism" (a brand of reporting that tells the truth excitedly, as if it were fiction), and his essay is marked by certain breathless features of style: long sentences full of parenthetical asides, ellipses (...), generous use of italics. Wolfe here coins a term to fit the blend of pornography and pandering to bloodlust that he finds in the media. Although not recent, his remarks have dated little since they first appeared.

Wolfe defines the word *pornoviolence* by drawing substantially on several other methods of development as well.

Narration (Chap. 1): paragraphs 10–16, 18, 20, 24
Example (Chap. 3): paragraphs 1–7, 8, 11–15, 18, 21–24, 27, 29–30
Comparison and contrast (Chap. 4): paragraphs 26, 30
Division or analysis (Chap. 6): paragraphs 22–26, 28–30
Cause and effect (Chap. 8): paragraphs 19, 27–28, 31
Definition (Chap. 9): paragraphs 16–17, 25–26, 28–31

"*Keeps His Mom-in-law in Chains,* meet *Kills Son and Feeds Corpse to Pigs.*" 1

"Pleased to meet you." 2

"*Teenager Twists Off Corpse's Head . . . to Get Gold Teeth,* meet *Strangles Girl Friend, Then Chops Her to Pieces.*" 3

"How you doing?" 4

"*Nurse's Aide Sees Fingers Chopped Off in Meat Grinder,* meet *I Left My Babies in the Deep Freeze.*" 5

"It's a pleasure." 6

It's a pleasure! No doubt about that! In all these years of journalism 7 I have covered more conventions than I care to remember. Podiatrists, theosophists, Professional Budget Finance dentists, oyster farmers, mathematicians, truckers, dry cleaners, stamp collectors, Esperantists, nudists, and newspaper editors—I have seen them all, together, in vast assemblies, sloughing through the wall-to-wall of a thousand hotel lobbies (the nudists excepted) in their shimmering gray-metal suits and pajama-stripe shirts with white Plasti-Coat name cards on their chests, and I have sat through their speeches and seminars (the nudists included) and attentively endured ear baths such as you wouldn't believe. And yet none has ever been quite like the convention of the stringers for the *National Enquirer*.

The *Enquirer* is a weekly newspaper that is probably known by sight 8 to millions more than know it by name. No one who ever came face-to-face with the *Enquirer* on a newsstand in its wildest days is likely to have forgotten the sight: a tabloid with great inky shocks of type all over the front page saying something on the order of *Gouges Out Wife's Eyes to Make Her Ugly, Dad Hurls Hot Grease in Daughter's Face, Wife Commits Suicide After 2 Years of Poisoning Fails to Kill Husband...*

The stories themselves were supplied largely by stringers, i.e., corre- 9 spondents, from all over the country, the world, for that matter, mostly copy editors and reporters on local newspapers. Every so often they would come upon a story, usually via the police beat, that was so grotesque the local sheet would discard it or run it in a highly glossed form rather than offend or perplex its readers. The stringers would preserve them for the *Enquirer*, which always rewarded them well and respectfully.

One year the *Enquirer* convened and feted them at a hotel in Man- 10 hattan. This convention was a success in every way. The only awkward moment was at the outset when the stringers all pulled in. None of them knew each other. Their hosts got around the problem by introducing them by the stories they had supplied. The introductions went like this:

"Harry, I want you to meet Frank here. Frank did that story, you re- 11 member that story, *Midget Murderer Throws Girl Off Cliff After She Refuses to Dance with Him.*"

"Pleased to meet you. That was some story." 12

"And Harry did the one about *I Spent Three Days Trapped at Bottom* 13 *of Forty-Foot-Deep Mine Shaft and Was Saved by a Swarm of Flies.*"

"Likewise, I'm sure." 14

And *Midget Murderer Throws Girl Off Cliff* shakes hands with *I* 15
Spent Three Days Trapped at Bottom of Forty-Foot-Deep Mine Shaft, and
Buries Her Baby Alive shakes hands with *Boy, Twelve, Strangles Two-
Year-Old Girl*, and *Kills Son and Feeds Corpse to Pigs* shakes hands with
*He Strangles Old Woman and Smears Corpse with Syrup, Ketchup, and
Oatmeal*...and...

...There was a great deal of esprit about the whole thing. These 16
men were, in fact, the avant-garde of a new genre that since then has
become institutionalized throughout the nation without anyone knowing its proper name. I speak of the new pornography, the pornography
of violence.

Pornography comes from the Greek word *porne*, meaning "harlot," 17
and pornography is literally the depiction of the acts of harlots. In the
new pornography, the theme is not sex. The new pornography depicts
practitioners acting out another, murkier drive: people staving teeth in,
ripping guts open, blowing brains out, and getting even with all those
bastards...

The success of the *Enquirer* prompted many imitators to enter the 18
field, *Midnight*, the *Star Chronicle*, the *National Insider*, *Inside News*, the
National Close-up, the *National Tattler*, the *National Examiner*. A truly
competitive free press evolved, and soon a reader could go to the newspaper of his choice for *Kill the Retarded!* (*Won't You Join My Movement?*)
and *Unfaithful Wife? Burn Her Bed!*, *Harem Master's Mistress Chops Him
with Machete*, *Babe Bites Off Boy's Tongue*, and *Cuts Buddy's Face to
Pieces for Stealing His Business and Fiancée*.

And yet the last time I surveyed the Violence press, I noticed a cu- 19
rious thing. These pioneering journals seem to have pulled back. They
seem to be regressing to what is by now the Redi-Mix staple of literate
Americans, mere sex. *Ecstasy and Me (by Hedy Lamarr)*,[1] says the *National Enquirer*. *I Run a Sex Art Gallery*, says the *National Insider*. What
has happened, I think, is something that has happened to avant-gardes
in many fields, from William Morris and the Craftsmen to the Bauhaus
group.[2] Namely, their discoveries have been preempted by the Establishment and so thoroughly dissolved into the mainstream they no
longer look original.

---

[1] *Ecstasy*, an early, European-made Hedy Lamarr film, was notorious for its scenes
of soft-core lovemaking. Later, paired with Charles ("Come with me to the Casbah")
Boyer, Lamarr rose to Hollywood stardom in *Algiers* (1938).—Eds.

[2] Morris (1834–96), an English artist, poet, printer, and socialist, founded a company of craftspeople to bring tasteful design to furniture (the Morris chair) and other
implements of everyday life. The Bauhaus, an influential art school in Germany
(1919–33), taught crafts and brought new ideas of design to architecture and to goods
produced in factories.—Eds.

Robert Harrison, the former publisher of *Confidential*, and later pub- 20
lisher of the aforementioned *Inside News*, was perhaps the first person to
see it coming. I was interviewing Harrison early in January 1964 for a story
in *Esquire* about six weeks after the assassination of President Kennedy,
and we were in a cab in the West Fifties in Manhattan, at a stoplight, by
a newsstand, and Harrison suddenly pointed at the newsstand and said,
"Look at that. They're doing the same thing the *Enquirer* does."

There on the stand was a row of slick-paper, magazine-size publica- 21
tions, known in the trade as one-shots, with titles like *Four Days That
Shook the World, Death of a President, An American Tragedy,* or just *John
Fitzgerald Kennedy (1921–1963).* "You want to know why people buy
those things?" said Harrison. "People buy those things to see a man get
his head blown off."

And, of course, he was right. Only now the publishers were in 22
many cases the pillars of the American press. Invariably, these "special
coverages" of the assassination bore introductions piously commemorating the fallen President, exhorting the American people to strength
and unity in a time of crisis, urging greater vigilance and safeguards for
the new President, and even raising the nice metaphysical question of
collective guilt in "an age of violence."

In the years since then, of course, there has been an incessant re- 23
play, with every recoverable clinical detail, of those less than five seconds in which a man got his head blown off. And throughout this
deluge of words, pictures, and film frames, I have been intrigued with
one thing: The point of view, the vantage point, is almost never that of
the victim, riding in the Presidential Lincoln Continental. What you
get is...the view from Oswald's rifle. You can step right up here and
look point-blank right through the very hairline cross in Lee Harvey
Oswald's Optics Ordinance in weaponry four-power Japanese telescope
sight and watch, frame by frame by frame by frame, as that man there's
head comes apart. Just a little History there before your very eyes.

The television networks have schooled us in the view from Os- 24
wald's rifle and made it seem a normal pastime. The TV viewpoint is
nearly always that of the man who is going to strike. The last time I
watched *Gunsmoke*, which was not known as a very violent Western in
TV terms, the action went like this: The Wellington agents and the
stagecoach driver pull guns on the badlands gang leader's daughter and
Kitty, the heart-of-gold saloonkeeper, and kidnap them. Then the badlands gang shoots two Wellington agents. Then they tie up five more
and talk about shooting them. Then they desist because they might not
be able to get a hotel room in the next town if the word got around.
Then one badlands gang gunslinger attempts to rape Kitty while the
gang leader's younger daughter looks on. Then Kitty resists, so he slugs
her one in the jaw. Then the gang leader slugs him. Then the gang

leader slugs Kitty. Then Kitty throws hot stew in a gang member's face and hits him over the back of the head with a revolver. Then he knocks her down with a rock. Then the gang sticks up a bank. Here comes the marshal, Matt Dillon. He shoots a gang member and breaks it up. Then the gang leader shoots the guy who was guarding his daughter and the woman. Then the marshal shoots the gang leader. The final exploding bullet signals The End.

It is not the accumulated slayings and bone crushings that make this 25 pornoviolence, however. What makes it pornoviolence is that in almost every case the camera angle, therefore the viewer, is with the gun, the fist, the rock. The pornography of violence has no point of view in the old sense that novels do. You do not live the action through the hero's eyes. You live with the aggressor, whoever he may be. One moment you are the hero. The next you are the villain. No matter whose side you may be on consciously, you are in fact with the muscle, and it is you who disintegrate all comers, villains, lawmen, women, anybody. On the rare occasions in which the gun is emptied into the camera—i.e., into your face—the effect is so startling that the pornography of violence all but loses its fantasy charm. There are not nearly so many masochists as sadists among those little devils whispering into one's ears.

In fact, sex—"sadomasochism"—is only a part of the pornography 26 of violence. Violence is much more wrapped up, simply, with status. Violence is the simple, ultimate solution for problems of status competition, just as gambling is the simple, ultimate solution for economic competition. The old pornography was the fantasy of easy sexual delights in a world where sex was kept unavailable. The new pornography is the fantasy of easy triumph in a world where status competition has become so complicated and frustrating.

Already the old pornography is losing its kick because of overexpo- 27 sure. In the late thirties, Nathanael West published his last and best-regarded novel, *The Day of the Locust,* and it was a terrible flop commercially, and his publisher said if he ever published another book about Hollywood it would "have to be *My Thirty-nine Ways of Making Love by Hedy Lamarr.*" He thought he was saying something that was funny because it was beyond the realm of possibility. Less than thirty years later, however, Hedy Lamarr's *Ecstasy and Me* was published. Whether she mentions thirty-nine ways, I'm not sure, but she gets off to a flying start: "The men in my life have ranged from a classic case history of impotence, to a whip-brandishing sadist who enjoyed sex only after he tied my arms behind me with the sash of his robe. There was another man who took his pleasure with a girl in my own bed, while he thought I was asleep in it."

Yet she was too late. The book very nearly sank without a trace. The 28 sin itself is wearing out. Pornography cannot exist without certified taboo

to violate. And today Lust, like the rest of the Seven Deadly Sins—
Pride, Sloth, Envy, Greed, Anger, and Gluttony—is becoming a rather
minor vice. The Seven Deadly Sins, after all, are only sins against the
self. Theologically, the idea of Lust—well, the idea is that if you seduce
some poor girl from Akron, it is not a sin because you are ruining her, but
because you are wasting your time and your energies and damaging your
own spirit. This goes back to the old work ethic, when the idea was to
keep every able-bodied man's shoulder to the wheel. In an age of riches
for all, the ethic becomes more nearly: Let him do anything he pleases, as
long as he doesn't get in my way. And if he does get in my way, or even if
he doesn't ... well ... we have *new* fantasies for that. *Put hair on the walls*.

"Hair on the walls" is the invisible subtitle of Truman Capote's   29
book *In Cold Blood*. The book is neither a who-done-it nor a will-they-
be-caught, since the answers to both questions are known from the outset. It does ask why-did-they-do-it, but the answer is soon as clear as it
is going to be. Instead, the book's suspense is based largely on a totally
new idea in detective stories: the promise of gory details, and the withholding of them until the end. Early in the game one of the two murderers, Dick, starts promising to put "plenty of hair on them-those
walls" with a shotgun. So read on, gentle readers, and on and on; you
are led up to the moment before the crime on page 60—yet the
specifics, what happened, the gory details, are kept out of sight, in grisly
dangle, until page 244.

But Dick and Perry, Capote's killers, are only a couple of Low Rent   30
bums. With James Bond the new pornography reached a dead center,
the bureaucratic middle class. The appeal of Bond has been explained
as the appeal of the lone man who can solve enormously complicated,
even world problems through his own bravery and initiative. But Bond
is not a lone man at all, of course. He is not the Lone Ranger. He is
much easier to identify than that. He is a salaried functionary in a bureaucracy. He is a sport, but a believable one; not a millionaire, but a
bureaucrat on an expense account. He is not even a high-level bureaucrat. He is an operative. This point is carefully and repeatedly made by
having his superiors dress him down for violations of standard operating procedure. Bond, like the Lone Ranger, solves problems with guns
and fists. When it is over, however, the Lone Ranger leaves a silver bullet. Bond, like the rest of us, fills out a report in triplicate.

Marshall McLuhan[3] says we are in a period in which it will become   31
harder and harder to stimulate lust through words and pictures—i.e.,
the old pornography. In the latest round of pornographic movies the

[3] Canadian English professor, author of *Understanding Media* (1964), *The Medium
Is the Message* (1967), and other books, McLuhan (1911–80) analyzed the effects on
world society of television and other electronic media.—EDS.

producers have found it necessary to introduce violence, bondage, torture, and aggressive physical destruction to an extraordinary degree. The same sort of bloody escalation may very well happen in the pure pornography of violence. Even such able craftsmen as Truman Capote, Ian Fleming, NBC, and CBS may not suffice. Fortunately, there are historical models to rescue us from this frustration. In the latter days of the Roman Empire, the Emperor Commodus became jealous of the celebrity of the great gladiators. He took to the arena himself, with his sword, and began dispatching suitably screened cripples and hobbled fighters. Audience participation became so popular that soon various *illuminati* of the Commodus set, various boys and girls of the year, were out there, suited up, gaily cutting a sequence of dwarfs and feebles down to short ribs. Ah, swinging generations, what new delights await?

QUESTIONS ON MEANING

1. Which of the following statements comes closest to summing up Tom Wolfe's main PURPOSE in writing "Pornoviolence"?

   Wolfe writes to define a word.
   Wolfe writes to define a trend in society.
   Wolfe writes to define a trend in the media that reflects a trend in society.
   Wolfe writes to explain how John F. Kennedy was assassinated.
   Wolfe writes to entertain us by mocking Americans' latest foolishness.

   (If you don't find any of these statements adequate, compose your own.)

2. If you have ever read the *National Enquirer* or any of its imitators, test the accuracy of Wolfe's reporting. What is the purpose of a featured article in the *Enquirer?*

3. According to Wolfe, what POINT OF VIEW does the writer or producer of pornoviolence always take? What other examples of this point of view (in violent incidents on films or TV shows) can you supply? (Did you ever see a replay of Jack Ruby's shooting of Oswald, for instance?)

4. "Violence is the simple, ultimate solution for problems of status competition" (para. 26). What does Wolfe mean?

5. Wolfe does not explicitly pass judgment on Truman Capote's book *In Cold Blood* (para. 29). But what is his opinion of it? How can you tell?

6. "No advocate of change for the sake of change, Tom Wolfe writes as a conservative moralist who rankles with savage indignation." Does this critical remark fit this particular essay? What, in Wolfe's view, appears to be happening to America and Americans?

QUESTIONS ON WRITING STRATEGY

1. On first reading, what did you make of Wolfe's opening sentence, "'*Keeps His Mom-in-law in Chains*, meet *Kills Son and Feeds Corpse to Pigs*'"? At what point did you first tumble to what the writer was doing? What IRONY do you find in the convention hosts' introducing people by the headlines of their gory stories? What advantage is it to Wolfe's essay that his INTRODUCTION (with its odd introductions) keeps you guessing for a while?

2. What is Wolfe's point in listing (in para. 7) some of the other conventions he has reported—gatherings of nudists, oyster farmers, and others?

3. What is the TONE or attitude of Wolfe's CONCLUSION (para. 31)? Note in particular the closing line.

4. **MIXED METHODS.** At what moment does Wolfe give us his short DEFINITION of *pornoviolence*, or the new pornography? Do you think he would have done better to introduce his short definition of the word in paragraph 1? Why, or why not?

5. **MIXED METHODS.** What do the EXAMPLES in paragraphs 21–23 and 30 (the latter instance developed by COMPARISON AND CONTRAST) contribute to Wolfe's definition of *pornoviolence*?

QUESTIONS ON LANGUAGE

1. What help to the reader does Wolfe provide by noting the source of the word *pornography* (para. 17)?

2. "The television networks have schooled us in the view from Oswald's rifle" (para. 24). What CONNOTATIONS enlarge the meaning of *schooled*?

3. Define *masochist* and *sadist* (para. 25). What kind of DICTION do you find in these terms? In "plenty of hair on them-those walls" (29)?

4. How much use does Wolfe make of COLLOQUIAL EXPRESSIONS? Point to examples.

5. What does Wolfe mean in noting that the fighters slain by the Emperor Commodus were "hobbled" and the cripples were "suitably screened" (para. 31)? What unflattering connotations does this emperor's very name contain? (If you don't get this, look up *commode* in your desk dictionary.)

SUGGESTIONS FOR WRITING

1. **JOURNAL WRITING.** Write about some recent examples of pornoviolence you have seen in the movies or on television or in newspapers or magazines. What, if anything, should be done about such examples?

   FROM JOURNAL TO ESSAY. Write an essay ARGUING why we should or should not try to regulate or otherwise censor violence in the media. Take into account who would set the standards, what the standards would be, and who would enforce the regulations. The issue of censoring media violence has received much attention in recent years, so you should be able to locate opinions and information easily in the *Readers' Guide to Periodical Literature* or *InfoTrac*.

2. Write an essay defining some current trend you've noticed in films or TV, popular music, sports, consumer buying, or some other large arena of life.

Like Wolfe, invent a name for it. Use plenty of examples to make your definition clear.

3. **CRITICAL WRITING.** Analyze Wolfe's distinctive journalistic style. In the note on the essay, we mention parenthetical asides (they appear between dashes as well as parentheses), three-dot ellipsis marks, and italics. Consider also his use of *I*, his piling up of detail (as in paras. 7 and 24), his informal diction ("losing its kick," "got his head blown off"), his choice of quotations, and any other features that strike you. What is the overall EFFECT of this style? What does it say about Wolfe?

4. **CONNECTIONS.** Read or reread Barbara Ehrenreich's "In Defense of Talk Shows" (p. 283). How is the problem she describes—exploiting people for entertainment—similar to or different from Wolfe's idea of pornoviolence? Write an essay comparing television talk shows and pornoviolence, considering their respective purposes, their methods (for instance, reliance on exploitation or spectacle), and their effects on their audiences.

5. **CONNECTIONS.** Spend some time watching one or more "real-life" television shows such as *Cops*, *World's Deadliest Car Chases*, or *When Animals Attack*. Then write a two-part essay in which you imagine the responses of Wolfe and then Marie Winn ("TV Addiction," p. 431) to these shows. Would Wolfe describe them as pornoviolence? Why, or why not? How would Winn explain their popularity, even addictiveness, for some viewers?

TOM WOLFE ON WRITING

"What about your writing techniques and habits?" Tom Wolfe was asked by Joe David Bellamy for *Writer's Digest*.

The actual writing I do very fast. I make a very tight outline of everything I write before I write it. And often, as in the case of *The Electric Kool-Aid Acid Test*, the research, the reporting, is going to take me much longer than the writing. By writing an outline you really are writing in a way, because you're creating the structure of what you're going to do. Once I really know what I'm going to write, I don't find the actual writing takes all that long.

The Electric Kool-Aid Acid Test in manuscript form was about 1,100 pages, triple-spaced, typewritten. That means about 200 words a page, and, you know, some of that was thrown out or cut eventually; but I wrote all of that in three and a half months. I had never written a full-length book before, and at first I decided I would treat each chapter as if it were a magazine article—because I *had* done that before. So I would set an artificial deadline, and I'd make myself meet it. And I did that for three chapters.

But after I had done this three times and then I looked ahead and I saw that there were *twenty-five* more times I was going to have to do this, I couldn't face it anymore. I said, "I cannot do this, even one more time, because there's no end to it." So I completely changed my system, and I set up a quota for myself—of ten typewritten pages a day. At 200 words a page that's 2,000 words, which is not, you know, an overwhelming amount. It's a good clip, but it's not overwhelming. And I found this worked much better. I had my outline done, and sometimes ten pages would get me hardly an eighth-of-an-inch along the outline. It didn't bother me. Just like working in a factory—end of ten pages, I'd close my lunch pail.

FOR DISCUSSION

1. In what way is outlining really writing, according to Wolfe? (In answering, consider the implications of his statement about "creating a structure.")
2. What strategy did the author finally settle on to get himself through the toil of his first book? What made this strategy superior to the one he had used earlier?

VIRGINIA WOOLF

Generally regarded as one of the greatest twentieth-century writers, VIRGINIA WOOLF earned her acclaim by producing uncommon fiction and nonfiction, the first sensitive and complex, the second poetic and immediate. Born Virginia Stephen in London in 1882, Woolf and her sister Vanessa were educated at home, largely by their father, Sir Leslie Stephen, an author and editor. The two sisters were central to the Bloomsbury Group, an informal society of writers and artists that included the economist John Maynard Keynes and the novelist E. M. Forster. Virginia married Leonard Woolf, a member of the group, in 1912, and the two soon founded the Hogarth Press, publisher of Virginia Woolf and many other notable writers of the day. Woolf's most innovative novels include *Mrs. Dalloway* (1925), *To the Lighthouse* (1927), *Orlando* (1928), *The Waves* (1931), and *Between the Acts* (1941). Her exemplary critical and meditative essays appear in *The Common Reader* (1925), *The Second Common Reader* (1933), and many other collections. Subject to severe depression all her adult life, in 1941 Woolf committed suicide.

The Death of the Moth

One of Woolf's most famous works of nonfiction, this essay was published in *The Death of the Moth and Other Essays* (1942). Though as brief as the life of the moth Woolf observes, the essay is typically evocative, intense, and enduring.

"The Death of the Moth" is a seamless blend of narration (Chap. 1) and description (Chap. 2). It is also implicitly a comparison and contrast (Chap. 4) between the moth in life and in death and between the author's responses to these states.

Moths that fly by day are not properly to be called moths; they do not excite that pleasant sense of dark autumn nights and ivy-blossom which the commonest yellow-underwing asleep in the shadow of the curtain never fails to rouse in us. They are hybrid creatures, neither gay like butterflies nor somber like their own species. Nevertheless the present specimen, with his narrow hay-colored wings, fringed with a tassel of the same color, seemed to be content with life. It was a pleasant morning, mid-September, mild, benignant, yet with a keener breath than that of the summer months. The plough was already scoring the field opposite the window, and where the share had been, the earth was pressed flat and gleamed with moisture. Such vigor came rolling in from the fields and the down beyond that it was difficult to keep the eyes strictly turned upon the book. The rooks too were keeping one of their annual festivities; soaring round the tree tops until it looked as if a vast net with thousands of black knots in it had been cast up into the air; which, after a few moments sank slowly down upon the trees until every twig seemed to have a knot at the end of it. Then, suddenly, the net would be thrown into the air again in a wider circle this time, with the utmost clamor and vociferation, as though to be thrown into the air and settle slowly down upon the tree tops were a tremendously exciting experience.

The same energy which inspired the rooks, the ploughmen, the 2 horses, and even, it seemed, the lean bare-backed downs, sent the moth fluttering from side to side of his square of the windowpane. One could not help watching him. One, was, indeed, conscious of a queer feeling of pity for him. The possibilities of pleasure seemed that morning so enormous and so various that to have only a moth's part in life, and a day moth's at that, appeared a hard fate, and his zest in enjoying his meager opportunities to the full, pathetic. He flew vigorously to one corner of his compartment, and, after waiting there a second, flew across to the other. What remained for him but to fly to a third corner and then to a fourth? That was all he could do, in spite of the size of the downs, the width of the sky, the far-off smoke of houses, and the romantic voice, now and then, of a steamer out at sea. What he could do he did. Watching him, it seemed as if a fiber, very thin but pure, of the enormous energy of the world had been thrust into his frail and diminutive body. As often as he crossed the pane, I could fancy that a thread of vital light became visible. He was little or nothing but life.

Yet, because he was so small, and so simple a form of the energy 3 that was rolling in at the open window and driving its way through so many narrow and intricate corridors in my own brain and in those of other human beings, there was something marvelous as well as pathetic about him. It was as if someone had taken a tiny bead of pure life and decking it as lightly as possible with down and feathers, had set it dancing and zigzagging to show us the true nature of life. Thus displayed one could not get over the strangeness of it. One is apt to forget all about life, seeing it humped and bossed and garnished and cumbered so that it has to move with the greatest circumspection and dignity. Again, the thought of all that life might have been had he been born in any other shape caused one to view his simple activities with a kind of pity.

After a time, tired by his dancing apparently, he settled on the win- 4 dow ledge in the sun, and, the queer spectacle being at an end, I forgot about him. Then, looking up, my eye was caught by him. He was trying to resume his dancing, but seemed either so stiff or so awkward that he could only flutter to the bottom of the windowpane; and when he tried to fly across it he failed. Being intent on other matters I watched these futile attempts for a time without thinking, unconsciously waiting for him to resume his flight, as one waits for a machine, that has stopped momentarily, to start again without considering the reason of its failure. After perhaps a seventh attempt he slipped from the wooden ledge and fell, fluttering his wings, on to his back on the windowsill. The helplessness of his attitude roused me. It flashed upon me that he was in difficulties; he could no longer raise himself; his legs struggled vainly. But, as I stretched out a pencil, meaning to help him to right himself, it came over me that the failure and awkwardness were the approach of death. I laid the pencil down again.

The legs agitated themselves once more. I looked as if for the enemy against which he struggled. I looked out of doors. What had happened there? Presumably it was midday, and work in the fields had stopped. Stillness and quiet had replaced the previous animation. The birds had taken themselves off to feed in the brooks. The horses stood still. Yet the power was there all the same, massed outside, indifferent, impersonal, not attending to anything in particular. Somehow it was opposed to the little hay-colored moth. It was useless to try to do anything. One could only watch the extraordinary efforts made by those tiny legs against an oncoming doom which could, had it chosen, have submerged an entire city, not merely a city, but masses of human beings; nothing, I knew had any chance against death. Nevertheless after a pause of exhaustion the legs fluttered again. It was superb this last protest, and so frantic that he succeeded at last in righting himself. One's sympathies, of course, were all on the side of life. Also, when there was nobody to care or to know, this gigantic effort on the part of an insignificant little moth, against a power of such magnitude, to retain what no one else valued or desired to keep, moved one strangely. Again, somehow, one saw life, a pure bead. I lifted the pencil again, useless though I knew it to be. But even as I did so, the unmistakable tokens of death showed themselves. The body relaxed, and instantly grew stiff. The struggle was over. The insignificant little creature now knew death. As I looked at the dead moth, this minute wayside triumph of so great a force over so mean an antagonist filled me with wonder. Just as life had been strange a few minutes before, so death was now as strange. The moth having righted himself now lay most decently and uncomplainingly composed. O yes, he seemed to say, death is stronger than I am.

QUESTIONS ON MEANING

1. Why does Woolf choose to write about something as insignificant as a moth's death? Does she have a PURPOSE other than relating a simple observation?
2. Why, in paragraph 2, does Woolf say that the moth was "little or nothing but life"? Why is the moth pitiable?
3. What does the moth in his square windowpane represent to the author? How does Woolf's DESCRIPTION in the essay make this clear?
4. How does Woolf's outlook change in paragraph 5? Why?

QUESTIONS ON WRITING STRATEGY

1. Is Woolf's essay an OBJECTIVE or a SUBJECTIVE description? Give details from the essay to support your answer.
2. What is the EFFECT of Woolf's scene-setting in paragraph 1? How does this description influence our perception of the moth?
3. **MIXED METHODS.** Which of the five senses does Woolf's description principally rely on? Why, do you think?
4. **MIXED METHODS.** This essay is a description in the framework of a NARRATIVE. Summarize the changes in Woolf's perceptions of the moth that occur in the narrative.

QUESTIONS ON LANGUAGE

1. Analyze the writing in paragraph 5. How do sentence structure and words create a mood different from that in earlier paragraphs?
2. Analyze Woolf's IMAGES in describing the moth and her substitutions for the word *moth*, such as "the present specimen" in paragraph 1. How do these reinforce Woolf's changing perceptions as you outlined them in question 4 on writing strategy?
3. You may find Woolf's vocabulary more difficult than that of some other writers in this book. Look up any unfamiliar words in the following list: rouse, hybrid, benignant, plough, share, down, rooks, clamor, vociferation (para. 1); zest, meager, pathetic, diminutive (2); decking, cumbered, circumspection (3); spectacle, futile, vainly (4); animation, righting, magnitude, minute, mean, antagonist (5).

SUGGESTIONS FOR WRITING

1. **JOURNAL WRITING.** Try thinking from Woolf's perspective, recognizing the struggle and life force within creatures we generally consider insignificant. In your journal, sketch out some ideas. What do you find admirable about turtles? mosquitoes? butterflies? minnows? ants?
   FROM JOURNAL TO ESSAY. Write a brief essay from your journal entry, using ample descriptive details to depict both the creature and its significance. What lessons does the creature have to offer?

2. Find a place to write, and begin working on this assignment. Examine your surroundings: What could conceivably distract you from your work? Peeling paint? An uncomfortable chair? A funny smell? A noise? The view out your window? Your blinking computer cursor? Write a description of what you see, hear, feel, smell, taste.

3. **CRITICAL WRITING.** Respond to the ideas about life and death in Woolf's essay. First explain what you understand these ideas to be. Then use EXAMPLES from your reading and experience to support or contest Woolf's ideas.

4. **CONNECTIONS.** Both Woolf's essay and Merrill Markoe's "Bob the Dog" (p. 116) describe an animal that has or acquires strong meaning for the author. The essays are quite different (Woolf is serious while Markoe is humorous; Woolf is explicit about a larger meaning while Markoe is not)— but they are also similar in what the authors see their subjects as representing. In a brief essay, explore how the moth and Bob the dog are alike.

5. **CONNECTIONS.** COMPARE Woolf's "The Death of the Moth" with Annie Dillard's "Lenses" (p. 547). Of these two highly subjective essays, which is the more personal? Write a brief essay answering this question, and support your answer with quotations and PARAPHRASES from both Woolf and Dillard.

VIRGINIA WOOLF ON WRITING

A diary keeper from her youth, Virginia Woolf used the form not only to record and reflect on events but also to do a kind of "rough & random" writing she otherwise had little chance for. (Today this kind of writing is often called *freewriting,* a term defined and illustrated on pp. 24–25.) Woolf wrote in her diary on April 20, 1919, that "the habit of writing thus for my own eye only is good practice. It loosens the ligaments. Never mind the misses & the stumbles. Going at such a pace as I do I must make the most direct & instant shots at my object, & thus have to lay hands on words, choose them, & shoot them with no more pause than is needed to put my pen in the ink. I believe that during the past year I can trace some increase of ease in my professional writing which I attribute to my casual half hours after tea."

Thirteen years later, Woolf felt just as strongly about the value of writing freely, without censorship. In "A Letter to a Young Poet," she advises against writing solely for "a severe and intelligent public." Follow the excitement of "actual life," she urges. "Write then, now that you are young, nonsense by the ream. Be silly, be sentimental, imitate Shelley, imitate Samuel Smiles; give the rein to every impulse; commit every fault of style, grammar, taste, and syntax; pour out; tumble over; loose anger, love, satire, in whatever words you can catch, coerce, or create, in whatever meter, prose, poetry, or gibberish that comes to hand. Thus you will learn to write."

FOR DISCUSSION

1. What does Woolf gain from diary writing? What does she mean when she says that such writing "loosens the ligaments"?

2. Do you think Woolf seriously believed that young writers should write "nonsense by the ream"? (A *ream*, incidentally, is about five hundred sheets of paper.) What might the young writer learn from such freedom?

3. These excerpts do not discuss the writer's work needed to turn the loose, private writing Woolf recommends into writing that can be understood and appreciated by others. In your view, what does that work consist of?

USING AND DOCUMENTING SOURCES

When you write about them, the essays in this book serve as your sources: Either you ANALYZE them or you use them to support your own ideas. Writing with sources will occupy you for much of your academic career, as you rely on books, periodical articles, interviews, electronic databases, and other materials to establish and extend your own ideas.

This appendix introduces the essentials of using sources: summarizing and paraphrasing (below), avoiding plagiarism (p. 670), integrating quotations into your own prose (p. 671), and documenting sources using the style of the Modern Language Association, or MLA (p. 672).

SUMMARIZING AND PARAPHRASING

To summarize or paraphrase is to express the ideas from a source in your own words. A SUMMARY condenses an entire passage, article, or even book into a few lines that convey the source's essential meaning. We discuss summary as a reading technique on pages 14–15, and the advice and examples there apply here as well. For another example, here is a summary of Barbara Lazear Ascher's "On Compassion," which appears on pages 145–47.

Ascher shows how contact with the homeless can be unsettling and depressing. Yet she also suggests that these encounters are useful because they can teach others to be more compassionate (145–47).

Notice how the summary identifies the source author and page numbers and uses words that are *not* the author's. (Any of Ascher's distinctive phrasing would have to be placed in quotation marks.)

In contrast to a summary, a PARAPHRASE usually restates a single idea, again in words different from those of the original author. Here is a quotation from Ascher's essay and a paraphrase of it:

> QUOTATION: "Could it be that the homeless, like [Greek dramatists], are reminding us of our common humanity? Of course there is a difference. The play doesn't end — and the players can't go home."

> PARAPHRASE: Ascher points out an important distinction between the New York City homeless and the characters in Greek tragedies: The homeless are living real lives, not performing on a stage (147).

As with the summary, note that the paraphrase cites the original author and page number. Here is another example of paraphrase, this from an essay about immigration by David Cole.

> QUOTATION: "If we are collectively judged by how we treat immigrants — those who appear to be 'other' but will in a generation be 'us' — we are not in very good shape."

> PARAPHRASE: Cole argues that the way native-born Americans deal with immigrants reflects badly on the native-born citizens themselves. He also points out that today's immigrants will be part of tomorrow's mainstream society (110).

AVOIDING PLAGIARISM

Take a look at another attempt to paraphrase the sentence above by David Cole.

> Cole argues that if we are judged as a group by how we treat immigrants — those who seem to be different but eventually will be the same — we are in bad shape (110).

This is PLAGIARISM — the theft of someone's ideas or written work. Even though the writer identifies Cole as the source of the information, the language essentially remains the same. It is not enough to change a few words — "collectively" to "as a group," "in a generation" to "eventually," "not in very good shape" to "in bad shape." A paraphrase must express the original idea in an entirely new way, both in word choice and in sentence structure. (Even more blatant plagiarism, of course, would have repeated Cole's statement exactly as he wrote it, without quotation marks *or* a source citation.) Plagiarism also occurs when a writer neglects to cite a source at all—if, for example, a writer paraphrased Ascher's comparison of the homeless with actors in a Greek drama, as on the previous page, but did not mention Ascher's name.

Not all information from sources must be cited. Some falls under the category of common knowledge—facts so widely known or agreed upon that they are not attributable to a specific source. The statement "World War II ended after the United States dropped atomic bombs on Hiroshima and Nagasaki, Japan" is an obvious example: Most people recognize this statement as true. But some lesser-known information is also common knowledge. You may not know that President Dwight Eisenhower coined the term *military-industrial complex* during his 1961 farewell address; still, you could easily discover the information in encyclopedias, in books and articles about Eisenhower, and in contemporary newspaper accounts. The prevalence of the information and the fact that it is used elsewhere without source citation tell you that it's common knowledge.

In contrast, a scholar's argument that Eisenhower waited too long to criticize the defense industry, or the President's own comments on the subject in his diary, or an opinion from a Defense Department report in 1959—any of these needs to be credited. Unlike common knowledge, each of them remains the property of its author.

USING AND INTEGRATING QUOTATIONS

Quotations from your sources can serve as EVIDENCE for your own ideas (see p. 456) and can enliven your subject—*if* they are well chosen. Too many quotations can clutter an essay and detract from your own voice. Choose quotations that are relevant to the point you are making, that are concise and pithy, and that use lively, bold, or original language. Sentences that lack distinction—for example, a statement providing statistics on economic growth between 1985 and 1995—should almost always be paraphrased.

When you do quote from a source, you want to integrate the quotation into your own sentences and also set it up so that readers know what you expect them to make of it. In the passage below, the writer drops the quotation awkwardly into her sentence and doesn't clarify how the quotation relates to her idea.

> NOT INTEGRATED: The problem of homelessness is not decreasing, and "It is impossible to insulate ourselves against what is at our very doorstep" (Ascher 147).

In the following revision, however, the writer indicates with "As Ascher says" that she is using the quotation to reinforce her point. These words also link the quotation to the writer's sentence.

INTEGRATED: The problem of homelessness is not decreasing, nor is our awareness of it, however much we wish otherwise. As Ascher says, "It is impossible to insulate ourselves against what is at our very doorstep" (147).

You can integrate a quotation into your sentence by interpreting the quotation and by mentioning the author in your text—both techniques illustrated above. The introductory phrase "As Ascher says" has many variations:

According to one authority...

John Eng maintains that...

The author of an important study, Hilda Brown, observes that...

Ascher, the author of "On Compassion," has a different view, claiming...

For variety, such a phrase can also fall elsewhere in the quotation.

"It is impossible," Ascher says, "to insulate ourselves against what is at our very doorstep" (147).

When you omit something from a quotation, use the three spaced periods of an ellipsis mark to signal the omission:

"It is impossible to insulate ourselves...," says Ascher (147).

In Ascher's view, "Compassion ... must be learned" (147).

CITING SOURCES USING MLA STYLE

On the following pages we explain the documentation style of the Modern Language Association, as described in the *MLA Handbook for Writers of Research Papers*, 5th edition (1999). This style—used in English, foreign languages, and some other humanities—involves a brief parenthetical citation in the text that refers to an entry in a list of works cited at the end of the text.

PARENTHETICAL TEXT CITATION

The homeless may be to us what tragic heroes were to the ancient Greeks (Ascher 147).

ENTRY IN LIST OF WORKS CITED

Ascher, Barbara Lazear. "On Compassion." The Bedford Reader. 7th ed. Ed. X. J. Kennedy, Dorothy M. Kennedy, and Jane E. Aaron. Boston: Bedford/St. Martin's, 2000. 145-47.

By providing the author's name and page number in your text citation, you're giving the reader just enough information to find the source in the list of works cited and then find the place in the source where the borrowed material appears.

MLA Parenthetical Citations

When citing sources in your text, you have two options:

- You can identify both the author and the page number within parentheses, as in the example at the bottom of the facing page.
- You can introduce the author's name into your own sentence and use the parentheses only for the page number, as here:

Wilson points out that sharks, which have existed for 350 million years, are now more diverse than ever (301).

A work with two or three authors

More than 90 percent of the hazardous waste produced in the United States comes from seven major industries, all energy-intensive (Romm and Curtis 70).

A work with more than three authors

With more than three authors, name all the authors, or name only the first author followed by "et al." ("and others"). Use the same form in your list of works cited.

Gilman herself created the misconception that doctors tried to ban her story "The Yellow Wallpaper" when it appeared in 1892 (Dock, Allen, Palais, and Tracy 61).

Gilman herself created the misconception that doctors tried to ban her story "The Yellow Wallpaper" when it appeared in 1892 (Dock et al. 61).

An entire work

Reference to an entire work does not require a page number.

Postman argues that television is destructive because of the nature of the medium itself.

A work in more than one volume

If you cite two or more volumes of the same work, identify the volume number before the page number. Separate volume number and page number with a colon.

According to Gibbon, during the reign of Gallienus "every province of
the Roman world was afflicted by barbarous invaders and military
tyrants" (1: 133).

Two or more works by the same author(s)

If you cite more than one work by the same author or authors, include the work's title. If the title is long, shorten it to the first one or
two main words. (The full title for the first citation below is <u>Death at
an Early Age</u>.)

In the 1960s Kozol was reprimanded by his principal for teaching the
poetry of Langston Hughes (<u>Death</u> 83).

Kozol believes that most people do not understand the effect that tax
and revenue policies have on the quality of urban public schools (<u>Sav-
age Inequalities</u> 207).

An unsigned work

Cite an unsigned work by using a full or shortened version of the title.

In 1995 concern about Taiwan's relationship with China caused in-
vestors to transfer large amounts of capital to the United States ("How
the Missiles Help" 45).

An indirect source

Use "qtd. in" ("quoted in") to indicate that you found the source
you quote within another source.

Despite his tendency to view human existence as an unfulfilling
struggle, Schopenhauer disparaged suicide as "a vain and foolish act"
(qtd. in Durant 248).

A literary work

Because novels, poems, and plays may be published in various edi-
tions, the page number may not be enough to lead readers to the
quoted line or passage. For a novel, specify the chapter number after
the page number and a semicolon.

Among South Pacific islanders, the hero of Conrad's <u>Lord Jim</u> found "a
totally new set of conditions for his imaginative faculty to work upon"
(160; ch. 21).

For a verse play or a poem, omit the page number in favor of line numbers.

In "Dulce Et Decorum Est," Wilfred Owen undercuts the heroic image of warfare by comparing suffering soldiers to "beggars" and "hags" (lines 1-2) and describing a man dying in a poison-gas attack as "guttering, choking, drowning" (17).

If the work has parts, acts, or scenes, cite those as well (below: act 1, scene 5, lines 16–17).

Lady Macbeth worries about her husband's ambition: "Yet I do fear thy nature; / It is too full o' the milk of human kindness" (1.5.16-17).

More than one work

In the post-Watergate era, journalists have often employed aggressive reporting techniques not for the good of the public but simply to advance their careers (Gopnick 92; Fallows 64).

MLA List of Works Cited

Your list of works cited is a complete record of your sources. Follow these guidelines for the list:

- Title the list "Works Cited."
- Double-space the entire list.
- Arrange the sources alphabetically by the last name of the first author.
- Begin the first line of each entry at the left margin. Indent the subsequent lines of the entry one-half inch or five spaces.

Following are the essentials of a works-cited entry:

- Reverse the names of the author, last name first, with a comma between. If there is more than one author, give the others' names in normal order.
- Give the full title of the work, capitalizing all important words. Underline the titles of books and periodicals; use quotation marks for the titles of parts of books and articles in periodicals.
- Give publication information. For books, this information includes city of publication, publisher, date of publication. For periodicals, this information often includes volume number, date of publication, and page numbers for the article you cite. For online sources such as Web sites, this information includes the electronic address and the date you consulted the source.
- Use periods between parts of each entry.

You may need to combine the models below for a given source — for instance, combine "A book with two or three authors" and "A book with an editor" for a book with two or three editors.

Books

A book with one author

Tuchman, Barbara W. The March of Folly: From Troy to Vietnam. New
 York: Knopf, 1984.

A book with two or three authors

Silverstein, Olga, and Beth Rashbaum. The Courage to Raise Good Men.
 New York: Viking, 1994.

Trevor, Sylvia, Joan Hapgood, and William Leumi. Women Writers of
 the 1920s. New York: Columbia UP, 1998

A book with more than three authors

You may list all authors or only the first author followed by "et al."
("and others"). Use the same form in your parenthetical text citation.

Kippax, Susan, R. W. Connel, G. W. Dowsett, and June Crawford. Gay
 Communities Respond to Change. London: Falmer, 1993.

Kippax, Susan, et al. Gay Communities Respond to Change. London:
 Falmer, 1993.

More than one work by the same author(s)

Kozol, Jonathan. Death at an Early Age: The Destruction of the Hearts
 and Minds of Negro Children in the Boston Public Schools. Boston:
 Houghton, 1967.

---. Savage Inequalities: Children in America's Schools. New York:
 Crown, 1991.

A book with an editor

Gwaltney, John Langston, ed. Drylongso: A Self-Portrait of Black America. New York: Random, 1980.

A book with an author and an editor

Orwell, George. The Collected Essays, Journalism and Letters of George
 Orwell. Ed. Sonia Orwell and Ian Angus. New York: Harcourt,
 1968.

A later edition

Mumford, Lewis. Herman Melville: A Study of His Life and Vision. 2nd
 ed. New York: Harcourt, 1956.

A work in a series

Hall, Donald. Poetry and Ambition. Poets on Poetry. Ann Arbor: U of
Michigan P, 1988.

An anthology

Glantz, Michael H., ed. Societal Responses to Regional Climatic Change.
London: Westview, 1988.

A selection from an anthology

The numbers at the end of this entry are the page numbers on
which the cited selection appears.

Kellog, William D. "Human Impact on Climate: The Evolution of an
Awareness." Societal Responses to Regional Climatic Change. Ed.
Michael H. Glantz. London: Westview, 1988. 283-96.

If you cite more than one selection from the same anthology, you
may give the anthology as a separate entry and cross-reference it by the
editor's or editors' last names in the selection entries.

Ascher, Barbara Lazear. "On Compassion." Kennedy, Kennedy, and
Aaron 145-47.

Kennedy, X. J., Dorothy M. Kennedy, and Jane E. Aaron, eds. The
Bedford Reader. 7th ed. Boston: Bedford/St. Martin's, 2000.

Quindlen, Anna. "Homeless." Kennedy, Kennedy, and Aaron 150-52.

A reference work

Cheney, Ralph Holt. "Coffee." Collier's Encyclopedia. 1993 ed.

"Versailles, Treaty of." The New Encyclopaedia Britannica: Macropae-
dia. 15th ed. 1990.

Periodicals:
Journals, Magazines, and Newspapers

**An article in a journal with continuous pagination
throughout the annual volume**

In many journals the pages are numbered consecutively for an entire annual volume of issues, so that the year's fourth issue might run
from pages 240 to 320. For this type of journal, give the volume number after the journal title, followed by the year of publication in parentheses, a colon, and the page numbers of the article.

Clayton, Richard R., and Carl G. Leukefeld. "The Prevention of Drug
Use Among Youth: Implications of Legalization." Journal of Primary Prevention 12 (1992): 289-301.

An article in a journal that paginates issues separately

Some journals begin page numbering at 1 for each issue. For this
kind of journal, give the issue number after the volume number and a
period.

Vitz, Paul C. "Back to Human Dignity: From Modern to Postmodern
Psychology." Intercollegiate Review 31.2 (1996): 15-23.

An article in a monthly or bimonthly magazine

Fallows, James. "Why Americans Hate the Media." Atlantic Monthly
Feb. 1996: 45-64.

An article in a weekly magazine

Gopnick, Adam. "Read All About It." New Yorker 12 Dec. 1994:
84-102.

An article in a newspaper

Gorman, Peter. "It's Time to Legalize." Boston Sunday Globe 28 Aug.
1994, late ed.: 69+.

The page number "69+" means that the article begins on page 69
and continues on a later page. If the newspaper is divided into lettered
sections, give both section letter and page number, as in "A7."

An unsigned article

"How the Missiles Help California." Time 1 Apr. 1996: 45.

A review

Bergham, V. R. "The Road to Extermination." Rev. of Hitler's Willing
Executioners, by Daniel Jonah Goldhagen. New York Times Book
Review 14 Apr. 1996: 6.

CD-ROMs, Diskettes, and Magnetic Tapes

For portable databases (CD-ROMs, diskettes, magnetic tapes), the
content of the citation depends on whether the database is a periodical
and whether it is also published in print.

For a periodical that is also published in print, provide full print information (following the models given earlier), the title of the electronic source, the medium (for instance, "CD-ROM"), the name of the distributor, and the date of electronic publication:

> Rausch, Janet. "So Late in the Day." Daily Sun 10 Dec. 1994, late ed.:
> C1. Daily Disk. CD-ROM. Cybernews. Jan. 1995.

If the periodical is published only as a CD-ROM, omit the publication information for a print version.

Treat a portable database that is not a periodical as if it were a book, but provide the version or release number and the medium after the title.

> Hardy, Joel P. Rose Quartz: A Study in Geology. Magnetic tape. Ver. 2.
> New York: Hestas, 1996.

Online Sources

Online sources vary greatly, and they may be and often are updated. Your aim in citing such sources should be to tell what version you used and how readers can find it for themselves. The basic MLA format for an online source includes (1) author's name, (2) the title of the work you used, (3) the title of the online site, (4) the date of electronic publication, (5) the date you consulted the source, and (6) the source's complete electronic address in angle brackets (< >).

> Valesquez, Joel. "Wearing Out the Internet." Internet Concerns. 15 Apr.
> 1996. 23 May 1999 <http://downtown.centaur.com/new/conc/
> internet/essay/valesquez.htm>.

The following models show various kinds of additional information to be inserted between these basic elements. If some information is unavailable, list what you can find.

A scholarly project or database

Include the names, if any, of the editor and of the institution or organization that sponsors the project or database.

> Bartleby Library. Ed. Steven van Leeuwan. 1999. Academic Information Systems, Columbia U. 3 Mar. 1999 <http://
> www.columbia.edu/acis/bartleby.html>.

A personal or professional site

Provide the date of electronic publication if it differs from the date of your access. If there is a sponsoring institution or organization, insert its name after the publication date.

McClure, Mark. "Speakers." <u>Online Calendar of Shakespeare Confer-</u>
    <u>ences</u>. 18 Apr. 1999. 23 May 1999 <http://www.mwc.edu/
    ~mcclure/sa_spkrs.html>.

A book

For a book published independently, after the title add any editor's
or translator's name, either the publication information for a print version (as in the following model) or the date of electronic publication,
and any sponsoring institution or organization.

Murphy, Bridget. <u>Fictions of the Irish Emigration</u>. Cambridge: Harvard
    UP, 1992. 5 Apr. 1999 <http://www.historicalfictions.unv.edu/
    irel_murph.html>.

For a book published as part of a scholarly project, give any information about print publication and then add the publication information for the project (including the date of publication). See the
previous page for a model of a scholarly project.

Frost, Robert. <u>Mountain Interval</u>. New York: Holt, 1920. <u>Bartleby Li-</u>
    <u>brary</u>. Ed. Steven van Leeuwan. 1999. Academic Information Sys-
    tems, Columbia U. 16 June 1999 <http://www.columbia.edu/
    acis/bartleby/frost/index3.html>.

An article in a journal

Base an entry for an online journal article on one of the models on
pages 677–78 for a printed journal article. If the journal does not number pages in sequence but does provide some indication of length
(pages, sections, paragraphs), provide the total for the article (for instance, "6 pp." or "15 paras.").

Zurbrugg, Nicholas. "Poetry, Entertainment, and the Mass Media." <u>The</u>
    <u>Chicago Review</u> 40.2 (1995). 7 July 1999
    <http://bug.chicago.edu:8080/CR4023/4023giorno.html>.

An article in a newspaper

Base an entry for an online newspaper article on the model on page
678 for a printed newspaper article.

Grady, Denise. "Trapped at the South Pole, Doctor Becomes a Patient."
    <u>New York Times on the Web</u> 13 July 1999. 14 July 1999

<http://www.nytimes.com/library/national/science/
071399hth-southpole-cancer.html>.

An article in a magazine

Base an entry for an online magazine article on one of the models on page 678 for a printed magazine article.

Brus, Michael. "Proxy War." <u>Slate</u> 9 July 1999. 12 July 1999
<http://www.slate.com/Features/profile/profile.html>.

A work from an online service

For a personal service, such as America Online, or a library service, such as Lexis-Nexis, give an electronic address if one is available. Otherwise, give the keyword or topic path you used to reach the source, as in this example.

"Morpheus." <u>Encyclopedia Mythica</u>. 1999. America Online. 3 July 1999.
    Path: Research & Learn; Encyclopedia; More Encyclopedias.

Electronic mail

Give as the title the text of the e-mail's subject line, in quotation marks. "To the author" in the example means to you, the author of the paper.

Dove, Chris. "Re: Bishop's Poems." E-mail to the author. 7 May 1999.

A posting to a listserv, newsgroup, or Web forum

For a posting to a discussion group, give the posting's subject line as the title, and follow the title with "Online posting," the date of the posting, and the title of the group (without underlining or quotation marks).

Forrester, Jane. "Embracing Mathematics." Online posting. 21 Sept.
    1998. Math Teaching Discussion List. 22 Sept. 1998
    <http://www.acc.edu/gargantuan/smart/mathteach.html>.

A synchronous communication

Cite a contribution to a MOO, MUD, or other form of synchronous communication with the name of the speaker, a description of the event, the date of the event, and the name of the forum.

Marvell, Peter. Interview. 20 May 1999. JeffersonMOO. 20 May 1999
    <telnet://jefferson.village.virginia.edu.osheim:8888>.

Other Sources

A film or video recording

Achbar, Mark, and Peter Wintonick, dirs. Manufacturing Consent:
    Noam Chomsky and the Media. Zeitgeist, 1992.

A television or radio program

"Cable TV Squeezes High Numbers and Aces Competition." All Things
    Considered. PBS. WGBH, Boston. 9 Feb. 1998.

A recording

Mendelssohn, Felix. A Midsummer Night's Dream. Cond. Erich Leins-
    dorf. Boston Symphony Orch. RCA, 1982.

A letter

List a published letter under the author's name, and provide full
publication information.

Hemingway, Ernest. Letter to Grace Hemingway. 15 Jan. 1920. In
    Ernest Hemingway: Selected Letters. Ed. Carlos Baker. New York:
    Scribner's, 1981. 44.

For a letter that you receive, list the source under the writer's name, add
"to the author," and provide the date of the correspondence.

Dove, Chris. Letter to the author. 7 May 1999.

An interview

Kesey, Ken. Interview. "The Art of Fiction." Paris Review 130 (1994):
    59-94.

Macedo, Donaldo. Personal interview. 13 May 1999.

USEFUL TERMS

Abstract and concrete   Two kinds of language. *Abstract* words refer to ideas, conditions, and qualities we cannot directly perceive: *truth, love, courage, evil, wealth, poverty, progressive, reactionary.* *Concrete* words indicate things we can know with our senses: *tree, chair, bird, pen, motorcycle, perfume, thunderclap, cheeseburger.* The use of concrete words lends vigor and clarity to writing, for such words help a reader to picture things. See IMAGE.

Writers of expository and argumentative essays tend to shift back and forth from one kind of language to the other. They often begin a paragraph with a general statement full of abstract words ("There is *hope* for the *future* of *motoring*"). Then they usually go on to give examples and present evidence in sentences full of concrete words ("Inventor *Jones* claims his *car* will go from *Fresno* to *Los Angeles* on a *gallon* of *peanut oil*"). Inexperienced writers often use too many abstract words and not enough concrete ones.

Allude, allusion   To refer to a person, place, or thing believed to be common knowledge (*allude*), or the act or result of doing so (*allusion*). An allusion may point to a famous event, a familiar saying, a noted personality, a well-known story or song. Usually brief, an allusion is a space-saving way to convey much meaning. For example, the statement "The game was Coach Johnson's Waterloo" informs the reader that, like Napoleon meeting defeat in a celebrated battle, the coach led a confrontation resulting in his downfall and that of his team. If the writer is also showing Johnson's character, the allusion might further tell us that the coach is a man of Napoleonic ambition and pride. To make an effective allusion, you have to be aware of your audience. If your readers do not recognize the allusion, it will only confuse. Not everyone, for example, would understand if you alluded to a neighbor, to a seventeenth-century Russian harpsichordist, or to a little-known stock car driver.

Analogy An extended comparison based on the like features of two unlike things: one familiar or easily understood, the other unfamiliar, abstract, or complicated. For instance, most people know at least vaguely how the human eye works: The pupil adjusts to admit light, which registers as an image on the retina at the back of the eye. You might use this familiar information to explain something less familiar to many people, such as how a camera works: The aperture (like the pupil) adjusts to admit light, which registers as an image on the film (like the retina) at the back of the camera. Analogies are especially helpful for explaining technical information in a way that is nontechnical, more easily grasped. In August 1981, for example, the spacecraft *Voyager 2* transmitted spectacular pictures of Saturn to Earth. To explain the difficulty of their achievement, NASA scientists compared their feat to a golfer sinking a putt from five hundred miles away. Because it can make abstract ideas vivid and memorable, analogy is also a favorite device of philosophers, politicians, and preachers. In his celebrated speech "I Have a Dream" (p. 567), Martin Luther King, Jr., draws a remarkable analogy to express the anger and disappointment of African Americans that, one hundred years after Lincoln's Emancipation Proclamation, their full freedom has yet to be achieved. "It is obvious today," declares King, "that America has defaulted on this promissory note"; and he compares the founding fathers' written guarantee—of the rights of life, liberty, and the pursuit of happiness—to a bad check returned for insufficient funds.

Analogy is similar to the method of COMPARISON AND CONTRAST. Both use DIVISION or ANALYSIS to identify the distinctive features of two things and then set the features side by side. But a comparison explains two obviously similar things—two Civil War generals, two responses to a mess—and considers both their differences and their similarities. An analogy yokes two apparently unlike things (eye and camera, spaceflight and golf, guaranteed human rights and bad checks) and focuses only on their major similarities. Analogy is thus an extended *metaphor*, the FIGURE OF SPEECH that declares one thing to be another—even though it isn't, in a strictly literal sense—for the purpose of making us aware of similarity: "Hope," says the poet Emily Dickinson, "is the thing with feathers / That perches in the soul."

In an ARGUMENT, analogy can make readers more receptive to a point or inspire them, but it can't prove anything because in the end the subjects are dissimilar. A false analogy is a logical FALLACY that claims a fundamental likeness when none exists. See pages 462–63.

Analyze, analysis To separate a subject into its parts (*analyze*), or the act or result of doing so (*analysis*, also called *division*). Analysis is a key skill in CRITICAL THINKING, READING, AND WRITING; see pages 15–17. It is also considered a method of development; see Chapter 6.

Anecdote A brief narrative, or retelling of a story or event. Anecdotes have many uses: as essay openers or closers, as examples, as sheer entertainment. See Chapter 1.

Appeals   Resources writers draw on to connect with and persuade readers:

- A **rational appeal** asks readers to use their intellects and their powers of reasoning. It relies on established conventions of logic and evidence.
- An **emotional appeal** asks readers to respond out of their beliefs, values, or feelings. It inspires, affirms, frightens, angers.
- An **ethical appeal** asks readers to look favorably on the writer. It stresses the writer's intelligence, competence, fairness, morality, and other qualities desirable in a trustworthy debater or teacher.

See also pages 456–57.

Argument   A mode of writing intended to win readers' agreement with an assertion by engaging their powers of reasoning. Argument often overlaps PERSUASION. See Chapter 10.

Assume, assumption   To take something for granted (*assume*), or a belief or opinion taken for granted (*assumption*). Whether stated or unstated, assumptions influence a writer's choices of subject, viewpoint, evidence, and even language. See also pages 16 and 457–60.

Audience   A writer's readers. Having in mind a particular audience helps the writer in choosing strategies. Imagine, for instance, that you are writing two reviews of a new movie, one for the students who read the campus newspaper, the other for amateur and professional filmmakers who read *Millimeter*. For the first audience, you might write about the actors, the plot, and especially dramatic scenes. You might judge the picture and urge your readers to see it—or to avoid it. Writing for *Millimeter*, you might discuss special effects, shooting techniques, problems in editing and in mixing picture and sound. In this review, you might use more specialized and technical terms. Obviously, an awareness of the interests and knowledge of your readers, in each case, would help you decide how to write. If you told readers of the campus paper too much about filming techniques, you would lose most of them. If you told *Millimeter*'s readers the plot of the film in detail and how you liked its opening scene, probably you would put them to sleep.

    You can increase your awareness of your audience by asking yourself a few questions before you begin to write. Who are to be your readers? What is their age level? background? education? Where do they live? What are their beliefs and attitudes? What interests them? What, if anything, sets them apart from most people? How familiar are they with your subject? Knowing your audience can help you write so that your readers will not only understand you better but more deeply care about what you say.

Cause and effect   A method of development in which a writer ANALYZES reasons for an action, event, or decision, or analyzes its consequences. See Chapter 8. See also EFFECT.

Chronological order   The arrangement of events as they occurred or occur in time, first to last. Most NARRATIVES and PROCESS ANALYSES use chronological order.

Claim   The proposition that an ARGUMENT demonstrates. Stephen Toulmin favors this term in his system of reasoning. See pages 457–60. In some discussions of argument, the term THESIS is used instead.

Classification A method of development in which a writer sorts out plural things (contact sports, college students, kinds of music) into categories. See Chapter 7.

Cliché A worn-out, trite expression that a writer employs thoughtlessly. Although at one time the expression may have been colorful, from heavy use it has lost its luster. It is now "old as the hills." In conversation, most of us sometimes use clichés, but in writing they "stick out like sore thumbs." Alert writers, when they revise, replace a cliché with a fresh, concrete expression. Writers who have trouble recognizing clichés should be suspicious of any phrase they've heard before and should try to read more widely. Their problem is that, so many expressions being new to them, they do not know which ones are full of moths.

Coherence The clear connection of the parts in a piece of effective writing. This quality exists when the reader can easily follow the flow of ideas between sentences, paragraphs, and larger divisions, and can see how they relate successively to one another.

In making your essay coherent, you may find certain devices useful. TRANSITIONS, for instance, can bridge ideas. Reminders of points you have stated earlier are helpful to a reader who may have forgotten them — as readers tend to do sometimes, particularly if your essay is long. However, a coherent essay is not one merely pasted together with transitions and reminders. It derives its coherence from the clear relationship between its THESIS (or central idea) and all its parts.

Colloquial expressions Words and phrases occurring primarily in speech and in informal writing that seeks a relaxed, conversational tone. "My favorite chow is a burger and a shake" or "This math exam has me wired" may be acceptable in talking to a roommate, in corresponding with a friend, or in writing a humorous essay for general readers. Such choices of words, however, would be out of place in formal writing — in, say, a laboratory report or a letter to your senator. Contractions (*let's, don't, we'll*) and abbreviated words (*photo, sales rep, ad*) are the shorthand of spoken language. Good writers use such expressions with an awareness that they produce an effect of casualness.

Comparison and contrast Two methods of development usually found together. Using them, a writer examines the similarities and differences between two things to reveal their natures. See Chapter 4.

Conclusion The sentences or paragraphs that bring an essay to a satisfying and logical end. A conclusion is purposefully crafted to give a sense of unity and completeness to the whole essay. The best conclusions evolve naturally out of what has gone before and convince the reader that the essay is indeed at an end, not that the writer has run out of steam.

Conclusions vary in type and length depending on the nature and scope of the essay. A long research paper may require several paragraphs of summary to review and emphasize the main points. A short essay, however, may benefit from a few brief closing sentences.

In concluding an essay, beware of diminishing the impact of your writing by finishing on a weak note. Don't apologize for what you have or have not written, or cram in a final detail that would have been better placed elsewhere.

Although there are no set formulas for closing, the following list presents several options:

- Restate the thesis of your essay, and perhaps your main points.
- Mention the broader implications or significance of your topic.
- Give a final example that pulls all the parts of your discussion together.
- Offer a prediction.
- End with the most important point as the culmination of your essay's development.
- Suggest how the reader can apply the information you have just imparted.
- End with a bit of drama or flourish. Tell an ANECDOTE, offer an appropriate quotation, ask a question, make a final insightful remark. Keep in mind, however, that an ending shouldn't sound false and gimmicky. It truly has to conclude.

Concrete   See ABSTRACT AND CONCRETE.

Connotation and denotation   Two types of meanings most words have. *Denotation* is the explicit, literal, dictionary definition of a word. *Connotation* refers to a word's implied meaning, resonant with associations. The denotation of *blood* is "the fluid that circulates in the vascular system." The word's connotations range from *life force* to *gore* to *family bond*. A doctor might use the word *blood* for its denotation, and a mystery writer might rely on the rich connotations of the word to heighten a scene.

Because people have different experiences, they bring to the same word different associations. A conservative's emotional response to the word *welfare* is not likely to be the same as a liberal's. And referring to your senator as a *diplomat* evokes a different response, from the senator and from others, than would *baby-kisser, political hack,* or even *politician.* The effective use of words involves knowing both what they mean literally and what they are likely to suggest.

Critical thinking, reading, and writing   A group of interlocking skills that are essential for college work and beyond. Each seeks the meaning beneath the surface of a statement, poem, editorial, picture, advertisement, Web site, or other "text." Using ANALYSIS, INFERENCE, SYNTHESIS, and often EVALUATION, the critical thinker, reader, and writer separates this text into its elements in order to see and judge meanings, relations, and ASSUMPTIONS that might otherwise remain buried. See also pages 15–17 and 267.

Data   The name for EVIDENCE favored by logician Stephen Toulmin in his system of reasoning. See pages 457–60.

Deductive reasoning, deduction   The method of reasoning from the general to the particular: From information about what we already know, we deduce what we need or want to know. See Chapter 10, pages 460–61.

Definition   A statement of the literal and specific meaning or meanings of a word, or a method of developing an essay. In the latter, the writer usually explains the nature of a word, a thing, a concept, or a phenomenon. Such a definition may employ NARRATION, DESCRIPTION, or any other method. See Chapter 9.

Denotation   See CONNOTATION AND DENOTATION.

Description   A mode of writing that conveys the evidence of the senses: sight, hearing, touch, taste, smell. See Chapter 2.

Diction   The choice of words. Every written or spoken statement contains diction of some kind. To describe certain aspects of diction, the following terms may be useful:

- **Standard English:** the common American language, words and grammatical forms that are used and expected in school, business, and other sites.
- **Nonstandard English:** words and grammatical forms such as *theirselves* and *ain't* that are used mainly by people who speak a dialect other than standard English.
- **Dialect:** a variety of English based on differences in geography, education, or social background. Dialect is usually spoken, but may be written. Maya Angelou's essay in Chapter 1 transcribes the words of dialect speakers: people waiting for the fight broadcast ("He gone whip him till that white boy call him Momma").
- **Slang:** certain words in highly informal speech or writing, or in the speech of a particular group—for example, *blow off, dis, dweeb.*
- **Colloquial expressions:** words and phrases from conversation. See COLLOQUIAL EXPRESSIONS for examples.
- **Regional terms:** words heard in a certain locality, such as *spritzing* for "raining" in Pennsylvania Dutch country.
- **Technical terms:** words and phrases that form the vocabulary of a particular discipline (*monocotyledon* from botany), occupation (*drawplate* from die-making), or avocation (*interval training* from running). See also JARGON.
- **Archaisms:** old-fashioned expressions, once common but now used to suggest an earlier style, such as *ere, yon,* and *forsooth.* (Actually, *yon* is still current in the expression *hither and yon*; but if you say "Behold yon glass of beer!" it is an archaism.)
- **Obsolete diction:** words that have passed out of use (such as the verb *werien*, "to protect or defend," and the noun *isetnesses*, "agreements"). *Obsolete* may also refer to certain meanings of words no longer current (*fond* for foolish, *clipping* for hugging or embracing).
- **Pretentious diction:** use of words more numerous and elaborate than necessary, such as *institution of higher learning* for college, and *partake of solid nourishment* for eat.

Archaic, obsolete, and pretentious diction usually has no place in good writing unless for ironic or humorous effect: H. L. Mencken delighted in the hifalutin use of *tonsorial studio* instead of barber shop. Still, any diction may be the right diction for a certain occasion: The choice of words depends on a writer's purpose and audience.

Discovery   The stage of the writing process before the first draft. It may include deciding on a topic, narrowing the topic, creating or finding ideas, doing reading and other research, defining PURPOSE and AUDIENCE, planning and arranging material. Discovery may follow from daydreaming or meditation, reading, or perhaps carefully ransacking memory. In practice, though, it usually involves considerable writing and is aided by the act of writing. The operations of discovery—reading, research, further idea creation, and refinement of subject, purpose, and audience—may all continue well into drafting as well. See also pages 24–26, 29–30.

Division   See ANALYZE, ANALYSIS.

Dominant impression   The main idea a writer conveys about a subject through DESCRIPTION—that an elephant is gigantic, for example, or an experience scary. See also Chapter 2.

Drafting   The stage of the writing process during which a writer expresses ideas in complete sentences, links them, and arranges them in a sequence. See also pages 26–27, 30–31.

Effect   The result of an event or action, usually considered together with CAUSE as a method of development. See the discussion of cause and effect in Chapter 8. In discussing writing, the term *effect* also refers to the impression a word, sentence, paragraph, or entire work makes on the reader: how convincing it is, whether it elicits an emotional response, what associations it conjures up, and so on.

Emotional appeal   See APPEALS.

Emphasis   The stress or special importance given to a certain point or element to make it stand out. A skillful writer draws attention to what is most important in a sentence, paragraph, or essay by controlling emphasis in any of the following ways:

- **Proportion:** Important ideas are given greater coverage than minor points.
- **Position:** The beginnings and ends of sentences, paragraphs, and larger divisions are the strongest positions. Placing key ideas in these spots helps draw attention to their importance. The end is the stronger position, for what stands last stands out. A sentence in which less important details precede the main point is called a **periodic sentence:** "Having disguised himself as a guard and walked through the courtyard to the side gate, the prisoner made his escape." A sentence in which the main point precedes less important details is a **loose sentence:** "Autumn is orange: gourds in baskets at roadside stands, the harvest moon hanging like a pumpkin, and oak and beech leaves flashing like goldfish."
- **Repetition:** Careful repetition of key words or phrases can give them greater importance. (Careless repetition, however, can cause boredom.)
- **Mechanical devices:** Italics (underlining), capital letters, and exclamation points can make words or sentences stand out. Writers sometimes fall back on these devices, however, after failing to show significance by other means. Italics and exclamation points can be useful in reporting speech, but excessive use sounds exaggerated or bombastic.

Essay   A short nonfiction composition on one central theme or subject in which the writer may offer personal views. Essays are sometimes classified as either formal or informal. In general, a **formal essay** is one whose diction is that of the written language (not colloquial speech), serious in tone, and usually focused on a subject the writer believes is important. (For example, see Bruce Catton's "Grant and Lee.") An **informal essay,** in contrast, is more likely to admit colloquial expressions; the writer's tone tends to be lighter, perhaps humorous, and the subject is likely to be personal, sometimes even trivial. (See Merrill Markoe's "Bob the Dog.") These distinctions, however, are rough ones: An essay such as Judy Brady's "I Want a Wife" may use colloquial language and speak of personal experience, though it is serious in tone and has an undeniably important subject.

Ethical appeal   See APPEALS.

Euphemism   The use of inoffensive language in place of language that readers or listeners may find hurtful, distasteful, frightening, or otherwise objectionable—for instance, a police officer's announcing that someone *passed on* rather than *died*, or a politician's calling for *revenue enhancement* rather than *taxation*. Writers sometimes use euphemism out of consideration for readers' feelings, but just as often they use it to deceive readers or shirk responsibility. (For more on euphemism, see William Lutz's "The World of Doublespeak" in Chap. 7.)

Evaluate, evaluation   To judge the merits of something (*evaluate*), or the act or result of doing so (*evaluation*). Evaluation is often part of CRITICAL THINKING, READING, AND WRITING. In evaluating a work of writing, you base your judgment on your ANALYSIS of it and your sense of its quality or value. See also pages 16–17 and 176.

Evidence   The factual basis for an argument or an explanation. In a courtroom, an attorney's case is only as good as the evidence marshaled to support it. In an essay, a writer's opinions and GENERALIZATIONS also must rest upon evidence. The common forms of evidence are **facts,** verifiable statements; **statistics,** facts stated numerically; **examples,** specific instances of a generalization; **reported experience,** usually eyewitness accounts; **expert testimony,** the opinions of people considered very skilled or knowledgeable in the field; and, in CRITICAL WRITING about other writing, **quotations** or **paraphrases** from the work being discussed. (See PARAPHRASE.)

Example   Also called **exemplification** or **illustration,** a method of development in which the writer provides instances of a general idea. See Chapter 3. An *example* is a verbal illustration.

Exposition   The mode of prose writing that explains (or exposes) its subject. Its function is to inform, to instruct, or to set forth ideas: the major trade routes in the Middle East, how to make a dulcimer, why the United States consumes more energy than it needs. Exposition may call various methods to its service: EXAMPLE, COMPARISON AND CONTRAST, PROCESS ANALYSIS, and so on. Most college writing is at least partly exposition, and so are most of the essays in this book.

Fallacies   Errors in reasoning. See pages 461–63 for a list and examples.

Figures of speech   Expressions that depart from the literal meanings of words for the sake of emphasis or vividness. To say "She's a jewel" doesn't mean that the subject of praise is literally a kind of shining stone; the statement makes sense because its CONNOTATIONS come to mind: rare, priceless, worth cherishing. Some figures of speech involve comparisons of two objects apparently unlike:

- A **simile** (from the Latin, "likeness") states the comparison directly, usually connecting the two things using *like, as,* or *than:* "The moon is like a snowball," "He's as lazy as a cat full of cream," "My feet are flatter than flyswatters."

- A **metaphor** (from the Greek, "transfer") declares one thing to *be* another: "A mighty fortress is our God," "The sheep were bolls of cotton on the hill." (A **dead metaphor** is a word or phrase that, originally a figure of speech, has come to be literal through common usage: "the *hands* of a clock.")
- **Personification** is a simile or metaphor that assigns human traits to inanimate objects or abstractions: "A stoop-shouldered refrigerator hummed quietly to itself," "All of a sudden the solution to the math problem sat there winking at me."

Other figures of speech consist of deliberate misrepresentations:

- **Hyperbole** (from the Greek, "throwing beyond") is a conscious exaggeration: "I'm so hungry I could eat a horse and saddle," "I'd wait for you a thousand years."
- The opposite of hyperbole, **understatement**, creates an ironic or humorous effect: "I accepted the ride. At the moment, I didn't feel like walking across the Mojave Desert."
- A **paradox** (from the Greek, "conflicting with expectation") is a seemingly self-contradictory statement that, on reflection, makes sense: "Children are the poor person's wealth" (wealth can be monetary, or it can be spiritual). *Paradox* may also refer to a situation that is inexplicable or contradictory, such as the restriction of one group's rights in order to secure the rights of another group.

Flashback   A technique of NARRATIVE in which the sequence of events is interrupted to recall an earlier period.

Focus   The narrowing of a subject to make it manageable. Beginning with a general subject, you concentrate on a certain aspect of it. For instance, you may select crafts as a general subject, then decide your main interest lies in weaving. You could focus your essay still further by narrowing it to operating a hand loom. You also focus your writing according to who will read it (AUDIENCE) or what you want it to achieve (PURPOSE).

General and specific   Terms that describe the relative number of instances or objects included in the group signified by a word. *General* words name a group or class (*flowers*); *specific* words limit the class by naming its individual members (*rose, violet, dahlia, marigold*). Words may be arranged in a series from more general to more specific: *clothes, pants, jeans, Levis*. The word *cat* is more specific than *animal*, but less specific than *tiger cat*, or *Garfield*. See also ABSTRACT AND CONCRETE.

Generalization   A statement about a class based on an examination of some of its members: "Lions are fierce." The more members examined and the more representative they are of the class, the sturdier the generalization. The statement "Solar heat saves homeowners money" would be challenged by homeowners who have yet to recover their installation costs. "Solar heat can save homeowners money in the long run" would be a sounder generalization. Insufficient or nonrepresentative EVIDENCE often leads to a hasty generalization, such as "All freshmen hate their roommates" or "Men never express their feelings." Words such as *all, every, only,* *never,* and *always* have to be used with care: "Some men don't express their feelings" is more credible. Making a trustworthy generalization involves the use of INDUCTIVE REASONING (discussed on pp. 460–61).

Hyperbole   See FIGURES OF SPEECH.

Illustration   Another name for EXAMPLE. See Chapter 3.

Image   A word or word sequence that evokes a sensory experience. Whether literal ("We picked two red apples") or figurative ("His cheeks looked like two red apples, buffed and shining"), an image appeals to the reader's memory of seeing, hearing, smelling, touching, or tasting. Images add concreteness to fiction — "The farm looked as tiny and still as a seashell, with the little knob of a house surrounded by its curved furrows of tomato plants" (Eudora Welty in a short story, "The Whistle") — and are an important element in poetry. But writers of essays, too, find images valuable to bring ideas down to earth. See also FIGURES OF SPEECH.

Inductive reasoning, induction   The process of reasoning to a conclusion about an entire class by examining some of its members. See pages 460–61.

Infer, inference   To draw a conclusion (*infer*), or the act or result of doing so (*inference*). In CRITICAL THINKING, READING, AND WRITING, inference is the means to understanding a writer's meaning, ASSUMPTIONS, PURPOSE, fairness, and other attributes. See also page 16.

Introduction   The opening of a written work. Often it states the writer's subject, narrows it, and communicates the writer's main idea (THESIS). Introductions vary in length, depending on their purposes. A research paper may need several paragraphs to set forth its central idea and its plan of organization; a brief, informal essay may need only a sentence or two for an introduction. Whether long or short, good introductions tell readers no more than they need to know when they begin reading. Here are a few possible ways to open an essay effectively:

- State your central idea, or thesis, perhaps showing why you care about it.
- Present startling facts about your subject.
- Tell an illustrative ANECDOTE.
- Give background information that will help your reader understand your subject, or see why it is important.
- Begin with an arresting quotation.
- Ask a challenging question. (In your essay, you'll go on to answer it.)

Irony   A manner of speaking or writing that does not directly state a discrepancy, but implies one. **Verbal irony** is the intentional use of words to suggest a meaning other than literal: "What a mansion!" (said of a shack); "There's nothing like sunshine" (said on a foggy morning). (For more examples, see the essays by Jessica Mitford, Linnea Saukko, and Judy Brady.) If irony is delivered contemptuously with an intent to hurt, we call it **sarcasm:** "Oh, you're a real friend!" (said to someone who refuses to lend the speaker the coins to make a phone call). With **situational irony,** the circumstances themselves are incongruous, run contrary to expectations, or twist fate: Juliet regains consciousness only to find that Romeo, believing her dead, has stabbed himself. See also SATIRE.

Jargon Strictly speaking, the special vocabulary of a trade or profession. The term has also come to mean inflated, vague, meaningless language of any kind. It is characterized by wordiness, ABSTRACTIONS galore, pretentious DICTION, and needlessly complicated word order. Whenever you meet a sentence that obviously could express its idea in fewer words and shorter ones, chances are that it is jargon. For instance: "The motivating force compelling her to opt continually for the most labor-intensive mode of operation in performing her functions was consistently observed to be the single constant and regular factor in her behavior patterns." Translation: "She did everything the hard way." (For more on such jargon, see William Lutz's "The World of Doublespeak" in Chap. 7.)

Journal A record of one's thoughts, kept daily or at least regularly. Keeping a journal faithfully can help a writer gain confidence and develop ideas. See also page 24.

Metaphor See FIGURES OF SPEECH.

Narration The mode of writing that tells a story. See Chapter 1.

Narrator The teller of a story, usually either in the first PERSON (*I*) or in the third (*he, she, it, they*). See pages 41–42.

Nonstandard English See DICTION.

Objective and subjective Kinds of writing that differ in emphasis. In *objective* writing, the emphasis falls on the topic; in *subjective* writing, it falls on the writer's view of the topic. Objective writing occurs in factual journalism, science reports, certain PROCESS ANALYSES (such as recipes, directions, and instructions), and logical arguments in which the writer attempts to downplay personal feelings and opinions. Subjective writing sets forth the writer's feelings, opinions, and interpretations. It occurs in friendly letters, journals, bylined feature stories and columns in newspapers, personal essays, and ARGUMENTS that appeal to emotion. Few essays, however, contain one kind of writing exclusive of the other.

Paradox See FIGURES OF SPEECH.

Paragraph A group of closely related sentences that develop a central idea. In an essay, a paragraph is the most important unit of thought because it is both self-contained and part of the larger whole. Paragraphs separate long and involved ideas into smaller parts that are more manageable for the writer and easier for the reader to take in. Good paragraphs, like good essays, possess UNITY and COHERENCE. The central idea is usually stated in a TOPIC SENTENCE, often found at the beginning of the paragraph that relates directly to the essay's THESIS. All other sentences in the paragraph relate to this topic sentence, defining it, explaining it, illustrating it, providing it with evidence and support. If you meet a unified and coherent paragraph that has no topic sentence, it will contain a central idea that no sentence in it explicitly states, but that every sentence in it clearly implies.

Parallelism, parallel structure A habit of good writers: keeping ideas of equal importance in similar grammatical form. A writer may place nouns side by side ("*Trees* and *streams* are my weekend tonic") or in a series ("Give me *wind, sea,* and *stars*"). Phrases, too, may be arranged in parallel structure ("*Out of my bed, into my shoes, up to my classroom*—that's my life"); or clauses ("Ask not what your country can do for you; ask what you can do for your country").

Parallelism may be found not only in single sentences, but in larger units as well. A paragraph might read: "Rhythm is everywhere. It throbs in the rain forests of Brazil. It vibrates ballroom floors in Vienna. It snaps its fingers on street corners in Chicago." In a whole essay, parallelism may be the principle used to arrange ideas in a balanced or harmonious structure. See the famous speech given by Martin Luther King, Jr. (p. 567), in which each paragraph in a series (paras. 11–18) begins with the words "I have a dream" and goes on to describe an imagined future. Not only does such a parallel structure organize ideas, but it also lends them force.

Paraphrase Putting another writer's thoughts into your own words. In writing a research paper or an essay containing EVIDENCE gathered from your reading, you will find it necessary to paraphrase — unless you are using another writer's very words with quotation marks around them — and to acknowledge your sources. Contrast SUMMARY. And see page 670.

Person A grammatical distinction made between the speaker, the one spoken to, and the one spoken about. In the first person (*I, we*), the subject is speaking. In the second person (*you*), the subject is being spoken to. In the third person (*he, she, it*), the subject is being spoken about. The point of view of an essay or work of fiction is often specified according to person: "This short story is told from a first-person point of view." See POINT OF VIEW.

Personification See FIGURES OF SPEECH.

Persuasion A mode of writing intended to influence people's actions by engaging their beliefs and feelings. Persuasion often overlaps ARGUMENT. See Chapter 10.

Plagiarism The use of someone else's ideas or words as if they were your own, without acknowledging the original author. See pages 670–71.

Point of view In an essay, the physical position or the mental angle from which a writer beholds a subject. On the subject of starlings, the following three writers would likely have different points of view: An ornithologist might write OBJECTIVELY about the introduction of these birds into North America, a farmer might advise other farmers how to prevent the birds from eating seed, and a bird-watcher might SUBJECTIVELY describe a first glad sighting of an unusual species. Furthermore, the PERSON of each essay would probably differ: The scientist might present a scholarly paper in the third person, the farmer might offer advice in the second, and the bird-watcher might recount the experience in the first.

Premise A proposition or ASSUMPTION that supports a conclusion. See page 461 for examples.

Process analysis A method of development that most often explains step by step how something is done or how to do something. See Chapter 5.

Purpose A writer's reason for trying to convey a particular idea (THESIS) about a particular subject to a particular AUDIENCE of readers. Though it may emerge gradually during the writing process, in the end purpose should govern every element of a piece of writing.

In trying to define the purpose of an essay you read, ask yourself "Why did the writer write this?" or "What was this writer trying to achieve?" Even though you cannot know the writer's intentions with absolute certainty, an effective essay will make some purpose clear.

Rational appeal See APPEALS.

Revision The stage of the writing process during which a writer "re-sees" a draft from the viewpoint of a reader. Revision usually involves two steps, first considering fundamental matters such as purpose and organization, and then editing for surface matters such as smooth transitions and error-free sentences. See pages 27–28, 31–34.

Rhetoric The study (and the art) of using language effectively. *Rhetoric* also has a negative CONNOTATION of empty or pretentious language meant to waffle, stall, or even deceive. This is the meaning in "The president had nothing substantial to say about taxes, just the usual rhetoric."

Rhetorical question A question posed for effect, one that requires no answer. Instead, it often provokes thought, lends emphasis to a point, asserts or denies something without making a direct statement, launches further discussion, introduces an opinion, or leads the reader where the writer intends. Sometimes a writer throws one in to introduce variety in a paragraph full of declarative sentences. The following questions are rhetorical: "When will the United States learn that sending people into space does not feed them on the earth?" "Shall I compare thee to a summer's day?" "What is the point of making money if you've no one but yourself to spend it on?" Both reader and writer know what the answers are supposed to be. (1) Someday, if the United States ever wises up. (2) Yes. (3) None.

Sarcasm See IRONY.

Satire A form of writing that employs wit to attack folly. Unlike most comedy, the purpose of satire is not merely to entertain, but to bring about enlightenment — even reform. Usually, satire employs irony — as in Linnea Saukko's "How to Poison the Earth" and Jonathan Swift's "A Modest Proposal." See also IRONY.

Scene In a NARRATIVE, an event retold in detail to re-create an experience. See Chapter 1.

Sentimentality A quality sometimes found in writing that fails to communicate. Such writing calls for an extreme emotional response on the part of an AUDIENCE, although its writer fails to supply adequate reason for any such reaction. A sentimental writer delights in waxing teary over certain objects: great-grandmother's portrait, the first stick of chewing gum baby chewed (now a shapeless wad), an empty popcorn box saved from the World Series of 1992. Sentimental writing usually results when writers shut their eyes to the actual world, preferring to snuffle the sweet scents of remembrance.

Simile See FIGURES OF SPEECH.

Slang See DICTION.

Specific See GENERAL AND SPECIFIC.

Standard English See DICTION.

Strategy Whatever means a writer employs to write effectively. The methods set forth in this book are strategies; but so are narrowing a subject, organizing ideas clearly, using TRANSITIONS, writing with an awareness of your reader, and other effective writing practices.

Style The distinctive manner in which a writer writes. Style may be seen especially in the writer's choice of words and sentence structures. Two writers may write on the same subject, even express similar ideas, but it is style that gives each writer's work a personality.

Subjective See OBJECTIVE AND SUBJECTIVE.

Summarize, summary   To condense a work (essay, movie, news story) to its essence (*summarize*), or the act or result of doing so (*summary*). Summarizing a piece of writing in one's own words is an effective way to understand it. (See pp. 14–15.) Summarizing (and acknowledging) others' writing in your own text is a good way to support your ideas. (See pp. 669–70.) Contrast PARAPHRASE.

Suspense   Often an element in narration: the pleasurable expectation or anxiety we feel that keeps us reading a story. In an exciting mystery story, suspense is constant: How will it all turn out? Will the detective get to the scene in time to prevent another murder? But there can be suspense in less melodramatic accounts as well.

Syllogism   A three-step form of reasoning that employs DEDUCTION. See page 461 for an illustration.

Symbol   A visible object or action that suggests some further meaning. The flag suggests country, the crown suggests royalty—these are conventional symbols familiar to us. Life abounds in such relatively clear-cut symbols. Football teams use dolphins and rams for easy identification; married couples symbolize their union with a ring.

In writing, symbols usually do not have such a one-to-one correspondence, but evoke a whole constellation of associations. In Herman Melville's *Moby-Dick,* the whale suggests more than the large mammal it is. It hints at evil, obsession, and the untamable forces of nature. Such a symbol carries meanings too complex or elusive to be neatly defined.

Although more common in fiction and poetry, symbols can be used to good purpose in nonfiction because they often communicate an idea in a compact and concrete way. For example, in Annie Dillard's essay on page 547, the lenses of the title could be said to symbolize insight.

Synthesize, synthesis   To link elements into a whole (*synthesize*), or the act or result of doing so (*synthesis*). In CRITICAL THINKING, READING, AND WRITING, synthesis is the key step during which you reassemble a work you have ANALYZED or connect the work with others. See page 16.

Thesis   The central idea in a work of writing, to which everything else in the work refers. In some way, each sentence and PARAGRAPH in an effective essay serves to support the thesis and to make it clear and explicit to readers. Good writers, while writing, often set down a **thesis sentence** or **thesis statement** to help them define their purpose. They also often include this statement in their essay as a promise and a guide to readers. See also pages 26–27.

Tone   The way a writer expresses his or her regard for subject, audience, or self. Through word choice, sentence structures, and what is actually said, the writer conveys an attitude and sets a prevailing spirit. Tone in writing varies as greatly as tone of voice varies in conversation. It can be serious, distant, flippant, angry, enthusiastic, sincere, sympathetic. Whatever tone a writer chooses, usually it informs an entire essay and helps a reader decide how to respond. For works of strong tone, see the essays by Barbara Huttmann; Roy Blount, Jr.; Jessica Mitford; Judy Brady; Joan Didion; Annie Dillard; and Martin Luther King, Jr.

Topic sentence   The statement of the central idea in a PARAGRAPH, usually asserting one aspect of an essay's THESIS. Often the topic sentence will appear at (or near) the beginning of the paragraph, announcing the idea and beginning its development. Because all other sentences in the paragraph explain and support this central idea, the topic sentence is a way to create UNITY.

Transitions   Words, phrases, sentences, or even paragraphs that relate ideas. In moving from one topic to the next, a writer has to bring the reader along by showing how the ideas are developing, what bearing a new thought or detail has on an earlier discussion, or why a new topic is being introduced. A clear purpose, strong ideas, and logical development certainly aid COHERENCE, but to ensure that the reader is following along, good writers provide signals, or transitions.

To bridge sentences or paragraphs and to point out relationships within them, you can use some of the following devices of transition:

- Repeat or restate words or phrases to produce an echo in the reader's mind.
- Use PARALLEL STRUCTURES to produce a rhythm that moves the reader forward.
- Use pronouns to refer back to nouns in earlier passages.
- Use transitional words and phrases. These may indicate a relationship of time (*right away, later, soon, meanwhile, in a few minutes, that night*), proximity (*beside, close to, distant from, nearby, facing*), effect (*therefore, for this reason, as a result, consequently*), comparison (*similarly, in the same way, likewise*), or contrast (*yet, but, nevertheless, however, despite*). Some words and phrases of transition simply add on: *besides, too, also, moreover, in addition to, second, last, in the end.*

Understatement   See FIGURES OF SPEECH.

Unity   The quality of good writing in which all parts relate to the THESIS. In a unified essay, all words, sentences, and PARAGRAPHS support the single central idea. Your first step in achieving unity is to state your thesis; your next step is to organize your thoughts so that they make your thesis clear.

Voice   In writing, the sense of the author's character, personality, and attitude that comes through the words. See TONE.

Warrant   The name in Stephen Toulmin's system of reasoning for the thinking, or ASSUMPTION, that links DATA and CLAIM. See pages 457–60.

Acknowledgments *(continued from p. iv)*

Barbara Ascher, "On Compassion," from *The Habit of Loving* by Barbara Ascher. Copyright © 1986, 1987, 1989 by Barbara Lazear. Reprinted by permission of Random House, Inc. "Barbara Lazear Ascher on Writing," excerpt from Barbara Lazear Ascher selection in *Contemporary Authors Online*. Copyright © 1999.

Russell Baker, "The Plot Against People." Copyright © 1951 by The New York Times Co. Reprinted by permission. "Russell Baker on Writing" previously appeared as "Computer Fallout" in *The New York Times Magazine*, 10/11/87. Copyright © 1987 by The New York Times Company. Reprinted by permission.

Dave Barry, "Batting Clean-Up and Striking Out," from *Dave Barry's Greatest Hits* by Dave Barry. Copyright © 1988 by Dave Barry. Reprinted by permission of Crown Publishers, Inc. "Dave Barry on Writing" excerpts from Dave Barry selection in *Contemporary Authors, New Revision Series*, Vol. 134. Published 1992. Copyright © 1992. Reprinted by permission of the Gale Group, www.galegroup.com.

Bruno Bettelheim, "The Holocaust." Excerpted from "The Holocaust," from *Surviving and Other Essays* by Bruno Bettelheim. Copyright © 1952, 1960, 1962, 1976, 1979 by Bruno Bettelheim and Trude Bettelheim as Trustees. Reprinted by permission of Alfred A. Knopf, Inc.

Elizabeth Bishop, "Filling Station." From *The Complete Poems 1927–1979* by Elizabeth Bishop. Copyright © 1979, 1983 by Alice Helen Methfessel. Reprinted by permission of Farrar, Straus and Giroux, LLC.

Roy Blount, Jr., "As Well as I Do My Own." Originally published in *The Atlantic Monthly*. Copyright © 1985 by Roy Blount, Jr. Reprinted with permission of the author. "Roy Blount, Jr. on Writing," excerpt from "Bittersweet," interview by Katie Bacon, *Atlantic Unbound*, 4/8/98, http://www.theatlantic.com/unbound/bookauth/ba980723.htm. Reprinted by permission.

Judy Brady, "I Want a Wife." Copyright by Judy Brady, 1970. Reprinted by permission of the author.

Suzanne Britt, "Neat People vs. Sloppy People." From *Show and Tell* by Suzanne Britt. Copyright © 1982 by Suzanne Britt. Reprinted by permission of the author. "Suzanne Britt on Writing," copyright © 1984 by St. Martin's Press, Inc.

Armin A. Brott, "Not All Men Are Sly Foxes." First published in *Newsweek* magazine in 1992. Reprinted by permission of the author.

William F. Buckley, Jr., "Why Don't We Complain?" by William F. Buckley, Jr. Copyright © 1960 by Esquire. Reprinted by permission of the Wallace Literary Agency, Inc. "William F. Buckley, Jr. On Writing," excerpts from *Overdrive* by William F. Buckley, Jr. Published by Doubleday. Copyright © 1981, 1983 by N. R. Resources, Inc. Reprinted by permission of Doubleday, a division of Bantam, Doubleday, Dell Publishing Group, Inc. Excerpt from *Hymnal: The Controversial Arts* by William F. Buckley, Jr. Copyright © 1978 by William F. Buckley, Jr. Reprinted by permission of G. P. Putnam's Sons.

Bernard Campbell, paragraph from *Humankind Emerging* 3rd ed. Copyright © HarperCollins, 1992. Reprinted by permission of HarperCollins.

Stephen L. Carter, "The Insufficiency of Honesty." From *The Atlantic Monthly*, February 1996. Reprinted by permission of the author.

Bruce Catton, "Grant and Lee: A Study in Contrasts." Copyright © 1956 by U.S. Capitol Historical Society. All rights reserved. Reprinted by permission. "Bruce Catton on Writing," excerpts from Oliver Jensen's introduction to *Bruce Catton's*

America. Reprinted by permission of American Heritage Magazine, a division of Forbes Inc. Copyright © 1979 by Forbes, Inc.

Curtis Chang, "Streets of Gold: The Myth of the Model Minority" and excerpts in "Curtis Chang on Writing" from Nancy Sommers and Donald McQuade, *Student Writers at Work and in the Company of Other Writers*, 3rd ed. Copyright © 1989 by St. Martin's Press, Inc. Reprinted by permission.

Sandra Cisneros, "Only Daughter." Copyright © 1990 by Sandra Cisneros. First published in *Glamour*, November 1990. Reprinted by permission of Susan Bergholz Literary Services, New York. All rights reserved. "Sandra Cisneros on Writing," excerpt from *Interviews with Writers of the Post-Colonial World* edited by Feroza Jussawalla and Reed Way Dasenbrock. Copyright © 1992 by the University Press of Mississippi. Reprinted by permission.

Judith Ortiz Cofer, "Silent Dancing" is reprinted with permission from the publisher of *Silent Dancing: A Partial Remembrance of a Puerto Rican Childhood*. Houston: Arte Publico Press—University of Houston, 1990. "Judith Ortiz Cofer on Writing," excerpt from Judith Ortiz Cofer selection in *Contemporary Authors, New Revision Series*, Vol. 115. Published 1985. Copyright © 1985. Reprinted by permission of the Gale Group, www.galegroup.com.

K. C. Cole, "Entropy." Copyright © 1982 by the New York Times Co. Reprinted by permission. "K. C. Cole on Writing," excerpt from "Mind Over Matter: A True-life Story: Why Science Writers Lie" by K. C. Cole, the *Los Angeles Times*, 11/20/97, p. B2. Copyright © 1997 by the *Los Angeles Times*. Reprinted by permission.

Meghan Daum, "Safe-Sex Lies." From *The New York Times Magazine* 1/21/96. Copyright © 1996 by Meghan Daum. Reprinted by permission of International Creative Management, Inc.

Joan Didion, "In Bed." From *The White Album* by Joan Didion. Copyright © 1979 by Joan Didion. Reprinted by permission of Farrar, Straus and Giroux, LLC. "Joan Didion on Writing," excerpts from "Why I Write," by Joan Didion. First appeared in *The New York Times Book Review*.

Annie Dillard, "Lenses," excerpt from *Teaching a Stone to Talk* by Annie Dillard. Copyright © 1982 by Annie Dillard. Reprinted by permission of HarperCollins Publishers, Inc. "Annie Dillard on Writing" copyright 1985 by St. Martin's Press, Inc.

Chitra Divakaruni, "Live Free and Starve." This article first appeared in Salon.com, at http://www.salon.com. An online version remains in the Salon archives. Reprinted with permission. "Chitra Divakaruni on Writing," excerpt from "Women's Places," interview by Katie Bolick *Atlantic Unbound*, 4/8/98, http://www.theatlantic.com/unbound/factfict/ff9804.html. Reprinted by permission.

Esther Dyson, "Cyberspace for All." First appeared as "If You Don't Love It, Leave It" in *The New York Times Magazine* on July 6, 1995. Reprinted by permission of the author. "Esther Dyson on Writing" copyright © 1996 by Bedford Books.

Barbara Ehrenreich, "In Defense of Talk Shows," *Time* December 4, 1995. Copyright © 1995 Time Inc. Reprinted by permission. "Barbara Ehrenreich on Writing" copyright © 1987, Foundation for National Progress.

Ralph Ellison, "On Being the Target of Discrimination," from *Collected Essays of Ralph Ellison* by Ralph Ellison. Copyright © 1970, by permission of Modern Library, a division of Random House, Inc. "Ralph Ellison on Writing," excerpt from *Shadow and Act* by Ralph Ellison. Copyright © 1953, 1964 by Ralph Ellison. Copyright © renewed 1981, 1992 by Ralph Ellison. Reprinted by permission of Random House, Inc.

Michael Kroll, "The Unquiet Death of Robert Harris" by Michael Kroll from the July 6, 1992 issue of *The Nation*. Reprinted with permission from *The Nation* magazine. © The Nation Company, L. P.

Christine Leong, "On Being a Chink." Reprinted by permission of the author. "Christine Leong on Writing" copyright © 1996 by Bedford Books.

Phillip Lopate, "Confessions of a Shusher," from *Portrait of My Body* by Phillip Lopate. Copyright © 1996 by Phillip Lopate. Used by permission of Doubleday, a division of Random House, Inc. "Phillip Lopate on Writing," excerpt from Phillip Lopate selection in *Contemporary Authors Online*. Copyright © 1999. Reprinted by permission of the Gale Group, www.galegroup.com.

William Lutz, "The World of Doublespeak." Excerpt from *Doublespeak* by William Lutz. Copyright © 1989 by Blond Bear, Inc. Reprinted by permission of HarperCollins Publishers, Inc. "William Lutz on Writing," excerpt from transcript of Booknotes, C-SPAN, 12/31/89, http://www.booknotes.org/transcripts. Reprinted by permission of C-SPAN.

Nancy Mairs, "Disability." Excerpt from *Carnal Acts* by Nancy Mairs. Copyright © 1990 by Nancy Mairs. Reprinted by permission of Beacon Press, Boston. "Nancy Mairs on Writing," excerpt from "When Bad Things Happen to Good Writers" by Nancy Mairs, *New York Times Book Review*, February 1993.

Brad Manning, "Arm Wrestling with My Father." Reprinted by permission of the author. "Brad Manning on Writing," copyright 1996 by Bedford Books.

Merrill Markoe, "Bob the Dog (1974–1988)", from *What the Dogs Have Taught Me* by Merrill Markoe. Copyright © 1992 by Merrill Markoe. Used by permission of Viking Penguin, a division of Penguin Putnam Inc. "Merrill Markoe on Writing," excerpt from "The Day I Turned Sarcastic" in *What the Dogs Have Taught Me* by Merrill Markoe. Copyright © 1992 by Merrill Markoe. Used by permission of Viking Penguin, a division of Penguin Books USA Inc.

John McPhee, "Silk Parachute." Originally in *The New Yorker*. Reprinted by permission; © 1997 John McPhee. All rights reserved. "John McPhee on Writing," excerpt from "The Strange Case of the Queen-Post Trust," by Douglas Vipond and Russell A. Hunt, *College Composition and Communication*, vol. 43, no. 3, pp. 202 and 203–4. Copyright © 1991 by National Council of Teachers of English. Reprinted by permission.

H. L. Mencken, "The Penalty of Death." Reprinted from *A Mencken Chrestomathy* by H. L. Mencken. Copyright 1926 by Alfred A. Knopf Inc. and renewed 1954 by H. L. Mencken. Reprinted by permission of the publisher. "H. L. Mencken on Writing," excerpts from "Addendum on Aims" by H. L. Mencken in *American Scene* and from "The Fringes of Lovely Letters" by H. L. Mencken in *Prejudices: Fifth Series*, all copyright © Alfred A. Knopf, Inc., a Division of Random House, Inc.

Horace Miner, "Body Ritual Among the Nacirema." Reproduced by permission of the American Anthropological Association from *American Anthropologist* 58:3, June 1956. Not for further reproduction.

Jessica Mitford, "Behind the Formaldehyde Curtain." Reprinted from *The American Way of Death*. Simon & Schuster © 1963, 1968 by Jessica Mitford, all rights reserved. Reprinted by permission of the Estate of Jessica Mitford. "Jessica Mitford on Writing," excerpts from *Poison Penmanship: The Gentle Art of Muckraking* by Jessica Mitford, copyright © 1979, and from *A Fine Old Conflict* by Jessica Mitford, copyright © 1977. Reprinted by permission of Random House, Inc.

N. Scott Momaday, "The Way to Rainy Mountain," The University of New Mexico Press © 1977. "N. Scott Momaday on Writing," excerpt from "Landscapes: N.

Acknowledgments

Scott Momaday" by William T. Morgan, Jr., *Sequoia*, vol. 19, no. 2 (winter 1975), copyright © Stanford University.

Gloria Naylor, "The Meanings of A Word." Reprinted by permission of Sterling Lord Literistic, Inc. Copyright 1986 by Gloria Naylor. "Gloria Naylor on Writing," excerpt from "A Talk with Gloria Naylor" by William Goldstein. Reprinted from the September 9, 1983 issue of *Publishers Weekly*. Copyright © 1983 by Publishers Weekly. Reprinted by permission.

Itabari Njeri, "When Morpheus Held Him." Originally published in *Harper's Magazine*. From *Every Goodbye Ain't Gone*. Copyright 1990 Itabari Njeri. Reprinted with permission of the author. "Itabari Njeri on Writing," excerpt from Itabari Njeri selection in *Contemporary Authors Online*. Copyright © 1999. Reprinted by permission of the Gale Group, www.galegroup.com.

George Orwell, "Shooting an Elephant." From *Shooting an Elephant and Other Essays* by George Orwell, copyright 1950 by Sonia Brownell Orwell and renewed 1978 by Sonia Pitt-Rivers, reprinted by permission of Harcourt, Inc. "George Orwell on Writing," excerpt from "Why I Write," from *Such, Such Were the Joys* by George Orwell, copyright © 1953 by Sonia Brownell Orwell and renewed 1981 by Mrs. George K. Perutz, Mrs. Miriam Gross, and Dr. Michael Dickson, Executors of the Estate of Sonia Brownell Orwell, reprinted by permission of Harcourt, Inc.

Heidi Pollock, "Welcome to Cyberbia." First appeared in *h2so4* no. 3 as "The Internet is Four Inches Tall," reprinted in the *Utne Reader*. Reprinted by permission of *h2so4*.

Emily Prager, "Our Barbies, Ourselves." Originally published in *Interview*, Brant Publications, Inc., December 1991. "Emily Prager on Writing," excerpt from "Focus on the United States: Will the Class of 2000 Be Able to Read?" by Emily Prager, the *Globe and Mail*, 1/14/89, p. D5.

William K. Purves and Gordon H. Orians, excerpt from *Life: The Science of Biology*. Copyright © 1983 by Sinauer Associates, Inc. Reprinted by permission of the publisher.

Anna Quindlen, "Homeless," from *Living Out Loud* by Anna Quindlen. Copyright © 1987 by Anna Quindlen. Reprinted by permission of Random House, Inc. "Anna Quindlen on Writing," excerpts from "In the Beginning" in *Living Out Loud* by Anna Quindlen. Copyright © 1987 by Anna Quindlen. Reprinted by permission of Random House, Inc.

Richard Rodriguez, "Aria," from *Hunger of Memory* by Richard Rodriguez (Boston: David R. Godine, Publisher, 1981) Copyright © 1981 by Richard Rodriguez. Reprinted by permission of George Borchardt, Inc. for the author. "Richard Rodriguez on Writing" copyright © 1985 by St. Martin's Press, Inc.

Scott Russell Sanders, "Homeplace." Copyright © 1992 by Scott Russell Sanders; first published in *Orion* (Winter 1992); reprinted by permission of the author. "Scott Russell Sanders on Writing," excerpt from Scott Russell Sanders selection in *Contemporary Authors Online*. Copyright © 1999. Reprinted by permission of the Gale Group, www.galegroup.com.

Linnea Saukko, "How to Poison the Earth" (and "Linnea Saukko on Writing") excerpts from *Student Writers at Work and in the Company of Other Writers*. Copyright © 1984 by St. Martin's Press, Inc. Reprinted by permission.

Gail Sheehy, "Predictable Crises of Adulthood," from *Passages* by Gail Sheehy. Copyright © 1974, 1976 by Gail Sheehy. Used by permission of Dutton, a division of Penguin Putnam Inc. "Gail Sheehy on Writing," excerpt from *New Passages* by Gail Sheehy. Copyright © 1995 by Penguin Books USA Inc. Excerpt from "Chronicler of Life's Cycles" by Regina Weinreich (NYT 7/23/95).

INDEX

Page numbers in bold type refer to definitions in
the glossary, Useful Terms.